New Testament Commentary

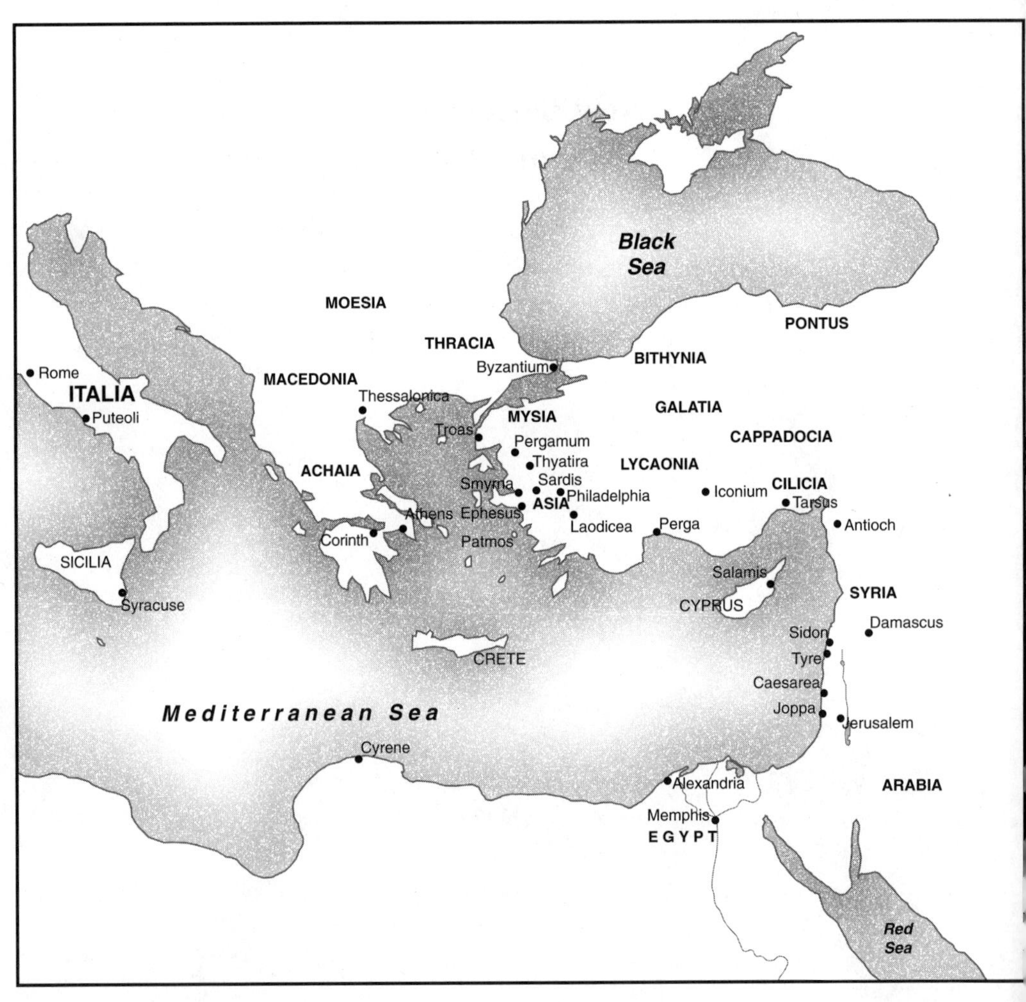
Black Sea
MOESIA
PONTUS
THRACIA
BITHYNIA
Rome
Byzantium
MACEDONIA
ITALIA
Thessalonica
GALATIA
Puteoli
MYSIA
Troas
CAPPADOCIA
Pergamum
Thyatira
LYCAONIA
ACHAIA
Sardis
Smyrna
Philadelphia
Iconium
CILICIA
ASIA
Tarsus
Athens
Ephesus
Laodicea
Antioch
Corinth
Perga
Patmos
SICILIA
Salamis
SYRIA
Syracuse
CYPRUS
Damascus
Sidon
Tyre
CRETE
Caesarea
Mediterranean Sea
Joppa
Jerusalem
Cyrene
Alexandria
ARABIA
Memphis
EGYPT
Red Sea

New Testament Commentary

Exposition of the

Book of Revelation

Simon J. Kistemaker

Published by Baker Academic
a division of Baker Book House Company
P.O. Box 6287, Grand Rapids, MI 49516-6287

Second printing, July 2002

12 volume set, first available 2002
ISBN 0-8010-2606-7

Printed in the United States of America

Library of Congress Cataloging-in-Publication Data

Hendriksen, William, 1900–1982.
New Testament commentary.

Accompanying Biblical text is author's translation.
Vols. 14– by Simon J. Kistemaker.
Includes bibliographical references and indexes.
Contents: [1] John I–VI — [2] John VII–XXI — [etc.] — [20] Exposition of Revelation.
1. Bible. N.T.—Commentaries. I. Kistemaker, Simon. II. Bible. N.T. English. Hendriksen. 1953.
BS2341.H4 1953 225.7′7 54-924
ISBN 0-8010-2252-5 (v. 20)

For information about academic books, resources for Christian leaders, and all new releases available from Baker Book House, visit our web site:
http://www.bakerbooks.com

Contents

Abbreviations

AB	Anchor Bible
ACNT	Augsburg Commentary on the New Testament
ANRW	*Aufstieg und Niedergang der römischen Welt*
AssembSeign	*Assemblées du Seigneur*
ASV	American Standard Version
ATR	*Anglican Theological Review*
AusBRev	*Australian Biblical Review*
AUSDDS	Andrews University Seminary Doctoral Dissertation Series
AUSS	*Andrews University Seminary Studies*
BASOR	*Bulletin of the American School of Oriental Research*
Bauer	Walter Bauer, W. F. Arndt, F. W. Gingrich, and F. W. Danker, *A Greek-English Lexicon of the New Testament,* 2d ed.
BBR	*Bulletin for Biblical Research*
BETL	Bibliotheca ephemeridum theologicarum lovaniensium
BF^2	British and Foreign Bible Society, *The New Testament,* 2d ed., 1958
BGBE	Beiträge zur Geschichte der biblischen Exegese
Bib	*Biblica*
BibSac	*Bibliotheca sacra*
BibToday	*The Bible Today*
BibTrans	*The Bible Translator*
BibZ	*Biblische Zeitschrift*
BIS	Biblical Interpretation Series
BJRL	*Bulletin of the John Rylands University Library of Manchester*
BofT	*Banner of Truth*
BTB	*Biblical Theological Bulletin*
BZNW	Beihefte zur Zeitschrift für die neutestamentliche Wissenschaft

Cassirer	Heinz W. Cassirer, *God's New Covenant: A New Testament Translation*
CBQ	*Catholic Biblical Quarterly*
Clem.	*(Epistle of) Clement* [of Rome]
ConcJourn	*Concordia Journal*
ConcThMonth	*Concordia Theological Monthly*
ConcTheolQuart	*Concordia Theological Quarterly*
ConNT	Coniectanea neotestamentica
CTJ	*Calvin Theological Journal*
Eccl. Hist.	Eusebius, *Ecclesiastical History*
EDNT	*Exegetical Dictionary of the New Testament*
EDT	*Evangelical Dictionary of Theology*
EphThL	*Ephemerides theologicae lovanienses*
EvQ	*Evangelical Quarterly*
ExpT	*Expository Times*
FilolNT	*Filología neotestamentaria*
FoiVie	*Foi et vie*
GNB	Good News Bible
GTJ	*Grace Theological Journal*
HDR	Harvard Dissertations in Religion
HeythJourn	*Heythrop Journal*
HNT	Handbuch zum Neuen Testament
HNTC	Holman New Testament Commentary
HTR	*Harvard Theological Review*
ICC	International Critical Commentary
Interp	*Interpretation*
ISBE	*International Standard Bible Encyclopedia*, rev. ed.
JB	Jerusalem Bible
JBL	*Journal of Biblical Literature*
JETS	*Journal of the Evangelical Theological Society*
JSNT	*Journal for the Study of the New Testament*
JSNTSup	Journal for the Study of the New Testament: Supplement Series
JSOT	*Journal for the Study of the Old Testament*
JTS	*Journal of Theological Studies*
KJV	King James Version (Authorized Version)
KNT	Kommentaar op het Nieuwe Testament
LCL	Loeb Classical Library
Liddell	H. G. Liddell, R. Scott, and H. S. Jones, *A Greek-English Lexicon*, 9th ed.
LXX	Septuagint

Merk	Augustinus Merk, ed., *Novum Testamentum Graece et Latine*, 9th ed.
MLB	The Modern Language Bible
MM	J. H. Moulton and G. Milligan, *The Vocabulary of the Greek Testament*, 1930
MNTC	Moffatt New Testament Commentary
Moffatt	James Moffatt, *The Bible: A New Translation*
MSJ	*The Master's Seminary Journal*
MT	Masoretic Text of the Hebrew Bible
NAB	New American Bible
NAC	New American Commentary
NASB	New American Standard Bible
NCB	New Century Bible
NCV	The Everyday Bible, New Century Version
NEB	New English Bible
Neotest	*Neotestamentica*
Nes-Al^{27}	Eberhard and Erwin Nestle, eds.; rev. Barbara and Kurt Aland et al., *Novum Testamentum Graece*, 27th ed.
NIBCNT	New International Biblical Commentary on the New Testament
NICNT	New International Commentary on the New Testament
NIDNTT	*New International Dictionary of New Testament Theology*
NIGTC	New International Greek Testament Commentary
NIV	New International Version
NIVAC	NIV Application Commentary
NJB	New Jerusalem Bible
NJBC	*New Jerome Biblical Commentary*
NKJV	New King James Version
NLT	New Living Translation
NovT	*Novum Testamentum*
NRSV	New Revised Standard Version
n.s.	new series
NTC	New Testament Commentary
NTS	*New Testament Studies*
NTT	*Nederlands theologisch tijdschrift*
Peterson	Eugene H. Peterson, *The Message*
Phillips	J. B. Phillips, *The New Testament in Modern English*
RB	*Revue biblique*
REB	Revised English Bible
RevExp	Review and Expositor
RevThom	*Revue thomiste*

RSV	Revised Standard Version
SB	H. L. Strack and P. Billerbeck, *Kommentar zum Neuen Testament aus Talmud und Midrasch*
SBL	Society for Biblical Literature
SJT	*Scottish Journal of Theology*
SNTSMS	Society for New Testament Studies Monograph Series
Souter	Alexander Souter, ed., *Novum Testamentum Graece*
SP	Sacra Pagina
StudTheol	*Studia Theologica*
SwJT	*Southwestern Journal of Theology*
Talmud	The Babylonian Talmud
TDNT	*Theological Dictionary of the New Testament*
Thayer	Joseph H. Thayer, *Greek-English Lexicon of the New Testament*
Theod.	Theodotion
ThLZ	*Theologische Literaturzeitung*
TNT	The New Translation
TNTC	Tyndale New Testament Commentaries
TR	*The Textus Receptus: The Greek New Testament according to the Majority Text*
TrinJ	*Trinity Journal*
TynB	*Tyndale Bulletin*
UBS[4]	United Bible Societies, *Greek New Testament*, 4th ed.
Vogels	H. J. Vogels, ed., *Novum Testamentum Graece et Latine*, 4th ed.
VoxEv	*Vox evangelica*
WBC	Word Biblical Commentary
WPC	Westminster Pelican Commentaries
WTJ	*Westminster Theological Journal*
WUNT	*Wissenschaftliche Untersuchungen zum Neuen Testament*
ZNW	*Zeitschrift für die neutestamentliche Wissenschaft*
ZPEB	*Zondervan Pictorial Encyclopedia of the Bible*

Introduction

Outline

A. Pattern
B. Figurative Language
C. Scripture Based
D. Author
E. Time, Place, and Setting
F. Modes of Interpretation
G. Unity
H. Acceptance in the Church
I. Recipients and Purpose
J. Theology
K. Summary
L. Outline

The Greek title of this book is *Apokalypsis* (that which is being uncovered), but readers may feel that not much is revealed. The Book of Revelation appears not to accomplish what its title promises, confusing its readers by all the images, figures, and numbers they encounter. Pastors usually preach only a sevenfold series on the letters to the seven churches in Asia Minor recorded in chapters two and three. People regard the book as Scripture, but they fail to make use of it as such. For many readers, Revelation is not revelation but rather a prophetic mystery that surpasses human understanding. Yet in this last book of the Bible, God permits us to see something of Christ and the church in heaven and on earth—and what we see is awesome indeed.

As we look carefully at this book, we begin to realize that it is not a mere human composition similar to the apocalypses of *1 Enoch,* 4 Ezra (= 2 Esdras in the OT Apocrypha), and *2 Baruch.* In Revelation the triune God is revealing his Word to the reader; that is, God himself is speaking to his people. This becomes evident in the introductory words "The revelation of Jesus Christ, which God gave him" (1:1), and in the letters to the seven churches. There we hear the voice of Jesus, who concludes each letter with the words "the Spirit says to the churches" (2:7, 11, 17, 29; 3:6, 13, 22). The last chapter records the voice of Jesus (22:7, 12–20), the voice of the Spirit (22:17), and the divine warning not to add or subtract from this book (22:18–19). Neglecting this message would be akin to detracting from the Scriptures. God tells us to regard Revelation as his holy Word, and he instructs us to read it reverently.[1] The warning Jesus utters in 22:18–19 can be compared to a copyright notice on the back of the title page in a modern book.

> I testify to everyone who hears these words of the prophecy of this book. If anyone adds anything to them, God will add to him the plagues written in this book. And if anyone takes anything away from the words of the prophecy of this book, God will take away his share in the tree of life and the holy city, which are described in this book.

The Book of Revelation throughout directs attention to its primary composer, God. He is the divine artist, the chief architect. It is a divinely constructed volume in which God shows his handiwork.

---

1. William Milligan, *The Revelation of St. John* (London: Macmillan, 1886), p. 6.

A. Pattern
1. Numbers

One of the first features of Revelation a reader notices is the use of numbers and their significance. To an amazing degree, the number seven is predominant both explicitly and implicitly. This number should not be taken literally but must be understood as an idea that expresses totality or completeness.[2] For instance, Jesus tells John to write letters to the seven churches of Ephesus, Smyrna, Pergamum, Thyatira, Sardis, Philadelphia, and Laodicea (1:11). These churches were located along an oval-shaped route going from the west to the north, then to the east and last to the south. But the church of Colosse, located in the vicinity of Laodicea, is omitted, and so is the neighboring congregation of Hierapolis (Col. 4:13). Papias, a student of the apostle John, served as pastor of the church in Hierapolis. Paul preached in the church of Troas (Acts 20:5–12; 2 Cor. 2:12) some seventy miles north of Pergamum, but Troas is not included in the list. Is Revelation addressed to only seven of the churches in the province of Asia (1:4)? The answer is no, for Jesus addresses the churches of all ages and all places. The number seven symbolizes completeness.[3]

The number seven precedes many nouns, including spirits (1:4; 3:1; 4:5; 5:6), golden lampstands (1:12; 2:1), stars (1:16, 20; 2:1; 3:1), lampstands (1:13, 20; 2:5; 11:4), seals (5:1; 6:1), horns (5:6), eyes (5:6), angels (8:2, 6; 15:1, 6–8; 16:1; 17:1; 21:9), trumpets (8:2, 6), thunder (10:3), crowns (12:3), heads (12:3; 13:1; 17:3, 7, 9), plagues (15:1, 6), bowls (15:7; 16:1), hills (17:9), and kings (17:10). In addition, there are seven thousand people killed because of an earthquake (11:13). In all these instances the number seven appears explicitly. But the implicit use of this number is even more striking. There are two passages that record songs of praise sung by a heavenly host. The first one is 5:12, with seven attributes, which I have italicized:

> Worthy is the lamb that was slain,
> to receive *power* and *wealth*
> and *wisdom* and *strength*
> and *honor* and *glory* and *thanksgiving!*

The second passage (7:12) also has seven attributes:

> Amen! *Praise* and *glory* and *wisdom* and
> *thanksgiving*
> and *honor* and *power* and *strength*
> be to our God for ever and ever. Amen!

2. The number seven appears fifty-four times in Revelation. See Stephen A. Hunter, *Studies in the Book of Revelation* (Pittsburgh: Pittsburgh Printing, 1921), p. 248.

3. William Hendriksen, *More Than Conquerors* (reprint, Grand Rapids: Baker, 1982), p. 42.

Further, there are seven beatitudes in Revelation, given here in abbreviated form:

- "Blessed is the one who reads" (1:3)
- "Blessed are the dead who die in the Lord" (14:13)
- "Blessed is the one who watches" (16:15)
- "Blessed are the ones who are called" (19:9)
- "Blessed and holy is the one who has part" (20:6)
- "Blessed is the one who keeps the words" (22:7)
- "Blessed are they who wash their robes" (22:14)

Also in this series, locusts, described as horses in 9:7–10, display seven distinguishing marks: (1) crowns of gold on their heads; (2) faces of men; (3) hair of women; (4) teeth of lions; (5) breastplates of iron; (6) wings that make the sound of thundering horses and chariots in battle; (7) tails and stings of scorpions. The Greek word *arnion* (lamb), referring to Christ, occurs twenty-eight times—the sum of seven times four. While the number seven signifies completeness, the number four is the numerical symbol of the created world. The expression *soon* or *quickly* with reference to the fulfillment of prophecy and Jesus' return appears seven times (1:1; 2:16; 3:11; 22:6, 7, 12, 20).[4] And last, the term *the word(s) of God* appears exactly seven times (1:2, 9; 6:9; 17:17; 19:9, 13; 20:4).[5]

The number four represents the four living creatures, four angels, four corners of the earth, four winds, and four angels bound at the Euphrates. Categories of four abound in Revelation:

- "tribe and language and people and nation" (5:9)
- "praise and honor and glory and power" (5:13)
- "sword, and famine, and disease, and by the wild beasts" (6:8)
- "peals of thunder and rumblings and flashes of lightning and an earthquake" (8:5;16:18)
- "their murders, their witchcraft, their fornication, and their thefts" (9:21)
- "many peoples and nations and languages and kings" (10:11)
- "harps and musicians and flutists and trumpeters" (18:22)

The number four describes God's creation: the four corners of the earth, that is, the four directions of the wind (7:1; 20:8). God is the ruler both of and in his creation, which is evident in the use of the relevant expression "the one who lives forever and ever" occurring four times (4:9, 10; 10:6; 15:7).

---

4. The reference in 11:14, "the third woe is coming soon," focuses not on Jesus' return but on his judgment.

5. Richard Bauckham, *The Theology of the Book of Revelation*, New Testament Theology (Cambridge: Cambridge University Press, 1993), p. 110; and idem, *The Climax of Prophecy* (Edinburgh: Clark, 1993), p. 35. The Greek word πορνεία (fornication) also occurs seven times, but this should be interpreted in the light of the great prostitute whose sins are piled up (literally, are cleaving) to heaven (18:5) and are complete. Also the word *sickle* occurs seven times (14:14–19) to signal the completeness of divine judgment.

The number three appears frequently: three quarts of barley (6:6); three angels (8:13); three plagues of fire, smoke, and sulfur (9:18); three unclean spirits (16:13); the great city split into three parts (16:19); three gates each to the east, north, south, and west (21:13). Series of three refer to the Deity with the triple shout of the living creatures saying "Holy, holy, holy" (4:8); and a description of God's power that was, is, and is to come (4:8; see 1:4, 8). Also, note the series of Jesus Christ, God, and his servants (1:1); Jesus Christ is the faithful witness, the firstborn from the dead, and the ruler of the kings of the earth (1:5).[6] Indeed, series of three occur throughout the book.

Ten is the number of completeness in the decimal system. This number in Revelation refers to ten days of persecution (2:10); a description of the dragon with ten horns (12:3); the beast coming out of the sea with ten horns and ten crowns (13:1); and the scarlet beast that had ten horns (17:3, 7, 12, 16).

As ten is a number that relates to Satan's servants and activities, the number twelve describes the elect of the twelve tribes (7:5–8); the woman, symbolizing the church, with twelve stars on her head (12:1); and the new Jerusalem with twelve gates, twelve angels, twelve tribes of Israel (21:12). This city has twelve foundations on which the twelve names of the apostles are written (21:14); it measures in length, breadth, and height twelve thousand stadia (21:16); and along both sides of the river flowing from the throne of God is the tree of life bearing twelve crops of fruit (22:2). Also, the term *elders* (Greek *presbyteroi*) appears twelve times. In Revelation the contrast between *ten* and *twelve* is striking indeed. The number twelve describes the people of God; the number ten is linked to Satan, his followers, and his actions.

2. Contrast

Revelation is a book filled with polarities: Christ versus Satan, light versus darkness, life versus death, love versus hatred, heaven versus hell. Throughout the book, this contrast appears even in all the details. John portrays the Trinity as Father, Son, and Holy Spirit (see the commentary on 1:4, 5); by comparison Satan's trinity is the devil, the beast, and the false prophet (chapters 12, 13). The words "who is, and who was, and who is to come" (1:4, 8; 4:8) are a paraphrase of the divine name (Exod. 3:14–15). But the beast is the one who "once was, and is not, and is about to go up from the Abyss and go to his destruction" or "the beast that was and is not and will come"(17:8). Good and evil are contrasted in God the Father versus Satan the dragon (1:4 and 12:3, 9); the Son of God versus the Antichrist (1:5 and 13:1–14); the Holy Spirit versus the false prophet (1:4 and 13:11–17; 19:20); the bride of Christ versus the prostitute (19:7–8; 21:9 and 17:1–18); and Jerusalem versus Babylon (21:9–27 and 16:19).[7]

---

6. Hunter (*Studies*, p. 246) describes the number three as the divine number. See J. P. M. Sweet, *Revelation*, WPC (Philadelphia: Westminster, 1979), p. 14.

7. See Howard W. Kramer, "Contrast as a Key to Understanding *The Revelation to St. John*," *ConcJourn* 23 (1997): 108–17.

God empowers his Son with authority to do his will (1:1), while Satan gives power and authority to the beast (13:2). Jesus sits on his throne (3:21), and likewise Satan has his throne (2:13; 16:10). The Son appears as the Lamb that was slain (5:6); by contrast the seven-headed beast has one head with a fatal wound that had healed (13:3). The Lamb has seven horns and seven eyes (5:6), whereas the beast coming up out of the earth is like a lamb with two horns (13:11). Jesus reveals himself as one who died but is alive forever and ever (1:18), which is parodied by the beast coming up out of the sea that was fatally wounded yet lived (13:3, 12, 14).

Conversely, Satan, the beast, and the false prophet are thrown into the lake of fire. This is the place of eternal death, where they are tormented forever and ever (20:10, 14). Jesus holds the keys of Death and Hades (1:18); Satan holds the key of the Abyss (9:1). Jesus is victorious and "destined to ultimate triumph," but Satan, who appears to be successful, "is doomed in reality to ignominious and everlasting defeat."[8]

The kingdom of Christ and the kingdom of Satan reveal additional contrasts: believers receive the seal of the living God on their foreheads (7:2–3); unbelievers have the mark of the beast on their right hand and forehead (13:16). Believers bear the name of the Lamb and the Father on their foreheads (14:1); unbelievers have the number 666, which is the name and number of the beast (13:17–18).[9] Note also the apostles of the Lord versus the false apostles in Ephesus (18:20 and 2:2); the angels serving God versus the demons controlled by Satan (12:7–9); the victory of Christ and the saints versus the defeat of the Antichrist and his followers (19:11–21).

3. Emphasis

When we stress something in print, we use an exclamation mark or we write in italic. But these conventions were unavailable to authors in biblical times. They employed the technique of repetition to hold the reader's attention. A few examples from the Scriptures make this point clear. God called Moses to the burning bush at Mount Sinai and said, "Moses, Moses" (Exod. 3:4); Jesus told Peter about Satan's request to sift the disciples as wheat and uttered the words, "Simon, Simon" (Luke 22:31); and the risen Lord called Paul near Damascus by saying, "Saul, Saul" (Acts 9:4). The double use of a name signifies emphasis.

Jewish people resorted to repetition in order to stress the intent of a concept. They would often do so by giving two examples that conveyed the same message. In Egypt, Joseph interpreted dreams: one for the cupbearer and another for the baker (Gen. 40:8–22), and two dreams for Pharaoh (Gen. 41:1–40). Moses was given the power to perform two miracles in the presence of the Israelites: turning his staff into a snake and making his hand leprous (Exod. 4:1–7). Wisdom

8. Milligan, *Revelation of St. John*, p. 111.

9. Refer to Didier Rochat, "La vision du trône: Un clé pour pénétrer l'Apocalypse," *Hokhma* 49 (1992): 7.

literature, especially from Psalms and Proverbs, is filled with parallelism that clarifies the point the writer intends to stress. Here is one example out of many: "In the way of righteousness there is life; along that path is immortality" (Prov. 12:28).

The same principle is woven into the structure of Revelation, where we encounter repetition for the sake of emphasis. John records the words of an angel who shouts in a loud voice, "Fallen, fallen is Babylon the Great" (18:2); and the kings of the earth, the merchants, and the seafarers cry out, "Woe, woe, the great city" (18:10, 16, 19). The letter to the church at Pergamum contains these lines:

> However, I have a few things against you in that you have there those who hold the teaching of Balaam, who taught Balak to put a stumbling block before the Israelites to make them eat food offered to an idol and commit fornication. So even you have those who similarly hold the teaching of the Nicolaitans. (Rev. 2:14–15)

Jesus is not saying that he refers to two classes of people in the church at Pergamum but rather that those who have followed erroneous teachings are all the same. There is no difference between the intent of Balaam and that of the Nicolaitans. Balaam intended to defeat the Israelites through deceptive prophecy; similarly, the Nicolaitans entered the church with deceptive doctrine.[10] The two parties reveal the same intention: to conquer God's people. Likewise, the teachings of Jezebel, who calls herself a prophetess, do not differ from that of Balaam and the Nicolaitans (2:20–23).

The song of Moses and the song of the Lamb are not two different hymns but one and the same, for they extol the deeds of the Lord God Almighty (15:3–4). Both the kings of the east and the kings of the whole world launch their war against Christ and his followers (16:12, 14). When John fell at the feet of an angel to worship him, the angel told him to worship not him but God (19:10). In the last chapter of Revelation John again relates that he fell down to worship at the feet of an angel and was told to worship not him but God (22:8–9). The repetition serves to emphasize the command to worship not the creature but the Creator.

4. Repetition

The principle of repetition for emphasis and clarity is also evident in the description of the woman's flight into the desert for 1,260 days to a place God prepared for her (Rev. 12:1–6). Eight verses later we again read that she flew to the desert to a place prepared for her for a time, times, and half a time (12:14). John gives two descriptions of the same event, for the place that God prepared for her is the desert, and the length of time is the same: 1,260 days equals 42 months (11:2–3) or 3½ years. Yet there is a difference, that of the ideal and the actual. For instance, the first few verses of chapter 12 depict the scene of the glorious

---

10. The term *Nicolaitan* is a combination of the Greek verb *nikaō* (I conquer) and the noun *laos* (people); that is, conqueror of the people. Compare Bauckham, *Theology*, p. 124.

woman "clothed with the sun and the moon under her feet, and a crown of twelve stars on her head" (12:1). She is pregnant and gives birth to a son who rules with a rod of iron and is snatched up to God's throne. This scene is an ideal that points to reality that is beyond the picture itself. That reality takes form with Christ's birth and includes his ascension to God's throne. Reality is depicted in the scene of warfare in heaven when Satan, now fully identified (v. 9), is hurled to the earth with his angels. The devil realizes that his time is short; he is enraged and wages war by pursuing the woman. This woman flees to a place prepared for her, and she receives help from the earth (v. 16). The rest of her offspring—the believers—are waging a spiritual war against Satan and individually endure the brunt of his wrath (v. 17). Thus, the first scene that depicts the exalted woman is idealistic, while the second scene describing the persecuted church is realistic.

Between the first and second scenes, John placed the report on the war that Michael with his angels fought against the dragon and his angels. When the dragon, namely Satan, is hurled to the earth along with his angels, the church not only endures his anger but overcomes him by the blood of the Lamb and by the testimony of God's Word (12:10–11). The placing of this battle account between the two scenes depicting the woman is to demonstrate that "the plan of redemption shall be achieved" among people, not angels.[11]

5. Parallels

All through the Book of Revelation are parallels presented in multiples of seven. There are seven letters to the churches in Asia Minor; there are seven seals followed by seven trumpets and concluded by seven bowls. To begin with the letters to the seven churches, we note parallels in their structure. Each letter consists of seven parts:

1. The address to each of the seven churches in Asia Minor (2:1, 8, 12, 18; 3:1, 7, 14).
2. An aspect of the Lord's appearance to John at Patmos (2:1, 8, 12, 18; 3:1, 7, 14).
3. An evaluation of the spiritual health of the individual church (2:2–3, 9, 13, 19; 3:1–2, 8, 15).
4. Words of praise or reproof (2:4–6, 9, 14–15, 20; 3:1–4, 8–10, 16–17).
5. Words of exhortation (2:5, 10, 16, 21–25; 3:2–3, 11, 18–20).
6. Promises to the one who overcomes (2:7, 11, 17, 26–28; 3:5, 12, 21).
7. A command to hear what the Spirit says to the churches (2:7, 11, 17, 29; 3:6, 13, 22).

In the first three letters, the sequence of points 6 and 7 is reversed. This makes for a division of the seven into three and four letters respectively. The second point in

11. Milligan, *Revelation of St. John*, p. 122.

each case presents a single aspect of Jesus' appearance. The table below shows how John's description of Jesus in chapter 1 is repeated in the letters to the churches:

Description	First In	Repeated In
Seven stars in his right hand	1:16	2:1
the golden lampstands	1:13	2:1
The first and the last, who died and came to life again	1:17–18	2:8
The double-edged sword	1:16	2:12
Eyes as blazing fire; feet as burnished bronze	1:14–15	2:18
Seven spirits and seven stars	1:4, 16	3:1
One who holds the key	1:18	3:7
Faithful witness	1:5	3:14

Next, the seven trumpets and seven bowls show distinct parallels, first, by listing individual parts, and second, by following an identical sequence (see the discussion in chaps. 8 and 16). The sequence of the parts in the seven seals is not as pronounced as in that of the trumpets and bowls.[12] But even in the flow of the seven seals we note an emphasis on both earth and heaven. The three series of seals, trumpets, and bowls each concludes with a reference to the consummation of the world. They reveal a progression that increases in intensity from the seals to the trumpets to the bowls.[13] The sixth seal and even the seventh introduce the great day of God's wrath and the wrath of the Lamb, which no one is able to endure. All classes of people cry out to the mountains and rocks to hide them from the face of the one who sits on the throne (6:15–17). The sounding of the seventh trumpet causes the twenty-four elders to worship God and say: "The nations were angry; and your wrath has come. The time has come for judging the dead" (11:18). And last, after the seventh angel pours out his bowl, a loud voice from the throne of God says: "It is done" (16:17). The fury of God's wrath causes every mountain and island to hide from his presence. All three series not only conclude with a description of the consummation but also demonstrate parallelism. The parallels feature expressions that include *hiding, the wrath of God, mountains, earthquakes, lightning,* and *voices.* The intent of these above-mentioned three passages is to refer to the Day of Judgment, when the end has come.

6. Division

The parallelism depicted in the three sets (seals, trumpets, and bowls) suggests that the writer is not presenting a chronological sequence but rather differ-

12. Compare Dale Ralph Davis, "The Relationship between the Seals, Trumpets, and Bowls in the Book of Revelation," *JETS* 16 (1973): 149–58.

13. Jon Paulien, *Decoding Revelation's Trumpets: Literary Allusions and the Interpretation of Revelation 8:7–12,* AUSDDS 11 (Berrien Springs, Mich.: Andrews University Press, 1987), p. 342.

ent aspects of the same events. This is even more pronounced when we notice the frequent indirect and direct references to the final judgment.

- Christ is coming with the clouds (1:7).
- Judgment for sinners is imminent, while the saints surround the throne (6:16; 7:17).
- The time for judging the dead has come (11:18).
- The coming judgment is symbolized as the Judge harvesting the earth (14:15–16).
- God's wrath is poured out as a description of the final judgment (16:17–21).
- This description is even more vivid with respect to the rider on the white horse coming to judge with justice and to make war on his enemies (19:11–21).
- The judgment comes to its climax when the books are opened and each person is judged (20:11–15).

William Hendriksen calls these seven references to the final judgment "progressive parallelism [that] divides the Apocalypse in seven parts."[14]

1. Christ in the midst of the seven golden lampstands (chaps. 1–3)
2. the book with seven seals (4–7)
3. the seven trumpets of judgment (8–11)
4. the woman and the male child persecuted by the dragon and his helpers (12–14)
5. the seven bowls of wrath (15–16)
6. the fall of the great harlot and of the beasts (17–19)
7. the judgment; the new heaven and earth (20–22)

7. Conclusion

The last book in Scripture is unique in its structure. It reveals a human author whom God inspired to write Revelation. John presents sets of illustrations that convey a number of events, yet these events must be perceived as different aspects of the same sequence of occurrence. With every additional set new light is cast on the illustrations, so that the reader gains a better understanding of the message of the Apocalypse. Not John but God, who has enhanced its composition with extraordinary care, proves to be the great architect of this remarkable

14. Hendriksen, *More Than Conquerors*, pp. 21, 36. Herman Bavinck writes, "The seven seals, the seven trumpets, and the seven bowls do not constitute a chronological series but run parallel and in each case take us to the end, the final struggle of the anti-Christian power" (*The Last Things: Hope for This World and the Next*, ed. John Bolt and trans. John Vriend [Grand Rapids: Eerdmans, 1996], p. 119). See S. L. Morris, *The Drama of Christianity: An Interpretation of the Book of Revelation* (Grand Rapids: Baker, 1982), p. 29; Craig S. Keener, *Revelation*, NIVAC (Grand Rapids: Zondervan, 2000), p. 34.

book. Revelation reveals unequaled precision and planning with respect to its structure, use of numbers and figures, and choice of words. The last book in the Bible demonstrates God's handiwork from beginning to end.

B. Figurative Language

As the prophetic books and the wisdom literature of the Old Testament are filled with signs, so the last book of the New Testament has its share of symbols. Sometimes, John interprets a symbol, as in the case of "that ancient serpent called the devil, or Satan" (12:9) and the waters that John observed as "peoples and crowds and nations and languages" (17:15).[15] At other times, the setting, usage, and characteristic of a given word provide an explanation. What we need to consider is an adequate description of figurative language.

1. Description

The world is filled with symbols that may convey diverse meanings to a viewer. For example, a flag of a particular nation is a source of pride to a national of that country who, traveling abroad, suddenly spots the emblem of his or her homeland. But for a citizen of a nation that has been treated unjustly by the government and armed forces of the first-mentioned country, the sight of its flag fills him or her with aversion and disgust. The cross is a symbol that speaks volumes to a Christian but creates antipathy in peoples of many other religions. To an observer, a symbol conveys meaning that is proportionate to the direct or indirect contact he or she has had with the field that a symbol represents. Here is a dictionary definition of a symbol: "Something that stands for or suggests something else by reason of relationship, association, convention, or accidental resemblance; *esp*[*ecially*] a visible sign of something invisible."[16]

Both the Old and New Testaments are full of symbolical language that relates to a variety of classes: nature, persons and names, numbers, colors, and creatures. Let us look at each more closely.

2. Nature

God warned Adam and Eve not to eat from the tree of the knowledge of good and evil, and he placed cherubim with a flaming sword at the entrance of the Garden of Eden to guard the way to the tree of life (Gen. 2:9, 17; 3:22, 24). References to the tree of life appear not only at the beginning but also at the end of God's written revelation (Rev. 2:7; 22:2, 14, 19). The symbolic language of the

15. Merrill C. Tenney (*Interpreting Revelation* [Grand Rapids: Eerdmans, 1957], p. 187) lists ten symbols that John explains in his Apocalypse: seven stars are seven angels of the churches (1:20); seven lampstands are seven churches (1:20); seven lamps are seven spirits of God (4:5); bowls of incense are prayers of the saints (5:8); the great multitude represents the ones coming out of the great tribulation (7:13–14); the great dragon is the devil or Satan (12:9); seven heads of the beast are seven mountains (17:9); ten horns of the beast are ten kings (17:12); waters represent peoples, multitudes, nations, tongues (17:15); the woman is the great city (17:18).

16. *Webster's New Collegiate Dictionary* (Springfield, Mass.: Merriam-Webster, 1981), p. 1172.

Apocalypse is evident in 22:2, "on either side of the river was the tree of life bearing twelve kinds of fruit, according to each month of the year it gave its fruit. And the leaves of the tree were to heal the nations" (compare Ezek. 47:12).

God told Elijah to stand on Mount Sinai, for the LORD was about to pass by. A great and powerful wind blew, an earthquake shook the mountain, and a fire burned, but God was not in any of them. He appeared as a gentle whisper (1 Kings 19:11–12). The Book of Revelation is filled with symbolic expressions relating to nature, including a strong wind (6:13; 7:1), an earthquake (8:5; 11:19; 16:18), a consuming fire (8:7; 20:9), and a period of silence (8:1).

Jesus instituted the sacrament of baptism with water and that of the Lord's Supper with bread and wine. His broken body and shed blood symbolize that the believer is forgiven, reconciled to God, and a partaker of eternal riches and glory. In his teaching about the law, Jesus used the symbol of the yoke (Matt. 11:30). And when Paul describes the Christian's spiritual armor, he refers to shoes of the gospel of peace, the belt of truth, the breastplate of righteousness, the shield of faith, the sword of the Spirit, the helmet of salvation, and communication in the Spirit (Eph. 6:13–18). The writer of the Apocalypse resorts to the symbolism of a voice like a trumpet (4:1), a sea of glass (4:6), the sky rolled up like a scroll (6:14), and a river of the water of life (22:1).

3. Persons and Names

The New Testament often employs names not to refer to persons as such but to their status, significance, and work. To illustrate, Abraham personifies the father of all believers and Moses personifies the law of God (Luke 13:16; 19:9; 24:27). Moses and Elijah are with Jesus on the Mount of Transfiguration, where Moses embodies the law and Elijah the prophets (Matt. 17:1–8). Paul designates Adam as the father of the human race (Rom. 5:14; 1 Cor. 15:22, 45), and James portrays Job as the embodiment of perseverance (James 5:11).

John's Revelation records names that illustrate faithfulness (Antipas; 2:13), deceit (Balaam; 2:14), and seduction (Jezebel; 2:20). He mentions Sodom and Egypt as symbols of immorality and slavery respectively (11:8). For him, Mount Zion is the symbol of the new Jerusalem, which comes down out of heaven as God's dwelling place with his people (Rev. 14:1; 21:2–3).

4. Numbers

We have already discussed certain numbers, but to be complete we also should look at the significance of individual numbers.[17] Thus, the number *one* denotes unity, which for the Jews was codified in their creed: "Hear, O

17. For a detailed study on the symbolic significance of numbers in Revelation, see James L. Resseguie, *Revelation Unsealed: A Narrative Critical Approach to John's Apocalypse*, BIS 32 (Leiden: Brill, 1998), pp. 48–69; Adela Yarbro Collins, "Numerical Symbolism in Jewish and Early Apocalyptic Literature," *ANRW*, II.21.2, pp. 1221–87.

Israel: the LORD our God, the LORD is one" (Deut. 6:4). *Two* is the number of persons needed to validate a testimony in a court of law; in the Apocalypse (11:3) two witnesses are God's representatives of the church on earth. The number *three* describes the triune God (1:4–5). *Four* refers to God's creation as is evident from the four directions of the winds and the four seasons of the year. *Five* is a round number and as such does not have much symbolic significance. Thus, five months (9:5, 10) means a period of indefinite duration. *Six* symbolizes Satan's reaching for completeness but always failing to achieve it; hence the number of the beast is a triple six (Rev. 13:18). Everywhere in Scripture, but especially in the Apocalypse, *seven* signifies completeness.[18] The number *ten* depicts fullness in the decimal system, the number *twelve* exemplifies perfection,[19] and the number *one thousand* intimates a multitude. Hence, the figure *12,000 stadia* describing the length, width, and height of the new Jerusalem relates to perfection in the form of a cube (21:16).[20] A cube has twelve edges, that is, four at the top and four at the bottom with four on the sides. An edge measures 12,000 stadia, which times twelve equals 144,000 stadia. The thickness or height of the city walls is 144 cubits, which is the square of twelve. Last, the twelve tribes of Israel each consisting of 12,000 make a total of 144,000 (7:4–8), which is also the number of the redeemed who stand before the Lamb (14:1, 3).[21]

John saw the number of mounted troops destroyed by four angels to be 200,000,000 (9:16). This number symbolizes an incalculable army of men and horses designated as the forces opposed to God, his Anointed, and his people. The angels are released to destroy these forces, so that a third of mankind is killed. The author's use of the expression "time, times and a half a time" (12:14) accords with 42 months and 1,260 days (11:2, 3; 12:6; 13:5). The expression "time, times and a half a time" derives from Daniel 7:25, which refers to a period of three and a half years. The numbers clearly convey a symbolic message, for no one is able to pinpoint the exact date of fulfillment.

18. The concept *seven* is prominent in the Old Testament: the word *good* occurs seven times in Genesis 1; God created a week of seven days. Seven priests blowing seven trumpets had to walk around the city of Jericho on the seventh day seven times (Josh. 6:4). And Daniel speaks of seven "sevens" (9:25).

19. Philo (*On Rewards and Punishments* 65) affirms that the number twelve as in the twelve tribes of Israel is "the perfect number."

20. Consult Sweet, *Revelation*, p. 15. Homer Hailey (*Revelation: An Introduction and Commentary* [Grand Rapids: Baker, 1979], pp. 46–47) calls the number twelve "a religious or spiritual idea." Gregory K. Beale (*The Book of Revelation: A Commentary on the Greek Text*, NIGTC [Grand Rapids: Eerdmans, 1998], p. 61) points out that this number occurs twelve times in the portrayal of the new Jerusalem (21:9–22:5).

21. Compare Henry Barclay Swete, *Commentary on Revelation: The Greek Text with Introduction, Notes, and Indexes* (1911; reprint, Grand Rapids: Kregel, 1977), p. cxxxv. He lists the numbers that occur in Revelation: 2, 3, 3½, 4, 5, 6, 7, 10, 12, 24, 42, 144, 666 (or 616), 1000, 1260, 1600, 7000, 12,000, 144,000, 100,000,000, and 200,000,000.

5. Colors

The shades of color that John mentions in Revelation are white,[22] red (6:4; 12:3), scarlet (17:3, 4; 18:12, 16), black (6:5, 12), pale and green (6:8; 8:7), blue (9:17), yellow (9:17), and purple (17:4; 18:12, 16). Gold is another color; it appears in this book numerous times either as a descriptive adjective or a noun.

For some of the colors mentioned in Scripture, the context appears to supply a symbolic meaning. For instance, white is the color that denotes holiness, purity, victory, and justice. God told the people of Israel: "Though your sins are like scarlet, they shall be as white as snow" (Isa. 1:18; see Ps. 51:7); at his transfiguration, Jesus' clothes became dazzling white (Mark 9:3); and the angel of the Lord at Jesus' tomb was dressed in white apparel (Matt. 28:3). Likewise, in Revelation, the robes of the saints in heaven are white (4:4; 6:11; 7:9, 13, 14; compare 3:4, 5, 18). The rider on the white horse is victorious and is accompanied by angels dressed in white garments and riding on white horses (6:2; 19:11, 14). The Son of Man, seated on a white cloud with a crown of gold on his head and a sickle in his hand, appears as a victorious conqueror who reaps a harvest (14:14); and last, the color of God's throne is white to express judgment and justice (20:11).

Red is the color of warfare, as is plain from the blood shed on the earth when the rider on the red horse wields his large sword (6:4). The red dragon is poised to kill the male child at birth and wages war against the archangel Michael and his angels (12:3, 7–9).

Black depicts famine, as illustrated by the highly inflated price for food: "A quart of wheat for a denarius [the daily wage of a workman] and three quarts of barley for a denarius, but do not damage the oil and the wine" (6:6). It also signifies darkness, when the sun fails to give its light (Isa. 13:10; Matt. 24:29; Rev. 6:12).

Of the colors John mentions in Revelation, white, red, and black are notable. Whereas purple attests to wealth (18:16), gold connotes heaven's perfection (21:18, 21).[23] Other colors occur infrequently in this book, and their contexts fail to clarify their use.

6. Creatures

From the animal world John has selected numerous representatives to illustrate certain concepts. The four-footed animals are a horse for riding purposes (6:2–9), a lamb for slaughter (5:6), a lion for its devouring mouth (13:2), a bear for its powerful feet (13:2), an ox for its strength (4:7), and a leopard for its speed (13:2). The reptiles are a serpent representing Satan (12:9, 15; 20:2), a scorpion because of its sting (9:3, 5, 10), and frogs to depict evil spirits (16:13). The birds are the vultures that gorge themselves on cadavers (19:17–18) and the eagle for its extended wingspan (8:13). The insects are represented by the lo-

22. Rev. 1:14 (twice); 2:17; 3:4, 5, 18; 4:4; 6:2, 11; 7:9, 13, 14; 14:14; 19:11, 14 (twice); 20:11.

23. Among others see Gervais T. D. Angel, *NIDNTT*, 1:205; and Joyce G. Baldwin, *NIDNTT*, 2:96.

custs to portray a plague (9:3). All these creatures in their own way add to the symbolism of Revelation.

7. Conclusion

No other book in the New Testament as the Book of Revelation has as many occurrences of the concept *great,* expressed by the Greek word *megas* and translated variously as "loud," "huge," and "intense." What John sees can be depicted only in terms of size, volume, intensity, and importance: angels with loud voices so that every creature is able to hear them (e.g., 6:10); huge hailstones weighing a hundred pounds each (16:21); intense heat (16:9); great authority (18:1); and Babylon the Great (18:2).

Nevertheless, not every detail is symbolic and in need of interpretation. Explaining the content of Revelation, we keep in mind the central message of a passage and consider details as pictorial and descriptive. The message is primary, the details secondary. Unless the message demands an interpretation of the individual parts, we should refrain from looking for a deeper meaning for each component.[24] Not all the information in the Apocalypse is symbolic. If the writer states that the grass is green (8:7) and that a breastplate is red, blue, and yellow (9:17), he merely describes the objects. When words like *green, blue,* or *yellow* occur only once in a given context, we have no basis to suspect symbolical language. Other passages relate to history, such as the author's exile on the island of Patmos (1:9); the Lord's Day (1:10); the letters to the seven churches (chapters 2 and 3); and the concluding verses of chapter 22. An allusion to history occurs in the birth of the male child that is snatched up to heaven (12:5). John presents the rest of the Apocalypse in visions introduced by the repetitive phrase *I saw.*

The conclusion we must draw is that the numbers, images, and expressions of greatness must be interpreted as symbols that present the idea of totality, fullness, and perfection. Much of John's symbolism derives from the Old Testament Scriptures and from the ecclesiastical context in which he spent his time. Let us note that the Jewish mind of the first century received and presented information by means of pictures, illustrations, and symbols. By contrast, the Greek mind of that era dealt with abstract concepts that it analyzed and explained with clear verbal exactness. Although John had spent considerable time in a Greek environment and wrote his book in the Greek language, his composition reflects an Eastern mindset that communicates revelation with the aid of pictorial images. The Hebrew mind sees God as a fortress, a rock, a shield, and a stronghold (Ps. 18:2). And these images must be viewed in their totality and not with respect to each individual detail. John writes the Apocalypse from an Old Testament perspective.

24. Hendriksen, *More Than Conquerors,* p. 40.

C. Scripture Based

By one count, the four hundred and four verses in Revelation divulge some five hundred allusions to the Old Testament.[25] To be precise, there are fourteen incomplete quotes from the Old Testament (a doublet occurs in 7:17 and 21:4). The verses from Revelation appear below, with the quoted portion in italics:

- 1:7 "Look, *he is coming with the clouds*, and every eye will see him and *those who pierced* him, *and all the tribes of the earth will mourn because of him*" (Dan. 7:13; Zech. 12:10).
- 2:27 *"He will rule them with an iron rod and as* the *earthen vessels are broken to pieces"* (Ps. 2:9).
- 4:8 *"Holy, holy, holy, Lord God Almighty"* (Isa. 6:3; Amos 3:13 LXX).
- 6:16 *"And they said to the mountains and to the rocks, 'Fall on us* and *hide us'"* (Hos. 10:8).
- 7:16 *"And they will neither hunger nor thirst* anymore *neither will the sun beat down on them nor* any *scorching heat"* (Isa. 49:10).
- 7:17 *"And God will wipe away every tear from* their *eyes"* (Isa. 25:8).
- 11:11 "The *breath of life* from God *entered them and they stood on their feet*" (Ezek. 37:5, 10).
- 14:5 "And *in their mouth is found no* lie" (Zeph. 3:13; Isa. 53:9).
- 15:3a "*Great and marvelous are your works*, Lord God Almighty" (Ps. 111:2).
- 15:3b *"Just and true are your ways, King of the nations"* (Deut. 32:4; Ps. 145:17; Jer. 10:7).
- 15:4 "*Who does not fear you,* O Lord, and glorify your name? For you alone are holy. *All the nations will come and worship before you*" (Jer. 10:7; Ps. 86:9).
- 19:15 "And *he will shepherd them with an iron rod*" (Ps. 2:9).
- 20:9 *"Fire came down from heaven and devoured them"* (2 Kings 1:10, 12).
- 21:4 *"And God will wipe away every tear from* their *eyes"* (Isa. 25:8).
- 21:7 *"I will be a God to him, and he will be a son to me"* (2 Sam. 7:14).

John alludes to nearly every book in the Old Testament canon. Most of the references come from the Psalms, Isaiah, Ezekiel, and Daniel. In addition, there are the five books of Moses; the historical books of Joshua, Judges, 1–2 Samuel, 1–2 Kings, 1–2 Chronicles, Ezra, Nehemiah, and Esther; the wisdom literature of Job, Proverbs, Song of Songs; the prophet Jeremiah; Lamentations; and all

25. Nes-Al[27], UBS[4]. Swete (*Revelation*, p. cxl) and Bruce M. Metzger (*Breaking the Code: Understanding the Book of Revelation* [Nashville: Abingdon, 1993], p. 13) note that of the 404 verses in the Apocalypse 278 verses allude to an Old Testament passage. Ferrell Jenkins counts 348 quotations and allusions in Revelation. See his *Old Testament in the Book of Revelation* (Grand Rapids: Baker, 1972), p. 24. See the tabulation by Jan Fekkes in his *Isaiah and Prophetic Traditions in the Book of Revelation*, JSNTSup 93 (Sheffield: JSOT, 1994), p. 62. Steve Moyise (*The Old Testament in the Book of Revelation*, JSNTSup 115 [Sheffield: Sheffield Academic Press, 1995], p. 14) asserts that "Revelation . . . does not contain a single quotation." And Elisabeth Schüssler Fiorenza (*The Book of Revelation: Justice and Judgment* [Philadelphia: Fortress, 1985], p. 135) states that Revelation never quotes the Old Testament.

the minor prophets except Haggai. Apart from Ruth, Ecclesiastes, and Haggai, John alludes to every book in the Old Testament.

John alludes to the New Testament in every chapter of his book. To illustrate, Jesus mentions the devil and his angels being cursed and consigned to eternal fire (Matt. 25:41); John refers to the dragon or devil and his angels being cast out of heaven and hurled to the earth (12:7–9; compare Luke 10:18). The author was familiar with most books of the New Testament, chiefly the Gospels, Acts, many of Paul's epistles, Hebrews, and the epistles of James, Peter, John, and Jude. He was also acquainted with apocryphal literature: 2 Maccabees, Tobit, 2 Baruch, Sirach, Wisdom of Solomon, and the Psalms of Solomon.

We do not expect that in exile on Patmos John had access to all the scrolls of biblical and extrabiblical literature. Nor do we expect that John rolled and unrolled a particular scroll to find passages for the writing of his Revelation. Instead, we infer from his allusions and incomplete quotations in the Apocalypse that he relied on his memory for the teachings of the Scriptures. From beginning to end, the entire fabric of Revelation is laced with thoughts and expressions taken from God's written Word. In it we see the artistic handiwork of God, the primary author of the Bible. John serves him as the secondary author filled with the Holy Spirit to pen the last volume of the canon.

The last book in the New Testament is also known as a doxological volume, for it lists numerous hymns and songs grounded in the Scriptures. They are the hymns sung by the four living creatures (4:8); the twenty-four elders (4:10–11); the creatures and the elders (5:9–10); the angels (5:12); all living beings (5:13); the great multitude (7:10); the angels, elders, and creatures (7:12); saints in white robes (7:15–17); the seventh angel (11:15); the twenty-four elders (11:16–18); the victorious saints (15:2–4); the third angel and a voice from the altar (16:5–6, 7); an angel with great authority (18:1–3); another heavenly voice (18:4–8); a vast multitude of angels and saints (19:1–3); the twenty-four elders and a voice from the throne (19:4, 5); and a great multitude (19:6–8).

We conclude that Revelation is truly the capstone of the entire canon of Scripture. As such the book must be seen in the light of the rest of the Bible. The Apocalypse unveils the teachings of God's Word by focusing attention on the coming of the Messiah. The first coming of the Christ is symbolized in the birth of the male child who was snatched up to heaven (12:5, 13). But fulfillment of Jesus' Second Coming is nowhere indicated. The book lists the promise of his return and the fervent plea of the Spirit and the bride (the church) for him to come quickly (22:7, 12, 17, 20).

D. Author

1. External Evidence

Nowhere in the Gospel of John is there any reference to John the son of Zebedee, Jesus' faithful disciple and apostle. Similarly, the three epistles attributed to John omit the name of the beloved disciple, although in two of them the writer refers to himself as "the elder" (2 John 1, 3 John 1). We could say that the author excludes his personal name out of modesty and refers to himself only as "the elder" because of his advanced age. But in Revelation the author is not afraid to use his personal name, for he identifies himself four times as John (1:1, 4, 9; 22:8). Could one and the same person pen literature of three different genres: Gospel, Epistle, and Apocalypse? The word choice, language, and diction of the Gospel and the Epistle are quite similar but that of the Apocalypse is completely dissimilar to the other writings.

Who is the author of Revelation? The New Testament lists at least five people with the name John: John the Baptist, John the son of Zebedee, Simon Peter's father (John 21:15–17), John Mark (Acts 12:12), and John who belonged to the high priest's family (Acts 4:6). The name was common in Judaism and in Hebrew was Yohanan and in Greek Ioannes or Ioanes. Could there be two different people with the same name responsible for the writing of the Johannine literature? The early church fathers ascribed the Book of Revelation to John the apostle. Thus, Justin Martyr in the first part of the second century (about 135) wrote, "There was a certain man with us, whose name was John, one of the apostles of Christ, who prophesied, by a revelation that was made to him."[26] The author of the Muratorian Fragment, dated approximately 175, attributed Revelation to John, whom he considered to be the apostle. About 180, Irenaeus commented that he knew of persons who had seen the author of the Apocalypse. We surmise that the persons he had in mind were Papias and Polycarp, disciples of the apostle John.[27] He also mentioned that John wrote during the reign of Emperor Domitian (81–96). And Melito, the bishop of Sardis and contemporary of Irenaeus, composed a no-longer extant commentary on the Apocalypse of John. Writers in the first few decades of the third century (Clement of Alexandria, Tertullian, Origen, Hippolytus, and Cypriot) credit the apostle John with the authorship of Revelation. In brief, support is strong for Johannine authorship from early writers of the second to the middle of the third century. Attacks on the integrity of Revelation in that era by the Alogi of Asia Minor and the followers of Gaius in Rome are insignificant.[28]

In the third century, Dionysius of Alexandria, who was active from 231 to 264, questioned the firmly established authorship of John the apostle. He had traveled to Ephesus, where he heard of two graves that were claimed as the burial places of John. He assumed that one of these belonged to the presbyter John

26. Justin Martyr *Dialogue with Trypho* 81, in *The Ante-Nicene Fathers,* ed. Alexander Roberts and James Donaldson, vol. 1, *The Apostolic Fathers, Justin Martyr, and Irenaeus* (reprint, Grand Rapids: Eerdmans, n.d.), p. 240. Note that the elapsed time between John's death (presumably in A.D. 98) and Justin Martyr's comment is less then forty years, when eyewitnesses could still testify to the veracity of his statement. Irenaeus (Eusebius *Eccl. Hist.* 3.39.5–6) writes that the apostle John lived "until the times of Trajan," who was emperor from 98 to 117.

27. See Irenaeus *Against Heresies* 3.11.3; 4.20.11; 4.35.2; 5.30.1; and Eusebius *Eccl. Hist.* 5.8.5.

28. Consult Swete, *Revelation,* p. cxiv. Ned B. Stonehouse (*The Apocalypse in the Ancient Church* [Goes, Netherlands: Oosterbaan & Le Cointre, 1929], p. 71), after examining the opposition from the Alogi and the Gaius party, concludes that there is no proof of any evidence of opposition to the Apocalypse in Asia Minor during the second century.

and the other to the apostle by that same name. Dionysius found no reference to apostolic authorship in Revelation. He studied the word choice, diction, style, and language of the Apocalypse, compared it with the Gospel and Epistles of John, and concluded that not the apostle but John the Elder was the author of this book. He did so on the basis of a statement made by Papias more than a century earlier[29] and later cited by Eusebius (*Eccl. Hist.* 3.39.4) in 325:

> But if ever anyone came who had followed the presbyters, I inquired into the words of the presbyters, what Andrew or Peter or Philip or Thomas or James or John or Matthew, or any other of the Lord's disciples, had said, and what Aristion and the presbyter John, the Lord's disciples, were saying. For I did not suppose that information from books would help me so much as the word of a living and surviving voice.[30]

The Greek clearly indicates that Papias uses the past tense (*had said*) to describe the apostles who had passed on and the present tense (*were* [lit., *are*] *saying*) for those who were still living. With the repetition of the phrase *the presbyter John*, Papias wants to communicate that he is thinking of the same person, namely, John the disciple and apostle of the Lord, who was the only one of the twelve apostles still alive.

There is more. In the early church, a particular chiliastic view met opposition: some writers, including Papias, Justin Martyr, and Irenaeus, held to the view of a thousand-year millennial reign of the Lord on this earth. But the Alexandrian leaders Dionysius and Eusebius rejected this teaching.[31] They repudiated the chiliastic view, and Eusebius in particular cast aspersions on Papias's character. What does this have to do with the authorship of Revelation? It lent support to the assumption that the author of the Apocalypse was not the apostle but the presbyter John. To Dionysius's credit, we note that he regarded this presbyter as "holy and inspired."[32] But his argument is weakened by his own statement that there were other persons in the province of Asia who bore the name John. He claims, "I hold that there have been many persons of the same name as John the apostle, who for the love they bore him . . . were glad to take also the same name after him."[33] But writ-

29. Papias composed a five-volume series *Interpretation of the Sayings of the Lord* in the years A.D. 95 to 110. The works are no longer extant, but fragments are preserved in the *Ecclesiastical History* of Eusebius. Robert W. Yarbrough, "The Date of Papias: A Reassessment," *JETS* 26 (1983): 181–91; Robert H. Gundry, *Matthew* (Grand Rapids: Eerdmans, 1982), pp. 610–11; John Wenham, *Redating Matthew, Mark, and Luke* (London: Hodder and Stoughton, 1991), p. 122.

30. *Eusebius: Ecclesiastical History*, trans. Kirsopp Lake and J. E. L. Oulton, 2 vols., LCL (Cambridge, Mass.: Harvard University Press, 1926–32), 1:293.

31. Eusebius *Eccl. Hist.* 3.39.12–13; 7.24.1. See Gerhard Maier, *Die Offenbarung und die Kirche*, WUNT 25 (Tübingen: Mohr, 1981), p. 107; Stonehouse, *Apocalypse in the Ancient Church*, p. 133; Compare Charles E. Hill, *Regnum Caelorum: Patterns of Future Hope in Early Christianity* (Oxford: Clarendon,1992).

32. Consult Eusebius *Eccl. Hist.* 7.25.7.

33. Ibid. 7.25.14.

ers in the early centuries of the Christian era know nothing of someone bearing the name John the Apostle, except the son of Zebedee. In addition, Dionysius's argument is weakened still further because he received the information on the two graves from hearsay.

The early church fathers are unable to confirm that a person called John the Presbyter existed. In fact, Dionysius expresses only an assumption, "But I think that there was a certain other [John] among those that were in Asia."[34] By contrast, we believe that the only person named John who could address the churches with the authority revealed in the Apocalypse is John, the apostle of Jesus Christ. Near the end of the fourth century, Jerome ascribes the last two epistles of John not to the apostle but to the presbyter; yet he affirms that the apostle wrote both the Gospel and the Apocalypse.[35] Further, in his advanced age, John could either identify himself as "the elder" (see 2 John 1; 3 John 1) or use his given name as he does in Revelation. No one but John could claim unchallenged authority in the church near the end of the first century.

The external evidence remains firm, because the criticism of Dionysius rests chiefly on the dogmatic basis of the millennial dispute, a multiplicity of people with the name John, and an unconfirmed report concerning two graves purportedly belonging to John.

2. Internal Evidence

Three times in chapter 1 (vv. 1, 4, 9) and once in chapter 22 (v. 8) the author identifies himself as John. He speaks as a person with unquestionable authority who is well known to all the churches in the province of Asia (western Turkey). Banished to the rocky island of Patmos to the west of the port city Miletus (near Ephesus), the writer uses only the name John. In his banishment, he pens the last book of the canon in an Aramaic type of Greek. For the question concerning the time of John's exile, consult the section on the date of the Apocalypse.

If we presume that John wrote his work near the end of Domitian's reign in 95, we infer that he himself was elderly. It may be that in his old age he reverted increasingly to using his mother tongue, Aramaic. When bilingual or multilingual people become old, they often resort to speaking their native tongue. John is no exception. An objection to this theory is that John's Gospel and Epistles, composed a few years prior to the Apocalypse, reveal acceptably good Greek free from the unusual constructions found in Revelation. But notice the difference in genre: the Gospel is a straightforward account of the life and teachings of Jesus, but Revelation is an unveiling of heavenly scenes. Com-

34. Ibid. 7.25.16.

35. Jerome *De viris illustribus* 9. Many scholars hold that one author composed all three epistles and that the verbal similarities in John's Gospel and Epistles unmistakably point to the same writer. But Gerhard A. Krodel (*Revelation*, ACNT [Minneapolis: Augsburg, 1989], pp. 61–62) writes, "Modern scholarship in general agrees with Dionysius but assigns the authorship of all Johannine writings to persons (plural) other than the apostle John."

ments William Hendriksen, "In this connection, let us not forget that when John wrote the last book of the Bible, his soul was in such a condition of deep, inner emotion, surprise and ecstasy (for he was 'in the Spirit'), that his earlier, Jewish training may have exerted itself more forcibly and may even have influenced his style and language."[36]

We suspect that in Ephesus, where John composed the Gospel and the Epistles, he had capable scribes to assist him. Employing scribes in the writing of letters and documents was a common practice during the first century, for Paul and Peter even mention their amanuenses by name: Paul refers to Tertius (Rom. 16:22) and Peter mentions Silas (1 Pet. 5:12). But as an exile, John was alone and had to rely on his own authorial ability and thus wrote Greek unaided by native speakers.

The vocabulary of Revelation differs strikingly from that of the rest of John's writings, and this point is crucial in regard to the question of authorship. Comparing the Gospel of John with the Apocalypse, Dionysius of Alexandria rightly commented that while the Gospel and the Epistles of John had much in common, this could not be said of the Gospel and the Apocalypse. He wrote, "But the Apocalypse is utterly different from, and foreign to, these writings; it scarcely, so to speak, has even a syllable in common with them."[37] This is a gross exaggeration, however, for substantiating evidence can be shown that there are many similarities. The expression *the Word of God* (19:13) is an indisputable reference to the introductory verse of the Fourth Gospel, "In the beginning was the Word, and the Word was with God, and the Word was God" (John 1:1). And a succession of terms in both Gospel and Apocalypse are the same:

- water of life (John 4:10, 11; 7:38; Rev. 21:6; 22:1, 17)
- vine (John 15:1, 4, 5; Rev. 14:18, 19)
- shepherd (John 10:11; Rev. 7:17)
- overcome (John 16:33; Rev. 2:7, 11, 17, 26; 3:5, 12, 21; 21:7)
- light (John 1:4, 5, 7, 8, 9, et al.; Rev. 18:23; 21:24; 22:5)
- love (John 13:35; 15:9, 10, 13; 17:26; Rev. 2:4, 19)
- to witness (John 1:7, 8, 15, 32, 34, et al.; Rev. 1:2; 22:16, 18, 20)

In his zeal to disclaim apostolic authorship for the Apocalypse, Dionysius has overstated his case and severely impaired his argument.[38] Swete writes, "Of the 913 words used in the Apocalypse 416 are found also in the Gospel, but the words common to both books are either of the most ordinary type, or are shared by other N[ew] T[estament] writers."[39] Differences concern such matters as the

36. Hendriksen, *More Than Conquerors*, p. 12.

37. Eusebius *Eccl. Hist.* 7.25.22.

38. For a detailed discussion on the vocabulary differences listed by Dionysius, see Robert L. Thomas, *Revelation 1–7: An Exegetical Commentary* (Chicago: Moody, 1992), pp. 5–7.

39. Swete, *Revelation*, p. cxxvii.

spelling of the term *Jerusalem* and a synonym for the word *lamb.*[40] They are insignificant, because they convey the same idea.[41]

Of greater divergence is the style of John's Gospel and the Apocalypse. Dionysius of Alexandria compared the style of each book and commented that the Gospel was "written in faultless Greek" that illustrated John's "greatest literary skill" with respect to diction, reasoning, and constructions. And concerning the author of Revelation he wrote: "I observe his style and that the use of the Greek language is not accurate, but that he employs barbarous idioms, in some places committing downright solecisms."[42] Dionysius was the first of many writers to note grammatical inconsistencies and rough structural breaks in the Apocalypse.[43] These solecisms are obvious in the Greek text but in translations fail to appear. They are grammatical errors: first, of the nominative case that follows the preposition *apo* (from) which governs the genitive case: "from him who is and who was and who is to come" (1:4). Next, the nominative case stands in apposition to other cases, as is evident in the greeting, "from Jesus Christ, the faithful witness" (1:5). Here, the Greek preposition governs the genitive case of the nouns *Jesus Christ;* but the next three words that should have been in the genitive are instead in the nominative case. And third, although in translation we notice no break in the sentence "To him who loves us and set us free from our sins by his blood, and made us a kingdom" (1:5b-6a), in Greek the author writes two participles *loves* and *set* followed by a finite verb *made.* These are just the first few inconsistencies of numerous others in the rest of Revelation.[44]

These discrepancies are not a case of ignorance or a lapse of memory but must be ascribed to John's deliberate intent. To illustrate, the writer breaks the grammatical rule of presenting the genitive case after the preposition *apo* in 1:4, but in the next clause, "and from the seven spirits that are before his throne," he correctly writes the genitive. Indeed, he uses this preposition thirty-one times in the Apocalypse, and in every instance it is written correctly, with the exception of the above-mentioned clause. We must conclude that John deliberately writes Aramaic Greek to approximate Hebrew idiom even to the point of breaking Greek grammatical rules.[45] Hence, the phrase *from him who is* relates to the structure of the Hebrew verb "I am" (Exod. 3:14;

40. The Fourth Gospel twice features the Greek word *amnos* (lamb, John 1:29, 36) spoken by John the Baptist, and once it has the term *arnion* (lamb, John 21:15) uttered by Jesus. This first word is absent in Revelation, but the second occurs there twenty-eight times referring to Jesus and once to the beast (13:11). We assume that this second term was precious to the apostle.

41. R. H. Charles, *A Critical and Exegetical Commentary on the Revelation of St. John*, ICC (Edinburgh: Clark, 1920), 1:xxx–xxxi. Charles lists some examples, and Swete (*Revelation*, p. cxxii) notes that *hapax legomena* are few.

42. Eusebius *Eccl. Hist.* 7.25.25–26.

43. "The Greek of the *Apocalypse* differs in an extraordinary degree from that of the Fourth Gospel. Not only does it display a greater freedom in copiousness of vocabulary and elaborate phraseology; it is simply defiant of the restraints of grammar." James Hope Moulton, *A Grammar of New Testament Greek*, vol. 2, part 1 (Edinburgh: Clark, 1908), p. 33.

44. Swete (pp. cxxiii–cxxiv) presents a list of peculiarities. So does Ernest B. Allo, *Saint Jean l'Apocalypse*, Études bibliques (Paris: Gabalda, 1921), pp. cxxxv–cxlvii.

45. Milligan (*Revelation of St. John*, p. 255) notes thirty-nine occurrences in the Apocalypse.

John 8:58). In fact, the Greek translation of the Old Testament has this expression *ho eimi ho ōn* (I am the one who is [Exod. 3:14 LXX]). And in the Greek text of Psalm 118:26 (117:26 LXX) the expression *ho erchomenos* (the one who is coming) appears. The saying "who is, who was, who is to come," with the addition of "the Almighty," occurs as a fourfold attestation of God's deity, eternity, presence, and power (1:8; 4:8). These four names of God are in John's mind as indeclinable nouns, not from a Greek perspective but from a Semitic standpoint.[46] And last, Jewish people were familiar with interpreting the Hebrew Bible aided by Aramaic Targums in synagogue worship. There the rabbi interpreted the Pentateuch and the Prophets from the Targums, Aramaic translations of the Old Testament Scriptures.[47]

The author of the Apocalypse has an enviable knowledge of the Old Testament Scriptures, and he reflects it in the style of this last book of the canon. Steeped in the wording of the Old Testament prophets, John purposely adopts their mode of expression even when it results in faulty Greek grammar.

3. Characteristics

John's literary works disclose certain characteristics of relatedness. One example of stylistic similarity is the coordinate clauses in John's literature. That is, while Luke generally composes his Gospel and Acts in a subordinate style of several clauses, John adopts a coordinate style of short and simple clauses that often begin with the conjunction *and.* This is true especially in the narrative sections of the Gospel and throughout Revelation.[48] John reflects a Semitic style of writing and Luke a Hellenistic one that at times borders on classical Greek.

Johannine literature in all three genres (Gospel, Epistles, and Revelation) displays a remarkable similarity in structure. A characteristic relevant to some parts of the Gospel is a spiral approach to the material at hand. An example is the Prologue, in which John develops a continuous theme by repeating his description of the *Logos* (the Word), as is evident in 1:1 and 14; his reference to John who came to testify in 1:6–9 and 15a; and the coming of Christ in 1:10–11 and 15b–17. The same spiral configuration marks the so-called farewell discourses of Jesus (chapters 14–17). For example, John writes about the Holy Spirit, who is the Counselor and the Spirit of truth sent in Jesus' name by the Father (John 14:16, 26). He repeats this information in the two succeeding chapters (John 15:26; 16:7, 13). With repetitive phraseology and increasing crescendo he writes about the Father-Son relationship, culminating with Jesus' high priestly prayer in chap-

46. Ruurd Jan van der Meulen, *De Openbaring in het Laatste Bijbelboek* (Utrecht: Den Boer, 1948), p. 17. Martin Kiddle (*The Revelation of St. John,* MNTC [London: Hodder and Stoughton, 1940], p. 7) writes, "Even a paraphrase of the name of the unchanging name of God must be preserved from declension."

47. Bruce K. Waltke, "The Textual Criticism of the Old Testament," in *Biblical Criticism: Historical, Literary and Textual,* ed. R. K. Harrison, B. K. Waltke, D. Guthrie, and G. D. Fee (Grand Rapids: Zondervan, 1978), p. 72. See also Sweet, *Revelation,* p. 40.

48. See Vern S. Poythress, "Johannine Authorship and the Use of Intersentence Conjunctions in the Book of Revelation," *WTJ* 47 (1985): 329–36.

ter 17. In John's First Epistle, we also notice a spiral approach in the composition. The concepts *sin* and *love* exemplify this spiraling style. Finally, the Apocalypse is filled with reiteration of themes.[49] For one, think of the repetitive elements in the seven letters, the seven trumpets, and the seven plagues.

The characteristics in the Johannine works are unique and seem to point to one and the same author. They form a substructure on which each individual genre is built and which hint at an identification of their author. We realize that not every question has been answered and not every problem has been addressed, yet that which has been presented aids us in establishing the identity of the writer of the Apocalypse.

4. Conclusion

In modern times many scholars have rejected the apostolic authorship of Revelation.[50] They do so, among other things, on the basis of the different genres with respect to the Fourth Gospel and the Apocalypse. Can one author compose books of different genres? The answer is affirmative and can be proved with many examples from both ancient and modern times, to mention only the works of C. S. Lewis.[51] In addition, we note that John's Apocalypse is unlike other Jewish apocalypses in regard to authorship: apocalypses are pseudonymous, but by his own testimony John is the author of Revelation. He prophesies not in the name of someone else, but in his own name. Comments Donald Guthrie, "[This was] a departure from tradition which could have arisen only through the conviction that the spirit of prophecy had once again become active and that there was no need for pseudonymous devices."[52] And Leonhard Goppelt concurs,

---

49. Refer to Schüssler Fiorenza, *Revelation*, p. 171.

50. Sweet (*Revelation*, p. 37) writes, "Most modern scholars hold, with Dionysius, that the author could not have written the Gospel and Epistles as well." And Wilfrid J. Harrington (*Revelation*, SP 16 [Collegeville, Minn.: Liturgical Press, 1993], p. 9) states, "Today it is widely accepted, or at least seriously argued, that any linkage of Revelation with the Fourth Gospel is, at best, tenuous." Concerning the view of Dionysius, Leon Morris (*Revelation*, rev. ed., TNTC [Leicester: Inter-Varsity; Grand Rapids: Eerdmans, 1987], p. 29) correctly observes: "Later scholars have scarcely done more than repeat and elaborate the position he took up." Other scholars take a neutral position by saying that the author was a Jewish-Christian prophet called John (commentaries of Kiddle, pp. xxxv–vi; Beasley-Murray, p. 37). But because of the solid external and supportive internal evidence favoring apostolic authorship, many scholars are persuaded that John son of Zebedee wrote the Apocalypse (among others, Donald Guthrie, William Hendriksen, Philip Edgcumbe Hughes, George E. Ladd, Leon Morris, Merrill C. Tenney, Robert L. Thomas).

51. Austin Farrer (*The Revelation of St. John the Divine* [Oxford: Clarendon, 1964], p. 49) writes: "Sonnet-writing and play-writing are very different *genres*, yet I suppose the critic might fairly claim to recognize the Shakespeare of the Sonnets in the Shakespeare of poetical speeches contained in the plays contemporary with them."

52. Donald Guthrie, *New Testament Introduction*, 4th ed. (Downers Grove: InterVarsity, 1990), p. 935. See also the discussion on the genre of Revelation in D. A. Carson, D. Moo, and L. Morris, *New Testament Introduction* (Grand Rapids: Zondervan, 1992), pp. 478–79. They view Revelation comprehensively "as prophecy cast in an apocalyptic mold and written down in a letter form" (p. 479). G. R. Beasley-Murray (*The Book of Revelation*, NCB [London: Oliphants, 1974], pp. 12–14) also calls it a letter. In effect, the Apocalypse has a name and a greeting at the beginning (1:4–5a) and a benediction at the end (22:21).

"On the Revelation of John: For an interpretation of the entire book, it is important to note that the seer, in conformity with the O[ld] T[estament] of which the description of his revelatory experiences is reminiscent, likens himself to the prophets of the O[ld] T[estament] without hiding behind the pseudonym of one of them as the other apocalyptic writers do."[53]

Another difference between Jewish apocalyptic writers and John is the time and place of composition, and the recipients. It is practically impossible to determine when and where and to whom the Jewish apocalypses were written and under what circumstances their authors lived. By contrast, John is open and direct when he informs his readers that he was on the isle of Patmos because of the word of God—a time of persecution and exile (1:9). In addition, the first three chapters of Revelation not only identify the recipients by place names, but they even describe circumstances that allude to a possible date.

Problems relating to theological emphases that touch on internal evidence are discussed in the introductory section on theology. Although there are significant difficulties with respect to the content of Revelation, I conclude on the basis of nearly solid external evidence and helpful internal evidence that the apostle John is the author of the Apocalypse.

E. Time, Place, and Setting

Scholars have defended either an early or a late date for the composition of the Apocalypse—early dating is in the mid-sixties and late dating in the mid-nineties. The early period would reflect the persecutions Christians endured during the last few years of Nero's reign (64–68); the later period would mirror the last years of Domitian (95–96).

Proponents of early and late dating for Revelation marshal the evidence they have gleaned from both external and internal sources: in other words, what writers of the first few centuries say about the dating of Revelation, and what the book itself indicates about a possible date of composition.

1. External Sources

A primary source for information is Irenaeus, who had been a disciple of Polycarp, who in turn was a disciple of the apostle John. Irenaeus served as bishop in Lyon, southern France, and wrote voluminously in defense of the Christian faith. Commenting on the Apocalypse with reference to the name of the beast (13:18), he writes:

> We will not, however, incur the risk of pronouncing positively as to the name of Antichrist; for if it were necessary that his name should be distinctly revealed in the present time, it would have been announced by him who beheld the apocalyptic

53. Leonhard Goppelt, *Typos: The Typological Interpretation of the Old Testament in the New*, trans. Donald H. Madvig (Grand Rapids: Eerdmans, 1982), p. 197 n. 81.

vision. For that was seen no very long time since, but almost in our day, towards the end of Domitian's reign.

The text is preserved in Latin by Irenaeus and in Greek by Eusebius.[54] In both the Latin and the Greek texts, the subject of the verb *was seen* is lacking and has to be provided. Did Irenaeus mean that the Apocalypse was seen? Or did he intend to say that John, the writer of Revelation, was seen? Some supporters of the early date for the Apocalypse stress that the subject of the verb is John. They argue on the basis of context that it is more logical to denote the writer than the writing as the leading subject. They claim that Eusebius facilitates their choice by quoting twice from Irenaeus: first, "As these things are so, and the number is found in all the approved and ancient copies, and those who saw John face to face confirm it"; and second, "For it was seen, not long ago, but almost in our generation, toward the end of the reign of Domitian."[55] They conclude that in these quotes the verb *to see* must have the same referent, so that not the Apocalypse but John is the subject of this verb. Thus, the apostle was seen in the last years of Domitian, while the Apocalypse had been in circulation for almost three decades.

The context of these passages in Irenaeus and Eusebius, however, shows that both authors had in mind the book and not the apostle. Irenaeus devotes an entire chapter (chap. 30) to the number and name of the Antichrist (Rev. 13:18), and in the course of his discussion he writes, "For that was seen no very long time since, but almost in our day, toward the end of Domitian's reign." This sentence is an explanation of the preceding one that ends with the expression "apocalyptic vision." Consequently, the subject is the same in both sentences. And Eusebius, noting the great cruelty of Domitian's persecution and the banishment of the apostle John to Patmos, mentions the Apocalypse and then quotes the above-mentioned words of Irenaeus. The context of these words in the writings of both Irenaeus and Eusebius intimates that not John but Revelation is the subject.[56]

Next, Domitian's name is absent from the writings of Clement of Alexandria and Origen when they mention John's banishment to Patmos. Clement says that John, who was exiled to Patmos, returned to Ephesus "after the death of the tyrant."[57] And Origen states, "The emperor of the Romans, as tradition teaches, condemned John to the isle of Patmos."[58] Advocates of an early date for Revelation claim that the words *tyrant* and *emperor* point not to Domitian

54. Irenaeus *Against Heresies* 5.30.3 (in *Apostolic Fathers*, pp. 559–60); Eusebius *Eccl. Hist.* 3.18.3; 5.8.6.

55. Eusebius *Eccl. Hist.* 5.8.5–6 (LCL); and Irenaeus *Against Heresies* 5.30.1, 3.

56. Ibid. John A. T. Robinson (*Redating the New Testament* [Philadelphia: Westminster, 1976], p. 221) notes that to make John the subject of the verb *was seen* "is very dubious."

57. Clement of Alexandria *Who Is the Rich Man That Shall Be Saved?* 42, in *The Ante-Nicene Fathers*, ed. Alexander Roberts and James Donaldson (reprint, Grand Rapids: Eerdmans, n.d.), 2:603; Eusebius *Eccl. Hist.* 3.23.6.

58. Origen *Matthew* 16.6. He writes the Greek word *basileus* (king), which means emperor (1 Pet. 2:13, 17).

but to Nero. They conclude that external tradition can only say with certainty that John was exiled to Patmos where he composed the Apocalypse but not when he wrote it. Because of indefinite statements from writers in the second and third centuries, so the proponents of an early date assert, the evidence for the dating of Revelation seems to favor the time of Nero's persecutions. But in the fourth century both Eusebius and Jerome write that John was banished to Patmos during the reign of Domitian. And Eusebius, who quotes Clement of Alexandria, "For after the death of the tyrant he [the apostle John] passed from the island of Patmos to Ephesus," mentions Domitian by name in the same chapter.[59]

Before Irenaeus wrote *Against Heresies* in approximately 185, a Christian historian named Hegesippus in the middle of the second century composed the book *Five Memoirs.* Only fragments of this work have been preserved by Eusebius and are reflected in the following statements that feature the term *story* and are attributed to Hegesippus:

> At this time, the story goes, the Apostle and Evangelist John was still alive, and was condemned to live in the island of Patmos for his witness to the divine word.
>
> After Domitian had reigned fifteen years, Nerva succeeded [96–98]. The sentences of Domitian were annulled, and the Roman Senate decreed the return of those who had been unjustly banished and the restoration of their property. Those who committed the story of those times to writing relate it. At that time, too, the story of the ancient Christians relates that the Apostle John, after his banishment to the island, took up his abode at Ephesus.[60]

Lawlor concludes, "But if the two passages referred to are really from Hegesippus we have this testimony that St. John the Apostle was banished to Patmos under Domitian, and resided at Ephesus under Nerva. That is to say, he must be added to the small band of early witnesses to the late date and apostolic authorship of the Apocalypse. And this is full of significance."[61] Hegesippus, who was born probably around 110, provides no evidence that John wrote the Apocalypse before the destruction of Jerusalem.

Even though authors in the early centuries were not as precise as we would expect them to be, we cannot say that the evidence points overwhelmingly in the direction of an early date. On the contrary, there is important evidence for a late date. Indeed, traditional late dating is a conceivable option that is further strengthened by the internal evidence of the Apocalypse.

---

59. Ibid.

60. Eusebius *Eccl. Hist.* 3.18.1 and 3.20.8–9 (LCL). See also H. J. Lawlor, *Eusebiana: Essays on the Ecclesiastical History of Eusebius Pamphili, ca 264–349 A.D. Bishop of Caesarea* (1912; reprint, Amsterdam: Philo, 1973), pp. 50–53.

61. Lawlor, *Eusebiana,* p. 95.

2. Internal Evidence

a. Measuring the Temple

One of the texts in Revelation that speaks about the temple and the holy city is crucial to those who hold to an early date, for it is claimed that by implication the temple in Jerusalem is still standing when the apostle John is told to measure it. These are the words in 11:1–3.

> And I was given a reed like a rod and was told, "Arise and measure the temple of God and the altar and those who worship there. But exclude the outer court of the temple and do not measure it because it has been given to the Gentiles, and they will trample the holy city for forty-two months. And I will give [power] to my two witnesses and they will prophesy for 1,260 days and be clothed in sackcloth."

The argument is that the entire New Testament is silent about the demise of the temple. This shocking event, predicted by Jesus in the Gospels and fulfilled forty years after his ascension, would presumably have been mentioned in Revelation if this book were written after the fall of Jerusalem. One writer concludes, "It has been shown that at the time of the writing of Revelation the Temple complex is spoken of as still standing. It is inconceivable that a book of the nature of Revelation could fail to mention its already having been destroyed, if Revelation were written after A.D. 70."[62]

The New Testament uses the Greek term *hieron* for the temple complex (e.g., Matt. 24:1; Acts 3:1) and the word *naos* for the inner sanctuary (see Matt. 27:51). Throughout Revelation John never uses the first term to refer to the temple but always the second one (sixteen times).[63] The inner sanctum was the place the high priest entered once a year on the Day of Atonement. There he was in the presence of Almighty God to sprinkle blood for himself and the people of Israel in remission of sins (Lev. 16:6–14). But when Jesus, the perfect sacrifice, shed his blood on the cross and died, the curtain of the Holy of Holies was split from top to bottom (Matt. 27:51). God made it known that no longer only the high priest but rather all God's people might freely enter his presence. The emphasis, then, is not on the temple complex in Jerusalem prior to its demise. Rather John accents the people of God who now with Jesus, their mediator, have the privilege of entering God's presence (Heb. 9:24). They are the temple of God and offer their sacrifices of praise on his altar. By contrast, the outer court where the altar of burnt offering stood is given to the Gentiles, the unbelievers, who are cast out from God's presence. They trample on the great city, which is no longer holy but unholy and figuratively called Sodom and Egypt (11:8; see also Luke 21:24).

62. Kenneth L. Gentry Jr., *Before Jerusalem Fell: Dating the Book of Revelation* (Tyler, Tex.: Institute for Christian Economics, 1989), p. 192.

63. Rev. 3:12; 7:15; 11:1, 2, 19 (twice); 14:15, 17; 15:5, 6, 8 (twice); 16:1, 17; 21:22 (twice). No other New Testament book has as many occurrences: there are nine in Matthew; four each in Luke and 1 Corinthians; three each in Mark and John's Gospel; two each in Acts and 2 Corinthians; and one each in Ephesians and 2 Thessalonians.

John intends to convey not a literal interpretation of the temple and the earthly city but rather a symbolical understanding of God's people who dwell in his presence, that is, in his temple.[64]

Next, if the period of forty-two months or 1,260 days refers to the beginning of the Jewish wars and ends with the destruction of Jerusalem, we would be able to determine the date for the composition of Revelation. This period lasted from the spring of 67 to the autumn of 70, until the fall of Jerusalem. The persecutions instigated by Nero also lasted that long: from the late autumn of 64 to the ninth of June, 68, when the emperor took his own life. An approximate date for Revelation would then be the middle or latter part of the 60s.[65]

Interpreting the time frame of forty-two months or 1,260 days not symbolically but literally creates a number of problems. First, these numbers also appear in contexts (12:6; 13:5) where a literal interpretation fails. Next, Nero set the city of Rome ablaze in July 64 and certainly did not wait until late autumn of that year to make the Christians a scapegoat. Third, the Jewish revolt against Rome broke out in the spring of 66 and came to an end with the destruction of Jerusalem in August–September 70. And last, the trampling of the holy city by the Gentiles could begin only when Jerusalem fell into the hands of the Roman soldiers. To place the forty-two months after September 70 is meaningless, for there is no historical incident that marks their termination.

John portrays the conflict between Christ and Satan, God's people and Satan's masses. He describes the scene of conflict symbolically, so that the numbers in the account of chapter 11 should be interpreted similarly. Furthermore, the other parts in this chapter receive a figurative interpretation: the measuring rod, the measuring, the two olive trees, and the two lampstands (11:1–4). Where a passage is filled with symbolism, one would not expect literalism. We conclude by saying that the text of 11:1–3 does not prove a date prior to the ruin of Jerusalem in 70.

b. The Number of the Beast

There is another passage that assumes a focal point in discussing the date of the Apocalypse: "Here is wisdom. Let anyone who has a mind calculate the number of the beast. It is the number of a man, and his number is 666" (13:18).

Let's begin with the mystery of the number 666, which numerous scholars ascribe to Nero, who is then designated as the Antichrist. Writing extensively about this number, Irenaeus points out the danger of knowing the name of the Antichrist: "Moreover, another danger, by no means trifling, shall overtake those who falsely presume that they know the name of the Antichrist."[66] He notes that there is no lack of names and mentions three that fit the number 666: Evanthas,

---

64. Consult Bauckham, *Climax of Prophecy*, p. 272.

65. Gentry, *Before Jerusalem Fell*, p. 256; David Chilton, *The Days of Vengeance: An Exposition of the Book of Revelation* (Fort Worth, Tex.: Dominion, 1987), p. 4.

66. Irenaeus *Against Heresies* 5.30.1.

Lateinos, and Teitan (that is, Titus, who destroyed Jerusalem). He calls attention to Teitan as a prospect, but he refrains from choosing any one of these names:

> We will not, however, incur the risk of pronouncing positively as to the name of Antichrist; for if it were necessary that his name should be distinctly revealed in this present time, it would have been announced by him who beheld the apocalyptic vision.[67]

At the end of the second century Irenaeus hesitated to venture an exact meaning for this mysterious number. Not until the 1830s did four German scholars propose the name Nero Caesar for the number 666.[68] In the twentieth century additional suggestions have been made: e.g., Vespasian, Titus, and Domitian.[69]

The choice of Nero Caesar for the name to interpret the number 666 requires the addition of the letter *n* to the name to make it Neron Caesar. This is the Hebraic (Aramaic) spelling of the name, which has been verified with a reading in a Murabbaʿat manuscript of the Dead Sea Scrolls.[70] If we assume that John had in mind Neron Caesar, we have to note that a textual variant that has the reading 616 spells Nero Caesar. But already in the second century Irenaeus discusses and rejects it. So, if we should understand the number 666 to refer cryptically to Nero, we have to ask why John writes openly about the "seven hills" (17:9); Roman writers commonly used this expression to designate Rome. And if we say 666 equals Nero as the beast, then the context presents difficulties. First, one of the beast's heads had received a mortal blow administered by someone else (13:3), but Nero committed suicide, while the beast continues to live. Next, the fatal wound that had healed symbolizes a return to life. This clearly is Satan's parody of seeking to imitate Christ's resurrection (compare 13:3 and 1:18). And the legend of Nero returning to life (Nero *redivivus*) "is adapted to give the beast a parodic counterpart of the future coming of Christ."[71] Third, in 13:16–17 the beast dictates that all his followers had to have this number stamped on their right hands and foreheads. Without this number no one could buy or sell. But Roman historians report nothing concerning such a decree in either Rome or the provinces. Yet the Apocalypse repeatedly mentions the mark of the

67. Ibid. 5.30.3.

68. O. F. Fritsche (1831); F. Benary (1836); F. Hitzig and E. Reuss (1837). Refer to D. Brady, *The Contribution of British Writers between 1560 and 1830 to the Interpretation of Revelation 13.16–18 (the Number of the Beast): A Study in the History of Exegesis,* BGBE 27 (Tübingen: Mohr, 1983), p. 292.

69. Respectively, W. G. Baines, "The Number of the Beast in Revelation 13:18," *HeythJourn* 16 (1975): 195–196; Ethelbert Stauffer, "666 (Apoc. 13, 18)," *ConNT* 11 (1947): 237–41.

70. Consult P. Benoit, J. T. Milik, and R. de Vaux, eds., *Discoveries in the Judaean Desert of Jordan* II (Oxford: Oxford University Press, 1961), p. 18, plate 29. Beale (*Revelation,* p. 24) queries "why the author would not use a Greek form instead of Hebrew form."

71. Bauckham, *Climax of Prophecy,* p. 437; see also Milligan, *Revelation of St. John,* p. 319.

beast or the number of his name (14:9; 15:2; 20:4). Even if we should identify the number of the beast with the name Nero, the question remains whether John wanted to convey a period in history or to contrast Satan and Christ, the vanquished and the victor. I suggest that a symbolic interpretation best fits the context.

Chapter 13 portrays the power of Satan over the world so that anyone who refuses to receive his mark will be shut out. In short, Satan appears to have conquered the saints: "If anyone goes into captivity, into captivity he goes. If anyone is to be killed with the sword, with the sword he will be killed. Here is the endurance and faith of the saints" (v. 10). John, however, shows a contrast in the next chapter, where the Lamb and the 144,000 saints are standing on Mount Zion with the Lamb's name and the name of his Father written on their foreheads (14:1). The followers of Satan have the number of his name marked on their right hand and forehead; the people of God have the names of the Lamb and the Father written on their foreheads (14:1).[72] John does not indicate that every follower of Satan has been branded with the number 666, and he does not say that all the followers of the Lamb have the number of Jesus' name indelibly written on their foreheads. John speaks symbolically. He contrasts Satan, who empowers the beast, and Christ, who leads his saints to victory. The saints "are the ones who are following the Lamb wherever he goes" (14:4). The message of chapters 13 and 14 is that Satan's power is limited, for Christ has overcome the world.

c. The Seven Kings

A related passage that intimates a time reference is found in chapter 17. "And there are seven kings: five have fallen, one is, another has not yet come. And when he comes, it is necessary that he remains a little while. And the beast that once was and now is, he is the eighth and is of the seven, and he goes to his destruction" (17:10–11).

Who are these seven kings or emperors? If we begin with Julius Caesar and add the names of his successors (Augustus, Tiberius, Caligula, Claudius, and Nero), then it is obvious that Nero is number six in the dynasty of the Caesars. But who is number seven and who is number eight? In the year after Nero's death (68–69), three successors ruled, each for a few months: Galba, Otho, and Vitellius. In the autumn of 69 Vespasian, general of the Roman forces besieging Jerusalem, was summoned to Rome, where he became the emperor and ruled for a period of ten years. Vespasian appointed his sons Titus and Domitian to succeed him. Titus reigned from 79 to 81 and Domitian from 81 to 96. Some interpreters are of the opinion that Augustus is the first emperor mentioned in Scripture and that the three pretenders to the throne (Galba, Otho, and Vitellius) should not be counted. This sequence places Vespasian as number six,

72. Refer to Bauckham, *Climax of Prophecy*, p. 399.

Titus as seven, and Domitian as eight.[73] Still others begin with Caligula, omit the three pretenders, and place Domitian as number six.[74]

Instead of counting Roman emperors, some scholars refer to chapters 2 and 7 in Daniel and on that basis speak of secular kingdoms that rise, flourish, and collapse. In sequence, these kingdoms are ancient Babylonia, Assyria, Neo-Babylonia, Medo-Persia, Greco-Macedonia, and Rome.[75] Rome is number six and fits the text, "five have fallen, one is." Rome is still the powerful empire, while the seventh empire has not yet come. The objection is that the text speaks not about kingdoms but kings. Although this is true, there is validation for the word *kingdoms.* The Hebrew text of Daniel 7:17 reads, "As for these four great beasts, four kings shall arise out of the earth" (NRSV). The term *kings* is translated in numerous versions, including the Septuagint, as "kingdoms," because kingdoms over which kings rule are greater and more enduring than their rulers. Rooted in the Old Testament Scriptures, John looks at the prophecies of Daniel and considers kings as representatives of their kingdoms. When he writes the verb *to fall* in "five [kings] have fallen," this verb applies more appropriately to empires that decline than to kings who are dethroned. Secular empires that are pitted against God's kingdom either collapse or are overthrown. Only the kingdom of heaven endures forever, while all other empires perish. The conflict portrayed in Revelation is that of Satan, who claims to have dominion over the kingdoms of this world (Luke 4:6), and Christ, who is King of kings and Lord of lords (17:14; 19:16).

Granted that John could have alluded to seven historical rulers of the second half of the first century, we would rather say that he writes the number seven as the symbol of completeness and refers to their totality. However, John writes about an eighth who is of the seven, "And the beast that once was and now is, he is the eighth and is of the seven, and he goes to his destruction" (17:11). The interpretation of this verse must be seen in the light of the preceding context where John speaks of the beast that "will come up out of the Abyss and go to his destruction" (17:8). This beast will come up out of the Abyss, which is the place where evil angels are kept who have their own place and assignment in their evil empire. The beast is not one of the seven rulers but is the concentration of the evil that is in them; it is greater than any one individual. This beast is the personification of the Antichrist (compare 2 Thess. 2:3–4); he arises from the pit but is on his way to destruction. Conclusively, the eighth personifies the Antichrist,

73. Friedrich Düsterdieck, *Critical and Exegetical Handbook to the Revelation of John* (New York and London: Funk and Wagnalls, 1886), p. 53.

74. E.g., Krodel, *Revelation*, p. 297.

75. Consult Hendriksen, *More Than Conquerors*, p. 171; S. Greijdanus, *De Openbaring des Heeren aan Johannes*, KNT (Amsterdam: Van Bottenburg, 1925), p. 349. Henry Alford has the same sequence of kingdoms but calls ancient Babylonia Egypt and Assyria Nineveh. See his *James–Revelation*, vol. 4, part 2 of *Alford's Greek Testament: An Exegetical and Critical Commentary* (1875; reprint, Grand Rapids: Guardian, 1976), p. 70. And see William Milligan, *The Book of Revelation* (New York: Armstrong and Son, 1893), p. 285.

who already has lost the battle against Christ even though the war itself is not yet over.

3. Settings in the Churches

John wrote seven letters to individual churches in the province of Asia. The contents of these letters reveal their setting and reflect the time in which they were composed. Even a cursory reading leaves the impression that their recipients were not first- but second-generation Christians. The conditions in the seven churches hardly confirm the notion that the people had only a short while ago received the gospel. We read of an abandonment of first love, practices of the Nicolaitans, persecution, martyrdom, teachings of Balaam, toleration of sexual immorality, learning Satan's deep secrets, and being rich in worldly wealth. Indeed, the setting of these churches does not comport with what we know of the churches founded and pastored by Paul in the 50s. For instance, Paul ministered for three years (53–56) in Ephesus and wrote epistles to Timothy, who was a pastor there in the 60s. Nothing in Acts or Paul's epistles corresponds to the conditions prevalent in the church of Ephesus when John wrote the epistle that Jesus dictated. Backsliding and degenerating faith had set in at Ephesus and the other churches. Neither the personal epistles addressed to Timothy in the mid-60s nor the general epistles of Peter sent to the same region at that time reflect the situation depicted in Jesus' letters to the churches in the province of Asia. Paul opposed Judaizers who slipped into the churches he had founded, but the seven letters of the Apocalypse disclose various adversaries including the Nicolaitans, followers of Balaam, and followers of Jezebel. "When we read the seven, especially the last four, Epistles in the Apocalypse, we are in a different atmosphere. Not the narrowness of Judaism, but the wild immorality and worldliness of heathenism is now striving to gain the upper hand; and the Christian has to overcome, not Judaism, but the world in its widest sense."[76]

If we opt for an early date for Revelation, we encounter problems because of factual material presented in Acts and the Epistles of Paul. As we already noted, Paul served the church in Ephesus in the mid-50s, and Timothy was the pastor there in the first half of the 60s. We lack any evidence that John was a pastor in Ephesus before the demise of Jerusalem; but even if he was in Ephesus, his time of service prior to his exile would have been short. Next, the seven letters to the churches in the province of Asia seem to show that John was well acquainted with the spiritual status of each one of them. But this seems hardly possible if John was there only briefly, apart from Jesus' instruction to write these letters. Third, we doubt that John could have come to Ephesus in the first part of the 60s, because addressing his letter to the Ephesians in 62, Paul would not have failed to mention John and commend him for his work. Fourth, in their writings both Peter and Paul are silent about John's labors in Ephesus. This appears to indicate that John did not come to Ephesus during their lifetime. And last, Polycarp

76. Milligan, *Revelation of St. John*, p. 334.

wrote a letter to the church in Philippi and indicates that when Paul composed his canonical letter to the Philippians in 62, the knowledge of Christ had not yet come to Smyrna.[77]

4. Persecution under Domitian

Throughout the Apocalypse, John alludes to the persecution that God's people had to endure. He himself experienced hardship by being banished to the island of Patmos "because of the word of God and the testimony of Jesus" (1:9). And he writes words of encouragement to the church in Smyrna, "Look, the devil is about to cast some of you into prison that you may be tested, and you will have tribulation for ten days" (2:10). He refers to saints who have been slain (2:13; see also 6:9–10; 16:6; 17:6; 18:24; 19:2; 20:4), and he alerts the readers to a time of trial (3:10). Certainly, Nero vented his rage on the Christians in Rome and put them to death. But is Domitian also known as a persecutor of God's people? Advocates of an early date opt for the Neronian persecutions of the 60s, while those who hold to a late date look at Domitian and the mid-90s. Evidence from secular and early Christian writers is lacking, however, to prove that persecutions instigated by either Nero or Domitian spread to the provinces. Clement of Alexandria at the beginning of the third century notes that Nero and Domitian were the only two emperors who slandered Christian teaching and falsely accused Christians.[78] And a century later, Eusebius writes that Domitian had become "the successor to Nero's campaign of hostility to God."[79] These references do not prove the point, yet it is undeniable that the content of Revelation speaks of persecution and suffering. The Apocalypse presents history and prophecy, realism and idealism, fact and uncertainty. The first recipients had experienced or were experiencing oppression, but they had to prepare themselves for more severe abuse.

Paul records one of the earliest Christian confessional statements, "Jesus is Lord" (1 Cor. 12:3). This declaration was in direct conflict with that of the Romans, "Caesar is Lord." The Romans regarded refusal to express their creed as a sign of insubordination to the emperor and the state. Repudiation of the highest authority in the empire was considered treason punishable by execution or exile. For the Christian, the highest authority on earth and in heaven was the Lord Jesus Christ. To pay homage to the emperor was abandoning the Master

---

77. Polycarp *To the Philippians* 11.3.

78. Recorded by Eusebius *Eccl. Hist.* 4.26.9. For a thorough study, see Leonard L. Thompson, *The Book of Revelation: Apocalypse and Empire* (New York and Oxford: Oxford University Press, 1990), especially pp. 95–115.

79. Eusebius *Eccl. Hist.* 3.17.1. For secular historians, see Tacitus *Annals* and *Histories* and Suetonius *Lives of the Twelve Caesars.* Consult also Albert A. Bell Jr., "The Date of John's Apocalypse: The Evidence of Some Roman Historians Reconsidered," *NTS* 25 (1977–78): 93–102. Bell states definitively, "Since the Apocalypse comes from the province of Asia, there must be some convincing evidence that action taken against the Christians in Rome was paralleled in Asia to provide John with his spark. And there is none" (p. 97). And see Krodel, *Revelation*, pp. 38–39.

who had redeemed them. To the Romans, Christianity had become an exclusive religion that brooked no compromise, for its followers spoke of the kingdom of God in which Jesus ruled as king. Because of their adherence to the Christian faith, Christians as a class had to endure persecution at the hands of the Roman officials who were appointed to enforce the state religion in every city and town. These officials had the authority to punish those people who refused to honor Caesar by executing or exiling them.[80]

During the reign of the emperor Trajan (98–117), Pliny the Younger served as governor of the province of Bithynia (110–113) and asked the emperor for advice on how to punish Christians who refused to obey Roman law on religious worship.[81] Pliny informed Trajan that he had asked defendants who were accused of being Christians at least three times to renounce their faith in Christ; and he had warned them that they would be punished. When they persisted, he would then give the order to have them executed.[82] Apparently Pliny did not initiate the persecution of Christians but merely followed standard procedure. He only asked advice because of the numerous cases before him. And when Trajan responded that Pliny had followed established Roman policy,[83] we ascertain that enforcing it had already begun by the last decade of the first century.

There is still further evidence relating to the province of Asia and in particular Ephesus in the time of Emperor Domitian. In 89–90 the temple of the Sebastoi (the family of Vespasian, Titus, and Domitian) was dedicated. It was customary to appoint temple wardens in cities that had dedicated a temple for the worship of emperors. S. Friesen writes,

> Neokoros [temple warden][84] therefore became a coveted title in spite of early efforts in Asia to moderate its impact. The explosive spread of the term indicates not merely a new city title of local significance, but a fundamental shift in the identification of these cities—a shift in which the worship of the emperors played a crucial role. The innovations that began with Asia's Temple of the Sebastoi in Ephesos changed the public discourse of religion and identity in the eastern Mediterranean for centuries to come.[85]

---

80. Ray Summers, *Worthy Is the Lamb: An Interpretation of Revelation* (Nashville: Broadman, 1951), pp. 92–93.

81. Pliny the Younger, *Letters and Panegyricus*, trans. Betty Radice, LCL (Cambridge, Mass.: Harvard University Press; London: Heinemann, 1962), 10.96 (2:285–91).

82. Pliny *Letters* 10.96.3.

83. Ibid. 10.97.

84. This Greek term occurs once in the New Testament (Acts 19:35).

85. S. Friesen, "The Cult of the Roman Emperors in Ephesos: Temple Wardens, City Titles, and the Interpretation of the Revelation of John," in *Ephesos, Metropolis of Asia: An Interdisciplinary Approach to Its Archaeology, Religion, and Culture,* ed. H. Koester, Harvard Theological Studies 41 (Valley Forge, Pa.: Trinity Press International, 1995), p. 236. I am indebted to my colleague Charles E. Hill for alerting me to this study.

The significance of temples dedicated to Roman emperors cannot be underestimated in relation to the Apocalypse. Pergamum, a city located to the north of Ephesus in the province of Asia, was known for emperor worship. Here the state religion was practiced and offerings were presented to the image of the emperor.[86]

Emperor worship of Domitian, who was honored as *dominus et deus* (Lord and God), was a prevailing phenomenon in Ephesus, and John encountered it in the 90s. "When John denounced imperial worship, he was not attacking a marginal socio-religious phenomenon. The developments in provincial worship of the emperors that are manifested in the Temple of the Sebastoi indicate that the worship of emperors played an increasingly important role in society at many levels."[87] In the light of emperor worship in Ephesus, dating the composition of Revelation to the last part of Domitian's reign is not at all unrealistic.

5. Jewish Opposition

For the first few decades after Pentecost and the founding of the church, Christians enjoyed the protection of Roman authorities because they placed them on the same level as the Jews. The Romans accorded the Jewish religion legitimacy, and its adherents were exempt from emperor worship. Followers of Christ found shelter under the umbrella the Romans had provided for the Jewish people. When Jerusalem and its temple were destroyed, the legal separation of Judaism and Christianity, which was already taking place gradually, became increasingly more permanent. Jewish people were among the first to bring charges against the Christians before the Romans, so that the Jews became a distinct threat to the church. The Jewish Council of Jamnia convened in the year 90 to acknowledge the extent of the Old Testament canon. At the same time, they added a curse on the Christians in the so-called Eighteen Benedictions prayer that was part of the synagogue liturgy. The Jews sought to expose the Christians by expelling them from their houses of worship and denying them civil protection. They were indeed the persecutors of the Christian community and became agents of Satan.

In his letters to the churches at Smyrna and Philadelphia, John notes these Jewish synagogues and associates them with Satan:

---

86. Consult William M. Ramsay, *The Letters to the Seven Churches of Asia and Their Place in the Plan of the Apocalypse* (London: Hodder and Stoughton, 1904; reprint, Grand Rapids: Baker, 1979), pp. 292–93. See also Colin J. Hemer, *The Letters to the Seven Churches of Asia in Their Local Setting*, JSNTSup 11 (Sheffield: JSOT, 1986), p. 84. Consult S. R. F. Price, *Rituals and Power: The Roman Imperial Cult in Asia Minor* (Cambridge: Cambridge University Press, 1984), p. 221.

87. Price, *Rituals*, p. 249. Consult also Isbon T. Beckwith, *The Apocalypse of John* (1919; reprint, Grand Rapids: Baker, 1979), p. 201; Thomas writes (*Revelation 1–7*, p. 184), "Emperor worship is constantly viewed as an agency of Satan's power." Coins that portray Domitian have been discovered; they bear the words *dominus et deus* (lord and god) with an image of the emperor's son, whose hand reaches out to seven stars (compare Rev. 1:20).

- "I know . . . the blasphemy from the ones who call themselves Jews and are not, but are the synagogue of Satan" (2:9).
- "I will make those of the synagogue of Satan and who call themselves Jews and are not but are lying—I will make them to come and bow down at your feet and admit that I have loved you" (3:9).

When Pliny executed numerous Christians whose names had been handed to him by an informant, we assume that among the informers were members of local synagogues. We conclude that in the last decade of the first century persecution was an undeniable reality and that Revelation reflects that period in which believers lived and died.

6. Conclusion

The Apocalypse notes that John was exiled to the island of Patmos because of the word of God (1:9). It notes that Antipas, the faithful witness of Jesus, was put to death in the city of Pergamum, "where Satan lives" (2:13). Even though the Apocalypse mentions only one exile and one execution, the historical, sociological, and religious settings in the latter part of the first century testify to the persecution of numerous Christians. Although many believers were put to death in Rome in the last years of Nero's reign, Christians also had to endure significant persecution throughout the Roman provinces of Asia Minor in the days of Emperor Domitian.

The veracity of Irenaeus may be questioned because of some doubtful stories about John. On the other hand, he was acquainted with Polycarp (69–155), who had been a disciple of the apostle and served as a bridge from the latter part of the first century to the latter part of the next. We would expect both Polycarp and Irenaeus to relate at least something about John that is historically verifiable. The reference of Irenaeus implies that John's Apocalypse dates from the time when Domitian's rule ended.

F. Modes of Interpretation

1. Methods

There are basically four methods of interpretation: preterist, historicist, futurist, and idealist. Some interpreters accommodate themselves to a combination of two or more views and argue that John wrote to his contemporaries, to believers throughout the ages, and to those who will be present at Jesus' Second Coming. Let us consider these four views separately and in depth.

a. Preterist

The name *preterist* is a combination of the two Latin words *praeter* (past) and *ire* (to go) meaning that which has gone past, that is, belongs to the past. According to this view, everything recorded in the Apocalypse was fulfilled in the first century at the time John wrote this book. The preterists teach that the symbolism in Revelation depicts historical events that took place during the second half of the first century; the Book of Revelation relates to that which occurred in the past but has no reference to the present and future.

A distinction must be made between a right wing and a left wing of the preterist school. The right wing teaches the inspiration of Revelation and thus holds to a high view of Scripture, while the left wing rejects the inspiration of this last book in the Bible.[88] Those of the right wing contend that most of Revelation was fulfilled in the days of the Roman empire of the first century. The preterists "look upon Revelation as a book for the day of persecution in Asia Minor but feel that it has only, at least to a great extent, a literary interest for people of our day."[89] And the left wing places the Apocalypse at the same level as any other apocryphal or pseudepigraphical apocalyptic.

In short, preterists either neglect or ignore the predictive element, for their focus is entirely on historical events of the first century.

Objections to the preterist view are these: First, although the preterists say that the message of Revelation can be applied to any age or generation, they fail to appreciate the progress in this book. The Apocalypse depicts progress in the predictive events that eventually culminate in the coming of the Judge with the attendant judgment on all people. This becomes plain in the accounts of the seven seals, seven trumpets, and seven bowls. It is difficult to see that the progressive sequence in each of these portrayals refers only to contemporary events in the latter half of the first century.

Next, the preterist view conveys the thought that the message of the Apocalypse was meant primarily for first-century believers; hence for believers in subsequent eras, this message has only secondary importance. Persecuted Christians at the time of Nero received words of comfort from John's Apocalypse when they heard the victorious Christ address them directly. But the universal church throughout cosmic time also hears that same voice of Christ speaking to them directly in their own circumstances. Likewise Paul wrote his epistles to specific churches and individuals, but the message of these letters is as relevant to the worldwide church today as it was to Christians in the middle of the first century.

Third, preterists identify the beast of Revelation 13 with Emperor Nero, especially in regard to the number 666 in verse 18 of that chapter. But the unnatural spelling of the name *Neron* in Hebrew required to achieve this number remains unconvincing. No doubt John was fully acquainted with the Neronian persecution, but to limit persecution to only one emperor in one particular period in history appears unrealistic.

---

88. Refer to Philip Schaff, *History of the Christian Church*, 3d ed. (1910; reprint, Grand Rapids: Eerdmans, 1950), 1:837–38. Schaff defines the right wing as those "who acknowledge a real prophecy and permanent truth in the book [of Revelation]" and the left wing as those who regard it as "a dream of a visionary which was falsified by events."

89. Summers, *Worthy Is the Lamb*, p. 44. Consult also Charles, *Revelation*, 1:clxxxiii; Harrington, *Revelation*, pp. 16–17.

Last, the seven letters to the seven churches in the province of Asia leave the distinct impression that Jesus addressed second- or even third-generation backsliding Christians. For instance, the church in Ephesus is commanded to "remember the place from which you have fallen, repent, and perform the works you did at first" (Rev. 2:5). Paul founded the church in Ephesus in 53 and labored there for three years. He wrote his epistle to the Ephesians in 62; and after his release from prison while Timothy was the pastor of the church in Ephesus, Paul in approximately 64 composed 1 Timothy, addressed to him and the local church. If, as the preterists say, the Apocalypse was written in about 65, then the letter to the church in Ephesus (Rev. 2:1–7) should show wholehearted devotion to the Lord. This is not the case. By contrast, both Ephesians and 1 Timothy reflect problems, but they are those of a growing and developing church.

b. Historicist

The Apocalypse, according to the continuous-historical approach, presents a concise outline of the church's development from the day of Pentecost until the consummation. Secular history and religious history are intertwined, and proponents have tried to interpret events of their own period in history as foretold in the Apocalypse. Henry Barclay Swete lists a few examples of bygone ages in which writers tried to find correspondence between Revelation and events in their own day. Thus, at the end of the twelfth century Joachim of Fiore, who died in 1202, considered the beast coming up out of the sea (13:1) to be Islam, which had been wounded by the Crusades. For him, Babylon was worldly Rome, and he identified some of the seven heads of the beast (17:3, 9–10) with rulers of his day. More than a century later, Franciscans of Paris saw the Antichrist as a pseudo-pope.[90]

The Reformers of the sixteenth century identified the pope and papacy as the Antichrist. Both Martin Luther and fellow Reformer John Calvin did not hesitate to call the pope the Antichrist.[91]

Still others regard the Apocalypse as a calendar of events that begins with the time of John on the island of Patmos in 96. They assign the seven seals and six trumpets to the early church and the Middle Ages, understand Revelation 10 and 11 as the time of the Reformation, and apply the message of the seventh trumpet to the true church. The two beasts in chapter 13 are the pope and papal power, the seven plagues are fulfilled in the French Revolution and modern upheavals, and the destruction of Babylon is the fall of the papacy.[92] The variations

---

90. Swete, *Revelation*, pp. ccxii–xiii; see also Alan F. Johnson, *Revelation*, in *The Expositor's Bible Commentary*, ed. Frank E. Gaebelein (Grand Rapids: Zondervan, 1981), 12:409.

91. Martin Luther, *The Catholic Epistles*, in *Luther's Works*, ed. Jaroslav Pelikan (St. Louis: Concordia, 1967), 30:252–53; John Calvin, *II Thessalonians* (reprint, Grand Rapids: Baker, 1981), pp. 330–31; and *The First Epistle of John* (reprint, Grand Rapids: Baker, 1981), p. 190.

92. Consult Albert Barnes, *Notes on the New Testament: Revelation*, ed. Robert Frew (reprint, Grand Rapids: Baker, 1949), pp. lvi–lxii.

to the method of applying the message of Revelation to history are numerous and self-defeating.

These are the objections to this historical view: For one, the text of the Apocalypse does not lend itself to a continuous historical presentation; history and apocalyptic literature are ill suited. Second, if Revelation were meant to be continuously historical, the early church and successive generations would have been unable to benefit from a message that did not apply to them. Also, interpreters apply the book to the Western church as if the church in the East does not exist. Further, the adherents of the historical view often resort to trivial interpretations that are not only fanciful but are dishonoring to Scripture. And last, the methods used to calculate epochs in history on the basis of numbers in Revelation are at best comical and at worst deceptive.

c. Futurist

The futurist approach to the interpretation of the Apocalypse is that most of the book, beginning at 4:1, belongs to the future. Proponents stress the prophecies in this book that, they say, will be fulfilled just before, during, and after Jesus' return to this earth. They are the vision of the throne, the scroll with the seven seals opened one by one, the seven trumpets, the two witnesses, the woman and the male child, the seven bowls, the great prostitute, the fall of Babylon. All these are events that occur before the coming of Christ.

Indeed, the writer of the Apocalypse points throughout this book to the day of Christ's return. The prophetic element is an undeniable component, for John writes the word *prophecy* seven times in Revelation (1:3; 11:6; 19:10; 22:7, 10, 18, 19). John writes in the light of the great and awesome day of Jesus' promised return. And in this respect, his message is prophetic.

The futurist compares the wording of Revelation 1:1 and 19 with that of 4:1. In the first two passages (1:1, 19), John stresses the things that must soon take place and writes down what he has seen of the things that are and will take place later. In the last passage John is told: "Come up here, and I will show you what must happen after these things" (4:1). The division, according to the futurist, falls into two categories: first, the things that belong to the time in which John lived; next, all the things that belong to the future. The futurist interprets the Apocalypse literally and considers the second part of this book as a witness to "those times of the end when cosmic issues are at stake and when supernatural forces shall be let loose."[93] This approach to the Apocalypse is eschatological and places the emphasis on the day of Christ's return.

There are, however, a few problems with this futuristic approach. One is that it makes "all but the first three chapters of Revelation irrelevant to the contemporary church."[94] Another problem is that the prophetic emphasis focuses on

93. Tenney, *Interpreting Revelation*, p. 140.

94. Johnson, *Revelation*, p. 409; consult also Robert H. Mounce, *The Book of Revelation*, rev. ed., NICNT (Grand Rapids: Eerdmans, 1998), p. 28.

Christ's return. No one will dispute that the church should eagerly expect this return, but this does not mean that the prophecies in Revelation will not be fulfilled until the Second Coming. If it were so, then the church from John's day to the present has not been able to apply the message of these prophecies to the time following the first century. Then the church must patiently wait and consider blessed those who will be present at the coming of the Lord, for only those saints will see the consummation (22:7, 10, 18, 19). John, however, is writing to his contemporaries and to believers in successive centuries; he has a message for the entire worldwide church in any age. The book is filled with words of comfort for God's people in every place and in all times.

d. Idealist

The last method for interpreting the Apocalypse is the idealist school. It interprets Revelation as a book of principles that contrasts the victorious Christ and his people with a defeated Satan and his underlings. John delineates this contrast from beginning to end of the book, from Jesus possessing the keys of Death and Hades in chapter 1 to the devil, Death, and Hades being thrown into the lake of fire in chapter 20.

When Jesus taught his discourse of the last things to his disciples (Matt. 24; Mark 13; Luke 21), he gave them principles that would give them and all believers throughout the ages the comfort and assurance that he is always with them. Similarly, John on the island of Patmos received not a vision of the church in subsequent time or at the end of time but ideals that encourage believers in the spiritual conflict they face. He describes Christ as setting forth principles that will ultimately eradicate evil from the world, and he points out opposing principles that Satan and his hordes put to use. The Apocalypse is not a history of events that have occurred in the past or a prophecy of events that will happen in the future. It is a book that fills God's people with comfort and motivation to endure to the end. Idealists stress the principles in this book so that its message is applicable to Christians of all generations, from John's time to the end of the ages.

Hendriksen sets forth the purpose of Revelation and stresses the comfort that the militant church receives in its fight against the forces of Satan. He writes that the book is

> full of help and comfort for persecuted and suffering Christians. To them is given the assurance that God sees their tears (7:17; 21:4); their prayers are influential in world affairs (8:3, 4) and their death is precious in His sight. Their final victory is assured (15:2); their blood will be avenged (19:2); their Christ lives and reigns forever and ever. He governs the world in the interest of His Church (5:7, 8). He is coming again to take His people to Himself in "the marriage supper of the Lamb" and to live with them forever in a rejuvenated universe (21:22).[95]

95. Hendriksen, *More Than Conquerors*, p. 7.

Believers who read the Apocalypse know that Jesus never forsakes them but is always near to his saints. They know that they are the bride and Jesus is the bridegroom (19:7; 21:2, 9). Therefore, as the Spirit and the bride petition him to come (22:17), Jesus assures them that he is coming soon (22:20).

God controls history from beginning to end and John reflects this in Revelation. Here John does not specify particular events but principles that apply to inherent tendencies and issues that appear in any age and place. The matter of time as such has little relevance in the Apocalypse, because it is not chronological time but an enduring principle that governs this book. Time is described in terms of forty-two months or 1,260 days (11:2, 3; 12:6; 13:5), and by the expressions *time, times, and half a time* (12:14) and *a short time* (6:11; 20:3). Time is presented as an idea in summary form that cannot be quantified in terms of years or centuries. Concludes Milligan, "We have no right, therefore, in interpreting the Apocalypse, to interject into it the thought either of a long or a short development of events. It is a representation in which an idea, not the time needed for the expression of the idea, plays the chief part."[96]

Revelation borrows images, signs, symbols, names, and numbers from the religious and cultural setting of the author and through them presents a message that is universal and abiding. That message is not bound to any particular time or place even though these terms and expressions represent scenes taken from countries surrounding the Mediterranean Sea and other places in the Middle East.

Objections to the idealist school concern the lack of emphasis on history and prophecy. These are legitimate concerns, for every careful exegete must see to it that no part of the Apocalypse is neglected. Indeed, God's curse is resting on all those who omit parts of his revelation (Rev. 22:19). The idealist, however, acknowledges that many parts of the Apocalypse lend themselves to historical settings but these may be applied to many epochs in the history of the Christian church. John was able to assign a number of visions to his own day, but likewise believers who have suffered or are suffering persecution even today have been able to see their situation mirrored in Revelation.

In respect to prophecies, idealists teach that these are being fulfilled in the course of time and will be fulfilled at the consummation when Jesus returns. They know that what he has promised he will fulfill in the time which the Father has set by his own authority (Matt. 24:36; Acts 1:7). But they also hold that the Apocalypse does not teach that the Second Coming of Christ has become a reality. The book teaches that he will return as he has promised, not that he has come.[97] The passage in 19:11–21 is a vision of an event that will come to pass.

A last word must be said concerning a contemporary idealist position. Not all interpreters hold to a high view of Scripture, and some use Revelation as a document

96. Milligan, *Revelation of St. John*, p. 153; compare S. L. Morris, *Drama of Christianity*, pp. 28–29.

97. Rev. 11:17 and 16:5 must be seen in their context, namely, John looks backward at the fulfillment of Jesus' promise to come quickly (see the commentary on these verses).

for specific causes. For these interpreters, the Apocalypse is a book filled with ethical principles that assist its readers in the day-to-day struggles in the areas of economics, race, and gender. They use Revelation as a source for teaching liberation theology to aid the poor in their struggle against economic oppression. They find in this book information suited to combat racial discrimination and the suppression of minorities. Some interpret the Apocalypse as a basis for constructing a feminist theology. Thus they see in chapters 10 through 15 a picture of a community and its oppressors, of prophets who are commissioned, of revealing enemies in the community, and of a liberation that appears at the time of the eschatological harvest.[98]

This emphasis stresses human needs and interests but does so at the expense of neglecting the eternal verities of God's revelation in Jesus Christ. The message of Revelation is much broader, for it points us to the victorious Christ and his followers who are more than conquerors.

2. Hermeneutical Interpretations

There are two distinct views on the timing of Jesus' Second Coming: both concern the thousand-year reign of Christ. Does that period take place between the end of the present age and the Judgment Day? Or does the period refer to an indefinite span that is current even now? A commentary does not lend itself to a lengthy discussion on the four millennial views: amillennial, postmillennial, premillennial, and dispensational. Specialized studies do that very well.[99] Thus, with due respect to other views, I limit myself to some points in the premillennial and amillennial beliefs.

a. Premillennialism

Jesus' return on the clouds of heaven inaugurates a thousand-year period of peace and prosperity. This is the premillennial view, which teaches that Jesus returns before a thousand-year period begins.[100] The view has many variations regarding sequence, number and classification of believers, conditions, and length of time. It holds that when Christ returns, Satan will be bound, and the saints will be raised and will reign with Christ a thousand years on this earth. "This millennial kingdom will end with a final rebellion and the last judgment."[101]

---

98. Elisabeth Schüssler Fiorenza understands the message of Revelation as a vision of "liberation from oppressive ecclesiastical structures and from the destructive domination of those who have power in this world." See her *Invitation to the Book of Revelation: A Commentary on the Apocalypse* (Garden City, N.Y.: Doubleday, 1981), p. 32; and her *Book of Revelation*, p. 199. See also Tina Pippin, *Death and Desire: The Rhetoric and Gender in the Apocalypse of John* (Louisville: Westminster/John Knox, 1992), pp. 70, 72, 80.

99. See among others Craig A. Blaising, "Premillennialism"; Kenneth L. Gentry Jr., "Postmillennialism"; and Robert B. Strimple, "Amillennialism," in *Three Views on the Millennium and Beyond*, ed. Darrell L. Bock (Grand Rapids: Zondervan, 1999); and C. Marvin Pate, ed., *Four Views on the Book of Revelation* (Grand Rapids: Zondervan, 1998).

100. The word comes from the Latin *pre* (before), *mille* (thousand), and *annus* (year).

101. George Eldon Ladd, *A Commentary on the Revelation of John* (Grand Rapids: Eerdmans, 1972), p. 261. See the chapter by Ladd, "Historic Premillennialism," in *The Meaning of the Millennium*, ed. Robert G. Clouse (Downers Grove: InterVarsity, 1977).

The resurrected saints will include both Jews and Gentiles, and they will be joined by those believers who are transformed to glory at the time Jesus returns. They will reign on this earth with truth and grace, though Jesus will rule over unbelievers with a rod of iron (2:27; 12:5; 19:15; Ps. 2:9). During this thousand-year reign, the blight of sin and death will still cover this earth. Yet evil will be kept in check, righteousness will prevail, and justice will be advanced. The earth will produce an abundance of food, and even the desert will blossom.[102]

Proponents of this view encounter some difficulties. One is that the picture of saints who are glorified in body and soul but living in a world that is still marred by sin and death fails to project perfection. How can saints live joyfully on an earth that is still groaning under the curse of sin, subjected to frustration with death in full control and the unbelieving world living in iniquity (Rom. 8:20–21)? How can the perfect live among the imperfect and the sinless among the sinners? Amillennialists assert that at Christ's return the saints are glorified and the non-Christians are condemned to eternal ruin. And these destinies are final.[103] Next, the number *one thousand* in respect to the end times occurs only in Revelation 20 and nowhere else in the Scriptures. Neither Jesus nor the apostles use a definitive time reference when they teach the doctrine of the last things. And last, how do we know that the number *one thousand* should be taken literally in chapter 20? If the answer is that this is prophecy, then we should turn to two passages in the prophecy of Ezekiel, where God speaks eschatologically:

- "Then those who live in the towns of Israel will go out and use the weapons for fuel and burn them up—the small and large shields, the bows and arrows, the war clubs and spears. For seven years they will use them for fuel" (39:9).
- "For seven months the house of Israel will be burying them [corpses] in order to cleanse the land" (39:12).

Both verses use the number seven, which should be interpreted not literally but symbolically. As a symbol, this number signifies totality and completeness of destruction and cleansing. In like manner, the number *one thousand* in the Apocalypse conveys not a literal but a symbolic meaning. It denotes the totality of time in which Satan is bound and the saints are reigning with Christ. It expresses not time but completeness.[104]

b. Amillennialism

The second view is known as amillennial. This term begins with the prefix *a* and leaves the impression that its proponents have no interest at all in a millen-

102. Anthony A. Hoekema, *The Bible and the Future* (Grand Rapids: Eerdmans, 1979), p. 181.

103. See Vernon S. Poythress, "2 Thessalonians 1 Supports Amillennialism," *JETS* 37 (1994): 529–38; Andrew Kuyvenhoven, *The Day of Christ's Return* (Grand Rapids: CRC Publications, 1999), pp. 92–93.

104. Consult Milligan, *Revelation of St. John*, p. 212; Patrick Fairbairn, *Ezekiel and the Book of His Prophecy* (Edinburgh: Clark, 1876), p. 423.

nial period. Such is not the case, for these proponents indeed believe in a millennium, although not in a literal but in a symbolical sense. They understand the term as a period of undetermined length. Amillennialist Hoekema notes that "the millennium of Revelation 20 is not exclusively future, but is now in the process of realization."[105]

Amillennialists stress the doctrine of Christ's kingdom that was heralded by John the Baptist and Jesus (Matt. 3:2; 4:23; Mark 1:14–15). Jesus is King in this kingdom, for his enthronement speech records the words, "All authority in heaven and on earth has been given to me" (Matt. 28:18). With the exception of Jude, all New Testament writers mention the kingdom of God. They portray the kingdom as spiritual (see John 18:36) yet tangibly present on this earth and manifested everywhere. They know that Jesus eventually hands over the kingdom to the Father at the consummation (1 Cor. 15:24). Therefore they teach, first, that the kingdom is present now; second, that after Christ's return the resurrection and judgment take place; and third, that Christ will eternally rule the kingdom on a new and perfected earth (compare Matt. 26:29; 2 Pet. 3:13; Rev. 19:9).

The scene depicted in Revelation 20:4 is heaven, where Christ reigns and where the saints are with him seated on thrones. In numerous passages throughout the Apocalypse Christ's throne is always placed in heaven and so are his people.[106] Further, in at least two verses the term *soul* signifies souls that are without a body (6:9; 20:4).

The passage 20:4–6 presents at least one difficulty, namely, the interpretation of the clause, "This is the first resurrection" (v. 5b). Premillennialists say that if there is a first resurrection, then by implication there is a second one. And if the second one is the physical resurrection of the body, then we may assume that the first one should be interpreted accordingly. A first resurrection is to be followed by a second resurrection, much the same as a second death is preceded by a first death. They conclude, then, that there is an interval of a thousand years between these two resurrections.[107]

This carefully reasoned argument, however, raises the interesting question: what is the meaning and sequence of the verb *come to life* in verses 4 and 5? If the souls of the ones who were beheaded (v. 4b) came to life and now reign with Christ in heaven (v. 4d), then John conveys not the thought of a physical resurrection but the passing from physical death to a glorified life in heaven. And those who died but did not come to life (v. 5a) experience the exact opposite of the saints who are with Christ. Unbelievers do not live and reign but are spiritually dead and with the second death are condemned forever (2:11; 20:6b, 14;

---

105. Hoekema, *Bible and the Future*, pp. 173–74. Beale (*Revelation*, p. 973) suggests the term "inaugurated millennialism."

106. Rev. 1:4; 3:21; 4:2–6, 9–10; 5:1, 6–7, 11, 13; 6:16; 7:9–11, 15, 17; 8:3; 11:16; 12:5; 14:3; 16:17; 19:4–5; 20:4, 11–12; 21:3, 5; 22:1, 3. The expressions *throne of Satan* (2:13), *the dragon's throne* (13:2), and *the throne of the beast* (16:10) refer to earthly thrones in contrast to the heavenly thrones.

107. Refer to Tenney, *Interpreting Revelation*, p. 154.

21:8). John writes about the unbelievers as a parenthesis (v. 5a); then he continues and says that believers who have come to life and reign with Christ have experienced the first resurrection. He adds that over such souls the "second death has no power."[108] In the context of verses 4–6, the first resurrection communicates a spiritual resurrection.

One commentator writes that if the first resurrection is interpreted spiritually (i.e., the souls who came to life) and the second literally(i.e., the dead who did not come to life), "then there is an end of all significance in language, and Scripture is wiped out as a definite testimony to any thing."[109] But note that John is not saying that the dead come to life; he only points out that souls come to life. The emphasis falls on the spiritual relation believers have with Jesus; unbelievers lack this relationship. Even though we say that by implication there is a second resurrection and a first death, it is significant that John omits both. He places a spiritual emphasis on the first resurrection and the second death. For believers the first resurrection is sharing the life that Christ gives through his resurrection. As Paul puts it:

- Or don't you know that all of us who were baptized into Christ Jesus were baptized into his death? We were therefore buried with him through baptism into death in order that, just as *Christ was raised* from the dead through the glory of the Father, *we too may live a new life* (Rom. 6:3–4, emphasis added).
- [You have] been buried with him in baptism *and raised with him* through your faith in the power of God, who raised him from the dead (Col. 2:12, emphasis added).

When believers die, their souls continue to live in heaven where they reign with Christ. They participate fully in Christ's resurrection, for "their living and reigning with him is interpreted by their incorporation into him."[110] Further, just as Christ was raised physically from the dead, so believers will be raised as Scripture attests (e.g., 1 Cor. 15:20–23). John teaches the physical resurrection in his Gospel (John 11:23–26), but in Revelation he enlightens believers about their spiritual resurrection (20:4–6). Only the believers receive everlasting life, while "the rest of the dead lived not until the thousand years were completed" (20:5a). Unbelievers are raised "to shame and everlasting contempt" (Dan. 12:2). The

108. See Hoekema, *Bible and the Future*, pp. 236–37. Consult also James A. Hughes, "Revelation 20:4–6 and the Question of the Millennium," *WTJ* 35 (1972–73): 281–302, especially 299–300.

109. Alford, *Revelation*, p. 732.

110. Philip Edgcumbe Hughes, *The Book of the Revelation: A Commentary* (Leicester: Inter-Varsity; Grand Rapids: Eerdmans, 1990), p. 214; compare Norman Shepherd, "The Resurrections of Revelation 20," *WTJ* 37 (1974): 34–43. For a debate on amillennial and premillennial views, see Meredith G. Kline, "The First Resurrection," *WTJ* 37 (1974): 366–75; J. Ramsey Michaels, "The First Resurrection: A Response," *WTJ* 39 (1976–77): 100–109; Meredith G. Kline, "The First Resurrection: A Reaffirmation," *WTJ* 39 (1976–77): 110–19.

Greek verb *ezēsan* (came to life) occurs in the context of Revelation 20:4–5. It also appears as a singular in the parable of the lost son (Luke 15:24, 32), where the father exclaims that his younger son is alive again, meaning that his son has experienced a spiritual rebirth.[111]

The apostle John has a penchant for using words with more than one meaning. For example, the term *world* can mean creation, humanity, and people either for or against God. Often without notice he switches from one connotation to another. He leaves it to the reader to understand the writer's intention of a particular word by carefully studying the context. This exegetical pursuit guarantees no unanimity among students of the Apocalypse, but it does present a challenge to each one to be diligent in the Word.

G. Unity

The author of the Apocalypse demonstrates from beginning to end a consistent unity in this book. He uses the same phrases and expressions in the parallels of the seven letters to the churches in the province of Asia. There is the same terminology with respect to the contrast between the Lamb and the Beast; and there are similar clauses that appear in individual chapters, especially those in the first three chapters (1–3) and the last three (20–22). Examples with minor variations abound. The phrase *will make war against them* occurs in many chapters (2:16; 11:7; 13:4, 7; 17:14; compare 19:19). Identical wording appears at the very beginning and near the end of Revelation, "to show his servants that which must soon take place" (1:1 and 22:6). And in 3:12 and 21:2 the author has nearly the same wording, "the new Jerusalem that is coming down out of heaven from my God." Identical wording appears more frequently in the first three chapters (1–3) and the last three chapters (20–22) of the Apocalypse, yet other chapters have their share of parallels. These incidents support the unity of this last book of the New Testament canon.

Nevertheless, Swete astutely observes that if we assume that the unity of the Apocalypse is the work of one author, then we ought to look at the reappearance of symbolical figures. Consider the imagery of Death and Hades in chapters 1, 6, and 20. Also, note the recurrence of unusual terms and forms in all components of Revelation: for example, *the Abyss* occurs seven times (9:1, 2, 11; 11:7; 17:8; 20:1, 3); *mid-heaven* three times (8:13; 14:6; 19:17); and the term *mark* seven times (13:16, 17; 14:9, 11; 16:2; 19:20; 20:4). The repetition of sevenfold incidents in relation to seals, trumpet blasts, and plagues is a characteristic hallmark. John's style, vocabulary, word choice, and syntax testify to the unity of this book.[112]

111. The Greek verb *ezēsen* (he lived) applies also to the beast coming up out of the sea that had the wound of the sword and yet lived (13:14). But the beast as the Antichrist models a ridiculous imitation of Christ, a parody. The beast received a fatal wound, was healed, and lived (13:3, 12, 14); Christ died and returned to life (Rom. 14:9). The beast is consigned to the lake of fire (19:20; 20:10), while Christ resides forever in the new Jerusalem with his saints (22:3–4).

112. Consult Swete, *Revelation*, pp. xlvi–xlix; Charles, *Revelation*, 1:lxxxviii; Beckwith, *Apocalypse*, pp. 22–24.

1. Compilation Theory

A brief look at the flow of thought may raise some questions, especially if the reader notices divisions in the Apocalypse. After the introduction and the seven letters (chaps. 1–3), there is a transition; then a segment of many chapters follows (chaps. 4–11); and the last segment is the largest (chaps. 12–22). Hence, scholars ask whether the author has used other apocalypses in the composition of his Apocalypse. There were such books available in the second part of the first century, written in Hebrew or Aramaic with translations in Greek. Could a Christian writer have taken material from these books and added his own apocalyptic material? Questions can be multiplied, but the issue centers on the use of sources.

Following scholars of the nineteenth century, one commentator has revived the compilation theory that bases Revelation on Jewish apocalypses and a Christian redaction. J. Massyngberde Ford proposes that Revelation should be divided into two parts. She writes that chapters 4–11 are derived from the circle of John the Baptist, because the phrase "he that cometh" reflects the expectation of the Baptist and his disciples. This part may be dated in oral form to the time of the Baptist and thus predates Jesus' ministry. The second part consists of chapters 12–22, which came from followers of the Baptist, who may or may not have become Christians. It dates from the second half of the 60s before the fall of Jerusalem. And last, she writes that "a Jewish Christian disciple of John the Baptist" supplied the first three chapters of Revelation and some verses in chapter 22.[113]

This theory fails on several counts. First, it is completely subjective. Next, there is no evidence either oral or written to support the theory. Third, the linguistic peculiarities appear to stem from the author rather than from an anonymous Christian editor. Finally, although the author of the Apocalypse may have used existing material, he developed the book in such a manner that it bears the stamp of his own personality.

2. Jewish Writings

John relied on the Old Testament books of Ezekiel, Zechariah, and Daniel and borrowed their imagery for his Apocalypse. He was also a contemporary of Jewish apocalyptic writers whose books were known in the days of the apostles. A number of features that characterize apocalyptic literature are peculiar to that period: eschatology, visions, concealed messages, literary dependence, and pseudonymity.[114] And at least three Jewish apocalypses show similarities with reference to the Messiah: *1 Enoch,* 4 Ezra (= 2 Esdras), and *2 Baruch.* The first

113. J. Massyngberde Ford, *Revelation: Introduction, Translation, and Commentary,* AB 38 (Garden City, N.Y.: Doubleday, 1975), pp. 3–4. She concludes, "Thus chs 4–11 and 12–22 should be placed earlier than the Gospels, perhaps earlier than most of the NT. They form a prophetic link between the Old and the New Covenants and prepare the way for the Gospels" (p. 37).

114. Consult Beckwith (*Apocalypse,* pp. 169–74) for an extensive discussion.

book (*1 Enoch*) dates from the first century before Christ and is quoted in Jude 14. Among the topics discussed in this book are passages relating to the person and office of the Messiah and the righteous eternally dwelling with God, the Messiah, and the angels. This book encouraged believers who eagerly expected the coming of the Messiah. The second book (4 Ezra [= 2 Esdras]) was written after the destruction of Jerusalem during the reign of Domitian. It reflects the pessimism of his day among the Jews. Nonetheless, it describes the reign of the Messiah, the coming judgment, and the rebuilding of a new Jerusalem. It depicts the Messiah meting out punishment, destroying his enemies, and gathering the tribes of Israel. The third book (*2 Baruch*) was composed after Jerusalem's destruction and has an optimistic view of the future. The writer looks forward to the rule of the Messiah, the judgment at which the righteous are commended and the wicked condemned, the resurrection, a renewed earth, and a heavenly Jerusalem.

Although these apocalypses share messianic features with Revelation, the differences between them and the last book in the canon are telling. John's Apocalypse is inspired and placed in the canon, the others are not inspired and lack canonical status; inspiration is one of the marks of canonicity. "The Apocalypse of John is differentiated from the Apocalypse of Baruch or of Ezra just as the Book of Daniel is differentiated from the Book of Enoch."[115]

3. Christian Apocalypses

There are a few apocalypses that originated in the centuries immediately following the apostolic period. Their composers gave these documents the names of certain apostles: The *Apocalypse of Peter*, the *Apocalypse of Stephen*, and the *Apocalypse of Thomas*. The last two were Gnostic and were regarded as apocryphal, but the first one appeared to be canonical because Clement of Alexandria seemed to regard it as a genuine work of Peter. But in time the *Apocalypse of Peter* was placed among the spurious and apocryphal books. In the fourth century, the *Apocalypse of Paul* surfaced as an explanation of the inexpressible things that cannot be told (2 Cor. 12:4). Swete, referring to Augustine, characterizes this work as folly "which is no less conspicuous than its presumption."[116] Of all the apocalypses, only the one John wrote has been received by the church as an inspired book that occupies a place in the canon. In it we find God's revelation as he brings to a close the sum total of his written Word.

H. Acceptance in the Church

Writers in the second century accepted Revelation as coming from the apostle John. They include Justin Martyr (see his *Dialogue with Trypho* 81.15) and his con-

---

115. Swete, *Revelation*, pp. xxix–xxx. Bauckham (*Climax of Prophecy*, p. 39) comments, "His [John's] distinctiveness may be comparable to that of one Jewish apocalypse in relation to others or it may be due to his deliberately Christian prophetic consciousness and message."

116. Swete, *Revelation*, p. xxxii.

temporary Irenaeus, who refers to Revelation as Scripture. By the end of the second century, the churches in the West had fully accepted John's Revelation, according to the Muratorian Fragment.[117]

At the beginning of the third century, Tertullian likewise attested to the apostolic origin of Revelation. He wrote in opposition to Marcion, who half a century earlier (150) had rejected the Apocalypse by leaving it out of his canon. Tertullian wrote, "We have also John's foster churches. For although Marcion rejects his Apocalypse, the order of their bishops when traced back to the beginning rests on John as the author."[118] In short, the evidence in the third century overwhelmingly supports Johannine authorship.

Objections to Johannine authorship in the last half of the second century came from a group of people known as Alogi. They rejected the Logos doctrine in the Prologue of John's Gospel and consequently renounced the Apocalypse; they ascribed the authorship of this book to Cerinthus the Gnostic. Eusebius cites Gaius of Rome, who wrote, "But Cerinthus by means of Revelations which he pretended to have written by a great apostle, falsely introduces wonderful things to us, as if they were shown him by angels."[119] Opposition to Johannine authorship of the Apocalypse came primarily from heretics and false prophets who wanted to discredit Christianity.

The church in Alexandria accepted John's Revelation. But after Dionysius became bishop in 248, he expressed his opposition to chiliasm by ascribing the Apocalypse not to the apostle but to the presbyter John. Thus, opposition to chiliastic teaching with reference to Revelation 20 entered into the debate about the authenticity of this book. Nearly a century later, the Alexandrian church historian Eusebius in 325 also questioned the authority of Revelation and expressed doubts about its place in the canon. He realized that the church at large accepted the book as genuine, yet he himself was not hostile to labeling it as spurious. At two places he qualifies Revelation's place in the canon by saying, "If this appears correct" and "If the opinion appears correct, the Revelation of John, which some reject, but others rank among the genuine."[120] By contrast, his contemporary Athanasius provided the church with a list of canonical Scriptures that included Revelation as the last book in the canon.

During the second half of the fourth century, ecclesiastical councils acknowledged the presence of the Apocalypse in the New Testament canon. The exception is the Council of Laodicea held in 360, which omits the book from its list of acknowledged canonical writings. This council followed the Eastern Church of the fourth century in precluding Revelation from the canon. But in other parts of the church, councils and church leaders recognized the Apocalypse as an in-

117. "For also John in the *Apocalypse*, although he writes to seven churches, nevertheless speaks to all." Consult Stonehouse, *Apocalypse in the Ancient Church*, p. 83.

118. Tertullian *Against Marcion* 4.5.

119. *Eccl. Hist.* 3.28.2.

120. Eusebius *Eccl. Hist.* 3.25.2, 4 respectively; see also 7.25.1–27.

spired book that belonged in the canon. The Council of Hippo Regius held in Numidia (modern Algeria), where Augustine was present as a presbyter in 393, agreed on the inclusion of the Apocalypse. So did the Council of Carthage in 397 and 419. Both Augustine and Jerome confirmed the decisions of the North African councils. In the East, the church's attitude toward including Revelation in the canon changed at the beginning of the sixth century. By 508, the Philoxenian Peshitta of the Syrian church contained Revelation as part of the New Testament canon.

When Martin Luther translated the Book of Revelation in 1522 into German, he put it with Hebrews, James, and Jude among the unnumbered books in his canonical list of the New Testament Scriptures. He listed all twenty-seven books as part of the canon, but because he placed a value judgment on each book, the four listed above were unnumbered. Luther claimed that these four did not preach Christ and the gospel of justification by faith. In the preface to his 1522 translation, he wrote, "About this book of the Revelation of John, I leave everyone free to hold his own ideas, and would bind no man to my opinion or judgment; I say what I feel. I miss more than one thing in this book, and this makes me hold it to be neither apostolic nor prophetic." He changed his mind on Revelation in the preface of the 1545 edition, where he writes concerning Revelation, "We can profit by this book and make good use of it."[121] Indeed he found the message of Christ in this book and therefore said, "Christ is near his saints and wins the victory at last." However, Luther left the Apocalypse among the unnumbered books of his canonical list.

John Calvin considered the Scriptures to be self-authenticating with respect to their divine origin, character, and authority. For him, the internal testimony of the Holy Spirit in the heart of the believer confirmed and sealed the inspiration of the canonical books. Although Calvin never wrote a commentary on Revelation, this is not to say that he rejected this book. On the contrary, a look at the Scripture indices of his commentaries and the *Institutes* corroborates the fact that the Reformer accepted the canonicity of the last book in the Bible.[122] Calvin wrote commentaries on most of the books in the Old and New Testament, composed his *Institutes*, preached daily in St. Peter's Church of Geneva, conducted correspondence with numerous people in and out of the church, and taught his students in the Geneva Academy. In poor physical condition, he kept a strenuous schedule that brought his life to an end at the age of 55. It is indeed amazing that he was able to do everything he accomplished in those years. Had he written a commentary on Revelation, he would have had it published.[123]

---

121. Martin Luther, *Works of Martin Luther* (Philadelphia: Holman, 1932), 6:488, 486.

122. Calvin quoted Revelation some forty times in his writings. See T. H. L. Parker, *Calvin's New Testament Commentaries* (Grand Rapids: Eerdmans, 1971), p. 78.

123. Parker states, "(1) No copy of a commentary is known. (2) The contemporary silence is stronger against than any statements for such a commentary." See his *Calvin's New Testament Commentaries*, p. 75.

I. Recipients and Purpose

To whom did John address his book? And what was his reason for composing it? These two questions are significant, for they address all the readers of the Apocalypse. The first three chapters of the Apocalypse inform the reader that Jesus addresses the members of the seven churches in the province of Asia: Ephesus, Smyrna, Pergamum, Thyatira, Sardis, Philadelphia, and Laodicea. But the congregations of Colosse and Hierapolis (Col. 4:13) are not mentioned, even though they were in the vicinity of Laodicea. Paul spent some time in the city of Troas (Acts 20:6; 2 Cor. 2:12), yet no letter is addressed to this place. About two decades after John composed Revelation, Ignatius of Antioch wrote letters to the established churches of Tralles and Magnesia in the province of Asia. We would expect that these churches were in existence near the end of the first century, but they are not mentioned in Revelation.

Why are only seven churches addressed? We can only surmise that the churches to which John sent letters are representative of the universal church of Jesus Christ. With respect to location, the seven congregations form an oval trajectory from which numerous other churches could be reached. In ever-widening circles the message has gone forth throughout the world, so that no church is bypassed. The number seven symbolizes completeness and suggests that Jesus appeals to all Christian believers of all places and all ages. The message of Revelation is for "everyone who hears the words of the prophecy of this book" (22:18). Also everyone who reads and studies this book is called blessed (1:3). And last, the repeated command, "He who has an ear, let him hear what the Spirit says to the churches," is addressed to everyone.[124] Every believer is urged to listen to Jesus' voice; and everyone who listens and obeys will receive the spiritual blessings Jesus promised.

The purpose of the Apocalypse is to encourage and comfort believers in their struggle against Satan and his cohorts. The book divulges that in this conflict between Christ and Satan, Christ is the victor and Satan the vanquished. Even though Satan and his army wage war against the saints on earth, who endure suffering, oppression, persecution, and death, Christ is victorious. It is Christ who encourages his people to withstand the onslaughts of the evil one, for they too will reign with Christ and will be seated with him on his throne (3:21). Jesus extends comfort to all believers, for God sees their tears and wipes them away (7:17; 21:4). God listens to their prayers and in response he will influence the course of history (8:3, 4). Saints who die in the Lord are called blessed, for their good deeds are not forgotten (14:13). The blood of martyrs will be avenged (19:2); saints clothed in white apparel are present at the wedding of the Lamb (19:7–9); and they will reign with Christ forever (5:10; 22:5).

This book of consolation, therefore, directs the attention of every believer to the judgment of the world and the ultimate victory for the church. Even though Satan opposes the march of the gospel and the growth of the church worldwide,

124. Rev. 2:7, 11, 17, 29; 3:6, 13, 22.

his power is limited and eventually will be brought to an end when he and his agents are cast into the lake of fire (20:10). Christ has won the victory for his church in his conquest over the forces of Satan and his cohorts. Consequently, the message of Revelation is a message of hope, for Christ who has overcome the world will vindicate his saints. He will lead his people into a state of eternal blessedness in which he is the bridegroom and they are the bride (19:1–9; 21:2, 9).

J. Theology

As the capstone of God's written Word, the Apocalypse consequently presents theological teaching on the following themes:

- God the Father as revealer and ruler;
- Jesus Christ in respect to his person and work;
- the Holy Spirit as the one who leads and guides;
- the saints on earth who suffer and those in heaven who triumph;
- the future of the world and its inhabitants.

1. Lord God Almighty

The first three chapters of the Apocalypse depict Jesus Christ, yet throughout the book the focus is on God. He is the central figure. He gave his revelation to Jesus to show his servants (1:1), reveals his word (19:13), prepares a place of safety for his people (12:6), and to him his servants ascribe glory and honor (1:2, 4–6).

The Book of Revelation features the name of God in every chapter, emphasizing from beginning to end God's rule, holiness, and justice. Writes Bauckham, "The theology of Revelation is highly theocentric. This, along with its distinctive doctrine of God, is its greatest contribution to New Testament theology."[125] At the outset, John describes God in the greetings to the seven churches in the province of Asia: "Grace and peace to you from him who is, and who was, and who is to come, and from the seven spirits before his throne" (1:4). Here is the first mention of God's throne, which is a pivotal expression in this book, occurring some forty-five times, because from this throne God rules the universe. Here is the seat of authority and power; here is holiness that prompts all God's creatures to worship him. Here justice is administered when everyone appears before the great white throne and all the books are opened (20:11–15).

John gives the most descriptive portrayal of God's throne in chapter 4, where in typical Jewish fashion he refers to the one who sits on the throne in heaven (4:2). John presents an array of symbols when he describes the central part of heaven: the throne. God has the appearance of jasper and carnelian; a rainbow with the green color of an emerald encircles the throne; twenty-four thrones occupied by twenty-four elders surround the throne (4:3). Then flashes of lightning are seen and peals of thunder are heard; seven blazing lamps and a sea of

125. Bauckham, *Theology*, p. 23.

clear glass are situated before the throne (4:5–6a); and four living creatures at the center and around the throne ceaselessly sing praises to God (4:6b–11).

In fifteen of the twenty-two chapters of the Apocalypse John mentions the *throne of God*, and in many of these chapters the word occurs repeatedly.[126] The one who is seated on the throne is the Lord God Almighty, who rules eternally with justice and truth (e.g., see 1:8; 4:8; 15:3; 16:7). The saints obey God's commandments (12:17; 14:12), for they make up the kingdom and priests for God (1:6; 5:10). All the saints and angels worship him and call him *our God* (5:10; 7:3, 10, 12; 12:10; 19:1). Even Jesus calls his Father *my God* (3:2, 12 [four times]).

The holiness of God permeates the entire book: the four living creatures sing, "Holy, holy, holy is the Lord God Almighty, who was, and is, and is to come" (4:8). The first part of this song is taken from Isaiah's vision in which the seraphs call out similar wording (Isa. 6:3). The Creator of this world must be worshiped by all his creatures (4:10; 5:14; 7:11; 11:1, 16; 14:7; 15:4; 19:4; 22:8, 9). The saints appear before him for worship (7:9–15), are privileged to enter the temple of God (3:12; 7:15), and are dwellers in the new Jerusalem (3:12; 21:2–3, 10, 27).

All those who blaspheme the name of God (13:6; 16:9, 11, 21) deserve the wrath of God (14:10, 19; 15:1, 7; 16:1; 19:15). Those who saw the effect of the plagues hardened their hearts and refused to repent, even though God gave them time to repent (2:21; 9:20; 16:9, 11). John mentions the wrath of God but does not expressly refer to the love of God.[127] Nonetheless, toward the saints God demonstrates his love by giving them life (11:11), preparing a place for them in the desert (12:6), fulfilling his promises (21:3, 7), and being a source of light for them (21:23; 22:5).

Satan proves to be the great imitator of God. He presents himself in threefold form: the devil, the beast, and the false prophet (16:13; 19:20; 20:10). The dragon, that is, Satan, stands at the shore of the sea as a beast comes forth out of the sea (13:1). All this is in imitation of God creating the world out of the primeval waters. The false prophet, that is, the beast coming forth out of the earth, deceives the inhabitants of the earth into paying homage to the beast (13:11, 14). Here is the imitation of God's Word and Spirit leading the saints to worship God.

Like God, Satan has his throne (2:13; 13:2); his subjects worship him (13:4, 8, 12, 15; 16:2; 19:20); and his kings serve him (17:12). These kings and the beast are given authority to rule only for as long as God has determined. Their demise is sure. The evil trio of Satan, the beast, and the false prophet meet their end in the lake of burning sulfur where they are tormented forever and ever (20:10). Evil personified in Satan comes to an end when the victorious Son of God appears and God renders judgment.

---

126. Rev. 1:4; 3:21 (twice); 4:2 (twice), 3, 4 (three times), 5 (twice), 6 (three times), 9, 10 (twice); 5:1, 6, 7, 11, 13; 6:16; 7:9, 10, 11 (twice), 15 (twice) 17; 8:3; 11:16; 12:5; 14:3; 16:17; 19:4, 5; 20:4, 11, 12; 21:3, 5; 22:1, 3, 4.

127. Consult Swete, *Revelation*, p. clx.

2. The Victorious Christ

More than sixty years after Jesus ascended to heaven, he showed himself to John on the island of Patmos. While he was on earth, he appeared in glorified form to the intimate circle of the three disciples, Peter, James, and John (Matt. 17:1–8). Peter writes about this event by saying that he and his fellow disciples "were eyewitnesses of [Jesus'] majesty. For he received honor and glory from God the Father when the voice came to him from the Majestic Glory" (2 Pet. 1:16–17). After his resurrection, Jesus appeared ten times to his followers, although at times they did not recognize him in his state of glory (e.g., Luke 24:16, 37; John 21:4). Similarly, Jesus' appearance to John was too much for the apostle to assimilate, for John fell at Jesus' feet "as though dead" (1:17).

John describes Jesus' glorified appearance in the same manner as he pictures the throne of God. He does not mention the name of Jesus, much as he avoids using the name of God in the description of the throne. In symbolic language he depicts the Son of Man as a person of supernatural brilliance: his face was as the sun; his head and his hair white as wool or snow; his eyes as a blazing fire; his feet like polished brass; his voice as the sound of rushing waters; his mouth as a sharp sword (the Word of God); and his apparel as a robe that reached down to his feet, with a golden sash around his chest (1:13–16). John describes the victorious Jesus as riding a white horse; wearing many crowns on his head; with eyes of blazing fire; being dressed in a robe dipped in blood; bearing the name of the Word of God and his title *King of kings and Lord of lords;* and with a sharp sword proceeding from his mouth (19:11–15).

John's description of Jesus is striking, for it is impossible for mortal eyes to look into the face of the glorified Christ that beams like the sun in all its brilliance. The blazing eyes of Jesus cause everyone to bow before him in worship. He rules in majesty and glory as one who has been crowned repeatedly with many crowns. The words of his mouth penetrate and judge all human thoughts and attitudes; nothing is hidden from him (Heb. 4:12–13). The color *white* depicts his head and hair and symbolizes purity and integrity, his seat on a white horse connotes the victory of a king, and the golden sash that encircles his chest denotes royalty.

The exalted Christ as the royal priest occupies the center of his church. There he holds the seven angels (messengers) of the seven churches in his protective right hand. There he addresses the seven churches in the province of Asia with messages that reach the church universal. There he enables every congregation to let the gospel light shine in a spiritually dark world. Also, as king he rules with a rod of iron (2:27; 12:5; 19:15) and judges with justice (19:11). He is the Lion of the tribe of Judah, the Root of David, which is a messianic title for the King of kings (5:5). His adversaries call on the mountains and the rocks to hide them from God who sits on the throne and from the wrath of the Lamb of God (6:16). Both God and the Lamb receive the praise and adulation from heavenly beings and glorified saints—the Lamb is praised because he was slain.[128] The Lamb

128. Rev. 5:6, 8, 12, 13; 7:9, 10, 14, 17; 15:3.

leads the saints he has purchased (14:4), while the saints under the altar who cry for justice over God's enemies are told to wait until the consummation (6:10–11). Those who have been invited to the wedding supper of the Lamb rejoice because they as the bride meet Christ, the bridegroom (19:7, 9; 21:9). Yet both the bride and the Spirit are calling on this royal priest to come quickly (22:17).

With God Jesus shares divine characteristics with respect to worship, authority, and a kingdom. God occupies the center of the throne, and the Lamb is standing in that same center (5:6; 7:17). While God is seated on the judgment throne (20:11), the Son is sitting with him on this throne (3:21). God in heaven rules supreme, but so does the Son of Man, whose everlasting kingdom will never be destroyed (Dan. 7:13–14; see Rev. 1:13; 14:14). God reflects his eternity in the words, "the one who is, and who was, and who is to come" (1:4, 8; 4:8; 11:17; 16:5). But Jesus also partakes of that same eternity; for he told the Jews, "Before Abraham was, I am" (John 8:58). Jesus' earthly life expired on the cross, and thus "he was." And people called him "the coming One," that is, the expected Messiah (compare Ps. 118:26; Matt. 11:3; John 11:27). Last, the words "I am the Alpha and the Omega, the beginning and the end" refer to both God and Christ (21:6 for God; 22:13 for Christ). The shorter version "I am the Alpha and Omega" for God (1:8) is echoed by Jesus in the words "I am the first and the last" (1:17).[129]

Nonetheless, nowhere in the Apocalypse does John designate Jesus as God, and so he avoids leaving the impression that he teaches the existence of two Gods. But although John never calls Jesus God, with the use of pronouns he places Jesus on the same level as God. In more than one passage where he mentions both God and the Lamb, he writes the singular pronouns *his* and *him.* For instance, with italics added, we read:

- "They will be priests of God and of Christ and will reign with *him* a thousand years" (20:6);
- "And the throne of God and of the Lamb will be in it, and *his* servants will serve *him,* and they will see *his* face. And *his* name will be on their foreheads" (22:3–4).

John calls Jesus the Son of God (2:18) and the Word of God (19:13). He notes that Jesus addresses God as "*my* God" (3:12 [four times]), implying the subordination of the Son to the Father. He describes Jesus as the firstborn of the dead, the ruler of the kings of the earth (1:5), the Root and Offspring of David (5:5; 22:16), the Lion of the tribe of Judah (5:5), and the bright Morning Star (22:16).[130] He ascribes divine characteristics to Jesus by placing him next to God, but he refrains from making God and Jesus exactly alike. Note that God is

129. Refer to Bauckham, *Climax of Prophecy*, pp. 33–34; and his *Theology*, pp. 25–28; Paulien (*Decoding Revelation's Trumpets*, p. 349) writes, "Language applied to Yahweh is freely applied to Christ."

130. Compare Swete, *Revelation*, pp. clxii–clxiii.

called the Creator of all things (4:11), while Jesus refers to himself as the "origin [Greek *archē*] of creation" (3:14). The word *origin* should not be interpreted in a passive sense as if Jesus were created or recreated, but in the active sense that he is the one who generates and calls creation into being (John 1:1; Col. 1:15–18; Heb. 1:2).[131] Jesus Christ receives God's revelation, which he passes on to John (1:1); he is the Lamb that was slain and with his blood he purchased the saints for God (5:6, 9); and as the Lamb he welcomes his bride, that is, the church, to the wedding feast (19:7–9; 21:9). John teaches that Christ is God's agent in creation, redemption, and consummation.

Furthermore, in chapter four, John relates that God receives unending praises (4:8, 11), but in the next chapter the saints and angels sing three songs adulating the Lamb (5:9–10, 12, 13b). Indeed in the last of these three songs they worship both "him who sits on the throne" and the Lamb. It is interesting to note that John speaks of the Lamb juxtaposed to God, for the doxologies are directed to both of them (7:10, 17; 14:4; 22:1, 3). The worship of Christ "leads to the joint worship of God and Christ, in a formula in which God retains the primacy."[132]

The name *Lamb of God* suggests both priesthood and kingship, as expressed in song by the heavenly multitude that worships the Lamb:

> because you were slain and with your blood
> you bought [men and women] for God
> out of every tribe and language and
> people and nation,
> and you made them for our God
> a kingdom and priests,
> and they will rule upon the earth. (5:9–10)

John also uses the name *Christ* in connection with power, authority, and kingdom. The kingdom of the world now belongs to Christ, who rules with power and authority (11:15; 12:10; compare 20:4, 6). This kingdom pertains to both Christ and God, for both will reign forever and ever (11:15, 17). Christ is the conquering ruler who sits next to his Father on the throne (3:21). Christ the Lamb is victor over the forces of the Antichrist, "because he is the Lord of lords and King of kings" (17:14).

Satan not only imitates God; he also mimics Jesus Christ in the appearance of a lamb. In Revelation, the word *lamb* occurs twenty-nine times, twenty-eight of which refer to the Lord and one to Satan's false prophet, namely, the beast coming up out of the earth (13:11). Satan's lamb speaks not the words of God but those of a dragon, that is, Satan (20:2). Satan's beast has a head with a fatal wound that had been healed (13:3), while Jesus is the Lamb that was slain (5:6). Further, Satan is ruler in his kingdom (16:10; 17:12) and the kings of this world

131. See Greijdanus, *Openbaring*, p. 106; Bauckham, *Theology*, p. 56.

132. Bauckham, *Climax of Prophecy*, p. 139. He points out that when John mentions God and Christ together, he writes a singular verb or singular pronoun (11:15 and 6:17; 22:3–4).

are subject to him.[133] Satan demands worship from his subjects, who must have the mark of the beast on their right hand and forehead.[134] But all those who have the mark of the beast encounter God's wrath, drink the cup of God's fury, and are tormented with fiery sulfur in the presence of the holy angels and of the Lamb (14:9–10). The beast, the false prophet, and Satan are thrown into the lake of burning sulfur (19:20; 20:10). Christ is the victor.

3. The Holy Spirit

Both Paul and Peter teach the doctrine of the Trinity in the introductory part of two of their epistles (Rom. 1:1–4; 1 Pet. 1:1–2). Be it more indirectly, John also notes the three persons of the Trinity. In the greeting to the seven churches in the province of Asia, he mentions God the Father as "him who is, and who was, and who is to come." He calls Jesus Christ by name and identifies him as "the faithful witness, the firstborn from the dead, and the ruler of the kings of the earth" (1:5). The Holy Spirit is described as "the seven spirits before [God's] throne." The term *the seven spirits of God,* also translated as "the sevenfold Spirit of God," denotes the completeness of the Spirit (3:1; 4:5; 5:6).

The Holy Spirit is God's Spirit, as is evident from the above-mentioned passages, but at the same time he is also the Spirit of Christ. John describes the Lamb in two passages as *holding* "the seven spirits of God" (3:1) and as *having* "seven horns and seven eyes, which are the seven spirits of God" (5:6).

The Holy Spirit dwelled in John to reveal to him spiritual truths in visions. Thus, John was in the Spirit on the Lord's Day (1:10); he was in the Spirit standing at the open door of heaven (4:2); an angel transported him into the desert while he was in the Spirit (17:3); and last, he was carried in the Spirit to a high mountain to see the Holy City, Jerusalem, coming down out of heaven (21:10). The question is whether John was in the Spirit on Patmos (1:10) and thus remained in the Spirit. If so, then the three following passages (4:2; 17:3; 21:10) depict the agency of the Spirit in transporting John to heaven, a desert, and a great and high mountain respectively. The prophecy of Ezekiel confirms this interpretation in many passages, for the Spirit of God lifted the prophet repeatedly. The Spirit brought Ezekiel to Jerusalem, Babylon, the valley of dry bones, and the temple of the Lord (Ezek. 3:12, 14; 8:3; 11:1, 24; 37:1; 43:5). Paul was caught up to the third heaven and was not permitted to tell anyone what he saw and heard (2 Cor. 12:2–4). But John, controlled by the Holy Spirit, had to make known God's revelation given to him through Jesus Christ (1:1).[135]

The role of the Holy Spirit is to reveal God's truth through Jesus Christ. He is the revealer and inspirer, as is evident from the repetitive concluding statement

133. Rev. 16:14, 16; 17: 2, 10, 12 (twice), 18; 18:3, 9; 19:19.

134. Rev. 9:20; 13:4 (twice), 8, 12, 15; 14:9, 11; 16:2; 19:20.

135. See Bauckham, *Climax of Prophecy*, p. 159; compare Jean-Pierre Ruiz, *Ezekiel in the Apocalypse: The Transformation of Prophetic Language in Revelation 16.17–19.10* (Frankfurt am Main: Peter Lang, 1989), pp. 300–303.

in the seven letters to the seven churches: "He who has an ear to hear, let him hear what the Spirit says to the churches."[136] The Spirit, then, speaks for the Lord Jesus Christ to the churches in the province of Asia in particular and the universal church in general. Concerning God's people, a voice from heaven tells John to write the second beatitude: "Blessed are the dead who die in the Lord from now on." To which the Holy Spirit adds, "Yes, that they may rest from their toils, for their works will follow them" (14:13). And the Spirit together with the church beseeches Jesus to come (22:17).

The Spirit speaks also through the messengers who witness for Jesus and who proclaim the testimony of Jesus. For instance, John was on the island of Patmos "because of the word of God and the testimony of Jesus" (1:9). The two witnesses who prophesy for 1,260 days finish their testimony when the beast attacks and kills them (11:3, 7). They are called *martyrs,* which word in Greek primarily means "witnesses," and they sacrificed their lives for Jesus in the battle against Satan (12:11, 17; 20:4). These witnesses are not only the ordained clergy who faithfully proclaim the gospel; they are the individual members of the church, the body of Christ, who bear witness wherever God has placed them. Writes Bauckham, "Those who bear the witness of Jesus are certainly not just the prophets (19:10) but Christians in general (12:17)."[137] They are instruments of the Spirit through which he makes known the testimony of and for Jesus; and that testimony is the work of the Holy Spirit.

Last, the Lord God employs the spirits of the prophets (22:6), but Satan has his unclean spirits to do his bidding (16:13, 14). These spirits come out of the mouths of the unholy trio: the dragon, the beast, and the false prophet. But when God sends his mighty angel, who, coming from the presence of God, illuminates the earth with his splendor (compare Ezek. 43:1–5), their doom is sealed (Rev. 18:2). Although the blood of the prophets and of the saints has been poured out on the earth (18:24), God avenges their blood (19:2). They are his saints who are invited to the wedding supper of the Lamb (19:9).

4. The Saints

The saints addressed in Revelation are both on earth and in heaven. The members of the seven churches in the province of Asia were in the church that fought against sin, had to cope with deceptive teachings and lifestyles, and had to endure oppression and persecution. Jesus encouraged them in their spiritual struggles; rebuked them for their slothfulness; called them to repentance; told them to be faithful unto death; and instructed them to hold on to what they had. Jesus has set the saints free from their sins (1:5), but not his adversaries, whose sins are piled up to heaven (18:4–5).

136. Rev. 2:7, 11, 17, 29; 3:6, 13, 22. See Beckwith, *Apocalypse,* p. 317; J. C. De Smidt, "The Holy Spirit in the Book of Revelation—Nomenclature," *Neotest* 28 (1994): 229–44.

137. Bauckham, *Climax of Prophecy,* p. 161.

Saints on earth present their prayers to God and do so not through intermediaries but directly. These prayers, presented not to saints or to angels but to God, are mingled with the incense that angels offer to him in golden bowls (5:8; 8:3, 4).[138] Further, the saints offer these prayers individually and collectively at a time when there is silence in heaven "for about half an hour" (8:1). God listens to the voices of his people on earth as they call on him in their afflictions. And the time for God's final response comes when Christ's kingdom has come and also when Christ begins to judge the wicked and reward the saints (11:18).

Also, the saints on earth must suffer persecution because of the word of God (1:9; 6:9; 20:4) and the testimony of and for Jesus.[139] Their blood is spilled on this earth to such an extent that the oppressors of the saints are pictured as drunk with it (17:6). While encouraging the martyrs on this earth, the Apocalypse commends the saints for their patience and faith in God (13:10; 14:12). The saints know that their perseverance and trust are never ineffective, for their righteous deeds will follow them (14:13). Although Satan, the beast, and the false prophet are formidable warriors and win battles, Christ is the Victor who leads the saints on earth to victory. Revelation ascribes victory to both Christ and his followers. Even though Satan's forces snuff out the lives of God's people who are faithful to the point of death, the final victory belongs to Christ and the saints.[140] God never abandons his own people; they belong in his camp (20:9).

John writes about the saints in heaven: they are exhorted to rejoice with apostles and prophets (18:20); their righteous acts are symbolized by fine linen (19:8); they have washed their garments white in the blood of the Lamb (7:14); and they sing praises to God and the Lamb (7:10). They are numberless, are dressed in white apparel, are holding palm branches of victory in their hands, and stand before the throne (7:9). With the angels and elders, saints worship God, who through his angel commands them to do so. For instance, John wants to pay tribute to the angel who instructed him to write another beatitude, "Blessed are the ones who have been called to the wedding banquet of the Lamb," to which the angel added, "These are the true words of God" (19:9). The angel, however, rebukes John for wanting to worship him and orders the seer to worship God. When John again wants to worship the angel who showed him heavenly words and visions, the angel points out that he like John is a servant and that worship should be rendered to God (22:9). No creature in heaven or on earth is worthy of worship. Only God and the Lamb receive tribute from angels, the four living beings, the twenty-four elders, and the countless multitude of saints in heaven and on earth. They must worship God the Creator and Redeemer, for he is holy. In fact, the saints in heaven who have been victorious over the beast sing the song of

138. Compare Luther Poellot, *Revelation: The Last Book in the Bible* (St. Louis: Concordia, 1962), p. 87.

139. Rev. 1:2, 9; 6:9; 12:17; 19:10; 20:4.

140. Rev. 1:18; 2:8; 11:7; 12:7–9; 13:7; 17:14; 19:11, 19. See Hendriksen, *More Than Conquerors*, pp. 8–9.

Moses and the Lamb and say, "Who does not fear you, O Lord, and glorify your name? For you alone are holy, because all the nations will come and worship before you" (15:4). God is called "the Holy One" (16:5); he is "holy and true" (6:10; and see 3:7), and his words are "trustworthy and true" (21:5).

The saints are privileged to be in the very presence of God. Repeatedly John uses the expression *before the throne of God* (e.g., 1:4; 7:15; 20:12). They have the freedom to be in God's very presence, because Christ has opened the way to the inner sanctuary. When the new Jerusalem comes down to earth, there is no temple in that city. The Lord God Almighty and the Lamb are its temple, because the saints are forever in their presence (21:22). There will be no night, for the glory of God and the Lamb are its light (21:23; 22:5). At the consummation, the future turns into God's eternal present where cosmic time is no more and perfection is complete.

By contrast, unbelievers cry out to the mountains and the rocks to cover them and hide them from the face of God and the wrath of the Lamb (6:16). They might even acknowledge that God is sovereign (11:13), but they refuse to repent (9:21; 16:9, 11). While saints in glory are always in God's presence, sinners are banished forever to the lake of fiery sulfur (21:8).

5. Prophecy

Revelation is a book of prophecy, as its first and last chapters indicate (1:3; 22:7, 10, 18, 19). But whereas Old Testament prophecies call attention to the first coming of Jesus Christ, the prophecies in Revelation focus on his Second Coming.

The word *prophecy* in the Apocalypse is at the same time comprehensive in scope, that is, it not only reveals the future but also encompasses revelation God has already given. This becomes clear with respect to the curse that is placed on anyone who adds to or subtracts from the prophecy in this book (22:18–19). Limiting the expression *the prophecy of this book* to Revelation is hardly adequate when we consider the hundreds of Old Testament and New Testament allusions in the Apocalypse. This book fully embodies "the word of God and the testimony of Jesus" (1:2).[141] Further, the words in 22:18–19 were spoken not by John but by Jesus, who voices his full authority emphatically demonstrated in the personal pronoun *I* in the clause "I testify to everyone who hears."[142] Biblical revelation in itself is prophecy and cannot be limited to prediction. Bauckham points out related elements of biblical prophecy: discernment of the situation in which the prophet lives and insight into God's nature and purpose; predicting what must come to pass by understanding how God fulfills the establishing of his universal kingdom; and the demand for the hearers of prophecy to respond by working out God's purpose in their contemporary world.[143] In addition, prophecy point-

141. Compare Beasley-Murray, *Revelation*, p. 347.

142. Swete, *Revelation*, p. 311; Robert L. Thomas, *Revelation 8–22: An Exegetical Commentary* (Chicago: Moody, 1995), p. 514.

143. Bauckham, *Theology*, pp. 148–49.

ing to future fulfillment is expressed in God's promises to his people (21:5–7); in the seven beatitudes (1:3; 14:13; 16:15; 19:9; 20:6; 22:7, 14); in Jesus' words to John and the seven churches (1:17–20; 2:1–3:22); and in angelic and heavenly announcements (10:6–7; 11:18; 17:7–18; 22:6).

The prophetic message of the Apocalypse reveals Christ's victory over evil and his reign with his people. His reign is now and not yet, now in principle and at the consummation in full reality (compare 11:15).

Revelation is a message of comfort and hope for Christians living between Jesus' ascension and his return on the clouds of heaven. It should not be limited to the first century in the days of John nor be restricted to the time immediately before and after the return of Christ. The message of the Apocalypse is for everyone reading and hearing the prophecy of this book, without limits of cosmic time.

K. Summary

This book is the conclusion of God's revelation, that is, the Scriptures. God completes divine revelation in this last book of the canon and gives the reader notice that nothing must be added to or subtracted from his written Word (22:18–19). In other words, the reader should note that the sixty-six books of Scripture are complete and present unity in message and content.

1. Synopsis

The Apocalypse consists of two parts: chapters 1–11 portray the church being persecuted by the world; chapters 12–22 depict Satan's attack on Christ and the church. The first part describes believers and unbelievers in conflict on earth; the second part illustrates the intensity of this conflict between Satan and Christ with his church. The dragon, the beasts, and the prostitute attack the church (chapters 12–20), but John lists their defeat in reverse order: the prostitute, the beasts, and the dragon. In the end, all these enemies are vanquished.[144]

Revelation unveils the battle between God and Satan, Christ and the Antichrist, the Holy Spirit and the false prophet, the saints and sinners, God's city and the world. The weapons Christ and his followers use in this conflict are truth and the Word of God; Satan and his cohorts resort to lying and deceit. In this conflict, Christ and the saints are victorious, while God's opponents face defeat and destruction.

2. Contents

The book begins with a prologue that succinctly states the origin of its contents: God makes his revelation known to Jesus Christ, who through an angel sends it to John for the benefit of the readers and hearers (1:1–3). Notwithstanding the name *Apocalypse*, the next few verses show the characteristics of a letter:

---

144. Refer to Hendriksen, *More Than Conquerors*, p. 22.

the sender, recipients, greetings, and doxology (1:4–8). After mentioning the addressees, John relates his experience as an exile on the island of Patmos one particular Lord's Day when Jesus appeared to him with a message to the seven churches in the province of Asia (1:9–20). Jesus sends a letter to every one of the seven churches (Ephesus, Smyrna, Pergamum, Thyatira, Sardis, Philadelphia, and Laodicea) in which he either commends or reproves them (2:1–3:22). These seven letters are a reflection of the universal church and have a relevant message for any church in whatever period of history it may be.[145]

Having recorded a description of the glorious Christ (1:12–16), John now sees an open door leading to heaven, where he is allowed to view God's throne. Twenty-four elders and four living creatures surround this throne and sing praises to God (4:1–11). The Lamb standing at the center of the throne is found worthy to break the seven seals of the scroll and look into it. Untold angels with elders, living creatures, and all other creatures adulate God and the Lamb (5:1–14). Then the Lamb opens four seals and four riders on four horses come forth representing victory, war, famine, and death (6:1–8). The fifth seal is a view of heaven, with souls asking God how long they have to wait before the Judgment Day; and the sixth seal is a view of earth, with God's enemies hiding themselves in caves and under rocks from the wrath of God and the Lamb (6:9–17).

Before John describes the opening of the seventh seal, he records the sealing of the 144,000 and the gathering of an innumerable multitude standing before the Lamb dressed in white robes that were washed in the Lamb's blood (7:1–17). After the opening of the seventh seal, the prayers of the saints ascend and the seven angels blow seven trumpets (8:1–5). The first six trumpets initiate plagues of burning, destruction, bitterness, darkness, suffering, and death (8:6–9:21). But before the seventh trumpet sounds, John depicts a mighty angel standing on the sea and on the land with a little scroll in his hand. The angel gives the scroll to John who is told to prophesy (10:1–11). Then John pictures two witnesses who prophesy and are killed; but they rise again from the dead while their enemies die in an earthquake (11:1–14). The seventh trumpet sounds, hymns are sung, and God's temple in heaven is opened (11:15–19). This marks the conclusion of the first half (chapters 1–11) of Revelation.

The second part of the Apocalypse includes an account of the birth of a male child, Satan losing his fight against Michael the archangel, and the dragon with his demons being hurled down to the earth (12:1–12). On the earth a war ensues between Satan and the woman with her offspring (12:13–13:1a); a beast coming out of the sea controls the world (13:1b–10) and a beast coming out of the earth controls the mind of the world (13:11–18). The scene changes from earth to heaven, where 144,000 saints worship the Lamb (14:1–5), while on earth the gospel is proclaimed, adversaries are punished, and saints are comforted (14:6–13). Also on earth the Son of Man and his angels reap a harvest, while God's winepress of wrath metes out judgment on the unbelievers (14:14–20). God's wrath

145. Compare David E. Aune, *Revelation 1–5*, WBC 52A (Dallas: Word, 1997), pp. lxxii–lxxv.

against his enemies is executed in seven plagues poured out of seven bowls: sores, sea becoming blood, rivers and springs becoming blood, scorching heat, ruin, drought, and utter destruction (15:1–16:21).

The next section portrays God's judgment on worldly Babylon: the prostitute rides the beast symbolizing worldly power, and the woman herself represents the great city that rules the kings of the world (17:1–18). This city falls while kings, merchants, and travelers weep over her, but they perish with her (18:1–24). Then follow sequentially the vindication of the saints (19:1–8), the wedding supper of the Lamb (19:9–10), and the victory of Christ over his enemies (19:11–21).

Chapter 20 features the thousand-year reign, Satan consigned to the lake of fire, the judgment of the dead, and Death and Hades cast into the lake of fire (vv. 1–15). With the elimination of God's foes, the time for renewal has come. John sees the new Jerusalem coming down from God, who will be forever with his people (21:1–8). The apostle presents a symbolic description of the Holy City by measuring its size, which is in the form of a cube; its foundations are decorated with precious stones and its gates with pearls, and its street are made of pure gold (21:9–21). The city has no need of a temple or of the light of sun or moon, for God and the Lamb are its temple and light (21:22–27). In it stands the throne of God and of the Lamb, and all the saints render homage (22:1–6). The Apocalypse ends with the plea for and the promise of Jesus' return (22:7–21).

L. Outline

In general, interpreters of Revelation are in one of two camps, adopting either a progressive or a cyclical approach to its structure. The progressive mode, also called successive or linear, presents a continuous development from the beginning to the end of the Apocalypse. The cyclical method, commonly known as the recapitulation theory, views the content of the book from various perspectives and points out its parallel segments.[146] The first approach interprets the book literally, wherever this is possible; the second approach advances a figurative interpretation. I have chosen the cyclical method, which evinces progressive parallelism in each successive cycle and reveals new perspectives on God's unfolding message to the church.

These two interpretive methods have a different view of the time frame depicted in the last book of the canon: chronological or symbolical time. Chronological time is only of passing significance in the Apocalypse, because not time but principle governs this book. But with symbolical time, parallel sections do not necessarily follow one another sequentially; instead they give the reader different perspectives of the same teaching that finally results in a definitive climax.

146. This theory goes back to the third century when Victorinus of Pettau in Pannonia (modern Hungary) wrote a commentary on Revelation (see J.-P. Migne, ed., Patrologia Latina [Paris, 1844–64], 5:281–344). See also Beale, *Revelation*, pp. 121–51; John M. Court, *Myth and History in the Book of Revelation* (Atlanta: John Knox, 1979), pp. 5–7.

In other words, progress in successive parallels relates not to temporal sequence but to intensity and emphasis.[147]

The symbolism of the number seven in the Apocalypse is of such importance, especially where it appears in parallel passages, that I have chosen the method of dividing the book into seven visions of the one encompassing panorama of God's revelation. These seven visions are preceded by an introduction and succeeded by a conclusion. Furthermore, visions 1, 2, 3, and 6 have introductory segments to enhance the setting of each individual vision and visions 2 and 3 have interludes. Where the biblical text clearly indicates seven parts to a vision, there I have listed them sequentially: seven letters, seven seals, seven trumpets, and seven bowls.

And last, the numerous occurrences of the phrase *and I saw* give the Apocalypse "an almost technical character."[148] The temptation is real to divide the book on the basis of these occurrences, but such attempts result in objectionable artificiality that I have tried to avoid. The outline below has seven visions with seven parts only in those visions where the biblical text permits it.[149]

- I. Introduction (1:1–8)
  - A. Prologue (1:1–3)
  - B. Greeting (1:4–5a)
  - C. Doxology (1:5b–6)
  - D. Prophecy (1:7–8)
- II. Vision 1: The Church on Earth (1:9–3:22)
  - A. Jesus' Glorious Appearance (1:9–20)
    - 1. Location (1:9–11)
    - 2. Appearance (1:12–16)
    - 3. Message (1:17–20)
  - B. Seven Letters (2:1–3:22)
    - 1. Ephesus (2:1–7)
      - a. Commendation (2:1–3)

147. Christopher R. Smith ("The Structure of the Book of Revelation in Light of Apocalyptic Literary Conventions," *NovT* 36 [1994]: 388) notes that the time reference of 1,260 days, 42 months, 3½ years occurs only after 10:8. "The 3½ year formula occurs seven times after 10:8, but *not* in the Babylon or Jerusalem visions" (his emphasis).

148. Leroy C. Spinks, "A Critical Examination of J. W. Bowman's Proposed Structure of the Revelation," *EvQ* 50 (1978): 18.

149. Refer to John Wick Bowman, *The First Christian Drama* (Philadelphia: Westminster, 1955); and his article, "The Revelation to John: Its Dramatic Structure and Message," *Interp* 9 (1955): 436–53; R. J. Loenertz, *The Apocalypse of Saint John* (London: Sheed and Ward, 1947); Spinks, "A Critical Examination"; Hendriksen, *More Than Conquerors*, p. 23; S. L. Morris, *Drama of Christianity*, p. 29; Elisabeth Schüssler Fiorenza, "Composition and Structure of the Book of Revelation," *CBQ* 39 (1977): 344–66; also as chapter 6 in her *Book of Revelation*; James L. Blevins, "The Genre of Revelation," *RevExp* 77 (1980): 393–408. See also the remarks by G. B. Caird, *A Commentary on the Revelation of St. John the Divine* (London: Black, 1966), pp. 105–6; Smith, "Structure of the Book of Revelation," pp. 373–93; Michael Wilcock, *The Message of Revelation: I Saw Heaven Opened* (Downers Grove: InterVarsity, 1975), pp. 15–18.

- b. Rebuke (2:4–5)
- c. Promise (2:6–7)
2. Smyrna (2:8–11)
3. Pergamum (2:12–17)
    - a. Violence (2:12–13)
    - b. Rebuke (2:14–16)
    - c. Promise (2:17)
4. Thyatira (2:18–29)
    - a. Address and Praise (2:18–19)
    - b. Reproof and Command (2:20–25)
    - c. Promise (2:26–29)
5. Sardis (3:1–6)
    - a. The Warning (3:1–3)
    - b. The Promise (3:4–6)
6. Philadelphia (3:7–13)
    - a. Address and Recognition (3:7–8)
    - b. Exhortation (3:9–11)
    - c. Promise (3:12–13)
7. Laodicea (3:14–22)
    - a. Description (3:14–16)
    - b. Reproof (3:17–18)
    - c. Admonition (3:19–20)
    - d. Promise (3:21–22)

III. Vision 2: God's Throne and the Seven Seals (4:1–8:1)

- A. The Throne of God (4:1–5:14)
    1. The Throne in Heaven (4:1–11)
        - a. On and before the Throne (4:1-6a)
        - b. Doxologies at the Throne (4:6b–11)
    2. The Sealed Scroll (5:1–5)
    3. Praise to the Lamb (5:6–14)
- B. The Seven Seals (6:1–8:1)
    1. The First Seal: The White Horse (6:1–2)
    2. The Second Seal: The Red Horse (6:3–4)
    3. The Third Seal: The Black Horse (6:5–6)
    4. The Fourth Seal: The Pale Horse (6:7–8)
    5. The Fifth Seal: The Patience of the Saints (6:9–11)
    6. The Sixth Seal: The Day of the Lord (6:12–17)
        - a. In Nature (6:12–14)
        - b. Toward Unbelievers (6:15–17)
    7. Interlude: The Saints (7:1–17)
        - a. The 144,000 Sealed (7:1–8)
        - b. The Great Multitude (7:9–12)
        - c. An Interview (7:13–17)
    8. The Seventh Seal: The Judgment of Unbelievers (8:1)

- IV. Vision 3: Seven Trumpets (8:2–11:19)
  - A. Introduction (8:2–5)
  - B. Seven Trumpeting Angels (8:6–11:19)
    - 1. The First Trumpet (8:6–7)
    - 2. The Second Trumpet (8:8–9)
    - 3. The Third Trumpet (8:10–11)
    - 4. The Fourth Trumpet (8:12)
    - 5. The Three Woes (8:13)
    - 6. The Fifth Trumpet (9:1–12)
      - a. The Abyss and Demonic Forces (9:1–6)
      - b. The Locusts (9:7–12)
    - 7. The Sixth Trumpet (9:13–21)
      - a. A Divine Command (9:13–16)
      - b. A Descriptive Vision (9:17–19)
      - c. Refusing to Repent (9:20–21)
    - 8. Interlude (10:1–11:14)
      - a. The Angel and the Little Scroll (10:1–11)
        - (1) A Mighty Angel (10:1–4)
        - (2) The Angel's Message (10:5–7)
        - (3) The Scroll and Its Purpose (10:8–11)
      - b. Two Witnesses (11:1–14)
        - (1) The Temple (11:1–2)
        - (2) The Power of Two Witnesses (11:3–6)
        - (3) The Death of Two Witnesses (11:7–10)
        - (4) The Resurrection of Two Witnesses (11:11–14)
    - 9. The Seventh Trumpet (11:15–19)
      - a. Two Hymns (11:15–18)
      - b. God's Covenant (11:19)
- V. Vision 4: Aspects of Warfare and Salvation (12:1–14:20)
  - A. The Woman and the Dragon (12:1–17)
    - 1. The Woman, the Son, the Dragon (12:1–6)
    - 2. Warfare in Heaven (12:7–9)
    - 3. A Song of Victory (12:10–12)
    - 4. Help and Safety for the Church (12:13–17)
  - B. The Beast from the Sea (13:1–10)
    - 1. The Description (13:1–4)
    - 2. Power and Authority (13:5–10)
  - C. The Beast from the Land (13:11–18)
    - 1. Parody of Christ (13:11–14)
    - 2. The Mark of the Beast (13:15–18)
  - D. The Lamb (14:1–5)
  - E. Four Messages (14:6–13)
    - 1. The First Angel (14:6–7)

- 2. The Second Angel (14:8)
- 3. The Third Angel (14:9–12)
- 4. A Heavenly Voice (14:13)

F. God's Wrath (14:14–20)

VI. Vision 5: Seven Bowls of Judgment (15:1–16:21)

A. The Setting (15:1–8)

1. The Saints and the Song (15:1–4)
   - a. Angels and Plagues (15:1)
   - b. Overcomers and Their Ode (15:2–4)
2. Temple, Angels, and Plagues (15:5–8)

B. The Seven Bowls (16:1–21)

1. The First Bowl (16:1–2)
2. The Second Bowl (16:3)
3. The Third Bowl (16:4–7)
4. The Fourth Bowl (16:8–9)
5. The Fifth Bowl (16:10–11)
6. The Sixth Bowl (16:12–16)
7. The Seventh Bowl (16:17–21)

VII. Vision 6: Victory for Christ (17:1–19:21)

A. Introduction (17:1–2)

B. Conflict and Judgment (17:3–19:10)

1. The Woman and the Beast (17:3–18)
   - a. The Seductive Temptress (17:3–6)
   - b. The Angel's Explanation (17:7–11)
   - c. The Sovereignty of the Lamb (17:12–14)
   - d. God's Purpose (17:15–18)
2. Songs of Doom and Destruction (18:1–24)
   - a. The First Lament (18:1–3)
   - b. The Command to Flee (18:4–8)
   - c. The Fall of Babylon (18:9–20)
     - (1) The Dirge of Royalty (18:9–10)
     - (2) The Lament of Merchants (18:11–17a)
     - (3) The Lament of Sea Captains (18:17b–19)
     - (4) Contrast (18:20)
   - d. A Symbol and a Song of Doom (18:21–24)
3. Songs of Praise, Wedding, and Worship (19:1–10)
   - a. Three Hymns and a Command (19:1–5)
   - b. The Wedding (19:6–9)
   - c. Worship (19:10)

C. The Decisive Battle (19:11–21)

1. The Rider and His Armies (19:11–16)
2. The Final Battle against the Antichrist (19:17–21)

VIII. Vision 7: New Heaven and New Earth (20:1–22:5)

A. Defeat of Satan and Death (20:1–15)

        1. The Binding of Satan (20:1–3)
        2. The Saints in Heaven (20:4–6)
        3. Satan's Defeat and Demise (20:7–10)
        4. The Judgment Day (20:11–15)
    B. The New Jerusalem and the Tree of Life (21:1–22:5)
        1. God and His People (21:1–8)
        2. The Holy City (21:9–14)
        3. The Adornment of the City (21:15–21)
        4. The Light of the City (21:22–27)
        5. The Tree of Life (22:1–5)
IX. Conclusion (22:6–21)
    A. Jesus' Return (22:6–17)
    B. Warning (22:18–19)
    C. Promise and Blessing (22:20–21)

Commentary

1

Introduction and Jesus' Glorious Appearance

(1:1–20)

Outline

- I. Introduction (1:1–8)
  - A. Prologue (1:1–3)
  - B. Greeting (1:4–5a)
  - C. Doxology (1:5b–6)
  - D. Prophecy (1:7–8)
- II. Vision 1: The Church on Earth (1:9–3:22)
  - A. Jesus' Glorious Appearance (1:9–20)
    1. Location (1:9–11)
    2. Appearance (1:12–16)
    3. Message (1:17–20)

1 1 The revelation of Jesus Christ, which God gave him to show his servants what must soon
take place. And he made it known by sending his angel to his servant John, 2 who testified
to the things he saw, that is, the word of God and the testimony of Jesus Christ. 3 Blessed
is the one who reads aloud and the ones who hear the words of this prophecy and heed
the things written in it. For the time is near.

4 John to the seven churches that are in [the province of] Asia. Grace to you and peace from him
who is and who was and who is to come, and from the seven spirits that are before his throne, 5 and
from Jesus Christ, the faithful witness, the firstborn from the dead, and the ruler of the kings of the
earth.

To him who loves us and set us free from our sins by his blood, 6 and made us a kingdom and
priests to his God and Father: to him be glory and power forever and ever. Amen.

> 7 Look, he is coming with the clouds,
>   and every eye will see him,
> even those who pierced him,
>   and all the tribes of the earth
>   will mourn because of him. Yes indeed, amen.

8 I am the Alpha and the Omega, says the Lord God, who is and who was and who is to come, the
Almighty.

I. Introduction
1:1–8

John's introductory words in his Gospel describe Jesus as the Word of God (John 1:1), and in the opening verse of his First Epistle, he introduces Jesus as the one from whom the disciples heard "the word of life" (1 John 1:1–3). In Revelation he states that God gave Jesus his revelation to make it known to John, who wrote it down and passed it on to the church. Although the title of the last book in the canon is often listed as *The Revelation of John,* it is in fact *The Revelation of Jesus Christ.* Furthermore, having received God's revelation, Jesus reveals himself to John on the island of Patmos. He tells him to write seven letters to the seven churches in the province of Asia. Jesus indeed is the living Word of God, and John is on the island because of the word of God and the testimony he has presented about Jesus. In short, John has been faithful in proclaiming God's revelation in Jesus Christ.

John begins the first chapter of Revelation with a twofold prologue in which he states first the origin and recipients of the Apocalypse and then the formulation of the first of seven beatitudes in this book.[1] Identifying himself as John, he addresses the seven churches in the province of Asia and greets them in the name of God, the Holy Spirit, and Jesus Christ (1:4–5). He purposely places Jesus last in this trinitarian greeting, because John makes Jesus known as the Redeemer who is coming back on the clouds.

A. Prologue
1:1–3

1. The revelation of Jesus Christ, which God gave him to show his servants what must soon take place. And he made it known by sending his angel to his servant John, 2. who testified to the things he saw, that is, the word of God and the testimony of Jesus Christ.

a. "The revelation of Jesus Christ." The term *Apocalypse* derives from the Greek word *apokalypsis,* which means an uncovering or revealing. Technically, as a heading, the term relates to only one book in the entire canon of the Scriptures, namely, Revelation, but the initial readers were not unacquainted with the Greek word *apokalypsis,* which occurs eighteen times in the New Testament, thirteen of them in Paul's epistles.[2] From time to time, God revealed messages to his people, but in the Apocalypse he presents an extended uncovering of his biblical revelation to Jesus. Hence a lengthy title for this book is "The Revelation of God to Jesus Christ."

When Jesus Christ imparts the revelation he has received, at that moment it becomes his own revelation. Indeed, the title of this book can also mean that Jesus Christ presents revelation about himself. This is so in the second half of the chapter and elsewhere, where he reveals himself to John and to the readers of the letters (1:12–13; 2:1, 8, 12, 18; 3:1, 7, 14). Jesus is both "the object and content of the revelation" that ultimately belongs to him.[3] He is not an angel who passed it on to John, but he is the revealer of and about himself. In short, Jesus' revelation is both subjective and objective.

The double name *Jesus Christ* is his given name and a description of his mediatorial office. In succeeding verses and chapters, the single name occurs either as *Jesus* (e.g., 1:9) or *Christ* (e.g., 11:15).[4] The double name tells the reader not only who Jesus is but also what he has done and continues to do as Lord and Savior. This combination appears at the beginning of the book to identify him fully

---

1. Rev. 1:3; 14:13; 16:15; 19:9; 20:6; 22:7, 14.

2. Luke 2:32; Rom. 2:5; 8:19; 16:25; 1 Cor. 1:7; 14:6, 26; 2 Cor. 12:1, 7; Gal. 1:12; 2:2; Eph. 1:17; 3:3; 2 Thess. 1:7; 1 Pet. 1:7, 13; 4:13; Rev. 1:1.

3. George Eldon Ladd, *Commentary on the Revelation of John* (Grand Rapids: Eerdmans, 1972), p. 21; Leon Morris, *Revelation,* rev. ed., TNTC (Leicester: Inter-Varsity; Grand Rapids: Eerdmans, 1987), p. 46; S. Greijdanus, *De Openbaring des Heeren aan Johannes,* KNT (Amsterdam: Van Bottenburg, 1925), p. 5.

4. Eugene H. Peterson (*Reversed Thunder: The Revelation of John and the Praying Imagination* [San Francisco: Harper & Row, 1988], p. 28) pointedly writes, "The Revelation gives us the last word on Christ, and the word is that Christ is center and at the center. Without this controlling center, the Bible is a mere encyclopedia of religion with no more plot than a telephone directory."

(see also 1:2, 5). He is the Son of God who appeared in human form to take upon himself the obligation to redeem and restore God's covenant people.

b. "Which God gave him to show his servants what must soon take place." Notice that Jesus Christ is subordinate to God, who by giving Jesus the revelation implicitly appoints him to an assignment. The verb *to give* is not merely a handing over of a gift, but rather it intimates the task of making God's revelation known to his people (John 12:49; 14:27; 17:8). Jesus Christ receives the task of showing it in the manner of a pictorial display. The book itself is an eloquent testimony that this display is given by signs, symbols, names, numbers, colors, and creatures. At the beginning of this book, its pictorial characteristics already become visible in the verb *to show.* It is a hint to the reader as to how the book should be read and understood.

The word *servants* denotes not slaves but God's people who obediently do his will (see 2:20; 7:3; 19:2, 5; 22:3, 6). Here the word bears a single message, whereas in two other places it has a dual message: "his [your] servants the prophets" (10:7; 11:18), which is a common Old Testament appellation (e.g., Jer. 7:25; Ezek. 38:17; Dan. 9:10; Amos 3:7). The single message states that God's servants withstand temptation, bear his seal on their foreheads, and sing his praises.

God's servants are to be informed about the things that must happen soon. What is the meaning of the word *soon*? To the recipients of the seven letters it meant that persecution would soon be reality. But this is only one aspect of the things that will come to pass. Throughout the ages, God's servants have experienced that the things Jesus made known to them truly occurred. Therefore, the church today is anxiously waiting for Jesus' promised return. The repetition of the words "what must soon take place" is significant because they are part of the last chapter of the Apocalypse (22:6) that features the promise of and petition for the Lord's return (compare also 4:1 and Dan. 2:28, 29). To quote a reassuring word from Peter, "The Lord is not slow in keeping his promise, as some understand slowness" (2 Pet. 3:9).

c. "And he made it known by sending his angel to his servant John." It is significant that the verb *to make known/to signify* in the Greek language is related to the noun *sign.* Here then is a foreshadowing of the method in which revelation is conveyed. The conveyor of the message is an angel, who differs from Jesus Christ, the revealer. An angel is a messenger, never a revealer (see 1 Pet. 1:12). And this angel conveys the message to John, the author of Revelation (22:6, 16). Here is John's first self-designation (1:1, 4, 9; 22:8), which he gives in the third person as "his servant."

d. "Who testified to the things he saw, that is, the word of God and the testimony of Jesus Christ." We would expect John to pen the present tense of the verb *to testify* as he did in the concluding words to his Gospel, "This is the disciple who testifies to these things, and who wrote them down" (John 21:24). But in the case of the Apocalypse, John is resorting to the technique of seeing himself from the perspective of his readers. They would realize that by writing the past tense "testified" John placed himself in the time when they received the Apocalypse.

This is the so-called epistolary aorist.[5] Some scholars are of the opinion that John wrote the past tense because he first wrote his Apocalypse and afterward added the prologue.[6] But this is unlikely because John wrote not on individual sheets of papyrus but on a scroll, which precludes adding a prologue. The author first had to see the things that were revealed to him before he could record them in a book.

"The word of God" does not mean the person of Jesus Christ (19:13; John 1:1) but refers to God's revelation. The Apocalypse originates not with John who is the writer but with God, who reveals his word to the readers through John (1:9). And "the testimony of Jesus Christ" is the completion of this clause, which in slightly altered form appears repeatedly throughout the book (1:9; 6:9; 12:17; 20:4). The question is whether the genitive in the phrase *testimony of Jesus Christ* is subjective or objective. Subjectively, the testimony belongs to Jesus who is the messenger of the word of God (see John 3:31–34). Objectively, the phrase points to God's faithful servants, including John, who proclaim the word and preach about Jesus. In this particular text, however, the choice is the subjective genitive because the context demands it. The first phrase *word of God* calls for it, and similarly the second requires it. Even though these phrases pertain to the Apocalypse, they embody the fullness of its content, namely, the numerous allusions to the Old Testament together with the earthly life and ministry of Jesus.

3. Blessed is the one who reads aloud and the ones who hear the words of this prophecy and heed the things written in it. For the time is near.

a. "Blessed is the one who reads aloud and the ones who hear the words of this prophecy." This is the first of seven beatitudes in the Apocalypse (1:3; 14:13; 16:15; 19:9; 20:6; 22:7, 14). The word *blessed* is sometimes translated as "happy," but its meaning is more than happiness. It points to "God from whom all blessings flow," to borrow the opening line of Thomas Ken's doxology. And in both the Old and New Testaments, the blessings of the Lord are reflected in the delightful faces of his faithful servants (see, e.g., numerous Psalms, Prophets, and the Beatitudes).[7]

The blessings of the Lord descend on both the person who reads aloud the words of this Apocalypse in the local worship service and the hearers who listen reverently and obediently to these words. In the ancient synagogues the Law and the Prophets were read on the Sabbath days (Luke 4:16; Acts 13:15; 15:21), and

---

5. See Morris, *Revelation*, p. 47; Henry Barclay Swete, *Commentary on Revelation* (1911; reprint, Grand Rapids: Kregel, 1977), p. 3; Greijdanus, *Openbaring*, p. 8; Robert L. Thomas, *Revelation 1–7: An Exegetical Commentary* (Chicago: Moody, 1992), p. 62.

6. Refer to Isbon T. Beckwith, *The Apocalypse of John* (1919; reprint, Grand Rapids: Baker, 1979), pp. 422–23; compare Robert H. Mounce, *The Book of Revelation*, rev. ed., NICNT (Grand Rapids: Eerdmans, 1998), p. 43.

7. Ps. 1:1; 112:1; 119:1; 128:1; Isa. 30:18; Jer. 17:7; Matt. 5:3–12. David E. Aune (*Revelation 1–5*, WBC 52A [Dallas: Word, 1997], p. 11) points out that the beatitude in Rev. 1:3 is unique because "it is formulated in *both* the third person singular ('the one who reads') and the third person plural ('those who hear'), thereby providing a blessing on the communication process itself."

in the churches the Gospels and the Epistles were added to the reading of the Scriptures (1 Tim. 5:18; Col. 4:16; 1 Thess. 5:27). The verb tense of *to read* and *to hear* is in the present to indicate that this is not merely a single exercise but rather that the religious exercise must be kept regularly, especially on the Lord's Day. This exercise is meant to worship God and to strengthen believers in their faith. The term *prophecy* appears seven times in Revelation (1:3; 11:6; 19:10; 22:7, 10, 18, 19) and does not necessarily refer to predictions. Prophecy in this book relates to God who through his messengers makes his truth known to his people. Prophecy means a continuation of God's word in the Old Testament Scriptures and indicates that God is its author who endows it with his authority. The prophetic message of the Apocalypse, therefore, assumes its rightful place among the other books in the canon.

b. "And heed the things written in it." Through these words of prophecy, God's messengers call people to a life of obedience and love for him. They are those who are the hearers of the words that are read; they must put these words into deeds to demonstrate that they are indeed children of God and followers of Jesus. They must keep these written words that never lose their power and authority.

"For the time is near." The Greek language has at least two words for time: first, *chronos,* from which we have the derivatives "chronic" and "chronicle," denotes calendar time of longer or shorter duration. Second, *kairos* signifies an opportune moment or a time of decision. This is the word used in the clause "for the time is near." For readers of Revelation, the time is at hand to make a decision. The word occurs seven times in the Apocalypse (1:3; 11:18; 12:12, 14 [three times]; 22:10).[8] With the composition of this book the *kairos* has come; aside from the *chronos,* it spans the passing of the ages. "Although the end has not yet come, and the *kairos* is still in progress, so much of what was to occur has already occurred, that now, surely, we may look the more eagerly for the end."[9]

The Book of Revelation repeatedly states that its contents relate to the time at hand (1:1, 3; 22:6, 10). It informs the readers that its message is applicable to the time in which they are living: the conflict between God and Satan, Christ and the Antichrist, the Holy Spirit and false prophets, the church and immorality is occurring in their lifetime. Consequently, every generation has to appropriate

8. Jörg Baumgarten, *EDNT,* 2:232–35. See additional time references in Rev. 2:16, 25; 3:11; 6:11; 10:6; 11:2–3; 12:6; 17:10; 22:7, 20. Consult M. Eugene Boring, *Revelation,* Interpretation (Louisville: John Knox, 1989), pp. 68–70.

9. R. C. H. Lenski, *The Interpretation of St. John's Revelation* (Columbus: Wartburg, 1943), p. 34. Consult Louis A. Vos, *The Synoptic Traditions in the Apocalypse* (Kampen: Kok, 1965), pp. 178–81; Sam Hamstra Jr., "An Idealist View of Revelation," in *Four Views on the Book of Revelation,* ed. C. Marvin Pate (Grand Rapids: Zondervan, 1998), p. 100. In the same volume, C. Marvin Pate ("A Progressive Dispensationalist View of Revelation," p. 136) observes, "For the early Christians, the Parousia was an epilogue, albeit an important one, to the first coming of Christ." By contrast, Gregory K. Beale (*The Book of Revelation: A Commentary on the Greek Text,* NIGTC [Grand Rapids: Eerdmans, 1998], p. 185) speaks of the "already-and-not-yet" aspect of the end-time.

and apply the message of the Apocalypse. And each generation of believers must wait with eager expectation for the Lord's return.

Greek Words, Phrases, and Constructions in 1:1–3

Verse 1

ἃ δεῖ γενέσθαι—"that which must take place." The word δεῖ denotes necessity that God controls. The aorist tense of the infinitive is constative to encompass time from beginning to end.[10]

Verse 2

ἐμαρτύρησεν, μαρτυρίαν—these two words (to testify; testimony) are typical Johannine expressions that frequently appear in the Gospel, Epistles, and Apocalypse. The verb is the aorist active indicative and its cognate the accusative noun.

Verse 3

οἱ ἀκούοντες—the definite article introduces a class of people. The verb *to hear* (in the present participle) is followed by the accusative that expresses the act of hearing and expects obedience.

γεγραμμένα—this is the perfect passive participle "has been written." The perfect tense implies that the action occurring in the past has lasting effect for the present and future.

καιρός—Augustine differentiated *kairos* and *chronos* by saying, "The Greeks indeed use *kairos* as a particular time—not however as one which passes in an alteration of divisions, but as one which is perceived . . . as time for harvesting, gathering grapes, warmth, cold, peace, war, and anything similar. They speak of *chronoi* as the very divisions of time."[11]

B. Greeting
1:4–5a

4. John to the seven churches that are in [the province of] Asia. Grace to you and peace from him who is and who was and who is to come, and from the seven spirits that are before his throne, 5a. and from Jesus Christ, the faithful witness, the firstborn from the dead, and the ruler of the kings of the earth.

a. "John to the seven churches that are in [the province of] Asia." This self-identification (see vv. 1, 9) presents the writer as a well-known person in the western part of Asia Minor (modern Turkey). He identifies himself in the Apocalypse because this genre differs from his Gospel and Epistles. The readers needed no further identification than the name John, because for the Christians throughout the province of Asia there was only one person who could

---

10. Refer to Lenski, *Revelation*, p. 29.

11. Augustine *Letters* 197.2. Richard C. Trench, *Synonyms of the New Testament*, ed. Robert G. Hoerber (Grand Rapids: Baker, 1989), p. 223.

speak with authority, namely, the apostle. As members of the seven churches residing in the province of Asia (the western region of Asia Minor), they knew the venerable John. When Jesus appeared to John on Patmos, he mentioned the seven churches by name: Ephesus, Smyrna, Pergamum, Thyatira, Sardis, Philadelphia, and Laodicea (v. 11). These seven churches receive greetings from the triune God and in addition they obtain the text of the Revelation. Notice that this is the first time the number seven appears in the Apocalypse—seven signifies completeness.

Beginning with the address, John demonstrates that the Apocalypse is written in epistolary form. In brief, the first line of verse 4 is equivalent to the address on an envelope.

b. "Grace to you and peace from him who is and who was and who is to come." The greeting of grace and peace also occurs in other New Testament epistles (Phil. 1:2; 1 Pet. 1:2); other letters add *mercy* (1 Tim. 1:2; Jude 2). The salutation grace (*charis*) is a variation of the Greek *chairein*, which was the common greeting of the Greek-speaking population (Acts 23:26); the word *peace* (Hebrew *šālôm*, expressed here by the Greek *eirēnē*) was used by Jewish people as a salutation.

Further, John differs from other letter writers in delivering greetings from all three persons of the Trinity. He describes the Father as "the one who is and who was and who is to come." This greeting is unique and reveals God's infinity with respect to present, past, and future. God is timeless from eternity to eternity.

The description of God would also be applicable to "Jesus Christ [who] is the same yesterday and today and forever" (Heb. 13:8). The Messiah was known as "the coming one" (Matt. 11:3; John 11:27). But in this trinitarian greeting, Jesus Christ has a place and so do the seven spirits, that is, the Holy Spirit.

Paul usually greets the recipients of his Epistles in the name of God the Father and the Son Jesus Christ; here, however, all three are mentioned preceded by the preposition *from*. At this point in Greek, the grammar is extremely awkward, which translators sidestep by providing a smooth translation. Critics are quick to declare that the author of Revelation cannot have been the writer of the Fourth Gospel, who writes acceptable Greek without grammatical errors. They conclude that if the apostle John penned the Gospel, another John must have written the Apocalypse. This is not necessarily so if we consider that the apostle John was surrounded by assistants in Ephesus where he wrote his Gospel but was alone on Patmos. Because of his Jewish heritage, John would not dare to bring any changes to the appellation "I am" by which God reveals himself (Exod. 3:14; see also John 8:58). The Greek translation of the Old Testament has the expression *ho ōn* (the one who is, Exod. 3:14 LXX), which is exactly what John writes in this text. John refuses to have the name of the "I am" conform to the rules of Greek grammar. Thus, he breaks grammatical rules so as not to discredit God's immutability. And John is consistent in his refusal, as is evident from other places where the same expression appears (1:8; 4:8; 11:17; 16:5). His wording "the one who was" refers to God, who existed in eternity before cosmic time came into being. And the futuristic phrase *the one who is to come* appears in the Greek text of Psalm 118:26 (117:26 LXX). So the entire clause "from the one who is and who was and who is to come" must be understood as an unalterable noun.[12]

c. "And from the seven spirits that are before his throne." John repeats the phrase *seven spirits* a few times in the Apocalypse (3:1; 4:5; 5:6) but does not explicate. Some translations have "sevenfold Spirit" or "seven Spirits" as the reading in either text or margin.

Interpretations of the expression *seven spirits* vary: First, some scholars say that they are seven angels because spirits are sometimes called angels (Heb. 1:7, 14).[13] But angels are created beings, subordinate to God, and in the Apocalypse are never called spirits. The term *seven angels* occurs frequently (15:1, 6–8; 16:1; 17:1; 21:9). Indeed, angels remain God's servants who can never fill the role of the third Person in the Trinity.

Second, others contend that the seven spirits are "symbols of divine majesty" as powerful beings through which God blesses the church.[14] These powerful beings, however, are inferior to God and thus cannot complete the fullness of the Trinity expressed in the greeting.

Third, the Apocalypse speaks of the Spirit but never uses the name *Holy Spirit.* Instead we assume that John employs the symbolism of the number seven and thus describes the Spirit. The seven spirits (1:4; 3:1; 4:5; 5:6) are sent out to all the nations of the world, so that through the church's faithful teaching of the Word, people everywhere may come to know and worship God.[15] The number seven signifies the fullness of the Holy Spirit in his person and work as exemplified in the prophecy of Zechariah 4:2, 6.[16] In the Holy Place of the temple, Zechariah sees a golden lampstand with seven lights each having seven spouts and wicks (v. 2). The abundance of oil symbolizes the Holy Spirit at work, as is evident from God's declaration, "'Not by might nor by power, but by my Spirit,' says the LORD Almighty" (v. 6). God rules this earth not by an earthly power but by his Spirit. In short, John relies on Zechariah's prophecy when he writes the greeting in his Apocalypse.

d. "And from Jesus Christ, the faithful witness, the firstborn from the dead, and the ruler of the kings of the earth." Once again (as in v. 1) John pens the full name Jesus Christ to stress the earthly life of Jesus and his messianic office. He is

---

12. John P. M. Sweet (*Revelation*, WPC [Philadelphia: Westminster, 1979], p. 65) cautions not to press this point. Likewise Beale, *Revelation*, pp. 188–89. They mention the irregularity of the devil's name (20:2). But John writes titles and descriptions in the nominative case (2:13, 20; 3:12; 20:2).

13. Boring, *Revelation*, p. 75; Josephine Massyngberde Ford, *Revelation: Introduction, Translation, and Commentary*, AB 38 (Garden City, N.Y.: Doubleday, 1975), p. 377. Ford calls them "throne angels." And see R. H. Charles, *A Critical and Exegetical Commentary on the Revelation of St. John*, ICC (Edinburgh: Clark, 1920), 1:12–13.

14. Martin Kiddle, *The Revelation of St. John* (reprint, London: Hodder and Stoughton, 1943), p. 8.

15. See Richard Bauckham, *The Climax of Prophecy: Studies on the Book of Revelation* (Edinburgh: Clark, 1993), p. 336. Refer to Eduard Schweizer, *TDNT*, 6:450.

16. Compare SB, 3:788.

the second Person in the Trinity, but John puts him in third place. John first sees the temple as the place where God the Father dwells in the Most Holy Place. Then in the Holy Place he notes the candelabra with the seven branches symbolizing the Holy Spirit. And last, at the altar blood was shed for remission of sins, pointing to the mediatorial work of Jesus Christ. This interpretation finds its basis in the expression "before his throne" (v. 4), referring to God on his throne. The candelabra in front of the Most Holy Place exemplified the Holy Spirit. And at the altar it is Jesus Christ who "set us free from our sins by his blood" (v. 5b).[17]

Three designations are given to Jesus Christ: he is the faithful witness, the firstborn from the dead, and the ruler of the kings of the earth. First, let us consider "the faithful witness," which in the Greek is rendered emphatically as *the witness, that is, the faithful one* (3:14). John may have taken the phrase from Psalm 89:36–37, where God mentions his faithfulness to David's lineage: "his line will continue forever and his throne endure before me like the sun; it will be established forever like the moon, the faithful witness in the sky." The throne typifies "divinely granted authority over the earth."[18] God swore an oath that David's lineage would be seated on the throne and now fulfilled it in Jesus Christ.

Jesus as the firstborn from the dead has conquered death and exercises absolute authority over both the living and the dead (Col. 1:18). He rules sovereignly over the kings of the earth. The wording derives from Psalm 89:27, where God says concerning David, "I will appoint him my firstborn, the most exalted over the kings of the earth." God's promise has been fulfilled in Jesus Christ, to whom everything has been subjected.

Greek Words, Phrases, and Constructions in 1:4–5a

Verse 4

ἀπό—this preposition governs the genitive case, but here it is succeeded by the nominative case ὁ ὢν καὶ ὁ ἦν καὶ ὁ ἐρχόμενος. The grammatical construction of this clause is incorrect in more than one sense. But John writes from a Jewish perspective according to which God's name might not be altered by grammatical rules. Swete notes that Philo (*Life of Abraham* 24 §121) writes that the name of God is ὁ ὤν and that Targum Pseudo-Jonathan on Deuteronomy 32:39 reads, "I am the one who is and who was and who will be." And even in Greek poetry, divine life is described as "Zeus was, Zeus is, and Zeus will be." Swete concludes, "Thus the Apocalyptist strikes a note familiar both to Jewish and Hellenic ears."[19]

John proves that he knows Greek grammar, for in thirty of the thirty-one times in the Apocalypse he correctly construes the preposition ἀπό with the genitive case. Clearly he shows deference to the divine name.

---

17. William Hendriksen, *More Than Conquerors* (reprint, Grand Rapids: Baker, 1982), p. 53.

18. Willem A. VanGemeren, *Psalms,* in *The Expositor's Bible Commentary,* ed. Frank E. Gaebelein (Grand Rapids: Zondervan, 1991), 5:582. Consult also Allison A. Trites, "*Martys* and Martyrdom in the Apocalypse: A Semantic Study," *NovT* 15 (1973): 72–80.

19. Swete, *Revelation,* p. 5. See Aune, *Revelation 1–5,* p. 30.

Verse 5a

ὁ μάρτυς, ὁ πιστός—"the faithful witness." John customarily writes titles and descriptions in the nominative, even though Greek grammar demands the genitive (e.g., 2:13, 20; 3:12; 20:2). The term μάρτυς primarily means one who testifies and secondarily one who suffers death. In this verse, both meanings are relevant even though the first meaning is stressed and the second implied.[20]

C. Doxology 1:5b–6

The paragraph division in the middle of verse 5 is necessary because of the subject matter. John moves from the trinitarian greeting to the doxology and applies it to Jesus and God the Father.

5b. To him who loves us and set us free from our sins by his blood, 6. and made us a kingdom and priests to his God and Father: to him be glory and power forever and ever. Amen.

a. "To him who loves us and set us free from our sins by his blood." John continues his comments on Jesus Christ by devoting praises to him. The graphic description of Jesus "who loves us" appears only here in the present tense. Notice that the present tense is juxtaposed with the past tense of "set us free" to heighten the contrast of a continuous act and a completed act. Jesus shows us his abiding love, which comes to expression in his finished work on Calvary's cross. There he released us from sin and guilt once for all. We see the vivid contrast between the ruler over the kings of the earth, who shows his love by shedding his blood for sins, and us, who are undeserving sinners. Robert Thomas correctly observes, "This is the only N[ew] T[estament] instance where His love is so described."[21]

Some translations read "washed us," which in the Greek differs from "set us free" by only one vowel (λούσαντι and λύσαντι) and has the same pronunciation. Whatever reading one prefers, the washing away of sin results in being set free.

b. "And made us a kingdom and priests to his God and Father." John had in mind an Old Testament passage that combines the concepts *kingdom* and *priests.* He reflected on the scene of Mount Sinai where God told the Israelites, "Although the whole earth is mine, you will be for me a kingdom of priests and a holy nation" (Exod. 19:5–6). Now he acknowledges Jesus as King and Priest who, having cleansed his people from sin, desired them to be a kingdom of priests worthy of presentation to his Father (5:10). These people are a holy priesthood in which they presently serve as priests of God and of Christ (20:6; 1 Pet. 2:9).

Jesus' kingdom differs from a worldly kingdom, as he told Pontius Pilate (John 18:36). He has citizens in every area, sector, and segment of life. These cit-

---

20. Refer to Trites, "*Martys* and Martyrdom in the Apocalypse," pp. 72–80.

21. Thomas, *Revelation 1–7*, p. 70.

izens seek to live obediently by the rules of Christ's kingdom; they pray for all those who are in authority and conduct themselves peaceably in godliness and holiness (1 Tim. 2:2). They demonstrate the love of the Lord Jesus by helping the poor and feeding the hungry (Matt. 25:37–40); they defend the rights of the disadvantaged (Deut. 24:17; 1 Tim 5:16); they care for needy people (Gal. 6:10); and they proclaim and teach the gospel of Jesus Christ (Matt. 28:19–20). As citizens of the kingdom, they testify to the present reign of Jesus in the world today.[22] Christ's followers, who make up his kingdom, honor him as Lord of lords and King of kings and utter their daily prayer, "May your kingdom come" (Matt. 6:10; Luke 11:2).

c. "To him be glory and power forever and ever. Amen." The exact wording of this doxology occurs only here in the Apocalypse and is almost the same as that of Paul's doxology in Romans 11:36. John records doxologies in other parts of Revelation with similar expressions (5:12–14; 7:12; 11:15), but note that in this verse he ascribes the doxology to Jesus Christ.

Greek Words, Phrases, and Constructions in 1:5b–6

Verse 5b

λύσαντι ἡμᾶς—"setting us free." This reading has the support of the better manuscripts (𝔓[18] ℵ A C 1611) and is reflected in the Old Testament (Isa. 40:2 LXX).[23] The other reading is λούσαντι ἥμας (washed us). It has been followed by the KJV and NKJV translators.

ἐκ—John uses this preposition 135 times in Revelation in a variety of ways. Here it occurs with the verb *set free.* Many witnesses, however, have the preposition ἀπό.

Verse 6

τῶν αἰώνων—although leading manuscripts omit these two words from the formula εἰς τοὺς αἰῶνας, scholars are reluctant to omit them here because of the frequent occurrence of the full construction elsewhere in this book.[24]

D. Prophecy
1:7–8

7. Look, he is coming with the clouds,
and every eye will see him,
even those who pierced him,
and all the tribes of the earth
will mourn because of him. Yes indeed, amen.

---

22. Andrew J. Bandstra, "'A Kingship and Priests': Inaugurated Eschatology in the Apocalypse," *CTJ* 27 (1992): 10–25.

23. See Bruce M. Metzger, *A Textual Commentary on the Greek New Testament,* 2d ed. (Stuttgart: Deutsche Bibelgesellschaft; New York: United Bible Societies, 1994), p. 662.

24. Rev. 1:18; 4:9, 10; 5:13; 7:12; 10:6; 11:15; 15:7; 19:3; 20:10; 22:5.

This verse appears to be a liturgical passage that was composed and circulated in the early Christian church. It is a stanza that in Greek New Testaments and modern translations is set off in four lines, followed by the concluding "Yes indeed, amen."

Here is a prophetic announcement based on Old Testament prophecies about the Messiah as the "son of man" (Dan. 7:13; Zech. 12:10) and New Testament references to Jesus' suffering and return (Matt. 26:64; John 19:34, 37; 1 Thess. 4:17). This is the first announcement of Jesus' return, which becomes more pronounced in the last chapter of Revelation (22:7, 12, 20). John not only speaks about Jesus' suffering and triumph, his priesthood and kingship, but also about his imminent return. John looks into the future and sees Jesus returning on the clouds of heaven, as he himself promised (Matt. 24:30). John calls his readers to the reality of Christ's coming by saying, "Look!" He follows it up with the present tense *he is coming*, which has a future and incontestable connotation, "he will come." For John himself, in a sense, these words were confirmed when Jesus appeared to him on the island of Patmos. Now he writes to tell the readers of the Apocalypse that the return of Jesus is truly imminent and everyone should look for his coming.

Scoffers say that Jesus' coming on the clouds is unrealistic because vast areas of the world are cloudless from time to time (2 Pet. 3:3–4). But John informs everyone that Jesus indeed returns seated on a cloud (14:14–16) and that his coming is sudden. Clouds are the visible signs by which God displays his majesty, and clouds surround Jesus and his angels (Exod. 13:21; Matt. 16:27; 24:30–31). In the words of the psalmist, "He makes the clouds his chariot" (Ps. 104:3).[25]

John borrows language from the messianic prophecy of Zechariah 12:10. Pointing to the visible return of Jesus, he declares that every eye will see him. He writes the singular adjective and noun *every eye* to indicate the inclusiveness of all people—believers and unbelievers alike. The clause *even those who pierced him* pertains not only to the Jews and Gentiles who surrounded Jesus' cross. It refers also to all people who despise, ridicule, and reject him. They are unable to escape, even though they call on the rocks and mountains to cover them (Rev. 6:16; Luke 23:30; Hos. 10:8). Revelation gives no indication that Christ's enemies come to repentance, so that all those who have refused to put their faith in Jesus will face the Judge of all the earth. John writes "all the tribes of the earth," which can refer to the tribes of Israel listed in 7:4–8 or to all the peoples and nations of the world.[26]

Further, the expression *will mourn because of him* means an outward display or lament but not necessarily an inner sorrow and genuine repentance. The

---

25. Consult R. B. Y. Scott, "'Behold He Cometh with Clouds,'" *NTS* 5 (1959): 127–32.

26. Norman Hillyer, *NIDNTT*, 3:871; Mounce, *Revelation*, p. 51; Greijdanus, *Openbaring*, p. 22; Alan Johnson remarks that although *tribes* is used of Israel in the Old and New Testaments, John "uses *phylai* in a number of places to refer more broadly to the peoples of all the nations (5:9; 7:9; 11:9; 13:7; 14:6)—a usage that seems natural here, also." See his *Revelation*, in *The Expositor's Bible Commentary*, ed. Frank E. Gaebelein (Grand Rapids: Zondervan, 1981), 12:423.

mourners will beat their chests with their fists and rue the life they led. They will be filled with remorse but not with penitence when they see Jesus. Because they do not repent, they face personal loss at the judgment.[27] In his eschatological discourse, Jesus speaks of the sign of the Son of Man appearing in the sky, "and all the nations of the earth will mourn" (Matt. 24:30). When they see him coming with power and glory, the people who have refused to acknowledge him will realize that it is too late to repent. John concludes these poetic lines with an affirmation: "Yes indeed, amen." The first part of this affirmation is a Greek idiom, the second a Hebrew idiom.

8. I am the Alpha and the Omega, says the Lord God, who is and who was and who is to come, the Almighty.

Here is the first self-designation of God, which John repeats with an addition in 21:6, "I am the Alpha and the Omega, the Beginning and the End." The question, however, is whether these words refer to God or to Christ. For one thing, the *I am* was spoken by God when he called Moses at the burning bush, "I am who I am" (Exod. 3:14). But in the Gospel of John, Jesus identifies himself repeatedly with the *I am* formula, for example, "Before Abraham was born, I am" (John 8:58). Both God and Jesus identify themselves as "I am the Alpha and the Omega." Notice these parallels:

God: I am the Alpha and the Omega (1:8).
Christ: I am the First and the Last (1:17).
God: I am the Alpha and the Omega, the Beginning and the End (21:6).
Christ: I am the Alpha and the Omega, the First and the Last, the Beginning and the End (22:13).[28]

The parallels are identical, yet not Jesus but God is called Almighty (1:8; 4:8; 11:17; 15:3; 16:7, 14; 19:6, 15; 21:22; and 2 Cor. 6:18).[29] Nonetheless, Christ is eternal and can say that he is the first and the last, the originator and the one who completes the work of creation and redemption. He is the first and the last letter of the Greek alphabet (i.e., everything from A to Z); he is fully the Word of God. Thus we see "Christ as the divine agent both in God's creation in all things and in God's eschatological fulfillment of all things."[30] Jesus is the one who was sent by God the Father to deliver the words of God (John 3:34).

This verse summarizes the first segment of chapter 1 by emphasizing the divinity of Jesus Christ as one with God the Father. The Lord Jesus Christ has been

27. Gustav Stählin, *TDNT*, 3:850.

28. Bauckham, *Climax of Prophecy*, p. 34; see also his *Theology of the Book of Revelation*, New Testament Theology (Cambridge: Cambridge University Press, 1993), pp. 26, 54–55.

29. Charles (*Revelation*, 2:387 n. 4) writes that verse 8 "is unquestionably interpolated" and must be rejected to restore the right order of thought. But he is unable to document this statement with manuscript evidence. Also, Jesus reveals himself as God and thus speaks these words and uses the appellation *the Almighty*.

30. Bauckham, *Theology*, pp. 56–57.

from eternity with the Father, has come to earth to pay the penalty of our sin through his death and resurrection, and is giving us the promise of his return. Jesus himself is uttering the words of this text, as is evident from a succeeding segment (vv. 17–18) where he identifies himself as first and last, the living one who was dead, but who lives eternally, holding the keys of Death and Hades. Jesus takes center stage in the first eight verses of this chapter:

- in the opening verses as God's agent of revelation (vv. 1–2);
- in the greeting as the faithful witness, the firstborn of the dead, and the ruler of the kings of the earth (v. 5a);
- in the doxology as the redeemer and king (vv. 5b-6);
- in the prophetic announcement of his return (v. 7);
- and in his declaration of his eternity, divinity, and power (v. 8).

John F. Walvoord rightly concludes, "If no more had been written than that contained in this introductory portion of chapter 1, it would have constituted a tremendous restatement of the person and work of Christ such as is found in no comparable section of Scripture."[31]

Greek Words, Phrases, and Constructions in 1:7–8

Verse 7

κόψονται—the future middle of the verb κόπτω indicates "beat one's breast as an act of mourning." It describes an outward display of sadness.

Verse 8

Ἄλφα . . . Ὦ—Metzger notes that the first letter of the alphabet is spelled out, but not the last one.[32] Some manuscripts add the words ἀρχὴ καὶ τέλος (the beginning and the end). Because it is easier to explain additions than omissions, editors of the Greek text dismiss the addition.

---

9 I, John, your brother and companion in the tribulation and kingdom and patient endurance that are in Jesus, was on the island called Patmos because of the word of God and the testimony of Jesus. 10 I was in the Spirit on the Lord's Day, and I heard behind me a loud voice like the sound of a trumpet 11 saying, "What you see, write in a book and send to the seven churches: to Ephesus, Smyrna, Pergamum, Thyatira, Sardis, Philadelphia, and Laodicea."

12 And I turned to see the voice that was speaking to me, and when I turned, I saw seven golden lampstands. 13 And in the midst of the lampstands was one "like a son of man," dressed in an ankle-length robe and a golden sash around his chest. 14 His head and his hair were white like white wool, like snow, and his eyes were like a flame of fire. 15 And his feet were like exquisite brass refined as in a furnace, and his voice was as the sound of many waters. 16 And in his right hand he held seven stars, and a sharp double-edged sword came out of his mouth, and his face was like the sun shining in its full strength.

---

31. John F. Walvoord, *The Revelation of Jesus Christ* (Chicago: Moody, 1966), p. 40.
32. Metzger, *Textual Commentary*, p. 663 n. 2.

17 And when I saw him, I fell at his feet as though dead. And he placed his right hand on me saying: "Fear not, I am the First and the Last. 18 And I am the living one and I was dead, and look, I am alive forever and ever. And I have the keys of Death and Hades. 19 Write, therefore, what you have seen and what is and what is about to take place after these things. 20 As for the mystery of the seven stars that you saw in my right hand and the seven golden lampstands: the seven stars are the angels of the seven churches, and the seven lampstands are the seven churches."

II. Vision 1: The Church on Earth
1:9–3:22

After the introduction to the Book of Revelation, John describes the first of seven visions that divide the Apocalypse. The other visions in sequence are

- God's Throne and the Seven Seals (4:1–8:1)
- Seven Trumpeting Angels (8:2–11:19)
- Aspects of Warfare and Salvation (12:1–14:20)
- Seven Bowls of Judgment (15:1–16:21)
- Victory for Christ (17:1–19:21)
- New Heaven and New Earth (20:1–22:5)

We begin with the first vision that includes the letters to the seven churches.

A. Jesus' Glorious Appearance
1:9–20

Decades after Jesus' ascension, Jesus appears to John on the island of Patmos and addresses him and the churches on the mainland. Here is the voice of Jesus, who now in glorified appearance speaks to the church of the first century and the centuries that follow. The messages that he brings are praise and rebuke, exhortation and promise. They fit the church of any place or time throughout the ages, for the recurring refrain to his people is to overcome by being faithful to the end.

1. Location
1:9–11

9. I, John, your brother and companion in the tribulation and kingdom and patient endurance that are in Jesus, was on the island called Patmos because of the word of God and the testimony of Jesus.

a. "I, John, your brother and companion in the tribulation and kingdom and patient endurance that are in Jesus." The writer of the Fourth Gospel and the Johannine Epistles refrains from identifying himself by name, but the author of Revelation leaves no doubt about his identity. Already in verses 1 and 4 his name appears, and now he writes "I, John, your brother and companion." He makes it clear who he is and where he is; that is, he is a spiritual brother and fellow sufferer who has been exiled off the coast of Asia Minor

(Turkey) to an isolated island called Patmos. The formula "I, [+ personal name]" is not limited to John. Paul refers to himself as "I, Paul" (Gal. 5:2; Eph. 3:1; Col. 1:23; 1 Thess. 2:18; Philem. 19), and in the Apocalypse Jesus says, "I, Jesus" (22:16).[33] The reason for the use of the emphatic pronoun *I* is to avoid any misunderstanding of identity and to affirm that the speaker's message is authentic.

John is well known to his readers, but they have to realize that in his exile something of extraordinary significance has happened: he has seen the Lord Jesus Christ and received messages from him to be delivered to the churches. Instead of calling himself *apostle,* he chooses the words *brother* and *companion* and thus places himself on the same level as his readers. Paul and Peter repeatedly placed themselves on that level (e.g., Acts 15:23; Rom. 15:14; 2 Pet. 1:10; 3:15). Even though the apostles received delegated authority from Jesus, they considered themselves spiritual brothers to all who serve and follow him.

John strengthens the concept *brother* with the word *companion,* which signifies more than partner or friend. He qualifies this term by adding the words "in the tribulation and kingdom and patient endurance that are in Jesus." As a companion he shares the suffering his readers have to endure in three areas: tribulation, kingdom, and patient endurance. Let us examine these three sequentially.

First, *tribulation.* Jesus told his disciples that they would experience great distress (Matt. 24:21; John 16:33). Paul similarly said to the Christians in Lystra, Iconium, and Pisidian Antioch, "We must go through many hardships to enter the kingdom of God" (Acts 14:22). These hardships inevitably must take place on account of the coming of God's kingdom. For Christians, hardships necessarily belong to the world in which God has placed them as his people.[34]

Next, *kingdom.* The expression *kingdom* is related to tribulation; in this world the one closely accompanies the other (see Acts 14:22). As citizens in God's kingdom, Christians experience constant pressure from people who are the enemies of God, his Word, and his people. Of all the books in the New Testament, the Apocalypse especially relates how that tribulation intensifies as the kingdom approaches the consummation.

Third, *patient endurance.* John mentions it frequently in the Apocalypse as one of the characteristic features of one who follows Christ.[35] But how do we explain the sequence of the three nouns we are examining? How does the kingdom relate to both tribulation and patient endurance? Members of this kingdom must of necessity suffer and endure, as is evident from the letters to the churches in Ephesus, Smyrna, Pergamum, Thyatira, and Philadelphia. On the one hand, Christians face tribulation because they are in the kingdom; on the other hand, they are told to

---

33. See also Dan. 7:15, 28; 8:1; Rev. 22:8.

34. Refer to Reinier Schippers, *NIDNTT,* 2:808; Heinrich Schlier, *TDNT,* 3:144.

35. Rev. 1:9; 2:2, 3, 19; 3:10; 14:12.

endure patiently so that the kingdom may come through their faithfulness to Christ. When thus we see the kingdom between tribulation and patient endurance, any tension is allayed.[36] A hymn on the suffering for Christ sung in the early church has this line, "If we endure, we will also reign with him" (2 Tim. 2:12).

b. "[I, John] was on the island called Patmos because of the word of God and the testimony of Jesus." Revelation is the only book in the New Testament that states the place where it was composed: on the island called Patmos. This island is located some forty miles to the southwest of Miletus (Acts 20:15), which served as a harbor for Ephesus. It measures ten miles from north to south and six from east to west and consists of hills that rise over eight hundred feet above sea level.

Patmos is a rocky, volcanic isle to which the Roman government in the first and second centuries banished exiles.[37] During the end of Emperor Domitian's reign (81–96), John was sent to this island, in his own words, "because of the word of God and the testimony of Jesus." The conjunction *because* is meaningful for it illustrates why John was on this island. He did not go there to start a church, for the population was sparse. He could have sent a coworker instead. And he did not visit Patmos because he expected Jesus to appear to him there. For John, Jesus' appearance was entirely unexpected. No, John was banished as the leader of the churches in the western part of Asia Minor. The Romans persecuted the Christians who acknowledged not Caesar but Jesus Christ as Lord; Roman officials considered John an instigator of the Christian religion. Tradition says that after Domitian's death, his successor Nerva released John and permitted him to return to Ephesus.[38]

John had faithfully proclaimed and taught the Word of God; he had written the testimony of Jesus (John 21:24); and he was known as the revered elder in the churches of Asia Minor (2 John 1; 3 John 1). No wonder that he was imprisoned when persecution struck in Ephesus. The phrase *testimony of Jesus* can be interpreted to mean either the gospel of Jesus or the preaching of that gospel for Jesus (compare v. 2).[39] Both interpretations are applicable in this instance.

---

36. Philip Edgcumbe Hughes, *The Book of the Revelation: A Commentary* (Leicester: Inter-Varsity; Grand Rapids: Eerdmans, 1990), p. 23. See also Lenski, *Revelation*, pp. 55–56; Walter Radl, *EDNT*, 3:406.

37. Pliny *Natural History* 4.12.23. In addition, see Irving A. Sparks, *ISBE*, 3:690. Aune (*Revelation 1–5*, p. 79) notes the Latin terms *relegatio* (temporary banishment) and *deportatio* (deportation). Pliny the Younger (*Letters* 10.56) mentions a three-year banishment as "relegatio." See also Gerhard A. Krodel, *Revelation*, ACNT (Minneapolis: Augsburg, 1989), p. 93.

38. Eusebius *Eccl. Hist.* 3.20.8–9: "After Domitian had reigned fifteen years, Nerva succeeded [96–98]. The sentences of Domitian were annulled, and the Roman Senate decreed the return of those who had been unjustly banished and the restoration of their property. . . . At that time, too, . . . the Apostle John, after his banishment to the island, took up his abode at Ephesus" (LCL).

39. The expression *the testimony of Jesus* appears six times in the Apocalypse (1:2, 9; 12:17; 19:10 [twice]; and 20:4). P. Vassiliadis ("The Translation of *Martyria Iēsou*," *BibTrans* 36 [1985]: 129–34) avers that the expression has martyrological overtones and means "witness (unto death) to Jesus" as an objective genitive.

10. I was in the Spirit on the Lord's Day, and I heard behind me a loud voice like the sound of a trumpet.

Both Peter and Paul were in ecstasy when the Lord spoke to them in a vision. Peter was in a trance on the flat roof of Simon the tanner in Joppa (Acts 10:9–10), and Paul experienced a trance in the temple of Jerusalem (Acts 22:17–18). John was not asleep but wide awake when the Lord addressed him. His senses were alert so that with a clear mind, focused eyes, and open ears he assimilated the information Jesus supplied and he later recorded. The phrase *in the Spirit* occurs also in 4:2 where John is invited to look into heaven, in 17:3 where an angel carries him into the desert, and in 21:10 where the angel brought him to a high mountain to see the new Jerusalem coming down out of heaven. These passages point to the close relationship between Jesus and the Holy Spirit in transmitting to John the content of the Apocalypse.[40]

John writes that he was in the Spirit on the Lord's Day. This is the only place in the New Testament where this day is so described, for elsewhere it is referred to as the first day of the week.[41] It is the day of the Lord's resurrection, and by the end of the first century Christians had begun to refer to it not as the first day of the week but as the Lord's Day (compare the expression *the Lord's Supper,* 1 Cor. 11:20). It is the day that is devoted to the Lord. The text refers not to the eventual return of the Lord and the Day of Judgment but to Jesus' appearing to John on the first day of the week—a day consecrated to Christ.

John hears behind him a loud voice that sounded like a trumpet. For him, the sound of this loud voice was unexpected and startling. The resonance of the trumpet, however, told him of its heavenly origin. John was reminded of God giving the Ten Commandments at Sinai where the Israelites heard a trumpet sound (Exod. 19:16, 19; 20:18). The beginning of the New Year was marked by trumpet blasts; indeed on the first day of the seventh month, the Jewish month Tishri (September–October), the people celebrated the Feast of Trumpets (Lev. 23:24; Num. 29:1–6). This was a prelude to the Day of Atonement on the tenth of Tishri. In his eschatological discourse, Jesus speaks about his return as accompanied by a loud trumpet call (Matt. 24:31; see 1 Thess. 4:16). In short, the sound of the trumpet introduced the advent of a new interval.

The trumpet sound in Revelation calls attention to an important message (e.g., 4:1), and the intensity of the voice demands alertness and obedience. Al-

40. Aune (*Revelation 1–5,* p. 82) prefers the translation, "I fell into a prophetic trance on the Lord's day." Although action of the Holy Spirit could be implied in his translation (p. 63, 10a), the fact that it is not stated weakens the wording of the Greek text. See R. Bauckham, "The Lord's Day," in *From Sabbath to Lord's Day,* ed. D. A. Carson (Grand Rapids: Zondervan, 1982), pp. 222–32.

41. Matt. 28:1; Mark 16:2, 9; John 20:1, 19; Acts 20:7; 1 Cor. 16:2. It is interesting to note that in Greece the first day of the week is called *hēmera kyriakē* (the Lord's day), with Monday being the second day, Tuesday the third, and Wednesday the fourth, etc. In Portuguese-speaking countries the same phenomenon occurs: Sunday is Domingo (Day of the Lord), Monday the second day, and Tuesday the third, etc. See also *Didache* 14.1; Ignatius *Magnesians* 9.1; Eusebius *Eccl. Hist.* 4.26.2; and consult Adolf Deissmann, *Light from the Ancient East* (reprint, Grand Rapids: Baker, 1978), pp. 361–63.

though in this verse the voice is unidentified, in subsequent verses the speech is that of Jesus, who calls himself "the First and the Last," the living One who is alive forever and ever (vv. 17–18).

11. Saying, "What you see, write in a book and send to the seven churches: to Ephesus, Smyrna, Pergamum, Thyatira, Sardis, Philadelphia, and Laodicea."

The divine voice addressing John tells him to take a pen and a scroll and write messages to seven churches that are in the province of Asia. These are churches that John has served before he was exiled to Patmos. Now Jesus has something to say to each of these seven congregations. John is told to write the epistles and see to it that they are sent and delivered to the respective addressees.

"What you see" refers not merely to the appearance of the Lord and the messages he must dispatch to the churches but to the entire content of the Apocalypse. All that he observes and hears must be recorded for the benefit of the whole church. The command to write is in the present tense, to indicate that he must continue to record until the end. He must take a scroll of adequate length (approximately sixteen feet), record God's revelation, and make it available to every congregation (compare 1:3). Although questions may arise concerning the structure of the Apocalypse, its content has always been presented as one book and has never appeared in individual parts.

The trajectory of the seven cities that are mentioned sequentially is oval in form and may have been a postal route. The route is from Ephesus in the center to Smyrna and Pergamum in the north, then on to Thyatira and Sardis in a southeasterly direction, and from there to Philadelphia and Laodicea in the south. William M. Ramsay conjectures that from these cities secondary messengers went out to neighboring towns with copies of the Apocalypse. These towns included Colosse, Hierapolis in the vicinity of Laodicea; then Tralles, Magnesia, and Miletus in the central part of the province; and last Troas to the north of Pergamum.[42] These seven letters, however, are for the church universal. It is more likely, then, that John is using the number seven symbolically to convey the idea of completeness. Hence, no church is ever left out, for Jesus has a message for each one.

Greek Words, Phrases, and Constructions in 1:9–11

Verse 9

τῇ θλίψει—the definite article controls three nouns: tribulation, kingdom, and endurance. They belong to the same category and follow in the given sequence.

τὴν μαρτυρίαν Ἰησοῦ—the genitive is either subjective (belonging to Jesus) or objective (for Jesus). Both are applicable here.

---

42. Refer to William M. Ramsay, *The Letters to the Seven Churches of Asia and Their Place in the Plan of the Apocalypse* (London: Hodder and Stoughton, 1904; reprint, Grand Rapids: Baker, 1979), pp. 191–92; Colin J. Hemer, *The Letters to the Seven Churches of Asia in Their Local Setting*, JSNTSup 11 (Sheffield: JSOT, 1986), pp. 14–15.

Verse 10

τῇ κυριακῇ ἡμέρᾳ—notice that the adjective signifies belonging to the Lord. In his letter to the Magnesians (9.1), Ignatius writes of "no longer observing the Sabbath, but living in the observance of the Lord's Day."

Verse 11

λεγούσης—grammatically this present participle should have been in the accusative to modify the noun *voice* and not the dependent genitive *trumpet*; this occurs again in 4:1.

---

2. *Appearance*
1:12–16

12. And I turned to see the voice that was speaking to me, and when I turned, I saw seven golden lampstands. 13. And in the midst of the lampstands was one "like a son of man," dressed in an ankle-length robe and a golden sash around his chest.

a. "And I turned to see the voice that was speaking to me." As in the first eight verses of this chapter, so in the rest of the verses, the accent falls on the Lord Jesus Christ. John's description of the glorified Jesus should be interpreted not literally but symbolically. It is impossible for John to express a heavenly appearance in exact human terms; thus, he employs the comparative term *like* (e.g., like a son of man, v. 13). Compare also Paul's hesitancy when, referring to his vision of paradise, he states his inability to express the things he had heard (2 Cor. 12:4).

John relates that upon hearing the voice that was speaking behind him, he turned around to identify the person who addressed him.[43] In Greek he writes the verb *lalein* (to talk) instead of *legein* (to speak), which means that he wants to identify the sound of the voice and not the content of the message. We ask whether John would have recognized the voice of Jesus after many decades had passed, but we have no answer. We know that the sound he compared to a trumpet alerted him to expect a voice from heaven.

b. "And when I turned, I saw seven golden lampstands." Instead of identifying a person, he describes first the surroundings and then the person himself. The surroundings are not one but seven golden lampstands. The tabernacle contained one lampstand made of pure gold with seven lamps (Exod. 25:31, 37). Solomon's temple had ten golden lampstands: five on the left and five on the right in front of the inner sanctuary (1 Kings 7:49); and Zechariah saw only one golden lampstand with seven lights with seven pipes supplying oil to the lights (Zech. 4:2). Even though John's imagery is based on the Old Testament, here he uses the word *lampstands*, to which he supplies the number *seven*. The lampstands are seven churches (Rev. 1:20), and seven denotes completeness. That is, John presents a picture of the entire church.

---

43. Compare James H. Charlesworth, "The Jewish Roots of Christology: The Discovery of the Hypostatic Voice," *SJT* 39 (1986): 19–41.

c. "And in the midst of the lampstands was one 'like a son of man'" (see also 14:14). What comfort for the church on earth! John first describes the church and then depicts her Lord, who always walks in her midst (2:1). Jesus as the Son of Man is walking among the churches, which brightly shine their light to dispel the darkness of this world. He has not withdrawn himself to heavenly realms; rather he is with the church on earth to be their source of light (John 8:12). The churches receiving their light from him must be light bearers; if they fail in this, Jesus will remove their lampstand from its place and they will cease to be his church (2:5).

By saying "like a son of man," John calls attention to Daniel 7:13–14, where this title describes the Messiah as ruler of this universe. The Son of Man is divine, dwells in eternity, possesses ultimate authority, and is the sovereign of an indestructible kingdom. This picture expresses majesty, power, and authority that no human being can equal. During his earthly ministry, Jesus applied the name *Son of Man* to himself for the purpose of identifying himself with fallen humanity to redeem his people. Here, then, is the majestic Lord walking among the churches to reprove and encourage, and to command and commend them.

d. "Dressed in an ankle-length robe and a golden sash around his chest." This sentence can mean that Jesus is high priest wearing a white ankle-length robe. Some commentators contend that the evidence to prove it is insufficient, for other dignitaries were also dressed in ankle-length garb. They conclude that the long robe and the golden sash mark the dignity of the person so adorned.[44] However, the description of the high priest's garment includes fine linen (white, Acts 23:3), a sash, and gold (Exod. 28:4–5; 29:5; Wisdom of Solomon 18:24). The Apocalypse presents Jesus as both king and priest who released his people from sin by his blood (1:5; compare 5:9). The feasibility of interpreting the sentence to refer to Jesus' priesthood cannot be excluded.

The sash of gold worn around the chest is also the apparel of seven angels who come out of the temple dressed in clean, bright linen with golden sashes around their chests (15:6; compare Dan. 10:5). John's wording, therefore, depicts the dignity and high standing of the Son of Man.

14. His head and his hair were white like white wool, like snow, and his eyes were like a flame of fire. 15. And his feet were like exquisite brass refined as in a furnace, and his voice was as the sound of many waters.

a. "His head and his hair were white like white wool, like snow." Again John can only describe Jesus' appearance by using the comparative terms *like* and *as* throughout these two verses. The terminology is reminiscent of Daniel's description of God, whom the prophet calls the Ancient of Days:

> And the Ancient of Days took his seat.
> His clothing was as white as snow;

44. Beckwith, *Apocalypse*, p. 438; Thomas, *Revelation 1–7*, pp. 99–100; Swete, *Revelation*, pp. 15–16; Charles, *Revelation*, 1:27–28.

> the hair of his head was white like wool.
> His throne was flaming with fire,
> and its wheels were all ablaze. (Dan. 7:9)

What Daniel in this passage ascribes to God, John with variation assigns to Christ. Jesus appears as God because he is one with the Father in regard to eternity, purity, and holiness. Daniel also notes that "a son of man . . . approached the Ancient of Days and was led into his presence" (7:13). The head and hair of Jesus are white as wool, to which John adds that they are white as snow.[45] It is obvious that John does not have the written scroll of Daniel at his disposal and, relying on memory, he attempts to approximate the biblical wording. White or gray hair demands respect and is to be regarded as a "crown of splendor" (Lev. 19:32; Prov. 16:31).

b. "His eyes were like a flame of fire." This clause again reflects an inexact memory of Daniel 7:9. In that passage God's throne was flaming with fire, but here John applies the flame to Jesus' eyes. He seems to have in mind the wording of a similar vision that reads, "his eyes like flaming torches" (Dan. 10:6). John's intent is to say that nothing escapes the penetrating eyes of Jesus. He corroborates this in the letter to the church in Thyatira (2:18), where Jesus says that he is the one "who searches the minds and the hearts" (2:23).

c. "And his feet were like exquisite brass refined as in a furnace." I admit that the translation "fine brass" is an approximation, because the Greek gives a name for "a metal or alloy, the exact nature of which is unknown."[46] The metal seems to have been similar to polished copper to which another metal contributed luster (compare Ezek. 1:7; Dan. 10:6). We have no further information whether John wishes to convey that the metal is still in the furnace or has been through it. Nor do we understand what polished brass is supposed to represent, except to say that it reflects divine glory. The Psalter teaches that the feet of Jesus trample down his enemies (Ps. 110:1).

d. "And his voice was as the sound of many waters." We picture John at the shoreline of Patmos, listening to the waves beating against the rocks. Elsewhere he uses similar wording (14:2; 19:6) to convey the image of the surging of the sea that is powerfully persistent and relentless. The Old Testament passage underlying this sentence is Ezekiel 43:2, where the prophet describes the glory of God

45. Charles (*Revelation*, 1:28) calls the words "white as snow" a marginal gloss that is "extremely awkward in its present context." That these three words are a gloss is unlikely, because John resorts to Hebraic parallelism that in this case he borrows from Daniel's prophecy. And arguments on accidental transpositions lack manuscript evidence. G. K. Beale observes, "About fifty percent of the OT references in vv. 7–20 are from Daniel, and of these the majority are from Daniel 7 and 10" (*The Use of Daniel in Jewish Apocalyptic Literature and in the Revelation of St. John* [Lanham, Md.: University Press of America, 1984], p. 171).

46. Bauer, p. 875. Hemer (*Letters to the Seven Churches*, p. 116) conjectures "an alloy of copper with metallic zinc" which he calls "copper-zinc."

and says, "His voice was like the sound of many waters" (NKJV). This passage is now ascribed to Jesus.

16. And in his right hand he held seven stars, and a sharp double-edged sword came out of his mouth, and his face was like the sun shining in its full strength.

This last verse in the passage on Jesus' appearance lists three physical features: his right hand, his mouth, and his face. These features ought to be understood not literally but symbolically; also an astrological interpretation of the seven stars must be rejected.[47]

a. "And in his right hand he held seven stars." John did not rely on phraseology taken from the Old Testament. Rather Jesus himself furnishes the explanation of the seven stars: "the seven stars are the angels of the seven churches" (v. 20). The angels are the messengers of God appointed to serve him in the seven churches (2:1, 8, 12, 18; 3:1, 7, 14).

The right hand can be interpreted as a source of power and protection. For instance, both the Old and the New Testaments speak of being seated at God's right hand as indicative of possessing authority (e.g., Ps. 110:1; Heb. 1:3). The psalmists mention safety by his right hand (see Ps. 44:3; 60:5). The expression, then, symbolizes shelter and security through the divine power that Jesus provides for his people who serve him as messengers. From him they receive delegated authority and can expect his ever-present nearness. Jesus Christ never forsakes his own, even when they go through the valley of death as in times of severe persecution (compare Acts 7:55).

b. "And a sharp double-edged sword came out of his mouth." The image of the sword symbolically represents Christ's spoken word. That word is sharper than a two-edged sword and is able to discern the thoughts and intentions of the heart (Heb. 4:12; see also Eph. 6:17). The sharpest weapon in the Roman arsenal was a double-edged sword, but whether this implement resembled a human tongue remains an open question.

At his return, Jesus will overthrow the lawless one with the breath of his mouth (2 Thess. 2:8). Jesus fights his enemies not with material weapons but with his word; the battle is not against flesh and blood but against spiritual forces of darkness (Eph. 6:12). In warfare, this word executes judgment and destroys the works of the evil one (2:12, 16; 19:15, 21; see also Isa. 11:4; 49:2). And last, in the Greek the verb *came out* is a present participle to denote that the divine word continuously comes forth from Jesus' mouth. It is constantly active, protecting his own and proving to be destructive to his opponents.

c. "And his face was like the sun shining in its full strength." The phraseology derives from Judges 5:31, where Deborah and Barak conclude their song by saying: "So may all your enemies perish, O LORD! But may those who love you be

---

47. A coin minted during the first part of Domitian's reign (A.D. 81–96) pictures his wife Domitia as queen of heaven and her son seated on a globe stretching out his hand toward seven stars. Ethelbert Stauffer, *Christ and the Caesars*, trans. K. and R. Gregor Smith (London: SCM, 1955), p. 152; Hemer, *Letters to the Seven Churches*, pp. 4, 214 n. 8; Walvoord, *Revelation*, p. 45.

like the sun when it rises in its strength." When Matthew records the transfiguration, he writes that Jesus' face shone like the sun (Matt. 17:2; compare 13:43).

John writes not the regular Greek word for face (*prosōpon*) but the expression *opsis,* which in classical Greek means appearance or face. Would John have in mind the face of Jesus after he described his hair, head, and eyes? Or does he mean the complete appearance of the Lord? We are unable to determine the exact meaning. What we can say is that from Jesus shines light as bright as the sun in full strength. In other words, it was humanly impossible to look Jesus in the face.

William Hendriksen writes that the description of Jesus must be taken in its entirety. I have presented a verse-by-verse interpretation, but it is helpful to see the full picture in his words:

> Notice that the Son of man is here pictured as clothed with power and majesty and with awe and terror. That long royal robe; that golden belt buckled at the breast; that hair so glistening white that like snow on which the sun is shining it hurts the eye; those eyes flashing fire, eyes which read every heart and penetrate every hidden corner; those feet glowing in order to trample down the wicked; that loud, reverberating voice, like the mighty breakers booming against the rocky shore of Patmos; that sharp, long, heavy great-sword with two biting edges; that entire appearance "as the sun shines in its power," too intense for human eyes to stare at—the entire picture, taken as a whole, is symbolical of Christ, the Holy One, coming to purge His churches (2:16, 18, 23), and to punish those who are persecuting His elect (8:5ff.).[48]

Greek Words, Phrases, and Constructions in 1:12–15

Verse 12

ἐλάλει—the Greek uses λαλεῖν to denote the act of speaking and λέγειν to emphasize the content of what is said (see v. 17, where the present participle λέγων occurs).

Verse 13

υἱὸν ἀνθρώπου—the definite articles that could precede the two nouns are lacking (so also Dan. 7:13 Old Greek and Theod.). Also, the adjective ὅμοιον should have been followed by the dative rather than the accusative.[49] Here and in 14:14 John writes a solecism.

Verse 15

πεπυρωμένης—the genitive case and not the dative case or nominative plural is the more difficult reading and hence preferred. The solution of inserting τῆς χαλκολιβάνου after the perfect passive participle is commendable (see the commentaries of Beckwith,

---

48. Hendriksen, *More Than Conquerors,* pp. 56–57.

49. See Rev. 1:15; 2:18; 4:3, 6, 7; 9:10, 19; 13:2, 4, 11; 18:18; 21:11, 18. Consult Friedrich Blass and Albert Debrunner, *A Greek Grammar of the New Testament,* trans. and rev. Robert Funk (Chicago: University of Chicago Press, 1961), §182.4; A. T. Robertson, *A Grammar of the Greek New Testament in the Light of Historical Research* (Nashville: Broadman, 1934), p. 530.

Greijdanus, Swete, and Thomas). As an alternative, it is possible to repeat mentally the word κάμινος in the genitive case and turn the participle into a genitive absolute, because κάμινος is feminine. In a genitive absolute construction, the noun or pronoun at times is lacking.[50]

---

3. Message
1:17–20

The last part of the chapter is Jesus' message to John. It serves as an introduction to the seven epistles that he must address to the churches in the province of Asia. Filled with dread at the sight of Jesus, John hears words of comfort as Jesus identifies himself as the risen Christ.

17. And when I saw him, I fell at his feet as though dead. And he placed his right hand on me saying: "Fear not, I am the First and the Last."

Seeing Jesus in glorified appearance proved to be too much for John, not so much because of human frailty as because of his awareness of his utter unworthiness to see Christ's glory. He fell to the ground at Jesus' feet, which is a common posture of the saints who are permitted to be in the presence of holiness. John had seen his glory on the mount of transfiguration, and when they heard the voice from heaven, he and his companions fell face down on the ground (Matt. 17:6). Scripture reveals that saints in both Old and New Testament eras had similar experiences.[51] The truth is that human beings are unable to face divine majesty: sinners prostrate themselves and acknowledge the presence of sinlessness.

Lying on the ground, John appeared to be dead. Yet his senses were alert, for he was fully aware of Jesus standing next to him. The Lord appeared to him, not to slay him, but to show him his divine power and majesty, which John should report to the churches. Both John and the churches had to become aware of Christ's awesome appearance and to do so in preparation for the message Jesus had for them.[52] Jesus placed his right hand on John and ordered him not to fear. The hand of the Lord touched John to establish physical contact and his voice told him not to be afraid. Daniel also was touched and raised after seeing heavenly visions, and he too was told not to fear (Dan. 8:18; 10:10, 12). By touching John, Jesus endowed him with strength to face the future; at the same time he spoke words that were an echo from the past: "Fear not." Jesus had often commanded his disciples to stop being afraid, whether it was on the stormy lake of Galilee (Matt. 14:27); on the mount of transfiguration (Matt. 17:7); on a missionary journey (Acts 18:9); or in custody (Acts 23:11). Jesus never deserts his own people.

---

50. See Aune, *Revelation 1–5*, pp. 65–66; compare Beckwith, *Apocalypse*, p. 439.

51. Gen. 17:3; Josh. 5:14; Judg. 13:20; Ezek. 1:28; 3:23; 43:3; 44:4; Dan. 8:17; 10:9; Matt. 17:6; Luke 5:8; Acts 9:4.

52. Compare Greijdanus, *Openbaring*, p. 36.

In the words "I am the First and the Last" John recognized Jesus, who is the "I am" (e.g., see John 8:58). Jesus is also the first as the Creator (John 1:1–3), the author of salvation (Heb. 2:10), and the firstborn from among the dead (Col. 1:18). He is the also the one who will bring all things to completion; thus by being the fulfillment of all things he is the end. He is the first and the last, the beginning and the end. What an encouragement to know that Jesus stands at the beginning and at the end of human history and that he is always with the saints.

18. "And I am the living one and I was dead, and look, I am alive forever and ever. And I have the keys of Death and Hades."

a. "And I am the living one and I was dead, and look, I am alive forever and ever." Jesus states that he is eternal, divine, and "the exact representation of God's being" (Heb. 1:3). He is the living one, in contrast to all the gods of paganism. Note, he does not now say that he is alive, but that he is the living one who possesses eternal life (John 5:26). He is the giver of life (John 6:33; 1 John 5:11), and the life he gives is eternal. Thus he is the great "I am" (John 8:58).

Jesus personifies life and at the same time he can say, "I was dead." He refers to his sacrificial death on Calvary's cross, where he conquered death for the sake of those held in the fear of death (Heb. 2:14–15). He speaks of an historical event when his body was lying lifeless in the tomb outside the city of Jerusalem. The contrast is telling, for the one who is life permits his body to submit to death. What he restores is a physical body that suffered death so that it could never die again. Hence, he triumphantly exults in life and exclaims, "Look, I am alive forever and ever" (Deut. 32:40; Dan. 4:34; 12:7; Rev. 4:9, 10; 10:6; 15:7). His body, which John saw and described, is alive and glorified in appearance. In this last clause, Jesus first tells John to look closely at the physical appearance of the Lord; next, he stresses that there is no time limit to the Lord's life, for he lives eternally. His life is immortal, indestructible, and unchangeable. The incontrovertible truth of Christ's resurrection causes every believer to rejoice in his power to open the graves and raise the dead.

b. "And I have the keys of Death and Hades." The one who has a key is able to unlock doors that give access to possessions, treasures, and secrets. Possessing a key means having power and authority. But no one on the face of this earth is able to claim power over Death and Hades. Jesus, who triumphed over death and the grave, possesses the keys to unlock them. Are these the keys that belong to Death and Hades (subjective genitive) or are they the keys that give someone power over them (objective genitive)? It stands to reason that Jesus, who has conquered Death and Hades, has power over them and thus possesses their keys also.[53] That is, both the objective and subjective genitives apply, for Jesus has complete power over death and the grave (John 5:28; compare also Matt. 16:19).

53. Jewish rabbis mention four keys in the hands of God, "the keys of life, the graves, food, and rain" (Targum Pseudo-Jonathan on Deut. 28:12); or three keys "of birth, rain, and the resurrection of the dead" (Babylonian Talmud, *Sanhedrin* 113a). Refer to SB, 1:737; and the commentaries of Swete (p. 20); Beckwith (p. 441); Charles (1:33).

Incidentally, the Old Testament frequently speaks about "the gates of death" (Job 17:16; 38:17; Ps. 9:13; 107:18).

What is the meaning of Hades? Is it different from death? Is it equivalent to the grave? Or is it the abode of the dead in the underworld? First, the Apocalypse personifies Death and Hades (6:8; 20:13–14). Next, Death is a state and Hades a place. Third, although Death and Hades are powerful forces (6:8), at the consummation their power comes to an end and both are cast into the lake of fire (20:14). Last, everyone faces death before Christ returns; believers do not enter Hades but enter the portals of heaven (Phil. 1:23; 2 Cor. 5:8).[54] But the ungodly are in Hades. All human beings will appear before the judgment seat of God and will be judged, but the saints whose names are written in the book of life will forever be with Christ. Hence, it is incorrect to interpret Hades as the grave, for everyone will return to dust (Gen. 3:19).

Jesus Christ has authority over Death and Hades, and when he speaks both of them submit to him. He is the Victor who has absolute power.

19. "Write, therefore, what you have seen and what is and what is about to take place after these things."

The command "Write, therefore, what you have seen" is a repetition of a preceding verse (v. 11). After John has described Jesus' appearance, the charge to write is given again, together with the clause "what you have seen," now in the past tense. Most scholars interpret the past, present, and future parts of this verse as a division of the Apocalypse.

- "What you have seen" points to Jesus' appearance to John (1:9–20).
- "What is" refers to the spiritual condition of the seven churches (chapters 2 and 3).
- "What is about to take place after these things" alludes to the period from the time of John to that of the Lord's return.

Others point out that the three time references (past, present, and future) derive from a formula that was in use for centuries in many cultures throughout the countries around the Mediterranean basin. This formula describing prophecy encompasses the totality of history and seeks to disclose its meaning.[55] We

54. Compare Hans Bietenhard, *NIDNTT*, 2:207; Joachim Jeremias, *TDNT*, 1:148–49.

55. Sweet, *Revelation*, p. 73; W. C. van Unnik, "A Formula Describing Prophecy," *NTS* 9 (1963): 86–94, and in *Sparsa Collecta: The Collected Writings of W. C. Van Unnik*, part 2 (Leiden: Brill, 1980), pp. 183–93; Gregory K. Beale, "The Interpretive Problem of Rev. 1:19," *NovT* 34 (1992): 360–87. It is interesting to note that the wording of the third part ("what is about to take place after these things") is an echo of what Daniel told King Nebuchadnezzar: "O king, your mind is turned to things to come, and the revealer of mysteries showed you what is going to happen," and, "The great God has shown the king what will take place in the future" (Dan. 2:29, 45; see especially v. 45 in the LXX [Theod.]). Geoffrey B. Wilson (*Revelation* [Welwyn, England: Evangelical Press, 1985, p. 25) observes, "Hence this verse does not announce the 'programme' of Revelation, except insofar as it constantly relates the present to the future."

might consider this formula to be a proverbial saying that transcends time and place and conveys the sense of comprising all of history.

The clause "what you have seen" should be understood in the light of verse 11, "What you see." John saw the awe-inspiring appearance of Jesus that stayed with him as he wrote his book. The impression he received can be formulated in one short sentence: "Jesus is in complete control of everything that has transpired, transpires, and will transpire."

We are unable to ascertain whether John wrote the Apocalypse piecemeal as he received instructions and visions from the Lord or whether he composed the entire book after he had received all the information. If we interpret the three clauses of verse 19 not sequentially but comprehensively, they take on an overall perspective. The things that John has seen, those that are, and those that will happen afterward—all these apply to all churches of the past, present, and future. Thus the clause "what you have seen" refers not necessarily to past time but to totality. Similarly the phrase "the things that are" is not limited to the present time of John's day but is all-inclusive. And the words "what is about to take place after these things" imply everything that will occur from the moment John receives the command to write until the end of cosmic time.[56] We conclude that the entire content of Revelation is meaningful to any and every church that has existed throughout the centuries, that exists today, and that will exist in the future. The message of Revelation, therefore, is one of comfort and assurance to all believers, past, present, and future.

20. "As for the mystery of the seven stars that you saw in my right hand and the seven golden lampstands: the seven stars are the angels of the seven churches, and the seven lampstands are the seven churches."

As readers of the Apocalypse, we look for hints as to how to interpret its symbols and understand its message. Scattered throughout the book are helpful clues that facilitate us in our interpretation. This is not to say that a particular symbol has only one explanation. John writes the expression *mystery*, which occurs four times in Revelation (1:20; 10:7; 17:5, 7). The first two relate to things pertaining to the church and to God, while the last two pertain to the great prostitute. Mysteries are secrets hidden from our understanding unless they are explained.

Jesus elucidates the symbols of the stars and the lampstands. He declares that the seven stars are angels and the seven lampstands seven churches. But are the angels heavenly beings sent out as God's messengers? Are they guardian angels, one for each congregation?[57] The term *angel* is common in the Apocalypse, occurring sixty-seven times. But it is impossible to maintain that in the Johannine literature a given word must have the same meaning throughout unless the au-

---

56. Beale, *Revelation*, pp. 152–70; see his "Interpretive Problem of Rev. 1:19," pp. 360–87. Also consult his *John's Use of the Old Testament in Revelation*, JSNTSup 166 (Sheffield: Sheffield Academic Press, 1998), pp. 169–71.

57. Refer to Daniel 10:13; 10:20–11:1; 12:1; Matt. 18:10; Acts 12:15.

thor indicates a change. To say that angels should mean ethereal beings and never human messengers runs counter to other passages in Scripture (Mark 1:2 [Mal. 3:1]; Luke 7:24; 9:52). From an analytical point of view, why would Jesus instruct John to write letters to seven individual angels? Note that in Greek the pronoun *you* (*your*) and the respective verbs in these letters are in the singular, which English is unable to transmit (e.g., 2:2). And would holy angels be held responsible for the sins of the people in the seven churches? Would it not make better sense if he told him to write to representatives of these churches who were responsible for the spiritual well-being of their members?[58] We know that Jesus is holding the seven stars (messengers) in his right hand (v. 16) to send them forth with authority and to protect them. The interpretation that the messengers to the congregations are their pastors makes sense if we view pastors as sent forth and commissioned by Christ. They are responsible for the spiritual development of God's people.

The seven lampstands are the seven churches. Notice the difference with respect to the first part of the explanation: the seven stars are angels of the seven churches. They are not called "seven angels," and in the Greek they are merely called "angels," without the definite article. The emphasis, therefore, falls not on the number of angels or the entire class of angels but on their capacity of being representatives. Pastors come and go but the pastoral responsibility remains.[59]

During the Old Testament era, Israel was undivided and represented a unity. In apostolic times, national identities emerged in forming synagogues, for example, the Synagogue of the Freedmen and Greek-speaking Jews (Acts 6:9). When churches were established, national and linguistic differences played a role. Yet all these churches confessing Jesus Christ as their Lord express basic unity. They are the golden lampstands that dispel the darkness of the world in which God has placed them.

Greek Words, Phrases, and Constructions in 1:17–20

Verse 17

μὴ φοβοῦ—the present imperative indicates John's continued terrified condition. Jesus tells John to cease being afraid.

Verse 18

ζῶν εἰμι—this is a periphrastic construction equivalent to the progressive present tense of the indicative "I am alive."

---

58. Hughes (*Revelation*, p. 31) writes, "Though it is possible to conceive of a guardian angel being assigned to each church, it is unlikely that the letters would have been addressed to these spirits. To understand these angels as human beings, whether local church leaders or appointed delegates, is therefore more satisfactory." Compare Hendriksen, *More Than Conquerors*, p. 58 n. 1.

59. See Greijdanus, *Openbaring*, p. 42.

Verse 19

ἅ εἰσίν—correct grammar demands a singular verb with a neuter plural subject, but in Koine Greek this rule is not always observed.

Verse 20

τὰς ἑπτὰ λυχνίας τὰς χρυσᾶς—commentators think that this phrase is dependent on the expression μυστήριον and should have been written in the genitive case. But John may have meant to place more emphasis on the seven stars as a mystery than on the seven lampstands. The accusative is an accusative absolute.

2

Letters to Ephesus, Smyrna, Pergamum, and Thyatira

(2:1–29)

Outline (continued)

B. Seven Letters (2:1–3:22)
   1. Ephesus (2:1–7)
      a. Commendation (2:1–3)
      b. Rebuke (2:4–5)
      c. Promise (2:6–7)
   2. Smyrna (2:8–11)
   3. Pergamum (2:12–17)
      a. Violence (2:12–13)
      b. Rebuke (2:14–16)
      c. Promise (2:17)
   4. Thyatira (2:18–29)
      a. Address and Praise (2:18–19)
      b. Reproof and Command (2:20–25)
      c. Promise (2:26–29)

2
1 "To the angel of the church at Ephesus write: The one who holds the seven stars in his
right hand and walks in the midst of the seven golden lampstands says this:
2 "I know your works and your toil and your patient endurance, and that you are not
able to tolerate evildoers; and you have tested those who call themselves apostles but are
not, and you have found them to be liars. 3 And you have endured and have tolerance because of my
name and have not become weary. 4 But I have this against you, that you have left your first love.
5 Therefore, remember the place from which you have fallen, repent, and perform the works you did
at first. If not, I will come to you and I will remove your lampstand from its place, unless you repent.
6 However, you have this [in your favor], that you hate the works of the Nicolaitans, which I also hate.
7 "Let anyone who has an ear listen to what the Spirit says to the churches. To everyone who overcomes I will give permission to eat from the tree of life, which is in God's paradise."

B. Seven Letters
2:1–3:22

In various ways, chapter 1 is introductory to the seven letters sent to the churches in the province of Asia. Jesus addresses John at Patmos and tells him twice to write letters to the seven churches on the mainland (1:11, 19). He reveals himself as the one who is the First and the Last, who is the living one who suffered death but is alive, and who has ultimate authority over Death and Hades. Also every letter following the address to each church has an opening line that is taken from the description of Jesus that John has recorded. Each of the seven churches presents a different aspect of Jesus' appearance, power, and authority.

Church	Text	Appearance of Jesus
Ephesus	2:1	Seven stars in his right hand; the golden lampstands (1:16, 13)
Smyrna	2:8	First and Last, who died and came to life again (1:17–18)
Pergamum	2:12	The double-edged sword (1:16)
Thyatira	2:18	Eyes as blazing fire; feet as burnished bronze (1:14–15)
Sardis	3:1	Seven spirits and seven stars (1:4, 16)
Philadelphia	3:7	Holding the key (1:18)
Laodicea	3:14	Faithful witness (1:5)

Also these seven letters reveal a parallelism that is unique: Some are longer, others are shorter in size, but each letter consists of seven parts:

1. The address to each of the seven churches in Asia Minor.
2. An aspect of the Lord's appearance to John at Patmos.
3. An evaluation of the spiritual health of the individual church.
4. Words of praise or reproof.
5. Words of exhortation.
6. Promises to the overcomer.
7. A command to hear what the Spirit says to the churches.

The first three churches (Ephesus, Smyrna, and Pergamum) close the individual letters with promises. The last four (Thyatira, Sardis, Philadelphia, and Laodicea) conclude with the command to listen attentively to what the Spirit says to the churches.

Jesus commends and rebukes four congregations: Ephesus, Pergamum, Thyatira, and Sardis. He praises two: Smyrna and Philadelphia. And he reprimands one: Laodicea. These seven are representative of the church universal; the seven letters are addressed to every place where God's people gather for worship, fellowship, and outreach.[1] Therefore, the number seven should not be taken in an absolute sense but rather as a symbol that stands for completeness. Conversely, while in Ephesus for some time John intimately knew the churches in the surrounding area. They were all within traveling distance of two to four days on foot, because Ephesus was conveniently located in an oval-shaped circle of these seven churches.

Did John send seven letters, one to each individual church that was addressed? R. H. Charles argues that the seven letters were written on a date prior to the composition of the entire Apocalypse, sent to the individual churches, and with later adaptation made part of Revelation.[2] But if we consider the evidence presented in the New Testament, we demur. First, even though Paul's letters were addressed to churches and individuals, the whole church shared them. Indeed, he instructed congregations to have his letters read by all others (Col. 4:16; 1 Thess. 5:27). The epistles in the New Testament that are called Catholic are actually letters meant for the universal church. Next, Jesus revealed himself to John and then instructed him to write, whereby he indicated that chapter 1 forms an inseparable introduction to the seven letters. In fact, Jesus himself addresses the seven churches, as is evident from the repetitive use of the personal pronoun *I*, while John with full apostolic authority serves as the secondary author of these letters. Third, Jesus instructs John to write not merely the letters but a book on what he observed and then to send the entire

1. The Muratorian Canon, dating from the last part of the second century, lists Revelation as follows: "John also, though he wrote the Apocalypse to seven churches, nevertheless speaks to them all." Refer to David E. Aune *Revelation 1–5*, WBC 52A (Dallas: Word, 1997), p. 130. In the early years of the second century, Ignatius wrote seven letters on his way to Rome. Among these are letters to the churches at Ephesus, Smyrna, and Philadelphia.

2. See R. H. Charles, *A Critical and Exegetical Commentary on the Revelation of St. John*, ICC (Edinburgh: Clark, 1920), 1:37.

Apocalypse to the churches (1:11).[3] These letters were composed as part of the Revelation that Jesus intended to be read and heard by all the members in the churches (1:3). Last, the Apocalypse is a unit from beginning to end in which the seven letters form an integral part.[4] Thus, Jesus' promise to all believers is that the overcomer will be blessed (2:7, 11, 17, 26; 3:5, 12, 21); they all hear Jesus say, "Look, I am coming soon. And my reward is with me to give to each according to his work. I am the Alpha and the Omega, the First and the Last, the Beginning and the End" (22:12–13). They may see the tree of life in paradise and eat from it (2:7; 22:2). And they who have the name of God and his city, the new Jerusalem, written on them are allowed to enter (3:12; 21:27; 22:14).

The seven churches faced dangers that were common to all of them. They had to endure opposition from forces outside and deception from movements inside the church. They were slandered by Jews (2:9); even Jesus' faithful witness Antipas was killed in the city where Satan lives (2:13). The prophetess called Jezebel wanted the followers of Christ to participate in her idolatry, immorality, and indulgence (2:20–25). The false apostles, that is, the Nicolaitans, introduced deceptive doctrines (2:2, 6, 15). The temptations to compromise were real, and yielding to them would prove deadly to the believers' faith. Then there were the allurements to become lax in their Christian conduct and the enticement to rely on earthly riches (3:1, 17). But Jesus commanded the readers and hearers of these letters to be faithful to the end and to hold on to what they had. If they did, they would have the privilege of sitting with him on his throne (3:21).

1. Ephesus
2:1–7
The City

The city of Ephesus had a varied history that went back centuries before this letter was addressed to the church that thrived within its walls. Riches gathered from commerce and religion enabled Ephesus to rebuild a temple destroyed by a fire. This temple was dedicated to the goddess Artemis (Diana for the Romans) and was served by countless priests and priestesses. It was considered one of the seven wonders of the world. The Ephesians constructed a theater that could seat an estimated twenty-four thousand people—the city may have accommodated a population in excess of two hundred thousand. Ramsay called Ephesus a city of change, because the Caÿster River along which it was located silted and eventually made its harbor useless.[5] This proved to be a setback to the commercial interests of the city, where the traffic of the land met the traffic of the sea. But

3. William M. Ramsay, *The Letters to the Seven Churches of Asia and Their Place in the Plan of the Apocalypse* (London: Hodder and Stoughton, 1904; reprint, Grand Rapids: Baker, 1979), p. 37.

4. Compare G. R. Beasley-Murray, *The Book of Revelation*, NCB (London: Oliphants, 1974), p. 71.

5. Ramsay, *Letters to the Seven Churches*, pp. 210–36.

throughout the first century after Christ, Ephesus continued to be an immense trading center, especially of religious artifacts, and to a degree an administrative center for the Roman government (Acts 19:24, 31, 38).

In addition, Ephesus had a temple built to further the imperial religion of Rome. The city dedicated the temple of the Sebastoi (the family of Vespasian, Titus, and Domitian) in A.D. 89–90, and, as was customary, it appointed temple wardens for the worship of the emperor.[6] In Ephesus the relationship between the worship of Artemis and the state religion of Rome was close. Further, Roman prefects forced the people to worship the emperor Domitian and to utter the statement "Caesar is Lord." Christians were unwilling to place Caesar above Christ, for they uttered the motto "Jesus is Lord" (1 Cor. 12:3). As a result they suffered persecution.

Christianity is exclusive, for it allows no compromise with other religions (John 14:6; Acts 4:12). In the latter part of the first century, it was on a collision course with Rome, which at first had allowed the Christians protection under the umbrella of the Jewish religion. But when the Roman authorities realized that Christianity was different from Judaism and would not deviate from the teachings of Christ, they were no longer tolerant of the Christians. They could not understand that these people separated themselves from the world to be a completely dissimilar society. Indeed they so abhorred the absolutism of this new religion that they sought to eliminate it by demanding observance of emperor worship. But the Christians rejected even a token obedience to the state religion, because they accepted no rival to Jesus Christ.

Numerous sources reveal that for centuries the temple of Artemis was declared a place of refuge for anyone who had committed a crime. Even parts of the city were at one time given the status of asylum. For instance, the area abutting the temple grounds even gave impunity to the criminal. At the time John wrote the Apocalypse in A.D. 95, the inner parts of Artemis's temple were a safe haven for any thief, robber, slave trader, and plunderer of a temple.[7]

The level of morality among the city's population was notoriously low. The people were licentious, superstitious, vile, and violent. The Greek philosopher Heraclitus, a resident of Ephesus, purportedly commented that "the morals of the temple were worse than the morals of beasts, for even promiscuous dogs do not mutilate each other."[8]

The Jewish residents in the city seemed to be numerous, rich, and influential.[9] They had established a Jewish community whose residents may have enjoyed the

6. S. Friesen, "The Cult of the Roman Emperors in Ephesos: Temple Wardens, City Titles, and the Interpretation of the Revelation of John," in *Ephesos, Metropolis of Asia: An Interdisciplinary Approach to Its Archaeology, Religion, and Culture,* ed. H. Koester, Harvard Theological Studies 41 (Valley Forge, Pa.: Trinity Press International, 1995), p. 236.

7. For references consult Colin J. Hemer, *The Letters to the Seven Churches of Asia in Their Local Setting,* JSNTSup 11 (Sheffield: JSOT, 1986), pp. 48–50.

8. See William Barclay, *Letters to the Seven Churches* (London: SCM, 1957), p. 18.

9. Josephus *Antiquities* 14.7.2 §§112–13; *Against Apion* 2.4 §39.

privilege of Roman citizenship. They had built their synagogue with legal protection from Rome to observe their own religion, including the keeping of the Sabbath. Although when Paul first came to Ephesus they welcomed the teaching of Christ (Acts 18:19–21), they soon rejected it and in time became virulently hostile to Christianity (Acts 19:23–41, especially 33). Yet Paul labored there for three years with positive results among both Jews and Greeks (Acts 19:17–20; 20:21). He sent an epistle to the church in Ephesus, probably in A.D. 62 during his Roman imprisonment. After his release he visited Ephesus, where Timothy had become the pastor (1 Tim. 1:2–3). Also John took up residence there and proved to be an influential force. But during the concluding years of Emperor Domitian's reign (the first half of the 90s), the pressure on the church increased because of emperor worship, with the result that John was banished to Patmos.

a. Commendation *2:1–3*

1. "To the angel of the church at Ephesus write: The one who holds the seven stars in his right hand and walks in the midst of the seven golden lampstands says this."

a. "To the angel of the church at Ephesus write." Jesus instructed John to write a short letter addressed to the pastor of the church in Ephesus. This church could be called the mother church in the province of Asia. Perhaps the God-fearing Jews from this province who returned home from their Pentecost visit to Jerusalem (Acts 2:9) may have been the first believers (disciples, Acts 19:1) in Ephesus. Paul and his associates came there to preach and teach the doctrines of Christ. And from Paul's rented quarters of the Tyrannus hall (Acts 19:9), students of the Word went forth to many cities in that area to further the spread of the gospel. In the early church, people considered Ephesus a leader in the province of Asia, and hence it was the first among the seven churches to receive a letter.

b. "The one who holds the seven stars in his right hand." The first identification of Jesus Christ given to the church is significant (1:16). Even though the church at Ephesus is first among the seven, her pastor is placed on the same level as the other six. Jesus says that he holds all of them in his protective hand, for he is not only their commissioner but also their guardian. The verb *to hold* means that Jesus has ultimate power and authority to safeguard his servants (compare John 10:29). Actually all his people are in his hand, for no harm shall come to any of them without his will.

c. "And [he who] walks in the midst of the seven golden lampstands says this." The golden lampstands are the members of the churches, on whom Jesus' eye constantly rests (1:12–13, 20). They represent the bride who awaits the coming of the bridegroom, and the bridegroom expects his bride to remain faithful, true, and pure. The symbolism of the text shows that Jesus wants the churches to let their light shine in the darkness where he has placed them. To give added meaning to the task of the churches, he tells them that he is walking among them. "For where two or three are assembled in my name, there am I in the midst of them" (Matt. 18:20). The light they spread passes from Jesus Christ to his servants who proclaim his Word. And pastors are not merely light bearers but like stars are light givers. They pass on the light to the members of the churches, who in turn dispel the darkness that surrounds them.

Jesus addresses the messengers of the local congregations, for they are responsible for bringing the message to the people. If they fail to do so, they shut out the light of the gospel and keep the members of the church in the dark. "And how can they hear without someone preaching to them?" (Rom. 10:14). Jesus speaks with authority and expects his servants of the Word to be his ambassadors.

2. "I know your works and your toil and your patient endurance, and that you are not able to tolerate evildoers; and you have tested those who call themselves apostles but are not, and you have found them to be liars."

a. "I know your works and your toil and your patient endurance." Jesus does not say that he is merely familiar with their works; he states that he has a detailed knowledge of everything they are doing, because nothing escapes his attention. He praises the Ephesians, as is evident from the three nouns *works, toil,* and *patient endurance.* Also the possessive pronoun *your* is significant and because of its repetition emphasizes their labor and attitude. This pronoun, however, is in the singular, which unfortunately English is unable to express. The use of the singular means that the pastor whom Jesus addresses is responsible for the spiritual well-being of the church. But also with this singular Jesus speaks to each individual church member.

The noun *works* is all-inclusive and can be interpreted to mean both good deeds and misdeeds. Here the stress is more on the positive than the negative aspect of the term.

Good works consist of toil on the one hand and patient endurance on the other. Toil includes physical and mental work—both of which are usually taxing and exhausting (compare Heb. 6:10; 10:32–34). Opposing wicked men, false apostles, and Nicolaitans in the community undoubtedly exhausted the members of the Ephesian church. Their attitude was one of patient endurance and steadfastness in the face of spiritual conflict. Incidentally, the Greek word *hypomonē,* which I have translated as "patient endurance," occurs seven times in Revelation and every time refers to the perseverance of the saints (1:9; 2:2, 3, 19; 3:10; 13:10; 14:12). What is patient endurance? It is an inner quality that is expressed in waiting for Jesus, in whose absence the believer steadfastly witnesses for him even to the point of suffering death through persecution.[10]

b. "And that you are not able to tolerate evildoers." A Christian who performs good works through external toil and internal patience is unable to put up with the deeds of evil people among them. The Greek verb *dynē* here translated as "are able" is singular in number. That is, the individual whose heart is truly de-

10. Refer to Friedrich Hauck, *TDNT,* 4:588.

voted to serve the Lord cannot yield place to evil and to those who purposely perpetrate it. The maxim that God loves the sinner but hates sin is valid and applies in this passage. But a follower of Christ cannot tolerate evildoers who refuse to repent but persist in doing evil.

Who are these evildoers? If we observe typical Hebraic parallelism that is used to stress or clarify a point, then we see the answer in the second part of this verse, namely, the false apostles. John does not convey the idea of two different types of evildoers, but of one. The liars are the evildoers.[11]

c. "And you have tested those who call themselves apostles but are not, and you have found them to be liars." The Ephesian Christians had to confront itinerant missionaries who entered the church and brazenly called themselves apostles. But the followers of Christ tested them and found them to be counterfeit. These so-called apostles preached a gospel that was not a gospel of Christ; they were not appointed by Jesus; and they lacked authority to serve the entire church (see 2 Cor. 11:13).[12] In Paul's days, false apostles came with fraudulent recommendations, and they demanded that he demonstrate his apostleship with an endorsement (2 Cor. 3:1). However, Paul laid down the marks of an apostle, namely, to preach Jesus and his gospel; to perform signs, wonders, and miracles; and to do them with perseverance (2 Cor. 11:4; 12:12). The Ephesians tested the doctrine and the works of these apostles and discovered that these people were imposters.

Because Jesus mentions the Nicolaitans by name (v. 6) and records their presence also in the church of Pergamum (2:15), the suggestion that these people were the false apostles is not at all unrealistic. Nevertheless we have no certainty that they originated in Palestine or were sent by Judaizers. Coming with pretense and fanfare, they met outright rejection from the Ephesians, who hated their practices. They were called liars.

3. "And you have endured and have tolerance because of my name and have not become weary."

a. *Stylistic composition.* Although much more so in Greek, even in translation the repetition of the same words is striking. Notice the terms *have endured* and *tolerance* in this verse; they also occurred in the preceding verse in the translation "patient endurance" and "tolerate." At the end of this verse John writes the phrase *have not become weary*, which has the same connotation as the noun "toil" (v. 2).

---

11. "The intolerance here commended is of evil-doers who claimed to be apostles," according to Charles, *Revelation*, 1:50; see also Henry Barclay Swete, *Commentary on Revelation* (1911; reprint, Grand Rapids: Kregel, 1977), p. 25; Alan F. Johnson, *Revelation*, in *The Expositor's Bible Commentary*, ed. Frank E. Gaebelein (Grand Rapids: Zondervan, 1981), 12:433; William Hendriksen, *More Than Conquerors* (reprint, Grand Rapids: Baker, 1982), p. 62.

12. Consult Simon J. Kistemaker, *Exposition of the Second Epistle to the Corinthians*, NTC (Grand Rapids: Baker, 1997), p. 376; C. K. Barrett, "ΠΣΕΥΔΑΠΟΣΤΟΛΟΙ (2 Cor. 11.13)," in *Essays on Paul* (Philadelphia: Westminster, 1982), p. 92.

b. *Praise.* Jesus commended the church in Ephesus for their deeds, hard work, endurance, testing false doctrine, and calling intruding teachers liars. Now he summarizes their stance by praising them for their perseverance to endure hardship for his name. These words should be understood as a reference to the disciplinary action the church took with reference to the intruders. They banned them from entering the church and they set an example to the other churches to do likewise. Yet the congregations in Pergamum and Thyatira failed to dismiss the interlopers (2:15).

c. *Name.* Not the witness for Jesus by a Christian is meant as much as the person of Christ. The name Christian implies that one belongs to and fully identifies with Christ. This means that if someone attacks a Christian, he attacks Christ himself (Acts 9:4). The converse is also true: when someone assaults Christ, he offends the Christian. "If you are insulted because of the name of Christ, you are blessed, for the Spirit of glory and of God rests on you" (1 Pet. 4:14).[13] If people reject the preaching of the gospel, they harden their hearts against Christ. When they attack his name, they besmirch his honor and they sin against the command not to use the Lord's name in vain (Exod. 20:7; Deut. 5:11). Also, the Christian who fails to defend Jesus' name is equally guilty in the sight of the Lord. The believers in Ephesus were zealous of that name and were tireless in promoting his honor. Over against the motto "Caesar is Lord," they boldly stated that "Jesus is Lord." By honoring Christ's name and readily enduring persecution and hardship, the Ephesians demonstrated that they had not become weary in their spiritual life.

b. Rebuke
2:4–5

4. "But I have this against you, that you have left your first love."

Instead of continuing his words of praise for the leading church in the province of Asia, Jesus chastised and admonished the Ephesian Christians. Notwithstanding their ceaseless efforts to oppose evil men who entered the church and subverted its members, to persevere tirelessly, and to endure hardship for the sake of Christ's name, something was amiss in Ephesus. They no longer demonstrated the love for Christ they had in the early years of their history. Those were the days when Paul preached that which was helpful to them and taught publicly from house to house for a period of three years (Acts 20:20–21, 31).

About a decade later, Paul wrote to Timothy, who was pastor in Ephesus, and told him that love from a pure heart, a good conscience, and sincere faith is the goal of God's work among them. He remarked that some false teachers in the congregation devoted themselves to myths and endless genealogies instead of the requirements of love (1 Tim. 1:4–6).

Is this love for each other in the Ephesian church or is it the Christian's love for the Lord? Jesus himself gives the answer in summarizing the Deca-

13. Compare also Isa. 66:5; Matt. 5:11; 10:22; 24:9; Luke 6:22; Acts 5:41.

logue by saying, "'Love the Lord your God with all your heart and with all your soul and with all your mind.' This is the first and great commandment. And the second is like it: 'Love your neighbor as yourself.' All the Law and the Prophets hang on these two commandments" (Matt. 22:37–40). With respect to the Decalogue, God is first and then his people, and the same thing is true regarding the Lord's Prayer. Genuine love for God instinctively leads to expressing love for the neighbor, while loving the neighbor is an expressing of love for God.

When Jesus says that the Ephesians have lost their first love, he does not mean to say that the Ephesians live and work without love for God or their neighbors. He stresses the adjective *first.* In effect a literal translation reads, "You have left your love, the first [love]." The lush green color of springtime in the congregation has disappeared, and the fading shades that characterize an early autumn are now prevalent. To put it differently, the church that Jesus addressed no longer consisted of first-generation believers but of second- and third-generation Christians. These people lacked the enthusiasm their parents and grandparents had demonstrated. They functioned not as propagators of the faith but as caretakers and custodians. There was an obvious deficiency in evangelistic outreach as a result of a status-quo mode of thought. They loved the Lord but no longer with heart, soul, and mind.

The first generation exerted extraordinary effort so that in Ephesus "the word of the Lord spread widely and grew in power" (Acts 19:20). In later years Paul addressed an epistle to them and praised them for their faith in the Lord Jesus and their love for fellow Christians (Eph. 1:15). The children and grandchildren of these people opposed heresy and demonstrated persistence in fulfilling the needs of the church, but they fell short of genuine enthusiasm for the Lord.

5. "Therefore, remember the place from which you have fallen, repent, and perform the works you did at first. If not, I will come to you and I will remove your lampstand from its place, unless you repent."

a. *Grammar.* The Greek verb tenses in this verse stand out from one another to emphasize the successive actions of the Ephesians. First, there is the command to remember, which is given in the present tense as "keep on remembering." Then, the verb *you have fallen* in the perfect tense indicates that considerable time has elapsed since the decline began. In passing, the tense seems to support not the early but the late dating for the Apocalypse. Next, the command to repent is in the aorist tense, signifying a single action that is to last once for all. Fourth, the same thing holds true for the command to perform the works the people did at first; their repentance must keep pace with their decision to work just as enthusiastically as their predecessors. Fifth, the threat *I will come,* although translated as a future, is actually in the present tense to indicate immediate action. Sixth, the verb *I will remove* in the future indicative connotes that the threat is not a possibility but a certainty if they fail to repent. And last, the verb *to repent*, in the second sentence, is given as an escape clause.

b. *Command.* The Lord does not only point to their shortcomings; he also shows them how to correct them. After negatively criticizing their spiritual status, he positively commands them to restore it. They must constantly recall their former position by reviewing their own ecclesiastical history and recollecting what their forebears did in the church forty years earlier; and as they recall their history, they must acknowledge that they have changed for the worse. The radiance of their spiritual ardor has vanished. Indeed their lackluster performance has caused them to forfeit a place of prominence among the churches. They have fallen from their former height and lost their moral standing.

When Jesus says, "Perform the works you did at first," he has in mind not the works the Ephesians have been doing all along but rather the works of love for Christ. The emphasis falls not on the word *works* but on the term *at first.* Just as he asked Peter on the shores of the lake of Galilee, "Simon son of John, do you truly love me more than these?" (John 21:15), so he is asking the members of the church in Ephesus for their undivided devotion. They must change their lifestyle and conduct, that is, they must repent and turn a complete 180 degrees to do so.

c. *Threat.* However, if they fail to respond to Jesus' repeated call to repentance, the Lord will take drastic measures. He is coming and is already on the way to visit them; he will not wait until his coming at the consummation. And even before his final coming, the Ephesians will no longer be a church.[14] Jesus will remove the lampstand from its place, which means that as a congregation they will experience a complete spiritual blackout. A church ceases to be a church when it no longer serves its Master with genuine love and dedication. There is hard evidence that nominal Christianity dies a natural death within a generation or two and consequently disappears completely from the scene.[15] The members may still come together, but they meet for social and not spiritual purposes.

A decade after John wrote the Apocalypse, Ignatius penned a letter to the church at Ephesus in which he praised the local Christians for their patient endurance and their resistance to deceit. He notes that some people from Syria had passed through Ephesus with evil teachings but that the Ephesians had refused to listen. He commends them for being of one mind with the apostles in

14. Gregory K. Beale, *The Book of Revelation: A Commentary on the Greek Text,* NIGTC (Grand Rapids: Eerdmans, 1998), p. 232.

15. In his own characteristic way, Martin Luther observed, "Hin ist hin, jetzt haben sie den Türken" (Gone completely, and now they have the Turks [that is, the Muslims of the sixteenth century]). Certainly today this prophetic observation is relevant and can be translated, "When the church disappeared, Islam took its place." With thanks to R. C. H. Lenski, *The Interpretation of St. John's Revelation* (Columbus: Wartburg, 1943), p. 89.

the power of Jesus Christ.[16] Apparently, the people had taken seriously the words of Jesus.

c. Promise
2:6–7

6. "However, you have this [in your favor], that you hate the works of the Nicolaitans, which I also hate."

The Ephesians had not wavered on doctrinal issues, for they remained true to the teachings of God's Word. Even though Jesus rebuked the members of the church at Ephesus, he pastorally lifts them up by commending them for their faithfulness to his Word. They opposed the false apostles and had sent these wicked men from their midst (v. 2).

Now Jesus inserts that the believers in Ephesus hated the works of the Nicolaitans, and he adds that he also hates these works. Note that hatred is directed toward works, not persons. Jesus hates sin but extends his love toward the sinner. While sin is an affront to his holiness, Jesus' mission is to bring sinners to repentance (Luke 5:32).

Who were the Nicolaitans? Three opinions on this matter remain conjectural because the details in Revelation are scanty. First, in the early church Irenaeus taught that the Nicolaitans were followers of Nicolaus, the convert to Judaism who was appointed a deacon (Acts 6:5).[17] Next, others see these people as a Gnostic sect that sought to infiltrate the churches.[18] Last, on the basis of exegesis, still others aver that the Nicolaitans were the people who followed the teachings of the false apostles and of Balaam. This assumption has merit, for in typical Hebraic style John writes parallelism to stress a point. The false apostles sought to capture the minds of the people with their deceptive doctrines, the followers of Balaam attempted to conquer the people through deceit, and the Greek name *Nikolaos* means "he conquers the people." By comparing what is said about the followers of Balaam (2:14) and the Nicolaitans (2:6, 15), we assume that these deceivers belong to the same group.[19] Yet I admit that there is no certainty on this point.

---

16. Ignatius *Ephesians* 3.1; 6.2; 8.1; 9.1; 11.2. Consult Ramsay, *Letters to the Seven Churches*, p. 241.

17. Irenaeus *Against Heresies* 1.26.3; and 3.11.1; see also Hippolytus *Refutation of All Heresies* 7.24.

18. Elisabeth Schüssler Fiorenza, *The Book of Revelation: Justice and Judgment* (Philadelphia: Fortress, 1985), pp. 116–17; Homer Hailey, *Revelation: An Introduction and Commentary* (Grand Rapids: Baker, 1979), pp. 123–24; Johnson, *Revelation*, p. 435. Other suggestions are made by R. Heiligenthal, "Wer waren die 'Nikolaiten'? Ein Beitrag zur Theologiegeschichte des frühen Christentums," *ZNW* 82 (1991): 133–37; W. M. Mackay, "Another Look at the Nicolaitans," *EvQ* 45 (1973): 111–15.

19. Charles, *Revelation*, 1:52–53; Philip Edgcumbe Hughes, *The Book of the Revelation: A Commentary* (Leicester: Inter-Varsity; Grand Rapids: Eerdmans, 1990), p. 37; Hemer, *Letters to the Seven Churches*, p. 89; Richard Bauckham, *The Theology of the Book of Revelation*, New Testament Theology (Cambridge: Cambridge University Press, 1993), p. 124. Compare Terence L. Donaldson, "Nicolaitans," *ISBE*, 3:534. Others demur. See Isbon T. Beckwith, *The Apocalypse of John* (1919; reprint, Grand Rapids: Baker, 1979), p. 460; also the commentaries of Lenski, p. 90; Swete, p. 28; Thomas, 1:149. Aune observes, "'Balaam' is a pejorative name, while 'Nicolaus' is a name of honor." See his *Revelation 1–5*, p. 149.

In view of the lack of information in the letters to the churches of Ephesus and Pergamum, we can only assume that the lifestyle of the Nicolaitans was characterized by immorality, participation in eating food offered to idols, and perversion of truth (2:14–16).

The Christians in Pergamum and Thyatira struggled with the same deceptive doctrines and lifestyles (2:14–16, 20–24). Yet in these churches many succumbed to the allurements of the intruders and subsequently received words of rebuke for their failure to follow Jesus.

7. "Let anyone who has an ear listen to what the Spirit says to the churches. To everyone who overcomes I will give permission to eat from the tree of life, which is in God's paradise."

a. "Let anyone who has an ear listen to what the Spirit says to the churches." The formula "Let anyone who has an ear listen" comes from the lips of Jesus during his earthly ministry.[20] Here an extended version appears with the words "what the Spirit says to the churches," occurring in every one of the seven letters (2:7, 11, 17, 29; 3:6, 13, 22). This saying precedes a promise in 2:7, 11, and 17 and follows a promise in 2:29; 3:6, 13, 22. The first part of this sentence is an idiomatic expression and refers to the capability of a person to hear and an accompanying willingness to listen. The second part is a command to listen attentively and obediently to the words of the Holy Spirit. Jesus speaks through the Spirit, as is evident in other passages of Scripture (John 14:26; 15:26; 16:13–14; Acts 2:33).

The message is directed not only to the congregation in Ephesus, but to all the churches. In other words, the message is for the universal church of all ages and places. Here then is further proof that the letter to Ephesus was not sent separately but together with the other letters was delivered to the entire church.

b. "To everyone who overcomes I will give permission to eat from the tree of life, which is in God's paradise."[21] A key word in this sentence is the expression *overcome*, which in the Greek is the present participle "the overcoming one." This is not a past or perfect tense as a completed action but current and continuous performance. That is, "the conflict and the trials of the present life in the world and in the churches are not final. The church's anticipated victory has its foundations laid in the victory already won by Jesus."[22] Christ won the battle, but the war is not over yet. Not only the martyrs but every believer is personally engaged in this war against Satan and his cohorts. Therefore, every follower of Christ receives the promise of eternal life and all the other promises that he grants the

20. Matt. 11:15; 13:9, 43; Mark 4:9, 23; Luke 8:8; 14:35; see also Rev. 13:9.

21. Charles, who conjectures that the individual letters were sent at an earlier date to the seven churches, states that this sentence was "added probably by our author when he edited the visions as a whole." See his *Revelation*, 1:53. Conjectures are worthy of consideration only when all solutions to a crux have failed. Here, however, we have not even a crux. See also S. Greijdanus, *De Openbaring des Heeren aan Johannes*, KNT (Amsterdam: Van Bottenburg, 1925), p. 62.

22. Walther Günther, *NIDNTT*, 1:651.

believer (2:10, 17, 26; 3:5, 12, 21). All these promises are given to the overcomer, namely, every true believer.[23]

Jesus promises the overcomer the right to eat from the tree of life. By referring to the tree of life, he effectively brings the reader back to the beginning of human history. After Adam and Eve sinned, God drove them out of the Garden of Eden and placed an angel with a flaming sword there to guard the tree of life (Gen. 2:9; 3:22, 24). By guarding that tree, God prevented our forebears from eating the fruit of the tree of life and thus living eternally in the unredeemable state in which the fallen angels exist. The redemption of his people, which Jesus Christ brings to completion at the consummation, includes the promise that everyone who overcomes will eat from the tree of life in paradise (Rev. 22:2, 14, 19).

The Greek term for *paradise* occurs only three times in Scripture (Luke 23:43; 2 Cor. 12:4; Rev. 2:7). In Genesis the expression *Garden of Eden* appears, which in the Greek translation of the Old Testament becomes *paradise.* Derived from Old Persian, this word depicts a walled park as a place of bliss. In the Old Testament it connotes a delightful place, unmarred by sin. It occurs at the beginning and the end of Scripture.[24] The word describes the blissful life that believers will have with Christ in a new heaven and a new earth. The paradise of God is similar to, but also much different from, the Garden of Eden God created for Adam and Eve.

Additional Note on 2:1–7

The church at Ephesus had been blessed with excellent pastors, of whom Paul and John were apostles of Jesus and Timothy an apostolic helper. We know that Paul was in Ephesus for three years (A.D. 52–55) and Timothy ministered there during the sixties. We surmise that John left Jerusalem in the late sixties and took up residence in Ephesus where he spent the rest of his days, except for his brief stay on the island of Patmos. Even though the believers were molded spiritually by three men, they began to decline in their love for Christ. And even though John as the apostle of love told the people to love one another (see 1 John 4:7–12), not he but Jesus addresses the Ephesians and rebukes them for departing from their first love. Jesus as the Chief Shepherd and Overseer of his flock (1 Pet. 2:25; 5:4) is walking in the midst of his church (2:1).

The body of Jesus Christ is the church and not a society; it is an organism and not an organization; it is a living being and not a formal entity. Whereas membership in a society or an organization can be terminated because of failure to pay dues or fulfill duties, the members of Christ's body are no longer a church when they cease to spread the light of the gospel. The word *church* in English (*Kirche* in German, *kerk* in Dutch) derives from the Greek term *kyriakē,* which means "belonging to the Lord." Romance languages use derivatives from the Greek *ekklēsia,* which signifies God's people *called out of* the world (*église* in

---

23. Refer to Beasley-Murray, *Book of Revelation,* p. 78; Stephen L. Homcy, " 'To Him Who Overcomes': A Fresh Look at What 'Victory' Means for the Believer according to the Book of Revelation," *JETS* 38 (1995): 193–201.

24. See also Gen. 2:15–16; 3:3, 8, 10, 24; 13:10; Ezek. 28:13; 31:8–9; Joel 2:3.

French, *iglesia* in Spanish, *igreja* in Portuguese, and *chiesa* in Italian). Hence, those people who make up the living body of Jesus Christ are the church, for they belong to him.

Greek Words, Phrases, and Constructions in 2:3–7

Verse 3

The verb tenses in this verse are significant: "you have [ἔχεις] patience" is present; "you have tolerated [ἐβάστασας]" is aorist; and "you have not become weary [κεκοπί-ακες]" is perfect. The aorist may be interpreted as constative, so that all three tenses show duration.

Verse 5

This verse features seven verbs of which only two have the same tense and mood. The first word in a Greek sentence always receives emphasis: μνημόνευε—remember! This is the imperative in the present tense to denote continued action. The second is πέπτωκας, which is in the perfect to imply that the fall of the Ephesians began in the past and continues to the present. The third and fourth verbs are in the aorist imperative and convey the command to obey once for all: μετανόησον (repent!) and ποίησον (do!). The fifth verb, which is in the present tense ἔρχομαι (I am coming) but denotes a future action, is followed by κινήσω (I will remove), which conveys the idea of certainty. The seventh verb, which stands last in the sentence for emphasis, is repetitious in a way (μετανοήσῃς, repent) but is given in the aorist subjunctive.

Verse 7

τοῦ ξύλου τῆς ζωῆς—"the tree of life." This phrase has been taken from the Septuagint version of Genesis 2:9; 3:22, 24. It should be understood as an eschatological phrase (Rev. 22:2, 14, 19; compare Ezek. 47:12). "A play on the cross of Christ is not yet evident in these passages in Revelation."[25]

---

8 "And to the angel of the church in Smyrna write: The First and the Last, who was dead and is alive, says this: 9 I know your tribulation, your poverty (but you are rich), and the blasphemy from the ones who call themselves Jews and are not, but are the synagogue of Satan. 10 And do not be afraid of anything you are about to suffer. Look, the devil is about to cast some of you into prison that you may be tested, and you will have tribulation for ten days. Be faithful unto death, and I will give you the crown of life.

11 "Let anyone who has an ear listen to what the Spirit says to the churches. Everyone who overcomes will not be hurt by the second death."

---

2. Smyrna
2:8–11
The City

Smyrna (modern Izmir), located on the west coast of Asia Minor, has a sheltered harbor that faces a bay whose breezes cool the city during the hot summer months and provide a pleasant climate. The harbor stimulated trade and com-

---

25. Heinz-Wolfgang Kuhn, *EDNT*, 2:487. Hemer (*Letters to the Seven Churches*, pp. 43–44) is not hostile to placing "the Cross in the Paradise of God."

merce that developed the city of Smyrna into a commercial metropolis. An estimate of its population in Paul's day reaches 250,000 inhabitants, which in modern times can be nearly doubled. It was a thriving city at the end of a major highway that cut through the fertile fields of the Hermus valley.

Politically the city sided with the Romans and became their faithful ally. Already in 195 B.C. it built a temple for Dea Roma, the goddess of Rome. In A.D. 26 it dedicated a temple to Emperor Tiberius and boasted to be first in emperor worship. This boast gratified Roman administrators, who fostered the peace and unity that characterized the spirit of Rome throughout the empire. William Barclay writes that to make the spirit of Rome tangible the Romans presented the emperor as its embodiment, and thus worship of the emperor arose. Although some of the first emperors disparaged this worship, the population energized it to the point that the emperor was considered to be divine.[26]

Writers in the ancient past extolled Smyrna as the city most beautiful in respect to its buildings, temples of Zeus and Cybele, and the layout of its streets. It was known as "the crown of Smyrna." The name originated from the city's buildings, whose symmetrical appearance was likened to a crown.[27] But in addition to the buildings and the design of the city, nature also contributed to the beauty of Smyrna. The city was blessed with many groves of trees, among them trees whose resin produced a brown to reddish or yellowish brown aromatic gum called myrrh. The word *myrrh* (Greek *smyrna*) appears in the New Testament as one of the precious gifts that the wise men from the East brought to Jesus and as an embalming ingredient Nicodemus brought for Jesus' burial (Matt. 2:11; John 19:39; see also Exod. 30:23; Ps. 45:8; Song of Songs 5:5, 13).

The Jewish population in Smyrna was sizable, for they are mentioned as a force that was hostile to the local church. They slandered the early Christians, called themselves Jews but really belonged to the synagogue of Satan, and abetted the persecution of Christ's followers (vv. 9–10). Why they were so adamantly set against the church cannot be answered. Whereas the members of the Smyrna church were poverty stricken, the Jews were wealthy. For instance, according to an inscription from the second century, Jews at one time donated the sum of ten thousand denarii for a project to beautify the city of Smyrna.[28]

Their opposition to Christianity is on record in connection with the martyrdom of Polycarp, who on February 23, 155, was killed for his refusal to deny the name of Jesus. He had been the bishop of Smyrna for many years. As an elderly saint, he responded to the proconsul who gave him the choice of cursing Jesus' name and living or confessing his name and dying: "Eighty-six years have I served Christ, and he has never done me wrong. How can I blaspheme my King who

26. Barclay, *Letters to the Seven Churches*, p. 32. Compare Edward M. Blaiklock, "Smyrna," *ZPEB*, 5:462.

27. Hemer, *Letters to the Seven Churches*, p. 60; Ramsay, *Letters to the Seven Churches*, pp. 256–57.

28. Ramsay, *Letters to the Seven Churches*, pp. 272, 444 n. 3; William Barclay, *The Revelation of John*, 2d ed. (Philadelphia: Westminster, 1960), 1:92.

saved me?"[29] Thereupon the proconsul sentenced him to die at the stake. The record indicates that the Jews were foremost in gathering wood for the fire. Even though it was the Sabbath, they deliberately carried burdens of wood and transgressed the law.[30]

A date for the founding of the Smyrna church cannot be firmly established. Devout Jews from the province of Asia were at the Pentecost feast in Jerusalem when the Holy Spirit was poured out (Acts 2:9), and some of these may have come from Smyrna and taken the gospel back to their hometown. Alternatively, when Paul came to Ephesus in the early fifties, he or his associates may have instituted the church at Smyrna. Polycarp's letter to the church at Philippi may indicate that the knowledge of Christ had not yet come to Smyrna when Paul in 62 wrote his letter to the Philippians: "for we did not yet know him [Christ]."[31] Ignatius, bishop at Antioch in Syria, was brought to Rome as a martyr in 110. On his way, he stopped at Smyrna where he wrote four letters to the various churches; and afterward when he rested at Troas, he wrote another three letters; one of these was addressed to the church in Smyrna.

The Letter

8. "And to the angel of the church in Smyrna write: The First and the Last, who was dead and is alive, says this."

Jesus commands John to write a letter to the pastor of the Smyrna church and identifies himself as "the First and the Last" (1:17; 22:13). This phrase is the self-identification of God who addresses Israel, "This is what the LORD says—Israel's King and Redeemer, the LORD Almighty: I am the first and I am the last; apart from me there is no God" (Isa. 44:6; 48:12; see also 41:4). With the expression "the First and the Last," Jesus defines his divinity as equal in power and authority to that of God. (Incidentally, apart from the words "for ten days" in verse 10, which are an echo of Daniel 1:12 and 14, there are no other allusions to the Old Testament in the letter to Smyrna.)

However, Jesus adds to his self-identification the clause "who was dead and is alive" (1:18). He is the one who died on Calvary's cross, conquered death, and is alive. Throughout the Apocalypse, the contrast between God and Satan, Christ and the Antichrist is spelled out. So the Antichrist, appearing as the beast coming up out of the sea, had a fatal wound and yet lived (13:3, 12, and 14). This description of the Antichrist reveals his insidious imitation of Christ's death and resurrection.[32] The difference between Christ and the Antichrist is that Christ conquered death, has the keys of Death and Hades, and as the living one gives life to his people. The beast, that is, the Antichrist, wounded by the sword is

---

29. Eusebius *Eccl. Hist.* 4.15.25.

30. *Martyrdom of Polycarp* (compare 8.1 with 13.1).

31. Polycarp *To the Philippians* 11.3.

32. Consult Richard Bauckham, *The Climax of Prophecy: Studies on the Book of Revelation* (Edinburgh: Clark, 1993), pp. 432–33.

thrown alive with the false prophet into the lake of fire and burning sulfur (13:14; 19:20).

9. "I know your tribulation, your poverty (but you are rich), and the blasphemy from the ones who call themselves Jews and are not, but are the synagogue of Satan."

a. "I know your tribulation, your poverty (but you are rich)." Jesus addresses the individual believer by using the singular possessive pronoun *your,* that is, he is fully aware of the tribulation and poverty each Christian in Smyrna has to endure for the name of Christ. The word *tribulation* actually means living in oppression, in narrow straits. Also, the one leads to the other: oppression results in poverty when work and resources are cut off because of one's testimony for Christ. The believers in Smyrna may have experienced the confiscation of their earthly belongings, for the expression *poverty* is the translation of the Greek term *ptōcheia,* which refers to the abject poverty of a beggar. Paul writes about this condition to the Corinthians when he notes that Jesus Christ, "though he was rich, yet for your sakes became poor, so that you through his poverty might become rich" (2 Cor. 8:2, 9). Jesus underscores these words by telling his people in Smyrna that they are spiritually rich. This does not mean that believers should invite persecution and hardships in order to become rich in spiritual possessions; rather, Jesus wants them to be faithful to him and his word even when they go through hardship and abuse, for then they will be blessed spiritually (Matt. 5:11–12; James 2:5).

b. "And the blasphemy from the ones who call themselves Jews and are not." Jesus spoke about blasphemy against himself and the Holy Spirit in the context of casting out a demon in a person who was blind and mute (Matt. 12:22–32). When the man could see, hear, and speak, the people asked their spiritual leaders whether Jesus could be the Son of David (the Messiah). But the Pharisees and teachers of the law told the crowd that "this fellow" (Jesus) was casting out demons in the name of Beelzebub (Satan). The clergy in Israel should have been the first to recognize the Messiah when Jesus healed a blind person. Isaiah repeatedly prophesied about the Messiah by saying that at his coming he would open the eyes of the blind (Isa. 29:18; 32:3; 35:5; 42:7; compare Matt. 11:5). Further, to the Jews were entrusted the very words of God (Rom. 3:2), so that they would see the messianic promises fulfilled in Jesus Christ. Instead they became, and many still are, vehemently opposed to him and his teachings. Knowing the truth about God and intentionally denying it is blasphemy.

Jews schooled in the rabbinic tradition knew the meaning of blasphemy: "The Holy One, blessed be he, pardons everything else, but on profanation of the Name [i.e., blasphemy] he takes vengeance immediately."[33] They circumvented uttering God's name by calling him Lord (Adonai). But Jesus as the Messiah enjoyed divinity and authority equal to God, so that anyone consciously rejecting him would be guilty of blasphemy. The Jews in Smyrna refused to acknowledge Jesus as their Messiah

33. *Sifre* on Deut. 32:28 (end); William L. Lane, *The Gospel according to Mark,* NICNT (Grand Rapids: Eerdmans, 1974), p. 145; Hans Währish and Colin Brown, *NIDNTT,* 3:344.

and cursed him and his followers. Jesus no longer called these people Jews, that is, spiritual sons of Abraham. Christians were now called sons and daughters of Abraham in their place, and Jews who rejected Jesus were in league with the devil.

c. "But [they] are the synagogue of Satan" (see 3:9). The Romans had granted the Jews in Israel and the dispersion exemption from Roman religious practices. They had given them the right to observe their own religion, which was known as a *religio licita* (an allowed religion). When Christianity came into being at Pentecost (Acts 2:1), Christians were safe under this Roman umbrella given to the Jews until the destruction of the temple in A.D. 70. From then on the Jews were among the first to accuse Christians to the Romans; they said that the Christians honored Jesus and not Caesar as Lord. Consequently, Christians no longer enjoyed civil protection but were slandered, persecuted, and often killed. Those Jews who falsely accused the followers of Christ to the Romans and purposely oppressed them were indeed agents of Satan, who had become the ruler of their synagogue. This is not to say that all Jews rejected Jesus and that Satan ruled all synagogues. In the province of Asia, Jesus portrayed Smyrna and Philadelphia as places where Satan instigated blasphemy and lying in the local synagogues (2:9; 3:9). Also in those two cities were churches that Jesus praised without uttering a word of reproof or correction. Truly in the darkest places the light shines brightest.

10. "And do not be afraid of anything you are about to suffer. Look, the devil is about to cast some of you into prison that you may be tested, and you will have tribulation for ten days. Be faithful unto death, and I will give you the crown of life."

a. "And do not be afraid of anything you are about to suffer." Once again Jesus utters the words "do not fear" (1:17). Now addressing each individual believer, he expands the saying to "don't be afraid of anything." He who is in full control of every situation knows what lies ahead of his people; he reveals that they are about to enter a period of suffering.

b. "Look, the devil is about to cast some of you into prison that you may be tested." The Christians in Smyrna must be fully aware that they are fighting a spiritual war in which they confront the devil. Hence, they are told to be alert, for the devil will incite the authorities so that some people of the congregation will be imprisoned with the distinct possibility of being put to death. This will strike fear into the hearts of the believers, who can expect to endure confiscation of property and goods, extreme poverty, and slander. But incarceration, at times without trial, may result in death. Jesus says that this threat to their lives is to test their faith in him.

Imprisonment may be a measure to subdue a rebellious person, an arrest while the guilty person is awaiting trial, or a prelude to his execution. The context of verse 10, "be faithful unto death," implies that incarceration of the Christian will be an "interim period of suffering in anticipation of martyrdom."[34]

c. "And you will have tribulation for ten days." This is the second time that the term *tribulation* occurs (v. 9). But here its duration is specified: for a ten-day pe-

34. Hemer, *Letters to the Seven Churches*, p. 68; see also Ramsay, *Letters to the Seven Churches*, pp. 273–74.

riod. In Revelation, the number ten conveys the meaning of fullness in the decimal system. It is a symbolical number to express the completeness of the period of suffering, which is neither long nor short but full, for its termination is sure.[35]

d. "Be faithful unto death, and I will give you the crown of life." Throughout the history of Smyrna her citizens had been faithful first to the Greeks and then to the Romans. Faithfulness to Rome was a well-known characteristic of the people in Smyrna, but now Jesus calls these followers to be faithful to him. Jesus is called "the faithful one" (1:5; 3:14; 19:11) and so is Antipas, the martyr in Pergamum (2:13). Now the saints in Smyrna are asked to pay the sacrifice to be faithful to death.

In view of Smyrna's city layout, commentators have no problem seeing a connection between the crown of the city and the crown promised to the faithful followers of Christ. But the words of Jesus are "the crown of life," which make them different and meaningful. The phrase probably was idiomatic—it occurs also in James 1:12—and can be translated "the crown, that is, fullness of life." It is emblematic of the "highest joy and gladness and of glory and immortality."[36] If the saints in Smyrna pay with their life for the testimony of Jesus, they will receive imperishable life in eternal glory.

11. "Let anyone who has an ear listen to hear what the Spirit says to the churches. Everyone who overcomes will not be hurt by the second death."

The repetition of the first sentence once more stresses the work of the Holy Spirit in conveying Christ's message to the churches. Notice that this letter is not addressed only to the congregation at Smyrna but to all the churches, so that the letter with the others is a universal message.

And once again the verb *to overcome* appears in a promise. The overcomer is given the promise of being unaffected by the second death. The first death pertains to one's physical demise, the second death to being cut off forever from God (see 20:6, 14; 21:8). The saints may suffer physical death at the hand of persecutors, but they will never be separated from God. By contrast, unbelievers will be cast into the lake of fire (20:14) and suffer eternal death. This means that they will experience not annihilation but never-ending punishment.

Greek Words, Phrases, and Constructions in 2:9–11

Verse 9

τὰ ἔργα καί—the Majority Text has added these words in conformity with 2:2, 19; 3:1, 8, 15. Their insertion, however, is easier to explain than their omission. Following the rule that the harder reading is likely the original, I have opted for their exclusion.

---

35. Refer to the commentaries of Beckwith (pp. 254, 454); Greijdanus (p. 69); Hailey (p. 127); Hendriksen (p. 65), among others.

36. Richard C. Trench, *Synonyms of the New Testament*, ed. Robert G. Hoerber (Grand Rapids: Baker, 1989), p. 94–95.

σου—the possessive pronoun controls the nouns *tribulation* and *poverty*. Preceding them, it gives added emphasis to these nouns: *your* tribulation and *your* poverty.

Verse 10

μηδέν—some manuscripts have the reading μή, but this undoubtedly is a revision based on similar wording in 1:17.

ἰδού—this aorist middle imperative, because of its frequent usage in Koine Greek, has become a demonstrative particle that calls the hearer or reader to pay attention: Look! It occurs twenty-six times in Revelation alone and most frequently in the Gospels of Matthew and Luke.

ἕξετε—there are variants that have the present tense either in the indicative ἔχετε or the subjunctive ἔχητε. The original reading is difficult to determine, for a good case can be made for each of the variants.

τὸν στέφανον τῆς ζωῆς—the genitive may express quality or apposition. Of the two, the latter is preferred: "the crown, namely, life."

Verse 11

ἐκ—with the verb *to be hurt* the preposition has a causal meaning.

---

12 "And to the angel of the church in Pergamum write: He who holds the sharp double-edged sword says this: 13 I know where you live, where Satan's throne is. Yet you are holding on to my name, and you did not renounce your faith in me, even in the days of Antipas, my faithful witness, who was killed among you where Satan lives. 14 However, I have a few things against you in that you have there those who hold the teaching of Balaam, who taught Balak to put a stumbling block before the Israelites to make them eat food offered to an idol and commit fornication. 15 So even you have those who similarly hold the teaching of the Nicolaitans. 16 Repent, therefore. If not, I will come to you quickly and make war against them with the sword of my mouth."

17 "Let anyone who has an ear listen to what the Spirit says to the churches. To everyone who overcomes, I will give hidden manna, and I will give a white stone; and on the stone is written a new name that no one knows except the one who receives it."

---

3. Pergamum
2:12–17
The City

Some sixty-five miles to the north of Smyrna and fifteen miles from the Aegean Sea lay the city of Pergamum (modern Bergama). Its name has been perpetuated in the English term *parchment* (French *parchemin*; Dutch *perkament*; Spanish *pergamino*). The expression illustrates the industry of ancient Pergamum, where due to a trade embargo its people, unable to buy paper products (made from Egyptian papyrus leaves), prepared animal skins for writing purposes. The city not only marketed these skins but also opened a library that eventually housed some two hundred thousand scrolls. It became a learning center where knowledge was accumulated, applied, and disseminated.

Located at an elevation of about one thousand feet, Pergamum served as a citadel that dominated the countryside. It was a city of prominence in the centuries before the Romans invaded and made it a capital. Pergamum was known as a religious center, with temples for Zeus Sōtēr, Athena Nicephorus, Dionysos Cathegemon, and Asclepius Sōtēr. Constructed on a ledge in front of the temple of Athena was the altar of Zeus. It was the most splendid of religious monuments because of its height—some forty feet. Asclepius was the god of healing and attracted the interest of countless people suffering physical ills. His symbol was the snake, which still decorates medical emblems today. After the Romans conquered Pergamum, they built a temple in 129 B.C. Later they dedicated the temple to Augustus and Rome,[37] and introduced the worship of Caesar. Temples dedicated to Trajan and Severus were constructed much later. Emperor worship had its center in Pergamum, and for some time the city rivaled Smyrna and Ephesus, for it was given the privilege of appointing a temple warden or temple sweeper (*neokoros*). It was also the first Roman administrative center in the province of Asia.[38] The proconsul who had his residence here held the power of the sword to determine whether a person should live or die.

Notice that the Greek word *sōtēr* applied to both Zeus and Asclepius means "savior." In view of their Savior Jesus Christ it was impossible for Christians to acknowledge these gods as saviors. In addition, they could never utter the motto *Caesar is Lord*, because for them the title *Lord* was reserved for Jesus only. Instead of the two hundred thousand or more volumes in the Pergamum library, they came only with the Scriptures. In place of numerous temples, they had no temple and said that their Christian fellowship and even their physical bodies served as the temple of the Holy Spirit (1 Cor. 3:16; 6:19). And in lieu of Asclepius's healing, the Christians taught that Jesus was their Great Physician. In brief, for Christians life in Pergamum was made nearly unbearable.

For their refusal to compromise, Christians were mocked by Romans and others who called them "christiani" and by Jews who labeled them "Nazarenes." They were charged with infidelity to Rome, scorned, accused of sedition, persecuted, and killed. In spite of persecution and even because of it, the Christian church continued to flourish and increase in number.

In Pergamum, Christians daily faced the pressures of a pagan society. If they refused to accept an invitation to attend a feast in honor of a pagan deity, they would not only be shunned, but they would lose their jobs or businesses. People would call them outcasts not fit to live on this earth. But for faithful believers there is no one higher than their Lord, no human law that takes precedence over God's law, and no teaching that supplants the gospel.

a. Violence
2:12–13

12. "And to the angel of the church in Pergamum write: He who holds the sharp double-edged sword says this: 13. I know where you live, where Satan's

37. Tacitus *Annals* 3.37.

38. For references see Barclay, *Letters to the Seven Churches*, pp. 46–53; and *Revelation of John*, 1:106–11; Charles, *Revelation*, 1:60–61; Ramsay, *Letters to the Seven Churches*, pp. 281–90; Swete, *Revelation*, pp. 34–35.

throne is. Yet you are holding on to my name, and you did not renounce your faith in me, even in the days of Antipas, my faithful witness, who was killed among you where Satan lives."

Except for the address, the introductory formula is the same as in all the letters to the churches in the province of Asia. Jesus' self-identification is a throwback to the description of his appearance (1:16). Even though the same words "the sharp double-edged sword" appear, the Greek has them in a sequence with definite articles for emphasis. Literally, the clause reads, "the one who has the sword, the double-edged one, the sharp one." It was not the Roman proconsul or the governor who decided on matters of life and death, but it was Jesus, with the sharp, double-edged sword of his word proceeding from his mouth. Jesus will indeed fight with this sword against his enemies (v. 16; 19:15, 21).

a. "I know where you live, where Satan's throne is." Fully aware of the situation in Pergamum, Jesus said to the local Christians, "I know where you live." He addressed not strangers, transients, or travelers (compare 1 Pet. 1:1), but permanent residents who were born and raised in Pergamum and had their roots in that city. God had called them out of their pagan environment to be his people.

Jesus explicates the clause "where Satan's throne is" with the words "where Satan lives." The verb *lives* signifies that his dwelling is permanent just as the local Christians are permanent inhabitants, but they are two opposing forces. Satan seems to have the upper hand until we realize that the Apocalypse contrasts God and Satan. Jesus sits on his Father's glorious throne in heaven (3:21) and Satan rules his kingdom in darkness (16:10). The word *throne* appears forty-two times in Revelation: forty refer to God's throne and two to the throne of Satan and the beast (2:13; 16:10). In other words, not Satan but God is in control.

What is the meaning of Satan's throne? There are at least five interpretations:[39]

- Pergamum was a center of pagan religion.
- To a traveler coming from the east, the acropolis had the appearance of a throne.
- The altar of Zeus Sōtēr seemed to be a throne.
- Asclepius Sōtēr was identified with the serpent.
- Pergamum was the center of emperor worship.

First, no doubt Pergamum was a religious center devoted to pagan idols. But the cities in the province of Asia were no different from Athens, for idol worship ruled the day in the pagan world of the first century. According to Paul, Athens was a city filled with idols and its people were very religious (Acts 17:16, 22).

The second interpretation closely follows the first and differs from it only in the appearance of the city, which was located on an elevated plateau. Even though the symbolism of its external appearance is striking, the internal dominance of Satan's rule in the lives of the people takes priority.

39. Hemer, *Letters to the Seven Churches*, pp. 84–85.

Third, Zeus's altar prominently placed above everything else is imposing.[40] But Zeus as chief god was worshiped everywhere in Greece, Macedonia, and Asia Minor—he was called Jupiter by the Romans (Acts 14:12 KJV).

The fourth explanation has merit, because the symbol of Asclepius is a serpent and in Scripture Satan is typified by the serpent symbol (Gen. 3:1; Rev. 12:9; 20:2). Personified in the god Asclepius, Satan proves to be the great deceiver as the healer of the sick and the savior of the people.

The fifth explanation is incisive. While the fourth interpretation calls attention to Satan's deception, the fifth stresses Satan's destructive power in persecuting God's people. Christians who refused to acknowledge Caesar as Lord and God (*dominus et deus*) faced confiscation of their property, exile, or death.[41] If we consider that Antipas was killed and John was exiled because of Jesus' testimony, then this fifth explanation fits the overall context.

b. "Yet you are holding on to my name, and you did not renounce your faith in me, even in the days of Antipas, my faithful witness, who was killed among you where Satan lives." Despite the hardships that the Christians in Pergamum endured, they remained faithful to their Lord and Savior Jesus Christ. They are commended for holding on to the name of Jesus. This action involves more than confessing his name: it includes living in harmony with the Scriptures and walking in Jesus' footsteps (1 Pet. 2:21). By making the Roman authorities enforce emperor worship and its subsequent oppression, Satan sought to exploit the weaknesses in the church of those members who might be tempted to renounce their faith in Jesus Christ. The believers, however, stood their ground and continued their loyalty to their Master.[42]

Persecution resulting in death was real, as is evident in the case of Antipas. We know very little about the man. His Greek name can either mean "against all" or be an abbreviated form of the name Antipater, but this has nothing to do with his life and death. His life is characterized by the designation "my faithful witness," which is the same ascription by which Jesus is known (1:5; compare 3:14). His death took place some time before the writing of the Apocalypse, and Antipas may have been representative of many others.

c. "Who was killed among you where Satan lives." These two clauses together evoke fear in the hearts of God's people. Living near the residence of Satan, followers of Jesus Christ can expect to endure both persecution and death. Their habitation and that of Satan happen to be the same, so that the evil one is always

---

40. See Adolf Deissmann, *Light from the Ancient East*, trans. Lionel R. M. Strachan (reprint, Grand Rapids: Baker, 1978), p. 281 n. 3.

41. Consult Ray Summers, *Worthy Is the Lamb: An Interpretation of Revelation* (Nashville: Broadman, 1951), p. 93. Aune (*Revelation 1–5*, p. 183) asserts that "there is no explicit evidence in 2:12–17 (or in Rev. 2–3) to suggest that the imperial cult was a major problem for the Christians of Asia." However, implicitly the problem was real for the early Christians. See S. R. F. Price, *Rituals and Power: The Roman Imperial Cult in Asia Minor* (Cambridge: Cambridge University Press, 1984), pp. 155–65, 221–22; Beale, *Revelation*, pp. 246–47.

42. See D. S. Deer, "Whose Faith/Loyalty in Revelation 2.13 and 14.12?" *BibTrans* 38 (1987): 328–30.

present. But Jesus told his disciples that they are in the world but not of the world (John 17:14–18). He assigns his people to take the redemptive message of salvation everywhere on this troubled earth. He as the Victor has said, "But take heart! I have overcome the world" (John 16:33). This victorious Jesus shares his victory with his followers, who go forth into the world with the knowledge that God's word never returns void, for that word is never bound (Isa. 55:11; 2 Tim. 2:9).

b. Rebuke
2:14–16

14. "However, I have a few things against you in that you have there those who hold the teaching of Balaam, who taught Balak to put a stumbling block before the Israelites to make them eat food offered to an idol and commit fornication. 15. So even you have those who similarly hold the teaching of the Nicolaitans."

a. "However, I have a few things against you in that you have there those who hold the teaching of Balaam." We would have expected words of encouragement from the lips of Jesus; instead we hear words of rebuke. Jesus reproves the Christians in Pergamum because of some weaknesses they displayed. The *few things* are not necessarily of little importance even though few in number. Jesus does not enumerate these things but mentions only one, namely, the lack of resistance to false teaching and conduct within the congregation. The believers have tolerated teachers who have spread their insidious doctrine and lifestyle, and they have failed to expel them from the church. Their influence is spreading like cancer cells in a healthy body; and radical measures must be taken before it is too late. While the church in Ephesus exercised discipline (2:2), the church in Pergamum did not.

Satan's servants entered the local congregation and sought to influence the members deceitfully with a lifestyle incompatible with those who follow Jesus. We have no information about the identity of the perpetrators. The words *you have there those* can mean that they had entered the church and had been accepted as bona fide members or that they were influenced by people from outside the church (2 Pet. 2:15; Jude 11). Jesus calls to mind the story of Balaam and Balak recorded in Numbers 22–25. We assume that the second- and third-generation Christians in Pergamum were sufficiently acquainted with the account of Israel's history that the writer did not need to spell it out in detail.

b. "[Balaam] taught Balak to put a stumbling block before the Israelites to make them eat food offered to an idol and commit fornication." We learn by inference that after Balaam's triple failure to curse the Israelites, he lured them into committing adultery with Midianite women, eating meat offered to idols, and worshiping pagan gods (see especially Num. 31:16 in the context of Num. 25). The teachings of Balaam were not so much doctrine as practice: indulging in sexual immorality with Moabite women, the eating of food sacrificed to idols, and the worship of these idols (Num. 25:1–3; Ps. 106:28). This was the stumbling block that Balak, following Balaam's advice, placed before the people of Israel to make them fall into sin.[43]

The Israelites were invited to participate in the pagan fertility rites of the Moabite people, whose women enticed the Israelite men to engage in sexually immoral acts. This stumbling block was similar to a trap commonly used for catching birds. The trap had a movable stick, so that a bird touching the stick would cause the trap to snap shut, with the result that the bird was caught and killed. This stumbling block brought about death for the Israelites: a plague struck and killed some twenty-four thousand of them (Num. 25:9; 1 Cor. 10:8).[44]

In Pergamum, people who followed the teachings of Balaam set a trap for the followers of Christ to seek personal safety by participating in the practices of those who assembled for emperor worship. First, they suggested that it was perfectly acceptable for Christians to eat meat that they knew had been sacrificed to idols. The believers knew that they should not question the origin of meat for sale at the meat market (1 Cor. 10:25), but that their consciences should not allow them to participate in a feast dedicated to an idol if the meat was eaten in one of the rooms of the temple (1 Cor. 10:19–22). Next, the Nicolaitans suggested that Christians engage in sexual immorality. However, the Christians knew that the law of God barred them from entering into any extramarital sexual relationships. They were fully aware of the numerous prostitutes in the temple precincts luring them under religious pretexts. And last, the followers of Balaam urged the Christians to sacrifice an animal in the worship of Caesar. This sacrifice, they said, would entail only the burning of an insignificant part of the animal and would leave the rest for a feast to be enjoyed by the Christians with family and friends. Again, the followers of Christ knew that they could not worship both Christ and Caesar.[45]

We know from Jesus' letter to the Ephesians (see my comments on 2:6) that the teachings and practices of the Nicolaitans were an abomination to Jesus. Even though the information concerning these people is scant, we assume that the lifestyle of the Nicolaitans was characterized by the sins of sexual immorality, eating food offered to idols, and perverting apostolic teachings (2:14–16). Stressing Christian liberty, they apparently taught that physical activities pertaining to sex and food were not sinful. In God's sight, however, engaging in sexual acts with temple prostitutes and entering pagan temples to eat food consecrated to a pagan god were violations of the Decalogue. God said:

---

43. Refer to Philo *Life of Moses* 1.54 §§295–97; Josephus *Antiquities* 4.6.6 §§126–28.

44. For the difference in total numbers (24,000 and 23,000), see Simon J. Kistemaker, *Exposition of the First Epistle to the Corinthians*, NTC (Grand Rapids: Baker, 1993), p. 330.

45. The Jerusalem Council exhorted Gentile Christians "to abstain from food sacrificed to idols, from blood, from the meat of strangled animals, and from sexual immorality" (Acts 15:29). Paul devoted the greater part of two chapters in his Corinthian correspondence to the question of eating food sacrificed to idols (1 Cor. 8:1–10; 10:14–33). Paul opposed Jewish legalism on the one hand and pagan practices on the other. See also Panayotis Coutsoumpos, "The Social Implication of Idolatry in Revelation 2:14: Christ or Caesar?" *BTB* 27 (1997): 23–27.

- "You shall have no other gods before me" (Exod. 20:3).
- "You shall not bow down to them or worship them" (Exod. 20:5).
- "You shall not commit adultery" (Exod. 20:14).

Likewise Paul warned the Corinthians that the body is not meant for sexual immorality but for the Lord; and he admonished God's people not to participate in sacrifices offered to an idol (1 Cor. 6:13; 10:20). As God is holy, so his people must strive for holy conduct (Lev. 11:44–45; 1 Pet. 1:15).

c. "So even you have those who similarly hold the teaching of the Nicolaitans." Once again (v. 6), Jesus mentions the Nicolaitans. Here he notes that the Pergamenes who practiced the sins of idolatry and sexual immorality were similar to the Nicolaitans who advocated them. Are the followers of Balaam and the Nicolaitans the same? We must see Satan at work as the great deceiver, because the intentions of Balaam and his followers and that of the Nicolaitans are identical: Balaam intended to defeat the Israelites with a deceptive lifestyle, and the Nicolaitans entered the church with deceptive teachings and practices. "Moreover, those who hold the teaching of Balaam (2:14) are probably the same people as those who hold the teaching of the Nicolaitans."[46]

We have no knowledge of the extent of the Nicolaitans' influence on the church, but we do know that the church was lax in discipline and permitted these antagonists to the Christian faith to be in their midst to the spiritual detriment of the believers. For this laxity, the church was reprimanded and told to repent. The Nicolaitans and those who had adopted their harmful teaching and practices had to face Jesus, who would come with the sword of the Spirit, that is, the word of God.

16. "Repent, therefore. If not, I will come to you quickly and make war against them with the sword of my mouth."

The verb *to repent* occurs twelve times in Revelation.[47] Eight of them are addressed to the churches in Ephesus, Pergamum, Sardis, and Laodicea as commands to repent; the other four are in the past tense and refer to unbelievers who refused to do so. The Christians of Pergamum had to repent of their failure to expel the Nicolaitans and their followers from among them. They had to see the error of their way, for if Jesus hated the works of the Nicolaitans (2:6) so should his people. So he called the Christians to turn their laxity into watchfulness, to enforce spiritual discipline, and to expel from among them the Nicolaitans and their adherents.

If the addressees refuse to obey, Jesus will come quickly (the Greek has the verb *to come* in the present tense; see v. 5). Christ's coming refers not to the Second Coming but to his imminent judgment that is swift and certain. The Nicolaitans would not have to wait until the Second Coming for Jesus to execute his

---

46. Schüssler Fiorenza, *Book of Revelation*, p. 116.

47. Rev. 2:5 (twice), 16, 21 (twice), 22; 3:3, 19; 9:20, 21; 16:9, 11.

threat.[48] As the Midianites and Balaam experienced God's judgment in their lifetime, so the Nicolaitans would soon encounter Jesus as warrior in their life span. During the battle that Israel fought against the Midianites at God's command, the Israelites killed Balaam (Num. 31:1–8; Josh. 13:22).[49]

Notice that the Lord calls the church to repentance but declares war on the Nicolaitans. He will fight them with the double-edged sword that proceeds from his mouth (see v. 12), and with this sword he slays the wicked. And that includes the Nicolaitans and their adherents. Those who are serving Satan and are bent on destroying the church meet the sword of her warrior and her victorious Lord.

The good news is that God works out all things for good to those who love and serve him (Rom. 8:28). All those who turn to the Lord and repent experience his love, grace, and mercy. By contrast, he forsakes all those who have forsaken him (2 Chron. 15:2; Isa. 1:28; 65:11–12).[50]

The Lord honors his promises and cancels his threats to the repentant sinner. But when there is no repentance, he fulfills his threats.

c. Promise
2:17

17. "Let anyone who has an ear listen to what the Spirit says to the churches. To everyone who overcomes, I will give hidden manna, and I will give a white stone; and on the stone is written a new name that no one knows except the one who receives it."

After the repetitive exhortation to listen to what the Spirit says to the churches, the overcomer receives the promise of receiving hidden manna and a white stone. What does the wording of these two gifts mean?

For forty years, manna was Israel's food in the wilderness until the people crossed the Jordan and entered Canaan. God instructed Moses to place a jar of manna in "the ark of the covenant," and thus it was hidden from sight (Exod. 16:32–34; Heb. 9:4). According to the writer of 2 Maccabees 2:4–7, at the destruction of Solomon's temple Jeremiah hid the tabernacle with the ark and altar of incense in a cave of Mount Nebo and sealed its entrance.

The Jews looked for the coming of the messianic age when they would eat the hidden manna.[51] The Christians, however, acknowledged Jesus as the Messiah who ushered in the messianic age. Ever since the coming of Jesus, his followers have eaten the hidden manna and enjoyed his blessings. Jesus called himself the bread of life and contrasted it with the manna that the Israelites ate in the desert (John 6:48–49). This life-giving bread is indeed the Christian's spiritual food and the hidden manna. It is hidden from view for the unbeliever but is available to all those who put their faith in Christ (Matt. 11:25; Col. 2:3; 3:3).

48. Lenski observes (*Revelation*, p. 108), "As in v 5, this refers to a preliminary judgment and not merely the final one." See also G. B. Caird, *A Commentary on the Revelation of St. John the Divine* (London: Black, 1966), p. 41.

49. Babylonian Talmud, *Sanhedrin* 90a, 105a. See also SB, 3:793.

50. Compare Greijdanus, *Openbaring*, p. 76.

51. SB, 3:793.

The meaning of the white stone remains a mystery, which commentators have tried to solve in numerous ways:

- Precious stones fell from heaven along with manna. But this is only a legend.
- White stones were cast in courts of justice to signify exoneration of the accused and black stones to condemn him. On the Judgment Day, a white stone would mark the Christian's acquittal. But the text does not say that the overcomer casts a white stone but that he receives a white stone. Also, the stones cast in a court case had no names inscribed on them.
- A white object made of steel, wood, or stone called *tessera* granted its possessor certain privileges in society. The durability of these substances is questionable, however.
- A white stone could be used as an amulet or charm. But this custom belongs to the practice of sorcery, not to the doctrine of salvation.
- Buildings in Pergamum in John's day were made out of dark brown stone. Inscriptions in these edifices were cut into blocks of white marble. Hemer observes, "Honorific decrees of the city repeatedly stipulate that the record of its benefactors shall be engraved on [white stone]."[52] The objection is that the Greek word *psēphos* in the text means "pebble," not "stone."
- The breastplate of the high priest had twelve stones, each of which had the name of a tribe written on it (Exod. 28:21). Similarly, a white stone with the name of the individual believer written on it is always in God's presence.
- The stone may be a translucent precious stone like a diamond on which the name of Christ is written. The name of Christ is written on the foreheads of the saints (3:12; 14:1; 22:4).[53]

The last two interpretations are the most helpful. In the context of Revelation, the last one seems the strongest and receives support from other passages. The name of Christ means that the saints belong to him. Already on this earth, believers are known as Christians, that is, followers of Jesus Christ, in whose footsteps they walk.

Greek Words, Phrases, and Constructions in 2:13–16

Verse 13

οἶδα—the Majority Text inserts the phrase τὰ ἔργα σου καί (your works and), which appears to be borrowed from a preceding text (v. 2). It is harder to explain the omission than the addition of this phrase and, therefore, it was probably not in the original text.

κατοικεῖς—the preposition κατά preceding the verb οἰκέω denotes permanence in a dwelling place, whereas the preposition παρά prefixed to that same verb denotes living somewhere temporarily.

---

52. Hemer, *Letters to the Seven Churches*, p. 244 n. 108.

53. Consult Hendriksen, *More Than Conquerors*, pp. 69–71.

παρ' ὑμῖν—in this context the preposition means "among" (compare Matt. 28:15; *1 Clem.* 1.3).[54]

Verse 14

κρατοῦντας—the present participle lacks the definite article and thus does not refer to a specific group or category but to "some who hold." It expresses an indefinite idea.

ἐδίδασκεν—the imperfect tense signifies repeated action on the part of Balaam. Notice that names in these two verses are indeclinable: Antipas, Balaam, Balak, Israel.

πορνεῦσαι—"to commit sexual immorality." Although this verb can be interpreted to refer to spiritual apostasy, the context of Numbers 25 and the overtones in this letter point first to sexual immorality and then to idolatry.

Verse 15

καὶ σύ—here is the ascensive use of the conjunction, "*even* you." The pronoun is in the singular to address the individual members of the church.

Verse 16

πολεμήσω μετ'—in this context the preposition μετά means not "with" but "against." The phrase should be translated "I will make war *against* them."[55] This construction occurs four times (2:16; 12:7; 13:4; and 17:14) and only in the Apocalypse; it is a Hebraism peculiar to Revelation.

---

18 "To the angel of the church in Thyatira write: The Son of God, who has eyes like a flame of fire and whose feet are like exquisite brass, says this: 19 I know your works, your love and faith and service and endurance; and [I know that] your last works are greater than your first. 20 However, I have this against you, that you tolerate that woman Jezebel, the one who calls herself a prophetess, and she teaches and deceives my servants to commit fornication and to eat food offered to an idol. 21 And I gave her time to repent, but she does not want to repent from her fornication. 22 Look, I will cast her on a bed [of suffering] and [I am casting] those who commit adultery with her into great tribulation, unless they repent of her deeds. 23 And I will kill her children with disease. And all the churches will know that I am the one who searches the minds and hearts, and I will give to each one of you according to your works. 24 And I am speaking to the rest of you who are in Thyatira, as many as hold not this teaching and who have not known the so-called depths of Satan. I place no other burden on you. 25 In any case, what you have, hold fast until I come.

26 "To everyone who overcomes and keeps my works until the end, I will give authority over the nations, 27 to rule them with an iron rod as earthen vessels that are broken to pieces. 28 And as I have received authority from my Father, I will give to every overcomer the morning star. 29 Let anyone who has an ear listen to what the Spirit says to the churches."

---

4. Thyatira
2:18–29
The City

Thyatira (modern Akhisar) was a fortified city located some forty miles southeast of Pergamum in a broad valley that leads to the Hermus River. It was near

---

54. A. T. Robertson, *A Grammar of the Greek New Testament in the Light of Historical Research* (Nashville: Broadman, 1934), p. 614.

55. Refer to C. F. D. Moule, *An Idiom-Book of New Testament Greek*, 2d ed. (Cambridge: Cambridge University Press, 1960), p. 61.

the border of the provinces Mysia and Lydia and was claimed by both. In 190 B.C. the Romans entered the valley and conquered the city, which, because of its location in the flat valley, had little protection against superior forces. Thyatira was situated along the trade route from Pergamum to Sardis; from Smyrna a leading artery led through the valley to this city. Hence, the location of Thyatira was along major trade routes that stimulated its economic growth. In addition, the local artisans produced a variety of merchandise, for they were bakers, painters, tanners, tailors, potters, and workers in wool, linen, and metal (chiefly copper); and there were slave dealers.[56] Thyatira was an industrial center controlled by guilds, that is, trade unions. These guilds paid homage to the pagan gods Apollo and Artemis (also known as Tyrimnos), and they worshiped at the shrine of Sabbathe. Members of the guild were obligated to attend festivals in honor of these gods, to eat meals in their temples, and to indulge in sexual promiscuity. Noncompliance with these rules meant expulsion from the trade union, lack of employment, and poverty. Christians who refused to honor pagan gods, eat meat sacrificed to an idol, and engage in sexual immorality jeopardized their material necessities. They were regarded as outcasts of society.

Lydia, a seller of purple, was a native of Thyatira but had moved to Philippi. Paul met her at worship and the Lord opened her heart as she heard the gospel (Acts 16:14). We assume that she became a God-fearer in Macedonia, and when Paul came to Philippi, she became a Christian.

a. Address and Praise
2:18–19

18. "To the angel of the church in Thyatira write: The Son of God, who has eyes like a flame of fire and whose feet are like exquisite brass."

The expression *Son of God* may mean that Jesus addresses Jews in Thyatira who rejected his divinity (compare Heb. 1:1–3). Although the letter gives no indication of a Jewish presence in this city, we cannot rule out their influence. The expression also is relevant to the pagan society of that day which regarded both Caesar and Apollo as sons of gods. But Jesus is the one and only Son of God, who is above all other gods. With eyes of flaming fire nothing escapes him, as he himself states that he searches the hearts and minds (v. 23). Into Jesus' holy presence nothing sinful can enter or be hidden. With his eyes of flaming fire he dispels the darkness and burns away impurities.

Jesus takes a stand in the city of Thyatira with feet like exquisite brass.[57] This alloy is durable, stable, and firm. The gleam of the metal attracts attention, so that the population takes note of Jesus' presence. As he takes up permanent residency in the city, so should his followers remain there without fear.

---

56. Ramsay, *Letters to the Seven Churches*, p. 325; Hemer, *Letters to the Seven Churches*, p. 246 n. 10.

57. Hemer (*Letters to the Seven Churches*, pp. 116, 250 n. 44) conjectures that the material was an alloy, a "copulative-compound," which he renders as copper-zinc.

19. "I know your works, your love and faith and service and endurance; and [I know that] your last works are greater than your first."

In at least four other letters (to the churches in Ephesus, Sardis, Philadelphia, and Laodicea), Jesus says that he knows their deeds.[58] He is thoroughly acquainted with the labors of love the believers in Thyatira have shown to God and to their neighbors. Their works include love and faith as internal qualities that come to expression in the external qualities of service and endurance. Note that Jesus summarized the Law in two commandments: to love the Lord God with heart, soul, and mind; and to love the neighbor as oneself (Matt. 22:37–40). Paul makes the second of these the primary rule (Rom. 13:9) and James calls it the royal law (James 2:8). The Christians in Thyatira visibly demonstrated love to their neighbors and faith and trust in God. Their service to others and their quiet endurance were exemplary in the face of hardship and opposition.

The church could receive no greater praise than that given in the words "your last works are greater than your first." This means that their works of love, faith, service, and endurance were constantly increasing. With respect to love, Thyatira received words of commendation, while Ephesus received words of condemnation. Jesus said to the Christians in Ephesus: "But I have this against you, that you have left your first love" (2:4).

b. Reproof and Command *2:20–25*

20. "However, I have this against you, that you tolerate that woman Jezebel, the one who calls herself a prophetess, and she teaches and deceives my servants to commit fornication and to eat food offered to an idol."

The switch from praise to rebuke is sudden and abrupt. Even though the believers had put forth a considerable effort to help needy people materially and trust God spiritually, they had tolerated a pernicious influence in the church. This influence was spreading like cancer so that in time the spiritual health of the congregation would be seriously jeopardized. The church at Ephesus hated the works of the Nicolaitans (2:6); the church at Pergamum allowed the Nicolaitans to live among them (2:15); the church at Thyatira tolerated deceptive teaching within the congregation.

The name Jezebel refers to the wife of King Ahab, who had married a princess from Sidon. Jezebel urged Ahab to worship the pagan god Baal and the goddess Asherah, and to construct a temple and a sacred pole (1 Kings 16:31–33; 21:25; see also 2 Kings 9:30–37). The woman in Thyatira is referred to by the name of the wife of King Ahab and called herself a prophetess.[59] The New Testament reveals that women prophesied (Luke 2:36; Acts 21:9; 1 Cor. 11:5). This woman held an influ-

58. On the variant reading of 2:9, see the relevant section on Greek words, phrases, and constructions.

59. Some commentators adopt the variant reading "your wife [or, the woman] Jezebel." See, e.g., Henry Alford, *James–Revelation*, vol. 4, part 2 of *Alford's Greek Testament* (1875; reprint, Grand Rapids: Guardian, 1976), p. 573.

ential post in the church because she was a teacher, but her instruction was deceptive. She persuaded the church to engage in illicit sexual relations at the pagan temples and there to eat the food that had been offered to an idol. No wonder that this woman is given the name Jezebel, because her namesake in the Old Testament persuaded Israel to worship Baal, the god of fertility, and Asherah, the goddess of fertility.[60] Under the guise of religion, the people fell into the sin of sexual immorality with all its dire consequences and into the sin of apostasy by eating food in pagan temples. Notice that the order of committing fornication and eating food offered to an idol is the reverse of the sequence in the letter to Pergamum (2:14).

We are unable to identify this Jezebel in Thyatira. She could hardly have been Lydia, the seller of purple, who was one of the first converts to the Christian faith in Philippi. Lydia became a Christian in 50 and Jezebel taught in Thyatira in the mid-nineties. Identifying the two women is pure speculation, for the New Testament and other literature provide no information. Undoubtedly, Lydia before her conversion was a guild member and had to resolve the problem of choosing for Christ or the guild. The woman called Jezebel may have had a business interest in Thyatira.[61]

The intent of the followers of Balaam (v. 14), the Nicolaitans (vv. 6, 15), and Jezebel is the same: to deceive God's people by persuading them to adopt a lifestyle that would allow them to be accepted in the world and to continue membership in the church. By accommodating themselves to the lifestyle that a guild required, the church members no longer had to fear being ostracized. But the Lord says, "No one can serve two masters" (Matt. 6:24; Luke 16:13). To which James adds, "Anyone who chooses to be a friend of the world becomes an enemy of God" (James 4:4).

21. "And I gave her time to repent, but she does not want to repent from her fornication."

The verbs in this verse (*gave* and *does not want*) and in the preceding one (*teaches* and *deceives*, v. 20) suggest that some time had passed since Jezebel entered the church. In other words, faithful servants of the Lord had warned her. John may very well have been one of the pastors who had counseled her. He knew that the Lord is not slow concerning his promise but exercises patience (2 Pet. 3:9) and always gives a sinner timely warnings and opportunity to repent. No one can say that God is acting hastily. The Scriptures teach repeatedly that God is a God of mercy who does not want the death of anyone. He wants the people to repent and live (see Ezek. 18:30–32). But when sinners refuse his pleas and warnings, they choose death. The woman called Jezebel was one of them.

22. "Look, I will cast her on a bed [of suffering] and [I am casting] those who commit adultery with her into great tribulation, unless they repent of her deeds.

---

60. Refer to Kurt Gerhard Jung, "Asherah," *ISBE*, 1:317–18; and "Baal," *ISBE*, 1:377–79.

61. Hemer, *Letters to the Seven Churches*, p. 121.

23. And I will kill her children with disease. And all the churches will know that I am the one who searches the minds and hearts, and I will give to each one of you according to your works."

The Greek text is given in abbreviated form and needs the additional wording within brackets to obtain a smooth translation. Behind this form we may detect Hebraic parallelism, which in its simple structure must be read as short clauses that repeat and reinforce one another.

- Look, I will cast her on a bed [of suffering].
- [I cast] adulterers into great tribulation, unless they repent of her deeds.
- [If not] I will kill her children with disease.

We see the parallel of the seducing woman and those seduced by her, the bed on which she suffers and the great distress her followers suffer.[62] The bed that Jesus has in mind is not a couch alongside a dining-room table that was customary in oriental homes of that day. Nor is it a bed for resting from one's daily labors. By implication, it is a bed for patients stricken by illness as the result of a licentious lifestyle. The woman Jezebel was reaping what she had sown: she was cast onto a bed of suffering that led to her eventual death (compare 1 Cor. 11:29–30).[63] She was not given another opportunity to repent because she refused to listen. However, her followers who committed adultery and practiced idolatry in a pagan temple are given time to repent from their erring ways. As the agent who seduced them, the woman receives the primary blame, while her followers are given time to repent. If they listen to Jesus, he will revoke his threat. But if they fail to heed his warning, he will strike them with disease and they will die. The parallelism in this passage suggests that we interpret the term *children* not literally but figuratively, for the children are the woman's followers. I have translated the Greek words that literally read "kill with death" as "kill with disease" to indicate the cause of death (compare Ezek. 33:27, "will die of a plague").[64]

All the churches (the seven and the universal church) will hear about the great distress with which these sinners are afflicted. They know that Jesus is the one who searches the hearts and minds of all people, for nothing in a human being is hidden from his sight. The Greek text literally reads, "he searches kidneys and hearts," which is a Hebrew idiom appearing in numerous passages (e.g., Ps. 7:9; Jer. 11:20; 17:10). The kidney and heart used synonymously re-

---

62. In the Apocalypse the writer uses the Greek word *megas* eighty times. It is variously translated as "great," "loud," "huge," and "intense." Here the word depicts the intensity of the punishment these adulterers will experience.

63. Interpretations of the Greek *klinē* are many: bed, dining couch, pallet, stretcher, funeral bier (Bauer, p. 436).

64. Gerhard A. Krodel, *Revelation*, ACNT (Minneapolis: Augsburg, 1989), p. 126. Beale (*Revelation*, p. 264) calls attention to God's judgment in Ezekiel, where the phrase "and they [you] will know that I am the LORD" (LXX) occurs some fifty times.

ferred to a person's innermost being that conceals one's morals, feelings, and thoughts. The English idiom, however, is "minds and hearts."

Jesus metes out both punishments and rewards (20:12; 22:12; see 2 Cor. 5:10). Here the judgment on Jezebel and her followers is swift, for the punishment is in accordance with sins of fornication, adultery, and idolatry. Because all the churches know about the judgment and its execution, the conclusion may be drawn that this text does not primarily refer to the final judgment.[65]

24. "And I am speaking to the rest of you who are in Thyatira, as many as hold not this teaching and who have not known the so-called depths of Satan. I place no other burden on you. 25. In any case, what you have, hold fast until I come."

The faithful followers of Christ now hear Jesus addressing them. They steadfastly rejected the teachings and lifestyle of the prophetess Jezebel and adhered to the teachings of the Scriptures. Her instructions and practices differed little from what the Nicolaitans taught and did in the churches of Ephesus and Pergamum (vv. 6, 15), so that this name may be applied to her followers.

What is the meaning of the phrase "the so-called depths [or, the deep things] of Satan"? Whose phraseology is this? Some suggest that the writer is scornfully accusing the erring members of the church of having fallen into the trap of knowing and practicing the deep things of Satan.[66] Others think that they are the deceitful words spoken by Jezebel and repeated by her adherents who say to the rest of the congregation, "You must know the depths of Satan." The pagan world in that era worshiped a serpent as the symbol of Satan; also Gnostics said that they knew the deep things and were the initiated ones. This is the opposite of Paul's teaching that the Spirit searches the deep things of God (1 Cor. 2:10). Knowing this, the faithful Christians in Thyatira would hardly be enticed by the bold invitation to know the depths of Satan. It remains difficult to determine the origin of these words.[67]

Jesus says, "I place no other burden on you." The apostolic decree formulated by the Jerusalem Council stipulated that Gentile Christians should "abstain from food sacrificed to idols, from blood, from the meat of strangled animals and from sexual immorality" (Acts 15:29). Of these four stipulations, the Christians in Thyatira are asked to observe two: to abstain from food sacrificed to idols and from sexual immorality.

The above-mentioned sentence, however, stands more or less by itself. Some translators have placed it in parentheses (NIV et al.), but then the first

---

65. Consult Charles, *Revelation*, 2:392–93 n. 7.

66. Compare, among others, John P. M. Sweet, *Revelation*, WPC (Philadelphia: Westminster, 1979), p. 95.

67. Leon Morris, *Revelation*, rev. ed., TNTC (Leicester: Inter-Varsity; Grand Rapids: Eerdmans, 1987), p. 72.

word in the next sentence must be deleted and that ought not to be. Beckwith presents a commendable translation of this and the next sentence, "I put upon you none other weighty admonition than this: Hold fast what you have."[68] And what do they have? The sum total of the Christian faith as deposited in the holy Scriptures, of which the apostolic decree was a part. With the inclusion of the Apocalypse, these people received the complete canon of the Old and New Testaments. They were the recipients of the full text of God's written revelation (compare Rom. 3:2). The promise "until I come" points to Christ's Second Coming.

c. Promise
2:26–29

26. "To everyone who overcomes and keeps my works until the end, I will give authority over the nations, 27. to rule them with an iron rod as earthen vessels that are broken to pieces."

As in all the letters to the seven churches, Jesus here speaks of the overcomer who is faithful to the end in doing the works of Christ (John 14:12). The juxtaposition of Jezebel's works (v. 22) and Jesus' works is striking. Doing the will of God as revealed in his Word is keeping Jesus' works to the end of cosmic time. That is Jesus' charge, given to the entire church.

Christ will not withhold his blessing from the one to whom he gives his promise: "I will give him authority over the nations." Only in this letter and in the one to Pergamum does Jesus give a twofold promise, which he introduces with the verb *I give:* he gives authority and the morning star (v. 28).

The authority that Jesus delegates to his followers is the same word used by Jesus before he ascended to heaven, "All authority in heaven and on earth has been given to me" (Matt. 28:18). Jesus rules on the face of this earth as King of kings and Lord of lords, for his name is known in every country of the world and his gospel is proclaimed in countless languages. We look at the growth of the church from our perspective. But from the perspective of the church in Thyatira, Jesus' words demanded faith that would triumph over opposition, deceit, and temptation.

The first promise to the overcomer is buttressed by an allusion and a citation from a messianic psalm: the allusion to exercising authority over the nations comes from Psalm 2:8, "I will make the nations your inheritance, the ends of the earth your possession"; the quotation derives from the succeeding verse. The wording and meaning of this psalm citation are troublesome. It is a free rendition of the Hebrew text of Psalm 2:9, "You will rule them with an iron scepter; you will dash them to pieces like pottery." The shift from the second to the third person aside, the Septuagint text of the first clause has the Greek verb *poimaneis,* which John has adopted and which could be translated "you will shepherd." But it is translated "you will rule" because the context suggests that the verb has a

68. Beckwith, *Apocalypse,* p. 470.

negative connotation.[69] The task of the shepherd is to care for his sheep and that includes protecting them from harm. Thus, he uses his rod made of oaken wood that is as hard as iron. With it he attacks anyone and anything bent on hurting his sheep.

The parallelism in the second part of the psalm quotation "as earthen vessels that are broken to pieces" strengthens the concept of ruling forcefully. Forces opposing the advancing gospel of Jesus will be dealt blows with the hard-as-iron rod in the hand of Christ. They will be dashed to pieces like pottery. The wording taken from this messianic psalm pictures a royal scepter of Christ that symbolizes his authority to rule, to exercise discipline, and to mete out judgment. With Christ the believer who overcomes will have the authority to rule, to discipline, and to judge (1 Cor. 6:2).

28. "And as I have received authority from my Father, I will give to every overcomer the morning star. 29. Let anyone who has an ear listen to what the Spirit says to the churches."

The second promise to the overcomer is the gift of the morning star. This term appears once more in the Apocalypse, where Jesus applies it to himself, "I am the root and descendant of David, the bright morning star" (22:16). How does Christ present this star to his faithful follower? There is a subtle connection between the reference to Psalm 2:8–9 and an allusion to Numbers 24:17, where Balaam prophesies, "A star will come out of Jacob; a scepter will rise out of Israel." The symbol of the scepter led to that of the star, for both are symbols of royalty that the believer shares. The saints rule with Christ and shine brightly as morning stars.[70]

The letter closes with the familiar call admonishing all the churches to listen carefully to the message the Holy Spirit is communicating.

Greek Words, Phrases, and Constructions in 2:20–25

Verse 20

τὴν γυναῖκα—to insert the possessive pronoun σου following the noun γυναῖκα lacks strong textual witnesses and "appears to be the result of scribal confusion arising from the presence of several instances of σου in verses 19 and 20."[71]

---

69. Aune, *Revelation 1–5*, p. 210. The translators of the Septuagint misunderstood the vowel pointing in the Hebrew word *tĕrōʿēm* (you will break them) and read it as *tirʿēm* (you will rule them). The Septuagint verb *poimainein* (to shepherd, rule) can also mean "to destroy," with an occurrence in Micah 5:5 (=5:6 English). Bauer (p. 683) comments, "The activity as 'shepherd' has destructive results." Hemer (*Letters to the Seven Churches*, pp. 124–25) sees the "rod of iron" to be synonymous with the sword at Pergamum (v. 12). The Micah passage also mentions a sword.

70. See Hemer, *Letters to the Seven Churches*, p. 126; and the commentaries of Alford (p. 578), Caird (p. 46), Hendriksen (p. 73), Hughes (pp. 52–53), and Sweet (p. 97). Others interpret it as referring to Lucifer (Isa. 14:12), but this does not fit the context; to the planet Venus, which was the symbol of Roman sovereignty, but this view clashes with Christ, who is the morning star; to the millennial reign of Christ on earth, but then the recipients of the letter receive no comfort and encouragement in their daily struggles.

71. Bruce M. Metzger, *A Textual Commentary on the Greek New Testament*, 2d ed. (Stuttgart: Deutsche Bibelgesellschaft, 1994), p. 664.

ἡ λέγουσα—the case should have been in the accusative in apposition to γυναῖκα, but the change to the nominative is common in writers with a Hebraic background.

Verse 22

κλίνην—a bed. Variants have the readings "prison," "oven," and "sickness." Some Latin manuscripts read *luctum*, "sorrow" or "affliction." All these readings are poorly attested and are glosses that are meant to exacerbate Jezebel's chastisement.

ἔργων αὐτῆς—the TR adopts the reading αὐτῶν in harmony with the plural subject of the verb *to repent.* The reading αὐτῆς has strong support from leading manuscripts.

Verse 23

ἀποκτενῶ ἐν θανάτῳ—"I will kill with death" appears to be a tautology, but this may refer to a slow but sure physical demise. The translation "disease" or "pestilence" for Θανάτῳ is appropriate.

Verse 24

λέγουσιν—"as some say" is used in general as an indefinite plural. The present tense is aoristic.[72]

Verse 25

κρατήσατε—the aorist imperative: Hold fast! Grammarians debate whether the aorist is constative, complexive, or terminative.[73] I prefer the constative, which comprises the entire range of action from beginning to end. The verbs *to have* and *to hold* are in the second person plural, while similar wording in 3:11 is in the singular.

72. Robertson, *Grammar*, pp. 406, 866.

73. Consult Friedrich Blass and Albert Debrunner, *A Greek Grammar of the New Testament*, trans. and rev. Robert Funk (Chicago: University of Chicago Press, 1961), §337.1.

3

Letters to Sardis, Philadelphia, and Laodicea

(3:1–22)

Outline (continued)

5. Sardis (3:1–6)
   a. The Warning (3:1–3)
   b. The Promise (3:4–6)
6. Philadelphia (3:7–13)
   a. Address and Recognition (3:7–8)
   b. Exhortation (3:9–11)
   c. Promise (3:12–13)
7. Laodicea (3:14–22)
   a. Description (3:14–16)
   b. Reproof (3:17–18)
   c. Admonition (3:19–20)
   d. Promise (3:21–22)

3
1 "And to the angel of the church in Sardis write: The one who has the seven spirits of God
and the seven stars says this: I know your works; you have a reputation that you are alive
but you are dead. 2 Be alert! Strengthen the things that remain and are about to die, for
I have not found your works brought to completion before my God. 3 Remember, therefore, how you received and heard [the message]; keep it and repent. Therefore, if you are not alert,
I will come like a thief, and you do not know at all in what hour I will come upon you. 4 However,
you have a few persons in Sardis who have not soiled their garments, and they will walk with me
[dressed] in white, because they are worthy. 5 The one who overcomes will thus be clothed in white
garments. I will never erase his name from the book of life, and I will confess his name before the
Father and before his angels. 6 Let anyone who has an ear listen to what the Spirit says to the
churches."

---

5. Sardis
3:1–6
The City

The city of Sardis (modern Sart) was located approximately thirty miles southeast of Thyatira and fifty miles east of Smyrna. The plural name *Sardis* refers, first, to the city as a fortress on top of a promontory, and next, to the prosperous city of commerce, agricultural products, and related industry positioned on a level plane of the valley below. Situated on a high and narrow strip, the fortress was militarily invincible. The city could be reached only from the south along this narrow and elevated strip that terminated at the promontory on which the fortress was built. Steep cliffs protected the city so that it could not be scaled. Because of its strong defenses, Sardis became the capital of Lydia, but its location precluded expansion and forced it to remain small. It was completely dependent on the fertile valley below for all the necessities of life, which had to be carried up to the city.

The second city was situated in the valley some fifteen hundred feet below. Many people settled there: farmers who produced and sold their agricultural products; workers in the wool industry; and merchants who bought and sold their goods. These people needed room to live and work. In times of peace they prospered along the trade routes that extended from the north to the south and from the east to the west in the provinces of Lydia and Asia. Sardis occupied the hub of these roads and increased in wealth.

The name *Croesus,* king of Lydia (560–546 B.C.), is part of the city's history. Whatever he touched, according to a legend, turned to gold. Even nature itself contributed to Sardis, for Herodotus writes concerning the River Pactolus that runs through the city, "The stream which comes down from Mount Tmolus and which brings Sardis a quantity of gold dust, runs directly through the market place of the city."[1] Its supply was soon depleted, certainly before the Romans occupied the area. But Croesus used wealth to extend his influence, which reached far to the east of Sardis. In a battle against Cyrus of Persia he relied on an oracle given to him by the priestess of Delphi, "If you cross the River Halys, you will destroy a great empire."[2] With his forces he crossed this river and destroyed not the Persian empire but his own.

Croesus thought that he would be safe in Sardis, his impregnable fortress. He did not expect Cyrus to follow him, and thus he failed to mobilize his forces. When the Persian armies came to Sardis, Croesus waited him out, believing that no one could scale the almost vertical walls of the promontory. But when one of his men accidentally dropped his helmet from one of the walls and went to retrieve it, he inadvertently demonstrated that the wall could be climbed. At night, Persian soldiers scaled the wall, met no opposition, and took the city.[3] Through one soldier's carelessness and a failure to guard the walls, Croesus lost the war.

When people pay no attention to their history, they must repeat the mistakes of the past. In the third century before Christ, Antiochus the Great of Syria sent his armies against Sardis (214 B.C.). His soldiers scaled the unguarded walls of the city and captured it in much the same way as the Persian warriors did in 546 B.C. Therefore, when Jesus said to the believers in Sardis, "Be alert!" (v. 2), they heard an echo from their own past that reinforced his warning.

Antiochus the Great caused some two thousand Jewish families to emigrate from Mesopotamia to Lydia and Phrygia in Asia Minor.[4] The Jews settled in many of the cities including Sardis, where archaeological research has shown that the Aramaic language was known. Josephus records that the Jews in Sardis enjoyed certain privileges like holding citizenship and filling leading positions as members of the city

---

1. Herodotus 1.93; 5.101 (LCL). See also William Barclay, *Letters to the Seven Churches* (London: SCM, 1957), 1:83; William M. Ramsay, *The Letters to the Seven Churches of Asia and Their Place in the Plan of the Apocalypse* (London: Hodder and Stoughton, 1904; reprint, Grand Rapids: Baker, 1979), p. 357; Colin J. Hemer, *The Letters to the Seven Churches of Asia in Their Local Setting*, JSNTSup 11 (Sheffield: JSOT, 1986), p. 131.

2. Herodotus 1.53. Consult William Barclay, *The Revelation of John*, 2d ed. (Philadelphia: Westminster, 1960), 1:143.

3. Herodotus 1.77–84. See E. M. Blaiklock, *Cities of the New Testament* (London: Revell, 1965), pp. 113–15; Colin J. Hemer, "The Sardis Letter and the Croesus Tradition," *NTS* 19 (1972): 94–97.

4. Josephus *Antiquities* 12.3.4 §149. There may be a hint of a Jewish settlement of earlier days in Obadiah 20, "This company of Israelite exiles who are in Canaan will possess the land as far as Zarephath; and exiles from Jerusalem who are in Sepharad will possess the towns of the Negev." Sepharad may be Sardis but certainty is elusive. Estimates on the total Jewish population in Asia Minor during the first century A.D. run as high as one million. Refer to P. W. van der Horst, "Jews and Christians in Aphrodisias in the Light of Their Relations in Other Cities of Asia Minor," *NTT* 43 (1989): 106–7.

council.[5] Excavations have unearthed the ruins of a sizable synagogue dating back to the third century of the Christian era. Admittedly, third-century ruins do not prove that Jews were in Sardis in the first century, yet they suggest that Jewish people may have lived there for some time previous to this and that they were wealthy, influential, and numerous enough to be able to build this synagogue complex.[6]

There is more. Jesus notes that a few people in Sardis had not soiled their clothes (v. 4). This means that these few kept themselves pure from outside influences and that they did not adapt to the religious practices of that day. While both the letters to the churches of Smyrna and Philadelphia mention the "synagogue of Satan" and people "who say they are Jews but are not" (2:9; 3:9), Sardis endured no opposition from the Jews. The gospel that the local Christians proclaimed and applied was too weak to be offensive to the Jews. Also, pagan temples dedicated to Cybele, Zeus Lydios, Heracles, and Dionysus were influential in the religion of the people. Again, the kind of gospel that the inhabitants of Sardis heard from the Christians posed no threat to their pagan religions.

Sardis was conquered by the Romans in 189 B.C. and suffered a devastating earthquake in A.D. 17, but Emperor Tiberius exempted the city from paying taxes for a period of five years. During these years its citizens rebuilt Sardis to rise from ruins to its former splendor. The Jews regularly sent money to Jerusalem for the maintenance of the temple. Josephus records that they addressed the city government about Caesar's decision not to hinder them from gathering the temple tax and sending it to Jerusalem.[7]

Of the seven churches Sardis was among the lowest in spiritual fervor. Its accommodation to its religious environment shielded the church from persecution, for hardly anyone took notice. Its inoffensive lifestyle yielded religious peace with the world but resulted in spiritual death in the sight of God. Apart from a few faithful members who kept the fire of the gospel burning, the church itself was gradually dying, like a fire that lacks fuel and air. Yet among the smoldering ashes were a few glowing embers.

a. The Warning
3:1–3

1. "And to the angel of the church in Sardis write: The one who has the seven spirits of God and the seven stars says this: I know your works; you have a reputation that you are alive but you are dead."

a. "The one who has the seven spirits of God and the seven stars says this." Jesus identifies himself differently in the opening sentence of each individual letter. Here he reveals himself with a combination of the initial greeting of the

---

5. Josephus *Antiquities* 14.10.17 §235; 14.10.24 §259. See Hemer, *Letters to the Seven Churches,* pp. 137–38, 143–44; Robert North, "Sardis," *ISBE,* 4:336–37; David E. Aune, *Revelation 1–5,* WBC 52A (Dallas: Word, 1997), pp. 218–19.

6. Aune, *Revelation 1–5,* p. 170.

7. Josephus *Antiquities* 16.6.6 §171.

book, "the seven spirits" (1:4), and a phrase taken from his appearance to John, "the seven stars" (1:16, 20; 2:1). The seven spirits describe the fullness of the Holy Spirit whom Jesus is sending forth from the Father (John 14:26; 15:26–27; Acts 2:33). Jesus says that he has the seven spirits, that is, he has received the fullness of the Holy Spirit and exercises authority over him. He commissions the Holy Spirit to make both believers and unbelievers know him and to fan the flames of renewal in churches that are waning. The Spirit, therefore, is the agent to blow new life into the dying church of Sardis and to stimulate indolent members to action.

The phrase *the seven stars* also occurs in the letter to the church at Ephesus (2:1), but there the believers had lost their first love and had fallen from their spiritual height (2:4–5); here they are declared spiritually dead, which is far worse. But through his life-giving Spirit Jesus is able and willing to revive the church. He holds the seven stars in his right hand (1:16), for they are his messengers appointed to proclaim the Word of God that generates new life within the church. Jesus gives these bearers of the good news both authority and protection. He commissions them to deliver not their own but God's message to the people.

b. "I know your works; you have a reputation that you are alive but you are dead." Jesus addresses the church members at Sardis and tells them that he is fully aware of their works, but he is unable to enumerate them because they are incomplete in God's sight (v. 2). God is not interested in halfhearted attempts to serve him. The summary of his law is "love the Lord your God with all your heart and with all your soul and with all your mind" (Matt. 22:37).

The church at large knew Sardis as a congregation that enjoyed the reputation of being alive. We assume that financial stature and influence may have contributed to giving the church the outward appearance of thriving spiritually. The external appearance may deceive fellow believers who take a superficial look, but Jesus examines the internal status of the church and finds an absence of vibrant faith that has resulted in spiritual deadness. Almost the entire church had capitulated to the surrounding world of pagan religion and Judaism, and instead of being an influence on the culture, it had become influenced by that culture. No wonder that Jesus described it as being dead. The church in Sardis had become a nonentity because it failed to contribute to the advance of the gospel. Jesus told the Ephesians that if they did not repent, he would remove their lampstand to preclude them from being a church (2:5). Similarly, Sardis would cease to be a church unless the members showed evidence of repentance.

2. "Be alert! Strengthen the things that remain and are about to die, for I have not found your works brought to completion before my God. 3. Remember, therefore, how you received and heard [the message]; keep it and repent. Therefore, if you are not alert, I will come like a thief, and you do not know at all in what hour I will come upon you."

a. "Be alert! Strengthen the things that remain and are about to die." The first command is to be vigilant. Hearing it, the inhabitants of Sardis would immediately recall their history. The Greek text stresses the continuous present to indicate that the church must always show itself to be alert to internal and external dangers: false teachers inside the church and false teaching coming to them from the outside (compare Acts 20:29–31; see also Matt. 24:24). Jesus' command to watchfulness reveals that some life is still present in the congregation, even though he described it as dead.

The second command is to begin the task of strengthening the people and the things that still function in the church. Although some members are still active, the works that they have undertaken are incomplete and in danger of becoming altogether inactive.[8] The emphasis in this sentence is on the verb *to strengthen,* so that both agents and activities still left in Sardis are reinforced. The works of faith and love practiced by a few devoted members have the potential of dying out. Incidentally, the wording of this clause echoes God's instruction to Israel, "You have not strengthened the weak" (Ezek. 34:4; compare also Luke 22:32).

b. "For I have not found your works brought to completion before my God." Jesus examines the activities of the church in Sardis as God weighed Belshazzar on the scales and found him wanting (Dan. 5:27). He desires not quantity but quality. That is, he wants that which is done in faith and with love for God and the neighbor. He wants the believer to be filled with the Holy Spirit and express to him works of gratitude. The expression *brought to completion* conveys the meaning of that which is perfect (see Matt. 5:48). No Israelite might offer a blemished animal to the Lord (Lev. 1:3; Deut. 15:21; Mal. 1:8), for an animal had to be without blemish, that is, whole. So the Christians in Sardis had to present their works before the Lord as perfect sacrifices. Jesus uses the possessive pronoun *my* five times when he speaks of God (3:2, 12 [four times]; see also John 20:17). Subordinate to God, he fulfills his mediatorial role.

c. "Remember, therefore, how you received and heard [the message]; keep it and repent." The verbs in this clause provide ample evidence that much time had elapsed since the people had first heard and believed the message of the gospel.[9] The verb *to remember* seems to point not to the immediate past of a few years ago but to the distant past of more than a generation. If the gospel was brought to Sardis in the mid-fifties and John wrote Revelation in the mid-nineties, forty years had passed. Next, the Greek has the perfect tense of the verb *to receive* to indicate that considerable time had elapsed.

The first-generation Christians had put their faith to work, but the second generation just rested on what had happened in the past. Hence, Jesus gives the command to keep on remembering what their parents had done, because the

8. Aune (*Revelation 1–5,* pp. 216, 219) in translation and interpretation singles out people rather than inanimate things. However, the succeeding clause has the expression "your works," which serves as an explanation of "the things." See also Hemer, *Letters to the Seven Churches,* pp. 143–44.

9. The object of the verbs *to receive* and *to hear* is the gospel. Consult Louis A. Vos, *The Synoptic Traditions in the Apocalypse* (Kampen: Kok, 1965), pp. 211–14.

first generation received the message of salvation, heard it, and obediently followed its instructions (see 2:5). The second generation still had the gospel message, but now they are told to safeguard it. Jesus is not saying that God's Word must be safely kept on the shelf or in a drawer, but that its teachings should be known, followed, and obeyed. Thus, he commands the readers and hearers to obey his gospel and to repent of their inactivity and indolence. The verb *to keep* relates to the gospel and the verb *to repent* to the radical change of the inner self.

Today, the Bible is a bestseller and millions of people purchase it. Although many people read it regularly, only some obey its teachings.

d. "Therefore, if you are not alert, I will come like a thief, and you do not know at all in what hour I will come upon you." The warning is straightforward, for neglecting to heed it inevitably results in the coming judgment of the Lord. Five of the seven epistles record his coming (Ephesus, 2:5; Pergamum, 2:16; Thyatira, 2:25; Sardis, 3:3; Philadelphia, 3:11); three of them have this information together with the stern warning to repent (Ephesus, Pergamum, and Sardis). This means that in these three instances the people's repentance and Jesus' coming ought to be interpreted against the historical backdrop of that time.

In the present context, the coming of Jesus appears imminent and unexpected. He is coming as a thief. This is a common theme in the New Testament, either referring to immediate punishment or to the Second Coming of Christ. Here the historical context points to impending judgment.[10] Failure to repent would inevitably lead to the Lord's swift reproof. The people in Sardis did not have to wait until Christ's promised return; should they fail to repent, his unexpected appearance would be like that of a thief whose coming can occur anytime.[11]

b. The Promise
3:4–6

4. "However, you have a few persons in Sardis who have not soiled their garments, and they will walk with me [dressed] in white, because they are worthy."

There is hope for the slumbering church in Sardis, where a few members are still faithful to the Lord. Among the ashes of the fire are a few glowing embers that with a draft of wind will burst into flame. The Greek reads "a few names" and conveys the idea that the Lord knows his faithful followers individually by name and cherishes their love for him.

The small number of faithful servants had not soiled their garments, which means that they had not been influenced by the secular culture of their day. The

10. Matt. 24:42–44; Luke 12:39–40; 1 Thess. 5:2; 2 Pet. 3:10; Rev. 16:15. See George E. Ladd, *A Commentary on the Revelation of John* (Grand Rapids: Eerdmans, 1972), p. 57; Gregory K. Beale, *The Book of Revelation: A Commentary on the Greek Text,* NIGTC (Grand Rapids: Eerdmans, 1998), pp. 275–76. The rearranging of the text from 16:15 to 3:3 by R. H. Charles (*A Critical and Exegetical Commentary on the Revelation of St. John,* ICC [Edinburgh: Clark, 1920], 1:80; 2:49) is unwarranted and has no manuscript support.

11. Consult Richard Bauckham, "Synoptic Parousia Parables and the Apocalypse," *NTS* 23 (1977): 162–76; and his "Synoptic Parables Again," *NTS* 29 (1983): 129–34.

word *clothes* is a symbol of their spiritual conduct and their moral lifestyle (Jude 23). They were not besmirched by the sins of adultery and idolatry; they had not undermined the message of the gospel; and they had refrained from compromise. They were true to their word given at their baptism to follow Jesus. Although these few believers might be regarded as odd and out of step with their culture, they steadfastly walked in the footsteps of apostles and other Christians who had brought and taught the gospel of salvation. Walking with the Lord God is exemplified in the life of Enoch (Gen. 5:22, 24) and in the lives of the disciples who with Jesus walked through Galilee and Judea.

The devoted followers of Jesus will walk with him and are dressed in white garments. The color *white* in this text signifies purity and holiness.[12] Their white garments are a covering that the Lord gives them as a robe of righteousness (see Isa. 61:10). These faithful few are worthy. That is, in the sight of Jesus they are declared worthy, not because of their own accomplishments but because of his. Their own so-called good works are nothing but filthy rags (Isa. 64:6). But by listening obediently to Jesus' voice and following in his footsteps (see Rev. 14:4), they through his atonement are declared worthy.

5. "The one who overcomes will thus be clothed in white garments. I will never erase his name from the book of life, and I will confess his name before the Father and before his angels 6. Let anyone who has an ear listen to what the Spirit says to the churches."

a. "The one who overcomes will thus be clothed in white garments." The typical Hebraic parallelism is evident as the writer links up the preceding reference to white garments with the concept *to overcome* (see 2:7). The person who endures to the end will be saved and will triumph in Christ (Matt. 24:13). The few faithful Christians in Sardis are the ones who overcome the temptations and trials on life's pathway. But what is the import of the word *thus*? It seems natural to take the adverb in its context of the preceding verse (v. 4b) and say that "thus" should be taken together with white garments as a consequence of walking with Jesus.[13]

Notice the passive voice in the verb *will be clothed*, which denotes that God has given the garments to the overcomer. The garments are the righteous acts of the saints (19:8). The color *white* denotes purity, and thus saints who are clothed in white garments are holy in God's presence (7:9, 13).

b. "I will never erase his name from the book of life." Here is a promise that is worded in strongly negative terms to assure faithful Christians in Sardis. It assures them that they are absolutely safe and secure. Their names have been recorded in the book of life and will never be erased. Elsewhere God testifies to his people, "See, I have engraved you on the palms of my hands" (Isa. 49:16). He is

12. Rev. 3:5, 18; 4:4; 6:11; 7:9, 13, 14; 19:14. See William Hendriksen, *More Than Conquerors* (reprint, Grand Rapids: Baker, 1982), p. 74.

13. Consult Aune, *Revelation 1–5*, p. 223. Beale (*Revelation*, p. 278) prefers to take "thus" with the present participle *ho nikōn* ("the one overcoming").

inseparably linked to them, for they are the apple of his eye (Deut. 32:10; Ps. 17:8; Zech. 2:8). John reveals that the names inscribed in this book of life were recorded from the foundation of the earth (17:8).

The Jewish people kept accurate records in regard to vital statistics. When the Jews returned from exile, lists were drawn up for the registration of families (Neh. 7:5–6; 12:22–24). Excluding people from the records of the house of Israel was practiced in the days of Ezekiel. False prophets were completely ostracized and banned from the land of Israel (Ezek. 13:9). The Romans would erase the name of a criminal from the records before they put him to death; Christians who refused to worship Caesar as Lord were considered convicts who would lose their citizenship. Jesus assures the faithful in Sardis that their names would never be erased from the book of life.[14] Those people who profess the name of Jesus but whose lifestyle fails to support their profession never had their names recorded in the "book of life." Jesus tells them that he never knew them and he orders them to depart from him (Matt. 7:21–23).

The wording "book of life" is significant because it differs from that of "civil register"; the one is in heaven, the other on earth. In Revelation, the *book of life* is where the names of those who have received the gift of eternal life are written (3:5; 13:8; 17:8; 20:12, 15; 21:27; and see Luke 10:20; Phil. 4:3; Heb. 12:23). In the Old Testament, "to be erased from the book" on earth means "to die," that is, to be blotted out from the civil register (Exod. 32:32–33; Ps. 69:28; Dan. 12:1).

c. "I will confess his name before the Father and before his angels." This is a word of Jesus, spoken during his earthly ministry and repeated with minor variations:

- "Whoever acknowledges me before men, I will also acknowledge him before my Father in heaven" (Matt. 10:32).
- "I tell you, whoever acknowledges me before men, the Son of Man will also acknowledge him before the angels of God" (Luke 12:8).
- "The one who confesses me before men, I will confess him before my Father" (*2 Clem.* 3.2).

An early Christian hymn states that Jesus will disown the person who disowns him (2 Tim. 2:12), and the parallel is that before God the Father, Jesus honors those who honor him (1 Sam. 2:30). In the highest courts of heaven before God and his angels, Jesus confesses the names of all those who confess his name on earth. Jesus is one with his people and is not ashamed to call them his brothers and sisters (Heb. 2:11).[15]

---

14. Isbon T. Beckwith, *The Apocalypse of John* (1919; reprint, Grand Rapids: Baker, 1979), p. 476; John P. M. Sweet, *Revelation,* WPC (Philadelphia: Westminster, 1979), p. 100; Alan F. Johnson, *Revelation,* in *The Expositor's Bible Commentary,* ed. Frank E. Gaebelein (Grand Rapids: Zondervan, 1981), 12:450; G. R. Beasley-Murray, *The Book of Revelation,* NCB (London: Oliphants, 1974), p. 98.

15. See the meaning of "name" in J. William Fuller, "'I Will Not Erase His Name from the Book of Life' (Revelation 3:5)," *JETS* 26 (1983): 297–306.

d. "Let anyone who has an ear listen to what the Spirit says to the churches." This is the repetitive refrain recorded in each of the seven letters. The Holy Spirit speaks to all the churches and not only to the congregation at Sardis.

Greek Words, Phrases, and Constructions in 3:1–6

Verse 1

ὄνομα—this word has a metaphorical meaning, "reputation."

Verse 2

γίνου γρηγορῶν—the verb *to be* with the present participle denotes a periphrastic construction, here in the imperative. The command reveals that the people are already alert and should continue to be so. But the imperative verb στήρισον is the ingressive aorist, "begin to strengthen."

ἔμελλον—this is an epistolary imperfect, because the writer places himself in the position of the reader, who when he reads the verb knows it is the past. It is translated as a present tense "are about to."

Verse 3

The verb tenses and moods in verse 3a vary: μνημόνευε (remember!) the present imperative; εἴληφας (you have received) the perfect active indicative; ἤκουσας (you heard) the aorist indicative; τήρει (keep!) the present imperative; μετανόησον (repent! see 2:5) the aorist imperative. The perfect tense of εἴληφας appears to take on an aoristic sense, "especially in view of the relatively few occurrences of the aorist indicative of λαμβάνω in Revelation."[16]

Verse 4

ὀλίγα ὀνόματα—"a few persons." The figurative meaning of the noun refers to persons who are each known by name (see Acts 1:15; Rev. 11:13; compare 18:15).

Verse 5

οὕτως—"thus." The TR has the reading οὗτος (this), which appears to be a correction of the adverb οὕτως, which was regarded as superfluous.[17] The manuscript evidence favors the reading "thus."

---

7 "To the angel of the church in Philadelphia write: He who is holy and true, who has the key of David, who opens and no one will shut and shuts and no one opens, says this: 8 I know your works. Look, I have set before you an open door, which no one is able to shut. I know that you have little strength and yet you have kept my word, and you have not denied my name. 9 Look, I will make those of the synagogue of Satan and who call themselves Jews and are not but are lying—look, I will make them to come and bow down at your feet and admit that I have loved you. 10 Because you have kept my command to persevere, I will keep you from the hour of trial that is about to come upon

---

16. Robert Hanna, *A Grammatical Aid to the Greek New Testament* (Grand Rapids: Baker, 1983), p. 445; A. T. Robertson, *A Grammar of the Greek New Testament in the Light of Historical Research* (Nashville: Broadman, 1934), p. 901.

17. Bruce M. Metzger, *A Textual Commentary on the Greek New Testament*, 2d ed. (Stuttgart: Deutsche Bibelgesellschaft, 1994), p. 665.

the whole world to try those who dwell upon the earth. 11 I am coming soon; hold on to what you have, so that no one takes your crown.

12 I will make the one who overcomes a pillar in the temple of my God. Never again will he go out of it. I will write the name of my God upon him and the name of the city of my God, the new Jerusalem that is coming down out of heaven from my God; and upon him I will write my new name. 13 Let anyone who has an ear listen to what the Spirit says to the churches."

---

6. Philadelphia
3:7–13
The City

Located nearly thirty miles to the southeast of Sardis and about sixty miles east of Smyrna, Philadelphia (modern Alaşehir) was founded in 140 B.C. by Attalus the Second.[18] His surname was Philadelphus, and out of love for his brother Eumenes he called the city Philadelphia, city of brotherly love. It was strategically located along a well-traveled highway that linked the east (Asia) with the west (Europe). It was a city with an open door through which trade, commerce, Greek language, and Greek culture spread from Greece and Macedonia to Asia Minor and Syria. Jesus' word "I have set before you an open door" (v. 8) was well received by the resident Christians who actively spread the gospel of Jesus Christ.

The area around Philadelphia was volcanic and known as "the burnt land." Volcanic ash fell on it and made the soil extremely fertile. In the fields around the city vineyards dotted the landscape, so that it became known for its wines and beverages. Nonetheless, because of volcanic activity earthquakes often struck this city. A severe quake devastated the city in A.D. 17, after which Emperor Tiberius exempted Philadelphia from paying taxes. He donated a sum of money to be used to rebuild the city. Its inhabitants out of fear of the repeated tremors preferred to live outside the city walls in the countryside. Thus, Jesus' promise was meaningful to his followers in that city: they would never have to go outside anymore (v. 12).

One other point of interest needs to be mentioned. The city devastated by the earthquake of A.D. 17 and aided financially by Tiberius wanted to honor the emperor by adopting the name *Neocaesarea* (the city of the new Caesar). The new name remained in vogue for some twenty-five to thirty years. Later, to honor Emperor Vespasian, whose reign lasted from 69 to 79, the city called itself "Flavia" and had a temple for emperor worship. Vespasian's full name was Titus Flavius Sabinus Vespasianus. Again, Jesus' promise to the Philadelphian Christians to give them a new name (v. 12) was meaningful.

Ramsay aptly summarizes the characteristics of Philadelphia: "First, it was the missionary city; secondly, its people lived always in dread of disaster, 'the day of

---

18. Another account states that the Egyptian Ptolemy Philadelphus founded the city in the third century B.C. Consult Joannes Lydus *De Mensibus* 3.32; Aune, *Revelation 1–5*, p. 234; Hemer, *Letters to the Seven Churches*, pp. 262–63 n. 3.

trial'; thirdly, many of its people went out of the city to dwell; fourthly, it took a new name from the Imperial god."[19]

Not only the church in Smyrna, but also the saints in Philadelphia were models of faithfulness to Jesus Christ. He praises them for their steadfastness and throughout this letter he speaks no word of reproof. Indications of the Christian influence in Philadelphia are many, for the church remained true to Jesus through the centuries, even when Islam became the dominant religion in the area. In the first part of the twentieth century, five Christian congregations were still flourishing in Philadelphia.[20] Of all the seven churches in the province of Asia, only the one in Philadelphia has spanned the centuries.

a. Address and Recognition
3:7–8

7. "To the angel of the church in Philadelphia write: He who is holy and true, who has the key of David, who opens and no one will shut and shuts and no one opens, says this: 8. I know your works. Look, I have set before you an open door, which no one is able to shut. I know that you have little strength and yet you have kept my word, and you have not denied my name."

a. "He who is holy and true, who has the key of David, who opens and no one will shut and shuts and no one opens." The self-description of Jesus is a fitting introduction of the letter to the Philadelphians, because Jesus counted on them to cherish both holiness and truth. Scripture teaches that because God is holy he expects all his people to be holy (Lev. 11:45; 19:2; 20:7). God is the Holy One (Isa. 40:25; Hab. 3:3), but here Jesus is called holy and true. In fact, both the demons and Jesus' disciples acknowledge Jesus as the Holy One of God (Mark 1:24; Luke 4:34; John 6:69). Of all the books in the New Testament, the Apocalypse most frequently calls God's people the holy ones, that is, the saints.[21] They have been cleansed by the blood of Christ and may enter God's presence as if they had never sinned at all. They are the bride of Christ from whom every spot or wrinkle has been removed (Eph. 5:26, 27).

Only twice in the New Testament are the two adjectives *holy* and *true* combined: once they are applied to Jesus (here) and once to God (6:10). *True* means that which is genuine as the opposite of fake. Jesus never breaks his word but fulfills all its implications. Those who called themselves Jews, but were not Jews, demonstrated the lie. By contrast, Jesus' word is trustworthy. The combination *faithful and true* is attributed to Jesus and to the words God speaks (3:14; 21:5; 22:6).

Jesus holds the key of David, which is a direct reference to his messianic lineage. The words are based on Isaiah 22:22, "I will place on his shoulder the key

---

19. Ramsay, *Letters to the Seven Churches*, p. 398.

20. Blaiklock, *Cities of the New Testament*, p. 122; Henry Barclay Swete, *Commentary on Revelation* (1911; reprint, Grand Rapids: Kregel, 1977), p. 53.

21. The expression for *saints* (*hagioi*) occurs 14 times in Revelation, 8 in Romans, 6 in 1 Corinthians, and lesser amounts in the other books.

to the house of David; what he opens no one can shut, and what he shuts no one can open." This is said to Eliakim son of Hilkiah, who served King Hezekiah as a faithful steward. Eliakim received royal emblems of authority: a robe with sash and the key of David's dynasty on his shoulder. He ruled over the house of David, Jerusalem, and Judah. He was a prototype of Jesus the Messiah (compare Isa. 9:6). Christ, on the other hand, holds the scepter of God's kingdom, is the Son over his house (Heb. 1:8; 3:6), and rules over all peoples.[22]

The expression *key* is in the singular preceded by the definite article and, thus, differs from the earlier portrayal of Jesus holding the keys of Death and Hades (1:18). Jesus is the one and only who holds absolute authority with that royal key of David (5:5; 22:16). He is the absolute ruler in heaven and on earth (Matt. 28:18), for what he opens no one can shut and what he shuts no one can open. His word and deed are final.

The opening and shutting of doors must be interpreted in the context of the Jews in Philadelphia (v. 9). They opposed the admission of Gentiles, whom Jesus warmly welcomed into the fellowship of the Christian church. The Jews themselves, however, were shut out of the kingdom of God even though they considered themselves God's chosen people (Matt. 8:12).

b. "[Jesus] says this: I know your works. Look, I have set before you an open door, which no one is able to shut." The Lord is thoroughly familiar with the works of the Philadelphians and need not list them (see 2:2, 19; 3:15). The two clauses about an open door and the inability to shut it seem to allude to the works performed by the church in Philadelphia. While the church in Sardis was idle, the Philadelphians were actively teaching and preaching Christ's gospel.

Scholars debate how to punctuate this verse. Some are of the opinion that the clause "I know your works" should be seen as a parenthesis. Others think that the sentence, "Look, I have set before you an open door, which no one is able to shut," is parenthetical. And still others make three separate sentences by repeating the words "I know" preceding the third sentence "that you have little strength, etc." The third option is preferable and is adopted by most translators.[23]

What is the meaning of the expression *an open door?* First, the Greek indicates that this door has been opened and remains open, although the Lord can shut it again. Next, traffic is not going out through the door into the world but rather it is coming through the door into the kingdom. Third, the Lord has to open the door to make the work of evangelism possible and effective. Paul and Barnabas reported to the church in Antioch how God "had opened the door

---

22. Beale, *Revelation*, p. 285. Ernst Lohmeyer (*Die Offenbarung des Johannes*, HNT 16 [Tübingen: Mohr, 1970], p. 35) applies the key of David to the new Jerusalem.

23. Aune (*Revelation 1–5*, p. 228) stays with the Greek text and refrains from repeating "I know." Thus, he translates *hoti* not as a conjunction ("that") but as causal ("because"). Similarly, R. C. H. Lenski, *The Interpretation of St. John's Revelation* (Columbus: Wartburg, 1943), p. 139. The GNB transposes the clauses "I have set before you an open door, which no one is able to shut" to the end of the verse as a concluding sentence.

of faith to the Gentiles" (Acts 14:27). God opens the door that no one is able to shut, so that the people may enter into his presence. Wherever he opens doors for his workers, there he blesses their work of presenting the gospel (1 Cor. 16:9; 2 Cor. 2:12; Col. 4:3). There the work of missions and evangelism flourishes when converts come to faith in Christ. In spite of fierce opposition by the Jews in the synagogue of Satan (v. 9), the little band of faithful Christians in Philadelphia were assured of a blessing because Jesus had opened the door to Gentile converts. In short, God is sovereign in the work of salvation, for he either closes or shuts the doors of service (compare Isa. 45:1). And the door that God opens is a stimulus to Christians to be actively engaged in the work of evangelism and missions.

c. "I know that you have little strength and yet you have kept my word, and you have not denied my name." Jesus emphasizes the word *little.* It precedes the noun *strength* and relates to the number of the saints in Philadelphia. In the eyes of the local Jews, these Christians were so insignificant that they could not even be regarded as meaningful. In the course of Jesus' earthly ministry, the Lord encouraged the disciples with these words: "Do not be afraid, little flock, for your Father has been pleased to give you the kingdom" (Luke 12:32).

Two commendations serve to bolster the spirit of this little group of believers: they had kept the word of Jesus, and they had not denied his name. These two are opposites in a Hebraic parallel setting: the first one is positive and alludes to Christ's gospel; the second is negative, with the word *name* embodying Jesus' revelation. Keeping the word of Jesus implies not that it should be hidden from view but that it should be guarded from subversion. Not denying the name signifies honoring it and at the same time making Jesus' revelation known to everyone (see v. 10; 2:13; John 8:51; 1 John 2:5). The *word* and the *name* of Jesus refer to God's special revelation that is expressed in both gospel and precept. His people observe this revelation in word and deed.

These two commendations imply that the faithful saints in Philadelphia had to endure opposition from Jews and Gentiles. Their adversaries opposed the name and message of Jesus and repudiated his followers because of their lifestyle. Yet the saints remained true to their Lord and, therefore, received his praise and blessings.

b. Exhortation
3:9–11

9. Look, I will make those of the synagogue of Satan and who call themselves Jews and are not but are lying—look, I will make them to come and bow down at your feet and admit that I have loved you.

a. The imperative *look!* appears twice for emphasis (see also v. 8). Notice the repetition of the first sentence, which occurs in the letter to the Christians in Smyrna (2:9). And note that the break in the middle of the verse causes the second part to strengthen the first. These two parts illustrate Hebraic syntax, with repetition used for emphasis.

b. "Look, I will make those of the synagogue of Satan and who call themselves Jews and are not but are lying." Translators have to depart from the literal version, "Look, I give those . . . ," and substitute the verb *to make* in the future tense for the reading "I give." In the second part of the sentence, the reading "I will make" appears again. The last three words "but are lying" are not in the letter to Smyrna that parallels this verse.

Revelation 2:9	**Revelation 3:9**
	I will make those of the synagogue of Satan
the ones who call themselves Jews	who call themselves Jews
and are not,	and are not
but are the synagogue of Satan.	
	but are lying.

The two congregations of Smyrna and Philadelphia are the only two of the seven that make specific reference to the Jewish people, their synagogue, and their master Satan. Yet these are also the only two churches that receive praise without a word of reproof.

Jewish people who converted to Christianity were no longer tolerated in synagogues after the destruction of the temple and city of Jerusalem in A.D. 70. Two decades later Jewish leaders met in Jamnia to acknowledge the canon of the Scriptures and to formulate the so-called Eighteen Benedictions. The twelfth petition in this prayer pronounces a curse on the apostates:

> For apostates let there be no hope, and the kingdom of insolence mayest thou uproot speedily in our days; and let Christians (*noṣerim*) and the heretics (*minim*) perish in a moment, let them be blotted out of the book of life and let them not be written with the righteous. Blessed art thou, O Lord, who humblest the insolent.[24]

Already in the middle of the first century, the Jews referred to Christianity as "the Nazarene sect" (Acts 24:5). After the curse on the heretics was formulated, the Jews denounced both Jewish and Gentile Christians during the worship services in the local synagogues. Even though no text dating from the first century has survived, we can safely state that Jewish hostility toward Christians became increasingly pronounced. We discover evidence of this in Christian writings dating from the last part of the first century to the beginning of the second and in scattered references to Christianity in Jewish literature.[25]

24. William Horbury, "The Benedictions of the *Minim* and Early Jewish-Christian Controversy," *JTS*, n.s. 33.1 (1982): 19–61, especially pp. 20–21 and 59–60. The quotation is from p. 20. See also SB, 4:208–49.

25. Ignatius *Philadelphians* 6.1. See also John 8:44; 2 Cor. 11:14–15.

Jesus called the Jewish assembly "the synagogue of Satan" (see the commentary on 2:9). As the Jews prided themselves on being God's chosen people with whom he had made a covenant, Jesus implied that they had forfeited the right to be called his people. They became instruments in the hands of Satan, who as their ruler used them to undermine and, if it were possible, to destroy the church. They rejected not only Jesus but also all his followers and, thus, indirectly acknowledged Satan as lord. Therefore, Jesus characterized them as liars because they no longer could claim to be God's people.

c. "Look, I will make them to come and bow down at your feet and admit that I have loved you." Israel as God's chosen nation was given the promise of restoration after the return from exile. God said: "Kings will be your foster fathers, and their queens your nursing mothers. They will bow down before you with their faces to the ground; they will lick the dust at your feet. Then you will know that I am the LORD; those who hope in me will not be disappointed" (Isa. 49:23; see also 60:14). Instead of the Jews being honored, Jesus predicts that they will honor Jesus' faithful followers and acknowledge that he truly loves his own. This suggests that God's promises to Israel have now passed on to Jesus' followers.[26] Admittedly, not all the Jews forfeit their claim to God's love. All those who repent and turn to him continue to experience his divine favor, for they are God's covenant people redeemed through Jesus Christ.

Jesus demonstrates his love to the Philadelphians by saying that even the opposing Jews will confess that he loves them (compare Isa. 43:4). As the apple of his eye, they are the recipients of his watchful care.

10. Because you have kept my command to persevere, I will also keep you from the hour of trial that is about to come upon the whole world to try those who dwell upon the earth. 11. I am coming soon; hold on to what you have, so that no one takes your crown.

a. "Because you have kept my command to persevere, I will also keep you from the hour of testing." Translations of verse 10 vary and consequently also the interpretations, cautioning the exegete not to be too dogmatic. Let us begin with the introductory word *because*; this conjunction reaches back to verse 8b ("you have kept my word, and you have not denied my name"), so that verse 9 serves as an explanatory note on the oppression the faithful believers had to endure.

Next, some commentators advocate continuity of verse 8b ("you kept my word") in verse 10. But the term *word* may have a different connotation when it is qualified by "to persevere," for then it takes on the meaning "command."

Third, there is the sequence of the verb *to keep* in verses 8 and 10, which can be interpreted as "to obey," as "you obeyed my word/command." But if the verb *to obey* is adopted, the verbal balance in verse 10 has been destroyed: "you have kept my command . . . I will also keep you." The choice, therefore, seems to lean toward the equilibrium of the verbs "kept" and "will keep."

26. Barclay, *Revelation of John*, 1:165; Johnson, *Revelation*, p. 453.

Fourth, there is the position of the possessive pronoun *my* that is taken either as "my word/command" (NRSV, NIV) or "the word of my endurance."[27] Even though a case could be made for either position (compare Heb. 12:1–3), the construction "my word" (see v. 8) calls for a measure of consistency in this matter. Nevertheless, Scripture teaches that having endured suffering himself, Jesus helps his people who now suffer because of their adherence to him (Heb. 2:18).

Last, does the preposition *from* mean preservation or evacuation? This preposition can be interpreted to mean "through" in the sense of God keeping the believer safe during a period of hardship. It can also be argued that God removes his child away from the difficulties that are encountered. However, in his high priestly prayer Jesus asks not that God take believers out of this world but that he protect them from the onslaughts of the evil one (John 17:15). Jesus sends his people into the world with the assurance that he will preserve them, as was evidenced in the life and ministry of Paul (see Acts 18:9–10). The Lord promises that he will preserve his people in the hour of testing.[28]

b. "The hour of trial that is about to come upon the whole world to try those who dwell upon the earth." The word *hour* is not limited to sixty minutes but rather denotes a period of time. But what does the word *trial* mean and to whom does it apply? This term can mean temptation, testing, or trial, of which the last one fits the context. Here the meaning of trial is associated with the adversities, afflictions, and troubles that God is sending to his people to test their faith, holiness, and character.[29] God is testing them and permits Satan to tempt them. For the Christians this means that in times of temptation they overcome through God's power and are strengthened in their faith.

Times of testing come to any church and to all believers in every age. As the church in Smyrna was cast into a period of persecution, so the church in Philadelphia experienced its hour of trial. This does not mean that Christians will not suffer physical death in these periods, but that God protects them from spiritual

---

27. Lenski, *Revelation*, p. 143. T. Mueller, "'The Word of My Patience' in Revelation 3:10," *ConcTheolQuart* 46 (1982): 231–34. Mueller interprets the pronoun objectively, "You have kept the faith with the result of perseverance in Me." Some commentators interpret "my patient endurance" subjectively to refer to the suffering and crucifixion Jesus endured, for his endurance was a stumbling block to the Jews. The question centers on the referent, that is, does the pronoun relate to Jesus' suffering on the cross or to his followers who are told to endure hardships for his name's sake? Consult S. Greijdanus (*De Openbaring des Heeren aan Johannes*, KNT [Amsterdam: Van Bottenburg, 1925], p. 100); Charles, *Revelation*, 1:89; Swete, *Revelation*, p. 56. The context appears to favor the second choice.

28. Robert H. Gundry, *The Church and the Tribulation: A Biblical Examination of Posttribulationism* (Grand Rapids: Zondervan, 1973), p. 57; Beale, *Revelation*, pp. 290–91. For other views see Charles C. Ryrie, "The Church and the Tribulation: A Review," *BibSac* 131, no. 522 (1974): 173–79; David G. Winfrey, "The Great Tribulation: Kept 'out of' or 'Through'?" *GTJ* 3 (1982): 3–18; Thomas R. Edgar, "Robert H. Gundry and Revelation 3:10," *GTJ* 3 (1982): 37–39; Robert L. Thomas, *Revelation 1–7: An Exegetical Commentary* (Chicago: Moody, 1992), pp. 286–88; John F. Walvoord, *The Revelation of Jesus Christ* (Chicago: Moody, 1966), p. 87.

29. Thayer, p. 498; Walter Schneider and Colin Brown, *NIDNTT*, 3:803; Aune, *Revelation 1–5*, p. 231 (10.h.).

death. They are the overcomers during their sojourn on this earth. "The hour of trial" is not limited to one particular event but gives a telescoped picture of the entire range of trials. It concerns not merely Philadelphia but "refers generically to all the trials that precede the return of Christ."[30] Furthermore, it encompasses the whole earth, so that the entire church at one time or another before Christ's return endures severe tribulation.

The phrase "those who dwell upon the earth" applies to unbelievers, as is evident from numerous passages in Revelation where it signifies the persecutors and enemies of believers.[31] God will test the unbelievers who persecute his people and will find them wanting. We conclude that in this verse the term *trial* and the verb *to try* point to both believers and unbelievers. "For Christians this tribulation, besides being a threat to their physical safety, will also be a test of their faith, which, by the Lord's help, they will be able to withstand. For the enemies of the church, however, whether Jews or Gentiles, it will come as the deserved punishment for their wickedness."[32]

c. "I am coming soon; hold on to what you have, so that no one takes your crown." Here is the recurring refrain that appears a number of times in the Apocalypse (2:16, 25; 22:7, 12, 20; see also Zech. 2:10). In Revelation not chronological time but its principle is significant. Centuries come and centuries go as the church continues to pray, "Maranatha, come, Lord Jesus!" There is no evidence when he will come, but the certainty of his return echoes throughout the Book of Revelation. Jesus comes both to comfort his people and to avenge his enemies.[33]

Jesus instructs the church in Thyatira to hold fast to what they have (2:25); he likewise exhorts the Christians in Philadelphia to guard their spiritual possessions. He promises the church in Smyrna "the crown of life" (2:10), but here he states that the believers in Philadelphia already possess this crown, which others would be able to take from them. They possess the crown of a victor. To hold on to it meant to continue their loyalty to the very end and thus be overcomers.

c. Promise
3:12–13

12. "I will make the one who overcomes a pillar in the temple of my God. Never again will he go out of it. I will write the name of my God upon him and the name of the city of my God, the new Jerusalem that is coming down out of heaven from my God; and upon him I will write my new name."

Notice the use of the possessive pronoun *my* that precedes the noun *God* four times and the new name of Jesus once (see also v. 2). Jesus emphasizes both his

30. Aune, *Revelation 1–5*, p. 240. See also Herman Hoeksema, *Behold, He Cometh! An Exposition of the Book of Revelation* (Grand Rapids: Reformed Free Publishing Association, 1969), pp. 132–33.

31. Rev. 6:10; 8:13; 11:10 (twice); 13:8, 14 (twice); 17:8; compare also 13:12; 14:6; 17:2.

32. Schuyler Brown, "The Hour of Trial (Rev 3:10)," *JBL* 85 (1966): 314. Refer also to Hughes, *Revelation*, p. 61.

33. Compare Robert L. Thomas, "The 'Comings' of Christ in Revelation 2–3," *MSJ* 7 (1996): 153–81.

subordination to his Father (John 20:17) and the authority he has received to write his new name on his people.

a. "I will make the one who overcomes a pillar in the temple of my God." Jesus promises to make the believer a pillar in the temple of God. There are at least two interpretations of the word *pillar.* One is that ancient temples had a number of pillars carved in the form of human beings that surrounded these structures. The second is that a pillar in a temple served to honor a distinguished person, much the same as plaques attached to pillars in European cathedrals. But these illustrations ought not to be taken seriously because the term *pillar* has a symbolical significance, much the same as James, Peter, and John were regarded as pillars in the church (Gal. 2:9; compare also 1 Tim. 3:15).

The passage speaks not of pagan temples or the Solomonic temple in Jerusalem (1 Kings 7:15–22; 2 Chron. 3:15–17) but of the new Jerusalem that is coming down out of heaven. This means that the saints are honored within that heavenly temple, which in fact is nothing less than the very presence of God. This rules out, then, any idea of supporting pillars as in ancient temples. In short, the expression *temple* must be interpreted figuratively. God intends to honor his people in his sacred presence.[34]

b. "Never again will he go out of it. I will write the name of my God upon him." The first clause was meaningful to the citizens of Philadelphia, who because of the frequent earthquakes preferred to live outside the city walls in the countryside. These people lived their whole lives in fear of natural catastrophes; by contrast, God's children abide safely forever in his presence (21:3).

Jesus promises that he will place the name of God on the Christian. In two other passages, John elaborates this thought by saying that the names of the Lamb and of the Father are written on the foreheads of the saints (14:1; 22:4). Note the recurring antithesis in the Apocalypse: the saints receive the names of God and the Lamb, while the unbelievers bear the name and the number of the beast (13:17–18).

c. "And the name of the city of my God, the new Jerusalem that is coming down out of heaven from my God; and upon him I will write my new name." Three times in this verse the word *name* occurs. In the third instance it is qualified by the adjective *new.* The Philadelphians could relate to these new names, for after the earthquake in A.D. 17 when Emperor Tiberius exempted them from paying taxes and donated money for rebuilding Philadelphia, they named their city Neocaesarea. Decades later, when they wished to honor Emperor Vespasian, they renamed it Flavia. Now the saints in Philadelphia are told that on them will be written the name of God, of the new Jerusalem, and of Jesus. These names serve them as a passport for entrance into God's presence and as a sign of citizenship of the Jerusalem that comes down from heaven.

---

34. Richard H. Wilkinson ("The στῦλος of Revelation 3:12 and Ancient Coronation Rites," *JBL* 107 [1988]: 498–501) calls attention to Solomon's temple where at a pillar kings were crowned or renewed a covenant (compare 2 Kings 11:14 and 23:3). But these references have little to do with a pillar in the new Jerusalem.

Although the new Jerusalem is mentioned here in passing, John provides a detailed description of this city in 21:2, 10–27.[35] This description is based on Ezekiel 48, where the details of the city are given with respect to dimensions, gates, tribes, and names. The prophet Ezekiel appropriately concludes this chapter by saying, "And the name of the city from that time on will be: THE LORD IS THERE" (48:35b). The new city is different from the old in regard to its form, appearance, and significance (see Gal. 4:25–26; Heb. 12:22). There God's throne is established, to which all the nations gather to honor the name of the Lord (Jer. 3:17; see also 33:16).

Believers in the city of Antioch were the first to receive the name *Christian*, that is, follower of Christ (Acts 11:26). To the world this was a name of derision (Acts 26:28; 1 Pet. 4:16). But by entering the new Jerusalem, the Christian receives Christ's new name. We are not told what this name is, but we are able to say that it pertains to the completion of Christ's redemptive work. This new name will no longer be mocked but will be honored and revered.

13. "Let anyone who has an ear listen to what the Spirit says to the churches."

These words are the same in all the seven letters to the churches in the province of Asia. And they once again stress the fact that the message of these letters is meant for all the churches in every age and place.

Greek Words, Phrases, and Constructions in 3:7–12

Verse 7

ἀληθινός—this adjective differs from ἀληθής, which means truthful; the reading in the text signifies "true to the idea."[36]

Verse 8

δέδωκα—notice that the verb *to give* must be translated as "to set." This is also true in verse 9, where it has the meaning "to make" as seen in the repetition in the second part of that verse. Here the perfect tense "I have set" reveals that considerable time has elapsed and that the sovereign Lord determines how long the door remains open.

αὐτήν—the personal pronoun is redundant because of the relative pronoun at the beginning of the clause (7:2, 9; 13:8, 12; 20:8).

Verse 9

διδῶ—this is the alternate form of δίδωμι (I give).[37]

---

35. The wording in Rev. 3:12; 21:2; and 21:10 is virtually identical:
"the city of my God, the new Jerusalem that is coming down out of heaven from my God" (3:12);
"the holy city, the new Jerusalem that is coming down out of heaven from God" (21:2);
"the holy city, Jerusalem that is coming down out of heaven from God" (21:10).

36. Beckwith, *Apocalypse*, p. 479.

37. Bauer, p. 192; Friedrich Blass and Albert Debrunner, *A Greek Grammar of the New Testament*, trans. and rev. Robert Funk (Chicago: University of Chicago Press, 1961), §94.1.

αὐτούς—the pronoun is the direct object of the verb ποιήσω (I will make) but the subject of the two verbs in the ἵνα clause.[38] This clause functions as an infinitive ("to come and bow down"). These two verbs, however, are in the future indicative and not the subjunctive like the verb γνῶσιν (they know).

Verse 12

ἐν τῷ ναῷ—"ναῷ signifies not the temple complex but the Holy of Holies; that is, God's very presence.

ἐπ' αὐτόν—the preposition and pronoun can refer to either "upon him" or "upon the pillar." Other passages in Revelation mention writing a name on the foreheads of God's people (14:1; 22:4), which argues in favor of ὁ νικῶν, the overcomer.

Ἰερουσαλήμ—this spelling occurs three times in the Apocalypse (3:12; 21:2, 10) and never in the Fourth Gospel; the alternate spelling Ἰεροσόλυμα occurs never in Revelation but twelve times in John's Gospel (1:19; 2:13, 23; 4:20, 21, 45; 5:1, 2; 10:22; 11:18, 55; 12:12). An attempt to distinguish authorship of these two books cannot be sustained because "several authors [Matthew, Luke, and Paul] use both forms interchangeably."[39]

---

14 "And to the angel of the church in Laodicea write: The Amen, the faithful and true witness, the origin of God's creation, says this: 15 I know your works; you are neither cold nor hot. I wish you were either cold or hot. 16 So because you are lukewarm and neither hot nor cold, I am about to spit you out of my mouth. 17 Because you say, 'I am rich and I have become wealthy and have need of nothing,' but you do not know that you are wretched, pitiable, poor, blind, and naked, 18 I advise you to buy from me gold refined by fire that you may be rich, and white garments to clothe yourself that the shame of your nakedness may not be revealed, and salve to anoint your eyes that you may see.

19 "Those whom I love I reprove and discipline. Be zealous, therefore, and repent. 20 Look, I stand at the door and knock. If anyone hears my voice and opens the door, I will come in to him and I will dine with him and he with me.

21 "To the one who overcomes, I will grant [the privilege] of sitting with me on my throne, just as I myself overcame and sat with my Father on his throne. 22 Let anyone who has an ear listen to what the Spirit says to the churches."

---

7. Laodicea
3:14–22
The City

Laodicea was located some forty-three miles to the southeast of Philadelphia, eleven miles west of Colosse and six miles south of Hierapolis (Col. 4:13) in the Lycus valley. It served as the gateway to Ephesus, due east about a hundred miles, which was the gateway to Syria. Until the middle of the third century before Christ, it was known as Diospolis (the city of Zeus) and Rhoas. But in approximately 250 B.C. the Syrian ruler Antiochus II extended his influence westward, conquered the city, and renamed it Laodicea in honor of his wife Laodice. The Romans entered the area in 133 B.C. and made the city a judicial and administra-

---

38. Blass and Debrunner, *Greek Grammar*, §476.1.

39. Aune, *Revelation 1–5*, p. 232 (12.g.).

tive center.[40] They built a road system from east to west and north to south. At the crossroads was the city of Laodicea, which expanded in size, became a leading commercial center, and gained wealth and influence. Its wool industry flourished through the production and export of black wool, the manufacturing of common and costly garments, and the invention of an effective eye salve. It had a flourishing medical school that specialized in ear and eye care and had developed an ointment for treating inflamed eyes. Because of this ointment, the school became world famous.

A devastating earthquake struck Laodicea in A.D. 17, and, like other cities in the province of Asia, it received financial aid from the Roman government. In A.D. 60 a second earthquake struck the city, and the Roman government offered financial aid to rebuild the city. But the city fathers sent the government a negative reply and made it known that they themselves had ample resources for reconstruction. In fact, they even contributed to the rebuilding of neighboring cities.[41]

Antiochus the Great (also known as Antiochus III) brought some two thousand Jewish families from Babylon to Lydia and Phrygia during the middle of the third century B.C.[42] The city of Laodicea, which bordered these two regions, became host to many of these families and prospered. When in 62 B.C. the Jews wanted to pay their annual tax for the upkeep of the temple in Jerusalem, their shipment of gold was confiscated by Proconsul Flaccus. Part of this shipment was from Laodicea and weighed more than twenty pounds. "It has been calculated that the amount from Laodicea would imply a population of 7,500 adult Jewish freemen in the district."[43] The letter to the church at Laodicea reveals nothing about a Jewish presence, which may mean that this church, like the one in Sardis, preached a gospel that was no threat at all to the Jews. Neither did the Laodicean Christians have to endure any persecution from the Gentile population, nor were there any false prophets, including the Nicolaitans, a Balaam, or a Jezebel, in the church. The temple for the worship of Caesar occupied a central place in the city of Laodicea. The church accommodated itself to other religions, basked in material wealth, was content to live a life of ease, and failed to press the claims of Christ. Consequently, Jesus has no word of praise or commendation for this church and similar churches that fail to proclaim his message of salvation.

One last item should be mentioned in this brief survey. The water supply for Laodicea came from a distance of six miles at Hierapolis via an aqueduct.[44] Its

---

40. Hemer, *Letters to the Seven Churches*, p. 181; consult also Ramsay, *Letters to the Seven Churches*, pp. 416–17; Barclay, *Letters to the Seven Churches*, 1:108–9; and his *Revelation of John*, 1:173–74; Gerald L. Borchert, "Laodicea," *ISBE*, 3:72–74.

41. Tacitus *Annals* 14.27: "One of the most famous cities of Asia, Laodicea, was in that same year overthrown by an earthquake, and, without any relief from us, recovered itself by its own resources."

42. Josephus *Antiquities* 12.3.4 §149.

43. Hemer, *Letters to the Seven Churches*, p. 182.

44. William M. Ramsay, *The Cities and Bishoprics of Phrygia*, vol. 1, parts 1 and 2 (1895; reprint, New York: Arno, 1975), pp. 48–49.

sources were hot water springs laden with calcium carbonate; when the water arrived in Laodicea, it was lukewarm. Although these hot springs themselves had medicinal value and as health spas attracted the people, Jesus compares the tepid waters near the city to the lukewarm spiritual life of the Laodiceans.

a. Description
3:14–16

14. "And to the angel of the church in Laodicea write: The Amen, the faithful and true witness, the origin of God's creation, says this: 15. I know your works; you are neither cold nor hot. I wish you were either cold or hot. 16. So because you are lukewarm and neither hot nor cold, I am about to spit you out of my mouth."

Apart from this text, the name *Laodicea* occurs only once in the entire New Testament (Col. 4:13). Its nearness to Colosse makes Epaphras the likely founder of the church in Laodicea (Col. 1:7; 4:12–13). Paul had sent a letter to this church, and he requested that the Colossians arrange that their letter be read in the church of the Laodiceans and they in turn read the Laodiceans' letter (Col. 4:16). We have no information that Paul ever visited this church.[45] Perhaps after his release from Roman imprisonment, he visited Colosse (Philem. 22) and neighboring Laodicea.

a. "And to the angel of the church in Laodicea write: The Amen, the faithful and true witness, the origin of God's creation, says this." Alone of all the seven letters to the churches in western Asia Minor, the description of Christ in this letter is not derived from Jesus' appearance to John on the island of Patmos (1:12–16). It comes from the greeting, which reads "and from Jesus Christ, the faithful witness, the firstborn from the dead" (1:5a).

Jesus' description of himself as the word *Amen* derives from the Hebrew text of the Old Testament. The "Amen" conveys the idea of that which is true, firmly established, and trustworthy. It was a word familiar to worshipers, who joined in a doxology uttering their confirmation to what they had heard (e.g., 1 Chron. 16:36; Ps. 106:48). It is the emphatic "Yes" as an affirmative response to a prayer or a conclusion to a doxology (Rom. 1:25; 9:5; 11:36; 16:27; Gal. 6:18; Rev. 1:7; 5:14; 7:12; 19:4).[46] Preceded by the definite article, the Amen has become personified in the Hebrew text as "the God of Amen," in translation, "the God of truth" (Isa. 65:16; compare 2 Cor. 1:20). Jesus takes this title for himself and interprets it in the next clause as "the faithful and true witness." The terms *faithful* and *true* are both translations of the same Hebrew expression *Amen.*

---

45. The Latin *Epistle to the Laodiceans* is apocryphal, for it has the wording taken from Paul's Epistle to the Galatians.

46. Refer to J. M. Ross, "Amen," *ExpT* 102 (1991): 166–71. L. H. Silbermann ("Farewell to *O AMEN:* A Note on Rev. 3:14," *JBL* 82 [1963]: 213–15) suggests that the original language of the Apocalypse was either Hebrew or Aramaic. However, the evidence fails to support this proposal. It is better to say that John was thoroughly familiar with Hebrew terms and readily used them. See Paul Trudinger, "*Ho Amēn* (Rev. 3:14), and the Case for a Semitic Original of the Apocalypse," *NovT* 14 (1972): 277–79.

This clarifying phrase *the faithful and true witness* is an echo of the trinitarian greeting (1:4b–5); without the term *witness* it is descriptive of the rider on a white horse (19:11). It means that whatever Jesus speaks is indubitably true, so that at the end of the Apocalypse we read the affirmation: "these words are faithful and true" (21:5; 22:6). For being a faithful witness, Antipas suffered martyrdom in Pergamum (2:13). Fulfilling the Old Testament prophecies (Isa. 43:10–13 and 65:16–18), Christ is the true Israel, because he is the "Amen, the faithful and true witness."[47]

When Jesus refers to himself as "the origin of God's creation," we see a close link to Paul's letter to the Colossians, which was read by the Laodiceans in worship services (Col. 4:16). The Lord calls himself the "origin [Greek *archē*] of God's creation." We should not interpret the word *origin* passively, as if Jesus were created or recreated, but actively, because Jesus is the one who generates and calls God's creation into being (John 1:1; Col. 1:15–18; Heb. 1:2).[48] What then is the purpose of this description? To show that Jesus Christ made all things and thus possesses and controls them. Also, all things were made to serve him. The message to the Laodiceans is that their boast in earthly riches is misplaced because all things belong to Jesus, who is worthy of praise and glory.

b. "I know your works; you are neither cold nor hot. I wish you were either cold or hot." The term *works* appears in the other letters too (2:2, 19; 3:1, 8). Here it means exactly the same thing as in the letter to the church in Sardis (v. 1): incomplete deeds that are not even worth mentioning. Jesus knew the works of both Sardis and Laodicea and for these two churches he had only sharp reproof. They were no longer active and alive: the few faithful in Sardis were like glowing embers amid a layer of ash; those in Laodicea were like their water supply—neither cold nor hot.

If the Laodiceans had never heard the gospel, they would have been cold in a spiritual sense. We assume that the first-generation Christians in Laodicea accepted the gospel and were glowing with a spiritual fire and enthusiasm. But their descendants were tepid. They had no interest in being a witness for Jesus Christ, in living a life of service for the Lord, or in preaching and teaching his gospel for the advancement of his church and kingdom. Although they possessed the Scriptures, they were apathetic, indifferent, and unconcerned about the things of the Lord (compare Heb. 4:2; 6:4). It is no wonder that Jesus said, "I know your works," with the implication that there were none.

c. "So because you are lukewarm and neither hot nor cold, I am about to spit you out of my mouth." The hot springs at a distance of six miles near Hierapolis sent water of medicinal quality down to Laodicea. By the time the water arrived there, it

47. Gregory K. Beale, "The Old Testament Background of Rev. 3:14," *NTS* 42 (1996): 133–52. And see his *John's Use of the Old Testament in Revelation*, JSNTSup 166 (Sheffield: Sheffield Academic Press, 1998), pp. 273–94.

48. See Greijdanus, *Openbaring*, p. 106; Richard Bauckham, *The Theology of the Book of Revelation*, New Testament Theology (Cambridge: Cambridge University Press, 1993), p. 56; Homer Hailey, *Revelation: An Introduction and Commentary* (Grand Rapids: Baker, 1979), p. 157.

had cooled considerably, and because of the calcium carbonate in the water, it had a nauseating effect on the people who drank it. By contrast, Colosse, eleven miles away, was blessed with springs producing refreshing water that was cold and pure.

Christ has no interest at all in lukewarm Christianity, because it is worthless. He prefers to work either with people who are aflame with energy to do his bidding or those who have never been told about the message of salvation and are willing to listen. Lukewarm water laced with calcium carbonate induces vomiting. Similarly nominal Christians void of spiritual works are utterly distasteful to the Lord, and he is about to spew them out of his mouth. Note that Jesus does not say, "I will spew you out of my mouth," but rather, "I am about to spew you out of my mouth." Here is the grace of the Lord Jesus as he is giving the Laodiceans time to repent after they have read his letter.[49] This epistle is meant to change the recipients' lukewarm attitude into an eagerness to work for the Lord, for grace always precedes condemnation (see v. 19).

The church in Laodicea "had not become indifferent because worldly interests had chilled its proper fervour, but it had become ineffective because, believing they were spiritually well-equipped, its members had closed their doors and left their real Provider outside."[50] They had excluded Christ (compare v. 20) and thought they could do without him. By doing so they had become utterly ineffective as a church. Without Christ the church is dead.

b. Reproof
3:17–18

17. "Because you say, 'I am rich and I have become wealthy and have need of nothing,' but you do not know that you are wretched, pitiable, poor, blind, and naked,"

a. "Because you say, 'I am rich and I have become wealthy and have need of nothing.'" The source of the saying seems to be the Hebrew text of Hosea 12:8, which shows distinct similarities:

> Ephraim boasts,
> "I am very rich; I have become
> wealthy.
> With all my wealth they will not find in
> me
> any iniquity or sin."

Although we cannot determine whether the members of the church in Laodicea were affluent or not, we do know that the local citizens were wealthy and pros-

49. Hendriksen, *More Than Conquerors*, p. 77; Beckwith, *Apocalypse*, p. 490; Lenski, *Revelation*, p. 155.

50. M. J. S. Rudwick and E. M. B. Green, "The Laodicean Lukewarmness," *ExpT* 69 (1957–58): 178. Consult also Stanley E. Porter, "Why the Laodiceans Received Lukewarm Water (Revelation 3:15–18)," *TynB* 38 (1987): 143–49; Peter Wood, "Local Knowledge in the Letters of the Apocalypse," *ExpT* 73 (1961–62): 263–64.

perous. The saying "I am rich and need nothing" also occurs in a diatribe of Epictetus, who records these words coming from an imperial bailiff.[51] Perhaps the saying was proverbial among the rich. But here the words come from the mouths of the Christians in Laodicea, who had adapted themselves completely to the citizenry. Thus, instead of the church influencing society, the reverse had taken place, with society leading the church.

Next, the word *rich* may point to either material or spiritual possessions. Did the members of the church identify with the local citizens who in A.D. 60 had rejected financial aid from Rome when Laodicea was devastated by an earthquake? Or does the context compel the reader to understand the word to refer to spiritual riches? The preceding passage (vv. 14–16) and the succeeding verse (v. 18) force commentators to adopt the second choice. The evidence indicates that the church had adopted the norms of Laodicea and carried them over into the spiritual realm. For instance, the city known as a financial center erected sizable buildings, gates, and towers soon after the quake that destroyed the city. It took pride in being independent and in its ability to help its neighbors suffering from the same disaster. The church members wholeheartedly approved of showing independence and helping one's neighbor. Consequently, they failed to see the difference between material and spiritual wealth. They boasted of their self-sufficiency and had no need of Christ. They were spiritually blind.

Third, from a logical point of view the order *being rich* and *having become wealthy* is reversed. After one becomes affluent, he or she can say, "I am rich." But this inversion of the expected sequence occurs more often in the Apocalypse (see 5:2, 5; 10: 9) and even appears in the Fourth Gospel, "angels of God ascending and descending on the Son of Man" (John 1:51).

Last, not to have need of anything is inconceivable for the true believer, who depends on God every moment day and night for food and drink, home, shelter, clothing, protection, spiritual nourishment, encouragement, comfort, love, joy, happiness, and numerous other blessings. To be self-sufficient is the height of spiritual arrogance, for faith and trust in the Lord no longer function.

b. "But you do not know that you are wretched, pitiable, poor, blind, and naked." The contrast introduced by the adversative *but* is striking indeed. Jesus said, "I know your works" (v. 15), and now he tells the Laodiceans that they lack knowledge of themselves. He uses the personal pronoun *you* for emphasis in the singular to address the church as a whole. He describes the church with five adjectives, of which the first one is *wretched* (see Rom. 7:24). It denotes the mundane condition of people who disregard divine essentials: a rich person who lacks the wealth that counts before God. In addition to being spiritually bankrupt, the wealthy are to be pitied. Paul uses the word *pity* in the superlative when he writes about people who doubt the resurrection. "If for this life only we have hoped in Christ, we are of all people most to be pitied" (1 Cor. 15:19 NRSV). Instead of being rich, the Laodiceans are spiritually poor because they are blinded

51. Epictetus *Diatribes* 3.7.29. See Aune, *Revelation 1–5*, p. 258.

by material possessions (compare 2 Pet. 1:9). And last, they stand naked before God and are unable to cover their shame. With only five adjectives, Jesus has described their miserable condition. The first two (wretched and pitiable) reflect the inner condition of the Laodiceans, while the last three (poor, blind, and naked) describe both their internal and external condition.

18. "I advise you to buy from me gold refined by fire that you may be rich, and white garments to clothe yourself that the shame of your nakedness may not be revealed, and salve to anoint your eyes that you may see."

This verse takes up the last three adjectives of the previous verse (v. 17), although out of sequence. When these three adjectives (poor, naked, and blind) are removed, the first two (wretched and pitiable) disappear. Also, these three comprise all the blessings a believer needs for his or her salvation: redemption, justification, and sanctification.

a. "I advise you to buy from me gold refined by fire that you may be rich." Instead of a harsh rebuke and sharp command, Jesus counsels the Laodiceans and demonstrates his divine grace. He borrows language from the marketplace and alludes to an Old Testament passage: "Come, buy wine and milk without money and without cost" (Isa. 55:1). Appealing to people who boldly stated that they had no needs, the Lord invites them to buy refined gold from him. By implication, he wants them to come to him as destitute beggars who would never be able to buy this precious commodity. The Greek word *gold* refers to finely crafted products as in jewelry or coins and not merely to the metal itself (compare 17:4; 21:18, 21 with 9:7; 18:12). The money changers at the Laodicean bank handled currency on a daily basis, but Christ is counseling the people to come to him and buy. Yet his advice purposely omits money, for the transaction must take place without legal tender. They can obtain the gold only from Jesus.

Notice, therefore, the kind of gold that Christ makes available to the Laodiceans: "gold refined by fire." It is gold that has been purified to such a degree that the glow of fire emanates from it (see 1 Pet. 1:7). These words hint at the fiery trial that the followers of Christ are to endure. *Gold* is actually another word for faith, which is far more precious than gold. Faith must be all-important to the Laodiceans, for they should realize that Jesus is speaking to them in spiritual terms. What is at stake here is that all their impurities are to be burned away, so that their faith comes out of the fire intact,[52] and as a consequence their love for Christ is pure.

b. "White garments to clothe yourself that the shame of your nakedness may not be revealed." In a city where the garment industry provided work and income for countless people, these words had a direct appeal. The black wool that the sheep produced was the color of the great majority of clothes manufactured there. Priests wore white garments, but now this attire is the eschatological attire of the saints who with the white color attest to holiness and purity.[53] There is an

52. Compare Swete, *Revelation*, p. 62; Barclay, *Revelation*, 1:181.

53. Rev. 3:4–5, 18; 4:4; 6:11; 7:9, 13, 14; 19:14.

allusion to the Ancient of Days, "His clothing was as white as snow" (Dan. 7:9; see Rev. 1:14).

The reason for clothing oneself with white garments is to cover the nakedness of sin and thus not be put to shame (compare 16:15). The Old Testament provides a number of instances where either the reality or the threat of utter humiliation centered on being stripped naked.[54]

The Christians in Laodicea were spiritually naked, "[for] all the looms in their city could not weave cloth to cover their sins. Laodicea might supply the whole world with her tunics and clothing materials; but righteousness was the white raiment which God demanded (see 19:8), and this they must get from Christ."[55] Only Jesus removes sin and guilt, for he alone can provide the white robe of righteousness.

c. "And salve to anoint your eyes that you may see." The medical school in Laodicea had become acquainted with the healing properties of the so-called Phrygian stone. This stone, which came from the nearby province Phrygia, was ground to powder and made into an ointment used to heal eye diseases.[56]

The Laodicean believers were blinded by self-deception, unable to see with spiritual eyes. With the eye salve that Jesus provides, the Laodiceans would be able to see their own sins in the light of God's Word and to walk with Jesus, who is the light of the world.

c. Admonition
3:19–20

19. Those whom I love I reprove and discipline. Be zealous, therefore, and repent. 20. Look, I stand at the door and knock. If anyone hears my voice and opens the door, I will come in to him and I will dine with him and he with me.

a. "Those whom I love I reprove and discipline." In these two verses, Jesus admonishes the church in Laodicea.[57] As with much of his teaching, he bases it on the Old Testament Scriptures. Thus, the words "Those whom I love I reprove and discipline" allude to Proverbs 3:12 (see also Heb. 12:6): "Because the LORD disciplines those he loves." Jesus changes the clause from the third person to the first person and adds the verb *to reprove.* Also, the Greek has the pronoun *I* at the beginning of the sentence for added emphasis. And last, the Lord speaks in gen-

54. Deut. 28:48; 2 Sam. 10:4; Isa. 20:2–4; 47:3; Ezek. 16:37–39; 23:10; Mic. 1:8, 11; Nah. 3:5.

55. Martin Kiddle, *The Revelation of St. John* (London: Hodder and Stoughton, 1940), p. 59.

56. Refer to Ramsay, *Letters to the Seven Churches,* p. 419; Hemer, *Letters to the Seven Churches,* pp. 196–99; P. R. Berger, "Kollyrium für die blinden Augen, Apk. 318," *NovT* 27 (1985): 174–95. Swete (*Revelation,* p. 62) comments that the word *collyrium* is a diminutive of the Greek *kollyra,* which is "(1) a small roll of bread, (2) from its roll-like shape, a kind of eye-salve made . . . from the poppy, the acacia, and other flowering plants; here possibly used with reference to the local powder."

57. Ramsay, in his epilogue to the seven letters (*Letters to the Seven Churches,* pp. 431–33), asserts that verses 19–22 apply not merely to the Laodicean congregation but to all seven churches. His contention is ably refuted by Hemer (*Letters to the Seven Churches,* pp. 201–7), who with historical evidence demonstrates that the message of these verses was directed to the church in Laodicea.

eral. He utters the pronoun "those" when he says, "those whom I love," to indicate that love and discipline go hand in hand in renewing their relationship.

Although the Greek verb *agapaō* can be translated "I truly love" and the verb *phileō* "I love" (John 21:15–17 NIV), these verbs are often seen as synonyms. The word *agapaō* appears in the letter to the church of Philadelphia, "I have loved you" (v. 9), but the verb *phileō* here. This does not mean that Jesus loved the Philadelphians with true love and the Laodiceans with affection.[58] Rather, it signifies that within the context of rebuke and discipline, Jesus addresses the church of Laodicea in love.

b. "Be zealous, therefore, and repent." Renewal takes place when the recipients of this letter obediently follow the twofold command: "be zealous" and "repent." Logically, the act of repenting precedes that of being zealous, but the oriental mind is interested in concepts, not analyses. The Greek shows a play on words: the adjective *zestos* (hot, vv. 15–16, from which we have the derivative "zest") and the verb *zēleue* (be zealous!) have the same root. Jesus tells them to begin being zealous for him with a passion that generates spiritual fervor. Zeal is a necessary component of love for God.[59]

Whereas being zealous is a command in the present tense to denote continuity, the imperative "repent" is a once-for-all action. That is, the Laodiceans must make a 180-degree turn by forsaking the past and wholeheartedly adopting their new life in Christ.

c. "Look, I stand at the door and knock." Being shut out from the spiritual life of the individual members of the Laodicean church, Jesus figuratively stands outside the door of their heart and knocks to gain entrance (compare James 5:9). He persistently knocks to gain their attention, so that no one will ever be able to say that the Lord failed to call them. He calls them individually by continually rapping on the doors of their hearts as though the owners are asleep. The stress is on human responsibility to go to the door and answer the one who is seeking entrance. The Lord opened Lydia's heart (Acts 16:14), but here he waits for the sinner to do so. Here is the crux of divine action and human responsibility. When these two appear with reference to God's electing grace in human beings, we encounter a mystery that defies human understanding. Scripture teaches God's intervention and human accountability as the two sides of the proverbial coin (Phil. 2:12–13).

Some scholars view this passage eschatologically as a parallel to the parable of the watchful servant (Matt. 24:33; Mark 13:29; Luke 12:36). They relate the text to the Second Coming of Christ and contend that an eschatological interpretation agrees with a similar motif in Revelation (2:5, 16, 25; 3:11).[60] But formidable

58. Hemer (*Letters to the Seven Churches*, pp. 281–82 n. 98) observes that "it is doubtful whether a rigid distinction of usage can be maintained" in view of the contrast in John 15:9 and 5:20.

59. See the commentaries of Sweet (p. 108); Swete (p. 63); Greijdanus (p. 111); and Charles (1:100).

60. Vos, *Synoptic Traditions*, pp. 94–100; Thomas, *Revelation 1–7*, pp. 321–22; Beckwith, *Apocalypse*, p. 491; Sweet, *Revelation*, p. 109; Swete, *Revelation*, p. 63.

objections dissuade other commentators from seeing this parable in the context of the church members in Laodicea whom Jesus told to repent. The Lord stands at the door of their heart, knocks repeatedly, and expects a response from them. The context of the watchful servant parable differs in its details from this passage.[61]

d. "If anyone hears my voice and opens the door, I will come in to him and I will dine with him and he with me." The term *anyone* indicates that the call to repentance is broad and inclusive. Jesus not only stands at the door of a sinner's heart and knocks repeatedly, but he also speaks and calls him or her to repent. As soon as a person responds to Jesus' voice (compare John 10:3; 18:37), Jesus enters his or her heart. Note well that Jesus is fully in control, for the emphasis in this sentence is on Jesus who speaks, enters one's heart, and dines with the person who responds. It is clear that the responsibility for listening and responding to Jesus' voice rests with the hearer.

This sentence teaches "a distinctively Johannine doctrine."[62] That is, Jesus desires to fellowship with us. In the Eastern mind, hospitality at mealtime demonstrates the host's trust in and respect for the guest (Ps. 41:9), for the host has opened his home to the guest and breaks bread with him. But here it is Jesus who assumes the role of host, for he says that he will enter and dine with his guest for the main meal of the day. This meal was enjoyed near the end of the day, after working hours, in an atmosphere of leisure and close fellowship. This was a time of conversation during which wholesome topics were discussed, laughter was heard, and counsel was given for solving problems. This passage speaks of union with Christ in a day-by-day walk with him. Although it hints at the celebration of the Lord's Supper and the wedding feast at the return of the Lord, especially in light of the eschatology of verse 21, that is not the main emphasis in verse 20.[63] The emphasis is on communion with Christ.

d. Promise *3:21–22*

21. "To the one who overcomes, I will grant [the privilege] of sitting with me on my throne, just as I myself overcame and sat with my Father on his throne. 22. Let anyone who has an ear listen to what the Spirit says to the churches."

John wrote the familiar words "the one who overcomes" as a repetition of the preceding letters and then writes the promise that Jesus gives to the overcomer. It indicates that Jesus gives this promise in the first place to the Laodiceans and

61. Consult Aune (52A, p. 251), Beasley-Murray (p. 107), Charles (1:100–101), Greijdanus (p. 112), Johnson (p. 321), Ladd (p. 67), Mounce (p. 114), Walvoord (p. 98).

62. Philip Edgcumbe Hughes, *The Book of the Revelation: A Commentary* (Leicester: Inter-Varsity; Grand Rapids: Eerdmans, 1990), p. 68. See John 6:56; 14:20; 15:4, 5; 1 John 3:24; 4:13, 15, 16.

63. See Robert H. Mounce, *The Book of Revelation*, rev. ed., NICNT (Grand Rapids: Eerdmans, 1998), p. 114. Aune (*Revelation 1–5*, p. 261) asserts that Jesus is not the host but the guest. But the emphasis in this passage is primarily on Jesus and secondarily on the person with whom he fellowships. Consult also Tim Wiarda, "Revelation 3:20: Imagery and Literary Context," *JETS* 38 (1995): 203–12.

then to all believers. What an astounding grace and mercy extended to a church that receives from the Lord no praise at all! Yet these people, provided they repent and overcome, will be given the privilege of being seated with Christ on the Father's throne (Matt. 19:28; Luke 22:28–30).

The language must be understood to convey a symbolical message. We are unable to comprehend the significance of the privilege to sit next to Jesus on the throne. Therefore, to ask whether the throne is large enough to accommodate Christ's followers is futile. The message supported by other passages in Scripture is that glorified believers have the honor and duty to judge the twelve tribes of Israel, the world, and angels (Matt. 19:28; Luke 22:30; 1 Cor. 6:2–3); and they will rule with Christ (2 Tim. 2:12; Rev. 5:10; 20:4, 6; 22:5). Jesus' promise is based on the vision that Daniel received: "Then the sovereignty, power and greatness of the kingdoms under the whole heaven will be handed over to the saints, the people of the Most High. His kingdom will be an everlasting kingdom, and all rulers will worship and obey him" (Dan. 7:27). Jesus looks backward to his suffering, death, and resurrection when he says that he too overcame. He remarks that he took a place on the throne at the right hand of the Father (Heb. 1:3; 8:1; 12:2; see also Mark 16:19; Eph. 1:20). Yet the difference is that Christ performed his mediatorial work on our behalf and has been given the honor of occupying the seat next to the Father. On the other hand, Jesus looks forward and tells us that when we overcome, we will take a place next to him at his invitation. That will be glory indeed.

The chapter concludes with the well-known refrain to hear what the Spirit says to the churches. And that means the entire church receives Christ's message of praise, reproof, and promise. Note also that at the end of the seven letters to the seven churches there is an indirect reference to the Judgment Day.

Greek Words, Phrases, and Constructions in 3:17–21

Verse 17

ὅτι—the first one is causal, "because," the second is recitative and is not translated, and the third one is the conjunction "that."[64]

πεπλούτηκα—the perfect active indicative of the verb πλουτέω (I am rich, prosper) shows action in the past that has relevance for the present.

οὐδέν—the verb *to have need* demands the genitive case οὐδένος, which some manuscripts have as a correction.

ὁ—this is the generic use of the definite article that with five adjectives describes the spiritual condition of the Laodicean Christians.[65]

Verse 18

The tenses in the ἵνα clauses show three verbs in the aorist (πλουτήσῃς, περιβάλῃ, φανερωθῇ) as a single action and one in the present (βλέπῃς) as a continuous action.

---

64. J. K. Elliott, "The Position of Causal ὅτι Clauses in the New Testament," *FilolNT* 3 (1990): 155–57.

65. See Thomas, *Revelation 1–7*, p. 311 n. 48.

"When the construction with ἵνα is continued in a further clause by μή, μή alone is repeated."[66]

Verse 19

Notice the difference between five verbs: four in the continuous present tense (I love, I reprove, I discipline, and be zealous), and one in the aorist (repent!) indicating a single act with lasting significance.

Verse 20

ἕστηκα—"I stand" is in the perfect tense that has been translated in the present to give it an enduring aspect.

καὶ εἰσελεύσομαι—the conjunction καί preceding the verb is awkward and probably stems from the coordinating Semitic style in the Apocalypse. Its inclusion is the harder reading that should be retained.

Verse 21

ὁ νικῶν--the present participle construction is the nominative absolute, because it stands alone at the beginning of the sentence (see also v. 12 and 2:26).

δώσω αὐτῷ—this is a Hebraic expression that is best interpreted in this context as "I permit him."

---

66. Robertson, *Grammar*, p. 1413. See Barclay, *Revelation of John*, 1:185–86.

4

The Throne in Heaven

(4:1–11)

Outline (continued)

III. Vision 2: God's Throne and the Seven Seals (4:1–8:1)
   A. The Throne of God (4:1–5:14)
      1. The Throne in Heaven (4:1–11)
         a. On and before the Throne (4:1–6a)
         b. Doxologies at the Throne (4:6b–11)

4 1 After these things I saw, and look, a door was opened in heaven, and the first voice which
I had heard as a trumpet talking to me said: "Come up here, and I will show you what must
happen after these things." 2 Immediately I was in the Spirit, and look, there was a throne
standing in heaven, and someone was sitting upon the throne. 3 And the one sitting was
like a jasper stone and a carnelian in appearance, and a rainbow encircled the throne like an emerald in appearance. 4 And around the throne were twenty-four thrones, and upon the thrones were
seated twenty-four elders clothed in white garments, and on their heads they had golden crowns.
5 And from the throne were proceeding flashes of lightning, and rumblings, and crashes of thunder,
and seven flaming torches were burning before the throne, which are the seven spirits of God. 6 And
before the throne was, as it were, a sea of glass like crystal.

And in the midst of the throne and around the throne were four living creatures full of eyes in
front and back. 7 And the first living creature was like a lion, the second living creature like an ox,
the third living creature had a face like a man, and the fourth living creature was like a flying eagle.
8 And each of the four living creatures had six wings, around and inside they were full of eyes, and
they had no rest day or night. They were saying,

> "Holy, holy, holy,
> Lord God Almighty,
> who was, and who is, and who is to come."

9 And whenever the living creatures give glory and honor and thanks to the one sitting on the
throne who lives forever and ever, 10 the twenty-four elders fall before the one sitting on the throne,
and they worship the one living forever and ever, and they cast their crowns before the throne saying,

> 11 "You are worthy, our Lord and God,
> to receive glory and honor and power,
> because you created all things,
> and because of your will they existed,
> that is, they were created."

III. Vision 2: God's Throne and the Seven Seals 4:1–8:1

The visions in the Apocalypse often come to an abrupt ending and do not flow from one into the next. Thus, vision 1 embodies the letters to the seven churches and ends with the one to the Laodiceans; the next verse (4:1) introduces vision 2 and concludes with the opening of the seventh seal (8:1). Indeed, after the sequence of Jesus instructing John to write seven letters to the churches in the province of Asia, the structure of the Apocalypse changes, and John features several direct and indirect contrasts.

First, there is the contrast between the sinful members of these seven churches versus the indescribable splendor and holiness of God. They are sinful human beings on a sinful earth over against a holy God in heaven.

Next, chapter 4 is a description of God's throne in heaven. God, who occupies this throne, is the Creator of the universe (v. 11). By contrast, chapter 5 describes the Lamb of God, who was slain, as the Redeemer of his people. It is the Lamb who is worthy to take the scroll and open its seals, for he is the Revealer.

Third, chapter 6 divulges the hostility that Satan and his cohorts direct against God. John concludes this chapter with a description of the horrors of divine judgments on these enemies. By contrast, chapter 7 discloses the sealing of God's people, who together with the angels and elders sing praises to God and the Lamb. The opening of the seventh seal is followed by a period of silence in heaven (8:1).

Fourth, in the first vision (1:9–3:22), Jesus reveals himself and addresses seven churches on earth. The second vision (4:1–8:1) is devoted to a description of God's throne. This throne in heaven is the center of the universe and this is the place where the Lamb opens seven seals.

And last, the message to the seven churches is direct and relatively simple, but the portrayal of the throne in heaven is given in symbolic language and so is the opening of the seven seals. This symbolism serves to tell the reader that God cannot be seen with human eyes and that the breaking of the seals to reveal what has been written cannot be understood without seeing the authority and power of the Lamb. The scroll for him is an instrument that has concealed the meaning of its content until the Lamb opened the seals.

John records what he is permitted to see and reveal to his brothers and sisters. He gives his report with the aid of the Holy Scriptures; these writings are part of his mental storehouse. For instance, the glorious privilege of viewing God's throne is recorded in many places.[1]

A. The Throne of God
4:1–5:14

Two relatively short chapters reveal the center of divine authority, namely, the throne of God and the power of his Son, who is King of kings and Lord of lords. These chapters teach the saints on earth that in spite of all the onslaughts of evil by Satan and his minions, God's rule is supreme. God assures us that he is working out his plan; he gives us his promise that he governs his entire creation through the Lamb. God rules from his throne.

1. The Throne in Heaven
4:1–11

a. On and before the Throne
4:1–6a

1. After these things I saw, and look, a door was opened in heaven, and the first voice which I had heard as a trumpet talking to me said: "Come up here, and I will show you what must happen after these things."

a. "After these things I saw, and look, a door was opened in heaven." The expression *after these things* appears ten times in the Apocalypse, of which five are

1. 1 Kings 22:19; Ps. 47:8; Isa. 6:1; 63:15; Ezek. 1:26; Dan. 7:9; Rev. 20:11.

followed by the verb "I saw."[2] There is no indication whether time has elapsed since the writing of the seven letters to the churches in the province of Asia, for that is not the point. John is seeing a different vision; he is given the unique opportunity to look into heaven and to describe what he heard and saw. Incidentally, Paul also was taken up to the third heaven in a vision, but he relates that "he heard inexpressible things, things that man is not permitted to tell" (2 Cor. 12:4). John observes and then in astonishment says, "Look!" as if the reader is able to see what he is permitted to view.

The report that John gives is couched in symbolic speech and should be interpreted accordingly. That is, the "door" to heaven is a figurative expression that conveys to John the limits of his heavenly observation. Not everything is visible to him. Notice the passive voice used here, perhaps as a linguistic device to avoid writing the name of God. The clause would then mean, "a door was opened in heaven by God." But the one seated on the throne is too awesome to describe. Hence the seer can only speak about someone sitting on the throne (vv. 2, 3, 9, 10; 5:1, 7, 13), and that someone is God Almighty. God had opened the portal of heaven and left it open so that John would be able to see the divine throne and reveal God's sovereignty to fellow believers.

John was not the first mortal who was permitted to see heaven. In a dream, Jacob saw a stairway reaching to heaven from where God addressed him. Jacob exclaimed, "This is none other than the house of God; this is the gate of heaven" (Gen. 28:17). Also Isaiah, Ezekiel, and Daniel were allowed to see God's celestial throne (Isa. 6:1; Ezek. 1:26; Dan. 7:9).

b. "And the first voice which I had heard as a trumpet talking to me said." The seer connects the first and second visions by identifying only the voice of Jesus.[3] When John encounters the divine, he avoids identifying either God or Jesus by name. Thus, the report of his first meeting on the Lord's Day lacks the name of Jesus (1:10–20); also here John identifies Jesus by calling him the voice like a trumpet. The reference to the trumpet is not only a connecting link for the two visions, but a Jew would immediately react to this sound because it meant that something important was to be heard. The trumpet sounded at the giving of the Decalogue (Exod. 19:16, 19; 20:18), the beginning of the New Year, and the onset of the Feast of Trumpets (Lev. 23:24). In addition, John also knew that it introduced the return of the Lord (Matt. 24:31; 1 Thess. 4:16). He knew by the trumpet sound that he would receive new revelation.

c. "'Come up here, and I will show you what must happen after these things.'" The voice of Jesus invites him to come up higher through the door and personally see the unfolding events that will occur in the future. Moses had received a similar command from God, who said to him, "Come up to me on the mountain"

2. Rev. 1:19; 4:1 (twice); 7:1, 9; 9:12; 15:5; 18:1; 19:1; 20:3. Of these 4:1; 7:1, 9; 15:5; 18:1 include the verb *I saw.*

3. David E. Aune (*Revelation 1–5*, WBC 52A [Dallas: Word, 1997], p. 282) calls this part of verse 1 "a redactional gloss" without providing evidence that John could not have written it.

(Exod. 24:12). Moses was with God on Mount Sinai, while John in a vision is permitted to enter heaven. Inviting John to come up to heaven, Jesus tells him that he will show him future events. That is, John is permitted to see the future unfolding before him from a heavenly perspective. He is told about things that *must* take place; they are predetermined by God and part of his divine plan (Ps. 103:19). God is busy working out his plan of salvation and John is given the privilege of seeing what is going to happen in the future on earth. In fact, the phrase *after these things* means "in the future" (compare 1:19). The visions that John is permitted to see include both realized and unrealized events. They refer to the past and present and comprise the future (see 1:19).[4]

2. Immediately I was in the Spirit, and look, there was a throne standing in heaven, and someone was sitting upon the throne.

The word *Spirit* should be capitalized in harmony with 1:10; 17:3; and 21:10. John's experience here echoes that of other saints who were in the Spirit (e.g., Isa. 61:1; Ezek. 11:1, 5). Some scholars use the lower case to refer to the human spirit or translate the Greek text with the phrase "in a prophetic trance."[5] But these translations miss the action of the Holy Spirit. Notice also that in an indirect manner John alludes to the three Persons in the Trinity (the Father on the throne, the voice of Jesus as a trumpet, and the agency of the Spirit).

John reports that he was immediately in the Spirit. This may signify that he was in that condition all along with an intermission but now again experienced the Spirit's power by which he was able to see and hear celestial sights and sounds. Writes William Hendriksen, "When a person is 'in the Spirit' and being in that state has a vision, there is a suspension of conscious contact with the physical environment."[6] Physical organs are not in use during the vision, for the soul assumes their functions. So John sees the throne of God and hears the voice of Jesus.

Jewish rabbis in ancient times seldom described God's throne for fear of desecrating the divine name. They were forbidden to speak openly about heavenly mysteries, and those who spoke about the throne ran the risk of profaning the Deity. Hence, few rabbis dared to write publicly on this topic.[7] But John is given the honor of ascending to the throne room, which is the very presence of God, and relating what he saw. Rather than give a description of God, which is forbidden (Exod. 20:4), or of heaven as such, John presents a symbolic portrayal of the divine throne and those who gathered around it: four living beings, twenty-four

4. Gregory K. Beale, *The Book of Revelation: A Commentary on the Greek Text,* NIGTC (Grand Rapids: Eerdmans, 1998), pp. 317–18.

5. Robert L. Thomas, *Revelation 1–7: An Exegetical Commentary* (Chicago: Moody, 1992), p. 338; John F. Walvoord, *The Revelation of Jesus Christ* (Chicago: Moody, 1966), pp. 103–4; Wilfrid J. Harrington, *Revelation,* SP 16 (Collegeville, Minn.: Liturgical Press, 1993), pp. 78–79; Aune, *Revelation 1–5,* p. 283; G. B. Caird, *A Commentary on the Revelation of St. John the Divine* (London: Black, 1966), p. 59.

6. William Hendriksen, *More Than Conquerors* (reprint, Grand Rapids: Baker, 1982), p. 82.

7. SB, 1:974–78; 2:338.

elders, many angels, and all other creatures from the entire universe. He sees the Lamb, seven lamps, and a sea of glass.

If there is one word that dominates this chapter, it is the term *throne,* which appears thirteen times in eleven verses. It occurs repeatedly in the Apocalypse, in total some thirty-seven times. But chapter 4 is the chapter that describes the throne of God. The purpose for this description is to demonstrate that God is the supreme ruler of this universe. He governs everything so that nothing happens without his will, whether good or evil. He assures them that he and not Satan is in control. "That is why this vision of the universe governed by the throne precedes the symbolic description of the trials through which the Church must pass, chapter 6."[8]

3. And the one sitting was like a jasper stone and a carnelian in appearance, and a rainbow encircled the throne like an emerald in appearance.

How does a mortal being who is privileged in a vision to see the throne of God speak about "the one sitting" on it? John gives his readers a sense of the majesty and beauty of the appearance of God and the throne by referring to three precious stones: the jasper stone, the carnelian, and the emerald. The jasper is also mentioned in the description of the new Jerusalem; there John, speaking of the glory of God, says, "Its brilliance was like a precious stone as a crystallized jasper stone" (21:11). It may be a variety of quartz that came in various colors, so that God's glory transmitted through this stone presented indescribable beauty. The jasper stone in antiquity (see Exod. 28:20; 39:13; Ezek. 28:13) may be different from what we call by that name today. In general, commentators compare its brilliance to that of a diamond.[9] This brilliance is a picture of the "unapproachable light" of God that allows no one to see him (1 Tim. 6:16). The second stone is called a carnelian; it is dark red, orange-red, or reddish-brown in color (Rev. 21:20; Ezek. 28:13).

A rainbow with the color of an emerald appeared around God's throne. We count seven hues in the spectrum of a rainbow, and one of these colors is green. An emerald as we know it is green. John, however, saw the entire rainbow as a shade of green. Likewise a precious stone in the fourth foundation of the new Jerusalem city walls was emerald (21:19). The rainbow is God's covenantal sign that he would not destroy the earth again with a flood (Gen. 9:15). John uses the word *iris* for rainbow, which was a nonbiblical word. But to be clear to his readers that he meant a rainbow, he was not afraid to adopt the term (see 10:1).[10] What is the significance of this semicircle over the throne of God? The symbolism of

8. Hendriksen, *More Than Conquerors,* p. 84.

9. Bauer, p. 368; Norman Hillyer, *NIDNTT,* 3:398; see also the entry in *EDNT,* 2:170. And see R. H. Charles, *A Critical and Exegetical Commentary on the Revelation of St. John,* ICC (Edinburgh: Clark, 1920), 1:114. In Revelation the NJB consistently translates "jasper" as "diamond."

10. See Leon Morris, *NIDNTT,* 3:1002; Karl Heinrich Rengstorf, *TDNT,* 3:341. Caird (*Revelation,* p. 63) comments, "But this is no prismatic bow in the sky; it is like an emerald—a statement that teases the imagination out of all thought."

the rainbow is not clear, except to say that it expresses God's faithfulness as he keeps covenant forever with his people; by it he expresses his grace and mercy.

4. And around the throne were twenty-four thrones, and upon the thrones were seated twenty-four elders clothed in white garments, and on their heads they had golden crowns.

The mental image we receive of the twenty-four thrones is that of a square with God's throne in the center and six thrones on each side of the square. In the canonical Scriptures the term *twenty-four* appears only in the Apocalypse and refers to either thrones or elders (4:4, 10; 5:8; 11:16; 19:4). This eliminates parallels that might cast light on the meaning of the number twenty-four.

On these thrones were twenty-four elders who had two distinguishing marks: being clothed in white garments and wearing golden crowns on their heads. These marks, together with the expression *thrones*, may aid the interpreter in explaining the meaning of this verse: for instance, the saints are invited by Jesus to sit with him on the throne (3:21) and the saints in heaven are given authority to judge by sitting on thrones (20:4). There is a distinct difference between angels and saints. First, not angels but saints receive this privilege (1 Cor. 6:2–3). Next, although angels appear in white garments (see 19:14; Matt. 28:2–3; Mark 16:5; John 20:12; Acts 1:10), the saints are dressed in white apparel that signifies the purity that comes from being cleansed from sin (3:4; 7:9). Third, crowns symbolize authority to rule with Christ (3:21; 5:10; 20:4, 6; 22:5; 2 Tim. 2:12); this is a privilege granted not to angels but to the saints.

God created Adam from the dust of the earth (Gen. 2:7), crowned him with glory and honor (Ps. 8:5), and appointed him to rule (Gen. 1:28). But God created angels as spirits to minister to and serve the needs of his people (Heb. 1:7, 14). Although Adam sinned, Jesus as the second Adam came to redeem him (Rom. 5:12, 19; 1 Cor. 15:45). But those angels who fell into sin are not redeemed by Jesus Christ (Heb. 2:16). Adam and Eve, with their offspring, are created in God's image (Gen. 1:27); angels are not created in his image but are only messengers (Ps. 104:4; Heb. 1:7).[11] When God's redeemed people are translated to glory, we know that they surround the throne of God and of the Lamb (Rev. 7:9). Their representatives are the twenty-four elders who occupy thrones to rule and to judge. They wear white garments to symbolize purity and wear crowns to indicate victory. They as covenant people are privileged to rule while angels as messengers serve. Hendriksen pointedly observes, "These twenty-four elders are mentioned first for the simple reason that they *are* first in importance and in glory of all creatures in heaven (Gen. 1:26; Heb. 2:8)."[12]

In chapters 4 and 5, John relates that around the throne are living beings, which are angelic beings, angels, and elders. We are led to believe that the elders

11. Refer to Simon J. Kistemaker, *Exposition of the Epistle of Jude*, NTC (Grand Rapids: Baker, 1987), pp. 387–88.

12. Hendriksen, *More Than Conquerors*, pp. 85–86.

are representative of the saints. If this were not the case, mention of the saints in heaven would have been neglected.

The traditional interpretation of the twenty-four elders is that this number is the total of twelve times two, namely, twelve Old Testament patriarchs and twelve New Testament apostles, the representatives of those redeemed by Christ. Victorinus of Pettau in Pannonia (modern Hungary), who died in 304, first suggested this view in his commentary on the Apocalypse. Many modern scholars have adopted this view as a symbolic interpretation of this passage, with variations.[13] Biblical evidence bolsters this interpretation, for elders were an integral part of Israel's religious life in the Old Testament era. In the days of Jesus and the apostles, elders were members of the Sanhedrin and prominent in local Jewish communities. Next, Paul appointed elders in the churches he had founded (Acts 14:23) and instructed Titus to appoint them in every town on the island of Crete (Titus 1:5). And in the postapostolic age elders took leadership in the government of the local churches. The Greek term *prebyterion* (presbytery) appears in Luke's writings and the Pastoral Epistles to designate a council of elders (Luke 22:66; Acts 22:5; 1 Tim. 4:14). The term *elders* (Greek *presbyteroi*) occurs twelve times in the Apocalypse: for example, they sit, fall down in worship, speak, and sing.[14]

The unity of the body of Christ is exemplified in the symbolism of the new Jerusalem. This city has a great, high wall with twelve gates. The names of the twelve tribes of Israel are written on these gates. And the wall of the city has twelve foundations. The names of the twelve apostles of the Lamb are written on these foundations (21:12, 14).

Another view interprets the expression *elders* as angelic beings.[15] These angels are dressed in white garments, as is evident from numerous passages (e.g., see John 20:12). In his epistles, Paul alludes to angelic hierarchies that Christ created with respect to thrones, powers, rulers, and authorities (Col. 1:16; see also Rom. 8:38; Eph. 3:10). Also the Old Testament refers to a council of heavenly beings consisting of an angelic host (Ps. 29:1; 89:7; 103:20; 148:2; Job 1:6). Perhaps the number *twenty-four* preceding the word *elders*, understood as angels, is derived from the twenty-four priestly orders that are mentioned in the Old Testament (1 Chron. 23:3–4; 24:4; 25:9–31).[16] But do angels have anything in com-

---

13. E.g., the commentaries of Alford (p. 596); Barclay (1:194); Greijdanus (pp. 122–23); Hailey (p. 168); Hoeksema (pp. 158–59); Hughes (p. 72); Lenski (pp. 174–75); Sweet (p. 118); Swete (p. 69).

14. Rev. 4:4, 10; 5:5, 6, 8, 11, 14; 7:11, 13; 11:16; 14:3; 19:4. A. Feuillet ("Les vingt-quatre vieillards de l'Apocalypse," *RB* 65 [1958]: 5–32) interprets the twenty-four elders as the great saints in the Old Testament and takes the number twenty-four from the orders of the priests, singers, and porters (1 Chron. 24:3–19; 25:6–31; 26:17–19). But are there no great saints of the New Testament era?

15. There are additional views. For a survey, see the commentaries of Aune (52A, pp. 288–92), Beale (pp. 323–26), and Charles (1:128–33).

16. Consult the commentaries of Thomas (*Revelation 1–7*, pp. 347–48); Beckwith (p. 498); Mounce (pp. 121–22); Johnson (p. 462); Morris (p. 86); Beasley-Murray (pp. 113–14). See also Ned B. Stonehouse, *Paul before the Areopagus and Other New Testament Studies* (London: Tyndale, 1957), pp. 88–108.

mon with priests? Are angels kings who wear crowns? Are angels given the duty to judge human beings? The answer to these questions is no. Angels do not sit on thrones, but elders do. Indeed if the elders are angels, then redeemed humanity is not represented at the throne.

I conclude, therefore, that in numerous respects elders are of greater importance and of higher rank than angels. The twenty-four elders represent the redeemed saints, and, with all the angels and all living creatures, these elders render praise, honor, and glory to the Lamb (5:12).

5. And from the throne were proceeding flashes of lightning, and rumblings, and crashes of thunder, and seven flaming torches were burning before the throne, which are the seven spirits of God. 6a. And before the throne was, as it were, a sea of glass like crystal.

a. "And from the throne were proceeding flashes of lightning, and rumblings, and crashes of thunder." In the opening words there is a resemblance to the last chapter of the Apocalypse, where John speaks about a river of the water of life. "It proceeds from the throne of God and the Lamb" (22:1). For John, God's throne depicts the majesty and grandeur of the Almighty. He writes with an Old Testament passage in mind, namely, the scene at Mount Sinai when God gave the Decalogue to the Israelites. "On the morning of the third day there was thunder and lightning, with a thick cloud over the mountain, and a very loud trumpet blast" (Exod. 19:16; compare Job 37:4, 5).

We must read this passage symbolically, because the throne of God is so awesome that John can portray it only with natural phenomena such as lightning, rumblings, and crashes of thunder. These phenomena are symbols that in nature display God's grandeur, power, and might (Job 36:29, 30; Ps. 18:13–15; 29:3–5).

b. "And seven flaming torches were burning before the throne, which are the seven spirits of God." Once again, the symbolism of this text is now expressed in the number *seven*, which occurs twice. It is the number of completeness and fullness. The seven torches represent an abundance of light at God's throne, and the seven spirits are a representation of the Holy Spirit's fullness (see the commentary on 1:4; and see 3:1; 5:6). John has taken his symbolism from the golden lampstand in the tabernacle (Exod. 25:31–40; 27:20–21; 40:24–25; Lev. 24:1–4) and from the prophecy of Zechariah (4:2). This lampstand of seven lamps stood in the area that was in front of the Holy of Holies. The display is much more that of blazing torches than of an oil-burning lampstand (compare Ezek. 1:13). The blazing fire of the torches provides light but also depicts God's holiness that brooks no sin in its presence (Ps. 18:8; 50:3; 97:3; Dan. 7:10).

These seven torches represent the seven spirits of God. The symbolism of the fullness of God's Spirit points to the work the Holy Spirit performs in regard to interpreting God's will, encouraging and comforting his people, sanctifying saints and reproving sinners (see John 16:7–11; Acts 2:17–21).[17]

17. Some commentators (e.g., Aune, Charles) consider the last clause in verse 5b to be an explanatory gloss, but this view is without justification.

c. "And before the throne was, as it were, a sea of glass like crystal." John qualifies what he observed by indicating that an area in front of the throne resembled a sea of glass similar to crystal. Crystal has the quality of perspicuity, so that everyone can see through it. This means that the saints in heaven are able to see God's wisdom in action. It is clear and yet profound (Exod. 24:9–10).

Interpretations of the "sea of glass" vary. Writes Caird, "The sea of glass is the reservoir of evil out of which arises the monster [that is, the beast rising from the sea] (13:1)."[18] But it is hard to imagine a pool of evil at the throne of God, where no sin is allowed to enter. Others compare the phrase to the bronze basin of water in use at the temple of Solomon (1 Kings 7:23–26; 2 Kings 16:17). The washing of feet and hands by priests in the Old Testament era is a symbol of the cleansing blood of Christ that washes away the sins of the saints in New Testament times.[19] Still other suggestions are the firmament that separates heaven and earth; a heavenly sea that separated a holy God from all that he had made; or a picture of the glassy Aegean Sea on a summer day seen by John exiled at Patmos. All these presentations have some value, but because John is describing heaven with symbols we must avoid being dogmatic on this point. Perhaps we do well to pay attention to the comparatives "as it were" and "like." Glass in ancient times was opaque, while crystal was clear. The emphasis appears to be on perspicuity to indicate God's infinite understanding and insight (see also 15:2).

Greek Words, Phrases, and Constructions in 4:1–4

Verse 1

φωνὴ . . . λέγων—the feminine noun is followed by a masculine participle to identify the Lord as the speaker.

λαλούσης . . . λέγων—the first present participle characterizes the act of speaking and the second the content of what is said. By contrast, Aune omits the first participle and calls the construction "a Hebraism that functions like ὅτι *recitative* to introduce direct speech."[20] He notes similar constructions in 10:8; 17:1; 21:9.

ἀνάβα—this is the alternate form of the second aorist active imperative that normally reads as ἀνάβηθι from the verb ἀναβαίνω (I go up).

Verse 2

καθήμενος—this present participle consistently functions substantively in the Apocalypse to refer to God seated on the throne and thus avoids using God's name. When this participle appears with the prepositional phrase *on the throne* ("the one sitting on the throne"), a curious case relationship occurs. If the participle is in the nominative case,

---

18. Caird, *Revelation*, p. 65. See M. Robert Mulholland Jr., *Revelation: Holy Living in an Unholy World* (Grand Rapids: Zondervan, Francis Asbury Press, 1990), pp. 150–54. Compare Gregory K. Beale, "The Problem of the Man from the Sea in 4 Ezra 13 and Its Relation to the Messianic Concept in John's Apocalypse," *NovT* 25 (1983): 182–88; Beale, *Revelation*, p. 327.

19. Refer to the commentaries of Greijdanus (pp. 124–25), Hendriksen (p. 86), Walvoord (pp. 108–9).

20. Aune, *Revelation 1–5*, pp. 269, 282.

throne is in the accusative case (ἐπὶ τὸν θρόνον/τοὺς Θρόνους, vv. 2, 4); if the participle is in the genitive case, the prepositional phrase is in the genitive (ἐπὶ τοῦ θρόνου, v. 10; 5:1); and when the participle is in the dative, the prepositional phrase is in the dative (ἐπὶ τῷ θρόνῳ, v. 9).[21] Since Greek syntax does not require the case of the prepositional phrase to change in tandem with the participle, the only explanation for this phenomenon is the stylistic choice of the author.

Verse 3

κυκλόθεν—"all around." Instead of being an adverb of place, it is put into service as a preposition that controls the genitive case. The enclitic -θεν means "away from" the circle.

Verse 4

πρεσβυτέρους—the accusative case can be explained as a direct object by mentally inserting the verb εἶδον (I saw) from verse 1.

---

b. Doxologies at the Throne
4:6b–11

6b. And in the midst of the throne and around the throne were four living creatures full of eyes in front and back. 7. And the first living creature was like a lion, the second living creature like an ox, the third living creature had a face like a man, and the fourth living creature was like a flying eagle.

a. "And in the midst of the throne and around the throne were four living creatures full of eyes in front and back." The imagery comes from the prophecy of Ezekiel, "in the fire was what looked like four living creatures. In appearance their form was that of a man, but each of them had four faces and four wings" (Ezek. 1:5–6; compare Isa. 6:2). John sharpens this prophecy by giving a clearer description of place and appearance than Ezekiel: the living creatures are in the midst of and around the throne. I suggest that these four living beings encircle the throne at four points that are equidistant from each other, so that from whatever angle we view the throne, one of these beings always occupies a central position. I admit that this is only a supposition, for no one including John can fully describe God's throne. Nonetheless, this explanation gives clarity.[22]

The four living beings are not immobile parts of the throne; rather, they serve God as messengers. In fact, Ezekiel calls them cherubim (Ezek. 10:20–21), who were high-ranking heavenly beings assigned to protect and guard, for instance, the tree of life (Gen. 3:24) and the ark of the covenant (Exod. 25:20). They are full of life, alert, and intelligent. They are covered with eyes in front and back (Ezek. 1:18), so that nothing escapes their attention. With the elders, they sing

21. Henry Alford, *James–Revelation*, vol. 4, part 2 of *Alford's Greek Testament* (1875; reprint, Grand Rapids: Guardian, 1976), p. 594.

22. It is not necessary to call the words "in the midst of the throne and" a gloss, as Charles does (1:118). It may mean in the middle of each of the four sides (Hendriksen, *More Than Conquerors*, p. 86). Robert G. Hall sees the living creatures as components of the throne. See his "Living Creatures in the Midst of the Throne: Another Look at Revelation 4:6," *NTS* 36 (1990): 609–13.

praises and say "Amen" (Rev. 5:6, 8, 11, 14). They speak at the opening of the first four seals (6:1, 3, 5, 7; 7:11; 14:3; 19:4). And one of them hands seven golden bowls of God's wrath to seven angels (15:7).

b. "And the first living creature was like a lion, the second living creature like an ox, the third living creature had a face like a man, and the fourth living creature was like a flying eagle." Ezekiel portrays the four living creatures as each having four faces: of a man, a lion, an ox, and an eagle (1:10). The order in John's vision is different, because the face of a man occupies third place. Also, Ezekiel's living beings have four faces each, while each of those in the Apocalypse has one face.

The church fathers (Origen, Victorinus, and Athanasius) saw the four Gospels depicted by these four symbols. However, whereas Origen said that Matthew is the man, Mark the eagle, Luke the ox, and John the lion, Victorinus had Matthew as the man, Mark as the lion, Luke as the ox, and John as the eagle, and Athanasius had Matthew as the lion, Mark as the man, Luke as the ox, and John as the eagle.[23] The confusion testifies to their imagination but not to a helpful understanding of Revelation. On the contrary, these four faces characterize the cherubim symbolically; they embody boldness and courage, strength and tenacity, intelligence and sagacity, dispatch and swiftness.[24] The four living creatures are sent out to serve the members of Christ's church (Heb. 1:14). Note that in the phrase "four living creatures," the number four is the numerical symbol for completeness in creation.

8. And each of the four living creatures had six wings, around and inside they were full of eyes, and they had no rest day or night. They were saying,

> **"Holy, holy, holy,**
> **Lord God Almighty,**
> **who was, and who is, and who is to come."**

a. "And each of the four living creatures had six wings." The resemblance to the visions of the prophets Isaiah and Ezekiel is clear, but there are differences. The living beings in the Old Testament passages are either seraphim or cherubim, while John refrains from giving them names. In the prophecy of Isaiah these angelic beings have six wings: two to cover their faces, two to cover their feet, and two for flying (Isa. 6:2), but in the Ezekiel passage they have four wings (Ezek. 1:6). The number six ought not to be interpreted as the sinister number of incompleteness but rather as three sets of two, with each set having a distinct function. These wings furnish cover when the angels stand before God, and in flight they provide speed.

Even though John echoes phrases taken from the prophecies of Isaiah, Ezekiel, and Daniel, he himself was given the privilege of looking into heaven to tes-

23. Charles, *Revelation*, 1:124. See also William Barclay, *The Revelation of John*, 2d ed. (Philadelphia: Westminster, 1960), 1:203.

24. In his *Commentary on Revelation* (1911; reprint, Grand Rapids: Kregel, 1977), p. 71, Henry Barclay Swete aptly concludes, "The four forms suggest what is noblest, strongest, wisest, and swiftest in animate Nature . . . including Man."

tify "to the things he saw" (1:2). We acknowledge that John's understanding of the heavenly things was illumined while he was "rapt in the Spirit."[25]

b. "Around and inside they were full of eyes." This is a throwback to verse 6, which describes the living creatures as covered with eyes. The question here concerns the word *inside.* The image of these angelic beings with eyes all around their body is clear, but a literal interpretation of eyes within their bodies is impossible. Perhaps the mental picture John wishes to convey is that of folded wings that kept eyes hidden, but when these wings were outstretched their eyes were on the underside (compare Ezek. 1:18).

c. "And they had no rest day or night." This clause should not be interpreted to mean that angels sing praises to God without ceasing. There is a difference between doing something continually and continuously. Although John introduces a time division of day and night (see 14:11), he employs human terminology in expressing the concept of eternity. Time and space limit human beings on earth but angels live in eternity. Angels worship God without rest day or night in heaven and, by contrast, worshipers of the beast have no rest day and night in hell (14:11).

d. "They were saying, 'Holy, holy, holy, Lord God Almighty, who was, and who is, and who is to come.'" Notice that this song mentions the holiness, exclusive power, and eternity of God but says nothing about the redemption of human beings. Chapter 4 depicts the throne and the holiness of God, while chapter 5 portrays the Lamb and the redemption of his people.

The angelic song recorded in Isaiah 6:3 is sung by seraphim. There is no reason to suggest that the four living creatures called cherubim cannot sing these words. Aune is of the opinion that this angelic song "may have been part of a hymn regularly chanted in the temple liturgy or at least a cultic liturgical formula."[26] Also in Christian hymnody the threefold use of the adjective *holy* is well known from the words of Reginald Heber,

> Holy, Holy, Holy! Lord God Almighty!
> Early in the morning our song shall rise
> to Thee;
> Holy, Holy, Holy! Merciful and mighty!
> God in Three Persons, blessed Trinity!

In this throne-room chapter, the words *Lord God Almighty* proclaim the truth of God's omnipotence. Nothing and no one in all creation can rival the Almighty. It is he who said, "I am the LORD, and there is no other" (Isa. 45:6). He is the one "who was, and who is, and who is to come." The sequence differs

25. Martin Kiddle, *The Revelation of St. John* (London: Hodder and Stoughton, 1940), p. 70.

26. Aune, *Revelation 1–5,* p. 303. Refer also to N. Walker, "The Origin of the 'Thrice-Holy,'" *NTS* 5 (1959): 132–33.

slightly from the earlier order, "who is and who was and who is to come" (1:4, 8; see also 16:5). These words describe God as timeless from eternity to eternity.

9. And whenever the living creatures give glory and honor and thanks to the one sitting on the throne and who lives forever and ever, 10. the twenty-four elders fall before the one sitting on the throne and they worship the one living forever and ever, and they cast their crowns before the throne saying,

This passage is introductory to the second hymn of praise sung in heaven (see v. 11) by the living creatures supported by the twenty-four elders at worship. These living creatures ascribe glory, honor, and thanks to God. While the combination "glory and honor" appears in the Old Testament (Ps. 8:5; Heb. 2:7, 9; see also Rev. 21:26), the noun "thanks" occurs chiefly in New Testament books (e.g., Acts 24:3; Eph. 5:4). Glory and honor relate to God's perfection, but thanksgiving to his gifts in both creation and redemption.[27]

John refers to God as the occupant of the throne and as the One who dwells in eternity. By resorting to circumlocution to avoid using the name of God, he denotes him as the possessor and giver of life, and he remarks that this life is eternal (10:6; 15:7; Dan. 4:34). The four living creatures receive their life from God, fulfill his commands, and joyfully sing his praises. The emphasis is on the number four, which relates to God's creation. Similarly, the clause "the one who lives forever and ever" appears four times in the Apocalypse (4:9, 10; 10:6; 15:7). God is the Creator who eternally rules over his creation.[28]

Also the twenty-four elders representing redeemed humanity worship God by falling on their faces before his throne. Falling prostrate in oriental manner, they render homage to the Almighty alone. No angel might be paid obeisance; indeed, an angel reproves John for falling at his feet and commands him to worship God (19:10; 22:8–9). It is remarkable how many times in the Apocalypse the twenty-four elders are mentioned falling before the one seated on the throne to worship him (5:8, 14; 7:11; 11:16; 19:4).

When Handel's *Messiah* was first performed in London in 1743 in the presence of King George II, the king rose from his seat when he heard the Hallelujah chorus.[29] By rising with bowed head, he indicated that not he but Jesus is King of kings and Lord of lords. The Messiah reigns forever and ever. The twenty-four elders cast their crowns before God's throne and render him the highest accolades in heaven and on earth. They had received these crowns from God for being overcomers, but they respectfully return them to God to assign to him all the glory and honor. They pay him obeisance, because he alone lives and rules forever.

27. See Swete, *Revelation*, p. 73.

28. Richard Bauckham, *The Climax of Prophecy: Studies on the Book of Revelation* (Edinburgh: Clark, 1993), pp. 31–32.

29. Compare Donna W. Payne and Fran Lenzo, *The Handel's Messiah Family Advent Reader* (Chicago: Moody, 1999), p. 99.

Satan tempted Jesus to bow down and worship him, but the Lord responded by quoting the Scriptures: "Worship the Lord your God, and serve him only" (Matt. 4:10; Luke 4:8; Deut. 6:13). Satan has his own throne (Rev. 2:13), but at the consummation he will be thrown into the lake of fire (20:10). Not Satan, although he is called the prince of this world (John 12:31), but God is in control and is worthy to receive glory, and honor, and power.

11. "You are worthy, our Lord and God, to receive glory and honor and power, because you created all things, and because of your will they existed, that is, they were created."

a. "You are worthy, our Lord and God, to receive glory and honor and power." Three successive songs in the Apocalypse have the adjective *worthy* as their opening word, which because of its position receives emphasis (4:11; 5:9, 12). No one in the entire universe is worthy of glory, honor, and power but God and the Lamb. God is worthy because of creation, and the Lamb is worthy because of his sacrificial death. Hence, the Lamb alone is worthy to execute God's plan of salvation and to fill the role of king in his kingdom.[30]

There is a difference between the song of the four living creatures (v. 8) and the song of the twenty-four elders. The angelic beings glorify God's holiness, exclusive power, and eternity, while the elders glorify God for his work of creation. Further, instead of the word *thanks* (v. 9), the song has the expression *power*.

b. "Because you created all things." God's power is revealed in creating all things in this vast universe. We as human beings are unable to absorb everything that exists, for we are limited by time and space. The universe that God created is so boundless that we marvel at God's power. The Creator has made all things from the smallest particle to the largest star. Thus, the work of creation is the reason for the elders expressing their praise to the Lord God. Notice that they call him "our Lord and God." In a succeeding song they praise the Lord Christ for purchasing them for God (5:9).

c. "And because of your will they existed, that is, they were created." The work of creation depends entirely on God's will; without his will nothing happens. In other words, this world did not come into being by evolving on its own, but God exercised his will (Heb. 11:3). Thus, humanity, the animal and plant worlds, and inanimate matter exist only because of the will of God. This means that everything created by God must serve him.

The last part of this verse has been interpreted in various ways, because the logical sequence should be "they were created, that is, they existed." Even that wording is imprecise, for the reading really ought to be in the present tense, "they exist," which is a reading supported by some manuscripts (see NKJV). Still other witnesses delete the words "they were created" to alleviate the problem

30. Erich Tiedtke, *NIDNTT*, 3:349.

entirely.[31] The most difficult reading is here, as often, likely the correct one; it forces us to accept the text as is and interpret it to the best of our ability.

The explanation suggested by a number of commentators is that the expression *they existed* looks back to the fact of creation and the expression *they were created* has to do with the beginning of their existence. The will of God is the cause of creation, and the Lord Christ is the agent of creation (John 1:1; Col. 1:15–18; Heb. 1:3).[32] This is a fitting conclusion to the account of God's throne room: God is sovereign in his creation.

Greek Words, Phrases, and Constructions in 4:6b–11

Verse 6b

ἐν μέσῳ—"in the midst of" is a literal translation of the Hebrew "out of the midst of [the fire]" (Ezek. 1:5).

Verse 7

ἔχων—the masculine singular participle in place of the neuter (because of ζῷον) indicates that the masculine gives the living being a personal identity.

Verse 8

ἀνά— the preposition has a distributive sense in connection with numbers, "six wings each."[33]

ἡμέρας καὶ νυκτός—the case in the two nouns is the genitive of time to express not length, which would have called for the accusative, but infinity.[34]

ἅγιος—this adjective occurs three times in succession for emphasis. Some manuscripts list the adjective nine times (see the Majority Text).

Verses 9–10

The future tenses in verses 9 and 10 in the verbs *give glory, fall,* and *cast* in the Greek text may be due to Semitic influence: the Hebrew imperfect tense in some cases can be translated as a future. But here the context demands a translation in the present instead of the future.

Verse 11

The definite article precedes each of the three nouns "glory and honor and power." See also the songs in 5:13; 7:12.

τὰ πάντα—the definite article with the adjective expresses universal totality: in the universe nothing exists that God has not created.

---

31. For instance, Charles (*Revelation,* 1:134) calls the last two words "an explanatory gloss added by a scribe who misunderstood ἦσαν."

32. Consult the commentaries of Alford (pp. 602–3), Barclay (1:207), Greijdanus (pp. 130–31), Hailey (p. 172), Hendriksen (p. 88), Hughes (p. 76), Johnson (p. 464), Düsterdieck (p. 202), Mounce (p. 127), Sweet (p. 121), Swete (p. 75), and Thomas (p. 368).

33. C. F. D. Moule, *An Idiom-Book of New Testament Greek,* 2d ed. (Cambridge: Cambridge University Press, 1960), p. 66.

34. Compare Thomas, *Revelation 1–7,* p. 362 n. 89.

ἦσαν καὶ ἐκτίσθησαν—some manuscripts insert the negative particle οὐκ before the first verb, while others have discarded the last two words to bring about a logical sequence. But the better manuscripts have the text presented here.

5

The Sealed Scroll and the Lamb

(5:1–14)

Outline (continued)

2. The Sealed Scroll (5:1–5)
3. Praise to the Lamb (5:6–14)

5 1 And I saw in the right hand of the one sitting on the throne a scroll written on the inside
and on the back sealed with seven seals. 2 And I saw a mighty angel proclaiming in a loud
voice, "Who is worthy to open the scroll, that is, to break its seals?" 3 And no one in heaven
or on the earth or under the earth was able to open the scroll or look inside it. 4 And I was
bursting into tears, because no one could be found to open the scroll and look inside it. 5 And one
of the elders was saying to me, "Weep not; look, the lion of the tribe of Judah, the root of David, has
overcome. He is able to open the scroll and its seals."

6 And I saw in the midst of the throne and of the four living creatures, and in the midst of the
elders a Lamb standing as though it had been slain. He had seven horns and seven eyes, which are
the seven spirits of God that are sent out into all the earth. 7 And he came and took the scroll out of
the right hand of him who is sitting on the throne. 8 And when he took the scroll, the four living
creatures and the twenty-four elders fell before the Lamb. Each had a harp and golden bowls full of
incense, which are the prayers of the saints. 9 And they sang a new song, saying,

"You are worthy to take the scroll
and open its seals,
because you were slain and with your blood
you bought men [and women] for God
out of every tribe and language and
people and nation,
10 and you made them for our God
a kingdom and priests,
and they will rule upon the earth."

11 And I looked and I heard the voice of many angels around the throne, the living creatures,
and the elders. And their number was myriads of myriads and thousands of thousands. 12 They were
saying in a loud voice,

"Worthy is the Lamb that was slain to receive
power and wealth and wisdom and strength
and honor and glory and thanksgiving."

13 And every creature in heaven and on earth and under the earth and on the sea, and all things
in them I heard saying,

"To the one sitting on the throne and to the
Lamb
be thanksgiving and honor and glory and
power
forever and ever."

14 And the four living creatures were saying, "Amen." And the elders fell and worshiped.

---

2. The Sealed Scroll
5:1–5

At the center of the universe, God is sitting on his throne to rule all that he has created. Although the earth is filled with turmoil and tumult, natural catastrophe of flood and earthquake, human suffering in terms of famine and disease, wars and conflicts, God is the ruler yet. He feeds the birds of the air and causes the lilies to grow in the fields (Matt. 6:26, 28–29). Nothing happens without his will. If then God takes care of his great creation, how much more does he take care of his people.

Chapter 4 describes God and his throne in heaven; the next chapter pictures the Lamb of God, who is known from the Old Testament Scriptures as the lion of the tribe of Judah and the root of David (Gen. 49:9–10; Isa. 11:1, 10). He was slain on Calvary's cross to redeem his people from sin and guilt; as God's spokesman he was sent to reveal his word (John 3:31–34). He fulfilled the priestly task to redeem the saints and the prophetic task to teach them God's revelation. As conqueror he fulfills his royal task.

Notice the verbal links between chapters 4 and 5:[1]

Revelation 4	Revelation 5
He who sits on the throne (vv. 2, 9)	He who sits on the throne (vv. 1, 7, 13)
The four living creatures (v. 6)	The four living creatures (vv. 6, 8, 11, 14)
The twenty-four elders (v. 4)	The twenty-four elders (vv. 6, 8, 14)
Fall . . . and worship (vv. 10, 11)	Fell and worshiped (vv. 8, 14)
Worthy (v. 11)	Worthy (vv. 9, 12)
You created all things (v. 11)	Every creature (v. 13)

The Lamb occupies the center of all God's decrees, for he is worthy and able to break the seal and open the scroll. Nothing comes to pass apart from the Lamb, for both creation and redemption begin and end with him. And last, the word *Lamb* should not be taken literally but symbolically.

1. And I saw in the right hand of the one sitting on the throne a scroll written on the inside and on the back sealed with seven seals.

John continues to reveal what he observed when he was permitted to look into heaven and see the throne of God. He relates what he saw at the throne but avoids the use of God's name. For a Jew, mentioning the name of God was forbidden, especially in connection with God's dwelling place, his throne (see the commentary on 4:2). So John writes about the one sitting on the heavenly throne and his right hand, which symbolizes divine power and authority.

The second part of this verse presents a number of difficulties for the interpreter: the appearance of the scroll, the message of the scroll, the place of the seven seals, and the symbolism of the sealed scroll.

a. *Appearance of the Scroll.* John says that the scroll was written on the inside and on the back to indicate that the message was so voluminous that

1. With thanks to J. Daryl Charles, "An Apocalyptic Tribute to the Lamb (Rev 5:1–14)," *JETS* 34 (1991): 462.

both sides of the writing material had to be used. The term he uses is "scroll," which normally had writing only on its smooth inner side. In the second century of our era the codex came into use; a codex consisted of individual leaves held together on one side in the form of a book. But the codex was not yet in use at the time of the writing of the Apocalypse. Also, we cannot expect that as an exile on a barren island John could have made use of a codex. Although individual leaves have writing on both sides, this kind of book would not fit John's observation of the scroll that had writing "on the inside and on the back." The volume is a scroll and not a codex as a manuscript in book form.[2] Prior to and during the first century, scrolls with writing on both sides were in use for both private and public purposes. They were called *opisthographs* (writing on the back; see Ezek. 2:9–10). John's account parallels an Old Testament prophecy of Ezekiel, but there is a remarkable difference.

Compare the verses.

Ezekiel 2:9–10	**Revelation 5:1**
Then I looked, and I saw a hand stretched out to me. In it was a scroll, which he unrolled before me. On both sides of it were written words of lament and mourning and woe.	And I saw in the right hand of the one sitting on the throne a scroll written on the inside and on the back sealed with seven seals.

In Ezekiel's vision, the scroll in the hand of God is not sealed but is spread out before him by God himself and is given directly to the prophet (Ezek. 2:9–10). By contrast, the scroll that John saw is sealed with seven seals. Only the Lamb is able to take it from the hand of God, and then by breaking the seven seals he opens it (vv. 1, 3, 5, 7, 9, 12; 8:1).[3]

Scrolls were made of either papyrus leaves grown in the Nile delta of Egypt or animal skins. They varied in length to accommodate the needs of the writer; for instance, the size of Paul's letter to the Romans and his letter to Philemon filled scrolls of 11½ feet and 1 foot respectively.[4] We are not told about the extent of this heavenly scroll, but the volume of writing on both sides may suggest a scroll of considerable length.

Another explanation is that of a document that was written twice: the first document was sealed with seven seals and the second one with the same text was unsealed and could be read (see Jer. 32:9–15). This procedure was common in the ancient world and such copies have been found; both the Greeks and the Ro-

2. Ernest B. Allo, *Saint Jean l'Apocalypse,* Études bibliques (Paris: Gabalda, 1921), p. 60.
3. Consult Richard Bauckham, *The Climax of Prophecy* (Edinburgh: Clark, 1993), p. 246.
4. William Barclay, *The Revelation of John,* 2d ed. (Philadelphia: Westminster, 1960), 1:208.

mans made use of such legal documents.[5] These manuscripts were sealed in the presence of seven witnesses. The similarity to the scroll in the hand of God is undeniable, but the objections to its explanation remain critical.

David Aune provides the following objections: First, a doubly written document had a summary statement on the outside, which anyone could read. This would make the sealing of the document unnecessary. Next, the contents of the second unsealed scroll are open to everyone, so that God's seven seals would lose their purpose. Why would John write the words "no one could be found to open the scroll and look inside it" (v. 4), if the unsealed document could be read? Third, there is no mention of seven witnesses in the scroll written on the inside and on the back in the Apocalypse. And last, the preferred reading of the text is "a scroll written on the inside and on the back," which fits our explanation, while the secondary reading "a scroll written on the inside and on the outside" suits the doubly written document theory.[6]

b. *Message of the Scroll.* First, the scroll lying visibly in the hand of God testifies that he is its author. Next, writing appears on its backside to such a degree that not a single line could be added. The extent of the written output is so voluminous that it comprises God's complete plan. Third, as the two tablets of stone on both sides had the writing of God (Exod. 32:15–16) as a symbol of completeness, so the scroll on both sides had God's writing of completeness. The opening of the seals in chapter 6 reveals that the contents of the scroll refer to a period of indefinite history. That is, the scroll reveals God's complete plan and purpose for the entire world throughout the ages from beginning to end. For us, the scroll with its seals is evidence of what God planned for the salvation of his people. This plan is a foreordained mystery, according to Paul, and is revealed in the fullness of time (Eph. 1:9–11; 3:9–11). Peter also speaks of this mystery of salvation through Christ and adds that angels long to look into it (1 Pet. 1:10–12).[7] God's plan of salvation is the coming of his kingdom to contest Satan's rule and to proclaim God as "the Lord God Almighty, who was, and who is, and who is to come" to establish his kingdom. I, therefore, conclude that the contents of the

5. O. Roller, "Das Buch mit den sieben Siegeln," *ZNW* 36 (1937): 98–113; R. H. Charles, *A Critical and Exegetical Commentary on the Revelation of St. John*, ICC (Edinburgh: Clark, 1920), 1:137. See Adela Yarbro Collins, *The Combat Myth in the Book of Revelation*, HDR 9 (Missoula: Scholars Press, 1976), p. 22.

6. David E. Aune, *Revelation 1–5*, WBC 52A (Dallas: Word, 1997), pp. 342–43; Colin J. Hemer, *Letters to the Seven Churches of Asia in Their Local Setting*, JSNTSup 11 (Sheffield: JSOT, 1986), pp. 218–19. Consult Gerhard A. Krodel (*Revelation*, ACNT [Minneapolis: Augsburg, 1989], pp. 161–62), who notes the difficulty of writing on the back side of an opisthograph. The papyrus fibers run horizontally (recto) on the one side and vertically (verso) on the other, which creates problems for writing neatly.

7. Refer to Homer Hailey, *Revelation: An Introduction and Commentary* (Grand Rapids: Baker, 1979), pp. 179–80; S. Greijdanus, *De Openbaring des Heeren aan Johannes*, KNT (Amsterdam: Van Bottenburg, 1925), pp. 132–33; Herman Hoeksema, *Behold, He Cometh! An Exposition of the Book of Revelation* (Grand Rapids: Reformed Free Publishing Association, 1969), pp. 166–68; William Hendriksen, *More Than Conquerors* (reprint, Grand Rapids: Baker, 1982), p. 89.

scroll pertain to God's secret purpose of establishing his kingdom on earth until the fullness of his glory is revealed.[8]

c. *Position of the Seven Seals.* Commentators are unable to explain with any degree of satisfaction how one can break the first seal and then read the document still firmly closed with six seals. Only when all seven are broken can the scroll be read. I suggest that John presents the general picture first and afterward relates the details. He speaks symbolically and does not expect his readers to interpret his words literally. Thus, he writes about opening the scroll, followed by the breaking of the seven seals (v. 2). John states the fact that the scroll is sealed and expects the reader to understand that when the Lamb takes the scroll out of God's right hand, Jesus breaks all the seals. Afterward John continues by elucidating what lies behind each seal.[9] In short, John expects the reader to fill in the details after the Lamb has broken the seven seals all at once.

d. *Symbolism of the Sealed Scroll.* The sealed scroll John presents is a symbol, which becomes evident when we read, first, that all available space on both sides of the document has been filled (something first-century scribes rarely did). Second, the Greek participle "sealed" is in a compound form to denote perfection: it is thoroughly sealed. In a word the picture John presents is permanence.[10] And last, the number seven represents completeness. John conveys the impression that the scroll with seven seals was completely sealed.

2. And I saw a mighty angel proclaiming in a loud voice, "Who is worthy to open the scroll, that is, to break its seals?" 3. And no one in heaven or on the earth or under the earth was able to open the scroll or look inside it.

The mighty angel spoke in a loud voice so that everyone throughout creation could hear him (for other appearances of a *mighty* angel, see 10:1 and 18:21). Notice the present tense of the participle "proclaiming" to indicate that he continued to call for anyone to step up to the throne of God. The implication is that no one touched by sin could approach the throne. Only those who are worthy may come. The emphasis on the term *worthy* is significant, for in the Apocalypse it is used exclusively of God and Jesus (4:11; 5:9, 12). The adjective does not mean "able." Ability refers to strength and skill, whereas worthiness relates to qualification for the purpose of fulfilling a task.

In all creation, no one can be found with the qualifications to open the scroll and break its seals. Incidentally, breaking the seals occurs prior to opening the scrolls; but John repeatedly reverses the logical sequence we expect.[11] In other words, the task is not merely the breaking of seals but the effective control of the

8. Consult Richard Bauckham, *Climax of Prophecy*, p. 249; see also his *Theology of the Book of Revelation*, New Testament Theology (Cambridge: Cambridge University Press, 1993), p. 80.

9. Gregory K. Beale (*The Book of Revelation: A Commentary on the Greek Text*, NIGTC [Grand Rapids: Eerdmans, 1998], p. 347) writes, "Indeed, the possible backgrounds of the 'book' show that such a progressive revealing may not be odd at all."

10. R. C. H. Lenski, *The Interpretation of St. John's Revelation* (Columbus: Wartburg, 1943), p. 192.

11. E.g., Rev. 3:3, 17; 10:4, 9; 22:14.

consequences of that action. The angel calls to those who dwell in all the parts of God's creation: in heaven, on the earth, and under the earth (see Exod. 20:4; Phil. 2:10). He wants to know if there is any creature anywhere worthy of breaking the seals and looking inside the scroll, that is, of reading it. The question arises whether a mighty archangel (Gabriel or Michael) could not have responded to the call. But angels are mere messengers who obediently listen to God's commands and fulfill them. They are unworthy because they cannot redeem fallen angels, not even to mention fallen humanity.

German theologian Zacharias Ursinus in 1563 asked the question, "Can there be found anywhere a mere creature able to satisfy for us?" He answered, "None; for, first, God will not punish any other creature for the sin man has committed; and, further, no mere creature can sustain the burden of God's eternal wrath against sin, and deliver others from it."[12]

When John writes the words "in heaven or on the earth or under the earth," he is not presenting a pagan view of a trilevel universe. Rather he conveys the picture of the totality of God's creation, that is, all angels and saints in heaven; all human beings on earth; and all fallen angels and people consigned to hell (Phil. 2:10; compare also Exod. 20:4; Deut. 5:8).[13]

4. And I was bursting into tears, because no one could be found to open the scroll and look inside it. 5. And one of the elders was saying to me, "Weep not; look, the lion of the tribe of Judah, the root of David, has overcome. He is able to open the scroll and its seven seals."

John shed copious tears in a demonstration of profound grief because of the sealed scroll that held the key to redemption of God's people. If the scroll remained sealed, God's plan of salvation would not be executed and the human race would be condemned forever.

No one in the entire universe was coming forward to answer the angel's call, break the seals, and open the scroll. No human being or angel was worthy; indeed their silence testified to their unworthiness. Even though human beings have tried and are trying repeatedly to bring about their own salvation, their obvious failure disqualifies them. Consequently, if the scroll remained closed, God's curse would continue to rest on sinful humanity, creation would not be set free from the bondage of decay (Rom. 8:21), and suffering would last interminably.

But note that one of the elders as representative of redeemed humanity addresses John (see 7:13). He tells him to stop weeping and focus his attention on "the lion of the tribe of Judah, the root of David, [who] has overcome." The verb *overcome* conveys good news. It links this verse to the letters to the seven churches, which have the recurring refrain "the one who overcomes" (e.g., 2:7), and also to Jesus who says "I have overcome" (3:21; John 16:33). This verb implies that

12. Heidelberg Catechism, Q. and A. 14.

13. See William Hendriksen, *Exposition of Philippians*, NTC (Grand Rapids: Baker, 1962), p. 115 n. 95.

Jesus is the conqueror over death and hell, the firstfruits of the dead, and the King who ascended to heaven and sits at God's right hand. As the conqueror, Jesus is worthy to break the seals and unroll the document. As the author of salvation, he received the honor and distinction to take the scroll out of God's hand and open it.

John uses Old Testament language to depict Jesus: "the lion of the tribe of Judah" is an echo of Jacob's words. The patriarch blessed his twelve sons and singled out Judah as the tribe from which a ruler should come forth. Jacob said to Judah, "You are a lion's cub, O Judah. . . . The scepter will not depart from Judah, nor the ruler's staff from between his feet, until he comes to whom it belongs, and the obedience of the nations is his" (Gen. 49:9–10; compare Heb. 7:14).[14] John calls Jesus "the root of David," which goes back to the prophets' saying that the Messiah will come up from the stump of Jesse and this root or branch of David will rule the peoples (Isa. 11:1, 10; Jer. 23:5; 33:15; Zech. 3:8). Jesus represents royalty, for these are messianic titles that attest to his royal status. As a descendant of David (Matt. 22:41–45) Jesus is human, and as Messiah he is divine.[15] He is worthy because of his role as mediator, and he is able because of his divinity. He is the God-man, and he is the one and only.

There is no one else in the entire universe worthy and able to open the scroll after breaking its seven seals. The sequence in the Greek text is reversed, but John seems to suggest that Jesus broke all seven seals to have access to the message of the scroll. This is implied from the wording of a succeeding verse, "You are worthy to take the scroll and open its seals" (v. 9). The verbs *to break* and *to open* combine the thoughts of being both worthy of and competent for this task.

Greek Words, Phrases, and Constructions in 5:1–4

Verse 1

ἐπὶ τὴν δεξιάν—the preposition followed by the accusative case signifies the place on which the scroll is found: on the right hand of God. Most English translations read "in the right hand," which could be interpreted not as enclosed by the hand but as lying on it (compare 1:20).

ὄπισθεν—instead of "on the back" a number of secondary manuscripts (TR, Latin, some Syriac and Coptic) have ἔξωθεν, "on the outside." Greek New Testaments feature the primary reading.

κατεσφραγισμένον—the prefix κατά of the compound intensifies the meaning of the participle. It is the perfective sense of the preposition, "thoroughly sealed."[16]

---

14. See SB, 3:801.

15. Consult Robert L. Thomas, *Revelation 1–7: An Exegetical Commentary* (Chicago: Moody, 1992), p. 388.

16. See A. T. Robertson, *A Grammar of the Greek New Testament in the Light of Historical Research* (Nashville: Broadman, 1934), p. 606; Thomas, *Revelation 1–7*, p. 380 n. 24.

Verses 3–4

In both verses the imperfect indicative tense occurs in the verbs ἐδύνατο (was able) and ἔκλαιον (I was weeping). They express continued action in the past.

---

3. Praise to the Lamb
5:6–14

The four living creatures praised God for his holiness and eternity and ascribed to him glory, honor, and thanksgiving. The twenty-four elders also sang his praises extolling him for his work of creation (4:8–11). Now the focus shifts from the one who sits on the throne to the Lamb who stands in the center of the throne. The Lamb is the one whom the four living beings and the twenty-four elders adore with songs of loudest praise. Three times in succession the heavenly companies jubilantly express their praises to the Lamb. First, the four living beings with the twenty-four elders sing a new song; then, innumerable angels sing in a loud voice glorifying the Lamb; and last, all the creatures that God has made ascribe praise, honor, glory, and power to the one who sits on the throne and to the Lamb. The conclusion is an amen from the four living creatures and worship from the elders.

6. And I saw in the midst of the throne and of the four living creatures, and in the midst of the elders a Lamb standing as though it had been slain. He had seven horns and seven eyes, which are the seven spirits of God that are sent out into all the earth.

a. "And I saw in the midst of the throne and of the four living creatures, and in the midst of the elders a Lamb standing as though it had been slain." The subject in this sentence is the Lamb, not the lion of the tribe of Judah nor the root or branch of David. The Lamb is the symbol of the lamb slain for the Passover feast of the Israelites. The blood of the lamb had to be put on the sides and top of the doorframes of their homes, so that the angel of death would pass over the Israelites and spare the lives of their firstborn (Exod. 12:1–13). Also, the Lamb is symbolized in the lamb that was led to the slaughter and stricken for the transgression of his people (Isa. 53:7–8; Acts 8:32). John the Baptist twice designates Jesus as the Lamb of God (John 1:29, 36). And last, Peter refers to the redeemed who were set free "with the precious blood of Christ, a lamb without blemish or defect" (1 Pet. 1:19).

Yet the symbol of the Lamb also depicts Jesus as leader and ruler. He is enthroned and sits on the throne of God (Rev. 7:17; 22:1, 3). As the Lamb, he occupies the throne and expresses his wrath to all his enemies (6:16).[17]

The Lamb was standing as though it had been slain, which signifies a body that had been cut to pieces but now was healed and able to stand. The marks of his wounds are still visible, as they were when Thomas was told to look at Jesus' hands and touch the scar in his side (John 20:27). The Lamb stood at the center

---

17. Consult Aune, *Revelation 1–5*, pp. 368–69.

of God's throne, slain, yet triumphant.[18] But how do we visualize the place Jesus occupied "in the midst of the throne and of the four living creatures, and in the midst of the elders"? This may be a Hebraic idiom (see Lev. 27:12 LXX): "Where we say 'between A and B,' Hebrew says 'between A and between B.'"[19] The Lamb was standing between the throne and the four living creatures on the one hand and between the throne and the elders on the other. This explanation finds support in verse 7, which says that the Lamb came and took the scroll out of the hand of him sitting on the throne. Elsewhere John places "the Lamb at the center of the throne" (7:17). But here the locale of the Lamb has no reference whatever to other beings. And last, in the letter to the Laodiceans Jesus notes that he sits on the throne (3:21), yet here he stands for the purpose of coming toward God and taking the scroll out of his hand.[20]

b. "He had seven horns and seven eyes, which are the seven spirits of God sent out into all the earth." The threefold use of the number seven emphasizes the symbol of completeness with respect to the Lamb. The horn is the symbol of might (e.g., see 17:12; Deut. 33:17), and with this might Jesus as King of kings promotes righteousness and justice. With seven horns he possesses all authority to rule in heaven and on earth (Matt. 28:18; John 17:2). With complete eyesight—seven eyes—he is able to observe everything that happens in the universe; nothing escapes his notice. Because of full vision he has perfect knowledge, discernment, and understanding; these are the eyes of the Lord that range throughout the entire world (2 Chron. 16:9; Job 24:23; Prov. 15:3; Jer. 16:17; Zech. 3:9; 4:10).

John provides an explanation of the significance of *seven eyes.* They are the seven spirits of God commissioned by him. Earlier we remarked that the expression *seven spirits* refers to the fullness of the Holy Spirit (see the commentary on 1:4; 3:1; 4:5). Both the Father and the Son commission the Spirit to go forth into all the earth (John 14:26; 15:26; 16:7; Gal. 4:6). Indeed, Jesus commissions the Holy Spirit to do the work of making known the Son of God and his message of redemption in all parts of the world. Here is an indirect reference to the outpouring of the Holy Spirit at Pentecost, in whose power the apostles were sent forth "to the ends of the earth" (Acts 1:8). The perfect tense of the Greek participle *sent* indicates the continuing presence and work of the Holy Spirit in the hearts and lives of God's people.

---

18. Refer to Donald Guthrie, "The Lamb in the Structure of the Book of Revelation," *VoxEv* 12 (1981): 64–71.

19. G. B. Caird, *A Commentary on the Revelation of St. John the Divine* (London: Black, 1966), p. 76; See also Charles, *Revelation,* 1:140; Aune, *Revelation 1–5,* p. 352; Greijdanus, *Openbaring,* p. 136; Henry Alford, *James–Revelation,* vol. 4, part 2 of *Alford's Greek Testament* (1875; reprint, Grand Rapids: Guardian, 1976), p. 607; Friedrich Düsterdieck, *Critical and Exegetical Handbook to the Revelation of John* (New York and London: Funk and Wagnalls, 1886), p. 209.

20. Some commentators (e.g., Thomas, *Revelation 1–7,* pp. 389–90; Swete, *Revelation,* p. 78) see the position of the Lamb at the centerpiece of concentric circles.

7. And he came and took the scroll out of the right hand of him who is sitting on the throne.

The Lamb came toward God seated on the throne (see the explanation of v. 6). He moved to the throne from his standing position between the four living creatures and the elders. From the right hand of God he took the scroll. Even though the expression *the scroll* occurs five times in the first five verses of this chapter, here in the Greek text the word is omitted and must be supplied. By omitting it the emphasis falls on the Lamb and not on the scroll.

It is the *right hand* of the one sitting on the throne[21] that supplies the scroll to the Lamb, connoting that God entrusts him with the authority to bring its contents to realization (compare 1:1). The right hand in oriental culture signifies success, while the left hand denotes something sinister. The Lamb is empowered to break the seals and open the scroll (see v. 9a).

8. And when he took the scroll, the four living creatures and the twenty-four elders fell before the Lamb. Each had a harp and golden bowls full of incense, which are the prayers of the saints.

a. "And when he took the scroll, the four living creatures and the twenty-four elders fell before the Lamb." The one and only person in the entire universe who is worthy and able to take the scroll from the hand of God is the Lamb. And when he takes the scroll and presumably breaks the seals to open it, the four living beings and the twenty-four elders as representatives of the angel world and redeemed humanity fall in worship before the Lamb.[22] They acknowledge his power and authority; they are jubilant that the contents of the scroll are now being revealed; they delight in the realization of God's plan and purpose; and they rejoice in the salvation of his people.

b. "Each had a harp and golden bowls full of incense." The angels and elders vocalize their song accompanied by a harp that each one of the elders possesses. Greek grammar favors the elders and not the four living creatures holding a harp and bowls. In addition, harps were held not by angels but by the Levites at worship (1 Chron. 25:1, 6); and elders not angels fulfill priestly duties. Yet all of them sing with the accompaniment of harps. We ought not to think of modern harps but rather of a "rectangular or trapezoidal instrument . . . with an average of eight to nine strings."[23] Scripture refers to the harp and lyre in both Old and New Testaments (2 Chron. 29:25; Ps. 33:2; 71:22; 92:3; 98:5; 147:7; 149:3; 150:3; Rev. 14:2; 15:2). The Jews used the harp as a conventional instrument for accompanying the singing of the Psalms. This is evident from the numerous references to it in the Psalter.

21. The phrase "the one who sits on the throne" occurs repeatedly in the Apocalypse: 4:2, 3, 9; 5:1, 13; 6:16; 7:10, 15; 19:4; 20:11; 21:5.

22. Although the text leaves out the verb "to worship," the word is implied, as is evident from verse 14 where it is used in combination with "to fall."

23. See Daniel A. Foxvog and Anne D. Kilmer, "Music," *ISBE*, 3:440. Consult also Harold M. Best and David K. Huttar, *ZPEB*, 4:320.

God instructed the Israelites to make bowls of pure gold for service in the tabernacle: "And make its plates and dishes of pure gold, as well as its pitchers and bowls for the pouring out of offerings" (Exod. 25:29; see also 37:16). These bowls were also used in the temple of Solomon (2 Chron. 4:22); they were taken to Babylon (2 Kings 24:13) and were eventually returned to Jerusalem (Ezra 1:10). The bowls were flat objects in the form of a pan or saucer to hold incense.[24]

c. "Which are the prayers of the saints." John provides an interpretation of the bowls of incense, relying on the Old Testament for the explanation. In one of his psalms David prays to God and says, "May my prayer be set before you like incense" (Ps. 141:2; see also Rev. 8:3). Are the prayers those of the saints in heaven or on the earth? The saints under the altar are calling out to God to judge those people who are hostile to him and to avenge those slain for his cause (6:10). If we limit the prayers to the saints in heaven, we are too restrictive. We must include the petitions and praises of thanksgiving from the saints on earth.

The expression *saints* occurs frequently in Acts, the Epistles, and Revelation; it means "the holy ones." In the Old Testament holy ones are God's companions (Dan. 7:21–22), but in the New Testament they are those who have been sanctified through Jesus Christ. The saints partake of God's holiness by entering into fellowship with him.[25]

9. And they sang a new song, saying,

> **"You are worthy to take the scroll and open its seals,**
> **because you were slain**
> **and with your blood you bought [men and women] for God**
> **out of every tribe and language and**
> **people and nation**
> **10. and you made them for our God**
> **a kingdom and priests,**
> **and they will rule upon the earth."**

a. "And they sang a new song." This is the first of the three hymns that exalt the Lamb for his redemptive work on the cross. The other two hymns are sung respectively by the angels and all creatures. Who are the singers of this first hymn? At least one scholar states that they are the twenty-four elders because they have harps.[26] Another argument is the reading of the line "you bought [men and women] for God," which in the TR reads, "you bought us for God" (see KJV, NKJV). The four living beings are unable to say that the Lamb had bought them with his blood. But these are questionable arguments grammatically and textually. Scholarly opinion favors the inclusion of the four living crea-

24. The Greek word φιάλη (bowl) appears only in Revelation (5:8; 15:7; 16:1, 2, 3, 4, 8, 10, 12, 17; 17:1; 21:9).

25. Refer to Horst Balz, *EDNT*, 1:20.

26. Charles, *Revelation*, 1:146.

tures, because with the elders they fell before the throne in worship (v. 8) and would be expected to express their worship in song.

Twenty-eight voices sing a new song. The adjective *new* suggests that the new has come forth out of the old as a separate entity. The Old Testament lists new songs celebrating God's wondrous deeds (Ps. 33:3; 40:3; 96:1; 98:1; 144:9; Isa. 42:10). But in the Apocalypse, the singers extol the redemption of God's people through the atonement of Jesus Christ. They praise not the one sitting on the throne but the Lamb who has accomplished his redemptive task. The Lamb deserves jubilant praise, because he triumphed over Satan by dying for the redeemed purchased from every tribe, language, people, and nation. The song is new not only "in point of time, but more important, it is new and distinctive in quality."[27] The Lamb is worthy of the highest praise.

b. "You are worthy to take the scroll and open its seals, because you were slain and with your blood you bought [men and women] for God out of every tribe and language and people and nation." The Lamb is worthy because of his willing sacrifice of his own life on the cross. His death was not a random casualty or an unavoidable tragedy. He voluntarily gave up his life to pay the penalty for sin, to satisfy God's justice, to remove the curse, to reconcile the world to God, and to restore his people to true fellowship with God (14:4; 1 Pet. 1:18–19). Because of his sacrificial death, the Lamb is worthy to take the scroll out of God's hand, to break its seals, and to make its contents reality (Rev. 13:8; Isa. 53:7).

The Lamb slain to redeem his people symbolizes the voluntary sacrifice of the crucified Christ[28] and at the same time the supremacy of the exalted Christ. As we shall see later, one of the heads of the beast coming up out of the sea was slain as a parody of Jesus' death (13:3). The difference is that Christ rose from the dead, while the beast is consigned eternally to the lake of fire (19:20). By shedding his lifeblood and dying on the cross, Christ Jesus paid for the sins of his people and set them free. By contrast, the beast, having suffered a fatal blow to one of his seven heads, enslaves his followers and continues to attack God, his name, his dwelling place, and his people (13:5–8).

Christ Jesus bought his people with his blood shed at Calvary. He did not pay Satan to redeem them, but with his death on the cross he satisfied the justice of God. He paid the penalty that God had placed on Adam and Eve and their descendants (Gen. 2:17) and set them free. God's people owe Jesus "an overwhelming religious debt" for his willingness to pay the price for their redemption.[29]

27. Robert H. Mounce, *The Book of Revelation*, rev. ed., NICNT (Grand Rapids: Eerdmans, 1977), p. 135.

28. Otto Michel (*TDNT*, 7:934 n. 42) notes that Christ's crucifixion "does not bear any close relation to slaughtering, so that theological interpretation rather than the historical event gives rise to the image of the slaughtered Lamb." See Elisabeth Schüssler Fiorenza, *The Book of Revelation: Justice and Judgment* (Philadelphia: Fortress, 1985), p. 73. Yet the historical fact of Christ's death on the cross as expressed in the Greek aorist tense of *esphagēs* (you were slain) remains unaltered.

29. Bauckham, *Theology*, p. 62.

The phrase "out of every tribe and language and people and nation" occurs repeatedly in Revelation with variations in word order (7:9; 10:11; 11:9; 13:7; 14:6; 17:15). The word *tribe* conveys the meaning of physical ties and descent, while the term *language* has a much broader connotation and points to linguistic communication. The word that I have translated as *people* relates to an ethnic group of common descent; and the expression *nation* refers to a political entity with distinct geographic boundaries. But because of the frequent appearance of these four categories in Revelation, it is better to interpret them as an all-encompassing idiom.[30] Jesus calls his followers, both Jews and Gentiles, from every possible place on the face of this earth, so that his people are the church universal.

c. "And you made them for our God a kingdom and priests, and they will rule upon the earth." Here is a parallel to the words in 1:6, "and made us a kingdom and priests to his God and Father," and 20:6, "they will be priests of God and of Christ and will reign with him a thousand years." John relies on Exodus 19:6, where God tells the people of Israel that they are to be for him a holy nation and a kingdom of priests (Isa. 61:6). As God called the Israelites to be a special people in their time, so he addresses his people today and instructs them to be citizens in his kingdom and serve him as dedicated priests. This charge is for time and eternity, for this present life and the life to come. The present rule of the saints on earth will continue with Christ on the renewed earth.

The text expresses three points: first, those who have been purchased are placed in God's kingdom; next, they are made priests; and last, they are given the privilege of ruling as kings.[31] The text reads that the Lamb *made* them priests, that is, they are priests already and are in the kingdom now and certainly in the future. Through their prayers, they even now rule on the earth.

11. And I looked and I heard the voice of many angels around the throne, the living creatures, and the elders. And their number was myriads of myriads and thousands of thousands.

John uses his senses of sight and sound as he is permitted to observe and hear in heaven countless angels surrounding God's throne. They form the second category of beings that sing praises to the Lamb. In concentric circles around the throne there are the four living beings, then the twenty-four elders, and last the innumerable multitude of angels (see 7:11, where the reverse order starts from the outside in and not from the inside out). Certainly the four living beings are angelic, but here the countless aggregation of angels is mentioned. We are told that their number is *myriads of myriads,* which literally translated is "ten thousands of ten thousands." It is better to think in terms of an immense number that no one can count. Also, the addition "thousands upon thousands" does not refer

30. Apparently, John uses the phraseology of Daniel 3:4 (Old Greek and Theod.), "nations and lands, languages and tribes." See Aune, *Revelation 1–5,* p. 361; Beale, *Revelation,* p. 359. Leon Morris (*Revelation,* rev. ed., TNTC [Leicester: Inter-Varsity; Grand Rapids: Eerdmans, 1987], p. 97) voices his objection because the wording in the two documents is not identical. But John writes the fourfold phrase seven times with variations. See Bauckham, *Climax of Prophecy,* p. 326.

31. Consult Düsterdieck, *Revelation,* p. 214.

to a lesser number but rather must be understood as a parallel to the "myriads of myriads" (see also *1 Clem.* 34.6).

John derives his wording from Daniel 7:10, where the seer records his vision of the attendants surrounding God's throne: "Thousands upon thousands attended him; ten thousand times ten thousand stood before him." We are not told anything about the outward appearance of these angelic hosts or any of their functions. What stands out in this verse is the vast multitudes of heavenly messengers (Heb. 12:22).[32]

12. They were saying in a loud voice,
"Worthy is the Lamb that was slain to receive
power and wealth and wisdom and strength
and honor and glory and thanksgiving."

No mention is made of harps or other musical instruments. We may assume that the heavenly host sang, but the text reads that they uttered a loud shout in unison so that the sound came as one voice.

The wording of this second hymn expresses much the same thoughts as the hymn sung by the four living creatures and the twenty-four elders (vv. 9–10). But the angels have no need of redemption; they have learned from the church about the mystery of salvation (Eph. 3:10; 1 Pet. 1:12). They stand in awe at the wonder of God's redeeming love in Christ Jesus. They are the ones who rejoice in heaven when one sinner on earth repents and cries out to God for mercy (Luke 15:7, 10). They are sent out as God's messengers (Ps. 104:4; Heb. 1:7), and they are servants of the saints who are to inherit salvation (Heb. 1:14). They sing loudest praises to the Lamb, for they themselves have an integral part in the process of salvation by conveying divine messages to God's people.

Thus the angels compose and sing a hymn, dedicated not to God but to the Lamb. Their song is more compact and even richer in attributes than the hymn sung by the cherubim and elders. It is unique because of its sevenfold construction: it lists seven nouns in succession that are ascribed to the Lamb: power, wealth, wisdom, strength, honor, glory, and thanksgiving. Seven is the number of completeness (compare 7:12). The four living creatures ascribed glory, honor, and thanksgiving to God seated on the throne (4:9), and the twenty-four elders do the same thing except that instead of *thanksgiving* they use the term *power* (4:11). Note, however, that the heavenly beings once call God worthy because of his work of creation, but twice they name the Lamb worthy because of his redemptive work (4:11 and 5:9, 12 respectively).

Some scholars divide the seven attributes into objective qualities (power, wealth, wisdom, and strength) and subjective qualities (honor, glory, and thanksgiving).[33] Even though this demarcation has merit, the question is whether John wished to convey a division of qualities. For instance, glory is a

32. On the background of Daniel 7 refer to Beale, *Revelation*, pp. 366–69.

33. Lenski, *Revelation*, p. 210; Greijdanus, *Openbaring*, p. 142.

heavenly attribute that people observe but are unable to increase. By contrast, honor is the act of people paying respect; and the act of thanksgiving "evokes man's thankful response for benefits received."[34] All the other qualities belong to God and the Lamb.

This song has its origin in heaven, yet the individual words reveal acquaintance with an Old Testament doxology composed by David: "Yours, O LORD, is the greatness and the power and the glory and the majesty and the splendor. . . . Wealth and honor come from you; you are the ruler of all things. In your hands are strength and power to exalt and give strength to all. Now, our God, we give you thanks and praise your glorious name" (1 Chron. 29:11–12). Hence the Old Testament is the basis for the New Testament, reflected even in this angelic hymn.

Qualities that belong to God are now ascribed to the Lamb. These qualities are power as inner strength; wealth that comes from God; and wisdom that God freely gives to his people. *Strength* is a synonym of *power*, and *honor* and *glory* frequently appear as a pair (e.g., Ps. 8:5). God grants these qualities to his people, and they in turn express their thanksgiving to him and the Lamb.

13. And every creature in heaven and on earth and under the earth and on the sea, and all things in them I heard saying,

> **"To the one sitting on the throne and to the**
> **Lamb**
> **be thanksgiving and honor and glory and**
> **power forever and ever."**

After the four living beings and the twenty-four elders have sung and similarly the countless angels, a third group of creatures utters a song of praise. This third group sums up the rest of God's created beings; the wording is a repetition of verse 3 with the addition of the two phrases "and on the sea, and all things in them" (see Exod. 20:11; Ps. 146:6). The last phrase comprises the totality of God's creatures, for nothing has been left out. I interpret the phraseology to be poetic language designed to incorporate everything God has made, for we cannot expect Satan and his followers in hell to utter praises to God.[35]

All intelligent beings in God's created universe sing his praises: the saints and angels in heaven, the birds in the sky, God's people on earth, and all living beings on land and in the sea. The overwhelming chorus of all these voices, in praise to God and to the Lamb, defies human imagination. God is the King of creation who delegated the work of creation and redemption to his Son. As God receives tribute from his creatures, so does the Lamb, for he has completed the tasks that God assigned to him.

---

34. Thomas, *Revelation 1–7*, p. 406.

35. Alford, *Revelation*, p. 611; George Eldon Ladd, *Commentary on the Revelation of John* (Grand Rapids: Eerdmans, 1972), p. 93. Compare Barclay, *Revelation of John*, 1:228–29.

All intelligent beings in the entire universe sing praises "to the one sitting on the throne and to the Lamb." The names *God* and *Jesus* are not mentioned. Instead the appellations *the one* and *the Lamb* show full respect to the Deity. They emphasize, first, God's absolute power over the universe and, second, the Lamb's victory over death and the grave. The hymn they sing is an affirmation and summary of those sung earlier (4:11; 5:12). This doxology evokes an affirmative "amen" from the representatives that surround God's throne.

14. And the four living creatures were saying, "Amen." And the elders fell and worshiped.

The four living creatures that are closest to the throne utter their affirmation by saying, "So be it!" Speaking on behalf of the rest of creation, they address God. They were the first to sing a hymn to God (4:8); they conclude the hymnody with a solemn "amen," which they utter again and again.

The elders pay homage to God and the Lamb by prostrating themselves before them. Theirs is the concluding act of praise and adoration. The writer of the Apocalypse is now ready to record the breaking of the seals and the opening of the scroll, and to reveal what is happening on the earth.

Greek Words, Phrases, and Constructions in 5:6–10

Verse 6

ἀρνίον—in the Apocalypse, this noun occurs twenty-eight times referring to Jesus, and once it appears denoting the beast coming up out of the earth (13:11). The synonym ἀμνός spoken by John the Baptist occurs only twice in Johannine literature (John 1:29, 36). Jesus uses the word ἀρνίον once when he tells Peter to feed his lambs (John 21:15). This word seems to have been precious to John.

ἑστηκός—this neuter perfect tense of the participle is translated as a present: "standing." The variant of the masculine perfect ἑστηκώς may have resulted from faulty hearing of the letters ο and ω.

The participle ἐσφαγμένον is an effective perfect of an action that occurred in the past with significance for the present. Similarly, the perfect passive participle ἀπεσταλμένοι denotes an action that happened in the past but has lasting significance for the present, "sent out." The masculine gender, as the harder reading, is preferred to the neuter reading, which is an adaptation to the preceding noun πνεύματα (spirits).

Verse 7

εἴληφεν—the perfect active of the verb λαμβάνω (I take, receive) should be understood as an aoristic perfect, "he took."[36]

---

36. Friedrich Blass and Albert Debrunner, *A Greek Grammar of the New Testament,* trans. and rev. Robert Funk (Chicago: University of Chicago Press, 1961), §343.1; James H. Moulton, *A Grammar of New Testament Greek* (Edinburgh: Clark, 1908), 1:145; Robertson, *Grammar,* p. 897.

Verse 8

αἵ εἰσιν—the feminine plural pronoun has its antecedent in φιάλας (bowls) and not in the neuter noun θυμιαμάτων (incense). Yet not the bowls but the incense is explained.

Verse 9

τῷ θεῷ—the TR, Majority Text, and Merk add the pronoun ἡμᾶς, which appears to be an emendation of scribes who supplied a direct object for the verb "bought," that is, "you bought us for God." But the addition is awkward because of the pronoun "them" in verse 10, "you made them." The reading "us" in verse 10 has insufficient textual support.[37] Following the rule that the harder reading is more likely original, I adopt the Greek text that has no pronoun and thus no direct object for the verb "bought." I have supplied the direct object (men and women) in brackets.

Verse 10

βασιλεύσουσιν—the manuscript evidence for the future tense (they will reign) rivals that for the present tense (they reign). Even though most translators prefer the future, the present tense can be interpreted as a futuristic present. Similarly, the future can be understood as having progressive qualities (e.g., Phil 1:18) that begin in the present and continue in the future. The reading "we will reign" (NKJV) has little manuscript support and appears to be an adaptation.

---

37. Bruce M. Metzger, *A Textual Commentary on the Greek New Testament*, 2d ed. (Stuttgart: Deutsche Bibelgesellschaft, 1994), p. 666.

6

The First Six Seals

(6:1–17)

Outline (continued)

B. The Seven Seals (6:1–8:1)
   1. The First Seal: The White Horse (6:1–2)
   2. The Second Seal: The Red Horse (6:3–4)
   3. The Third Seal: The Black Horse (6:5–6)
   4. The Fourth Seal: The Pale Horse (6:7–8)
   5. The Fifth Seal: The Patience of the Saints (6:9–11)
   6. The Sixth Seal: The Day of the Lord (6:12–17)
      a. In Nature (6:12–14)
      b. Toward Unbelievers (6:15–17)

6 1 And I saw when the Lamb opened one of the seven seals, and I heard one of the four
living creatures saying with a voice like thunder: "Come." 2 And I saw, and look, a white
horse, and he that sat on it had a bow and a crown was given to him, and he went out conquering and to conquer.

3 And when he opened the second seal, I heard the second living creature say, "Come." 4 And
another horse went out, a red one. And to him who sat on it authority was given to take peace from
the earth, so that they might slay one another; and there was given to him a large sword.

5 And when he opened the third seal, I heard the third living creature say, "Come." And I saw,
and look, a black horse, and he that sat on it had a pair of scales in his hand. 6 And I heard as it were
a voice in the midst of the four living creatures saying, "A quart of wheat for a denarius and three
quarts of barley for a denarius, but do not damage the oil and the wine."

7 And when he opened the fourth seal, I heard the voice of the fourth living creature saying,
"Come." 8 And I saw, and look, a pale horse, and he that sat on it had the name Death, and Hades
followed after him. And there was given to them authority over the fourth part of the earth to kill
with a sword, and famine, and disease, and by the wild beasts of the earth.

9 And when he opened the fifth seal, I saw under the altar the souls of the ones slain because of
the word of God and because of the testimony they were holding. 10 And they cried with a loud voice
saying, "How long, O Sovereign Lord, holy and true, will you not judge and avenge our blood on
those that dwell on the earth?" 11 To each one of them was given a white robe, and they were told to
rest a little while longer until the number was completed of their fellow servants and their brothers
[and sisters] who were about to be killed as they were killed.

12 And I saw when he opened the sixth seal, and there was a great earthquake and the sun became black as sackcloth made of hair, and the whole moon became as blood. 13 And the stars of
heaven fell to the earth as a fig tree casts its unripe figs when shaken by a strong wind. 14 And the sky
was receding as a scroll when it is being rolled up, and every mountain and island were moved out
of their places. 15 And the kings of the earth, and the great men and generals, and the rich and the
strong, and every slave and free person hid themselves in the caves and among the rocks of the mountains. 16 And they said to the mountains and to the rocks, "Fall on us and hide us from the face of
the one seated on the throne and from the wrath of the Lamb." 17 For the great day of their wrath
has come, and who is able to stand?

B. The Seven Seals
6:1–8:1

The section on the seven seals covers chapter 6 and the first verse of chapter 8. Six seals are listed sequentially in chapter 6, and the seventh (8:1) serves as a call to be silent at the judgment of the wicked. Between the sixth and the seventh seals, chapter 7 functions as an interlude. There is a similar interlude in the section on the seven trumpets (see 10:1–11:14). Chapter 7 gives a description of the saints, that is, the church on earth and in heaven. The present chapter, however, describes the history of the world and the church. The account is not a historical sequence of events or a prophecy that refers only to the return of Christ. It incorporates the period between Christ's ascension and return during which the gospel advances to the ends of the earth, wars devastate its populations, famine causes endless suffering, and death is the constant companion of those who dwell on the earth.

Chapter 6 is divided into three parts. The first four seals form a unit that features the symbolical figures of four colored horses. The second segment portrays the souls under the altar and represents people who died for their faith in the Lord. And the last section depicts the judgment and the terror of those who reject Christ.

The time element in the unit on the four horses can be interpreted either sequentially or simultaneously, of which the second is preferred. For instance, conquest, warfare, famine, and death are concurrent events in any given age or era. In world history, fraught with violence in one form or another, the church occupies a central position, and its people repeatedly suffer the brunt of injury and injustice for their witness to the Lamb. The followers of the Lord must tread "the same path he has trod: the path of faithful witness to the truth even to the point of death."[1] The opening of the seals implies that the saints on earth suffer from the anti-Christian forces until the day of Christ's return. It is no wonder that the martyrs in heaven cry out to God for justice. They are told to exercise patience and know that God sovereignly controls world history. His wrath and that of the Lamb are directed against those who have expressed their enmity to God, his Word, and his people. These enemies must face the Judge. Yet at the judgment they want to avoid meeting him by calling on the mountains and the rocks to cover them. The sixth seal with all its symbolism reveals the end time when the Lord returns and the time of judgment has come.

The Lamb opens the seals one after the other, so that the events described pictorially in the scroll might be fulfilled. By breaking the seals and opening the scroll, the Lamb inaugurates God's plan and reveals what must take place in the times before and at his coming. By breaking the seals one by one, the Lamb is repeatedly shown to be the initiator of the events in this chapter.

1. The First Seal: The White Horse
6:1–2

1. And I saw when the Lamb opened one of the seven seals, and I heard one of the four living creatures saying with a voice like thunder: "Come."

a. "And I saw when the Lamb opened one of the seven seals." John is still looking into heaven at the throne of God where the Lamb is standing with the seven-sealed scroll in his hand. We are not told about the contents of the scroll in the hand of the Lamb; we are only shown pictures of what is taking place. In other words, every time the Lamb breaks a seal, he gives John a drawing—a picture is worth a thousand words—so that John can relate in writing the series of visions

1. Richard Bauckham, *The Theology of the Book of Revelation*, New Testament Theology (Cambridge: Cambridge University Press, 1993), p. 145.

he saw. Each picture conveys a general idea, with a motif filling a central place in the illustration. The first of the seven representations is part of the subcategory of the four horsemen and is followed by three other judgments.

b. "And I heard one of the four living creatures saying with a voice like thunder: 'Come.'" *One of the living creatures* does not necessarily mean the first one in importance. Each of the four utters the summons to come forth, even though the first one speaks with a voice like a thunderclap. The volume with which he speaks is meant to call everyone to pay attention to the command to come.

Who is the one addressed in this command? Most translations and commentators say that not John but the horse and its rider are called to come. If we say that John is summoned to come, we have difficulty seeing him cross the sea of glass and approach the Lamb in the center of the throne. Presumably the rider is addressed, even though we are not told where horse and rider have come from. In any case, not John but the rider and horse come onto the scene and go forth upon the earth.

2. And I saw, and look, a white horse, and he that sat on it had a bow and a crown was given to him, and he went out conquering and to conquer.

Except for the first phrase "and I saw, and look," all parts in this verse are open to diverse interpretations and have given rise to at least four explanations of the meaning of the rider: the Antichrist, the Parthians, Christ, and the gospel as the Word of God. These views are not of recent origin; the last one goes back to the early church.

a. *The Antichrist.* The predominant view is that the white horse as the first one in a set of four horses must be seen as part of a destructive force of war, famine, and death. The horse was used in warfare and the bow signifies a weapon to kill people. The crown denotes victory, which is underscored by the double use of the phrase "conquering and to conquer." And the color white points to the ancient custom of having the victor ride on a white horse at his return from battle. Further, the image of a rider on a white horse in chapter 6 can be seen as Satan's parody of Christ and his warriors riding on white horses in 19:11, 14. Chapter 6 depicts the authority of the Antichrist with respect to conquering, killing, and starving God's people to death, to the point that the saints in heaven implore God to intervene. But the rule of the Antichrist has limits. Chapter 19 reveals the conquering and victorious Christ who casts the Antichrist and the false prophet into the lake of fire. And last, the text reads, "and a crown was given to him," with the implication that God as the supplier has set limits for the Antichrist.

Much can be said in favor of this interpretation, but difficulties encumber it. First, the color white elsewhere in the New Testament and especially in Revelation always denotes holiness, purity, victory, and justice. It is not used to describe Satan, his helpers, or his works. True, Satan imitates God and his works,[2] so that he mas-

2. Mathias Rissi ("The Rider on the White Horse: A Study of Revelation 6:1–8," *Interp* 18 [1964]: 407–18) applies the white-colored horse, the crown, and the victory to the Antichrist who imitates Christ. See also Louis A. Vos, *The Synoptic Traditions in the Apocalypse* (Kampen: Kok, 1965), pp. 187–91; Gregory K. Beale, *The Book of Revelation: A Commentary on the Greek Text,* NIGTC (Grand Rapids: Eerdmans, 1998), p. 377.

querades as an angel of light (2 Cor. 11:14). Yet in the Apocalypse, John alerts the reader to a depiction of Satan's parodies, which is illustrated, for instance, in 13:3 where one of the beast's heads was slain as a travesty of Jesus' death. But the account of the rider on the white horse provides no hint of any satanic imitation.[3]

Next, a crown was given to the rider on the white horse. This means that God is the agent who gives the rider a crown, for throughout the Apocalypse the passive verb "was given" relates to both the servants and the enemies of God. Some scholars argue that this passive voice must refer to an evil power as the recipient of the crown.[4] But the term *crown* (Greek *stephanos*) applies to divine and redeemed figures: the redeemed (2:10; 3:11), the elders (4:4, 10), the woman who gave birth to the male child (12:1), and the Son of Man (14:14). The one exception is the reference to locusts that had something like crowns of gold on their heads (9:7), but resemblance is not the real thing.[5] The text, therefore, does not unequivocally state that the picture of the rider on a white horse portrays an evil force.

Third, the phrase *conquering and to conquer* in Revelation never pertains directly to Satan. Even though the verb *to conquer* refers twice to the beast in the employ of Satan (11:7; 13:7), the rest of its occurrences apply to Christ and the redeemed.[6] By contrast, despite all his cunning, Satan is a constant failure; for example, in one particular chapter (chap. 12) John depicts him as a loser five times. Satan is unable to harm the male child (12:4b–5); he pursues the woman but God prepares a place for her in the desert (12:6, 14). He is cast out of heaven and thereafter wants to drown the woman in a torrent, which the earth swallows (12:9, 15–16). He realizes that persecuting the church is a failure (12:15–16). Again he loses when he wages war against the woman's offspring (12:17). In the Apocalypse, Satan is not the victor but the loser.

b. *The Parthians.* The Romans could never fully subdue the Parthians, who dwelled in an area now known as Iraq and Iran. In A.D. 62 they defeated the Romans. Their general was Vologäses, and his forces rode to victory on white horses. They used bows and arrows as primary weapons, and one of their leaders was called the Conqueror. The saying "a Parthian shot," still current today, indicates accurate marksmanship.[7]

---

3. Refer to David E. Aune, *Revelation 6–16*, WBC 52B (Nashville: Nelson, 1998), p. 394. He notes that there are no convincing arguments to support a satanic identification.

4. G. B. Caird (*A Commentary on the Revelation of St. John the Divine* [London: Black, 1966], p. 81) argues that it is "divine permission granted to evil powers." M. Robert Mulholland Jr. (*Revelation: Holy Living in an Unholy World* [Grand Rapids: Zondervan, Frances Asbury Press, 1990], p. 169) ably refutes the argument that a crown was given to an evil power.

5. The Greek synonym *diadem* applies twice to Satan and the beast (12:3; 13:1) and once to Christ, who wears many crowns (19:12).

6. Fourteen occurrences in Revelation relate to Christ and the saints: 2:7, 11, 17, 26; 3:5, 12, 21; 5:5; 6:2 (twice); 12:11; 15:2; 17:14; 21:7.

7. Tacitus *Annals* 15.13–17. Consult Caird, *Revelation*, p. 80; R. H. Charles, *A Critical and Exegetical Commentary on the Revelation of St. John*, ICC (Edinburgh: Clark, 1920), 1:163; James Moffatt, *The Revelation of St. John the Divine*, in *The Expositor's Greek Testament*, ed. W. Robertson Nicholl (reprint, Grand Rapids: Eerdmans, 1956), 5:389; William Barclay, *The Revelation of John*, 2d ed. (Philadelphia: Westminster, 1960), 2:5.

Attractive as an illustration, this reading encounters limits: the Parthians waged not offensive but defensive warfare, for they never conquered any of the Roman empire or invaded Rome. Also, the use of the bow was common in ancient battles. And for the Romans, victory was symbolized by the use of white horses in parades. Last, military leaders in any age or place did not hesitate to take the name *Conqueror.* Thus, the possibility that John has in mind the Parthians is indeed remote.

c. *Christ.* William Hendriksen lists seven reasons for interpreting Christ as the conqueror:

1. The context favors it, because John is told, "Weep not; look, the lion of the tribe of Judah, the root of David, has overcome" (5:5).
2. The symbolism of the color white in Revelation refers to that which is holy and pure; the crown refers to Christ, who is wearing a crown of gold (14:14); and the verb *to conquer,* with two exceptions (11:7; 13:7), always points to either Christ or his followers.
3. The parallel (19:11) of Christ riding on a white horse is clear, so that Scripture is its own interpreter.
4. Throughout the Apocalypse John unfolds the design that Christ is the one who has conquered, is conquering, and will conquer.
5. In the Gospels, Jesus teaches that Christ and the sword follow each other (Matt. 10:34), which is symbolized in the rider of the red horse who is given a sword (v. 4).
6. A messianic psalm (Ps. 45:3–5) describes the Christ as riding forth victoriously and with sharp arrows piercing the hearts of his enemies.
7. The parallel passage of the four horses (Zech. 1:8) insinuates that the rider is the angel of the Lord.[8]

This is a fine array of factual material to support the interpretation that Christ is the rider on the white horse. Yet there is one problem that surfaces, namely, Christ breaks the first seal and then he himself comes forth in obedience to the voice of one of the living creatures.[9] Even though John presents imagery, an interpreter must seek to avoid internal conflicts in the portrayal of this first seal. Hence, I am suggesting that Jesus, called the Word of God, is sending forth his gospel. Note also that from the mouth of Christ, who is riding on a white horse, protrudes a sharp sword as a symbol of both impending judgment and God's Word (1:16; 2:12, 16; 19:15; and compare Eph. 6:17; Heb. 4:12). This symbolic double-edged sword is a power that on the one side condemns and on the other

8. William Hendriksen, *More Than Conquerors* (reprint, Grand Rapids: Baker, 1982), pp. 93–96. Compare also Mulholland, *Revelation,* pp. 168–70. See M. Bachmann, "Der erste apokalyptische Reiter und die Anlage des letzten Buches der Bibel," *Bib* 67 (1986): 240–75.

9. Isbon T. Beckwith, *The Apocalypse of John* (1919; reprint, Grand Rapids: Baker, 1979), p. 518; G. R. Beasley-Murray, *The Book of Revelation,* NCB (London: Oliphants, 1974), p. 131; Leon Morris, *Revelation,* rev. ed., TNTC (Leicester: Inter-Varsity; Grand Rapids: Eerdmans, 1987), p. 101.

saves. Further, the bow with the arrows implied was an instrument in ancient warfare to hit an enemy at a distance.[10]

d. *The Gospel.* Here is the last interpretation in this series: Christ is sending forth his gospel that in the history of the church has always proved to be unstoppable. The Word of God cannot be bound (2 Tim. 2:9), for God is sending forth his Word to achieve his purpose (Isa. 55:11). This Word is set on conquering the world. The Greek text features the descriptive participle *conquering* in the present tense to denote continued activity and the verb *to conquer* as a stage that begins an action.[11]

I admit that the picture of the first seal does not say anything about Christ's gospel. Yet in Jesus' eschatological discourse, which serves as a parallel, the Lord speaks definitively about the gospel of the kingdom that must be preached to all nations (Matt. 24:14; Mark 13:10). In his discourse Jesus speaks also of war, famine, and death; all these have their counterpart in John's description of the four horsemen. The proclamation of God's Word creates reaction that results in clashes, strife, and hostility.[12]

This interpretation has its roots in the early church. Already in the third century Victorinus of Pettau in Pannonia (modern Hungary) wrote in his commentary on Revelation, "The white horse is the proclamation of the Word sent into the world with the Holy Spirit. For the Lord said: 'This gospel will be preached in the whole world as a witness to the Gentiles and then comes the end.' "[13] The Word of God goes forth conquering and to conquer, as is evident from the Book of Acts and church history. Indeed, the gospel is victorious from beginning to end.

Here are some concluding comments. John derives his pictorial information from two passages in the prophecy of Zechariah. The prophet relates a vision of a man riding a red horse, and there were also red, brown, and white horses (Zech. 1:8). In the other vision he saw four chariots drawn by horses that were distinguished by the colors red, black, white, and dappled. These horses were going out from the Lord throughout the whole world: black to the north, white to the west, and dappled to the south (Zech. 6:1–6). Aside from the number and color of four horses going into the whole world, there is little else that John has borrowed from Zechariah. The dappled horse appears as a pale horse in the

---

10. Friedrich Düsterdieck, *Critical and Exegetical Handbook to the Revelation of John* (New York and London: Funk and Wagnalls, 1886), p. 221.

11. Consult Richard A. Young, *Intermediate New Testament Greek: A Linguistic and Exegetical Approach* (Nashville: Broadman & Holman, 1994), p. 123.

12. George Eldon Ladd, *Commentary on the Revelation of John* (Grand Rapids: Eerdmans, 1972), p. 99; compare R. C. H. Lenski, *The Interpretation of St. John's Revelation* (Columbus: Wartburg, 1943), pp. 220–21; Theodor Zahn, *Die Offenbarung des Johannes*, Kommentar zum Neuen Testament 18 (Leipzig: Deichert, 1924–26), 2:352–53.

13. Henry Alford, *James–Revelation*, vol. 4, part 2 of *Alford's Greek Testament* (1875; reprint, Grand Rapids: Guardian, 1976), p. 614. John P. M. Sweet (*Revelation*, WPC [Philadelphia: Westminster, 1979], p. 138) suggests that the armies of heaven in 19:11–16 are the riders on white horses.

Apocalypse, and the sequence of the horses in Revelation differs from that in Zechariah's prophecy. Nonetheless, in both the prophecy of Zechariah and the Apocalypse, the horses and their riders go out into the world to do God's bidding: the black horses were going victoriously to the north country (Babylon) and pacified God's Spirit (Zech. 6:8). In the Apocalypse the horses and riders go forth for conquest, war, famine, and death. In short, John's message is more specific than the Old Testament prophecy.

Of the four horsemen, only the last one is given a name, namely, Death (v. 8). The other three have descriptions but no names. From these pictorial descriptions (white, red, black, and pale), interpreters must draw pertinent information but not necessarily names. These portrayals represent forces, conditions, or actions. The red horse symbolizes war, the black horse famine, and the pale horse death. These three are negative forces, but the white horse is a positive force: it symbolizes a power that is spiritual. I have interpreted this power as the gospel that is going forth "conquering and to conquer." Both the words *crown* and *white* strengthen this positive image.[14] And last, as the Apocalypse reveals contrast from beginning to end, similarly here the positive aspect of the first rider stands in contrast to the negative aspect of the other three riders.

Greek Words, Phrases, and Constructions in 6:1

φωνή—though there are variants in the genitive, dative, and accusative, the nominative is the most difficult to explain and is therefore likely to be the original reading. With the nominative, John draws attention to the majesty of the voice that speaks. The nominative is left hanging as "a pendent nominative."[15]

ἔρχου— in some manuscripts the present imperative is supplemented with καὶ ἴδε: "Come and see" (KJV, NKJV). Note that the shorter reading appears also in verses 3, 5, 7. This shorter text is well supported. Because not John is summoned but the four horsemen, translators favor it.

---

2. The Second Seal: The Red Horse
6:3–4

The next three horses and their riders symbolize waging war, causing famine, and effecting death. We find an echo of the sequence sword, famine, and plague in the prophecy of Jeremiah, who uses this triad fifteen times as an ominous poetic refrain.[16] John elaborates this feature by introducing sequentially a horse and rider to carry out each of these three calamities. We begin with the rider of the red horse. He represents warfare that is not limited to a specific period—for

---

14. Refer to M. Bachmann, "Noch ein Blick auf den ersten apokalyptischen Reiter (von Apk 6.1–2)," *NTS* 44 (1998): 257–78.

15. Alford, *James–Revelation*, p. 614. Robert L. Thomas, *Revelation 1–7: An Exegetical Commentary* (Chicago: Moody, 1992), p. 424.

16. Jeremiah 14:12; 21:7, 9; 24:10; 27:8, 13; 29:17–18; 32:24, 36; 34:17; 38:2; 42:17, 22; 44:13. Compare Ezek. 14:21.

example, the end time—but extends from the age in which the original readers lived until the end of time.[17]

3. And when he opened the second seal, I heard the second living creature say, "Come." 4. And another horse went out, a red one. And to him who sat on it authority was given to take peace from the earth, so that they might slay one another; and there was given to him a large sword.

The second living creature, having the appearance of an ox (see 4:7), which symbolizes strength and tenacity, spoke. No mention is made of the loudness of his voice as in the case of the first living creature (v. 1). Everyone is already paying close attention when the cry is heard, "Come." This summons means that the horse and rider appear and go forth.

a. "And another horse went out, a red one." While white stands for holiness, purity, and justice, the color red signifies bloodshed and points to warfare. The Greek word *pyr* (fire) has a related word *pyrros* that means fiery red. This derivative appears both here and in the description of the fiery red dragon bent on bloodshed and warfare (12:3). The conflict depicted in the Apocalypse is that of God versus Satan, Christ versus the Antichrist, and the Holy Spirit versus the false prophet. Wherever the gospel is introduced in areas where it has not yet been preached, this conflict is real and often leads to bloodshed. Jesus himself said, "Do not suppose that I have come to bring peace to the earth. I did not come to bring peace, but a sword" (Matt. 10:34). And he said, "You will hear of wars and rumors of wars. . . . Nation will rise against nation, and kingdom against kingdom" (Matt. 24:6, 7).

b. "And to him who sat on it authority was given to take peace from the earth." Translators generally insert the word *authority* or *power* to complete the concept of taking peace from the earth. The text literally reads, "It was granted to take peace from the earth" (NASB). The rider on this red-colored horse personifies evil that opposes God, his Word, and his people. Wherever this evil enters, peace vanishes. Opposition to the preaching and teaching of the gospel often results in serious conflict even in one's own family: "A man's enemies will be the members of his own household" (Matt. 10:36; see also Luke 12:49–53). Yet evil by itself has no inherent authority, for God grants evil the authority to take away peace. God is in control and sets the limits; in his hands "the control of human affairs remains."[18]

c. "So that they might slay one another; and there was given to him a large sword." Who are the people that take up arms and slay one another? Various interpretations could be mentioned: general warfare throughout the ages, civil war, Christians who are killed, Christians killing each other, and the enemies of God.

---

17. Refer to Beckwith, *Apocalypse*, p. 519.

18. Philip Edgcumbe Hughes, *The Book of the Revelation: A Commentary* (Leicester: Inter-Varsity; Grand Rapids: Eerdmans, 1990), p. 85.

There may be some evidence that the current passage alludes to the slaughter of God's people. The verb *to slaughter* occurs eight times in the Apocalypse, of which one pertains to the slain head of the beast as an imitation of the slain Lamb (13:3). The other passages refer to the slaughter of the Lamb and his followers.

- "A Lamb standing as though it had been slain" (5:6).
- "You were slain and with your blood you bought [them]" (5:9).
- "Worthy is the Lamb that was slain" (5:12).
- "I saw under the altar the souls of the ones slain" (6:9).
- "The Lamb that was slain" (13:8).
- "The blood of the prophets and the saints is found and of all who were slain on the earth" (18:24).

One other New Testament passage refers to being slain: 1 John 3:12 describes righteous Abel being killed by his brother. However, these texts fail to give specific information as to who were killed in Rev. 6:4.

We make two observations. First, although the slaughter of Christians is a proven fact throughout the ages in this continuous spiritual conflict, the reference in this verse to the large sword does not preclude general warfare. And second, John states that in addition to the prophets and the saints, other people are slain (18:24).[19] If the text is not clear, we do well not to rely on probabilities or dogmatic perspectives.

Greek Words, Phrases, and Constructions in 6:4

μάχαιρα μεγάλη—this is the short Roman sword, here modified by the adjective "great" to denote slaughter occurring in warfare. The ῥομφαία is the long sword (1:16). John appears to use the two words interchangeably, as is evident in verses 4 and 8.

---

3. The Third Seal: The Black Horse
6:5–6

5. And when he opened the third seal, I heard the third living creature say, "Come." And I saw, and look, a black horse, and he that sat on it had a pair of scales in his hand. 6. And I heard as it were a voice in the midst of the four living creatures saying, "A quart of wheat for a denarius and three quarts of barley for a denarius, but do not damage the oil and the wine."

The opening of the third seal evokes a cry from the third living creature addressed to a rider on a black horse: "Come!" which means come and go forth. This living creature, appearing with the face of a man (4:7), portrays intelligence and sagacity.

19. Otto Michel, *TDNT*, 7:935. Compare Richard Bauckham, *The Climax of Prophecy* (Edinburgh: Clark, 1993), p. 349 n. 22.

The horse on which the rider sits is black, depicting famine, as illustrated by the scales to measure the weight of food and by the highly inflated prices of wheat and barley. God said to the Israelites: "When I cut off your supply of bread, ten women will be able to bake bread in one oven, and they will dole out the bread by weight. You will eat, but you will not be satisfied" (Lev. 26:26; see also Ezek. 4:16).

A departure from the two preceding scenes is that in addition to the command "Come!" a voice speaks out and utters a message. It is possible to say that this voice does not belong to the third living creature alone but to all four speaking with one accord. John's words are vague, for he states that there was "as it were a voice in the midst of the four living creatures." Lenski suggests that the phrase *in the midst* is not spatial but relational.[20] But if we picture the four living creatures surrounding the throne of God, then the voice that speaks must be of either the Lamb or God in the midst of these four beings. From the one who sits on the throne comes the message of famine,[21] which in biblical times was heard repeatedly (2 Kings 8:1; Ps. 105:16; Isa. 14:30; Jer. 18:21; 24:10; 27:8; 34:17; 42:16; Ezek. 5:17; Amos 8:11). God, who often warned his people of famine, now once more informs them of shortages in the food supply.

God's voice cries, "A quart of wheat for a denarius and three quarts of barley for a denarius, but do not damage the oil and the wine." He informs the hearer and reader of four food items that are in short supply: wheat, barley, oil, and wine. The measure that is used (Greek *choinix*, a word found only here in the New Testament) is "a dry measure, oft[en] used for grain, almost equivalent to a quart."[22] The price of one quart of wheat for one denarius is highly inflated. The parable of the workers in the vineyard relates that a denarius is a workman's daily wage (Matt. 20:2). If one denarius would buy only one quart of wheat, the equivalent of one loaf of bread, a laborer would be unable to feed his family with that amount. He would have the choice of buying three quarts of barley for that same price, but barley lacks gluten, a protein substance in wheat flour that makes dough cohesive. Hence, barley is generally used for animal fodder. At the end of the siege of Samaria in the days of the prophet Elisha, seven quarts of wheat flour were sold for a shekel and thirteen quarts of barley for the same price (2 Kings 7:1, 16, 18). Jesus multiplied five barley cakes to feed five thousand men, besides women and children (John 6:9; see also Matt. 14:21). Regardless, if a laborer had to pay a denarius for one quart of wheat, he could barely keep himself alive and would have no money for other food items.

20. Lenski, *Revelation*, p. 226.

21. Consult Thomas, *Revelation 1–7*, pp. 431–32; Robert H. Mounce (*The Book of Revelation*, rev. ed., NICNT [Grand Rapids: Eerdmans, 1977], p. 144) notes that the voice comes from "the center of the throne room."

22. Bauer, p. 883. The Vulgate has *bilibris*, which is the equivalent of two pounds. The Spanish translation Cassiodoro reads "dos libras." See also Henry Barclay Swete, *Commentary on Revelation* (1911; reprint, Grand Rapids: Kregel, 1977), p. 88.

The message from the midst of the four living creatures spoke volumes to its readers and hearers. The Christians residing in the cities of Smyrna, Pergamum, Thyatira, and Philadelphia were forced to belong to guilds that required them to worship idols. When they refused and swore their allegiance to Christ, they would be unemployed and starve. They themselves experienced firsthand the effect of starvation.

What is the meaning of the command not to damage the oil and the wine? Some commentators refer to an edict issued by Emperor Domitian in A.D. 92 that no new vineyards be planted in Italy and that half of the vineyards in the Roman provinces be destroyed. The vine growers in Asia Minor were so upset with this decree that the order was revoked before it took effect.[23] This historical note would be a helpful insight into the time when John wrote the Apocalypse, except for two objections: the edict never took effect, and there is no mention of oil. These two reasons undo any attempt to put John's words in historical perspective.

The question is whether either the people or nature, symbolized by the black horse, should not harm the oil and the wine. Some scholars suggest that the rich were able to afford oil and wine while the poverty-stricken masses had to forego this luxury. But oil and wine were common staples in the days of John: oil was used for cooking purposes and wine was the daily beverage. Why would the rich damage these staples? Therefore, it is better to apply to nature the command not to harm the olive and grape crops. In other words, the command is "the limit of the plague ordained by the Lord."[24]

Greek Words, Phrases, and Constructions in 6:6

μὴ ἀδικήσῃς—"do not harm." The aorist subjunctive, functioning as an imperative and preceded by the negative particle, indicates not that harm is being done at the present but that harm is not to occur in the future.

---

4. The Fourth Seal: The Pale Horse
6:7–8

7. And when he opened the fourth seal, I heard the voice of the fourth living creature saying, "Come." 8. And I saw, and look, a pale horse, and he that sat on it had the name Death, and Hades followed after him. And there was given to them authority over the fourth part of the earth to kill with sword, and famine, and disease, and by the wild beasts of the earth.

When the Lamb has opened the fourth seal, the voice of the fourth living creature is heard. Earlier this creature was portrayed as a flying eagle (4:7). Like the other creatures this one utters the command, "Come!" (For an explanation of the shorter reading, see verse 1.)

---

23. Suetonius *Domitian* 7.

24. Düsterdieck, *Revelation of John*, p. 225.

a. "And I saw, and look, a pale horse, and he that sat on it had the name Death, and Hades followed after him." The fourth horse in the series of the first four seals is pale green in the Greek text. Translators usually omit the word *green*, while some qualify the term *pale* with the adjective *sickly* or *deathly*.[25] The yellowish green color (Greek *chlōros*) depicts death, and decomposition evokes abhorrence. Here then is the portrayal of the pale green horse of death.

Notice that of all the four horsemen only the rider of the fourth horse has a name: Death. Some interpreters call it *pestilence* on the basis of 2:23, where the Greek word *thanatos* (death) can be translated "disease." But here the context gives Death a much broader scope than merely pestilence, for its destructive methods include sword, famine, disease, and wild beasts.

Accompanying Death, although not riding on a separate horse, is Hades (see 1:18; 20:13–14).[26] We do not need to see him riding on the same horse or walking beside it; rather both Death and Hades symbolize termination of life and existence apart from God (compare Hos. 13:14). The Apocalypse mentions these two as companions: the one follows the other. Indeed, the imperfect tense of the Greek verb *akolouthein* (to follow) indicates a continuous activity of Hades. Wherever death strikes, Hades gathers its victims. Hades is not the grave, for all people who die before Jesus comes return to dust. Hades is the place where the souls of unbelievers are kept, while the souls of believers are and will be with Jesus in heaven (see 1:18).

b. "And there was given to them authority over the fourth part of the earth to kill with sword, and famine, and disease, and by the wild beasts of the earth." The passive voice "was given" points to God as the agent who grants them authority. Believers receive comfort from these words, for they know that God is fully in control even when a fourth part of the earth's population perishes (compare 9:18, where a third of humankind was killed). They belong to God and have been redeemed by the Lamb (5:9; 7:14, 15) and are safe. But Death and Hades kill and gather millions upon millions of people in various gruesome ways: first, violently with weapons of either individual or mass destruction; next, with shortages of food that result in gradual death; third, by rampant disease of one kind or another; and last, by wild beasts. John has taken the wording from Old Testament prophecies:[27]

> For this is what the Sovereign LORD
> says:
> "How much worse will it be when I
> send

---

25. *Phillips* has the reading "sickly green in color." See also "sickly pale" (NEB, REB) and "deathly pale" (NJB).

26. Charles (*Revelation*, 1:169–70; 2:402–3) regards the clauses "and Hades followed after him" and "to kill with a sword, and famine, and disease, and by the wild beasts of the earth" as glosses that should be omitted. Similarly, see Aune, *Revelation 6–16*, p. 401. But they fail to provide textual evidence to verify their statements.

27. See Ezek. 5:12, 17; 29:5; 33:27; Jer. 14:12; 15:2–3; 21:7. See also Beale, *Revelation*, p. 384.

against Jerusalem my four dreadful
judgments—
sword and famine and wild beasts and
plague—
to kill its men and their animals."
(Ezek. 14:21)

The first recipients of the Apocalypse could apply its message to their own circumstances. They constantly faced death by sword, starvation, and disease; and they awaited destruction by wild beasts. Roman power directly and indirectly threatened their existence, so that they lived constantly in the shadow of death. Yet throughout the centuries the extermination of large segments of the human race is attributed to warfare, hunger, and disease. The bubonic plague entered Europe in the fourteenth century and killed twenty-six million people between 1346 and 1352. During World War II, some twenty million people in Europe lost their lives, as did an equal number in Asia.

Numerous people die not accidentally or by common ailments and old age, but cruelly in wars, conflict, famines, and epidemics. However, the severity of eliminating life from a fourth part of the earth refers to a future catastrophic event and is a warning of God's forthcoming judgment.

Greek Words, Phrases, and Constructions in 6:8

ἐν ῥομφαίᾳ . . . ὑπὸ τῶν θηρίων—"by the sword . . . by the wild beasts." Three times the preposition ἐν occurs, with the nouns "sword," "famine," and "death [disease]." John relied on Ezekiel 14:21. The preposition ὑπό (by) "seems to fall outside the quotation" and is preceded by the verb "to kill" in the active voice instead of the passive voice, "so that in a sense the beasts are only the instruments wielded by the subject of that verb."[28]

---

5. The Fifth Seal: The Patience of the Saints
6:9–11

The opening of the fifth seal does not point to a specific moment in the history of the human race but parallels the scenes of the first four seals. That is, it occurs during the time between Jesus' ascension and return. The more severe the persecution of Christians becomes, the more urgently the saints in heaven call on God to judge the earth's inhabitants and to avenge the blood of his people.

9. And when he opened the fifth seal, I saw under the altar the souls of the ones slain because of the word of God and because of the testimony they were holding.

a. "I saw under the altar the souls of the ones slain." The scene that John sees when the fifth seal is opened takes place in heaven where the martyrs reside in the presence of God. But how do we interpret the word *altar*? The term occurs

28. C. F. D. Moule, *An Idiom-Book of New Testament Greek*, 2d ed. (Cambridge: Cambridge University Press, 1960), p. 66.

twenty-three times in the New Testament, of which eight are in Revelation (6:9; 8:3 [twice], 5; 9:13; 11:1; 14:18; 16:7). Does this verse refer to the altar of incense or the altar of burnt offerings? The time of sacrifices came to an end when Christ died on the cross (Heb. 9:26; 10:12); therefore, this is the altar of incense. Also, the smoke that ascends from this altar symbolizes the prayers of the saints (8:3).

John appears to present his vision in a Jewish context in which the blood of an animal, poured out at the altar of sacrifice, represented the life of the slain animal (Lev. 17:11; see also 4:7, 34). Similarly, the blood of martyrs was symbolically poured at God's altar in heaven, where their souls found a place to rest. A contemporary of John, Rabbi Akiba, taught that a Jew "buried in the land of Israel is as if he were buried beneath the altar; he who is buried beneath the altar is as if he were buried beneath the throne of glory."[29] John pictorially presents the souls of those slain as under God's altar, which is interpreted as being "at the bottom of God's throne." In this context he is not concerned about the martyrs' bodies. We see a similar wording in 20:4 of souls in heaven without any mention of bodies, "And I saw the souls of those who were beheaded because of their testimony of Jesus and the word of God."

b. "Slain because of the word of God and because of the testimony they were holding." These martyrs had been faithful to God and his Word and had been willing to die for him. Some commentators assert that the text speaks only of saints who had met a violent death because of their testimony. But then Stephen and the apostles James, Peter, and Paul would be included but not John, who presumably died a natural death in 98. Ladd pointedly writes, "Every disciple of Jesus is in essence a martyr; and John has in view all believers who have so suffered."[30] It is the Word of God that is their spiritual food and it is the Lord's testimony that they cherish from day to day.

The phrases *the word of God* and *the testimony* appear repeatedly in the Apocalypse.[31] The testimony is that of and about Jesus (e.g., see the commentary on 1:2). The phrase points to God's faithful servants who were holding on to that word and testimony. Facing persecution and death (12:11), they testified to the grace and love of the Lord. Polycarp, who died as a martyr at the stake on February 23, 155, in Smyrna, prayed to God that he might be received "as a rich and acceptable sacrifice."[32] All believers who in their hearts treasure God's revealed Word and the gospel of Jesus Christ by confessing his name (Rom. 10:9–10) view their testimony "as a badge of allegiance to Christ."[33] Holding God's truth in

29. *Aboth de Rabbi Nathan* 26 (7[c]); SB, 3:803. See also Babylonian Talmud, *Shabbath* 152b; *Ketuboth* 111a; Beasley-Murray, *Revelation*, p. 135; Charles, *Revelation*, 1:173.

30. Ladd, *Revelation*, p. 104.

31. Rev. 1:2, 9; 12:11, 17; 19:10; 20:4.

32. Eusebius *Eccl. Hist.* 4.15.34.

33. Thomas, *Revelation 1–7*, p. 444. See Homer Hailey, *Revelation: An Introduction and Commentary* (Grand Rapids: Baker, 1979), p. 194. Adela Yarbro Collins ("The Political Perspective on the Revelation of John," *JBL* 96 [1977]: 241–56) suggests that the death of each martyr causes the end to come closer.

one's heart and testifying to it with one's mouth identify the true believer who is willing to die for the faith.

10. And they cried with a loud voice saying, "How long, O Sovereign Lord, holy and true, will you not judge and avenge our blood on those that dwell on the earth?"

At the throne of God, the saints loudly cry out to the Judge of all the earth (Gen. 18:25) and here plead for justice. The volume of their plea indicates insistence and perseverance, much the same as the widow in the parable of the unjust judge. Jesus concludes this parable by asking, "And will not God bring about justice for his chosen ones, who cry out to him day and night?" (Luke 18:7; compare Ps. 79:10).

The martyrs' cry is addressed to the Sovereign Lord who is called "holy and true." The word *Sovereign* (Greek *despotēs*), as a strictly theological term, can be used in the New Testament to address God in praise, prayer, and petition (Luke 2:29; Acts 4:24; Rev. 6:10).[34] The phrase *holy and true* occurs only twice, here and in the letter to the church in Philadelphia, where it is applied to Jesus (3:7). *Holy* means entirely without sin and *true* signifies absolute trustworthiness. These two concepts are inseparable in their description of the Deity. The martyrs call on God to be holy and true to his being when their blood on earth is crying out for justice. God's name and honor are an unavoidable issue, for his people were made in his image and purchased for God by the blood of the Lamb (5:9). The saints are appealing to him to let his holiness and truth shine forth. Inattention to their plea would indeed mean a blot on his being.

"How long will you not judge and avenge our blood on those that dwell on the earth?" (compare Zech. 1:12). Is this a plea for revenge on the part of the martyrs? The answer is no, because this would be unworthy of the saints. The saints ask God for justice and petition him to avenge them. He himself has said, "It is mine to avenge; I will repay" and "The LORD will judge his people" (Deut. 32:35, 36; see also 32:43; Rom. 12:19; Heb. 10:30). This promise is solemn and sure, for God never breaks his word. The possessive pronoun *our* in "our blood" is telling, for God does not forget the spilled blood of his people and repeatedly utters his warning not to shed innocent blood.[35] God will vindicate his people and bring his enemies to justice. The phrase "those that dwell on the earth" refers not to every human being but rather to humanity that is hostile to God.

11. To each one of them was given a white robe, and they were told to rest a little while longer until the number was completed of their fellow servants and their brothers [and sisters] who were about to be killed as they were killed.

a. "To each one of them was given a white robe." The phrase *white robe* appears a number of times in the Apocalypse, signifying garments of righteousness. The

34. Refer to Günter Haufe, *EDNT*, 1:291; Karl Heinrich Rengstorf, *TDNT*, 2:48; Hans Bietenhard, *NIDNTT*, 2:509.

35. Gen. 4:10; Exod. 21:12; Num. 35:33; 2 Sam. 4:11; Ps. 9:12; 106:38; Heb. 12:24; Rev. 16:6; 19:2. The writer of *1 Enoch* 47.1–4 speaks three times of "the blood of the righteous."

color white denotes holiness (see 3:4, 5, 18; 4:4; 6:11; 7:9, 13). What does this robe symbolize? Some scholars take it to mean that saints who translated to glory receive a heavenly body, which here is expressed as a robe. They base this interpretation on Jewish apocalyptic writings that refer to resurrection bodies as "garments of glory" (*1 Enoch* 52.16; *2 Enoch* 22.8; *Ascension of Isaiah* 4.16; 9.6–7).[36] However, the wearing of a white robe is an anthropomorphic manner of speech, for there is no other way of depicting the saints in heaven. The white robe stands for purity.

b. "And they were told to rest a little while longer until the number was completed." John provides no information as to who addressed the martyrs, but because they pleaded with God for justice, we assume that the speaker is God himself. Their request is not denied, but they are told to rest and exercise patience for a little while. *Rest* must be understood as a time of blessedness and reinvigoration at the foot of the altar.

How long is "a little while"? Jesus referred to his imminent departure when he said, "Yet a little while am I with you" (John 7:33 KJV) and "Yet a little while is the light with you" (John 12:35 KJV). By contrast, the souls under the altar must wait as they call for judgment to take place at the consummation. No one, not even the Son of Man, knows when the culmination comes, for it is God the Father who sets the times and the seasons (Matt. 24:36; Acts 1:7). Admittedly, from our perspective we are inclined to think that "a little while" is a short period. We think in terms of chronological time, but the saints residing in eternity must look at that short interval from a heavenly perspective and wait. "The wait of a 'little longer' is in God's estimate but a fleeting moment, though for us it may stretch out for ages (cf. 12:12; 20:3)."[37]

The termination of the "little while" comes when the number of these saints in heaven is complete. No one on earth knows how many saints there will be, for John tells us that he saw "a great multitude that no one could number" (7:9). Only God knows the total number of his elect. Hendriksen notes that the exact number "has been fixed from eternity in His decree. Until that number has been realized on earth the day of final judgment cannot come."[38] At the conclusion of his discussion on the heroes of faith, the author of Hebrews writes about the consummation. "God had planned something better for us so that only together with us would they be made perfect" (Heb. 11:40).

c. "Of their fellow servants and their brothers [and sisters] who were about to be killed as they were killed." The closer we come to the end of time, the fiercer Satan rages against God's people. He knows that the "little while" is rapidly coming to a close. He attacks the saints on earth and even kills many of them as long as God gives him permission to do so. But when God's endurance has come to an end and the cup of his wrath is full, the time for judgment is near (Matt. 23:32; 1 Thess. 2:16).

---

36. Consult the commentaries of Caird (p. 86); Charles (1:176, 184–88); and Moffatt (p. 392). See also Murray J. Harris, *Raised Immortal: Resurrection and Immortality in the New Testament* (Grand Rapids: Eerdmans, 1983), pp. 98, 255.

37. Alan F. Johnson, *Revelation,* in *The Expositor's Bible Commentary,* ed. Frank E. Gaebelein (Grand Rapids: Zondervan, 1981), 12:475.

38. Hendriksen, *More Than Conquerors,* p. 106. Compare also the apocryphal literature of *1 Enoch* 47.4; 4 Ezra (=2 Esdras) 2:41; 4:36; *2 Baruch* 30.2.

Although John at times resorts to the use of a parallel, here the phrases *fellow servants* and *brothers [and sisters] about to be killed* can be interpreted that not all Christians meet a violent death in times of persecution. All true believers are God's servants and endure hardships. John, exiled to the island Patmos but not killed, is called a "servant" (1:1). Many Christians suffer in one form or another for their faithfulness to God and his Word, while others pay the ultimate price by being killed. "The faithful who were willing to die but were not put to death receive the same reward as those who suffered martyrdom."[39]

Greek Words, Phrases, and Constructions in 6:11

πληρωθῶσιν—the aorist passive subjunctive of the verb *to complete* is the better reading, over against πληρώσωσιν, which is the aorist active and would need an understood direct object, e.g., the course.[40]

καὶ οἱ σύνδουλοι αὐτῶν καὶ οἱ ἀδελφοὶ αὐτῶν—the double use of the conjunction καί may be translated "*both* their fellow servants *and* their brothers" to indicate two groups of people each introduced by a definite article.

---

6. The Sixth Seal: The Day of the Lord
6:12–17

In the scene of the fifth seal, the souls in heaven implore God to vindicate them and avenge their spilled blood; they are told to exercise patience. Then in the scene of the sixth seal John pictures the Judgment Day, when the unbelievers face the wrath of God and the Lamb.

Throughout the Apocalypse, John refers directly and indirectly to the judgment at the end of segments and cycles. For instance, at the conclusion of his introduction he alludes to the judgment that unbelievers face (1:7). At the end of the last of the seven letters, the one to Laodicea, he mentions that his followers will sit with him on his Father's throne, which is an indirect reference to the Judgment Day (3:21; 20:4). The sixth seal and the seventh are devoted to the judgment of the unbelievers. If we read the information John supplies in the next few verses, we understand that he is not speaking of an event that people can ignore. Rather, he points to the inescapable final judgment of which catastrophes in nature are harbingers.[41]

a. In Nature
6:12–14

12. And I saw when he opened the sixth seal, and there was a great earthquake and the sun became black as sackcloth made of hair, and the whole moon became

---

39. Hailey, *Revelation*, p. 196.

40. Consult Aune, *Revelation 6–16*, p. 385; Beale, *Revelation*, p. 395.

41. Compare Ernest B. Allo, *Saint Jean l'Apocalypse*, Études bibliques (Paris: Gabalda, 1921), p. 90; S. Greijdanus, *De Openbaring des Heeren aan Johannes*, KNT (Amsterdam: Van Bottenburg, 1925), p. 157.

as blood. 13. And the stars of heaven fell to the earth as a fig tree casts its unripe figs when shaken by a strong wind. 14. And the sky was receding as a scroll when it is being rolled up, and every mountain and island were moved out of their places.

After the opening of the sixth seal, John notices signs on the earth and in the sky. The first item he mentions is a *great earthquake,* a phenomenon not unknown to the original readers of the Apocalypse. For instance, in the first century earthquakes devastated the cities of Sardis, Philadelphia, and Laodicea. But notice that this earthquake is qualified by the adjective *great.* The sun is eclipsed and the moon has a reddish color. The stars are falling toward the earth, and the sky disappears. On the earth the landscape of mountains and islands completely changes (compare 16:18).

Are these phenomena to be taken literally or symbolically? True, an earthquake can change the contour of the land, and an eclipse can block the light of the sun and give the moon the color of blood. But stars, which are much larger than the earth, do not fall on it, the sky does not disappear as a scroll that is rolled up, and mountains and islands are not normally moved from their place. Before we answer the question mentioned above, let us first look at the rest of the Scriptures.

a. *Scriptural background.* Here are some passages that speak about natural phenomena (earthquake, eclipse of sun and moon, and falling stars) from both the prophets and Jesus' discourse on the last things.

- "In my zeal and fiery wrath I declare that at that time there will be a great earthquake in the land of Israel" (Ezek. 38:19).
- "The sun will be turned to darkness and the moon to blood before the coming of the great and dreadful day of the LORD" (Joel 2:31).
- "Before them the earth shakes, the sky trembles, the sun and moon are darkened, and the stars no longer shine" (Joel 2:10; see Isa. 13:10).
- "All the stars of the heavens will be dissolved and the sky rolled up like a scroll; all the starry host will fall like withered leaves from the vine, like shriveled figs from the fig tree" (Isa. 34:4).
- "Immediately after the distress of those days 'the sun will be darkened, and the moon will not give its light; the stars will fall from the sky, and the heavenly bodies will be shaken'" (Matt. 24:29; also Mark 13:24; see Isa. 13:10; 34:4).

Although there are other passages with similar wording (e.g., Hag. 2:6–7), we have sufficient evidence to see that John permits the Scriptures to speak on what will happen when the Judgment Day appears. The entire universe will be affected, and the earth will undergo a complete change. This is the day of the Lord in which catastrophic events of enormous proportions will take place.

b. *Imagery and reality.* John's wording reveals that he is thoroughly familiar with both the teachings of the Old Testament prophets and Jesus' discourse on the last things. On the one hand, the language he uses "can hardly be taken with stark literalness."[42] On the other hand, some unusual upheavals in nature will occur when cosmic time stops and eternity takes over. An earthquake shakes the universe to indicate that God's creation is intimately involved in the Day of Judgment. The darkening of the sun and moon is not the result of a temporary eclipse but rather signifies the end of their giving and reflecting light. Not light but darkness ruled at the beginning of creation (Gen. 1:2), and so it will be for unbelievers when the judgment comes. Stars falling from heaven are compared to unripe figs that the wind shakes from the trees. The image is falling stars; the reality is a complete dislocation of the stars in space. The atmosphere that gives us the appearance of a blue sky disappears and is removed like a curling sheet of paper. And last, the contour of this earth visible in mountains and islands changes completely.

For those people who reject Christ and curse God, the upheavals in nature are a picture of terror and dread they are unable to escape. Because John devotes the next chapter to the saints, now he focuses attention on the unbelievers.

c. *Additional comments.* John writes, "The sun became black as sackcloth made of hair." If there is no sunlight, there is no heat. This means that the phenomenon was not an ordinary eclipse, but a total blackout of the rays of the sun. In ancient days, sackcloth made of the hairs of a goat was black (compare Isa. 50:3). People in mourning wore sackcloth to demonstrate their sorrow, but the cloth also "suggested that society was out of balance and had to be righted" and indicated a threat of forthcoming judgment and a call to repentance.[43]

In the fading light of the sun, the moon became red like the color of blood. The scene portends the impending calamity that will fall upon the people. The falling of stars on the earth should be understood not literally but figuratively. John even uses the parallel of unripe figs that fall from the branches and cover the ground. It is another warning that the end has come. The atmospheric heaven is rolled up like a scroll, as a scroll that has been read is rolled up and put away in a closet. This heaven is replaced by a new heaven (21:1).[44]

b. Toward Unbelievers
6:15–17

15. And the kings of the earth, and the great men and generals, and the rich and the strong, and every slave and free person hid themselves in the caves and among the rocks of the mountains. 16. And they said to the mountains and to the rocks, "Fall on us and hide us from the face of the one seated on the throne and

---

42. Ladd, *Revelation*, p. 108.

43. Larry G. Herr, *ISBE*, 4:256; Gustav Stählin, *TDNT*, 7:63.

44. Verses 12–14 list six parts of God's creation: earth, sun, moon, stars, heaven, and "every mountain and island." Verses 15–17 enumerate six classes of human society facing judgment: kings, great men, generals, the rich, the strong, and "every slave and free person." Beale (*Revelation*, pp. 403–4) comments, "This parallelism could also support the suggestion . . . that the judgment of the cosmos in vv 12–14 is figurative for the judgment of sinners in vv 15–17. The parallel sixfold pattern may emphasize the imperfection of both inanimate and human creation."

from the wrath of the Lamb." 17. For the great day of their wrath has come, and who is able to stand?

a. "And the kings of the earth, and the great men and generals, and the rich and the strong, and every slave and free person hid themselves" (see the parallel in 19:18). Kings are the highest rulers in the land, with great men next to them as advisors and administrators. The generals represent the armed forces and the rich have economic influence. The strong men are powerful with respect to either mental or physical prowess. At the bottom of the social scale are the multitudes of slaves and those who had gained their freedom. Here is a portrayal of all the levels of humanity from top to bottom that face the coming judgment. Having rejected Jesus Christ as Lord and Savior, these multitudes are unable to escape the wrath of God and the Lamb.

b. "[They] hid themselves in the caves and among the rocks of the mountains." Attempts to escape from divine judgment end up in failure. The classes of people mentioned above try to hide in caves and among rock formations of mountainous areas. But when natural catastrophes strike, they have nowhere to conceal themselves. How do we understand this verse in harmony with the preceding passage where mountains are moved out of their place? John presents another aspect of this picture; to put it differently he shows a picture within a picture of events that are happening simultaneously. Bauckham notes that "Revelation's images are flexible, theologically significant and not intended to be pieced together into a single literal picture of what will happen at the End."[45]

c. "And they said to the mountains and to the rocks, 'Fall on us and hide us from the face of the one seated on the throne and from the wrath of the Lamb.'" In the eighth century before Christ, the prophet Hosea prophesied the fall of Israel. The destruction of Samaria would be so devastating that the people would call upon the mountains to cover them and on the hills to fall on them (Hosea 10:8; see also Isa. 2:19). On his way to Golgotha, Jesus quoted these words of Hosea when he addressed women who mourned and wailed for him (Luke 23:30). Thus, he predicted the destruction of Jerusalem, which would be so horrible that the people would call on mountains and hills to cover them.

In the Apocalypse, the enemies of God and the Lamb see the shaking mountains and falling rocks; in desperation they call on these inanimate objects to fall on them, for being crushed by them is preferred to facing divine wrath. God is depicted as the one seated on the throne in heaven from whose face no one can ever hide (Ps. 139:7–12).

The phrase *the wrath of the Lamb* occurs only here in the New Testament. This does not mean that wrath is limited to the Lamb and excludes God. Nor does it convey the thought that a meek animal like a lamb cannot be angry. The word *Lamb* is the symbol of the Christ who confronts his enemies at the end of the age. These people are the adversaries "[who] will make war against the Lamb and the Lamb will overcome them" (17:14). Further, the Lamb opens all the seven seals

45. Bauckham, *Climax of Prophecy*, p. 209.

of the scroll, and it is the Lamb who unleashes his fury against his opponents. The Lamb with the scroll of world history in hand is the Judge who directs his anger against his adversaries.

How should we understand the wrath of the Lamb? Is it an emotion of the Lord or is it his pronouncement of punishment on his enemies? The context is helpful in answering this question, for the word *wrath* is repeated in the next verse together with the phrase "the great day" (v. 17; see also Rom. 1:18; Heb. 3:11). These two expressions point to the Day of Judgment.[46]

d. "For the great day of their wrath has come, and who is able to stand?" The Greek text literally reads, "For there has come the day, the great day of their wrath." It places emphasis first on the verb *has come,* because it stands first in the sentence, and then on the noun *day,* which is followed by the descriptive adjective *great.* The Judgment Day is called "the great day" and in the Old Testament "the day of the LORD" (Isa. 13:9; Joel 2:11, 31; Zeph. 1:14, 15).

The verb *has come* is a past tense with a present connotation that awaits future realization.[47] John draws a picture of that day, even though the day itself is still to come. That is, all the terrible upheavals in nature and the universe usher in the great Day of Judgment, even though the fulfillment of this awesome portent must wait until the consummation.

Some Greek manuscripts read the singular possessive pronoun "*his* wrath" (followed by KJV and NKJV) instead of the plural "their wrath." This reading is grammatically correct because of the singular subject "the Lamb." But in the Apocalypse, John never calls Jesus God, but with the use of pronouns he places Jesus on the same level as God. For instance, we read: "they will be priests of God and of Christ and will reign with him a thousand years" (20:6); and "the throne of God and of the Lamb will be in it, and his servants will serve him" (22:3).

"And who is able to stand?" This rhetorical question has the implicit answer "No one but the innumerable multitude." The Old Testament psalmist and prophets asked the same question: "Who can stand before you when you are angry?" (Ps. 76:7b) and "Who can endure the day of his coming? Who can stand when he appears?" (Mal. 3:2; see Nah. 1:6). God's enemies are not asking for mercy and fail to show genuine repentance. On the contrary, they seek to hide from the Judge but are unable to escape.

Greek Words, Phrases, and Constructions in 6:17

ἦλθεν—the aorist tense conveys the meaning that the great day "'is already come' (that is, it came when the signs of the end described in verses 12–14 began)."[48]

---

46. Consult Gustav Stählin, *TDNT,* 5:424–25; Hans-Christoph Hahn, *NIDNTT,* 1:111; Wilhelm Pesch, *EDNT,* 2:529–30.

47. Bauer, p. 311.

48. Swete, *Revelation,* p. 95.

7

Interlude: The Saints

(7:1–17)

Outline (continued)

7. Interlude: The Saints (7:1–17)
   a. The 144,000 Sealed (7:1–8)
   b. The Great Multitude (7:9–12)
   c. An Interview (7:13–17)

7

1 After this I saw four angels standing at the four corners of the earth, holding the four winds of
the earth, so that no wind might blow upon the earth, the sea, or any tree. 2 And I saw another
angel coming up from the east having the seal of the living God, and he cried with a loud cry to
the four angels to whom was given power to harm the earth and the sea, 3 saying, "Do not harm
the earth, or the sea, or the trees until we have sealed the servants of our God on their foreheads."
4 And I heard the number of those who had been sealed to be one hundred and forty-four thousand sealed from every tribe of Israel.

5 From the tribe of Judah 12,000 were sealed,
from the tribe of Reuben 12,000
from the tribe of Gad 12,000
6 from the tribe of Asher 12,000
from the tribe of Naphtali 12,000
from the tribe of Manasseh 12,000
7 from the tribe of Simeon 12,000
from the tribe of Levi 12,000
from the tribe of Issachar 12,000
8 from the tribe of Zebulun 12,000
from the tribe of Joseph 12,000
from the tribe of Benjamin 12,000 were sealed.

9 After these things I saw, and look, a great multitude that no one could number, from every nation and all tribes and peoples and languages, standing before the throne and before the Lamb.
They were dressed in white robes with palm branches in their hands. 10 And they cried out with a
loud voice, saying,

"Salvation belongs to our God who is seated
on the throne and to the Lamb."

11 And all the angels stood around the throne, the elders, and the four living creatures; and they
fell before the throne on their faces and worshiped God, 12 saying,

"Amen! Praise and glory and wisdom and thanksgiving
and honor and power and strength be to our God
forever and ever. Amen!"

13 And one of the elders asked me, "These people who are dressed in white robes—who are they
and where did they come from?" 14 And I said to him, "Sir, you know." And he said to me, "These
are they who have come out of the great tribulation and have washed their robes and have made
them white in the blood of the Lamb.

15 "Therefore, they are before the throne of God
and serve him day and night in his temple,

and he who is seated on the throne will spread his tent
over them.
16 And they will neither hunger nor thirst anymore;
neither will the sun beat down on them,
nor any scorching heat.
17 Because the Lamb at the center of the throne will shepherd them,
and he will lead them to springs of living water,
and God will wipe away every tear from their eyes."

---

7. Interlude: The Saints
7:1–17
Preliminary Observations

a. *Intermission.* Many commentators see chapter 7 as a parenthesis or interlude between the sixth and the seventh seals (see also the interlude between the sixth and seventh trumpets, 10:1–11:14). This is correct, yet I must add that this chapter is the opposite of the immediately preceding seal (6:12–17), which discloses what is happening to God's enemies. Chapter 7 reveals what is happening to God's people. As the enemies face divine wrath and judgment, the saints sing praises of deliverance to God and the Lamb. The entire chapter, devoted to the saints, is more of a pinnacle than a pause.[1] To the question raised in the sixth seal, "Who is able to stand?" (6:17), John provides the answer: the 144,000 and the countless multitude. Not the people who ask the mountains and rocks to cover them from divine wrath, but the saints stand before the throne. They are the ones sealed by God, washed in the blood of the Lamb, clothed in white robes, and holding palm branches in their hands.

b. *Assembly.* Chapter 7 teaches that while God assembles his people, he suspends judgment until the last of the saints has been gathered and sealed (vv. 2, 3). The saints who gathered in the great multitude and include the 144,000 are the real Israel (vv. 4–9a). They celebrate the liturgy of the Feast of Tabernacles (vv. 9b–10; Lev. 23:40). In addition to the saints, all inhabitants in heaven worship God (vv. 11–12). The saints are portrayed as martyrs who are being gathered as a body until the end of time (vv.13–14).[2] And last, they are before the throne of God and the Lamb forever (vv. 15–17).

c. *Interpretation.* There are two ways of interpreting chapter 7, that is, it can be interpreted either literally or symbolically. The first interpretation explains the number 144,000 as the total number consisting of 12,000 sealed persons from each of the twelve tribes of Israel.[3] The group of people that no one could number taken from every nation, tribe, people, and language are the Gentiles, even

---

1. Refer to Hendrik R. van de Kamp, *Israël in Openbaring* (Kampen: Kok, 1990), p. 124.

2. Refer to J. Comblin, "Le réassemblement du peuple de Dieu: Ap 7.2–4, 9–14," *AssembSeign* 66 (1973): 42–49.

3. John F. Walvoord (*The Revelation of Jesus Christ* [Chicago: Moody, 1966], p. 143) notes that many more than 12,000 from each tribe will be saved, but the 144,000 are those who are protected during the time of tribulation. See also Robert L. Thomas, *Revelation 1–7: An Exegetical Commentary* (Chicago: Moody, 1992), pp. 477–78.

though the word itself is not used. The second interpretation teaches a symbolical approach to the numbers in this chapter. Throughout the Apocalypse, numbers have symbolical meaning, as is evident, for instance, in the number seven that conveys completeness. So it is more likely that the number 144,000 (twelve times twelve thousand) should be interpreted symbolically to express perfection.[4] This becomes evident with respect to the measuring of the new Jerusalem, which is 12,000 stadia in length, width, and height—a perfect cube and symbol of perfection (see the commentary on 21:16). Furthermore, the two scenes of the 144,000 and the incalculable multitude are two similar pictures that emphasize the same message. The first scene depicts idealism and the second realism. The second scene strengthens and amplifies the first one; "The two images depict the same reality."[5]

d. *Analogies.* The correlation between and development of chapters 7 and 21–22 is noteworthy:[6]

- the seal on the forehead (7:3 and 22:4)
- the twelve tribes of Israel (7:4–8 and 21:12)
- the nations (7:9 and 21:24, 26)
- the throne of God (7:9, 15 and 22:1, 3)
- the service rendered (7:15 and 22:3)
- the temple (7:15 and 21:22)
- the dwelling of God (7:15 and 21:3)
- thirst and springs of living water (7:16–17 and 21:6)
- the wiping of tears (7:17 and 21:4)

That is, if we explain the numbers and the names in chapters 21 and 22 symbolically, we expect that the names and numbers of chapter 7 must also be interpreted figuratively. Likewise in this chapter, John presents Revelation as a series of pictures from a symbolical perspective. William Milligan observes, "It is the custom of the Seer to heighten and spiritualize all Jewish names. The temple, the Tabernacle, and the Altar, Mount Zion, and Jerusalem are to him the embodiments of ideas deeper than those literally conveyed by them."[7]

---

4. Donald Guthrie, *New Testament Theology* (Downers Grove: InterVarsity, 1981), p. 640; Alan F. Johnson, *Revelation,* in *The Expositor's Bible Commentary,* ed. Frank E. Gaebelein (Grand Rapids: Zondervan, 1981), 12:481; Richard Bauckham, *The Climax of Prophecy* (Edinburgh: Clark, 1993), p. 218; Gregory K. Beale, *The Book of Revelation: A Commentary on the Greek Text,* NIGTC (Grand Rapids: Eerdmans, 1998), pp. 416–23; Kendell H. Easley, *Revelation,* HNTC (Nashville: Broadman & Holman, 1998), pp. 125–26.

5. Richard Bauckham, *The Theology of the Book of Revelation,* New Testament Theology (Cambridge: Cambridge University Press, 1993), p. 76. Mathias Rissi (*Time and History: A Study on Revelation* [Richmond: John Knox, 1966], p. 89) notes that "the designation of the 144,000 as 'servants of our God' is generally used for the church of Jesus."

6. Van de Kamp, *Israël en Openbaring,* p. 125.

7. William Milligan, *The Book of Revelation* (New York: Armstrong and Son, 1889), p. 118; Homer Hailey, *Revelation: An Introduction and Commentary* (Grand Rapids: Baker, 1979), p. 205.

e. *Sequence.* R. H. Charles advocates a number of transpositions in the Apocalypse; one of them is in chapter 7. He "restores" verses 5–6 "to their original order, in which the sons of Leah are followed by those of Rachel, and these in turn first by the sons of Leah's handmaid and then by Rachel's."[8] He is unable, however, to furnish proof for his transposition, because there are no textual witnesses to assist him in his work. His interpretation is strictly literal and does not take into account that John speaks not about physical Israel but spiritual Israel. For spiritual reasons Judah is mentioned at the head of the list and not Reuben, Jacob's firstborn. Judah is first because Jesus Christ descended from him; also the mixing up of the patriarchal names is designed to show that physical privileges and standings have ended.[9]

a. The 144,000 Sealed
7:1–8

1. After this I saw four angels standing at the four corners of the earth, holding the four winds of the earth, so that no wind might blow upon the earth, the sea, or any tree.

When John writes "After this," he is referring to the immediately preceding context, the opening of the sixth seal. The seventh seal (8:1) will be opened after he has described the two visions recorded in this chapter. John sees four angels, each occupying one of the corners of the earth. This should not be understood literally but rather symbolically, for it points to the totality of God's creation and the four directions: north, east, south, and west.

These four angels (see 9:14–15) have authority over the four winds that blow on the earth and are able to hold the destructive power of these winds in check. R. C. H. Lenski aptly remarks that the word *angels* in unmodified form is never used to refer to devils.[10] Angels are always God's messengers, sent out as his servants (Ps. 104:4; Heb. 1:7, 14). Again John is alluding to the Old Testament for the imagery. The expression *the four corners of the earth* appears in some passages (e.g., Isa. 11:12; Ezek. 7:2 KJV). And the phrase *four winds of heaven* occurs in Daniel 7:2; 11:4; Zechariah 6:5 (see Ezek. 37:9).[11] The text, however, reads *the four winds of the earth,* not *of heaven.* These four winds are God's agents to execute judgment.

The angels arrest the power of these four winds so that they do not destroy God's great creation with hurricanes, tornadoes, and storms (compare Jer. 49:36). The winds with their potentially destructive power are not yet given permission to harm anything in God's creation. His creation is summarized in the

---

8. R. H. Charles, *A Critical and Exegetical Commentary on the Revelation of St. John,* ICC (Edinburgh: Clark, 1920), 1:207–8; 2:405 n. 3.

9. S. Greijdanus, *De Openbaring des Heeren aan Johannes,* KNT (Amsterdam: Van Bottenburg, 1925), p. 169.

10. R. C. H. Lenski, *The Interpretation of St. John's Revelation* (Columbus: Wartburg, 1943), p. 245.

11. "The four winds of heaven" in Zech. 6:5 (NJB, NRSV, REB) can be translated "the four spirits of heaven." Because the Hebrew term *rûaḥ* can also mean "spirit," the question is whether it should be translated here as "winds" or "spirits." The LXX has the reading *anemoi* (winds). And last, to turn these four winds into four horses (6:2–7) on the basis of Zech. 6 is questionable.

interesting combination of *earth, sea,* and *tree.* It divides the land masses from the oceans, with the tree symbolizing the plant kingdom. Tall trees are exceptionally vulnerable to fierce winds.

Here are three observations: The imagery of the wind in the Apocalypse, apart from the illustration in 6:13, is limited to this particular verse. Next, we as humans are utterly unable to control the weather; it is God who sends forth the winds (John 3:8). And last, the imminent catastrophes caused by these winds are kept in abeyance.

2. And I saw another angel coming up from the east having the seal of the living God, and he cried with a loud cry to the four angels to whom was given power to harm the earth and the sea, 3. saying, "Do not harm the earth, or the sea, or the trees until we have sealed the servants of our God on their foreheads."

a. "And I saw another angel coming up from the east having the seal of the living God." The word *another* signifies an angel of the same kind as the preceding four who hold in check the four winds. We are unable to say much about this angel except for origin and identifying mark. His origin is the east, which means that he is approaching John from the rising of the sun, the source of light. To illustrate, the temple in Jerusalem faced east to focus attention on the rising of the sun and the presence of God (see Ezek. 43:2). The angel's mark of identity is "the seal of the living God." This mark appears to communicate God's protective care that no one is able to subvert or undo. The living God,[12] as the source of life dwelling in eternity, is sending forth the angel on a mission to stay the destructive power of the winds.

b. "And he cried with a loud cry to the four angels to whom was given power to harm the earth and the sea." Apparently, angels sent on a mission by God cry out their message in a loud voice, because this wording occurs repeatedly in Revelation (10:3; 14:7, 9, 15; 18:2; 19:17). The loud cry is necessary to reach to the limits of the earth, so that all four angels can hear the angel's message. The angels addressed are holding the destructive power to harm both land and sea.

c. "Saying, 'Do not harm the earth, or the sea, or the trees until we have sealed the servants of our God on their foreheads.'" The word addressed to these four angels who are occupying places at the four directions of north, east, south, and west is not to harm land, sea, and trees. They are not allowed even to begin their destructive work. God gave the angel the message because it is God who cares for his creation and especially his people (compare 9:4). Jesus said, "Are not two sparrows sold for a penny? Yet not one of them will fall to the ground apart from the will of your Father. And even the very hairs of your head are all numbered" (Matt. 10:29–30). When the angel uses the word *trees* in the plural, he indicates that God's eye is on everything in his creation.

Although the angel who announces the message is alone, he represents a multitude of helpers when he says, "Until we have sealed the servants of our

12. The expression *the living God* is prevalent in both Old and New Testaments: Deut. 5:26; Josh. 3:10; 1 Sam. 17:26, 36; 2 Kings 19:4, 16; Ps. 42:2; 84:2; Isa. 37:4, 17; Jer. 10:10; 23:36; Dan. 6:26; Hos. 1:10; Matt. 16:16; 26:63; Acts 14:15.

God." God sends forth his angels to seal his people, for his servants belong to him and are known by a seal.

What precisely is a seal? William Hendriksen notes first that "it is the most precious thing under heaven" and then provides three functions of the *seal.* For one, it prevents tampering; next, it ensures ownership; and last, on a document it certifies genuineness.[13]

How are God's servants marked with a seal? As in all parts of the Apocalypse, John relies on the Old Testament Scriptures. The people of Judah had turned their backs on God and his temple and instead were worshiping nature. In a vision, the prophet Ezekiel saw a man dressed in linen with pen and inkwell in his hand, who was told to go through Jerusalem and put a mark on the foreheads of all those who were grieving because of the idolatry in the land (Ezek. 9:4). All the people were slaughtered except those who had the mark on their foreheads. The symbol of God's people is the invisible mark of the Father and the Lamb (Rev. 14:1) to signify that the saints are members of God's family, purchased by the Son, and filled with the Spirit. By contrast, unbelievers have the mark of the beast on their right hand and forehead (13:16).

The servants of God are not only prophets, pastors, and church officials, but they include all believers. That is, those who faithfully serve God by loving him with heart, soul, and mind and by loving their neighbors as themselves are servants. The word *servants,* occurring in 2:20; 19:2, 5; 22:3, 6 and in the Old Testament expression *servants of God,* denotes the saints. Servants are those people who reflect God's glory in every aspect of their lives. Hence, the invisible mark on their foreheads becomes visible in the words and deeds of these devoted followers of Jesus, as they walk in his footsteps.

d. "Sealed." How does a seal relate to the saints? First, they are safe, and no one, not even Satan, can snatch them out of God's hand (John 10:28). Next, they belong to Jesus and are his possession. And third, his word to them is true and unchangeable, and his promises are genuine.

> The Christian is sealed in this threefold sense. The Father has sealed him, for the believer enjoys the Father's protection throughout life. The Son has sealed him, for he has bought and redeemed the believer with His own precious blood. He owns us. The Spirit had sealed him (Eph. 1:13), for He testifies that we are sons of God (Rom. 8:16).[14]

Nevertheless, they are not exempt from physical harm. To this fact many Christians in the seven churches of the province of Asia were able to testify (see 2:10). Throughout the centuries, innumerable believers have been and presently are persecuted, beaten, and killed because of their testimony of Christ. What, then, is the meaning of being sealed? The answer lies in the word *until*—"until we have

13. William Hendriksen, *More Than Conquerors* (reprint, Grand Rapids: Baker, 1982), p. 110; see also Beale, *Revelation*, pp. 409–15.

14. Hendriksen, *More Than Conquerors*, p. 110.

sealed the servants of our God on their foreheads." God postpones judgment, pictured here by the destructive power of the winds, until the last of the saints has been gathered and sealed. The angels who mark the believers with a seal protect them from the coming judgment (see 9:4). Thus, being marked with the seal of the living God means that he protects his own people from this judgment (3:10).[15] It also answers the question raised in 6:17, "For the great day of their wrath has come, and who is able to stand?" Not the unbelievers who seek cover from mountains and rocks, but believers who are covered with God's seal. They are able to stand before him and the Lamb, for they have no fear of the judgment to come.

All the saints, sealed with the seal of the living God, are acquitted; they rejoice in the presence of the Lamb. Conversely, the enemies of God face the wrath of God and the Lamb and are unable to escape (6:15–17).

4. And I heard the number of those who had been sealed to be one hundred and forty-four thousand sealed from every tribe of Israel.

Notice that John switches from the verb *to see* to the verb *to hear,* and he uses the past tense, "I heard." In other words, hearing the number of those who received the seal is an indication that the total sum is not a secret. This knowledge does not have to wait until the last person has been marked with the seal of the living God. Even though the information relates to the future, the verb *had been sealed* is in the past tense. God knows the number of those who receive the seals, and John communicates this symbolically to the readers.

The number of those who are sealed is 144,000, which is twelve times twelve times a thousand (twelve squared times ten cubed).[16] The number twelve in the Apocalypse always refers to that which is perfect: the saints (7:5–8), the woman with twelve stars on her head (12:1), the twelve tribes of Israel (21:12), the various aspects of the new Jerusalem (21:12, 14, 16), and the twelve fruit-bearing trees (22:2). And the number one thousand is ten times ten times ten, which is a multitude. Ten is the number of fullness in the decimal system. Hence, 144,000 is a symbolic number that expresses a multitude marked by absolute perfection.[17] Twelve tribes of Israel times the twelve apostles (21:12, 14) times a

15. Reinier Schippers, *NIDNTT,* 3:500; Gottfried Fitzer, *TDNT,* 7:951; Tim Schramm, *EDNT,* 3:317.

16. Easley, *Revelation,* p. 125.

17. Karl Heinrich Rengstorf, *TDNT,* 2:324. Richard Bauckham avers that the 144,000 are the Israelite army of the lion of Judah fitted to reconquer the promised land in the messianic war. See his "List of the Tribes in Revelation 7 Again," *JSNT* 42 (1991): 99–115; refer to his *Climax of Prophecy,* pp. 215–37. Although he sees a model in Numbers 1, Revelation 7 points to the Lamb, who has triumphed (5:5), and the victory which saints and angels share. Further, the numbers 144,000 and 12,000 are to be understood symbolically, not literally. Next, Rev. 7 does not speak about a messianic war; indeed the context mentions "servants of our God" (v. 3) not "soldiers of our God." Verses 4–8 are devoid of military terms. Levi's name is listed, for the context does not mention military service or the possession of land. And last, if the 144,000 are male soldiers, then women are excluded from that number. John mentions the army of the Lord in 19:19, but he gives no indication that the army itself participates in warfare. Compare David E. Aune, *Revelation 6–16,* WBC 52B (Nashville: Nelson, 1998), p. 436.

thousand equals perfection times perfection times a multitude. Here is the picture of the ideal that is followed by a picture of the actual in verse 9.

"From every tribe of Israel." An incalculable multitude conveys the concept of harmony, unity, and excellence. Although the temptation is real to take the term "from every tribe of Israel" literally, the New Testament teaches that the walls of racial distinctions have been broken down. All believers are one in Jesus Christ (Rom. 10:12; 1 Cor. 12:13; Gal. 3:28; Eph. 2:14–16; Col. 3:11). Harmony in Christ Jesus transcends all ethnic, racial, social, and sexual divisions. In short, the term *Israel* in this verse represents God's people.

5. From the tribe of Judah 12,000 were sealed,
from the tribe of Reuben 12,000
from the tribe of Gad 12,000
6. from the tribe of Asher 12,000
from the tribe of Naphtali 12,000
from the tribe of Manasseh 12,000
7. from the tribe of Simeon 12,000
from the tribe of Levi 12,000
from the tribe of Issachar 12,000
8. from the tribe of Zebulun 12,000
from the tribe of Joseph 12,000
from the tribe of Benjamin 12,000 were sealed.

a. *Difficulties.* The first problem we face is the wording of verse 4 "from every tribe of Israel," which is explicated with a list of twelve tribes. However, elsewhere in the New Testament the expression *twelve tribes* refers to Israel as a nation and not to twelve individual tribes (Acts 26:7; James 1:1). The twelve tribes form the basis on which the structure of the house of God is built and completed, and all the inhabitants of God's house form one family without any division. Believers of peoples other than Israel are grafted into the olive tree, to use Paul's illustration, and grow alongside the natural branches (Rom. 11:17). Jesus said, "I have other sheep that are not of this sheep pen. I must bring them also. They too will listen to my voice, and there will be one flock and one shepherd" (John 10:16).

b. *Structure.* The sequence of the twelve tribes listed here differs considerably from those recorded elsewhere in the Old Testament. For example, "These were the twelve sons of Israel: Reuben, Simeon, Levi, Judah, Issachar, Zebulun, Dan, Joseph, Benjamin, Naphtali, Gad and Asher" (1 Chron. 2:1–2; see also Gen. 35:23–26). But Judah precedes Reuben the firstborn, Dan is missing from the list, and in his place, to make the number twelve complete, the name of Manasseh appears as the grandson of Israel (compare the list in Ezek. 48:1–7, 23–29).

There are at least three similar features in the lists of Revelation and 1 Chronicles. First, apart from the initial two verses in chapter two, the Chronicler catalogues foremost the family of Judah (2:3–4:23); second, he lists the family of Manasseh (5:23–26; 7:14–19) but puts Ephraim in the place of Joseph (7:20–29); and, third, he omits the family of Dan.

The reason for deleting the name of Dan from the list goes back to a narrative in which the descendants of Dan committed idolatry (Judg. 18:30–31). They were also the first to perpetrate the sin of apostasy, for they accepted a golden calf that Jeroboam placed in the northern part of Israel as a center of worship. He chose this location so that the people of Israel could worship there and would not need to travel to Jerusalem (1 Kings 12:29–30). Because of their grievous sin, the tribe of Dan was among the first to be exiled.[18] After the period of exile came to an end, Scripture no longer mentions Dan.

John also excludes Ephraim from his list. This tribe likewise agreed with Jeroboam to place another golden calf at Bethel as a substitute for the true worship of God in Jerusalem (1 Kings 12:29). Ephraim, therefore, should not be subsumed under the name of Joseph, for Joseph has taken the place of Ephraim (see Ps. 78:67b; Hos. 5:3–5).

The arrangement of the twelve tribes in Revelation differs for various reasons. Judah is mentioned first because his is the tribe into which Jesus was born (Matt. 1:3; 2:6; Luke 3:33; Heb. 7:14; Rev. 5:5). Levi's name is included because the context has nothing to do with military service or the material possession of territory (Num. 1:47; Deut. 10:9). Scholars have proposed a number of solutions. For instance, Henry Barclay Swete suggests that the sequence of John's list originates partly in the birth order of the twelve patriarchs and partly in the geographical location of the twelve tribes.[19] Judah is the royal tribe, followed by Reuben the firstborn. The tribe of Gad was given the territory to the north of the tribe of Reuben, east of the Jordan (Josh. 13:24–28). The tribes of Asher and Naphtali were in the northern and central part of Galilee, with that of Manasseh in the center of Israel. Simeon and Levi as sons of Leah followed Reuben in their succession of birth. The tribes of Issachar and Zebulun occupied the southern part of Galilee. And Joseph and Benjamin were the sons of Rachel.

Similarly Richard Bauckham suggests that at the time Revelation was written, a modified list differed from the standard order by featuring the sons in relation to their mothers. The sons of Leah are Judah, Reuben, Simeon, Levi, Issachar, and Zebulun, of which the last four were placed in block form after the sequence Gad,

---

18. Thomas, *Revelation 1–7*, p. 481. The tribe of Dan became part of Syria during the reign of King Asa (1 Kings 15:20; 2 Chron. 16:4) and was returned to Israel when Jeroboam II conquered it (2 Kings 14:25); the Assyrian ruler Tiglath-Pileser II seized the area in 722 B.C. and exiled its people (2 Kings 15:29). However, Ezekiel prophesied that Dan will receive a territory (Ezek. 48:1). Irenaeus (*Against Heresies* 5.30.2) speculated that from the tribe of Dan the Antichrist was expected to come. And Dan 5.6 of the *Testaments of the Twelve Patriarchs* states that the tribe of Dan had Satan as the guardian prince. See also Charles E. Hill, "Antichrist from the Tribe of Dan," *JTS*, n.s. 46 (1995): 99–117.

19. Henry Barclay Swete, *Commentary on Revelation* (1911; reprint, Grand Rapids: Kregel, 1977), p. 98.

Asher, Naphtali, and Manasseh.[20] This indeed is a helpful explanation, even if questions remain about Joseph and Manasseh and the exclusion of Ephraim.

The sequence of these names as such is not important. "Suffice it to say that in general terms, it is virtually impossible to account for the unusual order and composition of the list of tribes by interpreting it as descriptive of ethnic Israel. But seeing in this list a portrayal of the church as the New Israel . . . resolves the difficulties quite simply."[21] Significant is the great multitude that no one can number; it comes forth out of the twelve tribes of Israel. In response to the Great Commission (Matt. 28:20), a worldwide multitude has come to faith in Christ that with the saints of the Old Testament constitutes the full number of God's servants (Heb. 11:40).

Greek Words, Phrases, and Constructions in 7:1–3

Verse 1

μήτε ἐπὶ πᾶν δένδρον—literally, "and not on any tree." The negative particle appears in a clause introduced by ἵνα and controls the negations that follow. Nestle-Aland[27] makes allowance for a paragraph division in the sense of a new segment, so that verse 1 stands as an introductory verse.

Verse 2

αὐτοῖς—the personal pronoun is superfluous because of the indirect object οἷς (to whom). The construction is a Semitism, appearing repeatedly in Revelation (3:8; 7:9; 13:8, 12; 20:8).

Verse 3

μὴ ἀδικήσητε—the aorist subjunctive serves as the aorist imperative for a negative prohibition whose action has not yet begun.

μετώπων—this expression has the sense of "the space between the eyes."[22]

---

b. The Great Multitude *7:9–12*

9. After these things I saw, and look, a great multitude that no one could number, from every nation and all tribes and peoples and languages, standing before the throne and before the Lamb. They were dressed in white robes with palm branches in their hands.

a. *Method.* By reading the Apocalypse, we become increasingly aware that John writes the Revelation from a Jewish perspective. The author repeatedly presents

---

20. Bauckham ("List of the Tribes," p. 113) uses a list from Pseudo-Philo and the *Testaments of the Twelve Patriarchs.* R. E. Winkle ("Another Look at the List of Tribes in Revelation 7," *AUSS* 27 [1989]: 53–67) proposes that Dan is omitted because Judas Iscariot was associated with that tribe.

21. Christopher R. Smith, "The Portrayal of the Church as the New Israel in the Names and Order of the Tribes in Revelation 7.5–8," *JSNT* 39 (1990): 117.

22. A. T. Robertson, *A Grammar of the Greek New Testament in the Light of Historical Research* (Nashville: Broadman, 1934), p. 609.

his material in seemingly repetitious form meant to stress a certain point: two similar accounts of the same thing often emphasize a specific revelation John records. The first account is the ideal while the second is reality.

The figure 144,000 (v. 4) and the subsequent summation of the twelve tribes with 12,000 persons each (vv. 4–8) understood symbolically represent the ideal. With the use of numbers, John illustrates perfection as the ideal. In the next illustration, he describes reality by what he is permitted to see in heaven, namely, the saints standing before the throne of God and the Lamb (vv. 9–12). He had depicted elders and angels surrounding the divine throne in preceding chapters (chapters 4 and 5), but now he notes that an innumerable multitude enters heaven and approaches the throne. The first picture portrays God's people from a historical perspective, while the second picture displays the incalculable throng as the completed product of Christ's redemptive work.[23]

b. *Characteristics.* The phrase *after this* introduces a new picture that pertains not to earth but to heaven. John heard the number 144,000 in the preceding scene (v. 4); now he sees a great multitude that no one could number. He first notes the tribes of Israel (vv. 5–8); next he depicts saints "from every nation and all tribes and peoples and languages." The word *nation* (Greek *ethnos*) means all the peoples that constitute a nation. Often several people groups make up an entire nation, so the Greek term should be understood as all-inclusive. These people groups include the Jewish believers as part of this countless throng. The sealing of all these saints is understood and therefore needs no second mention. Here is a picture of the universal church in its fullest sense fulfilling Jesus' word: "And this gospel of the kingdom will be preached in the whole world as a testimony to all nations, and then the end will come" (Matt. 24:14).

Isbon Beckwith asks the question, "Who then, in the author's intention, are the 144,00 that are to be sealed?" His answer is that these people "are *the whole body of the Church,* Jewish and Gentile alike."[24] He notes that this observation conforms with John the Apocalyptist, for it "does the least violence to the universalistic spirit of the book." Indeed, John mentions the 144,000 again in 14:1, where the saints have the name of the Lamb and the Father written on their foreheads. These saints constitute all the redeemed. With the divine names as a seal on their foreheads they represent the multitude that no one can number.

23. Craig S. Keener, *Revelation,* NIVAC (Grand Rapids: Zondervan, 2000), p. 212. Raymond E. Brown (*An Introduction to the New Testament,* Anchor Bible Reference Library [New York: Doubleday, 1996], p. 788) proposes that the church succeeds Israel and thus includes the whole world. The 144,000 on earth and the multitude in heaven "could be describing a church that is both earthly and heavenly, both militant and triumphant." See also Harry R. Boer, *The Book of Revelation* (Grand Rapids: Eerdmans, 1979), p. 59. J. Ramsey Michaels (*Revelation,* IVP NTC [Downers Grove: InterVarsity, 1997], p. 113) notes: "144,000 Jews are transformed into an innumerable multitude from every nation on earth!"

24. Isbon T. Beckwith, *The Apocalypse of John* (1919; reprint, Grand Rapids: Baker, 1979), p. 535 (his emphasis). See also Charles, *Revelation,* 1:199–201.

The sequence of words *nation, tribe, people, and language* occurs seven times in various orders in Revelation (5:9; 7:9; 10:11; 11:9; 13:7; 14:6; 17:15; see the commentary on 5:9). In this picture, all the saints stand before the throne of God and the Lamb, namely, before their Creator and Redeemer.

c. *Description.* The saints are dressed in white, which is a fulfillment of Jesus' promise to the church in Sardis that the faithful ones will be dressed in white (3:4, 5). The color white signifies holiness. Also the souls under the altar were given white garments (6:11; see also 3:18; 4:4; 7:13). Here is a scene of heaven at the throne of God and the Lamb.

The saints are holding palm branches in their hands as a sign of victory. Of the four evangelists only John notes that at Jesus' triumphal entry on Palm Sunday the people took palm branches to welcome him. The phrase *palm branches* occurs twice in the New Testament, here and in John 12:13 (see also Lev. 23:40; 1 Macc. 13:51; 2 Macc. 10:7).[25] The victory belongs to Jesus Christ, who conquered Satan, death, and the grave; joy belongs to the saints who celebrate this victory.[26] They are eternally thankful for the redemption Christ obtained for them.

10. And they cried out with a loud voice, saying,

"Salvation belongs to our God who is seated
on the throne and to the Lamb."

The saints in heaven sing a song with one accord, even though they came from many nations and spoke different languages. In heaven the confusion of Babel has ended and the speech of the saints is all the same. As in other places, John hears the dwellers in heaven speak in a loud voice, but here in jubilation. They sing a song in which the word *salvation* receives all the emphasis because of the work of redemption accomplished by the Lamb.

The redeemed are standing before the throne and before the Lamb. God who is seated on the throne planned the work of saving his people and commissioned his Son to initiate, execute, and complete it. With their song they express praise and thanks to God and the Lamb, who died, rose from the grave, and ascended to heaven to take his place at the right hand of God. They sing a song of victory which resembles the "Hosanna" (Lord, grant help) the people sang when Jesus came to Jerusalem (Matt. 21:9). Whereas the people surrounding Jesus at

25. J. A. Draper ("The Heavenly Feast of Tabernacles: Revelation 7:1–17," *JSNT* 19 [1983]: 133–47) suggests the possibility that some groups of Christians kept the Feast of Tabernacles, which gave impetus to the eschatological significance for the Apocalypse. But we do not have to infer that the palm branches point to a heavenly Feast of Tabernacles or a Feast of Dedication. "It is entirely sufficient . . . to regard the palm-branches as a sign of festal joy" (Friedrich Düsterdieck, *Critical and Exegetical Handbook to the Revelation of John* [New York and London: Funk and Wagnalls, 1886], p. 251). See also H. Ulfgard, *Feast and Future: Revelation 7:9–17 and the Feast of Tabernacles*, ConNT 22 (Stockholm: Almqvist & Wiksell, 1989).

26. Paul Ellingworth ("Salvation to Our God," *BibTrans* 34 [1983]: 444–45) asserts that the Greek word *sōtēria* conveys the Old Testament idea of "victory" in Rev. 7:10; 12:10; 19:1, and should be translated accordingly.

his triumphal entry were asking for salvation, the saints in heaven praise him for answering this request.

11. And all the angels stood around the throne, the elders, and the four living creatures; and they fell before the throne on their faces and worshiped God, 12. saying,

> **"Amen! Praise and glory and wisdom and thanksgiving**
> **and honor and power and strength be to our God**
> **forever and ever. Amen!"**

a. *Construction.* An innumerable multitude is singing praises of thanksgiving to God and the Lamb while the rest of the heavenly beings fall down worshiping God before his throne. The order is the reverse of that given in chapter 5, where the sequence of the worshipers is the four living creatures, the elders, all the angels, and last "every creature in heaven and on earth and under the earth and on the sea, and all things in them" (5:13). Here the progression is the multitude of saints, all the angels, the elders, and the four living beings.

The song of all the angels, the elders, and the living beings (5:12) is nearly the same as the one sung here. There they said, "Worthy is the Lamb that was slain to receive power and wealth and wisdom and strength and honor and glory and thanksgiving." Here they sing: "Amen! Praise and glory and wisdom and thanksgiving and honor and power and strength be to our God forever and ever. Amen!" Apart from sequence, the differences are that instead of "wealth" the present song has "thanksgiving" and the amen at both the beginning and the end. Note that the two songs have exactly seven attributes each—the number of completeness. The song of the redeemed in verse 10 is the last song dedicated to the Lamb in the Apocalypse, whereas this hymn is sung to worship God.

b. *Explanation.* The angels punctuate their song at the beginning and the end with the word *amen* (so be it). The duplication of this term intimates that their hymn was sung antiphonally in relation to the song of the saints. All of the angels wholeheartedly voice their agreement with the song of the countless multitude, because they rejoice over one sinner who repents (Luke 15:10) and they have stooped to look intently into the mystery of salvation (1 Pet. 1:12).

The sevenfold string of attributes is not meant to be exhaustive but highlights the praises sung by the psalmists in the Psalter. They sing of God's power, strength, splendor, glory, majesty, wealth, and honor (e.g., Ps. 24:8; 59:17; 62:11; 89:11; see 1 Chron. 29:11). All these virtues belong to God, whom the angels adore as "our God." To him they express their praises and thanksgiving forever and ever. The attributes of praise, glory, wisdom, thanks, honor, power, and strength occur repeatedly in the New Testament, some of them frequently, for example, the terms *glory* and *power.*

Greek Words, Phrases, and Constructions in 7:9

ἐκ παντὸς ἔθνους—"from every nation." Even though παντός is singular, the words "tribes," "peoples," and "languages" are in the plural and call for the plural form of the adjective ("all") to be supplied mentally.

περιβεβλημένους—the perfect passive participle of a compound verb, literally, "having been wrapped around [with robes]." The perfect tense indicates action in the past with lasting significance; the passive voice shows that God is the agent.

c. An Interview *7:13–17*

13. And one of the elders asked me, "These people who are dressed in white robes—who are they and where did they come from?" 14. And I said to him, "Sir, you know." And he said to me, "These are they who have come out of the great tribulation and have washed their robes and have made them white in the blood of the Lamb."

a. *Question.* Earlier an elder addressed John and told him not to weep, because the lion of the tribe of Judah, the root of David, had triumphed (5:5). Now for a second time one of them approaches John. The elder asks where the saints, dressed in white robes, come from. This inquiry is for the sake not of gathering knowledge but of teaching a fact. The link between the two appearances of elders instructing John is clear: in the first instance, John feared that the redemption of God's people would not be fulfilled (see 5:4). Now by questioning John, the elder points to the countless multitude dressed in white robes. He wants John to acknowledge that the lion of Judah has indeed fulfilled the Old Testament promises of salvation. The elder is the representative of the church in heaven and wants John to see promise and fulfillment. The saints in white robes are indeed the people whom the Lamb with his blood purchased for God (5:9). The color white denotes holiness and purity, for the blood of the Lamb cleansed the saints. Their robes are whiter than snow (Dan. 7:9).

"Who are they and where did they come from?" Here is a question that pertains to strangers who entered and needed identification. So Joshua asked the Gibeonites the same question (Josh. 9:8; and compare Jonah 1:8).

The question and answer technique is one of the oldest teaching methods. Not the student but the teacher is asking an obvious query that calls for an insightful reply. John should know the answer because he already witnessed the opening of the fifth seal, when the saints in heaven received white garments (6:11).

b. *Answer.* The answer John gives is short, to the point, and sufficient. "And I said to him, 'Sir, you know'" (compare Ezek. 37:3). With his brief reply, John implies that the elder is the one who should furnish a response, for as the representative of the church he knows exactly when and from where the saints have come. John may be perplexed when he observes the innumerable celestial throng. He places the burden of proof on his inquirer and forces him to answer. He defers to the elder, who has the response to his own query.

c. *Identification.* "And he said to me, 'These are they who have come out of the great tribulation.'" This part of the text is open to interpretations that depend on the theology and hermeneutics of a commentator.[27] It is impossible to interpret the Book of Revelation without an exegetical methodology, for it even affects translation, as is evident in this verse. The Greek verb form *erchomenoi* is a present participle ("the ones who are coming"), but it is translated "come" (NASB), "came" (KJV), or "have come" (NIV). Most scholars prefer the last one, "have come," because of the past tense in the following two verbs, "they have washed their robes" and "they have made them white." They define the present tense of the participle "coming" as timeless, so that John is able to look at the multitude apart from the action of the saints coming into heaven.

The verb *have come* is linked to the phrase *out of the great tribulation.* Some conclude that this phrase refers to the end time when believers will experience martyrdom just before Christ returns.[28] The context, however, indicates that the phrase relates to the innumerable multitude from all nations, tribes, peoples, and languages (v. 9). Here is a picture of all the saints clothed in white apparel standing before the throne and the Lamb. The expression *the great tribulation* includes all Christians who have experienced oppression and persecution everywhere throughout history. It is a universal and collective expression that encompasses all the saints throughout the ages. Everyone who has experienced the hatred and opposition of the evil one is included. The Scriptures teach that God's people of all places and of all times have encountered, do encounter, and will encounter persecutions, dangers, and hardships until the end of the age.[29] Old Testament saints suffered for the cause of their God (see Heb. 11:4–38). Christians in the early church suffered for the name of Christ; countless believers in the sixteenth and seventeenth centuries sustained persecution for their faith; and today more Christians lose their lives in persecutions than at any other time. All these saints have gone through the great tribulation. John presents a total picture of the celestial throng dressed in white robes.

In the Old Testament a prophecy speaks of a future "time of distress such as has not happened from the beginning of nations until then" (Dan. 12:1). This prophecy was fulfilled in the time of Antiochus Epiphanes, who defiled the temple in Jerusalem and brought about "the abomination that causes desolation" in 167 B.C. (Dan. 9:27; 11:31; 12:11). What Daniel predicted was fully accomplished (1 Macc. 9:27). Nonetheless, his prophecy also relates to other difficult times.

---

27. Compare Johnson, *Revelation,* 12:488.

28. John F. Walvoord, *The Revelation of Jesus Christ* (Chicago: Moody, 1966), p. 146; Thomas, *Revelation 1–7,* p. 497.

29. Refer to Van de Kamp, *Israël in Openbaring,* p. 144; Greijdanus, *Openbaring,* p. 175. Beale (*Revelation,* p. 434) remarks that the "'greatness' of the tribulation is the intensity of the seduction and oppression through which believers pass."

Jesus quoted Daniel's prophecy on "the abomination that causes desolation" (Matt. 24:15) and applied it to the destruction of Jerusalem in A.D. 70. In that same context, referring to the flight of its inhabitants in winter or on the Sabbath, he said: "For then there will be great distress, unequaled from the beginning of the world until now—and never to be equaled again" (Matt. 24:21, and see parallel passages). Jesus' prophecy came true forty years later when Jerusalem was taken, its people were killed or exiled, and its destruction became a byword. Even though no one doubts the severity of Jerusalem's demise and decimation of its inhabitants, this prophecy also comprises "the entire period beginning with the devastation in A.D. 70 and continuing on until Christ's return."[30] It is like seeing towering peaks, the one behind the other, in a mountainous landscape; the first one is high, but the second higher still.

d. *Symbolism.* John writes that these saints "washed their robes and have made them white in the blood of the Lamb." God told the Israelites at Mount Sinai to wash their clothes before coming before him (Exod. 19:10, 14). To stand before God in filthy garments is an abomination to him. The elder addressing John speaks symbolically not of the Israelites on earth but of the saints in heaven who appear in white robes (vv. 9, 13). These saints have washed their robes and made them white, not as two separate acts but as one procedure.

Note that the saints under the altar were given white robes (6:11), while here they *washed* them white. When sinners confess their sins, God forgives his people by making them pure. They purify their clothes, not through the blood of their own martyrdom but through the blood of the Lamb. Making one's garments white, that is, pure and holy, can be done without exception only through Christ's blood shed on Calvary's cross. It is his blood that removes the impurity of sin. "Without the shedding of blood there is no forgiveness [of sin]" (Heb. 9:22). We can interpret this passage only in symbolical terms, because it is impossible to think of red blood making clothes white (compare Gen. 49:11). The precious blood of Christ figuratively cleanses sinners from every sin to present them holy and spotless to God (Eph. 5:26–27; 1 John 1:7).

The next three verses appear to be a hymn sung in worship of God. It is a picture of heavenly bliss with the saints serving God continuously, free from earthly ills and pains. It is a picture of the Shepherd leading and feeding his sheep, an illustration of joy and eternal happiness. For this reason, editors and translators have presented the text in poetic form (e.g, Nes-Al[27], UBS[4], NIV, NRSV).

15. "Therefore, they are before the throne
of God
and serve him day and night in his temple,
and he who is seated on the throne will
spread his tent over them.
16. And they will neither hunger nor thirst
anymore

30. Craig L. Blomberg, *Matthew,* NAC 22 (Nashville: Broadman, 1992), p. 359.

neither will the sun beat down on them
nor any scorching heat."

a. "Therefore, they are before the throne of God and serve him day and night in his temple." This report of heavenly bliss is repeated in the last chapter of Revelation, "And the throne of God and of the Lamb will be in it, and his servants will serve him" (22:3). The scene is similarly described in 21:3–4, where a voice from the throne calls attention to God dwelling with his people to be their God; he cares for them by having removed from them death, grief, sorrow, and pain. The clause "before the throne of God" implies that the saints have direct access to the one who occupies that throne. Their relation to God is the same as it was in the Garden of Eden when God walked and talked with Adam and Eve.

Especially significant is the continuous service God's people render in his presence. The word *temple* refers not to the structure of a building but rather to the Holy of Holies, which is the place where God dwells. Some commentators see a conflict in this verse with Revelation 21:22, which reads that the new Jerusalem has no temple.[31] But John explains that "the Lord God Almighty and the Lamb are its temple," which means that because of the pervading presence of God and the Lamb the new Jerusalem is itself a sanctuary. Hence, being in the presence of God before his throne and serving him ceaselessly can be compared to the role of the high priest. Once a year the high priest entered God's sacred presence momentarily on the Day of Atonement, but the saints dwell in God's presence not for a few minutes but forever. They do not sprinkle the blood of a bull and a goat to be cleansed from sin, for they are sinless. And no longer do they petition God for remission of sin, for they are cleansed. Thus they serve him continually by praising and thanking him (22:3). The saints in heaven know no division of day and night; John remarks, "And there will be no night there" (22:5).

b. "And he who is seated on the throne will spread his tent over them." This sentence seems to be a poetic description of God protecting his people. *The one seated on the throne* is the phrase used to describe God,[32] and the clause *he will spread his tent over them* is significant theologically. Here is the divine promise that God grants his people security with his personal presence. This is a teaching that permeates Scripture from Leviticus to Revelation: God's desire to dwell with his people and to have them acknowledge him as their God. Notice the repeated wording of this desire in the following passages:

- "I will put my dwelling place among you, and I will not abhor you. I will walk among you and be your God, and you will be my people" (Lev. 26:11–12).

31. Charles (*Revelation*, 1:215) states, "In the *original* form of the vision, vii.9–17 . . . the phrase ἐν τῷ ναῷ αὐτοῦ was probably absent." But without manuscript evidence, his remark has lost its strength.
32. Rev. 5:1, 7, 13; 6:16; 7:10, 15; 19:4; 20:11; 21:5.

- "I will make a covenant of peace with them; it will be an everlasting covenant. . . . I will put my sanctuary among them forever. My dwelling place will be with them; I will be their God, and they will be my people" (Ezek. 37:26–27).
- "I will bring them back to live in Jerusalem; they will be my people, and I will be faithful and righteous to them as their God" (Zech. 8:8).
- "And I saw the holy city, the new Jerusalem, coming down out of heaven from God prepared as a bride adorned for her husband. And I heard a loud voice from the throne saying, 'Look, the tabernacle of God is with people, and he will dwell with them, and they will be his people, and God himself will be with them and be their God'" (Rev. 21:2–3).

This is covenant language that expresses God's desire for intimate communion with his people by dwelling with them in the same sanctuary. In the Garden of Eden God had fellowship with Adam and Eve. While sin disrupted this relationship, Christ Jesus restored it through his mediatorial work. The complete fulfillment comes at the renewal of God's creation.[33]

17. "Because the Lamb at the center of the throne will shepherd them,
and he will lead them to springs of living water,
and God will wipe away every tear from their eyes."

John's mind is fixed on the Old Testament Scriptures, particularly a passage that speaks of the restoration of God's people. "They will neither hunger nor thirst, nor will the desert heat or the sun beat upon them. He who has compassion on them will guide them and lead them beside springs of water" (Isa. 49:10; compare 4:5–6). God's people knew the deprivation of food and water when they had to travel through the deserts that bordered their land.

This Old Testament passage refers to the return from Babylonian captivity to the land of Israel. God told his people that they would be neither hungry nor thirsty. He would supply them with the basic necessities of life to still their hunger and quench their thirst at oases. There he would shield them from the heat of the sun and the scorching wind of the desert.

Further, this passage, taken from a chapter that depicts the Servant of the Lord, that is, the Messiah, predicts the restoration of Israel (Isa. 49). The Messiah will sustain God's people with spiritual and material blessings in this life and in the life to come. Here is a description of sustenance and solace for all the saints who put their trust in God. Jesus says, "Blessed are those who hunger and thirst for righteousness, for they will be filled" (Matt. 5:6).

---

33. Refer to Philip Edgcumbe Hughes, *The Book of the Revelation: A Commentary* (Leicester: Inter-Varsity; Grand Rapids: Eerdmans, 1990), p. 99.

a. "Because the Lamb at the center of the throne will shepherd them." The Lamb of God who was slain to redeem his people stands at the center, near the midpoint, of God's throne. He is between God, seated on the throne, and the four living beings. No being is closer to God himself than the Lamb, who is now given the role of Shepherd. This role change, like so many in the Apocalypse, should be understood symbolically. Peter meditates on the concept of the sacrificial Lamb when he quotes Isaiah 53:9, "He committed no sin, and no deceit was found in his mouth" (1 Pet. 2:22). Then he notes that the Lamb's wounds healed his readers. "For you were like sheep going astray, but now you have returned to the Shepherd and Overseer of your souls" (1 Pet. 2:25).

During his earthly ministry, Jesus revealed himself as the Shepherd of his people. He called himself the Good Shepherd and instructed Peter to shepherd his sheep (John 10:11, 14; 21:16). And in turn Peter calls Jesus the Chief Shepherd, while he and fellow elders serve him as shepherds of God's flock (1 Pet. 5:1–4).[34] These portrayals are taken from agricultural Israel. So David composed Psalm 23 and the prophet Ezekiel transmitted the word of God to his people, "I will place over them one shepherd, my servant David, and he will tend them; he will tend them and be their shepherd" (Ezek. 34:23). Jesus the Good Shepherd protects his sheep from danger and from harm, leads them to green pastures, and finds streams of refreshing water for them.

b. "And he will lead them to springs of living water." The Lamb who is now the Shepherd leads the sheep to springs of living water. The imagery is a clear reminder of the Samaritan woman who asked Jesus for living water so that she would no longer be thirsty and have to keep coming back to Jacob's well (John 4:15). Water symbolizes eternal life (Isa. 55:1; John 7:38, 39). Near the end of the Apocalypse, Jesus refers to himself as the Alpha and the Omega, the Beginning and the End. Then he offers to all those who are thirsty to drink freely from the spring of water of life (21:6; 22:17).

c. "And God will wipe away every tear from their eyes." If there is one text in Scripture that comforts the saints, it is this verse. Here we meet the infinite tenderness of our God, who is able to remove from our eyes every tear caused by suffering, death, and sorrow. John again quotes from the Old Testament, where God is saying to his people that he will swallow up death forever and will wipe away the tears from all faces (Isa. 25:8; see Jer. 31:16). And in John's vision of the new Jerusalem, God dwells with his people and as their God will wipe every tear from their eyes. "There will be no more death or mourning or crying or pain, for the old order of things has passed away" (Rev. 21:4). This is eternal bliss that can be portrayed only in pictures borrowed from this earthly scene—God bending down as a parent to wipe tears from the faces of his children.

34. As God's flock, Christians have spiritual shepherds. Refer to Matt. 26:31; Mark 14:27; Acts 20:28; 1 Pet. 5:2; *1 Clem.* 16.1; 44.3; 54.2; 57.2. See Joachim Jeremias, *TDNT*, 6:500–502; Aune, *Revelation 6–16*, p. 478.

The last line in this verse is a picture of joy and happiness, of deliverance from sin and guilt, of salvation full and free. It is a scene of life in the fullest sense of the word—to be forever in the presence of our covenant God, who dwells in the midst of the glorified saints. It is Paradise restored.

Greek Words, Phrases, and Constructions in 7:14–17

Verse 14

εἴρηκα—the perfect tense instead of the aoristic perfect, which is the "vivid, dramatic perfect in narrative."[35]

οἱ ἐρχόμενοι—some interpreters see the articular participle as a noun, "the comers," to eliminate a reference to time.[36]

Verse 15

The Greek of the New Testament has two words for the verb *to serve*: λατρεύειν, which denotes the general service of all the people, and λειτουργεῖν, which means service in a particular office such as the priesthood.[37] Here the present tense of λατρεύουσιν indicates that all the saints in heaven serve God and that the priesthood as such has come to an end. The family of λειτουργεῖν with nouns and adjective is absent from the Apocalypse.

Verse 16

πέσῃ ἐπί—Swete prefers the reading παίσῃ ἔτι (strikes continually) as "an attractive conjecture."[38] But unless a reading makes no sense at all, resorting to the use of a conjecture is not recommended. In this case, the text has a message.

---

35. Lenski, *Revelation*, p. 260; Robertson, *Grammar*, p. 902; Friedrich Blass and Albert Debrunner, *A Greek Grammar of the New Testament*, trans. and rev. Robert Funk (Chicago: University of Chicago Press, 1961), §343.1.

36. E.g., Beckwith, *Apocalypse*, p. 545.

37. Consult Richard C. Trench, *Synonyms of the New Testament*, ed. Robert G. Hoerber (Grand Rapids: Baker, 1989), pp. 137–39.

38. *Revelation*, p. 105.

8

The Seventh Seal and the First Four Trumpets

(8:1–13)

Outline (continued)

8. The Seventh Seal: The Judgment of Unbelievers (8:1)

IV. Vision 3: Seven Trumpets (8:2–11:19)
   A. Introduction (8:2–5)
   B. Seven Trumpeting Angels (8:6–11:19)
      1. The First Trumpet (8:6–7)
      2. The Second Trumpet (8:8–9)
      3. The Third Trumpet (8:10–11)
      4. The Fourth Trumpet (8:12)
      5. The Three Woes (8:13)

8

1 And when he opened the seventh seal, there was silence in heaven for about half an hour.

2 And I saw seven angels who stood before God, and they were given seven trumpets.

3 And another angel came and stood at the altar. He had a golden censer and was given much incense, to offer it with the prayers of all the saints on the golden altar before the throne.
4 And the smoke of the incense with the prayers of the saints went up out of the hand of the angel before God. 5 And the angel took the censer and filled it with fire from the altar and cast it on the earth. And there were claps of thunder and rumblings and flashes of lightning and an earthquake.

6 And the seven angels who held the seven trumpets prepared themselves to blow them. 7 And the first angel blew the trumpet, and there was hail and fire mixed with blood and it was cast upon the earth. And a third of the earth was burned, and a third of the trees were burned, and all the green grass was burned.

8 And the second angel blew the trumpet. And as it were a huge mountain burning with fire was cast into the sea, and a third of the sea became blood. 9 And a third of the living creatures in the sea died, and a third of the ships were destroyed.

10 And the third angel blew the trumpet. And a great star fell from the sky, burning as a torch, and it fell upon a third part of the rivers and upon the springs of water. 11 And the name of the star was Wormwood, and a third part of the water became wormwood, and many people died because of the water that had become bitter.

12 And the fourth angel blew the trumpet. And a third part of the sun and a third part of the moon and a third part of the stars were struck, so that a third part of them became dark and a third part of the day did not shine and likewise a third part of the night.

13 And I saw, and I heard an eagle flying in mid-heaven saying in a loud voice, "Woe, woe, woe to the inhabitants of the earth because of the trumpet sounds about to be blown by the other three angels."

---

8. The Seventh Seal: The Judgment of Unbelievers
8:1

1. And when he opened the seventh seal, there was silence in heaven for about half an hour.

The seventh seal follows the sixth one and is separated by the interlude of chapter 7. The two seals have a common purpose, namely, the portrayal of God judging the unbelievers. Notice that the sequence of the first four seals pictures horses and their riders. The fifth seal reveals the souls under the altar asking God to avenge their spilled blood. And the sixth seal depicts the wicked calling on the mountains and the rocks to cover them from the wrath of God and the Lamb. The seventh seal is a continuation of the sixth seal, but now there is a period of silence "either preceding or following *the* final judgment."[1]

---

1. Gregory K. Beale, *The Book of Revelation: A Commentary on the Greek Text*, NIGTC (Grand Rapids: Eerdmans, 1998), p. 448 (his emphasis).

Throughout the Apocalypse, John contrasts the bliss of the saints in heaven and the horror of the wicked when the wrath of God strikes them. This contrast is evident in the second half of the preceding chapter that describes the lot of the redeemed (7:9–17) and in the verses that reveal the lot of God's enemies on the Judgment Day (6:12–17).

"The opening of the seventh seal, however, cannot follow the sixth in chronological sequence, because the content of that seal portrayed the final day of wrath (6:12–17)."[2] The message of both seals relates to the same event, namely, the judgment of the wicked.

The structure of Revelation shows an ever-increasing, spiraling emphasis on the coming judgment. John pictures the wicked meeting their end when they face the wrath of God (6:17). Then in the interlude of chapter 7, he portrays the sealing of the 144,000 who, triumphing over their tribulation, enter the presence of God. Chapter 8 begins with a period of silence in heaven that is awe-inspiring with reference to God judging his enemies. God hears the ascending prayers of the saints and punishes the wicked. This theme occurring again and again imparts a telescopic structure to the Apocalypse. The recurring theme of the Judgment Day appears at the end of every cycle of the seven churches, the seven seals, the seven trumpets, and the seven plagues.

"The unity of John's book, then, is neither choronological nor arithmetical, but artistic, like that of a musical theme with variations, each variation adding something new to the significance of the whole composition. This is the only view which does adequate justice to the double fact that each new series of visions both recapitulates and develops the themes already stated in what has gone before."[3]

And last, the background to the silence in heaven in the presence of God comes from the Old Testament prophets (Hab. 2:20; Zech. 2:13). That silence expressed in human terms of cosmic time, "half an hour," is not an empty period but is a time of the outpouring of God's wrath. The time references that John mentions have little relevance in Revelation, because not chronological time but the abiding principle of time is significant. The silence observed in heaven is an awed hush while God executes justice.

IV. Vision 3: Seven Trumpets
8:2–11:19

The seven trumpets are divided over three chapters: chapter 8 features four trumpets, chapter 9 two, and the seventh trumpet is not introduced until 11:15. As the seventh seal comes after an interlude (7:1–17), so the seventh trumpet is

2. Geoffrey B. Wilson, *Revelation* (Welwyn, England: Evangelical Press, 1985), p. 77; see also R. C. H. Lenski (*The Interpretation of St. John's Revelation* [Columbus: Wartburg, 1943], p. 267), who writes, "What the seventh seal uncovers cannot chronologically follow what the sixth seal reveals." See also Gerhard A. Krodel, *Revelation*, ACNT (Minneapolis: Augsburg, 1989), pp. 189–90.

3. G. B. Caird, *A Commentary on the Revelation of St. John the Divine* (London: Black, 1966), p. 106.

separated from the preceding trumpets by an intermission that reveals the topics of the angel with the little scroll and the two witnesses (10:1–11:13).

The opening of the seventh seal introduces a series of plagues that again conclude with a message of judgment. The adversaries who wanted to destroy God's creation now face their own destruction, for the time of their judgment has come (11:18).[4] With every cycle of disasters in the Apocalypse, John provides more information and greater understanding of the final drama that unfolds in the consummation.

In the sequence of the seven angels who blow their trumpets, chapters 8 and 9 form a unit, while chapter 10 and the first half of 11 are an interlude. Yet the interlude shows a certain parallelism with chapters 8 and 9. The sound of the seven thunders corresponds to that of the seven angels blowing their trumpets (8:6 and 10:3–4); fire spews forth to devour the enemies of God (9:17–18 and 11:5); water turns into blood (8:8 and 11:6); and the first and second woes are followed by a third (8:13; 9:12; 11:14).

The recurring picture in 8:2 through 11:14 is that of impending judgment on unbelievers. This becomes evident in the trumpet sounds of the angels and the repeated call of the woes (8:13; 9:12; and 11:14). When plagues strike the world and its evil inhabitants, we see divine execution in response to the prayers of the saints (8:4–5). Because of the unbelievers' refusal to repent, God strikes them for committing theft and manslaughter, engaging in magic arts, and indulging in sexual immorality (9:21; 11:7–10). Incidentally, as the Apocalypse calls people to repentance, the saints obey while sinners harden their hearts and refuse to repent (9:21; 16:9, 11).

There is a parallel in the opening of the seals in 6:1–16 and the plagues described in 8:6–9:21: both the opening of the seals and the blowing of the trumpets reveal catastrophes. But the calamities connected to the seven seals pave the way for the rider on the white horse, which I have interpreted as the unstoppable advance of the Word of God on the face of the earth (see the commentary on 6:2).[5] When the trumpets are sounded, God's wrath is poured out on the wicked who have demonstrated their hatred toward him, his Word, and his people. The seven trumpet calls are divided into the first four, which affect the natural world, followed by the next two (the fifth and sixth trumpets), which harm and kill the inhabitants of the earth. The seventh trumpet ushers in the consummation of God's wrath. Indeed, "the judgments of the trumpets increase in intensity as they progress."[6]

4. Consult Martin Kiddle, *The Revelation of St. John* (reprint, London: Hodder and Stoughton, 1943), pp. 144–45.

5. Refer to S. Greijdanus, *De Openbaring des Heeren aan Johannes,* KNT (Amsterdam: Van Bottenburg, 1925), p. 179. See also E. Cuvillier, "Jugement et destruction du monde dans l'Apocalypse de Jean: Notes exégétiques sur Ap 8–9 et Ap 15–16," *FoiVie* 91 (1992): 53–67.

6. Jon Paulien, *Decoding Revelation's Trumpets: Literary Allusions and the Interpretation of Revelation 8:7–12,* AUSDDS 11 (Berrien Springs, Mich.: Andrews University Press, 1987), p. 325.

Chapter 6 lists the seals that introduce the persecution of the saints, chapter 7 depicts the saints protected from all harm because they have been sealed, and chapters 8 and 9 recount the sounding of the judgment trumpets that augur destruction for the wicked. Notice that the sounding of the trumpets constitutes warning signs to those people who oppose God. When they refuse to listen, then the bowls of wrath are poured out upon them. "The very function of the trumpets is to warn."[7] The warnings are preliminary to their impending doom.

A. Introduction
8:2–5

The Lamb opened the seven seals, but angels blow the trumpets. The emphasis, therefore, is on the task of the angels, who, though not mentioned by name, are given specific responsibilities. They do not serve as mediators between God and humans; their task is to serve (compare Heb. 1:14) and stand in God's presence.

The subtle contrast of verse 2 and verses 3–5 should not be overlooked. Seven angels are given seven trumpets with which they announce imminent destruction, while another angel mixes incense at the altar with the prayers of the saints and presents them to God. This section of chapter 8, then, is both explanatory and introductory to the rest of this chapter and the next.

2. And I saw seven angels who stood before God, and they were given seven trumpets. 3. And another angel came and stood at the altar. He had a golden censer and was given much incense, to offer it with the prayers of all the saints on the golden altar before the throne. 4. And the smoke of the incense with the prayers of the saints went up out of the hand of the angel before God.[8]

a. "And I saw seven angels who stood before God, and they were given seven trumpets." Scripture records only two names of archangels: Michael (Dan. 10:13, 21; 12:1; Jude 9; Rev. 12:7) and Gabriel (Luke 1:19, 26). Other traditional names are Uriel, Raphael, Raguel, Sariel, and Remiel. Note that all seven names of these archangels end in *-el*, which relates them to God, who is Elohim. Also, the concept of "the seven holy angels who present the prayers of the saints and enter into the presence of the glory of the Holy One" comes from Tobit 12:15 (RSV), which lists Raphael as one of them.[9] These seven angels are given trum-

7. William Hendriksen, *More Than Conquerors* (reprint, Grand Rapids: Baker, 1982), p. 116. Compare also William Barclay (*The Revelation of John*, 2d ed. [Philadelphia: Westminster, 1960], 2:52), who notes that a trumpet blast denotes (1) alarm, (2) arrival of royalty, and (3) summons to battle. Clearly the sound of the trumpet here is a warning of impending danger.

8. R. H. Charles (*A Critical and Exegetical Commentary on the Revelation of St. John*, ICC [Edinburgh: Clark, 1920], 1:218; 2:407–9) rearranges the text by placing verse 2 after verse 5 and verse 13 after verse 6. Consequently, when the rearrangement does not fit, he labels the text "hopelessly corrupt." Also Barclay (*Revelation of John*, 2:48) follows Charles in placing verse 2 after verse 6 and calls the present sequence "a copyist's mistake."

9. *1 Enoch* 20.2–8; 90.21, 22 mention seven names and call them archangels. Consult Henry Barclay Swete, *Commentary on Revelation* (1911; reprint, Grand Rapids: Kregel, 1977), p. 107. See also Charles, *Revelation*, 1:225; David E. Aune, *Revelation 6–16*, WBC 52B (Nashville: Nelson, 1998), p. 509; and Kendell H. Easley, *Revelation*, HNTC (Nashville: Broadman & Holman, 1998), p. 142.

pets (compare Matt. 24:31) and blow them to usher in God's initial judgment on his adversaries. Their final judgment comes when they stand before the great white throne (20:11–15). The expression "seven angels" reappears in the context of the seven plagues. Even though we could assume that they are the same group of seven, we have no certainty because countless angels surround God's throne. This is evident from other passages (v. 3; 7:2; 10:1; 18:1; 20:1). Also, the number seven conveys the meaning of completeness and need not be taken literally.

b. "And another angel came and stood at the altar." John wishes to show the reader another development that is taking place at the altar. Hence, the scene shifts not to indicate a delay in the sounding of the trumpets, but to reveal in the intervening paragraph the effect that the prayers of the saints have on the course of history. The focus is on an angel and the altar.

We are not told anything about the identity of this angel. If the text itself is not explicit, we ought not to read into it the identity of the Lord Jesus Christ. The context does not indicate that John is speaking of the Lord, though some may see the incense as a symbolic reference to Jesus Christ, who serves the saints as their intercessor in heaven (Rom. 8:34; Heb. 7:25; 9:24).[10] The multitude of angels is so large that this angel is only one of them. For instance, the expression *another angel* occurs elsewhere (10:1; 18:1); and the adjective *another* is meant to alert the reader to the mighty angel who sounded the call to break the seals of the scroll and open it (5:2). The angel, however, is only a servant who functions at the altar of incense; he is not a mediator and does not presume to take the place of Jesus.

The altar of incense in the tabernacle was a copy of the one in heaven.[11] This altar was most holy to the Lord God, because on its horns once a year the high priest made atonement with the blood of the sin offering (Exod. 30:10). With his sacrifice on the cross Jesus has fulfilled the need for atonement once for all. By it he removed the sins of his people (Heb. 9:28); and he perfected his people and their prayers.

c. "[The angel] had a golden censer and was given much incense, to offer it with the prayers of all the saints on the golden altar before the throne." A censer is a container with incense, which was often made from the aromatic gum of a frankincense tree. This incense was burned so that the smoke permeated the area with its fragrant aroma. Presumably God gave the angel a bountiful supply of incense. The multitude of prayers uttered by all the saints on earth had to be mixed with this sweet-smelling fragrance (compare 5:8).

10. See Philip Edgcumbe Hughes, *The Book of the Revelation: A Commentary* (Leicester: Inter-Varsity; Grand Rapids: Eerdmans, 1990), p. 104. However, Beale (*Revelation,* p. 454) identifies the angel as "'the angel of the presence' (as in Isa. 63:9; *Jubilees* 1.29) or even Christ himself." But Christ who created the universe, created also the angels who worship him (Heb. 1:2, 6). In the New Testament he does not appear as an angel.

11. Exod. 30:1–10; Heb. 8:5; and compare Rev. 9:13; 11:1; 14:18; 16:7.

Because of our sinful human nature, human prayers are incomplete and faulty. For this reason they must be presented with the fragrance of incense to make them acceptable to God. All our prayers show deficiency, with selfishness, formalism, and haste their major detractors. All our supplications and utterances of thanksgiving need to be sanctified and perfected to enter into God's presence. In one of his psalms David prays, "May my prayer be set before you like incense; may the lifting up of my hands be like the evening sacrifice" (Ps. 141:2). The presentation of all the prayers of the saints demonstrates unity, harmony, and strength. "The prayer of a righteous man is powerful and effective" (James 5:16). These united prayers rise up before the *throne*, a symbolic reference to God. This text twice mentions the expression *golden* to describe the censer and the altar. Gold alludes to heaven's perfection (see, e.g., 21:18, 21). In this context, the prayers of the saints are perfected and the response to the saints is at times astounding. For instance, Elijah's prayer influenced the weather so that the drought ended (1 Kings 18:42–45).

d. "And the smoke of the incense with the prayers of the saints went up out of the hand of the angel before God." The imperfections that were cleaving to the prayers of the saints were removed, symbolically, by the fragrant smoke, to make their intercessions, petitions, and praises ascend to God's throne. Whenever we pray, the exercise itself appears to be simple. Yet everyone who is seriously engaged in prayer knows that praying demands concentration and hard work. When our prayers ascend, they are placed on an altar. Then an angel takes our supplications, places them on a censer, and presents them to God. Again, the angel is not a mediator but only a servant in this process. Jesus Christ, as intercessor, perfects our prayers and petitions (Rom. 8:34).

5. And the angel took the censer and filled it with fire from the altar and cast it on the earth. And there were claps of thunder and rumblings and flashes of lightning and an earthquake.

At a first reading of this verse, we are perplexed and do not comprehend the flow of thought. When the angel presents our prayers to God, we are able to grasp the significance of this action because we realize the imperfections of human praises and petitions. But when that same angel takes fire from the altar of incense, puts it in the censer, and hurls it to the earth, we may fail to see the connection.

We have to discern the sequence of cause and effect. What we read in this verse is a consequence of the preceding verse. That is, God has heard the prayers of the saints and in response is sending judgment in the form of punishment upon the inhabitants of the world, all in his predetermined time. God has taken to heart the cry of the saints at the foot of the altar (6:9–10). He instructs the angel to take fire from that altar, to fill the censer, and to throw fire to the earth, where it causes death and destruction. Here is the fulfillment of Jesus' word of judgment, "I have come to bring fire on the earth, and how I wish it were already kindled" (Luke 12:49). "The saying of Jesus . . . seems, in the context where it is now found, to refer to the fire of discord (s[ee] vss. 51–3)."[12] The consequence of this action should serve as a warning to the

12. Bauer, p. 730.

wicked that the torments following the sounding of the trumpets are only the beginning of what is in store for them if they fail to repent.

The angel is only a servant sent forth by God to do his bidding. This becomes plain from the signs in nature that accompany the destructive fire: "peals of thunder and rumblings and flashes of lightning and an earthquake." In the thunder and lightning God reveals himself as he did at Mount Sinai (Exod. 19:16; compare Isa. 29:6). Also in the Apocalypse, three aspects of nature—thunder, rumbling, and lightning—are mentioned elsewhere (4:5; 11:19; 16:18), though the sequence differs.

Not an angel but the Almighty causes an earthquake, which in Revelation is mentioned seven times (6:12; 8:5; 11:13 [twice], 19; 16:18 [twice]) and is generally qualified by the adjective *great.* Through a great earthquake seven thousand people were killed (11:13).[13] Earthquakes are among all the other signs that usher in the end times. As Jesus said, "Nation will rise against nation, and kingdom against kingdom. There will be famines and earthquakes in various places. All these are the beginning of birth pains" (Matt. 24:7–8).

Greek Words, Phrases, and Constructions in 8:4–5

Verse 4

ταῖς προσευχαῖς— the dative can be construed as a temporal or associative usage.[14] "The temporal and associative rendering have a similar sense, such as 'together with prayers,' which appears to be the meaning in this verse; confer Acts 10:4 where prayers are offered with the giving of alms."[15]

Verse 5

εἴληφεν—this is the perfect active of the verb λαμβάνω (I receive, take) and is classified as a dramatic historical perfect translated as a past tense, "the angel took."

B. Seven Trumpeting Angels
8:6–11:19

After the angel at the altar presents the supplications of the saints to God and after God instructs the angel to cast fire in the form of punishments on the earth, the seven angels with the seven trumpets commence blowing their warn-

---

13. Consult Richard Bauckham, "The Eschatological Earthquake in the Apocalypse of John," *NovT* 19 (1977): 224–33; and see his *Climax of Prophecy* (Edinburgh: Clark, 1993), pp. 202–4. He avers that these phenomena in nature (8:5; 11:19; 16:18) are "a clear allusion to the Sinai theophany." But this may be mere conventional language that does not necessarily refer to Sinai. See Aune, *Revelation 6–16*, p. 518; Günther Bornkamm, *TDNT*, 7:198–99; Reinhard Kratz, *EDNT*, 3:237.

14. A. T. Robertson, *A Grammar of the Greek New Testament in the Light of Historical Research* (Nashville: Broadman, 1934), p. 529; C. F. D. Moule, *An Idiom-Book of New Testament Greek*, 2d ed. (Cambridge: Cambridge University Press, 1960), p. 43; Friedrich Blass and Albert Debrunner, *A Greek Grammar of the New Testament*, trans. and rev. Robert Funk (Chicago: University of Chicago Press, 1961), §188.1.

15. Robert Hanna, *A Grammatical Aid to the Greek New Testament* (Grand Rapids: Baker, 1983), p. 448.

ing sounds. The sound of the trumpets ushers in God's judgments in the form of punishments that affect the earth, the sea, the rivers and springs of water, the heavenly bodies, and the Abyss. The adversaries of God receive their due rewards. But notice the order of these seven trumpets. "The first four trumpets harm the wicked in their *physical* being; the last three bring *spiritual anguish*: hell itself is let loose!"[16] Chapter 8 has the first four, chapter 9 the next two, and chapter 11 the last one.

The parallel with the seven plagues in chapter 16 is unique in the Apocalypse. Apart from a few minor differences in wording, for example, the Abyss (9:1–2) and the throne of the beast (16:10), the headings are identical. Here are the parallel columns:[17]

Seven Trumpets	**Seven Bowls**
1. earth (8:7)	1. earth (16:2)
2. sea (8:8–9)	2. sea (16:3)
3. rivers, springs (8:10–11)	3. rivers, springs (16:4–5)
4. sun, moon, stars (8:12)	4. sun (16:8)
5. pit of the Abyss (9:1)	5. throne of the beast (16:10)
6. river Euphrates (9:13–14)	6. river Euphrates (16:12)
7. lightning, hail (11:15, 19)	7. lightning, hail (16:17, 21)

Further, the plagues, whether announced by the blowing of the trumpets or the pouring of the bowls, resemble the ten plagues endured by the Egyptians when God set Israel free (Exod. 7:8–13:16). The sequence and the details of the first four judgments differ remarkably from the plagues of Egypt, so that we can speak only of similarities.

1. The First Trumpet
8:6–7

6. And the seven angels who held the seven trumpets prepared themselves to blow them.

As a result of God's hearing and answering the petitions of the saints, the seven angels are given the task of sounding their individual trumpets. Now the seven plagues on the wicked can be executed. The prayers of the saints, therefore, prove to be a significant part in the history of mankind. "More things are wrought by prayer than this world dreams of," Alfred Tennyson said in *Idylls of the King* in the section on the death of Arthur. God does not impose and execute judgment unless and until the supplications of his people have been heard. Think, for instance, of Abraham's repeated pleas on behalf of Sodom (Gen.

16. Hendriksen, *More Than Conquerors*, p. 116.
17. For more extensive columns see Aune, *Revelation 6–16*, pp. 500–501.

18:16–33). But after these prayers have entered God's presence, the Almighty acts, sometimes swiftly, on other occasions in his own appointed time.

When each of the trumpets sounds, destruction comes to an area of God's creation that in this chapter is expressed as a third part. In chapter 8, the expression *a third* occurs twelve times, and once John refers to *the third angel* (v. 10). This is a common ordinal for division in both Jewish and Greek cultures; see Ezekiel 5:2, 12.[18]

7. And the first angel blew the trumpet, and there was hail and fire mixed with blood and it was cast upon the earth. And a third of the earth was burned, and a third of the trees were burned, and all the green grass was burned.

The first angel sounds the trumpet that results in the calamity of hail and fire mixed with blood cast upon the earth. The calamity is reminiscent of the seventh plague God brought upon Egypt, with two variations: in Exodus there is no reference to blood being mixed with the hail and fire, and the fire is described as lightning (Exod. 9:24–26; compare also Ezek. 38:22). We have no basis for interpreting the nouns *hail, fire,* and *blood* symbolically; hail and lightning are natural occurrences. They can maim and kill living beings, so that blood indeed mingles with the hailstones covering the landscape.[19] A frightful storm occasionally rages across the countryside and with hail and lightning destroys everything in its path. Human beings and animals often fall victim to the violence of a storm. The effect is divine judgment, since the passive construction *it was cast* intimates that God is the agent (compare Ps. 29:3–10).

Not only human beings and animals experience the brunt of nature's forces, but also "a third of the earth was burned, and a third of the trees were burned, and all the green grass was burned." The effect is truly devastating: three times in succession the verb *to burn* appears to indicate the severity of destruction. And twice the ordinal *a third* appears with reference to the earth and the trees. We include the phrase *all the green grass* in the third part that was burned. A total devastation of all grass including all the grain products in the world would mean an end to life for human beings and animals.

Even though God expresses his wrath in the ruin of his creation, he shows his mercy by destroying only a third part while keeping the rest of his creation intact. One commentator sees a contradiction, stating that the burning of the trees and all the grass "is absolutely in variance with ix.4."[20] In 9:4 the locusts are "told not to harm the grass of the earth, nor any plant, nor any tree, except people who did not have the seal of God on their foreheads." But we know that when

18. Refer to Colin J. Hemer, *NIDNTT,* 2:687; Wolfgang Feneberg, *EDNT,* 3:370; SB, 3:808. Babylonian Talmud, *Baba Metzia* 59b: "Then was the world smitten—a third of its olives, and a third of its wheat, and a third of its barley . . . the fire burned."

19. M. Robert Mulholland Jr. refers to Exodus 7:14–24, the changing of the waters of Egypt into blood. See his *Revelation: Holy Living in an Unholy World* (Grand Rapids: Zondervan, Frances Asbury Press, 1990), p. 191 n. 1. Swete (*Revelation,* p. 110) suggests that the blood was "red sand from the Sahara." Both interpretations lack cogency in the context of the passage.

20. Charles, *Revelation,* 1:233.

a firestorm burns away trees and vegetation, the rejuvenating force in nature sprouts fresh grass and even germinates seeds of trees. In brief, the wording of 9:4 does not contradict this passage at all.[21]

Greek Words, Phrases, and Constructions in 8:7

μεμιγμένα—"having been mingled." The perfect passive participle in the accusative neuter plural is to be preferred to the singular. Some witnesses have the neuter singular to agree with the noun πῦρ (fire), but the plural is the harder reading.

---

2. The Second Trumpet
8:8–9

8. And the second angel blew the trumpet. And as it were a huge mountain burning with fire was cast into the sea, and a third of the sea became blood. 9. And a third of the living creatures in the sea died, and a third of the ships were destroyed.

a. "And as it were a huge mountain burning with fire was cast into the sea." The preceding verses described devastation on the land, while these verses picture scenes on the seas. John has a vision and as he tries to verbalize what he sees he uses the expression *as it were;*[22] thus he approximates reality in symbolical terms. He mentions a huge mountain burning with fire that did not fall into the sea but was thrown into it. We ought not to make much of the mountain itself but rather of the vision's impact. The stress should fall on the horror that God's judgment has on his creation, which here is the sea. This is a calamity that defies description: an enormous mountain set ablaze and hurled into the sea. It may be compared to a meteorite of extraordinary proportions that upon entering earth's atmosphere is like a blazing fire; when it plunges into the sea, it causes a tremendous tidal wave that sweeps away coastal cities with untold loss of life.[23] John may also have memories of Mount Vesuvius's eruption on August 24, A.D. 70. But this tragedy was a local event, while this plague is an "announcement of a coming cosmic catastrophe that will affect the whole surface of the earth."[24] John portrays the reality of divine judgment on the wicked in symbols that convey spiritual validity.

The text of Jeremiah 51:25 only tangentially fits this situation. God says, "'I am against you, O destroying mountain, you who destroy the whole earth,' declares the LORD. 'I will stretch out my hand against you, roll you off the cliffs, and make you a burned-out mountain.'"[25] We conclude, therefore, that John reveals an in-

---

21. Compare Robert L. Thomas, *Revelation 8–22: An Exegetical Commentary* (Chicago: Moody, 1995), p. 18.

22. The repeated use in chapters 8 and 9 of the expressions *as it were, as,* and *like* suggests symbolism (see 8:8, 10; 9:2, 3, 5, 7–10, 17, 19).

23. Compare Gerhard A. Krodel, *Revelation,* ACNT (Minneapolis: Augsburg, 1989), p. 198.

24. Jürgen Roloff, *The Revelation of John,* trans. J. E. Alsup (Minneapolis: Fortress, 1993), p. 110.

25. Similar readings appear in *1 Enoch* 18.13, "I saw there seven stars like great burning mountains"; and *1 Enoch* 21.3, "Then shall come a great star from heaven into the divine sea."

cident that can only be explained symbolically as something extraordinary that God performs in the sight of his people.

God shows the apostle and the readers of the Apocalypse that this vision signifies divine judgment on his adversaries and serves as a call to repentance. People experience the effect of this colossal mountain that is flung into the sea, which douses the flames and fire. This is a picture of frightful punishment striking those who are on these waters.

b. "And a third of the sea became blood." That a third of the sea became blood is an implied reference to the first of the Egyptian plagues (Exod. 7:19–21; Ps. 78:43–44; 105:29). The difference is telling, however, because here a third of the sea turns into blood, but in Egypt it was the Nile, the streams, canals, ponds, and reservoirs that took on the color of blood. Yet there is resemblance that points to God striking Egypt with supernatural power because of Pharaoh hardening his heart (Exod. 7:22–23); in the Apocalypse God causes the death of human beings whose blood stains a third part of the sea (compare 16:3). The enormous loss of life, by whatever disaster God ordains, is a frightening judgment indeed.

c. "And a third of the living creatures in the sea died, and a third of the ships were destroyed." All along, God's mercy is evident in the repetitious use of the expression *a third.* Not all the seas turned to blood, not all the living creatures died, and not all the ships perished. Only a third of each were affected by God's wrath; the fish not affected by divine punishment continued to multiply and the traffic on the sea unhindered by maritime disaster continued to proceed normally. The catastrophes that God caused to fall on the sea are signs of the end times by which God tells the people to repent and live.

3. The Third Trumpet
8:10–11

10. And the third angel blew the trumpet. And a great star fell from the sky, burning as a torch, and it fell upon a third part of the rivers and upon the springs of water. 11. And the name of the star was Wormwood, and a third part of the water became wormwood, and many people died because of the water that had become bitter.

a. "And a great star fell from the sky, burning as a torch, and it fell upon a third part of the rivers and upon the springs of water." Subsequent to the judgment on the earth came the disasters on the sea. Now John reveals the third category to be divinely afflicted: the rivers and the inland bodies of water. God castigates his foes by causing a huge star to fall from heaven; it is a ball of fire that upon its descent pollutes the inland waters, bringing death to anyone drinking from them.

Outside of Revelation, Scripture does not provide any exact parallels to the phenomenon of a flaming meteorite falling from the sky (6:13; 9:1). The passage in Isaiah 14:12 speaks of a falling star: "How you have fallen from heaven, O morning star, son of the dawn. You have been cast down to the earth." But the passage in Revelation differs from this text in respect to the size of the star, its fiery appearance, the inland waters that are polluted by it, and its name.

God makes a star to fall from heaven and people can watch it approaching the earth. This is an awesome sight that can be explained only as a divinely ordained occurrence that is designed to call the wicked to repent from their evil ways and turn to God. There is nothing comparable in human experience. This burning star that falls on rivers, lakes, and ponds contaminates drinking water and consequently kills those who drink it. Once more we read of God's judgment on his adversaries expressed in symbolic language and conveying spiritual reality.

b. "And the name of the star was Wormwood." This expression *wormwood* (Greek *apsinthos*) appears only twice in the New Testament, both times in this verse. Some scholars translate its second appearance as "bitter." In the Old Testament it occurs seven times and is rendered in many translations as "gall" or "bitterness."[26]

Wormwood was grown in Israel and because of the camphor smell was used to deter moths from eating garments. This herb with its roots is very bitter. In the Old Testament it points to illicit sexual acts (Prov. 5:4), punishment for sin (Jer. 9:15), and corrupt justice (Amos 5:7). This means that sin usually leads to bitterness of the soul. Wormwood, therefore, exemplified in adversity and grief symbolizes damnation and justice.

Water mixed with wormwood tastes bitter but is not inherently poisonous. We expect that John has combined the concepts of wormwood and real poison (see Jer. 9:15), and in this manner he is able to declare that this combined substance has a fatal effect on the body (compare Exod. 15:23).[27]

c. "And a third part of the water became wormwood, and many people died because of the water that had become bitter" (compare Exod. 15:23). Again God's mercy is evident in the last part of this passage. The repetitive "a third" shows divine patience with the unbelievers. Not everyone suffers because of the water, for only a third part is affected by the plague and the rest of it is drinkable. Those people who died were a warning to the survivors to fear God and turn to him, for he will have mercy and freely pardon (Isa. 55:7).

Greek Words, Phrases, and Constructions in 8:11

ἐκ τῶν ὑδάτων—this prepositional phrase conveys a causal notion, "because of the waters."[28]

---

4. The Fourth Trumpet
8:12

12. And the fourth angel blew the trumpet. And a third part of the sun and a third part of the moon and a third part of the stars were struck, so that a third

---

26. Deut. 29:18; Prov. 5:4; Jer. 9:15; 23:15; Lam. 3:15, 19; Amos 5:7.

27. Consult W. E. Shewell-Cooper, *ZPEB*, 5:969; Leon Morris, *NIDNTT*, 2:29; and see his commentary *Revelation*, rev. ed., TNTC (Leicester: Inter-Varsity; Grand Rapids: Eerdmans, 1987), p. 121.

28. Robertson, *Grammar*, p. 598.

part of them became dark and a third part of the day did not shine and likewise a third part of the night.

The term *a third* appears six times in this verse in which the entire heavens are involved: the sun, moon, stars, and the division of day and night (see 6:12–13). The repetition emphasizes the severity of this celestial phenomenon. Its occurrence defies a natural explanation because an eclipse does not fit the description (compare 16:10).

The ninth plague striking Egypt turned it into darkness. Moses stretched out his hand toward the sky and the darkness that came on the land was so real that it could be felt. It covered Egypt for three days, while all the Israelites had light (Exod. 10:21–23). God could have used a sandstorm to block out the rays of the sun on the Egyptians but not on the Israelites in the land of Goshen. In Revelation a third part of the sun, a third part of the moon, and a third part of the stars turned into darkness; this is a supernatural intervention into the natural courses of these heavenly bodies. Geoffrey B. Wilson aptly remarks, "It should be obvious that John is painting a picture and not writing a treatise on astronomy."[29] When light is turned into darkness, there is a disruption of the cosmic order and dissolution of creation. The Old Testament frequently speaks about the disappearance of light when celestial bearers cease their normal functions.[30]

John writes that "a third part of them became dark and a third part of the day did not shine and likewise a third part of the night." He is not talking about eclipses that block the light of the sun or moon for less than an hour. These heavenly bodies fail to emit and reflect light for a third part of the day and a third part of the night. It is better to say that here we have an enigma that can only be interpreted and understood as a sign of divine judgment on a world that is reveling in sin. The symbolism of periods of darkness is meant to bring people to repentance and to declare their faith in God. These signs in nature, therefore, are expressions of God's grace and mercy by which he shows the coming of the Day of the Lord. Both believers and unbelievers hear the sound of the trumpets. Believers, guided by their knowledge of the Scriptures, recognize these signs, take refuge in God, and are safe. If God's adversaries ignore these signs in nature, they will face eternal darkness by being forever cut off from the source of light, namely, God. They may feel free to ignore the admonitions and scoff at the warnings concerning the Day of the Lord, but they will suffer the consequences.

Greek Words, Phrases, and Constructions in 8:12

μή—when the particle ἵνα with its result clause is followed by the negative particle μή with its clause, the sense remains the same.

---

29. Geoffrey B. Wilson, *Revelation* (Welwyn, England: Evangelical Press, 1985), p. 81.

30. Refer to Isa. 13:10; 24:23; 34:4; 50:3; Jer. 4:23; Ezek. 32:7–8; Joel 2:10, 31; Amos 8:9; Mic. 3:6.

5. The Three Woes *8:13*

After the first four trumpets usher in calamities in nature which everyone is able to observe, we would have expected the continuation of the remaining three trumpets. But here is an interruption in the sequence of the signs—interruptions happen often in the Apocalypse. Now nature itself coming in the form of an eagle warns God's opponents to pay attention to these signs that should be unavoidably clear in communicating divine judgment. The three trumpets that follow announce judgments that are even harsher than the four preceding ones. Demonic powers arise to attack human beings not merely physically but mentally and spiritually: people want to die but are unable to do so.

Hence, an eagle in the sky sounds the alarm in uttering a threefold woe to those inhabitants of the earth who have willfully ignored the first four trumpets. Again we have to interpret the loud call of the eagle in terms of God's compassion and mercy. He does not desire the death of the wicked but rather that the wicked live (Ezek. 18:32). Thus, the unbeliever will never be able to accuse God of having given insufficient warnings.

13. And I saw, and I heard an eagle flying in mid-heaven saying in a loud voice, "Woe, woe, woe to the inhabitants of the earth because of the trumpet sounds about to be blown by the other three angels."

a. "And I saw, and I heard an eagle flying in mid-heaven saying in a loud voice." John's senses are fully engaged, because he both sees and hears what is happening. He notices an eagle flying in mid-heaven, as an emblem of coming judgment and destruction (Deut. 28:49; Hos. 8:1; Hab. 1:8).[31] As a bird of prey an eagle with its keen eyesight is looking for carrion and game, its source of food (see Matt. 24:28; Luke 17:37). Looking from its lofty height, the bird cries out a threefold woe, implying that there will be plenty of food available. Flying in midair, the bird is right overhead and able to see far and wide (compare Prov. 30:18–19).

We need not argue about whether an eagle can speak, for the scene that John depicts is apocalyptic and symbolic. Note the beast that comes out of the sea is given a mouth to speak arrogant and blasphemous words (13:5). Similarly, the serpent spoke to Eve in Paradise (Gen. 3:1–5) and Balaam's donkey addressed her master (Num. 22:28–30). The eagle speaks in a loud voice so that everyone is able to hear its call of the threefold woe.

b. "Woe, woe, woe to the inhabitants of the earth because of the trumpet sounds about to be blown by the other three angels." The triple woe is unique in Revelation (see the double use in 18:10, 16, 19), for in both Old and New Testaments the single woe occurs. The woes are explained as the two trumpet blasts of the two angels in the next chapter. But two passages force the interpreter to enlarge the scope of the woes: "The first woe has come. Look, still two more

31. The term *eagle* appears in two other passages in the Apocalypse: 4:7 and 12:14. These passages stress the aspect of flying. See James L. Resseguie, *Revelation Unsealed: A Narrative Critical Approach to John's Apocalypse,* BIS 32 (Leiden: Brill, 1998), p. 89.

come after these things" (9:12) and "The second woe is past. Look, the third woe is coming soon" (11:14). John fails to mention the third woe, for the reference in 12:12 lacks enumeration, "Woe to the earth and the sea, because the devil has gone down to you." However, John seems to indicate that the blowing of the seventh trumpet is the introductory signal for the coming of the third woe (11:14–15a).

c. "The inhabitants of the earth." The Apocalypse features this term numerous times. In every case the term refers not to believers, who are sojourners, but to unbelievers, who try to make the earth their permanent dwelling.[32] The eagle warns the antagonists to pay attention to the warnings, for they will encounter God's punishments in the form of the forthcoming woes.

Greek Words, Phrases, and Constructions in 8:13

ἑνός—the number one in this clause is equivalent to the indefinite pronoun: "an eagle."[33] It should not be translated as "a solitary eagle" (*Phillips*). Two translations following weaker witnesses have the reading "an angel" (KJV, NKJV).

μεσουρανήματι—translated as "mid-heaven," the word refers to celestial bodies crossing the meridian.

οὐαί—the particle is followed by the accusative (although a variant reading has the dative), which may be classified as an adverbial accusative.

---

32. Rev. 3:10; 6:10; 8:13; 11:10 (twice); 13:8, 12, 14 (twice); 17:2, 8. See also the variant readings in 12:12 and 14:6 listed in Nes-Al^{27}.

33. Blass and Debrunner, *Greek Grammar*, §247.2.

9

The Fifth and Sixth Trumpets

(9:1–21)

Outline (continued)

6. The Fifth Trumpet (9:1–12)
   a. The Abyss and Demonic Forces (9:1–6)
   b. The Locusts (9:7–12)
7. The Sixth Trumpet (9:13–21)
   a. A Divine Command (9:13–16)
   b. A Descriptive Vision (9:17–19)
   c. Refusing to Repent (9:20–21)

9

1 And the fifth angel blew the trumpet. And I saw a star that had fallen out of the sky to the earth, and it was given the key to the pit of the Abyss. 2 And he opened the pit of the Abyss, and smoke from the pit went up as smoke of a great furnace, and the sun and the air were darkened because of the smoke of the pit. 3 And out of the smoke came forth locusts on the earth, and power was given to them as the scorpions of the earth have power. 4 And they were told not to harm the grass of the earth, or any plant, or any tree, except people who did not have the seal of God on their foreheads. 5 And they were given power not to kill them, but to torture them for five months, and their torment was like the torment of a scorpion when it strikes a man. 6 And in those days people will seek death and will not find it. And they will long to die and death flees from them.

7 And the appearance of locusts was like horses prepared for battle, and on their heads were something like crowns of gold. And their faces were like human faces, 8 and they had hair like hair of women, and their teeth were like those of lions. 9 And they had breastplates like the breastplates of iron, and the sound of their wings was like the sound of many chariots with horses racing into battle. 10 And they had tails and stings like scorpions, and in their tails they had power to harm people for five months. 11 They had a king over them, the angel of the Abyss; his name in Hebrew was Abaddon, and in Greek Apollyon.

12 The first woe has come. Look, still two more come after these things.

13 And the sixth angel blew the trumpet. And I heard a voice from the horns of the golden altar before God, 14 saying to the sixth angel, the one holding the trumpet, "Set free the four angels that are bound at the great river Euphrates." 15 And the four angels were set free, they who were prepared for the hour, day, month, and year to kill a third of the people. 16 And the number of the horsemen was two hundred million. I heard their number.

17 And thus in my vision I saw the horses and their riders. They had breastplates that were colored as fiery red, hyacinth blue, and sulfur yellow. The heads of the horses were like heads of lions, and out of their mouths came forth fire, and smoke and sulfur. 18 As a result of these three plagues a third part of mankind was killed by the fire, smoke, and sulfur that came out of their mouths. 19 For the power of the horses was in their mouths and in their tails, and their tails were like snakes. They had heads and with them they inflict harm.

20 And the rest of the people, who were not killed by these plagues, did not repent from the works of their hands or stop worshiping the demons and the idols made of gold, silver, bronze, stone, and wood. These idols are not able to see, hear, and walk. 21 And they repented not from their murders, their witchcraft, their fornication, and their thefts.

Whereas chapter 8 records the results of four trumpets blown by four angels, this chapter presents only two trumpets blown by the fifth and sixth angels respectively. (Incidentally, the seventh angel blows his trumpet to introduce the final judgment and to describe the worship that the saints render to God [11:15].) Notice the extensive description of the plagues that follow the trumpet calls of the fifth and sixth angels. The portrayal of the plague that occurs after the fifth trumpet is blown takes up two substantial paragraphs totaling eleven verses (vv. 1–11) and concludes with the words, "The first woe has come. Look, still two more come after these things" (v. 12). And the account of the blowing of the sixth trumpet comprises three lengthy paragraphs (vv. 13–21). Compared with the first four trumpet sounds, the effect of these next two trumpets depicted in protracted paragraphs indicates inconceivable severity.

The first four plagues describe calamities unleashed in nature: the earth, sea, rivers, springs of water, and the celestial bodies. The next two plagues describe the demonic forces that are unleashed by Satan, their king, to torment the people (v. 11). This is a description of hell itself in which people seek to die but realize that death is eluding them (v. 6). Their mental and spiritual suffering is without end.

The sixth plague involves all humanity, of which a third is killed (v. 15). Two hundred million warriors, representing demonic troops, wage war against the people. These forces symbolically depict a vast multitude of fallen angels (v. 16). They are bent on killing people with fire, smoke, and sulfur. But the sad result is that none of the unbelievers, although they experience agony and destruction, repents from their evil deeds of murder, witchcraft, fornication, and theft (v. 21).

The two judgments portrayed by the blowing of the fifth and sixth trumpets not only follow each other but are also closely related. Both illustrate the ruinous objective of the demons. In the first instance, they reside in the minds of the unbelievers and cause them mental torture. The second illustration shows the complete control demons have over human beings, who then perform every evil act imaginable.

I interpret the calamities described in chapters 8 and 9 not only as sequential but even in some aspects as simultaneous. That is, while the fifth and sixth trumpets usher in demonic forces, the calamities of the first four are already taking place. In other words, the references in both chapters to the death and dying of human beings overlap. The difference is that in addition to facing destructive powers in nature, humanity also encounters demonic powers that seek to destroy the body and ruin the soul.[1]

Last, my objective is to explain the content of this chapter not literally but symbolically. I am not looking for a specific time in history or the future in which the fifth and sixth plagues have been or will be fulfilled. "Rather, we need to see spiritual forces at work in the world of the unregenerated, wicked men—forces which are symbolized by these monsters of the infernal realm."[2]

6. The Fifth Trumpet
9:1–12

a. The Abyss and Demonic Forces
9:1–6

1. And the fifth angel blew the trumpet. And I saw a star that had fallen out of the sky to the earth, and it was given the key to the pit of the Abyss.

First, the effect of the fifth angel blowing his trumpet is that John has a vision of a star. But how do we interpret the expression *star*? In the first century some

1. S. Greijdanus, *De Openbaring des Heeren aan Johannes*, KNT (Amsterdam: Van Bottenburg, 1925), p. 194.

2. Homer Hailey, *Revelation: An Introduction and Commentary* (Grand Rapids: Baker, 1979), p. 225.

stars were given a figurative meaning; wandering planets were thought to have been cast into the Abyss (*1 Enoch* 21.6; 86.1; 88.1; compare Jude 13). The Old Testament poetically gives personality to stars by having them engage in battle or singing songs (Judg. 5:20; Job 38:7).[3]

John writes the past tense in the phrase "a star that had fallen" and says that he saw this star. He mentions the place where it had fallen, namely, the earth. At one time, then, this star had occupied a place in heaven but is now on the earth. I interpret the expression *star* symbolically, as is evident from John's description of this luminary. John gives it the characteristics of will and intellect. The star receives a key with which it opens the Abyss—these characteristics pertain to a rational being, not to an inanimate object. Hence, many interpreters identify this being as an evil angel, that is, Satan, who is given brief periods in history during which he can open the shaft of the Abyss.[4] The tense of the verb *had fallen* indicates that time had elapsed since its occurrence. Jesus says that he "saw Satan fall like lightning from heaven" (Luke 10:18). And John writes that Satan "was hurled to the earth, and his angels with him" (12:9).

The fifth angel blowing the trumpet presents a parallel to the fifth angel pouring out his bowl on the throne of the beast, whose kingdom was turned into darkness (16:10). Here the pit of the Abyss is the residence of a fallen star, namely, Satan; there his place of residence is the throne of the beast that occupies it in his name. But the king of this kingdom plunged into darkness is Satan himself, who aims to destroy God's kingdom. Note that the angel of the Abyss is called Abaddon in Hebrew and Apollyon in Greek (v. 11). In both languages the word means Destroyer (see Prov. 15:11).

If we identify this star with Satan, the prince of demons cast out of heaven to reside in the Abyss (compare Matt. 10:25; 12:24, where he is called Beelzebub), we need to understand that God is in complete control. Either Satan or one of his underlings receives the key to the Abyss, not in the sense of permanent possession but of momentary power. God allows the evil spirits temporary freedom to do their destructive deeds that are described in the succeeding verses of this chapter. God assigns the countless fallen angels to the Abyss, where they are awaiting the Judgment Day (Luke 8:31; 2 Pet. 2:4; Jude 6). He decrees the time of opening and closing of this place. He is the sovereign. Thus, I conclude that God holds the key to the Abyss; he gives it at times to the devil to fulfill his divine purposes.[5]

---

3. See Robert H. Mounce, *The Book of Revelation*, rev. ed., NICNT (Grand Rapids: Eerdmans, 1998), p. 185.

4. Consult Herman Hoeksema, *Behold, He Cometh! An Exposition of the Book of Revelation* (Grand Rapids: Reformed Free Publishing Association, 1969), p. 312; Henry Barclay Swete, *Commentary on Revelation* (1911; reprint, Grand Rapids: Kregel, 1977), p. 114; Henry Alford, *James–Revelation*, vol. 4, part 2 of *Alford's Greek Testament* (1875; reprint, Grand Rapids: Guardian, 1976), pp. 639–40; William Hendriksen, *More Than Conquerors* (reprint, Grand Rapids: Baker, 1982), p. 120; Hailey, *Revelation*, p. 225.

5. Some scholars interpret the star to be a good angel in harmony with 10:1; 18:1; and 20:1. But Gregory K. Beale (*The Book of Revelation: A Commentary on the Greek Text*, NIGTC [Grand Rapids: Eerdmans, 1998], p. 492) aptly observes that no scholar has "adduced one example where a fallen star metaphor is applied to a good angel." See also Otto Böcher, *EDNT*, 1:4; and consult Hans Bietenhard, *NIDNTT*, 2:205; Joachim Jeremias, *TDNT*, 1:9–10.

2. And he opened the pit of the Abyss, and smoke from the pit went up as smoke of a great furnace, and the sun and the air were darkened because of the smoke of the pit.

The expression *Abyss* in the New Testament refers to the abode of the evil spirits with the exception of Romans 10:6–7, where Paul uses the concept for the abode of the dead.[6] In Revelation, where the word occurs seven times,[7] the word uniformly signifies the place where Satan and his followers remain. After the judgment, they are cast into the lake of burning sulfur where they are tormented forever (19:20; 20:10, 14, 15). The demons whom Jesus cast out of the man called Legion beg him not to send them into the Abyss, because it is their prison (Luke 8:31).

The Abyss has a shaft that leads to the so-called bottomless pit. Out of this shaft fumes arise like smoke out of a great furnace. The picture John presents is that of thick smoke which obscures the light of day, obstructs breathing, contributes to illness, produces an unbearable stench, and besmirches everything on which it descends. It is as if hell itself breaks loose to mar, pollute, and defile God's creation. This enormous furnace serves to portray hell itself from which clouds of smoke ascend to darken the light of the sun and pollute the air, making breathing nearly impossible. Evil is like a dense cloud that turns the world into darkness and suffocates all those who are breathing its polluted air. But evil itself functions only with divine permission.[8] It arises, increases, and opposes all that is true, pure, good, and admirable. Evil never succeeds in conquering God's kingdom, because God not only permits but also controls its effect.

3. And out of the smoke came forth locusts on the earth, and power was given to them as the scorpions of the earth have power. 4. And they were told not to harm the grass of the earth, or any plant, or any tree, except people who did not have the seal of God on their foreheads.

The eighth Egyptian plague (Exod. 10:13–15) relates the destructive power of the locusts that devoured everything that was growing in the fields and stripped bare the trees (see also Joel 1:4, 6–7). So they deprive both people and animals of their food supply. But the locusts in this verse are entirely different:

- they come forth out of the infernal smoke that arises from the Abyss;
- they do not devour the green grass, plants, and trees;
- they attack people who are not part of God's kingdom;
- they strike the ungodly with the stings of scorpions.

---

6. By quoting Deut. 30:12–13, Paul contrasts heaven and its counterpart: "Who will ascend into heaven? . . . Who will descend into the deep?" (Rom. 10:6–7). The *deep* is another word for Hades.

7. Rev. 9:1, 2, 11; 11:7; 17:8; 20:1, 3.

8. James L. Resseguie, *Revelation Unsealed: A Narrative Critical Approach to John's Apocalypse*, BIS 32 (Leiden: Brill, 1998), p. 89.

Thus, the context itself forces the interpreter to explain the word *locusts* not literally but figuratively. These creatures coming forth from hell are demonic in appearance and action. But they can function only when God grants them power to sting like scorpions,[9] and they must do what God tells them, namely, to attack those people who lack his seal on their foreheads (compare the parallel in 7:3b). Not Satan but God is in charge, for he grants authority and sets its limits, and at the same time he protects his own people from spiritual harm (compare Ezek. 9:4, 6).

The sting of a scorpion is extremely painful but not necessarily fatal to humans. Henry Barclay Swete observes: "The scorpion takes its place with the snake and other creatures hostile to man, and with them symbolizes the forces of spiritual evil which are active in the world."[10] In both Old and New Testaments, scorpions and serpents are mentioned together (Deut. 8:15; Luke 10:19; and Sirach 39:30).

Who are these scorpions? The context of this chapter shows that we should not equate them with human beings but rather with demons. They are released from the Abyss when God gives Satan or a demonic underling permission to open this pit. And they can harm only those people who do not have God's seal on their foreheads. They strike those who love darkness instead of light, who have come to know the truth but reject it, and who willfully serve the evil one. They attack those people whom God has abandoned and given over to their sinful desires (Rom. 1:21, 24, 26, 28).

5. And they were given power not to kill them, but to torture them for five months, and their torment was like the torment of a scorpion when it strikes a man. 6. And in those days people will seek death and will not find it. And they will long to die and death flees from them.

These demons receive authority to torture human beings but not the power to kill. Once again the text clearly indicates that God is sovereign. We are reminded of God's permitting Satan to strike Job's flesh and bones but requiring him to spare his life. God set limits to Satan's power (Job 2:4–6). Not God but Satan is responsible for the evil in this world; yet God uses Satan's wickedness to punish recalcitrant sinners and call them to repentance (v. 21).[11]

Torture can be experienced physically or mentally. The centurion implored Jesus to heal his servant who was "paralyzed and in terrible suffering" (Matt. 8:6); Peter writes that Lot was tormented in his soul because of the lawless lives of the people in Sodom (2 Pet. 2:8). Also the demons themselves expressed fear of being tormented by Jesus in anticipation of the appointed time of torture (Matt.

---

9. The Greek verb *edothē* (was given) occurs numerous times in Revelation (e.g., 6:2, 4 [twice], 8, 11; 7:2; 8:3; 9:3, 5). The passive voice generally implies divine agency.

10. Swete, *Revelation*, p. 116; Philip Edgcumbe Hughes, *The Book of the Revelation: A Commentary* (Leicester: Inter-Varsity; Grand Rapids: Eerdmans, 1990), p. 109. David E. Aune (*Revelation 6–16*, WBC 52B [Nashville: Nelson, 1998], p. 527) adds that scorpions, in this case demonic locusts, are able to intimidate and terrorize their victims.

11. Hendriksen, *More Than Conquerors*, p. 120.

8:29; Mark 5:7; Luke 8:28). In the Apocalypse, however, the verb and the noun *torture* refer to divine judgment as a consequence of sin. John compares this acute torment to that of the scorpion's sting.

The demons are given power to afflict human beings for a period of five months. The life span of locusts coincides with the length of the growing season in Israel, from April to September. Here it points to a period of a relatively short duration, for the number five in the context of the decimal system is used as a round number. "There is no clear evidence that this number should be given any symbolical meaning in the N[ew] T[estament]."[12] In addition, the expression *five months* recurs in verse 10 with the same meaning.

The agony that people endure when they are stricken by a scorpion is so intense that they long to die but are prevented from doing so. Job speaks of people who long for death that does not come (Job 3:21; see 7:15), and the Lord God speaks of the survivors of the nation Judah who will prefer death to life (Jer. 8:3). Day after day they long for death to end their physical and even mental misery; instead they see that death eludes them. "Worse than any wound is to wish to die and yet not be able to do so," is the lament of the Latin writer Cornelius Gallus.[13]

These people are unable to die, not because of their inability to commit suicide but because the demons have been told not to kill them. R. C. H. Lenski perceptively writes, "The idea that the unsealed, ungodly, deluded might kill themselves is foreign to the picture. It is a well-known fact that despite all their wishing to be dead, when the most painful curse of their delusion strikes them like scorpion stings, the ungodly never have the courage to commit mass suicide."[14] The demons, lacking the power to kill, continue to vex the body and mind of the sufferers and drive them to utter despair.

By contrast, the followers of Christ have the seal of God on their foreheads and are safe. They have no fear of death, for even though they long to be with the Lord, they make it their goal to please him as long as they are on this earth (2 Cor. 5:8–9; Phil. 1:23–26). They are protected by the Lord himself, who has given his angels charge over them.

Greek Words, Phrases, and Constructions in 9:1–6

Verses 1–2

πεπτωκότα—the perfect active participle of the verb πίπτω (I fall). The perfect tense shows action that took place in the past with lasting significance for the present, illustrated by the phrase "out of the sky to the earth." In addition to the motion of falling, there is also the implied moral fall of the angel.

---

12. Colin J. Hemer, *NIDNTT*, 2:689–90.

13. With thanks to William Barclay, *The Revelation of John*, 2d ed. (Philadelphia: Westminster, 1960), 2:62.

14. R. C. H. Lenski, *The Interpretation of St. John's Revelation* (Columbus: Wartburg, 1943), p. 292.

τῆς ἀβύσσου—the Hebrew text of the Old Testament uses *tĕhôm* (the deep; Ps. 107:26), which in the Septuagint appears as ἄβυσσος, which means without depth or bottomless.[15] The adjective βύσσος (deep) functions as a noun because it lacks the term χώρα (region); the prefix α is a privative. Apocryphal literature also mentions the Abyss as the place where Satan and his followers are kept (*1 Enoch* 18.12–16; 21.7–10; 108.3–6).

Verse 4

ἵνα μὴ ἀδικήσουσιν—this construction serves as the subject of the verb ἐρρέθη (it was told [to them that]).[16] After the conjunction ἵνα the future indicative occurs, but in some manuscripts the aorist subjunctive. The writer often uses the future indicative (see v. 5 where ἵνα is followed by the future passive βασανισθήσονται), which varies little from the aorist subjunctive. This causes him to write οὐδέ (twice) instead of μηδέ, needed for the subjunctive.

Verse 6

ζητήσουσιν—the future tense with two other verbs (*to find* and *to long*) appears three times in verse 6 in a progressive sense: "will be seeking," etc. The emphatic negative οὐ μή means "in no way." It is impossible for them to find death. The present tense φεύγει (flees) is to be preferred to the future tense φεύξεται (will flee).

---

b. The Locusts *9:7–12*

John presents a vivid description of the locusts that must be understood in its entirety. He makes it clear that the word *locusts* should not be taken literally but symbolically, for these creatures

- have the power and grace of horses
- appear with the intelligence of human faces
- show charm with feminine hair but ferocity with lion's teeth
- come with armored protection ready for battle
- sting with the tails of scorpions

In the words of an Arabian proverb: "Locusts have the thigh of a camel, legs of an ostrich, wings of an eagle, breast of a lion, and a tail like vipers."[17] Here is a multifaceted symbol depicting demonic creatures seeking to wage war and overpower anyone and anything in their way.

---

15. Thayer, p. 2. Also see Robert L. Thomas, *Revelation 8–22: An Exegetical Commentary* (Chicago: Moody, 1995), p. 28.

16. A. T. Robertson, *A Grammar of the Greek New Testament in the Light of Historical Research* (Nashville: Broadman, 1934), p. 992.

17. R. H. Charles, *A Critical and Exegetical Commentary on the Revelation of St. John*, ICC (Edinburgh: Clark, 1920), 1:244. Mounce (*Revelation*, p. 189) presents a variation of this proverb: "The locust has the head like a horse, a breast like a lion, feet like a camel, body like a serpent, and antennae like the hair of a maiden." See also Isbon T. Beckwith, *The Apocalypse of John* (1919; reprint, Grand Rapids: Baker, 1979), p. 562; G. R. Beasley-Murray, *The Book of Revelation*, NCB (London: Oliphants, 1974), p. 162.

7. And the appearance of locusts was like horses prepared for battle, and on their heads were something like crowns of gold. And their faces were like human faces, 8. and they had hair like hair of women, and their teeth were like those of lions.

John partially borrows the imagery from the prophecy of Joel, who compares an invasion of locusts to a mighty army that destroys everything in its path. Indeed, this prophet writes that locusts have the appearance of horses, gallop like cavalry, resound with the noise of chariots, charge like warriors, and march straight ahead (Joel 2:2–11). Elsewhere the horse is compared to a locust (Job 39:20). This is the scene of battle that locusts wage on the ground by devouring the plant world and consequently rob the food supply of humans and animals. But John uses the imagery to depict symbolically the spiritual battle that demons wage against the human race. The demons released from the pit of the Abyss and coming forth out of billows of smoke have been given terrifying destructive powers. They are ready for battle and certain of victory; that is, John employs the symbol of horses prepared for battle with something like crowns exhibiting a golden appearance to mark impending triumph. The crown of gold serves as a parody of the golden crown on the head of Jesus the Son of Man (14:14).

The locusts appear with *human faces*, indicating intelligence, sagacity, and discernment. They are demonic creatures with the mental power of rational beings to inflict untold misery on those people who rebel against their Lord and Maker (Rom. 1:21). They purpose to delude the people who do not serve and worship him. They project demonic evil with a human face that is turned away from and is therefore without God.

John writes the phrases *hair of women* and *teeth like those of lions* to express figuratively demonic deception on the one hand and ferocious attack on the other. Female hair is pleasing to the eye; the contrast between its charm and the ferocity of the teeth is striking in its symbolism. The teeth of lions symbolize savagery and cruelty to satisfy a voracious appetite, for Satan and his demonic forces seek to entice human beings and ultimately destroy them.

Once again, John relies for this symbolism on the prophecy of Joel, "A nation has invaded my land, powerful and without number; it has the teeth of a lion, the fangs of a lioness" (1:6). Yet the demonic creatures in John's apocalyptic vision have not been given authority to kill but to torture unbelievers for a specified duration of five months (vv. 5, 10).

9. And they had breastplates like the breastplates of iron, and the sound of their wings was like the sound of many chariots with horses racing into battle. 10. And they had tails and stings like scorpions, and in their tails they had power to harm people for five months.

a. "They had breastplates like the breastplates of iron." These plates covered the front of ancient warriors much the same as bulletproof vests cover police officers today. An Aramaic commentary on the prophecy of Nahum 3:17 ("Your guards are like locusts") has an expanded reading, "Behold, your plates gleam like the locust." These words compare the iron breastplates of the Assyrian warriors, who were known for their inhuman cruelty, to the scaled breastplates of the locusts.[18] The text calls attention to physical warfare, which I interpret as spiritual combat.

The figurative presentation of these demonic beings points to their invincibility. No one on earth can rise up against these evil attacks that are designed to inflict untold harm on the human race. Only those people who have the seal of God on their foreheads are able to withstand the furious attacks of these monsters. Nonetheless, not even the holiest saint on earth can destroy a fallen angel, for as immortal beings they are invulnerable to ultimate destruction and death.

b. "The sound of their wings was like the sound of many chariots with horses racing into battle." John borrows his imagery from Joel's prophecy that compares the whirring sound of the wings of locusts in flight to horses that "gallop along like cavalry" (Joel 2:4). The thundering hooves of horses and the whirring wheels of chariots in ancient days turned the tide of battle when they outnumbered those of their opponents.[19] Here the innumerable locusts representing demonic forces are sure of their victory. The reference to the sound of battle should be interpreted not literally but symbolically. It depicts an imminent battle that fills human hearts and souls with unspeakable dread and fear.

c. "And they had tails and stings like scorpions, and in their tails they had power to harm people for five months." The verbal picture is that of horses followed by chariots with whirring wheels to harm hapless opponents. Similarly a scorpion takes hold of its prey and then with its tail administers a poisonous strike. As the chariot is the appendage to the horse so the tail is the appurtenance of the scorpion.[20]

In slightly different wording, John repeats what he wrote in verse 5, "And they were given power not to kill them, but to torture them for five months, and their torment was like the torment of a scorpion when it strikes a man." The sting of a scorpion usually does not kill a person but causes excruciating pain for a limited period. By repeating the same thought, John stresses the gravity of the attack. He indicates that the torment caused by demonic creatures is temporary. He mentions five months to convey a period of short duration.

11. They had a king over them, the angel of the Abyss; his name in Hebrew was Abaddon, and in Greek Apollyon.

The meaning of the text is clear, for locusts have no king, as the writer of Proverbs 30:27 notes. But demons pay allegiance to Satan, whom Jesus calls

18. Robert P. Gordon, "Loricate Locusts in the Targum to Nahum iii 17 and Revelation ix 9," *Vetus Testamentum* 33 (1983): 338–39.

19. Compare Luther Poellot, *Revelation: The Last Book in the Bible* (St. Louis: Concordia, 1962), p. 127.

20. Alford (*Revelation*, p. 643) bases this observation on the genitives in verse 9, which literally reads, "a sound *of* chariots *of* many horses" (i.e., the chariots are viewed as extensions of the horses).

"prince of this world" and whom Paul identifies as "ruler of the kingdom of the air."[21] Here the angel is either Satan or a demonic figure who represents the devil. He is called "the destroyer" in both Hebrew and Greek.

The New Testament assigns many names to Satan: devil, tempter, enemy, adversary, serpent, dragon, deceiver, accuser, evil one, Beelzebub, Belial, Apollyon.[22] The Hebrew name *Abaddon* and the Greek name *Apollyon* mean the same thing: Destroyer (compare Job 26:6; 28:22; Ps. 88:11; Prov. 15:11). Satan appointed himself as ruler; here he either functions as king over demons or he has delegated an underling to be called king and destroyer. The evil one rules all those people who do not have the seal of God on their foreheads; they are called "children of the devil" (1 John 3:10). This demonic figure called Destroyer is the exact opposite of the one who is called Savior. Why John used both the Hebrew name and the Greek name is difficult to determine. Some scholars say that he wrote the name Apollyon as a variation of the god Apollo, whose symbol was a locust. "There may be a punning dig at claims of Nero and Domitian to be incarnations of Apollo."[23] However, it is more prudent to assert that John's focus is on the spiritual destroyer, Satan or his minion, than on a veiled reference to an earthly despot, Nero or Domitian.

12. The first woe has come. Look, still two more come after these things.

John states that there are three woes, of which the first two are explained in this chapter. That is, the first woe relates to the locusts that have come to torment the people (vv. 1–11), and the second woe comprises the rest of chapter 9. I interpret 10:1–11:13 as a parenthesis, so that the text of 11:14 marks the conclusion of the second woe, "The second woe has come." Then John writes that the third woe is coming soon.

The three woes succeed one another in increasing intensity: the first woe follows the sounding of the fifth trumpet. It relates the release of demonic forces that are empowered to harm but not to kill for a specified duration. The second woe occurs when the sixth trumpet is blown. It reports that four angels are released to kill a third of the human race by fire, smoke, and sulfur. The calamities that occur are designed to bring the human race to repentance and faith in God; they call the people to change their sinful ways by turning back to God. These two woes also instruct the saints to observe the signs of the time, for the end is imminent. The third woe introduces God's judgment of the dead (11:15b–19).

---

21. Eph. 2:2; see also John 12:31; 14:30; 16:11; 2 Cor. 4:4; 1 John 4:4; 5:19.

22. Compare Daniel P. Fuller, "Satan," *ISBE*, 4:342; Hughes, *Revelation*, p. 111. Swete (*Revelation*, p. 120) observes, "It is unnecessary to enquire whether by Abaddon, the Destroyer, the Seer means Death or Satan." And see Thomas, *Revelation 8–22*, p. 38.

23. John P. M. Sweet, *Revelation*, WPC (Philadelphia: Westminster, 1979), p. 170; refer also to Aune, *Revelation 6–16*, p. 535; Beasley-Murray, *Revelation*, p. 162; Wilfrid J. Harrington, *Revelation*, SP 16 (Collegeville, Minn.: Liturgical Press, 1993), p. 110.

Greek Words, Phrases, and Constructions in 9:7–12

Verse 7

ὡς στέφανοι ὅμοιοι χρυσῷ—notice the words that indicate an approximation to the real thing: something like (ὡς), and similar to (ὅμοιοι). The demonic forces exhibit imitation crowns, gold, and human faces. In the same way, Paul speaks of masquerades that Satan uses to deceive the people (2 Cor. 11:14).

Verses 8–9

καὶ εἶχον—the imperfect tense at the beginning of both verses is descriptive: "they had." "The imperfect is here a sort of moving panorama."[24] Nonetheless, the next two verses (vv. 10, 11) have the present tense ἔχουσιν. The present tense is used to elicit vividness in the writer's description.

Verse 10

οὐρὰς ὁμοίας σκορπίοις καὶ κέντρα—this is a telescoped sentence that with supplied brackets reads "tails like [tails] of scorpions and stings [like stings of scorpions]."

τοὺς ἀνθρώπους—the noun with definite article is not contrasted to angels or animals but refers to humanity in general. Throughout the Apocalypse the term conveys a universalistic sense (e.g., 8:11; 9:6, 10, 15, 18, 20).[25]

Verse 11

βασιλέα—this noun without the definite article is the direct object of the verb *to have.* Although the translation is "they have a king," the lack of the definite article may indicate the absoluteness of this office, namely, king of demons.

Verse 12

μετὰ ταῦτα—should these words with or without the conjunction καί form the beginning of verse 13, as is evidenced in a number of minuscule manuscripts? The harder reading places these two words at the end of verse 12 and is adopted, even though John nearly always places them at the beginning of a sentence.[26]

7. The Sixth Trumpet *9:13–21*

The calamities affecting the world and the human race increase in intensity with the sounding of each successive blowing of a trumpet. In this segment, John reveals that a war will take place that has no parallel in the annals of human history. Calls for repentance go unheeded and God's revelation is deliberately rejected, so that a terrifying war ravages mankind as an outcome of divine wrath. The difference between earlier world wars and this one is the magnitude with

24. Robertson, *Grammar,* p. 883.

25. Richard Bauckham, *The Climax of Prophecy* (Edinburgh: Clark, 1993), p. 311.

26. For a detailed discussion see Bruce M. Metzger, *A Textual Commentary on the Greek New Testament,* 2d ed. (Stuttgart: Deutsche Bibelgesellschaft, 1994), pp. 669–70.

which hellish forces are unleashed and go unchecked. The powers of darkness rule supreme without any hindrance; they annihilate a third of the world's population. Demons inspire people to destroy fellow human beings with the most horrible weaponry at their disposal. Treaties and conventions that have served as barriers are ignored. This is God's judgment on a world that has abandoned him and his Word.

a. A Divine Command *9:13–16*

13. And the sixth angel blew the trumpet. And I heard a voice from the horns of the golden altar before God, 14. saying to the sixth angel, the one holding the trumpet, "Set free the four angels that are bound at the great river Euphrates."

a. *Observations.* Foremost, we see the parallel of the sixth angel blowing the trumpet to release four angels at the great river Euphrates and the sixth angel pouring out his bowl on the great river Euphrates (16:12). In addition, as the sixth trumpet reaches the climax of afflictions, so the opening of the sixth seal proved to be climactic (6:12–17). Here is explicit evidence of the parallelism that pervades the entire Apocalypse.

Next, some translations add the number *four* as a qualifier of "horns" in the first part of the second sentence: "the horns of the golden altar."[27] The addition of this number may be attributed to the parallel in the expression "four angels" (v. 14), or a scribe may have accidentally omitted it. Greek manuscripts are equally divided on this matter, so the choice is arbitrary; its inclusion or exclusion does not affect the message of the text.[28]

Last, the voice that speaks from the golden altar to the sixth angel blowing the trumpet is an answer to the prayers the saints in heaven and on earth have presented to God (6:9–10; 8:3–5). None of the other angels with trumpets receives such a direct communication from the presence of God himself.

b. *Interpretation.* "And I heard a voice from the horns of the golden altar before God." Even though John mentions God's name, he notes that the sound is coming from the altar, namely, the very presence of God. Thus, he avoids referring to God but reverently says that the voice originates from the golden altar. John used a similar method of indirect identification for Jesus when he called him the voice like a trumpet (1:10). And in 6:6 the voice coming from the midst of the four living creatures appears to be the voice of either the Lamb or God (compare 10:4, 8; 11:12). Swete comments that the voice is that of either the angel with the golden censer or represents the prayers of the saints (8:4–5).[29] Yet all the prayers of the saints come together before the Lord, who now responds to them with one voice. Is this the voice of an angel or of God?

Jewish tradition taught that an angel served God as an intermediary in conveying his word. Stephen, Paul, and the writer of Hebrews circumscribe the voice of

---

27. NCV, NEB, NIV, REB, *Peterson.* See also the commentaries of Thomas, Lenski, Harrington, Beckwith.

28. Consult Metzger, *Textual Commentary*, p. 670.

29. Swete, *Revelation*, p. 120.

God that utters the Ten Commandments at Mount Sinai; they state that the Law was given by angels (Acts 7:53; Gal. 3:19; Heb. 2:2).[30] Nevertheless, the introduction to the Decalogue reads, "And God spoke all these words" (Exod. 20:1). We surmise that John likewise circumscribes the voice of God by leaving the impression that an angel spoke on God's behalf.

The horns of the altar are not those of the altar outside the tabernacle or temple but of the altar of incense in front of the Most Holy Place. This altar was overlaid with gold (Exod. 30:1–6; 37:25–28). It was constructed according to the heavenly pattern Moses received from God on Mount Sinai (Exod. 25:9, 40; Heb. 8:5). In the Apocalypse, this altar serves as a place where the saints slain for the word of God plead with their sovereign Lord to avenge their blood (6:9–10). From this altar the smoke of incense mingled with the prayers of the saints rises up to God (8:4), and from this altar commands are given to commence the harvest that ushers in the end of the age (14:18–19).

c. *Instruction.* "[The voice was] saying to the sixth angel, the one holding the trumpet, 'Set free the four angels that are bound at the great river Euphrates.'" The sixth angel receives a command to release four angels. There is no indication that these four angels should be linked to those standing at the four corners of the earth (7:1). Here the angels are bound at the great river Euphrates, but in 7:1 the four angels hold the four winds of the earth. We face the question of whether the angels that are bound are good or evil.[31] We read that they are to be set loose, so that the plagues God has ordained to punish the godless may take effect. The fact that they *are bound,* which in the Greek is in the perfect tense to denote a lapse of time, signifies evil angels (see Jude 6). When they are released, the plagues that they have held in check are set in motion: the plagues of fire, smoke, and sulfur that will kill a third part of the human race (v. 18).

The expression *the great river Euphrates* occurs several times in the Old Testament.[32] It marked the boundary of the Promised Land that was not realized until the reign of King Solomon (1 Kings 4:21). In another century, it marked the eastern limit of the Roman empire.

Nevertheless, when the name Euphrates occurs in a chapter filled with symbolism, it is wise to affirm that next to a literal reading there is room for a figurative version. The name marks the boundary between good and evil, between the kingdom of God and that of Satan. The psalmist notes that the messianic kingdom fulfilled in Christ extends from the river Euphrates to the ends of the earth. And the effect of his rule makes the desert tribes to bow before him (Ps.

30. SB, 3:554–56; Greijdanus (*Openbaring,* p. 205) writes that the speaker is of the masculine gender as the participle *legonta* shows and therefore refers to God. But the word *angelos* is also of the masculine gender.

31. Alford (*Revelation,* p. 645) comments that the question of good or bad angels "does not enter in any way into consideration."

32. Gen. 15:18; Deut. 1:7; Josh. 1:4. See also Gen. 2:14; Deut. 11:24; Rev. 16:12.

72:8–9). Even the nations Assyria and Babylonia, which in the Old Testament era were the enemies of God's people, are subject to Christ.

The text reveals that when the four angels are released at the great river Euphrates, all hell breaks loose in a worldwide war. In Old Testament times, God used this river figuratively to overrun the land of his people with their enemies (Isa. 8:7–8).[33] He now commands the sixth angel to set free the four angels which have been bound and thus rendered unable to stop the march of the gospel (Matt. 24:14). When the moment comes for their release, evil forces are loosed against a world that has forsaken God and his Word. We can be sure that the forces of the Antichrist are also pitted against the citizens of the kingdom of heaven, even though they bear God's seal and receive his spiritual protection (vv. 4–5). Jesus said that if the days of great distress were not shortened, "no one would survive." But "for the sake of the elect those days will be shortened" (Matt. 24:22).

15. And the four angels were set free, they who were prepared for the hour, day, month, and year to kill a third of the people. 16. And the number of the horsemen was two hundred million. I heard their number.

The passive construction of the verb *to set free* means that God is the agent who commands the release of these four angels. The number four signifies worldwide impact, as is evident from the destruction that these angels induce: a third part of the world's population perishes. This is a picture of a war that encompasses the entire world as it faces God's judgment. All along God had kept in check the forces of global destruction of humanity, albeit he had sent calamities on a third of the earth, trees, the creatures of the sea, the ships, the waters, and the heavenly bodies (8:7–12). He also increases the intensity of his judgments. Following the opening of the fourth seal, Death and Hades are given "authority over *the fourth part* of the earth to kill with a sword, and famine, and disease, and by the wild beasts of the earth" (6:8, emphasis added). But now we read that a third part of the earth's population is slain. To be precise, after the plagues that affect a third of creation, God releases a plague on ungodly people. This scourge is so severe that these people long to die but cannot because death slips away from them. Then as a result of the next plague a third of mankind perishes.

God releases four angels who were ready and equipped with instruments to execute their horrifying task. John even mentions the exact time for which they have been prepared: *the hour, day, month, and year.* This means that God determines the exact moment and extent of the chastisement he metes out on one third of the human race. He sets the very hour of the plague. He also makes it known that this devastation on humanity is not for a fleeting moment but will last for the duration he has decided in his wisdom.

A global war breaks out in which both the godly and ungodly are involved to the point that one third of the world's inhabitants die. God uses war as an instru-

33. George Eldon Ladd, *Commentary on the Revelation of John* (Grand Rapids: Eerdmans, 1972), p. 136; compare Lenski, *Revelation*, p. 302, who does not call the Euphrates a geographical river or place but "the fountain of world dominance."

ment to warn the ungodly to repent, yet countless multitudes refuse to heed God's warning. John writes, "And the rest of the people, those who were not killed by these plagues, did not repent" (v. 20). He depicts warfare in terms of his day with horsemen, namely, troops of cavalry.[34] He specifies that their number is two hundred million; and he adds that he heard this number mentioned. In other words, it came to him from an outside source and not necessarily from seeing them (v. 17). John describes the number of angels as "myriads of myriads and thousands of thousands" (5:11), which amounts to an incalculable number. Similarly, "200 million (200 x 1000 x 1000) is an overwhelmingly large number of troops amassed against humanity."[35]

The Old Testament speaks of God's heavenly hosts of angels as numbering "tens of thousands and thousands of thousands" (Ps. 68:17; and see Dan. 7:10). In the Old Testament passages, the subject is God's angels, but here it is mounted troops.

Greek Words, Phrases, and Constructions in 9:13–16

Verse 13

φωνὴν μίαν—the number one is best translated as an indefinite article (see 8:13; 18:21; 19:17), yet the singleness of the voice that speaks in answer to the multiplicity of prayers (8:3) should not be minimized.

τοῦ . . . τοῦ . . . τοῦ—with the triple use of the definite article preceding three nouns, John seems to indicate that the voice comes from the very presence of God (8:3 also features the definite article τό three times).

ἐπί—with the dative case, this preposition has a locative meaning, "at the great river."

Verse 15

εἰς τὴν ὥραν—the preposition governs the accusative case of the four successive nouns (ὥραν, ἡμέραν, μῆνα, ἐνιαυτόν). One definite article precedes all four nouns to indicate one group of nouns specifying a moment in time.

Verse 16

ἤκουσα—followed by the accusative case τὸν ἀριθμόν denotes that John both heard and understood the significance of "the number."

---

b. A Descriptive Vision
9:17–19

In the preceding section, John describes what he heard: the sound of a trumpet blown by an angel; a voice coming from the golden altar; the command to

---

34. Bauer, p. 380.

35. Resseguie, *Revelation Unsealed*, p. 61. Bauer (p. 199) interprets it as "an indefinite number of incalculable immensity." Ladd (*Revelation*, p. 137) observes, "It is difficult to believe that a literal number is intended." But in their respective commentaries, Thomas (p. 46) pleads for "an exact number," and Walvoord (p. 166) notes that "the literal interpretation is not impossible."

release four angels; and the number of the mounted troops. Now he describes in detail what he saw: the color of breastplates; the appearance of the horses; the killing of a third of humanity; and the power of these horses.

17. And thus in my vision I saw the horses and their riders. They had breastplates that were colored as fiery red, hyacinth blue, and sulfur yellow. The heads of the horses were like heads of lions, and out of their mouths came forth fire, and smoke and sulfur.

Steeped in the Old Testament, John writes, "In my vision I saw," employing vocabulary taken from Daniel 7:2; 8:2. He uses this phrase only here in the Apocalypse apparently to stress the contrast between having heard the number of the riders on horses and now seeing them.[36] He wishes to convey a full account of what he heard and saw, because the multitude of horsemen portended nothing but fear and terror to an unrepentant world.

John writes that they "had breastplates that were colored as fiery red, hyacinth blue, and sulfur yellow."[37] The sequence of the Greek text indicates that the description of breastplates qualifies the riders and not the horses, even though in ancient warfare horses at times were also shielded with metal armor in the form of links and plates.

The colors of these breastplates are illustrative: red refers to fire, blue to the hyacinth plant, and yellow to sulfur. The Septuagint mentions the expression *hyacinth* in connection with a dye that was used to give a blue color to fine linen and the curtain of the tabernacle (Exod. 26:1; 27:16; 28:8). Swete notes that the expression "doubtless meant to describe the blue smoke of a sulfurous flame."[38] The descriptions match the fire, smoke, and sulfur in the next line and are repeated in connection with the three plagues (v. 18).

After describing the riders, the author writes about the heads and mouths of the horses: "The heads of the horses were like heads of lions, and out of their mouths came forth fire, and smoke and sulfur." Comparing the horses' heads to those of lions, John depicts ferocious destructiveness. The description of fire, smoke, and sulfur coming forth from their mouths fits the ancient stories of dragons spewing forth fire. The flow of these three elements is portrayed as one continuous stream of devastation. This picture evokes terror and represents evil stalking the globe with brute force. The horses and their riders are controlled by demonic beings that are bent on causing death and destruction.

---

36. Charles (*Revelation,* 1:252) calls the last clause in verse 16 and the first clause in verse 17 "a confused gloss." However, Greek manuscripts lend no support to this assertion. Beckwith (*Apocalypse,* pp. 567–68) calls the addition of the verb *I saw* superfluous. But Aramaic idiom demands the verb *to see,* in, for instance, "I lifted up my eyes and saw."

37. See the NKJV, NJB, *Cassirer.* MLB, RSV, and NRSV use the word *sapphire* to describe the blue tint. Likewise M. Robert Mulholland Jr., *Revelation: Holy Living in an Unholy World* (Grand Rapids: Zondervan, Frances Asbury Press, 1990), p. 198. And William Barclay (*Letters to the Seven Churches* [London: SCM, 1957], 2:65) calls it "smoky blue."

38. Swete, *Revelation,* p. 123.

18. As a result of these three plagues a third part of mankind was killed by the fire, smoke, and sulfur that came out of their mouths. 19. For the power of the horses was in their mouths and in their tails, and their tails were like snakes. They had heads and with them they inflict harm.

Here is an interesting poetic layout of verses 17b and 18 in a chiastic arrangement:[39]

A [17b]from their mouths
B proceeded
C fire and smoke and sulfur
D [18a]From these three plagues a third of humanity was killed,
C′ [18b]from the fire and smoke and sulfur
B′ which proceeded
A′ from their mouths

John enumerates the three plagues that destroy a third of the human race (v. 15); they are *fire, smoke, and sulfur* discharging from the mouths of devilish monsters. These three natural elements are symbols that represent war, desolation, and destruction.

First, the Old Testament teaches that fire refers to war, for "burning a city with fire was a basic principle of ancient total warfare."[40]

Next, the fire of warfare includes the smoke that obscures the light of the sun, pollutes the air, and suffocates every being that has breath. In the Old Testament, smoke is a manifestation of God's fierce wrath directed against his enemies (Judg. 20:40; 2 Sam. 22:9; Ps. 18:8; Isa. 30:27).

Last, sulfur, also known as brimstone, in Scripture represents God's punishment of the wicked, as is clearly seen in the destruction of Sodom and Gomorrah (Gen. 19:24).[41] When deposits of sulfur begin to burn, toxic gasses are released, especially in volcanic eruptions. A combination of hot lava and burning sulfur results in painful agony and death for all those in its destructive path.[42]

The writer relates that the power to kill human beings resides in both the front and the back of the horses, that is, in their mouths and tails (compare v. 10). Their mouths figuratively spew forth fire, smoke, and sulfur, while their

39. With thanks to Aune, *Revelation 6–16*, p. 540.

40. Harold Van Broekhoven Jr., *ISBE*, 2:305. Consult Judg. 1:8; 9:49; 18:27; 20:48; 1 Sam. 30:1–4; 1 Kings 9:16; 2 Chron. 36:19; Jer. 17:27; 21:10; 22:7; 32:29; 43:12–13; 49:27; Amos 1:4–14; 2:2, 5.

41. See Deut. 29:23; Job 18:15; Ps. 11:6; Isa. 30:33; Ezek. 38:22; Luke 17:29; Rev. 9:17–18; 14:10; 19:20; 20:10; 21:8.

42. Hoeksema (*Behold, He Cometh!* pp. 328–30) interprets fire, smoke, and sulfur as symbols of war, famine, and pestilence respectively. He links fire to the second horseman representing war; smoke to the third horseman; and sulfur to the fourth horseman (6:3–8). However, from Scripture it is difficult to prove that smoke represents famine.

tails resemble snakes that bite. John does not say that the riders of these horses kill human beings, but that the horses have that power. The text, then, is highly symbolic, so that we have to think in terms of demonic forces that are given authority to kill God's adversaries. With both heads and tails, these demons inflict untold harm.

c. Refusing to Repent
9:20–21

20. And the rest of the people, who were not killed by these plagues, did not repent from the works of their hands or stop worshiping the demons and the idols made of gold, silver, bronze, stone, and wood. These idols are not able to see, hear, and walk.

These two verses serve as a brief summary of the catastrophes God has sent, including calamities in both nature and warfare. The word *plagues* in the Greek text conveys the sense of God administering blows. Even though plagues destroy a third of the world's inhabitants, survivors appear to become inured to the repeated calamities. If terms like *tidal wave, earthquake, genocide,* and *ethnic cleansing* become common expressions, the population at large begins to take them in stride and refuses to consider the impact and message they convey. God uses these disasters to call human beings to their senses and does not limit adversities to those resulting from armed conflict.

These concluding verses relate not to God's people but rather to unrepentant sinners. This passage, therefore, emphasizes not adversities but recalcitrant unbelievers. In spite of the traumatic loss of life, the rest of humanity refused to repent from the works of their hands. This is not because God had not given them time and reason for repentance. For example, Jesus told the church of Thyatira that he had given the prophetess Jezebel "time to repent, but she does not want to repent from her fornication" (2:21). Likewise the people on whom God's wrath was poured out cursed God's name and refused to repent (16:9, 10). God employed plagues to cause people to change their ways and convert; instead they repudiated him.

What are "the works of their hands" that the unbelievers refused to abandon? They are worthless handmade idols of gold, silver, bronze, stone, and wood (Jer. 1:16; 16:19–20; Dan. 5:23; Mic. 5:13). Westerners do not typically worship images of the Buddha or other gods, but the idols of material possessions, especially money (Matt. 6:24; Luke 16:13), are omnipresent as visual images of false gods. The psalmists eloquently attest to the impotence of false gods:

> They have mouths, but cannot speak,
>   eyes, but they cannot see;
> they have ears, but cannot hear,
>   noses, but they cannot smell;
> they have hands, but cannot feel,
>   feet, but they cannot walk;

nor can they utter a sound with their throats.
(Ps. 115:5–7; see also 135:15–17)

Paul notes that to worship idols is the equivalent of worshiping demons. Idols embody the concept of worshiping demons that demand unquestionable devotion. The Song of Moses records these words about Israel's relation to God: "They made him jealous with their foreign gods and angered him with their detestable idols. They sacrificed to demons, which are not God" (Deut. 32:16–17a). An idol made of gold, silver, bronze, stone, and wood is and remains a dead object, but demons persuade people to worship it (1 Cor. 10:20). Hence, presenting homage to an idol is the same as professing allegiance to demons, and demons promote not the well-being of their devotees but their destruction. They induce the idolaters to transgress God's commandments.

21. And they repented not from their murders, their witchcraft, their fornication, and their thefts.

Idolaters daily witnessed death and destruction as reminders that penalties inevitably follow the transgressing of divine commandments. In a direct affront to God, they served idols. They committed murder, witchcraft, adultery, and theft—sins perpetrated against society. These sins violate the Decalogue: not to serve other gods and make idols; not to kill; not to commit adultery and fornication; and not to steal (Exod. 20:3–4, 13–15). Throughout the Old and New Testaments, idolatry is mentioned repeatedly because it replaces the worship of God. Related to idolatry is the sin of magic spells and witchcraft, which are an abomination to the Lord God (Deut. 18:10–12). Indeed, God instructed Moses to put to death those who consulted soothsayers and those who practiced witchcraft (Exod. 22:18; Lev. 20:6, 27). Paul combines idolatry and witchcraft as works of the flesh (Gal. 5:20). And John lists sorcerers, fornicators, murderers, and idolaters among those who are consigned to everlasting doom (21:8; 22:15).[43]

The people refused to repent and thus at the Judgment Day must take full responsibility for their deeds. Six trumpets, blown as warning signs of impending judgment, are designed to call sinners to repentance, conversion, and a new life. But when hardened sinners ignore the trumpet calls, they will be unable to blame anyone but themselves.[44] The six trumpet sounds are preludes to the seventh, which records the song of the twenty-four elders representing the countless saints:

And the time has come to judge the dead
and to reward your servants the prophets,

43. Consult Thomas, *Revelation 8–22*, p. 54. See also J. Stafford Wright (*NIDNTT*, 2:558), who comments that "there has always been a magical tradition of herbs gathered and prepared for spells, and also for encouraging the presence of spirits at magical ceremonies."

44. Beale (*Revelation*, p. 518) states that God's warning to "the remaining unbelievers is not to accomplish actual repentance among the majority, since they did not have it in them, so to speak, to repent." Instead God demonstrates his sovereignty and his justice.

and the saints and those who fear your name,
the small and the great,
and to destroy those who are destroying the
earth. (11:18)

Greek Words, Phrases, and Constructions in 9:20–21

Verse 20

ἵνα μή—these particles introduce "the idea of conceived result."[45] That is, if the people had repented, the result would have been a renouncing of the worship of demons and idols. The future προσκυνήσουσιν takes the place of the subjunctive, which is common in the Apocalypse.

Verse 21

φαρμάκων—"magic potion, charm."[46] The fact that this noun occurs only here suggests that it is the original reading. Copyists would be more inclined to change it to the noun φαρμακεία (sorcery, magic, 18:23; Gal. 5:20) than to let it stand.[47] The derivative *pharmacy* is a link to the concept of *drugs that induce magic spells.*

---

45. Robert Hanna, *A Grammatical Aid to the Greek New Testament* (Grand Rapids: Baker, 1983), p. 449; Robertson, *Grammar*, p. 998.

46. Bauer, p. 854.

47. Metzger, *Textual Commentary*, p. 670.

10

The Angel and the Little Scroll

(10:1–11)

Outline (continued)

8. Interlude (10:1–11:14)
   a. The Angel and the Little Scroll (10:1–11)
      (1) A Mighty Angel (10:1–4)
      (2) The Angel's Message (10:5–7)
      (3) The Scroll and Its Purpose (10:8–11)

10 1 And I saw another mighty angel coming down from heaven clothed in a cloud. And the
rainbow was on his head, and his face was like the sun, and his legs as pillars of fire. 2 And
he held a little scroll, unrolled in his hand. He placed his right foot on the sea and his left
on the land, 3 and he cried with a loud voice as a lion roars. And when he cried, the seven
peals of thunder raised their voices. 4 And when the seven peals of thunder spoke, I was about to
write, and I heard a voice from heaven saying, "Seal the things which the seven peals of thunder said,
and do not write them."

5 And the angel, whom I saw standing on the sea and on the land, raised his right hand to heaven.
6 And he swore by the one who lives forever and ever, who created heaven and the things in it, the
earth and the things in it, and the sea and the things in it, and said, "There will no longer be a delay."
7 However, in the days when the voice of the seventh angel is about to blow his trumpet, the mystery
of God will be accomplished, as he proclaimed to his servants the prophets.

8 And the voice that I heard speaking with me again from heaven said, "Go, take the scroll that
is unrolled in the hand of the angel who stands on the sea and on the land." 9 And I went to the angel
and asked him to give me the little scroll. And he said to me, "Take it and eat it, and it will turn your
stomach sour, but in your mouth it will be as sweet as honey."

10 And I took the little scroll out of the hand of the angel and ate it. And it was in my mouth as
sweet as honey, and when I had eaten it, my stomach turned sour. 11 And I was told, "You must
prophesy again against many peoples and nations and languages and kings."

---

8. Interlude
10:1–11:14
a. The Angel and the Little Scroll
10:1–11

Once again, John writes an interlude, just as he did in chapter 7. After the sixth seal, he digresses to show the reader a picture of the saints in heaven. The sixth seal revealed the scene of unbelievers facing the wrath of God and the Lamb (6:15–17); the subsequent interlude of chapter 7 presented the saints in glory, who are sealed by God and are a prelude to the opening of the seventh seal (8:1). Similarly, the sounding of the sixth trumpet depicts the unbelievers who refuse to repent from their evil works, even though they have witnessed divine judgment in a series of plagues (8:6–9:21). But before the seventh trumpet sounds, John presents the saints on earth who are instructed to present the Word of God to the world. In short, this interlude of chapter 10 is not an interval of ease but a time to receive and proclaim the gospel.

In the sequence of sevens (seals, trumpets, and bowls), there is an interlude after the sixth seal and the sixth trumpet, but not after the sixth bowl. This signifies that in addition to the church preaching the gospel to the world, there is nothing else believers can do as they wait for the consummation that ends in the final judgment. John presents a series of sevens in the context of seals, trumpets, and bowls that show progressive parallelism. These sets of seven reveal pictures within pictures that are neither rigorously contemporaneous nor successive. It is better to say that the sets of seven are realized both simultaneously and successively.[1] As the sets of pictures unfold, the focus on Christ's victory and Satan's defeat becomes increasingly clearer. These sets, each in its own way, point to the consummation.

John hears a voice from heaven saying, "Seal the things which the seven peals of thunder said, and do not write them" (v. 4). As elsewhere in the Apocalypse, he couches the vision in the language of the Old Testament, taking some words from Daniel's prophecy. Daniel is told to seal up his visions because they pertain to the future (8:26; 12:4, 9; contrast Rev. 22:10).[2] Likewise John's visions become reality when God's time has come. The reading "a breath of life from God entered them, and they stood on their feet" (11:11) seems to echo Ezekiel 37:10, "and breath entered them; they came to life and stood up on their feet."[3] The angel's instruction to have John eat the little scroll, which tasted like honey, echoes the Psalms and the Prophets (Ps. 19:10; 119:103; Jer. 15:16; Ezek. 2:8; 3:3–13).

What is the meaning of the expression *little scroll?* There are some interpreters who state that the expression refers to the scroll that the Lamb took from the right hand of God (Rev. 5:1–9). They point out that here the adjective *little* has lost its meaning since in the Greek the word *scroll* is itself a diminutive. Indeed, some examples prove that a diminutive at times loses its characteristics.[4] The context of this chapter shows that John sometimes uses the terms *scroll* and *little scroll* interchangeably (see vv. 2, 8, 9, 10). These interpreters conclude that the two words signify the same thing and that not much weight should be placed on a distinction between the scroll in 5:1–9 and the *little* scroll in 10:2, 9–10.[5] But is it John's intention to identify the two scrolls mentioned in chapters 5 and 10?

We note that in regard to these words John makes a few distinctions. First, he writes the term *book* in the phrase *the book of life,* which book contains the names of God's people (3:5; 20:15). He seems to convey the idea that this is an all-inclusive volume. Next, he pens the word *scroll* for the volume that is so full that it has

---

1. Refer to Herman Hoeksema, *Behold, He Cometh! An Exposition of the Book of Revelation* (Grand Rapids: Reformed Free Publishing Association, 1969), p. 335.

2. Richard Bauckham, *The Climax of Prophecy* (Edinburgh: Clark, 1993), p. 251.

3. Consult Steve Moyise, *The Old Testament in the Book of Revelation,* JSNTSup115 (Sheffield: Sheffield Academic Press, 1995), p. 105.

4. E.g., Hermas *Vision* 2.1, 4 shows that the two Greek words *biblaridion* and *biblidion* are synonyms of *biblion,* and all of them mean "little book."

5. Frederick D. Mazzaferri, *The Genre of the Book of Revelation from a Source-Critical Perspective,* BZNW 54 (Berlin and New York: de Gruyter, 1989), pp. 265–79; Bauckham, *Climax of Prophecy,* pp. 243–57; and see his *Theology of the Book of Revelation,* New Testament Theology (Cambridge: Cambridge University Press, 1993), pp. 80–84. David E. Holwerda, "The Church and the Little Scroll (Revelation 10, 11)," *CTJ* 34 (1999): 148–61. Holwerda agrees with Bauckham and suggests that "both scrolls could be coextensive with each other and with the book of Revelation after the opening of the seals" (p. 153).

writing on the inside and on the back (5:1). With this term, he appears to say that the scroll is of considerable length. Third, when he uses the expression *little scroll,* he calls attention to an unsealed roll lying open in the hand of an angel (10:2). By contrast, the scroll that the Lamb took from the hand of God was sealed with seven seals. Fourth, if the two scrolls were the same, we would have expected John to add the definite article before the word *scroll* to alert the reader to the previous references in chapter 5, which is not the case in 10:2 ("a little scroll"). Then in 10:8 the definite article appears ("the little scroll") referring to 10:2.[6] From an exegetical perspective, the arguments against identifying the two scrolls are impressive.[7]

This little scroll links chapters 10 and 11. Its content seems to be the gospel that the church proclaims to the world (11:3–7). The church must prophesy God's word and the testimony of Jesus, which is exactly the reason that John is on the island of Patmos (1:9). In obedience to Jesus' mandate to be witnesses before the end comes (Matt. 28:19–20), this gospel must be proclaimed to "many peoples, nations, languages, and kings" (10:11).[8] The task of the two witnesses, namely the church, is to proclaim the message of salvation in a hostile world (11:3). The period during which this message is preached "relates not to the time of the last trumpet, as many have held, but to the entire period with which this book is concerned."[9]

(1) A Mighty Angel
10:1–4

1. And I saw another mighty angel coming down from heaven clothed in a cloud. And the rainbow was on his head, and his face was like the sun, and his legs as pillars of fire.

When John writes that he saw another mighty angel, he is no longer in heaven but back on earth. He saw the angel coming down from heaven to earth and was "standing on the sea and on the land" (v. 5). Earlier John was in heaven observing a scroll in God's right hand and a mighty angel asking anyone who would be worthy to break its seals and open it (5:1–2). With a slight variation, the adjective

6. See Robert H. Mounce, *The Book of Revelation,* rev. ed., NICNT (Grand Rapids: Eerdmans, 1998), p. 202. The Syriac version has the expression *sephrâ dᵉḥayê* (the book of life) in 3:5, and *sephrâ* appears also in 20:12. The word *kᵉthābhâ* (book, record) appears in 5:1–9, but in chapter 10 the word *kᵉthābhûnâ* (booklet, pamphlet) consistently appears (vv. 2, 8, 9, 10). The Syriac provides insight into the relevance of the diminutive *booklet.*

7. David E. Aune, *Revelation 1–5,* WBC 52A (Dallas: Word, 1997), p. xcix; Gregory K. Beale (*The Book of Revelation: A Commentary on the Greek Text,* NIGTC [Grand Rapids: Eerdmans, 1998], p. 531) notes "the stubborn fact" that the word *biblaridion* occurs only here and therefore cannot be without significance.

8. Compare Martin Kiddle, *The Revelation of St. John* (reprint, London: Hodder and Stoughton, 1943), p. 167; R. H. Charles, *A Critical and Exegetical Commentary on the Revelation of St. John,* ICC (Edinburgh: Clark, 1920), 1:260; Charles R. Erdman, *The Revelation of John* (Philadelphia: Westminster, 1936), p. 99.

9. G. R. Beasley-Murray, *The Book of Revelation,* NCB (London: Oliphants, 1974), p. 169.

mighty is used for the voice of an angel who had great authority (18:1–2).[10] But what is the meaning of the adjective in this context? We are unable to identify the angel with Jesus Christ, for nowhere in this chapter do we read anything about worshiping or adoring him, which would be true for the Lord. The New Testament in general and the Apocalypse in particular do not call Jesus an angel. The writer of Hebrews teaches that angels are creatures in submission to Jesus. Indeed he says, "For surely it is not angels he helps, but Abraham's descendants" (2:16). Whereas Jesus is divine and human, angels are only spirits. Therefore, it stands to reason that if Jesus had been an angel, he would be expected to aid fellow angels. But this is not the case, for fallen angels cannot be redeemed; they are condemned and chained in the Abyss.[11] Also, this angel swears by the one who lives forever and ever (v. 6), which seems more appropriate for an angel than for Jesus. And last, to identify the angel with archangels (for instance, Michael or Gabriel) is only an assumption.[12]

John describes this angel as mighty because of the physical appearance of his head, face, and legs; this colossal figure stands on sea and land, and with his reverberating voice he reaches everyone in God's creation. In addition, he possesses the enormous power needed to execute God's purpose. There may be similarities between the portrayal of the mighty angel (vv. 1–6) and the description of the bronze statue of Colossus at Rhodes, an island to the southeast of Patmos.[13] This figure, erected about 280 B.C., reached a height of 105 feet (32 meters). But an earthquake more than fifty years later destroyed it, and thus the statue lost its significance. There is no indication that John thought of an icon dedicated to a sun god.

This mighty angel comes directly from the presence of God and the Lord Jesus Christ. He is clothed in a cloud to demonstrate his eminence and majesty. Scripture speaks poetically of clouds as vehicles God uses to progress (Exod. 13:21; Deut. 33:26; Ps. 104:3; Isa. 19:1). So the Son of Man is coming with a cloud (Dan. 7:13 and see Rev. 1:7; 14:14). Around the angel's head is a rainbow as a symbol of God's faithfulness to keep his covenant promises with his people (Gen. 9:12–16). This does not mean that God appears in the form of an angel but that God sent this angel as his messenger to communicate his sovereignty and his trustworthiness.

---

10. In his excursus on angels, M. Robert Mulholland Jr. avers that in numerous places where angels are mentioned in Revelation (7:2; 8:3; 10:1; 18:1; 20:1; 22:6–9) they are identified with Christ. See his *Revelation: Holy Living in an Unholy World* (Grand Rapids: Zondervan, Frances Asbury Press, 1990), pp. 62–64. Likewise Beale (*Revelation*, p. 525) writes that "the angel is the divine Angel of the Lord, as in the OT, who is to be identified with Christ himself."

11. Simon J. Kistemaker, *Exposition of the Epistle to the Hebrews*, NTC (Grand Rapids: Baker, 1984), p. 76.

12. Refer to George Eldon Ladd, *Commentary on the Revelation of John* (Grand Rapids: Eerdmans, 1972), p. 141; Alan F. Johnson, *Revelation*, in *The Expositor's Bible Commentary*, ed. Frank E. Gaebelein (Grand Rapids: Zondervan, 1981), 12:496; Charles, *Revelation*, 1:258; Robert L. Thomas, *Revelation 8–22: An Exegetical Commentary* (Chicago: Moody, 1995), pp. 59–60.

13. David E. Aune, *Revelation 6–16*, WBC 52B (Nashville: Nelson, 1998), pp. 556–57.

The colorful rainbow results from a refraction of the brilliant beams radiating from the angel's face (compare Ezek. 1:28). As Jesus' face "was like the sun shining in its full strength" (1:16), so the reference to the angel's face beaming like the sun means that the angel came from the presence of Jesus. While Jesus' feet were like fine brass refined as in a furnace (1:15), the angel's legs are like pillars of fire. The description is meant to convey the magnitude and magnificence of the angel's appearance. The imagery of the angel's legs as pillars of fire refers indirectly to God's providential care. God protected the Israelites during chilly nights in the desert with the warmth and light from a pillar of fire, and with it he shielded them from the Egyptian army, thus showing his constant nearness and power (Exod. 13:21–22; 14:24).

2. And he held a little scroll, unrolled in his hand. He placed his right foot on the sea and his left on the land, 3. and he cried with a loud voice as a lion roars. And when he cried, the seven peals of thunder raised their voices.

a. "And he held a little scroll, unrolled in his hand." John again relies on the Old Testament for his descriptive material by turning to the prophecy of Ezekiel. The prophet writes that a hand, stretched out to him, held a scroll that was unrolled in front of him (Ezek. 2:9). Of significance is the term *unrolled*, which suggests that the volume is small in size so as to give the reader full view of the written message. John, therefore, qualifies the scroll with the adjective *little* to convey the idea of "a small papyrus roll."[14] The contrast between this scrap of paper and the scroll that was sealed (Rev. 5:1) is clear. The message of the sealed scroll revealed God's plan for the entire world throughout cosmic time from beginning to end. But the scrap of papyrus lying open in the hand of the angel is apparently a gospel message relating the testimony of Jesus. Although the text itself is brief, the context of this chapter and the next shed light on the significance of the little scroll. That is, after John consumes the booklet, he is told to prophesy (v. 11); similarly the two witnesses prophesied until they finished their testimony (11:3, 6, 7).

b. The angel "placed his right foot on the sea and his left on the land." Here is a picture of an angel that is colossal in appearance and controls God's creation on both sea and land. With a written message in hand, he takes possession of sea and land—the sea comes first as being the greater of the two bodies. Note the repetition of the phrase "standing on the sea and on the land" (vv. 5 and 8). I do not think that the placing of the left foot on the land symbolizes something sinister and the right foot on the sea something blissful. Furthermore, there is no need to say that John wrote from his point of view on the island Patmos as he saw the angel's right foot on the Mediterranean Sea and his left foot on Asia Minor.

14. Henry Barclay Swete, *Commentary on Revelation* (1911; reprint, Grand Rapids: Kregel, 1977), p. 126. Isbon T. Beckwith (*The Apocalypse of John* [1919; reprint, Grand Rapids: Baker, 1979], p. 580) comments, "Apparently the word is meant to distinguish this roll from the great scroll of chapt[er] 5." Similarly, Jürgen Roloff, *The Revelation of John*, trans. J. E. Alsup (Minneapolis: Fortress, 1993), p. 123.

The verse communicates the authority of this gigantic angel over both land and sea, for he comes with a message that proclaims salvation to those who obey and judgment to those who reject this message.

c. "And he cried with a loud voice as a lion roars." Once again John relies on Old Testament prophets. The wording "roar as a lion" comes from Hosea 11:10, where the Lord God roars to tell the Israelites who are scattered in various countries to return from exile. And Amos 3:8 reads: "The lion has roared—who will not fear? The Sovereign LORD has spoken—who can but prophesy?" When the Lord roars from Zion, his people are warned of coming judgment should they fail to listen. Likewise, Jeremiah writes this word of prophecy:

> The LORD will roar from on high;
> he will thunder from his holy dwelling
> and roar mightily against this land.
> (Jer. 25:30; see Amos 1:2)

Peter speaks descriptively about Satan going around like a roaring lion (1 Pet. 5:8). But here the picture refers to the voice of a mighty angel who calls out with such volume that his voice is heard throughout God's creation. In brief, the illustration of a roaring lion is a symbol of a sound that reverberates.

d. "And when he cried, the seven peals of thunder raised their voices." John writes poetic parallelism, in both the preceding line and this one. As the lion roars on the earth, so thunder rumbles in the sky. To give it special emphasis, he notes that there were seven peals of thunder. The number seven has no literal meaning but only symbolic significance. Seven stands for completeness, so that the noise of thunder is overwhelming to the people living on earth. Both the roaring of the lion and the peals of thunder induce fear and trepidation in the hearts of earth's inhabitants.

John and his readers were familiar with one of the psalms of David that extols God's glory, majesty, and power. "The voice of the LORD is over the waters; the God of glory thunders, the LORD thunders over the mighty waters. The voice of the LORD is powerful; the voice of the LORD is majestic" (Ps. 29:3–4). John's allusion to Psalm 29 is even more meaningful when we see that in this psalm David mentions the phrase "the voice of the LORD" seven times. Also, in the Apocalypse John repeatedly mentions thunder as "a sign of the divine presence and judgment."[15] But in Psalm 29 and in Revelation the peals of thunder are not simply noise but articulate speech.

---

15. John P. M. Sweet, *Revelation*, WPC (Philadelphia: Westminster, 1979), p. 138. See also Friedrich Düsterdieck, *Critical and Exegetical Handbook to the Revelation of John* (New York and London: Funk and Wagnalls, 1886), p. 300; Leon Morris, *Revelation*, rev. ed., TNTC (Leicester: Inter-Varsity; Grand Rapids: Eerdmans, 1987), p. 135; William Hendriksen, *More Than Conquerors* (reprint, Grand Rapids: Baker, 1982), p. 124 n. 2; Bauckham, *Climax of Prophecy*, p. 259.

4. And when the seven peals of thunder spoke, I was about to write, and I heard a voice from heaven saying, "Seal the things which the seven peals of thunder said, and do not write them."

When Scripture uses the word *thunder*, nearly without exception it brings a message of divine power and judgment. In the Apocalypse thunder repeatedly accompanies divine activity and messages (e.g., 4:5; 6:1; 8:5; 11:19; 16:18). The noise of thunder is a symbol of judgment.

Sevenfold thunderous noise comes to John in the form of spoken words, but we are not told what was said. I assert that John emphasizes the act of speaking and not the message it conveyed. And therefore, I assume that these spoken words differ from the message of the scroll (v. 2). The scroll contains a prophetic message, while the communication of the seven thunders cannot be made known. Even though John wishes to be obedient to the voice of Jesus who first called him to write (1:11, 19), he is now told by a voice from heaven not to do so. This voice speaking to him is perhaps the voice of Jesus Christ, who in the Apocalypse quite often addresses John (see 9:13–14; 10:8; 11:12).

John says that he was about to write. While pen in hand ready to record, he hears a divine voice saying: "Seal the things which the seven peals of thunder said." Words can be sealed when they are written down, but before the author begins to pen the words he is told to seal them. What precisely is the meaning of the command? This verse communicates that the words of the seven-thunder voice must not be revealed. And the reason that this action is even mentioned is to differentiate between the things that are sealed and those that are revealed (see Deut. 29:29). We are not allowed to speculate and surmise what the message of the sevenfold thunder may have been. This remains a mystery that we must leave unexplained.

The verb *to seal* appears again in the last chapter of the Apocalypse, where John is told not to seal the words of the prophecy of this book (22:10). This contrasts with the instruction Daniel received to seal up his vision and the writing on a scroll. That restriction would be lifted at the end time (Dan. 8:26; 12:4, 9). Similarly the message that came to John from the seven thunders will have to wait until cosmic time has come to an end. We realize that visions and words about heaven and the future often cannot be expressed intelligibly to human beings; our capacity for comprehending heavenly portents is severely limited in the sinful state that is ours.

Greek Words, Phrases, and Constructions in 10:1–4

Verse 1

ἡ ἶρις—the word *rainbow* is in the nominative case instead of the accusative as object of the verb "I saw." But John writes an Aramaic coordinate style consisting of clauses that take the place of sentences. The same thing is true for the nominative singular participle ἔχων (having), which should have been in the accusative.

Verse 2

βιβλαρίδιον—"booklet." This word occurs three times in this chapter (vv. 2, 9, 10) and nowhere else. It is a diminutive, which is also true for βιβλίον (v. 8). The manuscripts vary between these two words in all these verses, but the manuscript evidence best supports the readings in the text.

Verse 3

μυκᾶται—"he roars." This verb appears only here in the New Testament. In classical Greek it is used of animal sounds: the bellowing of oxen, the braying of donkeys, and the growling of dogs.

Verse 4

μὴ αὐτὰ γράψης—the aorist subjunctive serves as a prohibition to indicate that the act of writing had not yet begun. So John is told, "Do not begin to write."[16]

---

(2) The Angel's Message
10:5–7

5. And the angel, whom I saw standing on the sea and on the land, raised his right hand to heaven.

The author resumes his identification of the angel. He leaves the impression that the angel who descended from heaven must be distinguished from Jesus. By mentioning again the angel's stance on the sea and on the land, John wishes to stress the power and authority of this particular servant of God.

Raising one's right hand at the taking of an oath is customary today in courts of law and at inaugurations. It indicates appealing to God as the highest power in heaven and on earth; often the appeal is concluded with the phrase, "So help me God."

Scripture provides references to people and God lifting their hands to heaven as they swear an oath. To illustrate, Abraham raised his hand to the Lord God when he took an oath in the presence of the king of Sodom (Gen. 14:22). Daniel saw a man dressed in linen who lifted both hands to heaven and swore by him who lives forever (Dan. 12:7). And God swears by himself and raises his hand to heaven (Exod. 6:8; Deut. 32:40).

6. And he swore by the one who lives forever and ever, who created heaven and the things in it, the earth and the things in it, and the sea and the things in it, and said, "There will no longer be a delay."

There is a link between the preceding verse (v. 5) and this one in the threefold division of the created world. Verse 5 gives the sequence sea, land, and heaven; here the order is reversed: heaven, earth, and sea.

The angel swears by the one who lives forever and ever. When he swears by the living God, he testifies that the spoken words are absolutely sure and reliable.

---

16. A. T. Robertson, *A Grammar of the Greek New Testament in the Light of Historical Research* (Nashville: Broadman, 1934), p. 853.

Further, whereas a law can be changed or repealed, an unconditional oath cannot be altered but remains in effect. As the angel swears by God who lives forever and ever, he calls on his eternity by applying it to the oath. The phrase *forever and ever* occurs more often in Revelation (1:6, 18; 4:9, 10; 15:7) than in any other New Testament book.

Next, the angel swore because God is the creator of the world and watches over everything that heaven, earth, and sea contain. That is, he appeals to God's providential care over all his creatures (Exod. 20:11; Neh. 9:6; Ps. 146:6; Acts 4:24) and relates the entire world with all its fullness to the oath which he swears.

The oath reveals a time limit, for the angel says, "There will no longer be a delay." A literal translation is, "Time will be no more," which means that a period of waiting is past, so that without any further delays God's judgments will begin to take place. Concerning Jezebel Jesus says, "And I gave her time to repent, but she does not want to repent from her fornication" (2:21). When time for repentance is past, delay is ruled out. But how do we understand the concept *delay* when chronological time continues to its inevitable end? Is there a conflict with the plea of the souls at the altar who cry out, "How long, O Sovereign Lord, holy and true, will you not judge and avenge our blood on those that dwell on the earth?" And the Lord tells them to wait a little while longer (6:10–11). The answer lies in the fact that the interlude of chapter 10 occupies a place between the blowing of the sixth trumpet (9:13) and that of the seventh (11:15). This interlude presents a picture within a picture. It shows an occurrence presented not necessarily in chronological sequence but concurring with the events in the era before the Lord's return and even before the angel blows the seventh trumpet. Then the plagues will take place. They will be completed when the seventh angel pouring out his bowl of God's wrath speaks the brief utterance "It is done" (16:17). As a last remark, bear in mind that the words spoken by the mighty angel (v. 1) are said in the context of swearing a solemn oath.

7. "However, in the days when the voice of the seventh angel is about to blow his trumpet, the mystery of God will be accomplished, as he proclaimed to his servants the prophets."

a. "However, in the days when the voice of the seventh angel is about to blow his trumpet." The adversative *however* links this verse to the last line of verse 6, where John notes that there will be no more delay. The division between verses 6 and 7 is infelicitous, for the preceding sentence should be taken together with verse 7.

We would have expected the seventh angel to blow his trumpet to introduce the series of seven plagues. This is not the case here, because John is writing only a preliminary reference to this event and not the event itself, which will take place in 11:15. With this reference he tells the reader to wait until he has completed the writing of his interlude that describes the task of God's people on earth.

In other words, the blowing of the seventh trumpet will not occur immediately during or after John's lifetime. When this trumpet sounds, the days of the end have arrived and are made visible by several visions.[17] The trumpet blast announces the message that the end is at hand and the consummation of this age is near. And when this trumpet is heard, the second woe belongs to the past (11:14). The third woe encompasses the judgment (11:15b–19).

b. "The mystery of God will be accomplished, as he proclaimed to his servants the prophets." What is the meaning of the expression *the mystery of God?* John relies on the Old Testament prophets Daniel and Amos for the setting of this verse. Nebuchadnezzar asked Daniel to interpret a dream he had, to which the prophet replies that no one is able to do so. "But," Daniel said, "there is a God in heaven who reveals mysteries" (2:28). And as God's messenger he interpreted the king's dream in regard to future events. Next, Amos assured the people of Israel that "the Lord GOD does nothing, without revealing his secret to his servants the prophets" (3:7 NRSV). God reveals his mystery to his spokesman John relative to the events that must occur in the last days.

The events take place in the future, at the time when the mystery of God will be accomplished. Interestingly, whereas in translation the future tense of the verb *to accomplish* is used, the Greek text shows the past tense. In Greek the past tense has a futuristic connotation that should be understood not from the author's point of view but from God's eventual fulfillment. When delay has run its course (v. 6), the trumpet of the seventh angel will sound and God will cause his mysterious plan to become reality. When this trumpet sounds, the time has come for God and his Christ to rule the kingdom of the world and to judge the dead (11:15–18). The cry of the souls under the altar asking for judgment will be fulfilled on the Judgment Day (6:10; 20:11–15), and the blowing of the seventh trumpet is a sign of that day. During the time preceding the Judgment Day, however, God's prophets must proclaim his message of salvation to the world. God does not want "anyone to perish, but everyone to come to repentance" (2 Pet. 3:9).

Who are God's prophets? The term *his servants the prophets* appears frequently in the Old Testament.[18] It includes the prophets of both the Old and New Testament eras, of which John is the last one with respect to recording God's Word. John does not distinguish between the prophets of the two eras: all the people commissioned to write the divine Word are prophets, and that includes the apostles and their helpers (Eph. 3:4–5). And John himself has the honor of revealing to the church God's apocalypse concerning the end time.

Last, God proclaimed the good news of his revelation to his servants the prophets. It is the message of God's redemption to those who love him and judgment for those who hate him. God gives this message to his servants, whom he expects to pass it on to all people (vv. 10–11; 11:3, 10).

---

17. James L. Resseguie, *Revelation Unsealed: A Narrative Critical Approach to John's Apocalypse*, BIS 32 (Leiden: Brill, 1998), p. 164.

18. 2 Kings 17:13, 23; 21:10; Ezra 9:11; Jer. 7:25; 25:4; 26:5; 29:19; 35:15; 44:4; Dan. 9:6, 10; Amos 3:7.

Greek Words, Phrases, and Constructions in 10:6–7

Verse 6

ὤμοσεν ἐν—"he swore by." The preposition ἐν used with the verb *to swear* reflects Hebraic syntax (Matt. 5:34, 36; 23:16).[19] In Greek grammar this verb is followed by the accusative case (James 5:12), the preposition κατά (Heb. 6:13, 16), or the preposition εἰς (Matt. 5:34–35).

Verse 7

εὐηγγέλισεν—this is the aorist active of the verb *to bring good news.* In the New Testament the active appears only here and in 14:6; everywhere else it is in the middle voice. The active is prevalent in later Greek and in essence is nearly the equivalent of the much more common middle voice εὐαγγελίζομαι.[20]

(3) The Scroll and Its Purpose
10:8–11

The announcement on imminent judgment is moderated by additional insights into the unfolding of world history. First, the conflict between good and evil leads inevitably to its final end. Next, during the interlude God does not forsake his own but makes his revelation known. And last, revelation must be proclaimed to all people throughout the world.

8. And the voice that I heard speaking with me again from heaven said, "Go, take the scroll that is unrolled in the hand of the angel who stands on the sea and on the land."

The first time the voice from heaven spoke, it told John to seal the things the seven peals of thunder said and not to write them down (v. 4). The voice apparently is the voice of Jesus Christ.

The voice utters a clear command by saying "Go!" This word is followed by a second imperative, "take!" The object John must take is the scroll, which is now qualified by the phrase "that is unrolled in the hand of the angel." Here is the little scroll or booklet that can be read at a glance (v. 2).

The angel is identified as the one who controls sea and land, that is, God's creation and all those who live in it. This mighty angel, therefore, comes with a message from God Almighty. Three times in succession the writer describes the stance of this angel on sea and land (vv. 2, 5, 8).

9. And I went to the angel and asked him to give me the little scroll. And he said to me, "Take it and eat it, and it will turn your stomach sour, but in your mouth it will be as sweet as honey."

Standing on the earth, John approached the angel with the little scroll lying open in his hand and asked him for it. The angel's response to him was, "Take

19. C. F. D. Moule, *An Idiom-Book of New Testament Greek,* 2d ed. (Cambridge: Cambridge University Press, 1960), p. 183.

20. Bauer, p. 317.

it and eat it." The wording is taken from the Book of Ezekiel, where a voice from heaven instructs the prophet to eat an unrolled scroll and to fill his stomach with it. Ezekiel did so and discovered that it was sweet like honey in his mouth (Ezek. 2:8; 3:1–3). The prophet saw the unrolled scroll and noticed that on both sides there were words of lament, mourning, and woe (Ezek. 2:10).

John is told to eat the little scroll that will be sweet as honey in his mouth but bitter in his stomach. He is now personally involved in knowing the booklet. By eating and swallowing it, he realizes its effect in his inward being. This is God's Word that is sweeter than honey in his mouth (Ps. 19:10; 119:103). It is indeed a joy to take the words of God into one's mouth and to sing his praises. But that same Word when it is proclaimed creates inner tension that is bitter. First, it uncovers hidden sins in the closet of one's heart. Next, the world rejects God's Word and demonstrates opposition by attacking its messengers. Third, whatever gift God gives his people is always good. Although his people endure oppressions and persecution because of his Word, God blesses them by drawing them ever closer to himself.

Nonetheless, as the gospel brings life, light, and joy to believers, it causes unbelievers to react with indifference, antipathy, and enmity. Both the prophets in the Old Testament era and the apostles in New Testament times experienced opposition from the people of Israel and the world. They brought the message of redemption which was a stumbling block to the Jews and foolishness to the Gentiles (1 Cor. 1:23). The gospel of Christ turns the members of one's own household against one another (Matt. 10:35–36), and the unbelieving world hates the servants of the Lord (John 15:18–19). In fact, this is what the two witnesses in the Apocalypse encountered when they prophesied to the world in the name of the Lord: they were killed (Rev. 11:3–10).

10. And I took the little scroll out of the hand of the angel and ate it. And it was in my mouth as sweet as honey, and when I had eaten it, my stomach turned sour. 11. And I was told, "You must prophesy again against many peoples and nations and languages and kings."

a. "And I took the little scroll out of the hand of the angel and ate it." The sequence of action of "my stomach turned sour" and "in my mouth as sweet as honey" (v. 9) is now reversed to the normal process of eating and digesting. Some commentators interpret this passage literally by stressing that the natural flow from mouth to stomach suggests a literal eating of the booklet.[21] I prefer to say that John mentally appropriated the message of the little scroll so that he completely mastered it. He tasted its sweetness in his mouth when he proclaimed the message; but noticing the opposition this word created among the people, he had to endure bitterness in his inward being.

Witnessing for the Lord calls for unflinching courage and gracious tact. Anyone who speaks the Word of God in a hostile world will be opposed, scorned, and ridiculed. But that person ought to have fully absorbed the Word so that it has

21. Thomas, *Revelation 8–22*, p. 74; Düsterdieck, *Revelation*, p. 304.

become an inseparable part of his or her being. He or she must appropriate God's message by faith, obey it fully, be totally controlled by it, always remain true to its message, speak judiciously, and not become silent.[22]

b. "And I was told, 'You must prophesy again against many peoples and nations and languages and kings.'" Almost every word in this sentence presents interesting perspectives and even some difficulties. We begin with the introductory formula "And they said to me." We assume that the pronoun *they* points to heavenly voices that speak to John. But he fails to identify them. Therefore, the indefinite subject allows us to translate the formula as a passive, "And I was told." The use of the passive voice hides the identity of the agent.

Next, a moral obligation lies on John's shoulders. When heavenly voices tell him to prophesy, he knows that he must obey God's will. Prophesying does not merely mean to foretell what is going to happen; it also means to propagate all the other visions and divine disclosures John had received. In short, he must proclaim God's full revelation. The adverb *again* signifies that John earlier had received some information that he had to make known. And now, possessing the message of the little scroll, he is told to make its message known to the world.

Third, one Greek word is open to various translations; it is the preposition *epi* which in this verse can mean "before" (KJV), "against" (NJB), "concerning" (NASB), "over" (REB), and "about" (NIV, NRSV).

Most translators have interpreted the Greek preposition as "about." Thus, John is told to prophesy "about many peoples and nations and languages and kings." Although this translation is good, the question must be asked concerning the recipients of this message. Are these four groups receptive to the gospel (5:9; 7:9) or are they hostile? John appears to use the phrase for unbelievers who are to be judged because of their identification with Babylon and the beast (11:9; 13:7–8; 14:6; 17:15). Therefore, the translation *against* is preferred and can be supported by Jeremiah 25:30 (32:30 LXX), "Now prophesy all these words against them."[23]

John categorizes humanity in four ways: peoples, nations, languages, and kings; the number four symbolizes the world. He writes a fourfold grouping of people seven times in the Apocalypse: five have the same categories although in different sequence (5:9; 7:9; 11:9; 13:7; 14:6) and two with variations (10:11, "kings" in place of "tribes"; 17:15, "crowds" instead of "tribes"). Regarding these seven occurrences, remember that the number seven signifies completeness. John alludes to the Book of Daniel, where a threefold phrase (peoples, nations, languages) occurs six times.[24] The Old Greek translation of Daniel, however, adds the word *regions* to the phrase in Daniel 3:4 and thus provides a list of four categories (see also Gen. 10:20, 31).[25]

---

22. Compare Hoeksema, *Behold, He Cometh!* p. 357.

23. Aune, *Revelation 6–16,* pp. 573–74; Beale, *Revelation,* p. 554. Mounce (*Revelation,* p. 210 n. 52) takes *epi* "in the sense of 'to' or 'about' rather than 'against.'"

24. Dan. 3:4, 7; 4:1 (Theod. only; = 3:31 MT); 5:19; 6:25; 7:14.

25. Refer to Bauckham, *Climax of Prophecy,* pp. 326–28.

God wants all humanity to hear and respond to his message. He is concerned about all people, for all of them individually are his image bearers (Gen. 1:27). The Lord God has no desire that anyone should die a spiritual death: "I take no pleasure in the death of anyone, declares the Sovereign LORD. Repent and live!"(Ezek. 18:32). He wants all people everywhere "to be saved and to come to a knowledge of the truth" (1 Tim. 2:4).

Greek Words, Phrases, and Constructions in 10:8–11

Verse 8

λέγουσαν—grammatically this participle should be in the nominative, but is in the accusative case by attraction to the present participle λαλοῦσαν. It may also be that the last letter of λέγουσαν is the movable ν to separate it from the present imperative ὕπαγε (go!).

τὸ βιβλίον—the manuscript support for this word in chapter 10 is divided. Manuscripts A, C, and 1006 have this reading in verse 8, and manuscripts 𝔓[47], ℵ, and 1006 have it in verse 9. The TR and the Majority Text have the diminutive βιβλιδάριον in both verses. The two words in this verse are identical in meaning because of the qualifying phrase "unrolled in the hand of the angel," which indicates it is the booklet mentioned in verse 2.[26]

Verse 10

The reading βιβλαρίδιον (v. 10) instead of βιβλίον is decided "on the weight of external evidence."[27]

Verse 11

λέγουσιν—the variant reading is the present singular λέγει, which obviously is a textual corrective. The more difficult reading is the original.

ἐπί—with the genitive the preposition means "before"; with the accusative, "against"; and with the dative, "in regard to."[28]

---

26. J. Ramsey Michaels (*Interpreting the Book of Revelation* [Grand Rapids: Baker, 1992], p. 61) links 10:8 to 5:1. He interprets 10:8 by saying, "Go take *the* scroll [with the definite article recalling the scroll described in chapter 5]. . . ." But this exegesis can hardly be correct in view of verse 2, which has the noun *scroll* without the definite article; this occurrence of the word serves as the more immediate, and hence more likely, antecedent for the article that appears in v. 8.

27. Bruce M. Metzger, *A Textual Commentary on the Greek New Testament*, 2d ed. (Stuttgart: Deutsche Bibelgesellschaft, 1994), p. 671.

28. S. Greijdanus, *De Openbaring des Heeren aan Johannes*, KNT (Amsterdam: Van Bottenburg, 1925), p. 224. In the Old Testament the phrase *to prophesy against* is common in the major prophets (Jer. 25:13; Ezek. 4:7; 11:4; 25:2).

11

Two Witnesses and the Seventh Trumpet

(11:1–19)

Outline (continued)

- b. Two Witnesses (11:1–14)
  - (1) The Temple (11:1–2)
  - (2) The Power of Two Witnesses (11:3–6)
  - (3) The Death of Two Witnesses (11:7–10)
  - (4) The Resurrection of Two Witnesses (11:11–14)

9. The Seventh Trumpet (11:15–19)
   - a. Two Hymns (11:15–18)
   - b. God's Covenant (11:19)

11 1 And I was given a reed like a rod and was told, "Arise and measure the temple of God
and the altar and those who worship there. 2 But exclude the outer court of the temple
and do not measure it, because it has been given to the Gentiles, and they will trample the
holy city for forty-two months.

3 "And I will give [power] to my two witnesses and they will prophesy for 1,260 days and be
clothed in sackcloth." 4 These are the two olive trees and the two lampstands that are standing before
the Lord of the earth. 5 And if anyone wants to harm them, fire comes forth out of their mouth and
devours their enemies. And if anyone should wish to harm them, he must be killed in this manner.
6 These have power to shut up the sky so that it will not rain during the days of their prophecy, and
they have power over the waters to turn them into blood and to strike the earth with every kind of
plague as often as they wish.

7 And when they finish their testimony, the beast that comes up out of the Abyss will make war against
them and will overcome and kill them. 8 And their bodies will lie in the street of the great city that spiritually is called Sodom and Egypt, where also their Lord was crucified. 9 And the [citizens] from the peoples and tribes and languages and nations look at their bodies for three and a half days, and they do not
permit their bodies to be placed in a tomb. 10 And the inhabitants on the earth gloat over them and celebrate and exchange gifts, because the two prophets tormented those who dwell on the earth.

11 And after three and a half days the breath of life from God entered them and they stood on their
feet, and great fear fell on those who saw them. 12 And they heard a loud voice from heaven saying to
them, "Come up here." And they came up to heaven in a cloud, and their enemies saw them. 13 And
in that hour, there was a great earthquake and a tenth of the city fell and seven thousand people were
killed in the earthquake, and the rest were terrified and gave glory to the God of heaven.

14 The second woe is past. Look, the third woe is coming soon.

---

b. Two Witnesses
11:1–14

The second part of the interlude could have been covered in chapter 10 much the same as chapter 7 has a two-part interlude. This second part is a continuation of the first segment with respect to the message of the scroll that is sweet to the taste but bitter to digest. In this part, the two witnesses proclaim their testimony but experience opposition, warfare, and death. However, their death does not spell defeat, for they will be raised from the dead and ascend to heaven.

Before John writes about the two witnesses, he relates his assignment to measure the temple of God but not the outer court.[1] He mentions the location as the

---

1. R. H. Charles (*A Critical and Exegetical Commentary on the Revelation of St. John*, ICC [Edinburgh: Clark, 1920], 1:270–73), adopting the views of Wellhausen, asserts that 11:1–2 and 11:3–13 are two loose fragments that have no connection with the preceding and following context; they point to a different authorship. This is nothing but a guess. The fact of the matter is that the one passage depends on the other and thus supports the unity of the text.

holy city and the duration as 42 months or 1,260 days. Much has been written about the place and the time that John mentions:

a. The first view is a literal interpretation of the temple in Jerusalem before its destruction in A.D. 70.[2] But the name *Jerusalem* does not appear in this chapter; instead we read the words "the holy city." A survey of this expression in Revelation conveys not a literal but a symbolic meaning. We notice that in the Apocalypse the expression *the holy city* is used figuratively to identify the new Jerusalem and the believer's eternal abode (21:2, 10; 22:19). Similarly, the term *the great city* is figurative language for Sodom and Egypt to indicate moral corruption and slavery (v. 8). Also, John writes this term to identify Babylon as a city of immorality (14:8; 16:19; 17:18; 18:2, 10, 16, 19, 21). If the writer explains these expressions figuratively all through Revelation, we do well not to take them literally.

b. A second view sees a literal temple that will become reality just before and during the time of Christ's return.[3] But nowhere in the entire New Testament do we read that a physical temple will be renewed in the city of Jerusalem. Jesus predicted the destruction of the temple, but he never spoke about rebuilding it (Matt. 24:2). The tearing of the curtain in front of the Holy of Holies was God's sign that the era of the temple and its services had ended (Matt. 27:51). Paul uses the word *temple* to describe God's spiritual dwelling, namely, the church (1 Cor. 3:16; 2 Cor. 6:16; Eph. 2:20–22). The writer of the Epistle to the Hebrews explicitly states that believers "have come to Mount Zion, to the heavenly Jerusalem, the city of the living God [namely] . . . to the church of the firstborn, whose names are written in heaven" (12:22–23). Notice that he writes about the church, not the temple. The death and resurrection of Jesus brought to an end the Old Testament era. By bringing the ultimate sacrifice, Jesus had fulfilled God's demand for atonement. Hence, the temple no longer needed to function as a place of sacrificing animals to atone for sins. The temple in Revelation serves a symbolic purpose (e.g., 3:12; 7:15; 21:22). But the new Jerusalem has no temple, "For the Lord God Almighty and the Lamb are its temple" (21:22). I conclude that from the New Testament no evidence can be adduced to support the restoration of a physical temple in Jerusalem.[4]

c. A third approach is a prophetic interpretation with a message of hope and salvation for the Jewish Christian community in John's day.[5] The question is

2. Theodor Zahn, *Die Offenbarung des Johannes,* Kommentar zum Neuen Testament 18 (Leipzig: Deichert, 1924–26), 2:419–20; Ernst Lohmeyer, *Die Offenbarung des Johannes,* HNT 16 (Tübingen: Mohr, 1970), p. 87. Kenneth L. Gentry Jr., *Before Jerusalem Fell: Dating the Book of Revelation* (Tyler, Tex.: Institute for Christian Economics, 1989), p. 192; David Chilton, *The Days of Vengeance: An Exposition of the Book of Revelation* (Fort Worth, Tex.: Dominion, 1987), p. 4.

3. Robert L. Thomas, *Revelation 8–22: An Exegetical Commentary* (Chicago: Moody, 1995), p. 82; John F. Walvoord, *The Revelation of Jesus Christ* (Chicago: Moody, 1966), p. 176.

4. Herman Hoeksema, *Behold, He Cometh! An Exposition of the Book of Revelation* (Grand Rapids: Reformed Free Publishing Association, 1969), pp. 364–65; Gregory K. Beale, *The Book of Revelation: A Commentary on the Greek Text,* NIGTC (Grand Rapids: Eerdmans, 1998), p. 568.

5. George Eldon Ladd, *Commentary on the Revelation of John* (Grand Rapids: Eerdmans, 1972), p. 150; Isbon T. Beckwith, *The Apocalypse of John* (1919; reprint, Grand Rapids: Baker, 1979), pp. 588–90.

whether this chapter mentions anything at all about a literal Israel, that is, a Jewish remnant that must be saved. That question receives a negative answer, because in writing the Apocalypse John is addressing the church universal.

d. A last view is a figurative explanation that sees the temple of God as the church at worship. This exegesis fits the context of the Apocalypse that repeatedly and consistently presents numerous pictures through symbolism. Indeed the context of verses 1 through 13 is symbolical: the temple and the holy city, the time component of 1,260 days, the two witnesses, and the earthquake that destroyed a tenth of the city and killed seven thousand people. Robert H. Mounce judiciously comments, "Symbolism is not a denial of historicity but a figurative method of communicating reality. Apocalyptic language has as one of its basic characteristics the cryptic and symbolic use of words and phrases."[6]

If the late date of the Apocalypse near the end of the first century is correct, then in exile on the island of Patmos John would hardly be referring to the temple in Jerusalem already lying in ruins for more than two decades. The imagery of the temple presented in terms of the sanctuary, the altar, worshipers, and the outer court lends itself to symbolism instead of literalism. Because the second half of the interlude is phrased in symbolic terms, it would be contrary to expectations to understand the first two verses literally. An interpretation that focuses attention on a symbolic sanctuary and altar has merit. This is especially true for two reasons: the time in which John wrote Revelation when the destruction of the temple was a distant memory, and the worshipers within God's temple.[7] The era of the old covenant came to an end and the time of the new covenant arrived. Not the temple but the church is the place where God dwells. Even though at the conclusion of his third missionary journey Paul went to the temple in Jerusalem to appease his opponents (Acts 21:23–29), he taught the church in Corinth that they themselves were God's sacred temple; he called their body the temple of the Holy Spirit (1 Cor. 3:17; 6:19). God dwells in the hearts of believers, so that their bodies are sacred temples.

Nonetheless, for this imagery John uses the familiar structure of the temple in Jerusalem: the sanctuary, the altar, the worshipers, and the outer court. The temple destroyed by Roman forces could still serve him as a teaching model.

---

6. Robert H. Mounce, *The Book of Revelation*, rev. ed., NICNT (Grand Rapids: Eerdmans, 1998), p. 212. Most scholars espouse a figurative interpretation: among others, Leon Morris, *Revelation*, rev. ed., TNTC (Leicester: Inter-Varsity; Grand Rapids: Eerdmans, 1987), pp. 140–41; Henry Barclay Swete, *Commentary on Revelation* (1911; reprint, Grand Rapids: Kregel, 1977), pp. 132–33; R. C. H. Lenski, *The Interpretation of St. John's Revelation* (Columbus: Wartburg, 1943), pp. 328–32; G. B. Caird, *A Commentary on the Revelation of St. John the Divine* (London: Black, 1966), p. 132; Richard Bauckham, *The Climax of Prophecy* (Edinburgh: Clark, 1993), p. 272; David E. Aune, *Revelation 6–16*, WBC 52B (Nashville: Nelson, 1998), p. 598.

7. Compare Michael Bachmann, "Himmlisch: Der 'Tempel Gottes' von Apk 11.1," *NTS* 40 (1994): 474–80.

(1) The Temple
11:1–2

1. And I was given a reed like a rod and was told, "Arise and measure the temple of God and the altar and those who worship there."

a. *Reed.* John received a measuring rod and a command to measure the temple of God. We are not told who gave him the reed and the command, but we assume that an angel as a heavenly messenger supplied it and gave him instruction concerning its use. An Old Testament reference lies back of this text, for God gave the prophets Ezekiel and Zechariah a vision of the new temple area. There was a man with a measuring rod that was about 10½ feet (3.2 meters) long, who surveyed the temple buildings and grounds (Ezek. 40–43; see also Zech. 2:1–2). In the New Testament an angel measures the new Jerusalem (city, gates, and walls) with a rod of gold (Rev. 21:15).[8]

b. *Command.* The writer is told to get up and measure three parts: the temple of God, the altar, and the people worshiping there. He fails to identify the speaker. The purpose of making these measurements is to delimit the area that is holy from that which is profane; measuring means to protect God's temple, altar, and people. John's task is to safeguard that which God has set aside as holy and to shield it from intrusion and desecration. The destroyer cannot enter the place that God has marked off as holy and within whose boundaries his people are secure.

The place where the people are safe is God's temple, which throughout the Apocalypse means not the temple complex but the temple building, which includes the Holy of Holies and the Holy Place. God opened to full view the inner sanctuary when at the time of Jesus' death the curtain separating these two places was torn from top to bottom (Matt. 27:51). This area is the very presence of God, where he welcomes and dwells with the saints after Jesus offered himself as the perfect sacrifice and removed the sins of his people (Heb. 9:12). The temple of God, therefore, is a symbol of the true church that worships the triune God.[9] In the church God meets his people, accepts their praise and adoration, listens to their petitions and confessions, and acknowledges their expressions of gratitude. As the saints in heaven are always in God's presence, so the saints on earth have the divine promise: "for where two or three are gathered together in my name, there am I in the midst of them" (Matt. 18:20 KJV).

John presents a picture of the inner sanctuary he must measure. No measurements are listed because the assignment of measuring an area where the saints

---

8. Kenneth A. Strand ("An Overlooked Old Testament Background to Revelation 11:1," *AUSS* 22 [1984]: 317–25) argues that the more likely background passage is not Zechariah 2:1–5 and Ezekiel 40–48 but Leviticus 16. This chapter outlines the Day of Atonement but says nothing about the command "measure the temple." See also Frederick D. Mazzaferri, *The Genre of the Book of Revelation from a Source-Critical Perspective,* BZNW 54 (Berlin and New York: de Gruyter, 1989), pp. 319–21.

9. William Hendriksen, *More Than Conquerors* (reprint, Grand Rapids: Baker, 1982), p. 127; Caird, *Revelation,* p. 132; Lenski, *Revelation,* pp. 326–30; Gerhard A. Krodel, *Revelation,* ACNT (Minneapolis: Augsburg, 1989), pp. 219–21.

meet their God proves to be an impossible task. The saints are a great multitude that no one can number (7:9). Measuring the temple of God symbolizes the knowledge and care God provides for his people.

What is the significance of the altar? It can be either the altar of sacrifice or the incense altar in front of the curtain. The altar of burnt offerings stood outside the temple building in the outer court. Because John is told not to measure the outer court (v. 2), which was the court of the priests, I interpret the altar to be the one on which incense was offered. This is the altar in the heavenly sanctuary (6:9; 8:3 [twice], 5; 9:13; 14:18; 16:7). By contrast, there are no references to the altar of burnt offerings, for the death of Jesus terminated its usefulness. The incense offered is the prayers of the saints (8:3, 5), and measuring the altar's dimensions signifies that the saints have access to God and enjoy his protective care.[10] At the altar they are safe.

The multitude of saints, counted in chapter 7 and measured in chapter 11, are worshiping in Christ's church anywhere and everywhere. Jesus told the Samaritan woman at the well of Jacob that the time had come that true worshipers would neither worship on Mount Gerizim nor in Jerusalem, but everyone would worship the Father in spirit and truth (John 4:21–24). Christians worship anywhere, and wherever they are God shields them from spiritual harm. Although from time to time they endure physical suffering, they will never experience spiritual death. They are safe and secure in the hollow of God's hand. "The 'measuring' of the temple is a variant of the 'sealing' of the Church in 7:1–8."[11] Only God's people are measured or counted, not the profane, who are in the outer court outside the church and are doomed.

2. "But exclude the outer court of the temple and do not measure it, because it has been given to the Gentiles, and they will trample the holy city for forty-two months."

At first sight, this appears to be a puzzling passage, for a literal translation reveals an apparent redundancy: "And the court of the temple, the one outside, cast it outside." But not really so. God makes a clear division between the saints who worship him in spirit and truth and those people who pay him lip service but whose hearts are far from him (Isa. 29:13; Matt. 15:8–9). The first group of people worships in holiness and receives his blessing; the second must be cast out because of their hypocrisy. The first group is in the presence of God and is alive; the second is outside God's sphere and is dead. Here is the contrast between holy and profane that John describes all through the Apocalypse. The saints are those who have God's seal on their foreheads (9:4); they are measured, that is, protected. The profane are the people who refuse to repent of their evil

10. James L Resseguie, *Revelation Unsealed: A Narrative Critical Approach to John's Apocalypse*, BIS 32 (Leiden: Brill, 1998), p. 94. A number of commentators interpret the altar as the altar of burnt offerings (Aune, 52B, p. 606; Swete, p. 132; Beckwith, p. 590; Zahn, 2:424). Beale (p. 563) avers that believers sacrifice themselves "on the altar of the gospel."

11. Wilfrid J. Harrington, *Revelation*, SP 16 (Collegeville, Minn.: Liturgical Press, 1993), p. 119.

deeds (9:20–21); they are not to be measured, that is, they are rejected.[12] Jesus notes that God's people enter the gates of the holy city (22:14), but outside are those who are unclean (22:15).

The temple of Solomon had an inner court for the priests and an outer court (1 Kings 6:36; 7:12; 2 Chron. 4:9; Ezek. 10:5; 40:17–47). When Herod the Great built the temple, the outer court was divided into three parts: the court of the women, of the Israelites, and of the priests. Beyond the three-part court was the court of the Gentiles. But in Revelation John speaks symbolically of the outer court of the temple and thus refers to those people who are within the outer perimeter of the church but not part of it (1 John 2:19). These people are part of the world; they have joined arms with the Gentiles bent on destroying the church, if possible. They are those who in John's day were members of Satan's synagogue and were indistinguishable from the Gentiles (Rev. 2:9; 3:9). All of them are driven by the spirit of the Antichrist set on trampling and desecrating everything that is holy.

The last part of this verse raises questions concerning place and time. How do we interpret "the Gentiles . . . will trample the holy city for forty-two months"? Is John alluding to the holy city, namely, Jerusalem, destroyed by the Gentiles in the second half of the first century? Should the period of forty-two months be taken literally?

First, let us study the expression *holy city* in scriptural context. The Old Testament calls Jerusalem the holy city because it was the place God had chosen to dwell with his people (Ps. 48). The Jews in Jerusalem called themselves "citizens of the holy city" (Isa. 48:2) even though they refused to live in truth and righteousness. Daniel spoke prophetically about the holy city (Dan. 9:24), and Nehemiah noted the restoration of Jerusalem when the Jews resettled in the holy city (Neh. 11:1, 18). In the New Testament, however, the appellation occurs at the beginning of Jesus' ministry when the devil tempting him takes him to the holy city (Matt. 4:5). When Jesus died on Calvary's cross, some graves were opened and those who were raised appeared in the holy city (Matt. 27:53). These references are to the beginning and the end of Jesus' earthly ministry. After that period, the term *holy city* no longer occurs. For God took up residence not in Jerusalem but in the church; at Pentecost the Holy Spirit filled not the temple or Jerusalem but the apostles and all those who repented and were baptized (Acts 2:1–4, 38–39). This exegesis is confirmed in Revelation where John describes the new Jerusalem as the holy city (21:2, 10; 22:19).[13] He explains that this is "the camp of the saints and the beloved city" (20:9), which Jesus calls "the city of my God" (3:12). The holy city is the spiritual Jerusalem of the saints.

12. Consult A. Feuillet, "Essai d'interprétation du chapître XI de l'Apocalypse," *NTS* 4 (1957–58): 186–87. And see Adela Yarbro Collins, *Crisis and Catharsis: The Power of the Apocalypse* (Philadelphia: Westminster, 1984), p. 66.

13. Refer to Hendrik R. van de Kamp, *Israël in Openbaring* (Kampen: Kok, 1990), pp. 174–75; Homer Hailey, *Revelation: An Introduction and Commentary* (Grand Rapids: Baker, 1979), p. 252; Martin Kiddle, *The Revelation of St. John* (reprint, London: Hodder and Stoughton, 1943), p. 184.

In short, the New Testament shows that earthly Jerusalem lost its claim to be called the holy city when the Holy Spirit changed his dwelling place from Jerusalem to the hearts of God's people, the saints. They are persons of every nation, tongue, tribe, and people; together they are residents of the holy city, the new Jerusalem. The Christian church is symbolically called the holy city, for in that place God dwells with his covenant people (21:3).

Next, Jesus predicted the destruction of Jerusalem forty years before it happened. He said, "Jerusalem will be trampled on by the Gentiles until the times of the Gentiles are fulfilled" (Luke 21:24; compare Isa. 5:5; 63:18; and Dan. 8:13).[14] Jesus defines the length of time as "the times of the Gentiles," while John writes "forty-two months." The Apocalypse makes this period equal to 1,260 days or "time, times, and a half time," which is three and a half years (11:3; 12:6, 14). The three and a half years comprise the period of the Maccabean war when the temple was desecrated from June 167 to December 164 B.C. (compare Dan. 7:25; 12:7). Swete offers the following equation: "the duration of the triumph of the Gentiles = the duration of the prophesying of the Two Witnesses = the duration of the Woman's sojourn in the wilderness."[15] In short, these periods showing harmony in duration and extent appear to refer to an interval of undetermined length that extends from Jesus' ascension to his return.[16]

Last, some interpreters apply the period of forty-two months to the years immediately preceding the destruction of the temple in Jerusalem. But the length of time does not fit the record. The Jewish revolt against Rome began in the late spring of 66 and ended with the destruction of Jerusalem in August-September 70. Also, the trampling of the holy city by the Gentiles began after Jerusalem fell into the hands of the Romans. Placing the forty-two months after September 70 is pointless, for then there is a beginning without an end.

Accordingly, John takes this prophecy of Jesus and applies it not to the earthly Jerusalem but to the church, which is the image of the new Jerusalem. The Gentiles are not non-Jews but rather non-Christians who trample all that is holy and make it profane. The trampling of the holy city refers to a period of persecution that Christians suffer throughout the ages. But remember that God sets the limit for its duration. Indeed, this period spans the time from the ascension to the return of Jesus. I conclude that in Revelation time is an idea presented in summary form that should not be expressed in literal terms of years or even centuries. Chronological time is of fleeting importance in this book, because not time but principle governs the Apocalypse.

---

14. Louis A. Vos, *The Synoptic Traditions in the Apocalypse* (Kampen: Kok, 1965), pp. 120–25.

15. Swete, *Revelation*, p. 134.

16. Beale, *Revelation*, p. 567; Mathias Rissi, *Time and History: A Study on the Revelation*, trans. Gordon C. Winsor (Richmond: John Knox, 1966), p. 40.

Greek Words, Phrases, and Constructions in 11:1–2

Verse 1

λέγων—the present participle stands by itself although the speaker is the one who gives John the measuring rod. The attempt to add a phrase and thus provide a subject for the participle is evident in a number of manuscripts supporting the TR, "And the angel stood." The more difficult reading, however, is to be preferred.[17]

τὸν ναόν—throughout the Apocalypse, not ἱερόν (temple complex) but ναός is the word for temple, and indicates the presence of God.

Verse 2

τὴν ἔξωθεν—the repetition of this adverb "outside" signifies emphasis; it is the finality of God rejecting that which is profane.

(2) The Power of Two Witnesses
11:3–6

3. "And I will give [power] to my two witnesses and they will prophesy for 1,260 days and be clothed in sackcloth." 4. These are the two olive trees and the two lampstands that are standing before the Lord of the earth.

From the preceding paragraph (vv. 1 and 2), we learn that God's people are spiritually safe and divinely protected. Now we read that they as the church are given a task here on earth: they are to be witnesses for God, who is arming them with his power to fulfill this task. Incidentally, the word *power* or something similar needs to be supplied from the context because it is lacking in the original Greek.

Who are the two witnesses? Scholars have suggested names taken from both the Old and the New Testaments. Tertullian and Irenaeus mentioned Enoch and Elijah because these two did not see death (Gen. 5:24; 2 Kings 2:11). But would these two glorified saints who did not die return at the same time and would they oppose the beast that comes up out of the Abyss and suffer martyrdom (v. 7)?[18] Others say that the witnesses are Moses and Elijah. These two appeared with Jesus on the Mount of Transfiguration (Matt. 17:3). Moses represented the Law and Elijah the Prophets. Scripture stated that God would raise up a prophet like Moses (Deut. 18:15, 18) and Elijah would reappear (Mal. 4:5).[19] Still others propose the names of Jeremiah and Elijah, Joshua and Caleb,

17. Consult Bruce M. Metzger, *A Textual Commentary on the Greek New Testament*, 2d ed. (Stuttgart: Deutsche Bibelgesellschaft, 1994), p. 671.

18. See Bauckham, *Climax of Prophecy*, p. 276. He writes, "There is no good evidence of traditions from before the time of Revelation in which returning prophets were expected to suffer martyrdom."

19. William Barclay, *The Revelation of John*, 2d ed. (Philadelphia: Westminster, 1960), 2:86–87; Thomas, *Revelation 8–22*, p. 89; Caird, *Revelation*, pp. 134–36.

Peter and Paul, John the Baptist and Jesus of Nazareth, John and his brother James, Stephen and James of Zebedee, to mention no more.[20]

However, I suggest a symbolic interpretation, namely, that the two witnesses represent the church of Christ that by proclaiming the gospel calls the world to repentance. First, the witnesses must address all the inhabitants of the world: peoples, tribes, languages, and nations (v. 9), which can hardly be done by only two witnesses. Second, the pairing of the witnesses is reminiscent of Jesus' sending out his disciples two by two (Mark 6:7; Luke 10:1). The apostles also go out two by two (Acts 3:1; 8:14). Third, in Israel a verdict was confirmed on the testimony of two or three witnesses (Deut. 17:6; 19:15), and the church exerts discipline on that same basis (Matt. 18:16). Indeed, the witness of one man can be disregarded, but on the testimony of two men truth is validated (John 8:17).

Last, John relies on an Old Testament prophecy, for he describes the two witnesses as two olive trees and two lampstands (v. 4). The prophet Zechariah mentions two olive trees and a solid gold lampstand (Zech. 4:2–3); olive oil placed in the lampstand functions to spread the light and dispel the darkness. And symbolically, a lampstand is the church (1:20) made up of believers who live by the word of God and the testimony of Jesus. Thus, Zechariah identifies the two olive trees as anointed servants who serve the Lord of all the earth (Zech. 4:3, 11, 14). They seem to be Joshua the high priest and Zerubbabel the governor (Zech. 4:14), who represented the Jewish community of returnees. Similarly, I interpret the two witnesses in the Apocalypse to be representative of the entire church.[21]

John notes that the two witnesses are *clothed in sackcloth.* Although the sackcloth made of goat or camel hair was a garment worn by both men and women in distress (2 Kings 19:2; Judith 9:1), its use often assumed symbolic significance. This was true especially when prophets wore sackcloth to point out a disrupting sin in society, to call the people to repentance, or to warn them of imminent judgment and punishment.[22] Men like Elijah in the Old Testament era and John the Baptist in New Testament times recalled society to its God-given moorings. Symbolically dressed in sackcloth as a sign of repentance, the church has been called to prophesy the Word of God, the content of the little scroll, to the world. It is the duty of the church to call people everywhere to repentance and faith in Christ (10:11).

The voice from heaven tells John that the two witnesses receive power to prophesy 1,260 days. This number divided by thirty equals forty-two months, which is the same period as that during which the Gentiles profane the outer court (v. 2). It is the period from the Great Commission to the consumma-

20. Refer to Van de Kamp, *Israël in Openbaring*, pp. 183–86; Josephine Massyngberde Ford, *Revelation: Introduction, Translation, and Commentary*, AB 38 (Garden City, N.Y.: Doubleday, 1975), pp. 177–78.

21. See G. R. Beasley-Murray, *The Book of Revelation*, NCB (London: Oliphants, 1974), p. 184; Alan F. Johnson, *Revelation*, in *The Expositor's Bible Commentary*, ed. Frank E. Gaebelein (Grand Rapids: Zondervan, 1981), 12:504; Aune, *Revelation 6–16*, pp. 602–3; Beale, *Revelation*, pp. 574–75.

22. See Larry G. Herr, "Sackcloth," *ISBE*, 4:256; Gustav Stählin, *TDNT*, 7:63.

tion, from the birth of the New Testament church to the end of the age (Matt. 28:19–20).

5. And if anyone wants to harm them, fire comes forth out of their mouth and devours their enemies. And if anyone should wish to harm them, he must be killed in this manner.

First, note the parallelism in the two clauses that begin these sentences, "If anyone wants to harm them." The symmetry is designed to stress the weight of John's words. Those who go forth witnessing for the Lord receive his power that is able to protect them. "For the word of God is living and active," writes the author of the Epistle to the Hebrews (4:12).

Next, as elsewhere in the Apocalypse, John bases his message on the Old Testament, where he reads about Elijah, who called down fire from heaven successively on two companies of fifty soldiers and their captains to destroy them (2 Kings 1:10, 12). David says in the Psalter that as he meditated, fire burned when he spoke (Ps. 39:3; compare 18:8; 97:3), and God told Jeremiah that his words would be a fire in the prophet's mouth (Jer. 5:14; 23:29).

Third, John's words cannot be taken literally, because no Christian witness can call down fire from heaven to destroy God's adversaries. Like the rest of this chapter, the text has a figurative meaning: God's Word cannot be stopped even though God's messengers may be persecuted and even killed. When someone tries to harm these messengers, this does not mean physical harm but rather spiritual harm by silencing their prophetic voice. It signifies the intent to lead the messengers astray so that they deny their Master who sent them and whose Word they must proclaim. That is how messengers can be harmed. But God's Word rises in judgment against his enemies and destroys them by casting them into the lake of fire (20:15).

Last, the enemies of God, his Word, and his people ought not to underestimate the power given to God's witnesses whose prayers he answers. When these enemies hear the Word of God and repudiate it and its messengers, they stand condemned before the Judge of heaven and earth. The witness of the saints on earth against their adversaries is recorded in heaven as a testimony from which they are unable to escape.

6. These have power to shut up the sky so that it will not rain during the days of their prophecy, and they have power over the waters to turn them into blood and to strike the earth with every kind of plague as often as they wish.

The allusion to Elijah is undeniable, for he prayed that it might not rain, and the drought lasted three and a half years (Luke 4:25; James 5:17; 1 Kings 17:1). The phrase *the days of their prophecy* is an implicit reference to that period of time. Jewish sources provide the interpretation of this phrase, circulating in the first century of our era, as an idiom that signified an indefinite length of time.[23]

23. Refer to SB, 3:760–61; and see Simon J. Kistemaker, *Exposition of the Epistle of James*, NTC (Grand Rapids: Baker, 1986), p. 181.

James compares Elijah to any believer who prays in faith: "The prayer of a righteous man is powerful and effective" (James 5:16). A believer who prays in full confidence that God hears and answers prayer can indeed move mountains, figuratively speaking (Matt. 17:20; 21:21; 1 Cor. 13:2). Believers pray the Lord's Prayer and petition God that his kingdom may come, and in answer to that petition God restricts the power of the evil one and raises up men and women to speak for him in every area and sector of society.

Next, John alludes to Moses and Aaron, who changed the water of Egypt into blood (Exod. 7:17, 19–20). The plague left nothing untouched, for blood was everywhere throughout the land. This was the first of ten plagues God sent the Egyptians and which were well known in later years, even by the Philistines in the days of Samuel. The Philistines who captured the ark of the covenant were afraid and recalled that the Egyptians were struck with all kinds of plagues (1 Sam. 4:8).

This does not mean that Christians control the weather, water supply, and devastation caused by natural causes. God controls all these forces, but his people possess the power of prayer as they petition the Almighty to intervene in respect to climate, life-sustaining necessities, and environmental disasters. The saints under the altar asked, "How long, O Sovereign Lord, holy and true, will you not judge and avenge our blood on those that dwell on the earth?" (Rev. 6:10). So the church on earth petitions God to judge and avenge them, for God has said, "It is mine to avenge; I will repay" (Deut. 32:35; Heb. 10:30). In no way should Christians take revenge, for they must leave room for God's wrath (Rom. 12:19).

Greek Words, Phrases, and Constructions in 11:5–6

Verse 5

καὶ εἴ τις θελήσῃ—the translation should be "and if anyone may wish," not "even if. . . ." Although the Majority Text adopts the present tense reading θέλει in harmony with the preceding sentence, the harder reading is the aorist subjunctive. Charles thinks that the second sentence in verse 5 "seems to be the weak gloss of a scribe based on the preceding clause."[24] But he is unable to provide substantiating proof. I propose that the repetition in this verse is a Semitic emphasis.

Verse 6

ἵνα μὴ ὑετὸς βρέχῃ—"that no rain may rain" reveals redundancy. The construction is unusual, but the use of βρέχω in Luke 17:29 ("fire and sulfur rained down from heaven") suggests that the verb can be used with other forms of "precipitation."

ὁσάκις ἐάν—this combination followed by the subjunctive occurs three times in the New Testament with the meaning "as often as" (here and in 1 Cor. 11:25, 26).

---

24. Charles, *Revelation*, 1:284.

(3) The Death of Two Witnesses
11:7–10

7. And when they finish their testimony, the beast that comes up out of the Abyss will make war against them and will overcome and kill them. 8. And their bodies will lie in the street of the great city that spiritually is called Sodom and Egypt, where also their Lord was crucified.

a. "And when they finish their testimony, the beast that comes up out of the Abyss will make war against them." This verse projects a picture of the end times when the church has completed the task of proclaiming the gospel of the kingdom to all the nations in the world (Matt. 24:14). All along in history, the faithful in the church have preached and taught the Word of God and the testimony of Jesus. But while they complete their work, the beast declares war on the church. We have to realize, however, that whenever and wherever the gospel is proclaimed, it encounters opposition. Here and there the evil one has been waging war against the followers of Jesus with intermittent oppression and persecution. John identifies the evil force as *the* beast, even though this is the first time he mentions him. Prior to writing the Apocalypse, John had seen the entire revelation. Thus, he was fully aware of *the* beast, even if he had not yet mentioned him.[25] He gives a further description of this creature when he writes, "The beast which you saw was and is not and is about to go up from the Abyss and go to his destruction" (17:8). Here is a picture of the evil one imitating God's infinity with respect to present, past, and future: the Antichrist was, and is not, and is about to go up from the Abyss. The Antichrist is constantly opposing Christ and his church every day and every step of the way.

Paul alludes to the Antichrist when he writes that the "man of lawlessness" cannot exert his full power and authority until the time has come, for God holds him back.

> That day will not come until the rebellion occurs and the man of lawlessness is revealed, the man doomed to destruction. He will oppose and will exalt himself over everything that is called God or is worshiped, so that he sets himself up in God's temple, proclaiming himself to be God. (2 Thess. 2:3–4)

When the volume of wickedness has reached its peak, then the Antichrist takes over and as a consequence the witness of the church comes to an end. The Antichrist is not Satan but is closely allied to him and is sent forth by him. He appears as the lamb with two horns that speaks like the dragon (Rev. 13:11; see also Dan. 7:1, 19–28). John takes his reference to warfare directed against God's people from the Old Testament, where Daniel writes, "As I watched, this horn was waging war against the saints and defeating them" (7:21). In subsequent chapters and verses, the writer of the Apocalypse expands his information on the war

25. Van de Kamp, *Israël in Openbaring*, p. 191 n. 54.

the beast wages against the church (12:17; 13:7; 16:14; 19:19). At the end of the age just before the Lord returns, the Antichrist will rule supreme.

b. "[The beast] will overcome and kill them." In his discourse on the end time, Jesus encourages the believers by saying, "For then there will be great distress, unequaled from the beginning of the world until now—and never to be equaled again. If those days had not been cut short, no one would survive, but for the sake of the elect those days will be shortened" (Matt. 24:21–22). The beast's primary attack is on the message and secondarily on the messengers; he kills the messengers to silence the message. When at the end of time unbelievers reject the message, God withdraws both message and messengers, permitting the Antichrist to kill the saints. "It is not a literal prediction that every faithful Christian will in fact be put to death. But it does require that every faithful Christian must be prepared to die."[26]

c. "And their bodies will lie in the street of the great city that spiritually is called Sodom and Egypt." In civilized cultures, the burial of the dead is a solemn rite performed with dignity and respect. To leave corpses unburied and in public view is the height of indignity and shame. Here we are told the bodies of the two witnesses are left unburied on the main street of the great city as objects of contempt.

This text calls for a choice between a literal interpretation or a figurative portrayal. Scholars who offer a literal explanation assert that the great city is Jerusalem and adduce the last clause of this verse to prove their point, "where also their Lord was crucified."[27] Further, some interpret John's reference to the great city (Jer. 22:8; *Sibylline Oracles* 5.154, 226, 413) prophetically and say that he looked forward to a rebuilt and inhabited Jerusalem in the last days.[28] But John looks forward to the holy city, the new Jerusalem that comes down out of heaven (21:3, 10).

A symbolic interpretation of this chapter states that the term *Jerusalem* conveys a spiritual, that is, a figurative meaning. Notice that John uses the adjective *great* and not *holy* to refer to the city. This suggests that he is speaking not about its character but about its size. As in all of Revelation, so also here there is a point of contrast between that which is holy and that which is profane. There are only two cities: the holy and the profane. It is the division between the people of God in the holy city and his adversaries in the great city. God's people inhabit the holy city, the spiritual Jerusalem of the saints. His enemies live in the great city, not in one particular place but in "the worldwide structure of unbelief and defi-

26. Richard Bauckham, *The Theology of the Book of Revelation*, New Testament Theology (Cambridge: Cambridge University Press, 1993), p. 93.

27. The NLT substitutes "Jerusalem" for "the great city." Scholars who identify Jerusalem as "the great city" are Beckwith, *Apocalypse*, pp. 591, 601; Friedrich Düsterdieck, *Critical and Exegetical Handbook to the Revelation of John* (New York and London: Funk and Wagnalls, 1886), p. 317; Walvoord, *Revelation*, p. 181; C. van der Waal, "The Last Book of the Bible and the Jewish Apocalypses," *Neotest* 12 (1978): 111–32; Aune, *Revelation 6–16*, p. 619; Lohmeyer, *Offenbarung*, p. 93.

28. Thomas, *Revelation 8–22*, p. 94.

ance against God."[29] The great city is identified with Sodom, a place of immorality with fewer than ten righteous people (Gen. 18:32), and with Egypt, a land symbolizing the enslavement of the Israelites. The prophets Isaiah and Ezekiel address the people residing in Jerusalem and Judah and compare them to the inhabitants of Sodom (Isa. 1:9–10; 3:9; Ezek. 16:46, 48–49), but nowhere in the Old Testament is Jerusalem identified with Egypt.

d. "Where also their Lord was crucified." The great city where their Lord was crucified is not an earthly city called Jerusalem; rather, it is contrasted with the holy city where God's people reside. The great city is the place where people living contrary to the will of God have crucified and continue to crucify the Lord all over again (Heb. 6:6). In Revelation, the expression *the great city* refers consistently to Babylon, a symbol for the world's opposition to God (14:8; 17:18; 18:2, 10, 16, 18–19, 21). When Jerusalem took its place next to Babylon in a defiant stance against God, his message, and his messengers, it lost its name as the holy city (see commentary on v. 2). The great city "is any and every city in which the church bears its prophetic witness to the nations."[30]

To whom does the pronoun *their* allude in the expression *their Lord?* John could not have applied the pronoun to the Jews who crucified Jesus, for they refused to acknowledge him as Lord. The pronoun refers to the two witnesses whom Jesus calls "my witnesses" (v. 3), that is, the church.

9. And the [citizens] from the peoples and tribes and languages and nations look at their bodies for three and a half days, and they do not permit their bodies to be placed in a tomb.

Now citizens from all over the world (peoples, tribes, languages, and nations) view the corpses of the witnesses. These people represent the world set against the saints (10:11; 13:7; 14:6; 17:15). Their implied numbers indicate that they did not come to view two corpses lying in a particular street of Jerusalem: they view the demise of the church in all its worldwide structures. The witness of the church has been completed, God has withdrawn his word and testimony, and the world now views the lifeless frame of the Christian religion.

The people of the world look at the corpses for a period of three and a half days (see v. 11). This period corresponds with the three and a half years of the two witnesses (v. 3). But these two are not identical. Three and a half days denotes a brief period compared with the much longer time during which the witnesses proclaim the gospel to the world. After God withdraws his word, the interval of the world's triumph is momentary. Its duration is short, for God determines its length when after three and a half days the witnesses are raised from the dead (v. 11).

29. Philip Edgcumbe Hughes, *The Book of the Revelation: A Commentary* (Leicester: Inter-Varsity; Grand Rapids: Eerdmans, 1990), p. 127. Consult the commentaries of Morris, p. 146; Mounce, p. 221.

30. Bauckham, *Theology*, p. 86; Martin Kiddle, *The Revelation of St. John* (reprint, London: Hodder and Stoughton, 1943), p. 184.

The world refuses to grant the saints permission to place the bodies in a tomb (compare Ps. 79:2–3). The word *tomb* refers not merely to a grave; it is a place with a tombstone inscription to remember the dead. In short, the forces of the Antichrist want to erase the memory of Christianity. The Greek text has the plural form "bodies" to convey the idea of the church in its totality. By refusing burial ceremonies, the world shows thorough disrespect for that which is sacred, but by their refusal unbelievers exhibit their inability to forget about the church. They spurn God and his Word but at the same time use his name in cursing while uttering derogatory remarks about his message.

10. And the inhabitants on the earth gloat over them and celebrate and exchange gifts, because the two prophets tormented those who dwell on the earth.

Who are the *inhabitants on the earth*? The expression appears frequently in Revelation; each time it denotes those people who have made earth their home without any thought of an eternal home with the Lord.[31] This does not mean a complete absence of believers on the face of this earth, because in the preceding text (v. 9) the believers by implication were not permitted to attend to funeral arrangements. We conclude that the saints number so few that they are not even mentioned.

John describes the citizens of the world with three verbs: *gloat, celebrate,* and *exchange.* The first verb has a negative connotation in the sense that they were filled with wicked satisfaction. The unbelievers celebrate victory over God's people by rejoicing and giving one another gifts. Scripture relates a parallel account with a positive connotation. When the Jews in Persia experienced relief from their enemies in the days of Queen Esther, they observed a day of celebration during which they exchanged food and presented gifts to the poor (Esther 9:19, 22).

The stated reason for this celebration is that "the two prophets tormented those who dwell on the earth." This statement unveils the twisted thinking of the world: God's messengers spiritually tormented the unbelievers.[32] The message God sent them by way of his envoys pricked their consciences and denied them peace of mind. The Word of God exposed their sins, and they were called to repentance, faith, and a life of service to God. They were told of God's wrath and the Day of Judgment. But they silenced God's message by killing his witnesses; consequently they thought to calm their fears and soothe their conscience. Lenski aptly comments, "Hell fills the whole world with jubilation when the Word of the prophets at last lies forever silent in the streets."[33] They may rejoice now, but they are unable to escape the inevitable Day of Judgment, at which time God will destroy those who are destroying the earth (v. 18).

---

31. Rev. 3:10; 6:10; 8:13; 11:10 (twice); 13:8, 14 (twice); 17:2; 17:8; compare also 13:12; 14:6.

32. Compare Werner Stenger (*EDNT,* 1:200), who remarks that the text does not refer to the torments after the Judgment Day. They suffer not physically but spiritually.

33. Lenski, *Revelation,* p. 347.

An interesting parallel can be drawn between the two prophets who represent God and the false prophet who represents Satan. Here is the paradigm.[34]

Two Witnesses	**Second Beast**
1. Prophets (11:10)	1. False prophet (16:13; 19:20; 20:10)
2. Perform signs (11:6)	2. Performs signs (13:13, 14; 19:20)
3. Receive authority from God (11:3)	3. Receives authority from the first beast (13:12)
4. Torment the inhabitants of the earth (11:10)	4. Deceives the inhabitants of the earth (13:14)
5. Two olive trees; lamps (11:4)	5. Two horns (13:11)
6. Breath of life from God (11:11)	6. Breathes into the image of first beast (13:15)

Greek Words, Phrases, and Constructions in 11:7–10

Verse 7

μετ᾽ αὐτῶν—the translation should not be "with them" but "against them." See also 2:16; 11:7; 13:4, 7; 17:14; compare 19:19.

Verse 8

τὸ πτῶμα—the singular "body" has the support of many manuscripts, while the plural is a correction—the plural appears in verse 9. The singular may be interpreted as denoting totality.

ὁ κύριος αὐτῶν—some Greek manuscripts feature the pronoun ἡμῶν in an effort to eliminate misunderstanding; others have deleted the pronoun altogether.

Verse 9

ἐκ—the preposition introduces a partitive genitive for which the word "citizens" or "persons" should be supplied.

Verse 10

ἐπί (twice)—the first one is with the genitive and means "on (the earth)." The second one is with the dative and is translated "over (them)."[35]

(4) The Resurrection of Two Witnesses *11:11–14*

The word of Jesus that "no servant is greater than his master" (John 13:16) is applicable to the two witnesses, the church. As Jesus died at the hands of wicked men, so his servants die. As Jesus was raised from the dead,

34. Resseguie, *Revelation Unsealed*, p. 128.

35. A. T. Robertson, *A Grammar of the Greek New Testament in the Light of Historical Research* (Nashville: Broadman, 1934), p. 565.

so his servants rise again.[36] As Jesus ascended to heaven and a cloud hid him from the apostles (Acts 1:9), so his servants ascend in a cloud in the sight of their enemies.

11. And after three and a half days the breath of life from God entered them and they stood on their feet, and great fear fell on those who saw them.

The demise of the Christian witness is of short duration because God intervenes. The world gloats over the corpses of the witnesses for three and half days (vv. 9–10). When this period comes to an end, God as the author of life breathes life into the corpses of these two witnesses (Job 33:4; Ezek. 37:5–14). As God breathed the breath of life into Adam's nostrils (Gen. 2:7), so he makes the dead come alive (Job 19:25–27).

"And great fear fell on those who saw them." Suddenly the tables are turned when God brings to life the witness of the church and confronts the world. This witness is not raised from the dead to convert the unbelievers, for the period of grace has come to an end when divine judgment is pending. The world that gloated over the demise of God's servants instantly realizes that its punishment is approaching. As a result, the adversaries of these witnesses are filled with dread and fear.

What is the meaning of this resurrection? The information John supplies is scant, so that we only assume what may happen. It may refer to the general resurrection of the dead when Jesus returns (1 Thess. 4:16–17), namely, to the great and glorious day that precedes the consummation. But it is also possible to say that this resurrection should be understood symbolically. Ezekiel speaks figuratively about the resurrection of the dead (37:10–13), so also here the return of God's witness can be interpreted metaphorically.[37]

12. And they heard a loud voice from heaven saying to them, "Come up here." And they came up to heaven in a cloud, and their enemies saw them.

The loud voice from heaven is divine and belongs to Jesus. John avoided using Jesus' name when he first heard a loud voice like a trumpet on the Lord's Day at Patmos (1:10). Then he heard the same voice again when he saw the door to heaven opened, and it said, "Come up here, and I will show you what must happen after these things" (4:1). And now once more, John heard the loud voice of Jesus giving the same command to tell God's resurrected witnesses to ascend.

The ascension of the saints is similar to that of Jesus, who went up into heaven "and is at God's right hand—with angels, authorities and powers in submission to him" (1 Pet. 3:22). The saints ascend *in a cloud,* which means that they are transformed at the coming of the Lord and will be caught up in the clouds to meet him in the air (1 Thess. 4:17). When Jesus ascended, the

---

36. Jesus remained in the tomb for three days, while the two witnesses were dead for three and a half days. These two are not identical. The first is a literal reckoning of time, but the second is utterly symbolical.

37. Consult the commentaries of Beale (p. 597); Mounce (pp. 222–23); Hailey (p. 259).

apostles saw him rise. But when the saints are caught up in the air, God's enemies watch them go up to heaven. Their ascension signifies full and complete victory over the evil one. There is an indirect parallel that relates to Christ's return, "Look, he is coming with the clouds, and every eye will see him" (Rev. 1:7; compare Zech. 12:10b). Our idiom uses the indefinite "in a cloud" in translations, but the Greek literally says, "in the cloud." This undoubtedly is a specific reference to the glory cloud which appeared when Jesus was transfigured (Matt. 17:5) and which enveloped him when he ascended from the Mount of Olives (Acts 1:9).

Twice in as many verses (vv. 11, 12) the phrase *saw them* occurs. John emphasizes that God's enemies see the risen and glorified saints ascend to heaven. Those adversaries filled with fear of the approaching judgment watch the ascension of God's people. At the end of time, the contrast of God's enemies and God's saints is striking indeed.

13. And in that hour there was a great earthquake and a tenth of the city fell and seven thousand people were killed in the earthquake, and the rest were terrified and gave glory to the God of heaven.

a. "And in that hour there was a great earthquake." We should understand the last few verses (vv. 11–13) in the framework of the period immediately preceding and during the Lord's return. This verse speaks about the unbelieving world that faces divine wrath in the form of a great earthquake that shakes the earth to indicate God's involvement in the Day of Judgment (see 6:12). At the moment the saints ascend to heaven, God strikes the earth with a great tremor to reveal his anger against the unbelievers who killed his people. He often uses this phenomenon in nature to indicate an unusual event. Earthquakes occurred when Jesus died and rose from the dead (Matt. 27:51; 28:2). Similarly, a great earthquake accompanied both the resurrection and the ascension of the saints.

b. "And a tenth of the city fell and seven thousand people were killed in the earthquake." Most commentators infer a total population of seventy thousand from the phrase *tenth of the city*. If we take the text literally, a tenth of the city's population equals seven thousand, so that the total number of inhabitants is seventy thousand. History provides numerous examples of thousands being killed in an earthquake devastating a midsize city. Although the loss of life is telling, it is difficult to assert that it is extraordinary.

The use of symbolism in this text is obvious.[38] The city is the place which the Gentiles will trample under foot and where the Lord was crucified (see the commentary on vv. 2, 8). It is the profane place that contrasts with all that is holy. This profane place, encompassing a worldwide structure set in unbelief and defiance against God, is now stricken with a great earthquake that vibrates its foundations. So it seems best to interpret the number seven thousand symbolically, as *seven*

38. Eduard Lohse (*Die Offenbarung des Johannes,* Das Neue Testament Deutsch 11 [Göttingen: Vandenhoeck & Ruprecht, 1960], p. 64) interprets the verse literally by applying it to Jerusalem.

signifies completeness and *one thousand* as ten times ten times ten (ten denotes fullness in the decimal system) indicates a multitude. The term *a tenth* is an indication of God's plan that the earthquake not kill all unbelievers.

c. "And the rest were terrified and gave glory to the God of heaven." Those who are not killed are filled with fear and consternation. They realize that the saints' ascension to heaven is going to be followed by punishment, judgment, and doom for them. It is no wonder that terror fills their hearts and minds, for their time on earth has run out.

Commentators are divided on the interpretation of the words, "And the rest . . . gave glory to the God of heaven." The words *gave glory to God* cause us to ask whether this is a matter of true repentance or fictitious remorse.

Many scholars are of the opinion that the unbelieving world not killed by the earthquake turned to God, repented of their wicked deeds, and glorified God.[39] In other words, these evil people were converted at the last possible moment and God in his grace and mercy accepted them into his family. The evidence for this position lies in these people giving glory to God, which is interpreted as "a form of relig[ious] devotion."[40]

Other scholars argue that not the death of the martyrs but their resurrection "struck terror to the hearts of their enemies and caused them to give glory to God."[41] There is a difference between remorse and repentance: Judas showed remorse and hanged himself, but Peter repented and was restored. There is a difference between concession and contrition; Achan gave glory to God and conceded that he had sinned against God (Josh. 7:19–20), but David confessed his sin with contrite heart (Ps. 51:4). Further, the next to the last verse of this chapter (v. 18) indicates a description of the last judgment that is reminiscent of verse 13 and confirms the conclusion of a last judgment scene and not one of repentance. Therefore, genuine conversion is no longer possible, "since it would have to be placed *after* the commencement of the last judgment, which is signaled in v[erse] 13a."[42] After God passes judgment, the time for repentance is over.

As long as the church proclaims the Word, there is time for salvation. But when the witnesses ascend to heaven, their message is no longer heard. The time of repentance comes to an end, because without the power of the Word there are no conversions. Also, John reveals a cyclical approach in his Apocalypse, whereby the topic of God judging unbelievers appears repeatedly. For instance, there is the imminent judgment for sinners (6:16) and the time for judging the

39. See the following commentaries: Aune (52B, pp. 628–29); Beasley-Murray (p. 187); Caird (pp. 139–40); Harrington (p. 123); Krodel (pp. 227–28); Ladd (pp. 159–60); Johnson (pp. 507–8); Thomas (*Revelation 8–22*, pp. 98–99). See also Bauckham, *Climax of Prophecy*, pp. 278–79, 282–83.

40. Bauer, p. 204. Compare the uses of this phrase in Acts 12:23; Rom. 4:20; Rev. 14:7; 16:9; 19:7.

41. Mounce, *Revelation*, p. 224. See the commentaries of Beale (p. 607); Hailey (p. 260); Hendriksen (p. 132); Hoeksema (p. 397); Hughes (p. 130); Kiddle (p. 206); Lenski (p. 351); Walvoord (p. 183).

42. Beale, *Revelation*, p. 607 (his emphasis).

dead (11:18). The Judge harvests the earth (14:15–16); after the outpouring of the seven bowls there is the coming judgment (16:17–21); and the rider on the white horse comes to judge the wicked (19:11–21). In all these instances, there is no mention of unbelievers being converted.

John borrowed the phrase *God of heaven* from the Old Testament (Ezra 1:2; Neh. 1:4; Dan. 2:18–19; Jonah 1:9). In Revelation it occurs only twice, here and in 16:11.

14. The second woe is past. Look, the third woe is coming soon.

John mentioned the end of the first woe in 9:12; at that time he announced that there were two more to come. Here then is the end of the second woe, but John fails to tell us what segment of the Apocalypse comprises the third woe. Some scholars think that the substance of chapter 16 that reveals the seven plagues makes up this last affliction.[43] The objection to this interpretation is its distance from the announcement that the third woe is at hand. Therefore, it is better to see the last part of this verse introducing the next segment (vv. 15b–19) as the content of the third woe. The scene of the seventh trumpet "is a more severe woe than the fifth and sixth trumpets, since it represents the climactic final judgment."[44] The seventh trumpet permits us a view subsequent to the final judgment when the wicked face destruction. Thus, the woe speaks to the devastation of those people who have been destructive during their time on earth (v. 18).

Greek Words, Phrases, and Constructions in 11:12–13

Verse 12

ἤκουσαν—the third person plural form is to be preferred to the first person singular ἤκουσα on the basis of external evidence.

Verse 13

ὀνόματα—"names," but translated as "people" or "persons." The word indicates that these people are known individually by name (see 3:4; Acts 1:15).

---

15 And the seventh angel blew the trumpet. And there were loud voices in heaven saying, "The kingdom of the world has become the kingdom of our Lord and his Christ. And he will reign forever and ever." 16 And the twenty-four elders, those who were seated on their thrones before God, fell on their faces and worshiped God, 17 saying:

> "We give thanks to you, Lord God, Almighty, the one who is and who was, because you have assumed your great power and have begun to reign. 18 And the nations were angry, but your wrath has come.

---

43. Consult Beckwith, *Apocalypse*, pp. 608, 669–71; Thomas, *Revelation 8–22*, p. 100; Johnson, *Revelation*, p. 508.

44. See the commentaries of Beale (p. 610), Lenski (p. 360), Hughes (p. 131), and Hoeksema (p. 402).

And the time has come to judge the dead
and to reward your servants the prophets,
and the saints and those who fear your
name, the small and the great, and to destroy those who are destroying the earth."

19 And the temple of God in heaven was opened and his ark of the covenant appeared in his temple. And there were flashes of lightning and rumblings and an earthquake and a great hailstorm.

---

9. The Seventh Trumpet
11:15–19

The two-part interlude (10:1–11:14) has come to an end, and John continues with the series of trumpets, of which the seventh is next. The seventh trumpet shows similarities with the seventh seal and the seventh bowl. All three place their scenes in heaven, where silence is observed (8:1), loud voices are heard (11:15), and there is a voice saying, "It is done" (16:17). All three are at the end of seven-part cycles and provide information on the end of time. Yet the differences are telling, for the seventh seal ushers in the seven trumpets. The seventh trumpet reveals a victory celebration as if the battle against the enemy is won. And the seventh bowl marks the final plague in nature so severe that it has no equal (16:18, 21).

The last segment of this chapter, introducing the final judgment, contains two hymns, one on the kingdom and the other on thanksgiving for what God has done. The first one mentions Christ as the everlasting ruler in his kingdom in the sense that the war with Satan is over. The second one, addressed to God, speaks of divine power, judging the dead, rewarding prophets and saints, and destroying the destroyers. This second hymn that the twenty-four elders sing regards the Judgment Day as if it already belongs to the past. Both hymns are paeans of victory that bring the series of trumpets to a climax. Concisely, the seventh trumpet gives us a heavenly vision in which Christ triumphs over his enemies.

Verse 19 seems to be out of place, for the nearest passages that have similar wording are 15:5 (the temple) and 16:18, 21 (lightning, rumblings, thunder, earthquake, and hail).[45] It alludes, however, to the covenant relation God has with his people and to his awesome power in nature, and thus it forms a fitting conclusion to the first part of Revelation. In addition, the sequence of flashes of lightning, rumblings, thunder, earthquake, and hail occurs four times with variations (4:5; 8:5; 11:19; and 16:18). These references show an expanding formula that relates to the severity of God's judgment depicted in the progress of the Apocalypse.

---

45. Michael Wilcock (*The Message of Revelation: I Saw Heaven Opened* [Downers Grove: InterVarsity, 1975], pp. 110–15) places 11:19 at the head of the next section (11:19–15:4). We would expect an introductory verse to summarize what the section teaches. But this is not the case, for chapter 12 introduces the second half of the Apocalypse. M. Robert Mulholland Jr. (*Revelation: Holy Living in an Unholy World* [Grand Rapids: Zondervan, Frances Asbury Press, 1990], p. 214) calls 11:19–15:5 the "centerpiece of Revelation."

a. Two Hymns
11:15–18

15. And the seventh angel blew the trumpet. And there were loud voices in heaven saying, "The kingdom of the world has become the kingdom of our Lord and his Christ. And he will reign forever and ever."

Earlier John wrote about the seventh angel sounding his trumpet to indicate that the end of time is near (10:7). And now he describes the angel blowing the trumpet and its setting. The backdrop is heaven, where loud voices are singing praises to God and his Christ. We are not told who were singing. What we can say is that the voices belong to all those who dwell in heaven.

These voices declare that the kingdom of the world now belongs to "our Lord and his Christ." This means that Satan, who tempted Jesus by offering him the kingdoms of the world, no longer possesses them (Matt. 4:8–9; Luke 4:5–6). Relying on the Old Testament, John reveals that the kingdom belongs to God and his Christ (Ps. 2:2, 8–9; 22:28; Dan. 7:14; Obad. 21).[46] There is one kingdom, not two. There is one God, not two. Notice how in the Apocalypse John ascribes divinity to Jesus when he mentions him together with God. Here are two examples, with italics added:

- "They will be priests of God and of Christ and will reign with *him* a thousand years" (20:6).
- "The throne of God and of the Lamb will be in it, and *his* servants will serve *him*" (22:3).

In the Apocalypse, John teaches that both God and Christ are called King, for they are worthy of praise and adoration. For instance, the trinitarian greeting depicts Jesus Christ as "ruler of the kings of the earth" (1:5). The song of Moses and of the Lamb is addressed to God as "the King of the ages" (15:3). Christ made his people to be a kingdom and priests (1:6; 5:10), yet the kingdom belongs to both Christ and God (11:15; 12:10). The rule of Christ and God is the same, because God rules his kingdom through his Son.

Christ has been king in his kingdom all along (Ps. 110:1); he uttered his enthronement speech prior to his ascension, "All authority in heaven and on earth has been given to me" (Matt. 28:18). When the last enemy is destroyed, namely death, then comes the end, and he will hand over the kingdom to God the Father (1 Cor. 15:24–28). This does not mean that then he will cease to rule; he will reign forever and ever.

The text looks at the victory Christ has achieved and simply states, "The kingdom of the world has become the kingdom of our Lord and his Christ." From John's perspective, the utter defeat of Satan and his cohorts has taken place. They were usurpers of world power; now Christ is the victor and will reign eter-

---

46. John P. M. Sweet (*Revelation*, WPC [Philadelphia: Westminster, 1979], p. 191) observes that the themes of Psalm 2 repeatedly appear in Revelation (12:5; 14:1; 16:14; 17:18; 19:15, 19).

nally. "His dominion is an everlasting dominion that will not pass away, and his kingdom is one that will never be destroyed" (Dan. 7:14; see also 2:44; 7:27; Ps. 10:16).

16. And the twenty-four elders, those who were seated on their thrones before God, fell on their faces and worshiped God.

The twenty-four elders seated on twenty-four thrones represent the saints in heaven (Rev. 4:4, 10; 5:8; 11:16; 19:4). They have been given the privilege of surrounding God's throne and are closer to this throne than angels. Redeemed humanity seated on thrones before God is privileged to rule with Christ (3:21). These twenty-four elders lead in worship by prostrating themselves in the presence of God. They are the ones who express thanksgiving and praise for the redemption accomplished on their behalf by God's Son.

While the chorus in heaven sings a victory paean to God and Christ for rightfully claiming the kingdom of the world, the twenty-four elders sing their own hymn of praise to express their thanks. The work of redemption has been completed and the time has come to render honor, praise, and glory to the Lord God Almighty.

17. Saying: "We give thanks to you, Lord God, Almighty, the one who is and who was, because you have assumed your great power and have begun to reign."

The twenty-four elders as representatives of the church are expressing their gratitude not to Christ but to the Father, who is called the *Lord God, Almighty*. He commissioned the Son to redeem his people, to forgive their sins, to grant them eternal life, and to teach them his Word. Now the elders thank God, who is their sovereign and all-powerful Lord. Their words of thanks show a typical Jewish background demonstrated in David's Psalm of Thanks and in the Psalter (1 Chron. 16:8, 26; Ps. 105:1; 106:1, 47; 136:1–4).[47]

The phrase "the one who is and who was" is reminiscent of 1:4, 8; 4:8, but lacks the third part "and who is to come." John took this third part from the Old Testament (e.g., Ps. 96:13; 98:9), where God comes to save and judge. The early Christians identified his coming with that of Jesus Christ as they looked forward to Christ's return.[48] Its omission signals that God has indeed come as John now looks backward at the fulfillment of Jesus' promise to come quickly (also compare 16:5). That is, this paean of praise sung by the twenty-four elders omits the phrase *who is to come* as if his coming had already occurred. They looked back at the battle against Satan, the Antichrist, and the inhabitants of Babylon. God revealed his power, defeated his enemies, and destroyed the oppressors of his people.

The next clause, "because you have assumed your great power and have begun to reign," is an affirmation of God defeating his adversaries and taking his rightful governing power over his creation in heaven and earth. Notice that the

47. The verb *to give thanks* occurs thirty-eight times in the New Testament, twenty-four of them in Paul's Epistles. John has three occurrences in his Gospel (6:11, 23; 11:41) and one in Revelation (11:17). See Hermann Patsch, *EDNT*, 2:88; Hans-Helmut Esser, *NIDNTT*, 3:818.

48. Refer to Bauckham, *Theology*, pp. 28–29; and his *Climax of Prophecy*, pp. 32–33.

perfect tense is used in the verb *to assume.* This means that no power will ever again rise against God to take away from him authority as in the case of Satan, called "the prince of this world" (John 12:31; 14:30; 16:11; 2 Cor. 4:4; Eph. 2:2; 1 John 4:4; 5:19).

In Greek, John stresses the adjective *great* as he writes "great power." God's power directed against his opponents is awesome, for "it is a dreadful thing to fall into the hands of the living God" (Heb. 10:31). Swete writes, "It is not the normal exercise of Divine power, but that final and overwhelming display to which all prophecy points."[49]

At the demise of his enemies, the Lord God begins his unrestricted reign. The twenty-four elders, looking back on the accomplished work of redemption, rejoice in Christ's triumph and absolute rule over the entire universe. This rule signals that Satan's reign has ended and that the time for judgment has come.

18. "And the nations were angry, but your wrath has come. And the time has come to judge the dead and to reward your servants the prophets, and the saints and those who fear your name, the small and the great, and to destroy those who are destroying the earth."

a. "And the nations were angry, but your wrath has come." Two parallel clauses, which reflect the words of David in Psalm 2, speak about anger and wrath. This psalm relates that nations rebel against God and his Anointed. But "the one in heaven laughs," for he "rebukes them in his anger and terrifies them in his wrath" (Ps. 2:1–5, 12; Acts 4:25–27; compare Jer. 30:23–24). Israel and the Roman empire, represented by the high priest with the Sanhedrin and Pontius Pilate respectively, nailed Jesus to the cross and afterward persecuted his followers. But the anger and wrath of God differ from the anger and wrath of God's enemies. While they direct their ire against God to destroy his kingdom and trample all that is holy (Ps. 2:2), God directs his vengeance against the nations to bring them to justice and their destined end.

b. "And the time has come to judge the dead." John is not alluding to chronological time but to the right moment that God ordained for the Day of Judgment. It is the time God has appointed for the last judgment. The sixth seal (6:17), the seventh trumpet (11:18), and the sixth bowl (16:14) all refer to the moment when the great Day of Judgment comes. John presents his Apocalypse in a cyclical manner and looks at God's revelation from different perspectives.

The term *the dead* occurs eight times in the Apocalypse and signifies all those who have died. More specifically it can mean either believers or unbelievers. For example, "Blessed are the dead who die in the Lord from now on" (14:13) and "And the rest of the dead lived not until the thousand years were completed" (20:5a). Here as well as in 20:12–13 the term alludes to all people: some receive rewards and others condemnation.

---

49. Swete, *Revelation,* p. 143.

c. "And to reward your servants the prophets, and the saints and those who fear your name, the small and the great." A reward is not something that is earned, for it comes to the believers as a gift from God. The concept *reward* and *conduct* are connected, but not in the sense of cause and effect. Rewards are given as tokens of God's free grace.[50]

A preliminary reading leaves the impression that John has in mind three classes of people: servants who are prophets, saints, and God-fearers both small and great. This is not necessarily so, because the expression *your servants the prophets* already appeared in 10:7 (see the commentary). They are God's servants, prophets or apostles and their helpers, who were commissioned to convey his revelation and often were told to write it down. They are a special class of people. In addition there are the *saints*, who are the God-fearers both the small and the great (19:5; Ps. 115:13). The word *saints* occurs fourteen times in the Apocalypse; they are the holy people whom God has sanctified through the blood of Christ.[51] They suffer for his name, exercise patience and faithfulness for his cause, present prayers to God, and are killed for being his people. They are those who fear God worldwide whether they are beginners or giants in the faith.[52] I suggest, therefore, that there are two classes of people: God's special servants, who fulfill a particular task, and the saints, who are all those who revere God's name.[53]

d. "And to destroy those who are destroying the earth." The twenty-four elders petition God to destroy those wicked persons who are constantly engaged in morally ruining the inhabitants on the earth.[54] This is precisely what "the great prostitute, who ruined the earth with her fornication," had done (19:2). God's wrath is poured out upon those who lead astray the people and now are destroyed themselves.

b. God's Covenant
11:19

19. And the temple of God in heaven was opened and his ark of the covenant appeared in his temple. And there were flashes of lightning and rumblings and an earthquake and a great hailstorm.

a. "And the temple of God in heaven was opened and his ark of the covenant appeared in his temple." The twenty-four elders have concluded their hymn of praise, and now John responds by describing the temple of God in heaven. This is the holy place where God dwells and which is his sacred presence. Since the curtain separating the Holy of Holies from the Holy Place has split, the ark of

---

50. Paul Christoph Böttger, *NIDNTT*, 3:144.

51. Rev. 5:8; 8:3, 4; 11:18; 13:7, 10; 14:12; 16:6; 17:6; 18:20, 24; 19:8; 20:9; 22:21 (variant).

52. The phrase *small and great* occurs also in 13:16, where John mentions sociological categories of unbelievers, but here he emphasizes the spiritual dimensions of the saints.

53. Consult the commentaries of Greijdanus (pp. 243–44); Ladd (p. 163); Lenski (pp. 356–57); Mounce (pp. 227–28); and Thomas (*Revelation 8–22*, p. 11).

54. Bauer, p. 190. See also Günther Harder, *TDNT*, 9:103.

the covenant is open to view. We understand the vision symbolically, for the temple on earth no longer existed at the time John wrote Revelation (7:15; 15:5, 8). The expression *temple* in this book signifies the very presence of God, and John looks at the temple from his earth-to-heaven perspective.

The *ark of the covenant* in the tabernacle and later in the temple of Solomon was the place where God dwelled. This sacred box symbolized God's presence, and into that sacred presence the high priest might enter once a year to atone for his own sins and the sins of the people. On its lid animal blood was sprinkled; and in the ark were the two tablets on which God had written the Decalogue (1 Kings 8:9; 2 Chron. 5:10; Heb. 9:4). This ark, now open to all, is God's viewable demonstration that he keeps covenant with his people. At that place filled with glory, God meets with them and establishes his law among them (Exod. 25:22; 29:42–43). And the words of his law that were inscribed on stone tablets in the ark reflect God's sacred presence in the lives of his people. With them he has a covenantal relationship so that the knowledge of God's law fills the earth "as the waters cover the sea" (Isa. 11:9; Hab. 2:14). "Hence, when this ark is now seen, that is, fully realized, the covenant of grace (Gen. 17:7) in all its sweetness is realized in the hearts and lives of God's children."[55]

Even though the ark and the tablets of stone were destroyed by the Babylonians when they conquered Jerusalem on August 14, 586 B.C. (2 Kings 25:9), the practice of observing the law remained intact.[56] The fact that John speaks of a heavenly ark, although symbolically, shows that the relevance of God's moral law endures and is everlasting. There is no place for sin and lawlessness in the presence of the Almighty, for on the one hand his redeemed covenant people are forgiven and on the other the people who deliberately break his law are condemned.

b. "And there were flashes of lightning and rumblings and an earthquake and a great hailstorm." The phenomena that occur in nature are a flashback to the giving of the Decalogue at Mount Sinai, where God caused thunder, lightning, and a tremor (Exod. 19:16–18). The writer of Revelation repeatedly records these natural occurrences (4:5; 8:5; 11:19; 16:18, 21). Here and in 16:21 he adds the falling of hailstones. These phenomena are reminders of the Sinai event and suggest that God's judgment has come. "John uses the allusion to Sinai to suggest that the End has been reached, though not yet exhaustively described."[57] Indeed, at this point in the Apocalypse John portrays the end of time. We cannot, however, simply go on to the next chapter as if the one flows into the other. Chapter 11 marks the coming of the Judgment Day, while chapter 12 describes a woman and the birth of a male child—a new start.

---

55. Hendriksen, *More Than Conquerors*, p. 133.

56. According to a tradition recorded in 2 Macc. 2:4–8, the prophet Jeremiah took the tent and the ark to Mount Nebo and hid them in a cave that he sealed. God would reveal the tent and the ark at the time he gathers his people and shows his mercy. Even if this tradition circulated among the Jews, John is not thinking of a restoration of temple and ark on earth. His vision of a heavenly ark points to the fulfillment of Christ's redemptive work.

57. Bauckham, *Climax of Prophecy*, p. 204.

Greek Words, Phrases, and Constructions in 11:17–18

Verse 17

ὁ ὢν καὶ ὁ ἦν—many minuscule manuscripts add ὁ ἐρχόμενος, which is "a typical Byzantine accretion, in imitation of the tripartite expression in 1.4, 8."[58] The TR and two translations feature this addition (KJV, NKJV).

Verse 18

τοὺς μικροὺς καὶ τοὺς μεγάλους—external support for this reading is strong, whereas the use of the dative case appears to be a correction.[59]

---

58. Metzger, *Textual Commentary*, p. 672.

59. Thomas (*Revelation 8–22*, p. 115) calls the use of the accusative case an anacoluthon (i.e., an abrupt shift in syntax). Swete (*Revelation*, p. 144) writes that the accusative "must be explained by supposing that the writer has forgotten that he started with δοῦναι μισθόν." It is also possible to construe the accusative case with the preceding clause "to judge the dead" (compare 20:12), even though the sequence remains problematic.

12

The Woman and the Dragon

(12:1–17)

Outline (continued)

V. Vision 4: Aspects of Warfare and Salvation (12:1–14:20)
  A. The Woman and the Dragon (12:1–17)
    1. The Woman, the Son, the Dragon (12:1–6)
    2. Warfare in Heaven (12:7–9)
    3. A Song of Victory (12:10–12)
    4. Help and Safety for the Church (12:13–17)

12 1 And a great sign appeared in heaven: a woman clothed with the sun and the moon under her feet and a crown of twelve stars on her head. 2 She was pregnant, and she cried out in birth pains and in anguish to give birth. 3 And there appeared another sign in heaven. And look, there was a great red dragon that had seven heads and ten horns and seven crowns on his heads. 4 And his tail swept away a third of the stars of heaven and he cast them to the earth. And the dragon stood before the woman who was about to give birth, so that when she gave birth he might devour her child. 5 And she gave birth to a son, a male child, who is about to rule all the nations with an iron rod. And the child was snatched to God and to his throne. 6 And the woman fled into the desert, where she had a place prepared by God, so that there she might be nourished for 1,260 days.

7 And there was war in heaven. Michael and his angels fought against the dragon. And the dragon and his angels fought back 8 and did not prevail, and a place in heaven was no longer found for them. 9 And the great dragon was cast down, that ancient serpent called the devil and Satan, the deceiver of the whole world. He was cast down to the earth, and his angels were cast out with him. 10 And I heard a loud voice in heaven saying,

> "Now have come the salvation, power, and kingdom of our God, and the authority of his Christ, because the accuser of our brothers [and sisters] has been cast out; he is the one accusing them before our God day and night. 11 And they have overcome him by the blood of the Lamb and by the word of their testimony, and they did not love their lives even in the face of death. 12 Therefore, rejoice, O heavens, and they who dwell in them! Woe to the earth and the sea, because the devil has gone down to you! He is very angry, because he knows that his time is short."

13 And when the dragon saw that he was cast down to the earth, he pursued the woman who gave birth to the male child. 14 And two wings of a great eagle were given to the woman, so that she might fly into the desert to her place, where she might be nourished for a time, times, and a half time away from the presence of the serpent. 15 And the serpent cast out of its mouth water like a river after the woman, so that she might be swept away by the river. 16 And the earth helped the woman, and the earth opened its mouth and swallowed up the river that the dragon cast out of its mouth. 17 And the dragon became furious at the woman, and he went out to fight against the rest of her offspring, those who were keeping the commandments of God and held to the testimony of Jesus.

V. Vision 4: Aspects of Warfare and Salvation 12:1–14:20

We have now come to the center of the book and are entering the second part of Revelation. There is no close connection between the content of chapter 11 and that of chapter 12. Here is a new beginning, for Revelation basically has two main parts. These parts are divided into Christ's church persecuted by the world (chapters 1–11) and Christ with the church persecuted by Satan (chapters 12–22).[1] In addition, chapter 1 features an introduction to this book and chapter 22 a conclusion.

First, we note that the structure of Revelation tends to teach us a cyclical instead of a linear approach. This approach explains the apparent break in the middle of the Apocalypse, where the writer calls attention to Christ and his church persecuted by Satan (vv. 3–6, 13–17). Being cast out of heaven with his angels, the devil gives authority to the Antichrist and the false prophet—the beast coming out of the sea and the beast coming out of the earth. All who do not have the mark of the beast or the number of his name are unable to buy or sell (13:1–18). But Christ takes on Satan and his cohorts, namely, the Antichrist and the false prophet. He appears as the Son of Man to inaugurate the Judgment Day (14:14–20).

After these three chapters, John continues with his series of sevens, namely, the seven bowls of wrath (chapters 15–16). Divine wrath poured out on God's enemies is a description of the final judgment (16:17–21). The woman called Babylon and all those who follow her are thrown down (17:1–18:24). The rider on a white horse comes to judge with justice and to make war on his enemies (19:11–21); and God's judgment reaches its completion when the books are opened and each person is judged (20:11–15). In brief, the Apocalypse reveals parallels that develop progressively with each cycle.

Next, chapter 12 reflects typical Johannine repetition that serves to emphasize his unique presentation. For instance, the time period of 1,260 days appears in verse 6, where God prepared a place for the woman in the desert. And in verse 14 this woman flew to a place prepared for her in the desert "for a time, times, and a half time." These two time references are the same in duration: twelve hundred sixty days equals forty-two months (11:2–3) or three and a half years.

Third, the chapter pictures both an ideal situation and a present reality.[2] The symbolism of the glorious woman "clothed with the sun, the moon under her feet, and a crown of twelve stars on her head" (v. 1) is an ideal picture of this woman having reached the zenith. Back of this ideal picture lies reality; it is the reality that takes form in the birth and ascension of Christ. It includes heavenly

---

1. William Hendriksen, *More Than Conquerors* (reprint, Grand Rapids: Baker, 1982), p. 23. Jon Paulien (*Decoding Revelation's Trumpets: Literary Allusions and the Interpretation of Revelation 8:7–12*, AUSDDS 11 [Berrien Springs, Mich.: Andrews University Press, 1987], p. 344) divides Revelation into a historical division (seals and trumpets) and the end-time crisis (chapters 12–14 and the bowls). David E. Aune (*Revelation 6–16*, WBC 52B [Nashville: Nelson, 1998], p. 661) regards 11:19 as an introduction to 12:1–17.

2. Compare George Eldon Ladd, *Commentary on the Revelation of John* (Grand Rapids: Eerdmans, 1972), p. 167; Isbon T. Beckwith, *The Apocalypse of John* (1919; reprint, Grand Rapids: Baker, 1979), pp. 617, 621–22; Robert H. Mounce, *The Book of Revelation*, rev. ed., NICNT (Grand Rapids: Eerdmans, 1998), p. 231.

warfare, when the archangel Michael hurls Satan with his angels to the earth (v. 9). It points to the wrath of the devil, who pursues the woman as she flees to a place prepared for her while receiving help from the earth (v. 16). It portrays the followers of Christ waging a spiritual war against Satan and enduring the devil's wrath (v. 17). Conclusively, the scene that depicts the exalted woman is idealism; the scene that describes the persecuted church is realism.

Last, chapter 12 stresses the defeat of Satan. His defeat is highlighted by the verb *cast out/down,* which appears five times in succession (see vv. 9 [three times], 10, 13). Throughout this chapter, Satan is portrayed as a five-time loser, while Christ and his church are victorious.

- The devil attempted to devour the male child, but God snatched him up to his throne (v. 5).
- Satan fought against Michael and his angels but lost (v. 9).
- The dragon pursued the woman, but God prepared a place for her in the desert (vv. 6, 14).
- The serpent wanted the woman to drown in a torrent, but the earth swallowed the river (vv. 15–16).
- Satan lost when he waged war against the woman's offspring, who kept on obeying God's commands and holding on to Jesus' testimony (v. 17).

A. The Woman and the Dragon
12:1–17

Did John borrow material from pagan mythology, which seems to provide parallels to this passage (vv. 1–6) in a number of accounts? There is the Greek myth of Apollo born of the goddess Leto; it also mentions the dragon Python. Next, there is the Babylonian creation myth about Tiamat and the seven-headed monster slain by the god Marduk as Tiamat swept a third of the stars from the sky. Third, there are Persian and Egyptian myths with similar stories. And last, there are coins with messages: one portrays Emperor Domitian with an image of his son whose hand reaches out to seven stars; then a coin with an image of this son with the moon and six stars; also one with the son and his mother Domitia, who is depicted as a goddess.[3]

Even though John was familiar with various mythological stories of the pagan world, we still must reject any suggestion that he borrowed from these sources to create the Apocalypse. God revealed the content of Revelation to Jesus, who in turn told John to write down what he has observed (1:1–2, 11, 19). Therefore, the Apocalypse is a God-given book. This does not mean that John mechanically wrote

3. See the commentaries of G. R. Beasley-Murray, *The Book of Revelation,* NCB (London: Oliphants, 1974), pp. 192–93; Alan F. Johnson, *Revelation,* in *The Expositor's Bible Commentary,* ed. Frank E. Gaebelein (Grand Rapids: Zondervan, 1981), 12:512–13. See also the doctoral dissertation of Adela Yarbro Collins, *The Combat Myth in the Book of Revelation,* HDR 9 (Missoula: Scholars Press, 1976), pp. 63–67, 70–71; Aune, *Revelation 6–16,* pp. 667–74.

down what he was told, but rather that he wrote the visions he saw in the framework of symbols. The sun, moon, and crown of twelve stars adorn the woman to make her appearance beautiful and mighty. At the same time, these heavenly bodies are subordinate to her; she is far greater than they are. We see a parallel in Joseph's dream of the sun, moon, and eleven stars bowing before him (Gen. 37:9).

John shows the reader a picture of the struggle between a woman and Satan, which is a throwback to the beginning of human history when God addressed both the woman and the serpent (Gen. 3:14–16). It depicts the spiritual warfare that God's people have faced ever since Adam and Eve fell into sin. This warfare becomes acute with the woman's delivery of a male child whom the serpent stands ready to devour at the moment of birth (vv. 1–6). Following the birth of the child, John describes warfare in heaven (vv. 7–9). As an interlude (vv. 10–12), John records a heavenly hymn. Then he concludes this chapter with a second report on Satan's war against the woman and her offspring (vv. 13–17).

1. The Woman, the Son, the Dragon
12:1–6

1. And a great sign appeared in heaven: a woman clothed with the sun and the moon under her feet and a crown of twelve stars on her head.

a. "And a great sign appeared in heaven." Translators differ in expressing the meaning of the words *great sign.* Here are two examples: "a great wonder" (KJV, NCV) and "a great and wondrous sign" (NIV). The sign is a portent marvelous to behold, for it is large and visible in heaven. The word *sign* appears seven times in Revelation to portray the work of either God or Satan and his fallen angels (12:1, 3; 13:13, 14; 15:1; 16:14; 19:20). And the adjective *great* describes the "sign" here and in 15:1, where it refers to seven angels with seven plagues that fulfill God's wrath. The adjective and noun also occur in 13:13, where the second beast (the false prophet) performs great signs for the devil in full view of the people on earth.

b. "A woman clothed with the sun and the moon under her feet, and a crown of twelve stars on her head." This sentence can be understood only symbolically. Yet we have to ask the identity of this woman. Who is she?

Is she Mary the mother of Jesus? Early Christian literature lists no references to that effect. Epiphanius of Salamis, approximately in the middle of the fourth century, is the first one to note that "some individuals [unnamed] were identifying the woman with Mary."[4] But the New Testament speaks against this exegesis, because for herself Mary assumes a modest place in society and church. Also, during the Middle Ages the majority of writers equated the woman not with Mary but with the church.

Other scholars interpret the woman to be Israel, regarded by God as his wife (Isa. 54:3–6; Jer. 31:32; Ezek. 16:32; Hos. 2:16).[5] When John composed the Apoc-

---

4. Raymond E. Brown, ed., *Mary in the New Testament* (Philadelphia: Fortress, 1978), p. 235 n. 512.

5. John F. Walvoord, *The Revelation of Jesus Christ* (Chicago: Moody, 1966), p. 188; and Robert L. Thomas, *Revelation 8–22: An Exegetical Commentary* (Chicago: Moody, 1995), p. 120.

alypse, however, many Jews in the dispersion were members of the synagogue of Satan; they persecuted the Christians (2:9; 3:9). Further, the Jewish people, unable to rebuild Jerusalem after its destruction in August 70, have left no record of a national conversion after that date.

Still others see that Satan attacks God's covenant people from the time of the fall into sin to the consummation, so that the woman he assaults represents the covenant community of both the Old Testament and New Testament eras (Heb. 11:39–40). The people of these two eras demonstrate a oneness by calling her mother. She gave birth to the Messiah (Isa. 7:14), for she represents Christ's human ancestry that incorporates Gentile Christians of the new covenant (Rom. 9:5; 11:11–21). The woman's children, John intimates, are "those who were keeping the commandments of God and held to the testimony of Jesus" (v. 17).[6] John teaches the unity of the people of God.

The *crown of twelve stars* represents God's people exemplified in the twelve patriarchs of the old covenant era and in the twelve apostles of new covenant times. The number twelve is a description of God's people. Notice the difference between the cosmic glory of this woman and the human glitter of the great prostitute (17:4).

2. She was pregnant, and she cried out in birth pains and in anguish to give birth.

This glorious woman was clothed with the brilliance of the sun as a source of light that was reflected by the moon. She had a crown of twelve stars on her head that symbolized complete victory. She was pregnant and about to give birth, which symbolizes the coming of Jesus in the flesh. Indeed, this verse is a reflection of the entire Old Testament period in which Satan displays his enmity toward God. He attacks the saints whom God places in the world to occupy a central position. They have been and are a source of light that they received from their Maker and Redeemer. Thus, God's people through his Word reflect his brilliance to dispel the darkness of the world.

The woman is in pain and anguish as she is giving birth (compare Isa. 26:17; 66:7; Mic. 4:10; Gal. 4:19).[7] When John wrote the last book in the Bible, the birth of Jesus had taken place a century earlier. But the author highlights this text in the period of Jesus' birth to stress the severe conflict Satan has fomented and continues to foment against God and his people.

---

6. See Johnson, *Revelation*, p. 514; S. Greijdanus, *De Openbaring des Heeren aan Johannes*, KNT (Amsterdam: Van Bottenburg, 1925), p. 250; Mounce, *Revelation*, p. 232; Michael Wilcock, *The Message of Revelation: I Saw Heaven Opened* (Downers Grove: InterVarsity, 1975), p. 119; Gregory K. Beale, *The Book of Revelation: A Commentary on the Greek Text,* NIGTC (Grand Rapids: Eerdmans, 1998), p. 630.

7. Beckwith (p. 622) comments, "No special symbolism, such as Israel's long history of suffering before the advent of Christ, is contained in the words; all such reference is remote from the purely idealistic passage." But this view is hard to maintain in view of Satan's aim to thwart God's purposes.

3. And there appeared another sign in heaven. And look, there was a great red dragon that had seven heads and ten horns and seven crowns on his heads.

Chapter 12 is the first chapter in the Apocalypse that juxtaposes the woman and the dragon. It is also the first chapter that introduces two signs in heaven, one for each, with the difference that the adjective *great* describes the woman's sign. The sign of the dragon is not called great; instead the imperative "Look!" alerts the reader's attention to a horrific dragon. Not the sign but the dragon is great, that is, enormous in size.

The dragon's color is red, which symbolizes the color of warfare. The Greek word *pyrros* (fiery red) is used both here and for the rider on the red horse (6:4).

Although mythology has numerous accounts of dragons, John himself explains the meaning of the word *dragon*: "And the great dragon was cast down, that ancient serpent called the devil and Satan, the deceiver of the whole world" (v. 9; 20:2). Satan came to Eve in Paradise in the form of a serpent to deceive her (Gen. 3:1; 1 Tim. 2:14). But the deceiving serpent has become a powerful dragon that instills fear and dread in his opponents. Notwithstanding, God's people know that Jesus Christ has conquered this dragon, even if his force and fury continue to be overpowering. Wherever the dragon goes, he wages war aimed at gaining victory.

Note that this beast is depicted with seven heads, ten horns, and seven crowns. These numbers ought not to be taken literally but symbolically. The number seven signifies completeness, and the number ten is the number of fullness in the decimal structure. The seven heads and ten horns refer to completeness in conquering the world, which is evident in the appellation applied to Satan, *prince of this world* (John 12:31; 14:30; 16:11). After the fall into sin, Adam no longer ruled in God's creation but Satan ruled by usurping that power (Luke 4:6). The dragon dominates the world by governing global empires, principal authorities, political movements, and philosophical ideas. An angel interprets for John the significance of the seven heads and ten horns by saying, "The seven heads are seven hills on which the woman sits. And they are seven kings" (17:9–10). These heads give leadership in their respective kingdoms, that is, the number seven signifies complete control, as John explains in the next chapter (see 13:1–9). The expression *ten horns* appears in Daniel 7:7 and 24, where it portrays a beast that terrifies humanity and personifies ten kings. Last, the term *seven crowns* (also translated "diadems"; see 13:1; 19:12 NASB, NRSV, REB) symbolizes his complete control in respect to royal supremacy and majestic sovereignty. Satan's crowns, however, represent nothing but pretended royalty. As R. C. H. Lenski puts it, Satan wears "symbols of arrogated dominion."[8] The devil exercises fearsome power; nonetheless, the saints in heaven and on earth know that his power comes to an end at the consummation. They are able to sing joyful praises to Jesus because he rules supreme (vv. 10–12).

8. R. C. H. Lenski, *The Interpretation of St. John's Revelation* (Columbus: Wartburg, 1943), p. 365. See also Hendriksen, *More Than Conquerors*, p. 136.

4. And his tail swept away a third of the stars of heaven, and he cast them to the earth. And the dragon stood before the woman who was about to give birth, so that when she gave birth he might devour her child.

a. "And his tail swept away a third of the stars of heaven and he cast them to the earth." Is this sentence referring to Satan disturbing the starry heavens or causing the fall of a third of the angel world? Many scholars understand these words literally because of 8:12, where the phrase "a third part of the stars was struck" calls for a plain interpretation. They also direct attention to Daniel 8:10, "[The horn] threw some of the starry host down to the earth and trampled on them." The starry host refers not to an angelic host but to the godly Jews who obeyed God's law and were slain by the armed forces of Antiochus IV Epiphanes (168–164 B.C.). Is John in the Apocalypse suggesting a literal interpretation of stars being hurled out of the heavens toward the earth?

Ladd comments, "The dragon is such a colossal creature that with one sweep of his tail he can brush a third of the stars out of their natural position."[9] Even though Satan's power is indisputable, a literal sense encounters the difficulty of explaining how colossal stars can land on the earth.

A second view interprets the stars symbolically as angels whom Satan swept along with him into sin. These angels have been consigned to the bottomless pit, which a star (i.e., an angel) opens (9:1–2).[10] God prepared this horrible place for the devil and his angels (Matt. 25:41; 2 Pet. 2:4; Jude 6). The number of angels is incalculable, so that the expression *a third* alludes to a large aggregate of demons that with Satan were cast out of heaven (vv. 7–9). But also note that a third is the lesser part of the division, and that the majority of angels remained faithful to God.

b. "And the dragon stood before the woman who was about to give birth, so that when she gave birth he might devour her child." This story of Satan seeking to exterminate Eve's godly offspring is repeated all through the centuries. Influenced by Satan, Cain killed his brother Abel, and Pharaoh drowned the male children of the Hebrews. With murderous intent King Saul hurled his spear at David, and Haman plotted to annihilate the Jewish people living in the provinces of Persia. In New Testament times, Herod the Great slew the baby boys up to two years old in Bethlehem. Whenever a new development was about to take place in the history of God's people, in this verse symbolized by the woman, Satan stood ready to thwart God's purposes and tried to eliminate his Son. Satan's attacks on the woman continue until Christ returns.

In Paradise, God put enmity between the serpent and the woman and between his offspring and hers. He said that the woman's offspring would crush the serpent's head (Gen. 3:15; see Rom. 16:20). This divine prophecy was fulfilled in the birth, life, and ascension of Jesus, as the next verse indicates.

---

9. See the commentaries of Ladd (p. 169); Johnson (p. 515); and Mounce (p. 233).

10. This is the view of numerous commentators, including Beasley-Murray, Greijdanus, Hendriksen, Hughes, Lenski, Poellot, and Thomas.

5. And she gave birth to a son, a male child, who is about to rule all the nations with an iron rod. And the child was snatched to God and to his throne.

a. "And she gave birth to a son, a male child." Here is the fulfillment of the messianic prophecies that predict the coming of the Christ (Isa. 7:14; 66:7). The woman, representing the church of Old Testament believers, gave birth to her Son, the Messiah. John's wording seems redundant: a son, that is, of the male gender. But John is purposely explicit to highlight the relationship of the woman and the son. We must see the woman as the church that bore the Son; and in time, we must see the Son redeeming the church, which then becomes his bride (19:7; 21:2, 9; 22:17).[11]

b. The Son "is about to rule all the nations with an iron rod." John often alludes to the Psalter and especially to the messianic psalms. Three times in Revelation he quotes words from Psalm 2:9, "You will rule them with an iron scepter" (2:27; 12:5; 19:15). That is, Jesus rules over unbelievers with an iron rod, which he applies to anyone who rises up against him. He is the Shepherd who cares for his sheep and protects them from harm. On the one hand, in Revelation the words *all the nations* can refer to the world that Satan leads astray. An angel announces, "Fallen, fallen is Babylon the Great, which made all the nations drink the raging wine of her fornication" (14:8). On the other hand, God gathers his own from all the nations, so that they come and worship before him (15:4). Indeed, Christ rules by establishing his kingdom and applying his rule over all the nations of the world (Matt. 24:14). He rules supreme with justice and love as King of kings and Lord of lords.

c. "And the child was snatched to God and to his throne." John writes nothing about the suffering, death, and resurrection of the Lord. But why does John omit these redemptive events? He telescopes Jesus' earthly life for several reasons. First, he calls attention to Satan's defeat at the Lord's birth and ascension. Next, he links Jesus' ascension to his rule over the nations. Third, he uses the ascension as a prelude to the next segment, namely, warfare in heaven (vv. 7–9). And last, John mentions two main redemptive facts: he stresses Jesus' birth *on earth* that includes his ministry and his ascension *into heaven* that includes his majestic rule.

God is in control, for at the right moment he intervenes to safeguard his Son and causes Satan's strategies to collapse. God is the agent in the passive voice of the phrase "the child was snatched to God." When Jesus took his rightful position on God's throne, Satan and his angels lost their place in heaven.

11. Compare Herman Hoeksema, *Behold, He Cometh! An Exposition of the Book of Revelation* (Grand Rapids: Reformed Free Publishing Association, 1969), p. 419. Four women appear in Revelation: Jezebel (2:20), the mother of the son (12:1–6), the great prostitute (17:1), and the bride (21:2, 9). Jezebel and the prostitute are Satan's representatives. By contrast, the mother and the bride are God's people. Two women are profane and two are holy.

6. And the woman fled into the desert, where she had a place prepared by God, so that there she might be nourished for 1,260 days.

Through the Antichrist, Satan directs his wrath primarily against the Christ, whom he seeks to eliminate and whose place he wants to usurp. Before the birth of the Messiah, the devil had tried to destroy the line of believers out of which Jesus would be born, but he failed. Then he attacked Jesus, but realized that this assault also ended in failure. After that he began to persecute his followers who proclaimed and continue to proclaim the name of their Lord. All these efforts, too, result in failure because God protects his people.

The woman represents Christ's church on earth whose members flee to a place that God has prepared for them: the desert.[12] The image of the desert evokes the account of Israel's forty-year stay in the Sinai peninsula (Deut. 8:2–4), Elijah's flight to that same desert (1 Kings 19:3–8), and John the Baptist's sojourn in the desert of Judea (Luke 1:80). Paul also spent time in a desert, the one in Arabia (Gal. 1:17–18). Three factors emerge from spending time in a desert: a person is completely dependent on God to provide the material and spiritual necessities of life; the desert is always a temporary place; and last, the desert is a place where God trains his people spiritually and prepares them for service. Thus, the members of the church depend on God to be their provider and protector; they also realize that their stay on earth is but temporary; and they know that they are being trained for more extensive duties. Just as Israel's time in the desert of Sinai was temporary while the Israelites longed for permanence in the Promised Land, so the church today waiting on earth longs to be with Christ forever (see 2 Cor. 5:6–8).

God prepares a place of protection and nourishment for the church for 1,260 days. Even though her members suffer oppression and persecution, God never allows the annihilation of the church. The number 1,260 applies to the two witnesses who received power to prophesy for that length of time (11:3). Thus, the reference to the woman in the desert harmonizes with the prophesying of the two witnesses, which means that the witnesses and the woman represent the church.[13]

The number 1,260 divided by thirty equals forty-two months, which is the length of time allotted to the Gentiles to trample on the outer court of the temple (11:2). The period during which the church is able to witness for the Lord is from the day of Jesus' ascension to the time of his return. The beast of the earth has been given a mouth to blaspheme God's name and to exercise authority for a period of forty-two months (= 1,260 days). The devil, therefore, has been given

12. John F. Walvoord (*Revelation*, p. 191) writes, "There is obviously a tremendous time lapse between verses 5 and 6, but this is not an uncommon occurrence in prophecy; the first and second comings of Christ are frequently spoken of in the same sentence." Would the first readers and hearers of this passage have understood the verse in this manner? Verses 5 and 6 refer not to the two comings of Christ but to his ascension and God's care for the church.

13. Henry Barclay Swete, *Commentary on Revelation* (1911; reprint, Grand Rapids: Kregel, 1977), p. 152.

exactly the same length of time the church on earth has received. In short, the meaning of these numbers in chapters 11 and 12 is the same.

Greek Words, Phrases, and Constructions in 12:6

ἀπό—this preposition signifies either agency (by) or source (from). "The construction here appears to mean 'prepared by God's command' not by himself, with ἀπό denoting that God was the source of the command."[14]

τρέφωσιν—the primary meaning of this verb is "to nourish"; the secondary definition is "to rear, bring up," which is appropriate here and in verse 14.[15]

---

2. Warfare in Heaven
12:7–9

Peter, writing about the ascension of the Lord, says that Jesus Christ "has gone into heaven and is at God's right hand—with angels, authorities and powers in submission to him" (1 Pet. 3:22). Jesus proclaimed victory over the spiritual forces that opposed him; these forces are Satan and his evil angels. Paul calls these powers "the spiritual forces of evil in the heavenly realms" (Eph. 6:12). Victory came when the archangel Michael and his angelic hosts conquered these evil forces by casting them out of heaven and hurling them to earth.

7. And there was war in heaven. Michael and his angels fought against the dragon. And the dragon and his angels fought back 8. and did not prevail, and a place in heaven was no longer found for them.

a. "And there was war in heaven." All through history until Jesus' ascension, Satan could appear in God's presence (Job 1:6; 2:1). Satan, whose name means "the accuser," could even accuse the high priest Joshua in the presence of God, but the Lord rebuked him (Zech. 3:1–2). Also, Jesus told the seventy-two disciples who returned from their mission assignment, "I saw Satan fall like lightning from heaven" (Luke 10:18; see John 12:31). In other words, Satan had not yet been denied access to God's presence but could accuse God's people day and night (v. 10).

When Jesus completed his mediatorial work on earth, he ascended to heaven and took his seat at God's right hand. His entry into heaven made it impossible for Satan to come before God to accuse the saints. Jesus assumed the role of the attorney-at-law, the advocate with the Father (1 John 2:1). He paid the price to set his people free, and as a result Satan has been unable to bring slanderous accusations against God's people (see Rom. 8:34; Jude 9).[16] Thus, Satan and his hosts were denied a place in the presence of the Almighty.

---

14. Robert Hanna, *A Grammatical Aid to the Greek New Testament* (Grand Rapids: Baker, 1983), p. 450. See also C. F. D. Moule, *An Idiom-Book of New Testament Greek*, 2d ed. (Cambridge: Cambridge University Press, 1960), p. 74.

15. Bauer, p. 825; Josephus *Against Apion* 1.19 §141. See also *EDNT*, 3:369.

16. Consult Geoffrey B. Wilson, *Revelation* (Welwyn: Evangelical Press, 1985), p. 106; Werner Foerster, *TDNT*, 7:157.

b. "Michael and his angels fought against the dragon. And the dragon and his angels fought back." The name Michael means "Who is like God?" As one of the archangels, he wages war against the archangel Satan, who wants to be like God. Michael is mentioned in the Old Testament as a prince and protector of God's people (Dan. 10:13, 21; 12:1). It is he who with his angels attacked and fought the dragon and his cohorts. The grammatical construction indicates that the dragon is an angel, for he fights at the head of his multitude of angels. Note that not Satan but Michael is the one who leads the attack; he forces the evil one into battle, which is an indication that he has the upper hand and is sure of the victory.

c. "And did not prevail, and a place in heaven was no longer found for them." Satan and his cohorts had to acknowledge Jesus' victory and their defeat when the Lord ascended to the throne. Far from accepting the reality of their overthrow, they faced Michael and his formidable hosts of angels, who drove them out of heaven and into a fierce battle. Satan's war with God began when the human race was plunged into sin. When believers in the Old Testament era were taken to heaven, Satan accused them before God of being unworthy sinners. As accuser of the saints, he had free access to God's presence.

The devil was not alone in his opposition to the saints entering heaven. He employed fallen angels to work for him. For instance, the Old Testament relates the account of a lying spirit standing before God, who gave him permission to put a lie in the mouths of the prophets as they counseled the kings of Judah and Israel (1 Kings 22:17–23). Since Christ's victory over sin and death, these evil spirits can no longer appear before God to accuse the saints. Indeed, not a single accusation can be brought against them, for God listens only to their praises, confessions, gratitude, and petitions. Hence, a new era has dawned in which Satan with his angels have lost their place in heaven and are restricted to a place on earth. On that same earth, God gave the woman a place and protected her. "Wherever Jesus reigns, wherever the world domination of the lamb is already established, there the adversary of God has neither place nor rights."[17]

9. And the great dragon was cast down, that ancient serpent called the devil and Satan, the deceiver of the whole world. He was cast down to the earth, and his angels were cast out with him.

A good teacher repeats the points he wishes to make. So John mentions the downfall of Satan a total of five times in three verses (vv. 9 [three times], 10, 13). The great dragon and his followers are cast down to the earth, for heaven is now off limits to them. The series of names (great dragon, ancient serpent, devil, Satan, and deceiver) is given for at least three reasons: to identify the one whom Christ has conquered; to alert the dwellers on earth of the devil's grim power; and to illustrate this monster's capability to both destroy and deceive.

17. Jürgen Roloff, *The Revelation of John*, trans. J. E. Alsup (Minneapolis: Fortress, 1993), p. 148.

a. *The great dragon.* Here is "a picture of the primeval power of chaos."[18] That is, the dragon is called *great* because of his enormous power. He gives his power, throne, and authority to the beast that rises up out of the sea (13:1–2).[19]

b. *That ancient serpent.* The adjective *ancient* is a reference to Satan, who in the form of a serpent deluded Eve in Paradise (Gen. 3:1–7). John uses the term *serpent* as a synonym for dragon. In fact, it appears five times in Revelation (9:19; 12:9, 14, 15; 20:2). Paul even warns the church not to listen to the serpent's whispers and so being led astray to depart from Christ (2 Cor. 11:3).

c. *The devil.* The Greek term *diabolos* comes from the preposition *dia* (through) and the verb *ballein* (to throw) and means "to throw over or across, to divide, set at variance, accuse, bring charges, slander, inform, reject, misrepresent, deceive."[20] This is an accurate description of the devil's activities. John warns the believers not to yield to his temptations, for then they will be numbered among the children of the devil (John 8:44; 1 John 3:8, 10). And both James and Peter instruct their readers to resist the devil, for he will flee from them (James 4:7; 1 Pet. 5:8–9; see also Eph. 4:27; 6:11).

d. *Satan.* This name is a synonym of *the devil,* and the terms are used interchangeably in the New Testament. The name derives from the Hebrew *haśśāṭān* and signifies "the adversary." Satan is at enmity with God and all those who serve and worship him. He is the accuser and slanderer of God's people. Through him the Antichrist appears as "the lawless one," whom Jesus will overthrow with the breath of his mouth (2 Thess. 2:3–4, 7–9).

e. *The deceiver.* Satan deceives the *whole world,* which does not mean that the elect are also led astray (Matt. 24:24). He is no longer able to accuse the elect in the presence of God; he is confined to do his evil work on the face of the earth. He seeks to blind the minds of the unbelievers to prevent them from understanding the good news of Jesus Christ (2 Cor. 4:4).

Satan and his evil angels are confined to this earth to carry out their deceptive and destructive work, and even here they cannot do whatever they please but can only go so far and do only as much damage as God allows. Satan not only must abide by God's decrees but must also realize that his schemes against God end in failure. Not Satan but God is the ruler in this world.

Greek Words, Phrases, and Constructions in 12:7

πόλεμος ἐν τῷ οὐρανῷ—this phrase is deleted by Friedrich Düsterdieck as a conjecture to improve the grammar in the sentence. Without it, the verb ἐγένετο can be taken to introduce the articular infinitive τοῦ πολεμῆσαι (to make war). The infinitive needs a preceding finite tense to complete the sentence. Düsterdieck is of the opinion that the

---

18. Hans Bietenhard, *NIDNTT,* 1:507; see also Nikolaus Walter, *EDNT,* 1:353; Werner Foerster, *TDNT,* 2:283.

19. In chapter 12, the word *dragon* occurs eight times (vv. 3, 4, 7 [twice], 9, 13, 16, 17).

20. Hans Bietenhard, *NIDNTT,* 3:468; Otto Böcher, *EDNT,* 1:297–98.

phrase is a "marginal note that has entered into the text."[21] However, it is possible to insert mentally the verb ἐγένετο before ὁ Μιχαήλ, which would then preclude the use of a conjecture.[22]

---

3. A Song of Victory
12:10–12

This hymn announces the triumphal conquest of God and Christ, and includes the saints who share in this victory. Afterward the heavens and its inhabitants are told to rejoice; and, last, the people on earth and the sea are alerted to the great wrath of the devil, whose time is short.

10. And I heard a loud voice in heaven saying, "Now have come the salvation, power, and kingdom of our God, and the authority of his Christ, because the accuser of our brothers [and sisters] has been cast out; he is the one accusing them before our God day and night."

a. "And I heard a loud voice in heaven saying." John reports that he heard a loud voice in heaven, but he fails to identify the speaker or singer, indicating that it is not a matter of importance. Even though angels often sing hymns of praise, the use of the possessive pronoun *our* together with the noun *brothers* [*and sisters*] rules out the angels. Some exegetes point to Revelation 19:10 and 22:9, where an angel uses the words "your brothers." But these passages do not prove the point that angels call redeemed saints their brothers and sisters. Angels can never regard human beings as brothers and sisters. They differ from the saints in many respects: they lack physical bodies, have not been redeemed, are not heirs of salvation, have not been created in the image of God, and do not have a covenant relationship with God. The voice represents a group of singers, possibly the saints in heaven who sing this song of victory (compare 11:15).

What does John wish to convey with the time reference *now*? Revelation stresses not chronological time, which is of fleeting consequence, but the governing principle of time. Here the adverb points to the dividing line in human history, Christ's death and resurrection, which resulted in his victory over Satan. The words of the song anticipate the final overthrow of Satan (20:10).

b. "Now have come the salvation, power, and kingdom of our God and the authority of his Christ." The words of the song honor God by ascribing to him the salvation of his people accomplished in Christ, the power Jesus received to overcome Satan, and the kingdom which the Lord handed over to him (1 Cor. 15:24–28). God is supreme in his kingdom. Although Jesus has been given full authority, it is God who rules his kingdom through his Son (Rev. 11:15). Jesus told

---

21. Friedrich Düsterdieck, *Critical and Exegetical Handbook to the Revelation of John* (New York and London: Funk and Wagnalls, 1886), p. 344.

22. Beale, *Revelation*, p. 654. Other solutions are presented by A. T. Robertson, *A Grammar of the Greek New Testament in the Light of Historical Research* (Nashville: Broadman, 1934), p. 1066; Moule, *Idiom-Book*, p. 129; and R. H. Charles, *A Critical and Exegetical Commentary on the Revelation of St. John*, ICC (Edinburgh: Clark, 1920), 1:321–22.

the disciples: "All authority in heaven and on earth has been given to me" (Matt. 28:18).

c. "Because the accuser of our brothers [and sisters] has been cast out; he is the one accusing them before our God day and night." It is not Michael and his angels who receive praise for the overthrow of Satan, but Christ, who exercises supremacy in his kingdom. When Jesus ascended to the throne with full authority to rule, Satan was cast out of heaven. The phrase *the accuser of our brothers* [*and sisters*] characterizes the devil's activity in the presence of God (see Job 1:6–12; 2:1–5). This activity has now come to an end, because Jesus is the intercessor for the saints, and that precludes anyone from bringing a charge against them (Rom. 8:33–34).

What is the significance of the present tense of the participle in *the one accusing them*? Cast down to earth, Satan can no longer accuse the believers before God's throne. But he does not accept defeat so as to desist from his evil works. On the contrary, Satan continues his attacks day and night by constantly accusing the followers of Christ and torturing their consciences.[23] He does so by first enticing a person to sin; next, if he is successful, he taunts the sinner with accusations. However, he fails miserably in his endeavors in view of God's forgiving grace through the shed blood of Christ Jesus (Heb. 9:22).

11. "And they have overcome him by the blood of the Lamb and by the word of their testimony, and they did not love their lives even in the face of death."

John presents a picture that portrays the redeemed people of God—a picture that is not limited by chronological time. He is concerned with the past but at the same time with the present and future.[24] So he writes in the past tense as if all God's children have already entered into glory. John writes confidently about the victory of the saints even though the time of Christ's return has not yet come. On the other hand, countless multitudes have already been victorious and are now with the Lord. They claim victory with Christ on the basis of his shed blood that has redeemed them from sin and set them free from Satan's accusations. They are "more than conquerors through him who loved [them]," for the Lord Jesus Christ gives them the victory (Rom. 8:37; 1 Cor. 15:57). John's perspective is not from earth—still without victory—to heaven, but rather from heaven—triumphant in victory—to earth. He sees the triumph of Christ with all the heavenly saints who overcame Satan and share in that victory. Whereas Satan seeks to accuse the saints on earth day and night, the saints in heaven sing God's praises day and night in thankfulness for their redemption.

The phrase *the blood of the Lamb* is a repetition of an earlier description of the saints in heaven who have experienced the great tribulation. These are they who

---

23. Greijdanus, *Openbaring*, p. 260.

24. G. B. Caird comments: "John's vision . . . is equally concerned with the interpretation of past and present and the anticipation of the future" (*A Commentary on the Revelation of St. John the Divine* [London: Black, 1966], p. 26). See also James L. Resseguie, *Revelation Unsealed: A Narrative Critical Approach to John's Apocalypse*, BIS 32 (Leiden: Brill, 1998), p. 46.

"have washed their robes and have made them white in the blood of the Lamb" (7:14). In other words, the power in Christ's blood has made them victorious; they conquered because they proclaimed and taught the gospel, that is, the *word of their testimony.* They received the gospel and passed it on, so that it was their testimony on behalf of Jesus.[25]

The blood of Christ is the key to this passage, for the believers redeemed through Christ's sacrifice fearlessly and without any hesitation have been his witnesses (6:9). These redeemed believers did not value their lives more than the message of the gospel; they were willing to offer their lives for the sake of Christ. Jesus says to his followers, "Whoever finds his life will lose it, and whoever loses his life for my sake will find it" (Matt. 10:39; see 16:25 and parallels). The Lord repeatedly teaches the principle of losing one's life for his sake (see, e.g., John 12:25). Paul demonstrates it when he addresses the Ephesian elders. He said, "However, I consider my life nothing to me, if only I may finish the race and complete the task the Lord Jesus has given to me—the task of testifying to the gospel of God's grace" (Acts 20:24).

Believers express gratitude to him in their willingness to suffer for him even to the point of death. The preservation of one's life is a natural proclivity in human beings, but the love for the Lord Jesus overrules it.

12. "Therefore, rejoice, O heavens, and they who dwell in them! Woe to the earth and the sea, because the devil has gone down to you! He is very angry, because he knows that his time is short."

a. *Rejoice!* The voice calls the heavens in general and the dwellers in particular to express their joy in the victory Jesus has achieved. The adverb *therefore* links the preceding verses (vv. 10–11) to the injunction to be glad in the triumph of the Lord. Delivered from the accuser's constant intrusion into God's presence, the heavens now rejoice. Numerous times the heavens are exhorted to express their joy.[26] The twenty-four elders, the four living beings, and all the angels experienced Satan's intrusions that have now come to an end. Thus, neither the heavens nor the saints dwelling there will hear Satan's slanderous accusations any longer. Through Christ's victory heaven itself has been cleansed.

b. *Lament!* Here is the dividing line between the triumphant church in heaven and the militant church on earth that resists sin and evil. Now that Satan and his cohorts have been denied entrance into heaven and have been cast down to the earth, the devil is filled with wrath against God's people. He realizes that he has been defeated, that he has been given a limited time here on earth, and that in the short period allotted to him he must unleash his fury. On both land and sea he seeks to deceive and destroy the saints.

The "woe" addressed to the dwellers on earth should not be considered the third woe that is mentioned in 11:14. This woe stands by itself and lacks the differentiation of the definite article (see 9:12 and 11:14). It is used in a general

---

25. Compare Louis A. Vos, *The Synoptic Traditions in the Apocalypse* (Kampen: Kok, 1965), p. 207.

26. Deut. 32:43 LXX; Ps. 96:11; Isa. 44:23; 49:13; Dan. 3:59 Old Greek and Theod.; Rev. 18:20.

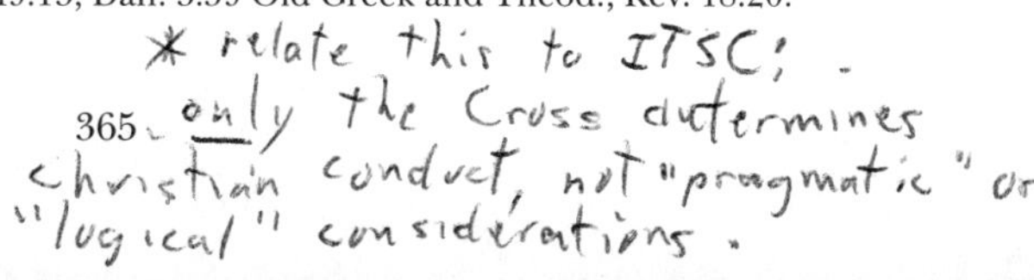

sense, much the same as the double woes uttered by kings, merchants, and seafarers (18:10, 16, 19). The heavenly voice warns the earth and the sea that anguish and distress are coming upon them because of the devil's defeat in heaven. Defeated by the victorious Christ, he now vents his rage against the Christians (compare v. 17).[27]

Satan knows that the opportunity God has given him is of short duration. It is the same as the three and a half years, the forty-two months, or the 1,260 days mentioned elsewhere (11:2–3; 12:6, 14; 13:5); these indications of time are not to be taken literally but figuratively. The Apocalypse features time not in terms of chronology but as an ideal. This book presents time as an idea in summary form without quantifying it in terms of years or centuries. Not Satan but God controls time and place. Therefore the saints on earth know the limitations of the devil as they rely on God's protective care.

Greek Words, Phrases, and Constructions in 12:10–12

Verse 10

ὁ κατήγωρ—"the accuser." The word in this exact form occurs only once in the New Testament, whereas the other spelling κατήγορος is more familiar (Acts 23:30, 35; 24:8 [variant]; 25:16, 18). The first one is the more original reading and is favored.[28]

Yarbro Collins delineates several features in this hymn, including rhyming with respect to the repetition of ἡμῶν at or near the end of the lines, the nouns ἀρνίου and θανάτου, and the parallels of ὁ κατήγωρ and ὁ κατηγορῶν.[29]

Verse 11

διά—this preposition followed by the accusative case should be translated as "by" and not "through." It has the sense of "by force of" as an efficient cause.[30]

Verse 12

οὐαί—the interjection governs the accusative nouns "the earth and the sea" as direct objects. Notice that the interjection appears without the definite article, which makes it general, while the three woes feature the article (9:12; 11:14).

ὀλιγὸν καιρόν—note the construction χρόνον μικρόν (6:11; reversed in 20:3), which is translated exactly the same as this entry, namely, "a short time." While καιρός means opportunity, season, fixed or favorable time, χρόνος denotes chronological time.

---

27. Martin Kiddle writes that the devil cannot hurt believers but only "unregenerate mankind." See his *Revelation of St. John* (reprint, London: Hodder and Stoughton, 1943), p. 235. But in this chapter Satan and his minions war against the saints on earth.

28. Refer to Bruce M. Metzger, *A Textual Commentary on the Greek New Testament*, 2d ed. (Stuttgart: Deutsche Bibelgesellschaft, 1994), p. 673; Adolf Deissmann, *Light from the Ancient East*, trans. Lionel R. M. Strachan (reprint, Grand Rapids: Baker, 1978), p. 93.

29. Yarbro Collins, *Combat Myth*, p. 137.

30. Moule, *Idiom-Book*, p. 55; Hanna, *Grammatical Aid*, p. 451.

4. Help and Safety for the Church *12:13–17*

Here is the last part of the account that began with a portrayal of a woman clothed with the sun, the moon under her feet, and a crown of twelve stars on her head (v. 1). The woman gave birth to a male child who was snatched up to heaven, while she herself was cared for in a desert place prepared for her by God (v. 6). The second part of the account describes Satan's defeat followed by a heavenly victory song, and in the third segment John continues his account of the woman pursued by the dragon.

13. And when the dragon saw that he was cast down to the earth, he pursued the woman who gave birth to the male child.

This verse is filled with symbolism: the dragon is the symbol of Satan, the woman is the church, and the male child is Christ. Unable to attack the exalted Lord in heaven, the devil on earth seeks to destroy the church, the body of Christ. Jesus and his followers are one body, as Saul learned when Jesus asked him, "Why do you persecute me?" (Acts 9:4). Christ is the head and we are his body (Eph. 1:22; 4:15; 5:23; Col. 1:18; 2:19). If Satan is powerless to assail Jesus, he vents his wrath on his followers. He persecutes Christians, as is evident not only throughout the centuries but also today.

The words *cast down/out* appear here for the fifth time (see vv. 9 [three times], 10, 13). These words sound a note of victory over Satan's defeat even though the church on earth must endure his wrath. They refer to the devil's painful fall and his bloodied head (13:3a) that was predicted at the onset of human history (Gen. 3:15). Satan has power on earth and is intent on destroying the church. But he does not seem to realize that because God vigilantly protects his people as the apple of his eye (Deut. 32:10), Satan himself will be defeated in the end.

The term *male child* is preceded by the definite article to indicate the Lord Jesus Christ who ascended to his Father's throne. That same term appearing without the article in verse 5 to designate "the newly born male" marks the beginning of Jesus' earthly life.[31]

14. And two wings of a great eagle were given to the woman, so that she might fly into the desert to her place, where she might be nourished for a time, times, and a half time away from the presence of the serpent.

John relies on the Old Testament for symbolic pictures. God told the Israelites at Mount Sinai that he had carried them on the wings of an eagle and brought them to himself (Exod. 19:4). The Israelites had just escaped from the clutches of Pharaoh's soldiers and could testify that God had safely carried them across the Red Sea. Other passages speak of the protective wings of the eagle (Deut. 32:11; Isa. 40:31). Indeed God applies to himself the image of wings that serve as a place of refuge (Ps. 91:4).

With the two wings of the great eagle that the woman receives from God, she no longer flees but literally flies to the place prepared for her in the desert. The

31. Consult Lenski, *Revelation*, p. 382.

church has wings to fly away and safely escape from the attacks of the devil. It is obvious that with all his resources in the world, Satan is unable to annihilate the church. God has given her a place and lavishly provides her with daily necessities much the same as he gave the Israelites manna, quail, and water during the wilderness journey. The Israelites were given physical health; their clothes and their shoes did not wear out; they were shielded from the hot desert sun during the day and were kept warm by the pillar of fire by night. God protected them from the stings and bites of natural enemies, from scorpions and snakes. Hence, God shields the church from the attacks of the devil by providing his covenant people with spiritual armor (Eph. 6:10–18). He nourishes and trains them in their spiritual service.

John writes that the woman is kept from the presence of the serpent for a specified period: "for a time, times, and a half time," which is three and a half years. This reference is taken from Daniel 7:25 and 12:7 and is a time span which equals that of the forty-two months and the 1,260 days mentioned by John elsewhere (see v. 6; 11:2–3; see 13:5). In a historical setting there is a literal period of three and a half years during the time of Elijah, who prayed that it might not rain (1 Kings 17:1; James 5:17). There was a literal period of three and half years when the temple was desecrated during the Maccabean war from 167 to 164 B.C. (1 Macc. 1–3; 2 Macc. 5); the prophecies of Daniel 7:25 and 12:7 refer to it.[32] In Revelation, this period refers not literally but symbolically to the interval between Jesus' first and second comings as the interim of the forty-two months or the 1,260 days. It is the period in which the serpent of deception rules the world; this time definitively comes to an end when God intervenes.[33]

15. And the serpent cast out of its mouth water like a river after the woman, so that she might be swept away by the river. 16. And the earth helped the woman, and the earth opened its mouth and swallowed up the river that the dragon cast out of its mouth.

This is now the third time in this chapter that John writes the word *serpent* (vv. 9, 14, 15). His choice is not merely stylistic; it attests to the craftiness of Satan, who has been losing the battle against God and the church. He is trying once more with trickery to overwhelm the woman and bring her to ruin. He does this by unleashing a stream of water in the desert where God placed her. Note that this water like a river comes forth from the mouth of the serpent, which can be interpreted to mean a flood of deceptive words.

Already in the earlier part of the Apocalypse, we read that Satan had his own synagogues in the cities of Smyrna and Philadelphia (2:9; 3:9). The leaders of these synagogues subjected the followers of Christ to slander, seduction, and per-

32. Josephus (*War* 1 proem 7 §19; 5.9.4 §394) notes a period of three and half years from June 167 to December 164 B.C.

33. Hoeksema (*Behold, He Cometh!* p. 446) interprets the number seven symbolically as a configuration of completeness and its two parts of three and a half symbolically as the eras before and after Christ. See also Beale, *Revelation*, pp. 646–47.

secution. And voices of deception via the media today engulf the members of the church, so that they are in danger of being swept away. But the believers are always aware of Satan's parody that Revelation displays: the river of deception and death is contrasted to the river of the water of life flowing from God's throne (22:1).

God constantly encourages his people not to fear even when the floodwaters threaten to overwhelm them. He comforts them by saying, "When you pass through the rivers, they will not sweep over you" (Isa. 43:2). The floodwaters of falsehood, malice, crime, and suffering will not be able to overtake them, for God is in charge. His people are not swept away by the torrents swirling around them but are kept safe. God causes the earth to swallow up the waters that come forth out of the serpent's mouth. His people sang the song of Moses in praise to God, "You stretched out your right hand and the earth swallowed them" (Exod. 15:12). Even though they may suffer physically in many ways, God protects his own from permanent harm, spiritually speaking.

Satan loses out once again. At the beginning of this chapter, the dragon stood in front of the woman ready to devour her child (v. 4). After he has been hurled to the earth, he pursues the woman, who flies away with the wings of a great eagle (vv. 13–14). Now he stands far away from the woman, whom he wants to destroy with a flood, but his efforts end in failure (vv. 15–16). His own territory, the earth, turns against him when it helps the woman. The deluge wanted to swallow the woman, but instead the earth now swallows the deluge. The word *earth* need not be taken literally as in the case of Korah, Dathan, and Abiram, who were swallowed by the earth (Num. 16:30, 32; see also Deut. 11:6). Symbolically the earth stands for the structure of society that by God's intervening grace reaffirms morality, abolishes evil, and establishes truth.[34]

17. And the dragon became furious at the woman, and he went out to fight against the rest of her offspring, those who were keeping the commandments of God and held to the testimony of Jesus.

Satan, called "the dragon," never concedes defeat; every time he is vanquished, he returns with vengeance and fury. He is unable to reach the victorious Christ and thus turns his wrath on the church. He is unable to swallow the church as a whole and thus fights Christians faithful to their Lord. Satan faces a losing battle, which by itself is a source of comfort for those who feel the brunt of his anger in days of persecution and physical abuse.

What is the meaning of the phrase "he went out to fight against the rest of her offspring"? If we take the development of this chapter sequentially, we could infer that Satan has been successful in destroying the church and now wants to conquer the individual believers who form the remnant.[35] The context, how-

34. See J. Dochhorn, "Und die Erde tat ihren Mund auf: Ein Exodusmotiv in Apc 12,16," *ZNW* 88 (1997): 140–42.

35. Swete, *Revelation*, p. 160; Johnson (*Revelation*, p. 519) writes, "The church, then, is paradoxically both invulnerable (the woman) and vulnerable (her children)." Kiddle (*Revelation*, p. 240) comments, "The distinction between the woman and her *offspring* is simply that of the messianic community as a whole, and the noblest of her sons—'the conquerors' in the seven letters."

ever, reveals that Satan has not been able to remove the church because the earth absorbed the flood he sent to swallow her (v. 16). "The rest of her offspring" points to the church as a whole, which remains intact until the return of Christ. God will never, no never, leave or forsake her (Heb. 13:5).

John has come to the end of the chapter and now summarizes the contents of verses 13–16. The author, steeped in the Old Testament, goes back to the beginning of human history where the words *serpent* and *offspring* already appear. God said to the serpent, "And I will put enmity between you and the woman, and between your offspring and hers" (Gen. 3:15). Yet this passage is not the only Old Testament reference John has in mind. If it were so, the italicized words in "*the rest of* her offspring" would not be explained. John alludes to the prophecy in Isaiah 66:7 and 8. There the prophet writes of Zion:

> Before she goes into labor,
> she gives birth;
> before the pains come upon her,
> she delivers a son. . . .
> Yet no sooner is Zion in labor
> than she gives birth to her children.

Two words stand out in this prophecy: *son* and *children*. The virgin gave birth to a son (Isa. 7:14) and Zion brought forth children; the son is the Messiah and the children are his followers. All along, but especially at the end of time, the dragon attacks not the woman but "the rest of her offspring." "The equation of singular 'male' with plural 'children' and collective 'seed,' all alluding to the same offspring from Zion, is virtually identical to the phenomenon in Revelation 12."[36] The contrast, therefore, is that of Christ the Son and of all the offspring identified with him.

John describes the followers of Christ with the clause, "those who were keeping the commandments of God and held to the testimony of Jesus." The characteristics of these people are faithfulness and obedience with respect to God's law and the gospel of the Lord. The law denotes the Old Testament and the gospel the New Testament. Faithfully and obediently they continue to keep the teachings of God's Word; as long as they do so, Satan is unable to touch them. These followers advance the cause of Christ's kingdom in this world wherever they are.

Verse 17 reveals the dragon's aim to destroy those who are Christ's followers. At the same time, it forms a bridge to chapter 13 that introduces the dragon giving power to the beast from the sea and the beast from the earth. Every time the dragon plots against God and his people, he faces inevitable defeat. This fact indeed comforts and assures all believers of their safety and spiritual welfare.

36. Beale, *Revelation*, p. 677.

A last remark. Some translations number the verse that follows 12:17 as verse 18. But this verse should be combined with the first verse of the next chapter. Chapter 13 begins a new segment on the dragon and the beast coming up out of the sea.

Greek Words, Phrases, and Constructions in 12:14–17

Verse 14

καιρόν—note that the expression *time* is not chronological time but a fixed or favorable time, so that "time, times, and a half a time" does not add up to precisely three and a half years, but rather to an indeterminate season.

Verses 15–16

στόμα—in verses 15 and 16 the word *mouth* appears three times, referring twice to the serpent and once to the earth.

Verse 17

ποιῆσαι πόλεμον μετά—"to make war with." However, this literal translation fails to communicate the correct meaning; hence I prefer the reading "to make war against."

13

The Beasts from the Sea and the Land

(13:1–18)

Outline (continued)

B. The Beast from the Sea (13:1–10)
   1. The Description (13:1–4)
   2. Power and Authority (13:5–10)

C. The Beast from the Land (13:11–18)
   1. Parody of Christ (13:11–14)
   2. The Mark of the Beast (13:15–18)

13 1 And the dragon stood on the shore of the sea.
And I saw a beast coming up out of the sea. And he had ten horns and seven heads,
and on his horns he had ten crowns and on his heads blasphemous names. 2 And the beast
that I saw was like a leopard, and his feet like a bear, and his mouth like the mouth of a
lion. And the dragon gave the beast his power and his throne and great authority. 3 And one of the
beast's heads was as if it had been mortally wounded, and the mortal wound was healed.
And the whole earth marveled, following the beast. 4 And they worshiped the dragon, for he gave
authority to the beast, and they worshiped the beast, asking, "Who is like the beast, and who is able
to make war against him?"
5 And the beast was given a mouth to speak great things and words of blasphemy, and he was given
authority to do so for forty-two months. 6 And he opened his mouth for blasphemies against God to
blaspheme his name and his tabernacle and those who dwell in heaven. 7 And he was given power to
make war against the saints and to overcome them, and he was given authority over every tribe, people,
language, and nation. 8 And all those living on the earth will worship the beast, everyone whose name
was not written in the book of life of the Lamb that was slain, from the foundation of the world.
9 If anyone has an ear, let him hear.
10 If anyone goes into captivity, into captivity he goes.
If anyone is to be killed with the sword, with the sword he will be killed.
Here is the endurance and faith of the saints.
11 And I saw another beast coming up out of the earth, and he had two horns like a lamb and
spoke like a dragon. 12 And he wields all the authority of the first beast in its presence, and he makes
the earth and those dwelling in it to worship the first beast, whose mortal wound was healed. 13 And
he performs great signs so that he even makes fire to come down out of heaven onto the earth before
people. 14 And he deceives the inhabitants on the earth because of these signs that were given him
to perform in the presence of the beast. He told the inhabitants on the earth to make an image in
honor of the beast that had the wound of the sword and yet lived.
15 And he was given power to give breath to the image of the beast, so that the image of the beast
might both speak and cause as many as do not worship the image of the beast to be killed. 16 And he
causes all, both small and great, both rich and poor, both free persons and slaves, to receive a mark on
their right hand or on their forehead. 17 And no one was able to buy or sell except the one having the
mark, that is, the name of the beast or the number of his name. 18 Here is wisdom. Let anyone who
has a mind calculate the number of the beast. It is the number of a man, and his number is 666.

B. The Beast from the Sea
13:1–10

The connection between chapter 12 and this one is evident in the word *dragon.* Satan appearing as the dragon dominates the scene in both chapters. In the one (chapter 12) he persecutes the church, and in the other (chapter 13) his helpers are portrayed. The beast arising out of the sea as the Antichrist reveals brute force, and the beast coming out of the earth appears as the false prophet who discloses the power of deception. In short, chapter 13 is an explication of the preceding chapter.

This chapter portrays the designs of Satan to wage war against God's people. Through the beast as the Antichrist he literally desires to take the place of Christ. This becomes evident in his repeated attempts to take on the appearance of the Christ. Here are seven examples indicative of satanic parody.

- "And the dragon gave the beast his power and his throne and great authority" (v. 2).
- "And one of the beast's heads was as if he had been mortally wounded, and the mortal wound was healed" (v. 3).
- "And the whole earth marveled, following the beast. And they worshiped the dragon" (vv. 3b–4a).
- "He was given authority over every tribe, people, language, and nation" (v. 7).
- "And I saw another beast coming up out of the earth, and he had two horns like a lamb and he spoke as a dragon" (v. 11).
- "He makes the earth and those dwelling in it to worship the first beast, whose mortal wound was healed" (v. 12).
- "He told the inhabitants of the earth to make an image in honor of the beast that had the wound of the sword and yet lived" (v. 14).[1]

This is also a chapter on the followers of Satan. Notice the repetition: they worship the beast (vv. 4, 8, 12, 15), are representative of the whole world (vv. 3, 7, 8, 14, 16), and have a distinguishing mark and number (vv. 16–18). The saints, however, have their names written in the book of life and belong to the Lamb (vv. 8, 10).

1. The Description
13:1–4

1. And the dragon stood on the shore of the sea.

And I saw a beast coming up out of the sea. And he had ten horns and seven heads, and on his horns he had ten crowns and on his heads blasphemous names.

a. *Textual Variant.* "And the dragon stood on the shore of the sea." The reading in the first line is either "he [the dragon] stood" or "I [John] stood." In Greek the difference is only one letter, *estathē* or *estathēn* respectively. The extra letter *n* may have slipped in because of a scribe's faulty hearing or may have been an accommodation to the verb "I saw." Of course, the reverse could also be true, namely, that the subject in the immediately preceding verse is the dragon. In addition, the better Greek manuscripts have the reading "he stood." If we adopt the reading "I stood," this is the only place in Revelation where John changes his physical position without having received instructions to do so. For this reason,

1. Compare Richard Bauckham, *The Climax of Prophecy* (Edinburgh: Clark, 1993), p. 431. He notes that "the emphasis in chapter 13 is on the similarity between the beast's 'death' and 'resurrection' and Christ's" (p. 437).

I prefer the reading "he stood."[2] Nonetheless, the problem still remains whether the first line of this verse should be part of the last text in the preceding chapter or be combined with the first verse of this chapter. I have chosen the second option, believing that the dragon is and remains the subject in both chapters. I suggest, therefore, that the line in question can stand by itself as a heading to the first part of chapter 13.

b. *Interpretation.* If the dragon stands on the sandy beach of the sea, how do we interpret the word *sea*? Before we answer this intriguing question, we must view the dragon standing on the shore as a dividing line between sea and land. He employs two helpers in the form of two beasts; he first calls forth a beast out of the sea and then summons the beast out of the earth. These two beasts work together in their effort to destroy God's people. The context clearly shows that the whole world and all its inhabitants worship the first beast (vv. 4, 8). John himself interprets the term *sea* symbolically in 17:15, where the angel told him, "The waters that you saw on which the prostitute sat, they are the peoples and the crowds and nations and languages." Similarly, Old Testament prophecies support a symbolical interpretation; Isaiah 17:12 mentions raging nations like the raging sea; and Daniel 7:3 describes four beasts coming up out of the sea, as an allusion to humanity (see Jer. 51:13, 42, 55, 56; Ezek. 26:3). We also note that John already had written that the beast came forth out of the Abyss (11:7); that place is the beast's environment and incorporates sacrilegious humanity. The interpretation that the beast represents Rome is too restrictive in view of the totality of the human race worshiping him.

c. *Symbolism.* "And I saw a beast coming up out of the sea. And he had ten horns and seven heads, and on his horns he had ten crowns and on his heads blasphemous names." If we interpret the term *sea* figuratively, it follows that the rest of this verse should be explained likewise. Alluding to the Daniel 7:3 passage, John observes not four beasts but one beast as a combination of four coming up out of the sea.[3] This beast has ten horns and seven heads, but these numbers should not be taken literally to refer to seven kings (17:9–10). For instance, the enumeration of seven kings is so diverse that an indisputable explanation is out of the question: some begin their count of the Roman emperors with Julius Caesar, others with Augustus, and still others with Caligula.[4] Even if a satisfactory exposition could be given, the interpreter would have difficulty explaining the literal meaning of ten horns and ten crowns. It is wise to understand the numbers seven and ten symbolically as figures of completeness and fullness,[5] and to

---

2. John P. M. Sweet, *Revelation,* WPC (Philadelphia: Westminster, 1979), p. 205; David E. Aune, *Revelation 6–16,* WBC 52B (Nashville: Nelson, 1998), p. 716.

3. William Hendriksen, *More Than Conquerors* (reprint, Grand Rapids: Baker, 1982), p. 146.

4. J. H. Ulrichsen, "Die sieben Häupter und die sieben Hörner: Zur Datierung der Offenbarung des Johannes," *StudTheol* 39 (1985): 1–20.

5. Homer Hailey, *Revelation: An Introduction and Commentary* (Grand Rapids: Baker, 1979), p. 283; Philip Edgcumbe Hughes, *The Book of the Revelation: A Commentary* (Leicester: Inter-Varsity; Grand Rapids: Eerdmans, 1990), pp. 145, 185–87.

apply them to the combined forces of world governments set against the saints on earth.

The seven heads form a united front against God, his Word, and his people, and they attack with the complete power of ten horns. The seven heads and the ten horns are those of Satan himself, who already has been described as the gigantic red dragon (12:3). Though staying in the background, Satan is using the beast—an image of world governments—to do the work for him. Notice that the dragon had seven heads with seven crowns on his heads, but the beast has ten horns with ten crowns on his horns. These are all figurative portrayals of earthly powers; the numbers, the heads, the horns, and the crowns—all of these together exemplify a tremendous force that no one should take for granted. Satan uses world powers to advance his cause on earth, for he knows that his time is short (12:12).

The term *blasphemous names* displayed on the seven heads of the beast points to a motto, slogan, or creed a government has adopted. In John's day, Caesar was revered as *dominus et deus* (Lord and God), which no Christian could confess. For the Christian, only Jesus was Lord and God (1 Cor. 12:3). Other governments have made their anti-Christian teachings known by various slogans; for instance, during the French Revolution the slogan *ni Dieu ni maître* (neither God nor master) was blasphemously touted. Blasphemy is the ridiculing of all that is holy. John says that blasphemy is the slandering of God's name, his abode, and those who are in heaven (v. 6). He mentions blasphemous names again when he describes the woman sitting on the scarlet beast (17:3). John may have had in mind the prophecy of Daniel 11:36 that speaks about the king who exalts himself above every god and speaks blasphemous things against God.

2. And the beast that I saw was like a leopard, and his feet like a bear, and his mouth like the mouth of a lion. And the dragon gave the beast his power and his throne and great authority.

For his imagery in this chapter, the author of Revelation relies on Daniel 7. This verse also has its origin in that chapter. In it Daniel portrays four beasts, of which three are named—a lion, a bear, a leopard (vv. 4–6)—and the fourth is described as terrifying (v. 7). These beasts depict four successive world empires: Neo-Babylonia, Medo-Persia, Greece, and Rome. But John combines them into one beast to denote all the world powers hostile to Jesus Christ.

The first portrayal is that of the leopard, noted for stalking its prey, its amazing speed in capturing prey, and its swiftness in dealing the deathblow. The second picture is that of a bear, who with its powerful paws is able to tear its victims apart. And third, the lion's mouth symbolizes cruelty as it kills and devours wild animals. The three pictures of these beasts are a depiction of force, speed, and savagery.

The object of this portrayal is to show that the dragon, namely, Satan himself, stands behind the beast coming up out of the sea. John writes, "The dragon gave the beast his power and his throne and great authority." The use of the expression *dragon* in this chapter (vv. 2, 4, 11) corroborates its close relationship to the preceding chapter (chap. 12). That is, Satan is empowering the Antichrist to take the place that belongs to God and his Christ. He is the lawless one who sets himself up in God's temple and proclaims himself to be God. He receives power from Satan to be able to do all kinds of counterfeit miracles, signs, and wonders (2 Thess. 2:6, 9). In addition, Satan gave the beast his throne, which is not limited to any one permanent location on earth. For example, Jesus told the church in Pergamum that Satan's throne was in their locale (2:13). Also, we read that an angel poured the fourth bowl of God's wrath on the throne of the beast and thereby cast Satan's kingdom into utter darkness (16:10). Last, Satan gave great authority to the beast, which means that he has granted him authority over all the kingdoms of this world (compare Luke 4:6). Through the beast, Satan rules this world as its titular head; Jesus acknowledges that the devil is the prince of this world.[6]

3a. And one of his heads was as if it had been mortally wounded, and the mortal wound was healed.

The agent who inflicted the mortal wound is not mentioned, but the Scriptures relate how God pronounced a curse on the serpent in the Garden of Eden, whereby the seed of the woman would crush his head (Gen. 3:15). John relates that the wound was caused by the sword (v. 14), which is indicative of a battle that had taken place. This spiritual battle took place when Jesus died on the cross and rose from the dead; thus he defeated Satan. Although Satan's wound had been fatal, it had healed (v. 12). With this description of Satan, John delineates a parody of the death and resurrection of Jesus, whose place the beast wants to usurp.

Many scholars understand the fatally wounded head to be the first of seven Roman emperors, possibly Nero (compare 17:9–10). The healing of the mortal wound would then refer to the legend of *Nero redivivus,* coming back to life.[7] But this interpretation meets objections; for one, why would John allude to a legend in a chapter filled with symbolism? If in this chapter we interpret the number seven as literally referring to seven kings (17:9–10), what interpretation is there for the number ten? Next, the text intimates that an outside agent administered the fatal wound to one of the heads, but history records that Nero himself inflicted the wound that resulted in his death. Last, as I mentioned above, the parallels between Christ and the beast are numerous in this chapter. This signifies that the author is not interested in identifying one of the heads of the beast with one particular Roman emperor or even one empire. John identifies the beast with God's opponent, Satan himself.[8] His purpose throughout Revelation is to show contrast; here it is the contrast of the Lamb that was slain (5:6, 9) and the

6. John 12:31; 14:30; 16:11. See also 1 Cor. 2:6; 2 Cor. 4:4; Eph. 2:2.

7. Consult Aune, *Revelation 6–16,* pp. 736–40; Adela Yarbro Collins, *The Apocalypse* (Wilmington: Glazier, 1979), p. 91; Gerhard A. Krodel, *Revelation,* ACNT (Minneapolis: Augsburg, 1989), p. 249.

8. Gregory K. Beale, *The Book of Revelation: A Commentary on the Greek Text,* NIGTC (Grand Rapids: Eerdmans, 1998), pp. 690–91.

beast who has one head that was mortally wounded. The emphasis is not on the one head that was wounded and healed; instead John states that the beast was wounded and lived (vv. 12 and 14). The world of unbelief worshiped not the head that was slain and healed but the beast that was alive and well.

3b. And the whole earth marveled, following the beast. 4. And they worshiped the dragon, for he gave authority to the beast, and they worshiped the beast, asking, "Who is like the beast, and who is able to make war against him?"

Not just single individuals—believers are excluded—but the whole world of unbelievers marveled and worshiped the beast. This interpretation is supported in 17:8b, where John comments: "And the inhabitants of the earth will be astonished, those whose names are not written in the book of life from the foundation of the earth. They see the beast that was and is not and will come." Each passage must be seen in its own context, however, for the two do not relate the same event.[9]

The world worships the dragon. This is evident in that people believe the lie instead of the truth; they uphold the death of innocents instead of the sanctity of life; and they practice immorality instead of striving to live a moral and upright life.

Even though there is repetition in verse 4 of the phrase *they worshiped the*, there is no reason to delete the first part of the verse "they worshiped the dragon, for he gave authority to the beast."[10] John intends to make it clear that the worship of the dragon is the same as the worship of the beast, that is, the beast is the instrument in the hand of the dragon. Throughout this chapter the dragon is present but always in the background; the beast is doing the work for him. The dragon empowers the beast with authority, which again is an imitation of Jesus, who shortly before his ascension said, "All authority in heaven and on earth has been given to me" (Matt. 28:18). Notice that in this chapter the verb *to worship* occurs five times, of which one refers to the dragon and four to the beast (vv. 4 [twice], 8, 12, 15).

The question asked by the people is, "Who is like the beast, and who is able to make war against him?" The readers and hearers of the Apocalypse were familiar with the hymnody derived from the Old Testament and would recognize that the question raised by unbelievers is a parody of the songs of Zion. "Who among the gods is like you, O LORD? Who is like you—majestic in holiness, awesome in glory, working wonders?" (Exod. 15:11; Ps. 35:10).[11] Satan, who wants to occupy God's place, appears in the form of the beast. Brazenly he queries whether there is anyone like the beast. This question expects a negative answer, for with the authority the beast has received there is no one on earth who is able to oppose him. With the second part of the question, the beast challenges God's people to engage him in battle. His aim is to overpower them, lead them into captivity, and

9. See Bauckham, *Climax of Prophecy*, p. 440; Beale, *Revelation*, p. 693.

10. Aune (*Revelation 6–16*, pp. 740–41) suggests its deletion.

11. See also Exod. 8:10; Deut. 3:24; Ps. 18:31; 35:10; 89:6, 8; 113:5; Isa. 40:18, 25; 44:7; 46:5.

kill them (vv. 7, 10). Does the lie triumph over truth, evil over good, injustice over justice, dishonesty over honesty, vice over virtue? The answer is no, because God is in control. Through his Son, God establishes justice, truth, righteousness, and peace. The beast and ultimately Satan will face the wrath of God and the Lamb (17:14; 19:19–21; 20:10).

Greek Words, Phrases, and Constructions in 13:1–3

Verse 1

ὄνομα—this is the reading supported by 𝔓[47] ℵ C 1006. The last two letters of the plural ὀνόματα (A 2053) may have been omitted accidentally, but these two could also have been added to the singular.[12] Although the plural construction occurs in 17:3, the original reading is difficult to determine.

Verse 3

μίαν—this feminine number in the accusative case modifying κεφαλή is probably the direct object of the verb "I saw" (v. 1).

ὅλη ἡ γῆ—this nominative subject is preceded by the verb "to marvel" in the singular but followed by the verb "to worship" in the plural. Collectively the people marvel, but they worship individually.

2. Power and Authority
13:5–10

5. And the beast was given a mouth to speak great things and words of blasphemy, and he was given authority to do so for forty-two months.

Four times in two verses the phrase *was given* appears (vv. 5, 7). Satan is the one who gave the beast power and authority (vv. 2, 4), yet the ultimate Sovereign is God Almighty. In his inscrutable wisdom, God allows the beast to blaspheme, exercise authority, and wage war against the saints.

The background for the phrase "a mouth to speak great things and words of blasphemy" is Daniel 7:8, 11, 20. Daniel mentions a little horn, namely, the Antichrist, who had a mouth and spoke boastful words. He describes the work of the Antichrist in great detail by revealing that a king will speak words of blasphemy against God, exalt himself above all gods, make war against mighty fortresses, and appoint rulers over many people (Dan. 11:36–39).

Arrogant with power and authority, the beast uses modern means of communication to spread the lie, subvert justice, teach false doctrines, and revile the name of God and his Christ. He thinks himself to be in full control yet knows that he is unable to subvert God's people, that he is accountable to God, and that his time is short. God allots him a total of forty-two months to rule on the face of this earth.

12. Bruce M. Metzger, *A Textual Commentary on the Greek New Testament*, 2d ed. (Stuttgart: Deutsche Bibelgesellschaft, 1994), p. 673.

Forty-two months or three and a half years is the same as 1,260 days. These references appeared earlier in two preceding chapters where John noted that the Gentiles would trample the holy city for forty-two months and the two witnesses would prophesy for 1,260 days (11:2–3). And he related that the woman (the church) would be cared for in the desert by God for 1,260 days or time, times, and a half time, namely, three and a half years (12:6, 14). These references signify the entire period during which the gospel is proclaimed, from the time of Jesus' first coming to his promised return. In that period, Satan through the beast blasphemes God's name, bans the preaching of his Word, and attempts to destroy the church.

6. And he opened his mouth for blasphemies against God to blaspheme his name and his tabernacle and those who dwell in heaven.

The words *he opened his mouth* reflect an Aramaic idiom. We are reminded of the Gospel writer's idiom "he opened his mouth and said" (Matt. 5:2 KJV), which simply means "he said." So here the meaning is that the beast spoke words of blasphemy toward God. His sole purpose of existence is to be in opposition to God and his Christ. He wants to occupy the place of God and thus speak constantly against his name, his dwelling place, and his people. We examine these three items successively.

a. *His name.* The names of God are the same as the revelation of God, for the Almighty makes himself known to us through his names. The beast denies that God and his Son have anything at all to say in the world in which Satan functions as prince. Thus, in Satan's kingdom the written Word of God may not be read, heard, or distributed. God's commandments may not be observed as rules of life in society; and the name of Jesus must be confined at best to private worship and under no circumstances can enter the numerous spheres of life. The beast teaches that everything in the world has come into existence by human power and serves to glorify human achievements.[13]

b. *His dwelling.* The choice of words is interesting, for the literal translation is "tent," that is, "tabernacle." The word appears only three times in the Apocalypse and refers to God's dwelling in the midst of his people (13:6; 15:5; 21:3). The image of the Old Testament tabernacle in the desert comes to mind when a cloud covered this tent and God's glory filled it (Exod. 40:34–35). It is the tabernacle with its two compartments: the Holy Place and the Holy of Holies (Lev. 16:2–3; Heb. 9:12; 10:19). Into the Holy of Holies the high priest entered once a year as representative of God's people to atone for sins by the sprinkling of animal blood. The beast desires to occupy God's place and dwell in the midst of humanity on this earth, ruling over mankind.

c. *His people.* John uses the noun *tent* for God's dwelling place and the verb *to tent* for God's people. The Greek literally reads, "and his tent and those who tent in heaven." Once again we must call to mind the Sinai desert scene of God dwell-

---

13. Consult Herman Hoeksema, *Behold, He Cometh! An Exposition of the Book of Revelation* (Grand Rapids: Reformed Free Publishing Association, 1969), p. 461.

ing in the tabernacle surrounded by his people who dwelled in tents. It is a picture of harmony and peace, which John in similar wording expresses about the consummation (see 21:3). But there is more. We can extend the illustration by saying that God spreads his tent over his people, so that they live together in God's abode. The italicized words in the phrase "those who dwell *in heaven*" remind us that blasphemers on earth are not afraid to slander celestial beings (2 Pet. 2:10b; Jude 8). The beast blasphemes God's people, whose citizenship is in heaven (Phil. 3:20). At the same time, the saints on earth are one with those in heaven, yet only those on earth experience the wrath of the devil (12:12; see also Dan. 7:25). And they are the people whom the beast persecutes, as the next verse reveals.

7. And he was given power to make war against the saints and to overcome them, and he was given authority over every tribe, people, language, and nation.

The first part of the text is a repetition of 11:7, "the beast that comes up out of the Abyss will make war against them and will overcome and kill them." It is also language borrowed from Daniel 7:21, "As I watched, this horn was waging war against the saints and defeating them." The incongruity of this warfare is that the one who conquers is defeated and those who are defeated by him are in the end designated as conquerors. The saints indeed are more than conquerors in Christ Jesus. They may lose their lives while on earth in their opposition to the powers of the Antichrist, but they will spend eternity with Christ living and reigning with him. Of the saints it is said that they have overcome the Antichrist "by the blood of the Lamb and by the word of their testimony, and they did not love their lives even in the face of death" (12:11).

The passive voice "he was given" intimates that in his providence God permits the beast to exercise authority over the saints and to rule the people on the earth. It is true that it is Satan who gives the beast authority and power (v. 2), but it is God who is in control and allows this transaction to take place. As in verse 5 so here we twice read the words *he was given.* God's people realize that although the forces of the evil one are strong and able to overcome them, deliverance comes from God. Satan increasingly governs every tribe, people, language, and nation; nonetheless, even if the devil seems to have power over the saints on earth, he is unable to separate them from the love of God in Christ Jesus (Rom. 8:38–39). Jesus told his followers that no one is able to snatch them out of the Father's hand (John 10:28).

Once again we see the beast as the Antichrist seeking to usurp the place of Christ. The Son of Man was given authority, and "all peoples, nations and men of every language worshiped him" (Dan. 7:14). The Antichrist "was given authority over every tribe, people, language, and nation," and they worship the beast. God is the one who assigns authority to both the Christ and the Antichrist, with the distinction that the Christ is victorious over the beast.[14]

14. See Beale, *Revelation*, p. 700; Bauckham, *Climax of Prophecy*, p. 264.

8. And all those living on the earth will worship the beast, everyone whose name has not been written in the book of life of the Lamb that was slain, from the foundation of the world.

a. "And all those living on the earth will worship the beast." John looks to the future and predicts that the population of this earth will follow the directions of the beast and worship him. On all the continents, the people as a whole will obey and venerate the Antichrist. The Greek text indicates the masculine pronoun *him* for the Antichrist to indicate that he will appear in human form. This person will receive the adulation of all the people on the earth, except the saints. John clearly divides humanity into those who worship the beast and those whose names are recorded in the book of life. It is the division of the unregenerate over against the regenerate, the unbelievers opposite the believers, the ungodly versus the godly. The Antichrist seeks to imitate Christ, who purchased his people from every tribe, language, people, and nation (5:9). The beast desires world domination by having everyone not written in the book of life follow him.

b. "Everyone whose name has not been written in the book of life." This book belongs to the Lamb who died for all those whose names have been recorded in it. These people belong to him since the time of creation, and therefore he protects and delivers them from the evil one. He has given the solemn assurance that he will never erase their names from this book (3:5). John writes the noun *name* and the verb *written* in the singular to indicate that he is not referring to the group as a whole but to the individual believer who receives the assurance that he or she is a child of God.

Unbelievers, those who reject God's Word and the testimony of Jesus, never had their names recorded in the book of life. They are the followers of the beast and they worship him instead of the Lord of lords and King of kings. Thus they are followers of the devil whose final destiny they share (20:10, 15). The names of the believers, however, have been recorded in the Lamb's book of life from eternity.

c. "The Lamb that was slain, from the foundation of the world." How do we interpret these words? Should the phrase "from the foundation of the world" be taken with "slain" or "written"? The answer to this question lies in reading other passages that shed light on this matter. John says, "And the inhabitants of the earth will be astonished, they whose names are not written in the book of life from the foundation of the earth" (17:8). Here he omits the reference to the slain Lamb and thus indicates that God's elect were chosen in eternity. Paul also testifies that God chose his people in Christ before the creation of the world (Eph. 1:4). Having said that, we should note that God chose Christ for the task of redeeming his people before the world was created (1 Pet. 1:20). And this task implies that he eventually would be slain at the time God had appointed for him.

On balance, the evidence John supplies in 17:8 is telling, for there he connects the phrase "from the foundation of the world" with "written." The objection can be raised that the phrase is too far removed from the verb in question.[15] This objection may be valid, yet the fact remains that in John's writing this phe-

15. G. B. Caird, *A Commentary on the Revelation of St. John the Divine* (London: Black, 1966), p. 168.

nomenon occurs often when he wishes to qualify a noun in greater detail. He explains the phrase "the book of life" with the modifiers "of the Lamb that was slain." In short, the book of life with all the names of God's people belongs to the slain Lamb of God.[16] Here is a word of comfort for the saints on earth who experience the onslaughts of the evil one. Their names are recorded in the book of life and the Lamb who was slain on their behalf has purchased them to live with him eternally (5:9).

9. If anyone has an ear, let him hear.

The message of the preceding verse is loud and clear: the Lord is on the side of his people on earth. Let all those who hear these comforting words take note, for through his servant John the Lord addresses them. The saying "If anyone has an ear, let him hear" is common and reminds us of the letters Jesus sent to the seven churches (chapters 2 and 3) and the teachings of Jesus (Matt. 11:15; 13:9, 43). These words pertain first to what has been said in the preceding verses and, next, they serve as a bridge to what follows. The message is addressed to the individual believer, who must take a stand for Jesus. Amid deceit and falsehood, persecution and death, the Christian occupies a lonely position of being the target of the Antichrist and his subordinates. Experiencing the severest hardships, the elect know that God is on their side and will avenge his adversaries.

10. If anyone goes into captivity, into captivity he goes.
If anyone is to be killed with the sword, with the sword he will be killed.
Here is the endurance and faith of the saints.

The first two lines are loosely taken from the prophecy of Jeremiah. God said through the prophet, "Those destined for death, to death; those for the sword, to the sword; those for starvation, to starvation; those for captivity, to captivity" (Jer. 15:2; see also 43:11). Jeremiah wrote this passage to the wicked people in Jerusalem and Judah who no longer could count on divine help and deliverance. God would no longer listen to intercessions for his sinful people but was about to punish them with death, the sword, famine, and exile. By contrast, John addresses suffering Christians who are experiencing the scourge of imprisonment and loss of life. He writes to encourage the saints in their suffering for the Lord.

The sayings are difficult to interpret because of the variants. The first line has the variant reading, "If you lead [a Christian] into captivity, [you yourself will] go into captivity," which would fulfill the law of retribution. But a fundamental rule is that the shorter reading of a verse is generally to be preferred, for scribes were apt to augment a text. The shorter reading is "Those for captivity, to captivity go." This text is the stronger of the two and therefore the more acceptable as the original.

The second line also shows variants: "If you kill with the sword, with the sword you must be killed" (KJV, NRSV, NASB), and "If anyone is to be killed with the sword, with the sword he will be killed" (NIV, NCV, REB). The first one is active in meaning,

16. See L. van Hartingsveld, *Revelation* (Grand Rapids: Eerdmans, 1985), p. 53. In the Apocalypse, the concatenation of nouns, pronouns, and adjectives in the genitive is common. See, e.g., the Greek text of 14:10 and 21:9, where John lists successive series of qualifying genitive cases.

the second passive. The first one expresses the law of retribution, the tit-for-tat law. What you sow, you will also reap. Jesus told Peter in the Garden of Gethsemane, "All who draw the sword will die by the sword" (Matt. 26:52). In other words, do not engage in active resistance by trying to defend yourself against the onslaughts of the enemy. Numerous commentators support this reading.[17]

The second variant calls for patient endurance and harmonizes with the first line of the Old Testament allusion. The subjects in both lines are the Christians who suffer loss of freedom and loss of life. These two lines express that Christians experience hardships when the devil unleashes his fury against them. The lines are not addressed to Satan's henchmen who face God's retribution. Instead, the Lord addresses the saints and exhorts them to endure hardships and exercise their trust in him.[18]

But do Christians have to suffer passively without defending themselves? If this is the case, it seems that the evil one would have the freedom to wipe out all the followers of Christ. This is exactly the point, however, for Satan does not have this prerogative. He can only do what God permits him to do. Christians must not take up the sword but permit God to be their defender. It is not Satan but God who rules on this earth: "Vengeance is mine," says the Lord (Deut. 32:35; Rom. 12:19; Heb. 10:30). We should also consider that the insignificant group of Christ's followers during the first century would not have had a chance had they taken up arms against all-powerful Rome. The Lord called them not to active resistance but to patient endurance.

The third line, "Here is the endurance and faith of the saints," depends on the first two lines and is a summary. It properly fits the shorter readings of the text. Not the persecutors and executioners but the suffering saints are called to submit to and rely on the Lord. They have been called to exercise endurance in the earlier chapters and verses of the Apocalypse (1:9; 2:2, 3, 19; 3:10; see also 14:12). Similarly, the faith of the readers has been expressed earlier (2:13, 19; and see 14:12).

Greek Words, Phrases, and Constructions in 13:6–10

Verse 6

τοὺς . . . σκηνοῦντας—although some manuscripts delete these two words, there is good textual support for them, and they appear to be the harder reading.[19] If the words should be omitted, the phrase ἐν τῷ οὐρανῷ would then be taken with the words "and his tent."

---

17. William Barclay, *The Revelation of John*, 2d ed. (Philadelphia: Westminster, 1960), 2:126; Henry Barclay Swete, *Commentary on Revelation* (1911; reprint, Grand Rapids: Kregel, 1977), p. 168; Isbon T. Beckwith, *The Apocalypse of John* (1919; reprint, Grand Rapids: Baker, 1979), p. 638; Leon Morris, *Revelation*, rev. ed., TNTC (Leicester: Inter-Varsity; Grand Rapids: Eerdmans, 1987), p. 165; Louis A. Vos, *The Synoptic Traditions in the Apocalypse* (Kampen: Kok, 1965), pp. 104–9.

18. Refer to Hughes, *Revelation*, p. 150; Robert L. Thomas, *Revelation 8–22: An Exegetical Commentary* (Chicago: Moody, 1995), p. 168; Robert H. Mounce, *The Book of Revelation*, rev. ed., NICNT (Grand Rapids: Eerdmans, 1998), p. 253; George Eldon Ladd, *Commentary on the Revelation of John* (Grand Rapids: Eerdmans, 1972), p. 182. Jürgen Roloff, *The Revelation of John*, trans. J. E. Alsup (Minneapolis: Fortress, 1993), p. 159.

19. Metzger, *Textual Commentary*, p. 674.

Verse 7

καὶ ἐδόθη . . . νικῆσαι αὐτούς—the omission of this clause in some leading manuscripts is due to an error of the eye. Because of the similar reading καὶ ἐδόθη αὐτῷ in the first line, a scribe overlooked the first line and skipped over to the second occurrence.[20]

The omission of the words καὶ λαόν probably stems from doctrinal considerations, that is, not God's covenant people but the nations are under the beast's authority. However, the fourfold formula of "tribe, language, people, and nation" with internal variations appears seven times in the Apocalypse (5:9; 7:9; 10:11; 11:9; 13:7; 14:6; 17:15). Bauckham observes, "The order of the list is not varied haphazardly, . . . but is varied according to certain principles of order."[21] In other words, the context determines the meaning of each verse.

Verse 8

αὐτοῦ—this personal pronoun is redundant because of the personal pronoun at the beginning of the clause (see also v. 12; 3:8; 7:2, 9; 20:8).

Verse 10

The repetition of εἰς αἰχμαλωσίαν has led to its omission in the second clause, "the result of accidental oversight in transcription."[22]

ἀποκτανθῆναι αὐτόν—this difficult reading finds its origin in a Hebrew idiom that in translation reads, "If anyone is to be slain with the sword, he is to be slain with the sword."[23] Some manuscripts read the future tense ἀποκτενεῖ, δεῖ (he will kill, it is necessary) or the present tense ἀποκτείνει, δεῖ (he kills, it is necessary). Nevertheless these two readings appear to have entered the text on the basis of Jesus' word to Peter not to take up his sword (Matt. 26:52).[24] A scribe has added the word δεῖ to ease the awkwardness of the clause. Its presence is more likely due to insertion than its absence to omission. On the whole, the shorter text is probably the original one that in its brevity harmonizes with the Greek text of Jeremiah 15:2.

C. The Beast from the Land
13:11–18

Satan uses the beast coming up out of the sea as the Antichrist and the beast coming out of the earth as the false prophet. The one represents physical force and raw power, for he comes up out of the sea of humanity; the other stands for deceit, because he presents himself as possessing intellectual acumen and rational philosophy. The one attacks the external part of a human being, that is, the physical body, with destruction and death; the other influences the inner part of a person, namely, the mind. The second one is even more fearful than the first;

---

20. Ibid.

21. Bauckham, *Climax of Prophecy*, p. 327.

22. Metzger, *Textual Commentary*, pp. 674–75.

23. R. H. Charles, *A Critical and Exegetical Commentary on the Revelation of St. John*, ICC (Edinburgh: Clark, 1920), 1:355.

24. Metzger, *Textual Commentary*, p. 675.

he is able to make the inhabitants of the earth worship the beast that came out of the sea. He is a symbol of false religion and fallacious philosophy.

These verses clearly exhibit Satan's design to imitate Christ. The parody is evident throughout the next verses: the mention of a lamb, the granting of all authority, the worship of the beast, the fatal wound that was healed, the mark on the forehead, and the name of the beast.

1. Parody of Christ *13:11–14*

11. And I saw another beast coming up out of the earth, and he had two horns like a lamb and he spoke like a dragon.

a. "And I saw another beast coming up out of the earth." The second beast comes not from the sea of people as a symbol of brute force but arises from the earth in contrast to heaven. This beast stands in direct opposition to everything that comes from heaven and is devoid of anything that is heavenly. He is therefore the aggregate of sin that reaches from earth to heaven, and, as the false prophet, he stands completely in the service of the Antichrist.[25] The false prophet is mentioned three times in the Apocalypse (16:13; 19:20; 20:10). He personifies secular philosophies, that is, the worldly theories of knowledge that influence the thinking and actions of the masses. His purpose is to set the whole world against God and his Christ, revelation, and people. Briefly, his aim is to be victorious in this endeavor, but in reality, as Revelation shows, Christ is the victor and he the vanquished.

b. "And he had two horns like a lamb." Once again John relies on the prophecy of Daniel. He alludes in the Apocalypse to some twenty-seven verses from this prophecy,[26] among which is the one from 8:3, "I looked up, and there before me was a ram with two horns." The lamb of the male gender appears with two horns as symbols of power and might. He had not ten horns like the dragon (12:3) but only two. The number two signifies sufficiency in respect to spreading the lie and wielding authority throughout the world. The appearance of the lamb is not merely a parody of the Lamb of God; it also appears as the embodiment of deception—harmless, lovable, and attractive.[27] It is the proverbial iron fist in a velvet glove or the wolf in sheep's clothing (Matt. 7:15). This beast is instigated by the father of lies (John 8:44).

c. "And he spoke like a dragon." In the Greek text the verb "had" in the preceding clause and the verb "spoke" are in the imperfect tense to indicate the continuation of an act. That is, the lamb all along was seen with the two horns and

---

25. S. Greijdanus, *De Openbaring des Heeren aan Johannes*, KNT (Amsterdam: Van Bottenburg, 1925), p. 277; Charles, *Revelation*, 1:357.

26. Consult Steve Moyise, *The Old Testament in the Book of Revelation*, JSNTSup 115 (Sheffield: Sheffield Academic Press, 1995), p. 45; Charles, *Revelation*, 1:lxviii–lxxxi.

27. J. Massyngberde Ford, *Revelation: Introduction, Translation, and Commentary*, AB 38 (Garden City, N.Y.: Doubleday, 1975), p. 213. It is difficult to understand why Ford writes, "The second beast is a parody not of the Lamb but of the two witnesses."

it kept on speaking like a dragon. The dragon relates to the previous chapter, where he is identified as that ancient serpent called the devil and Satan (12:9). The word then intimates that he can speak deceptively, like the serpent who addressed Eve in Paradise (Gen. 3:1).[28]

12. And he wields all the authority of the first beast in its presence, and he makes the earth and those dwelling in it to worship the first beast, whose mortal wound was healed.

a. "And he wields all the authority of the first beast in its presence." The beast of the sea has received delegated authority that he shares with the beast out of the earth. The first one demonstrates power; the second one displays propaganda. But the second should never be underestimated, for he enjoys the same supremacy as the first beast, in whose interest he works. These two anti-Christian forces are united in their effort to overthrow the rule of Christ. This powerful combination of thought and authority rules on the face of the earth and controls the minds and bodies of untold millions of people.

Authority implies that the earthly beast shares the power and the throne Satan has made available (vv. 2, 4, 7). Thus, standing in the very presence of the first beast, he has awesome forces at his disposal to attack and overthrow the followers of Christ.

b. "And he makes the earth and those dwelling in it to worship the first beast." Everything on the face of the earth is to serve the interest of the Antichrist, the first beast. All the institutions of communication, all the resources of governments and administrations, all the educational resources, and all the commerce and industry must stand at the beck and call of the Antichrist. For that reason, the false prophet as the mouthpiece of the Antichrist must control and govern the human mind. This feat can be accomplished only when human beings turn away from their former allegiances and worship the Antichrist.

The act of worship in the province of Asia meant to acknowledge the Roman emperor as Lord and God (chapters 2 and 3). When Christians entered a pagan temple and participated in meals offered to an idol, they were in fact participating in the worship of demons (1 Cor. 10:20–21). The number of people who through the centuries have turned away from Christ to follow idols is definitive proof of the nefarious work of the second beast. The Antichrist wants all people to worship him and thus supplant the worship of Christ.

c. "Whose mortal wound was healed." Together with the clause, "[He] had the wound of the sword and yet lived" (v. 14), these words are a parody of Jesus' suffering, death, and resurrection. The Antichrist seeks to imitate Christ with a semblance of fatal wounds and a subsequent revival. But he will be thrown into the lake of fire, where he will experience the second death (19:20; 20:14).

28. Compare the commentaries of Sweet (p. 215), Beckwith (p. 630), and Beale (p. 708).

13. And he performs great signs so that he even makes fire to come down out of heaven onto the earth before people.

The great imitator accomplishes miracles comparable to those done by God's servants. For example, the signs Elijah performed were marvelous indeed. He called to God and fire came down from heaven, burning the sacrifice and the wood on the altar and its stones, and even licking up the water in the trench that surrounded the altar (1 Kings 18:38). And he called down fire from heaven to consume two captains with fifty men each (2 Kings 1:10, 12; see also Luke 9:54–55).

Paul warns his readers that "the coming of the lawless one will be in accordance with the work of Satan displayed in all kinds of counterfeit miracles, signs and wonders" (2 Thess. 2:9; see Matt. 24:24). The two prophets whom God sends forth to present his testimony to the world had the power to spew fire from their mouths to devour their enemies (11:5). God's people, however, should be able to discern the true prophet from the false one. God instructs Moses to tell the Israelites that they must reject the false prophet who announces miraculous signs and wonders for the purpose of worshiping other gods. This prophet must be put to death (Deut. 13:1–5).

The acts of performing false miracles and barring people from the worship of God go hand in hand. With their tricks, magicians incited Pharaoh to harden his heart and not let God's people go (Exod. 7:11); on the island of Cyprus, Elymas the sorcerer tried to hinder the proconsul from worshiping God and his Christ (Acts 13:6–8). Magicians who performed the hoax of having fire come down from heaven tried to influence the Christians in the first century to worship the emperor. By contrast, accompanying the spread of the gospel, "God also testified to it by signs, wonders and various miracles, and gifts of the Holy Spirit distributed according to his will" (Heb. 2:4).[29] Hence, Christians must clearly and carefully distinguish between genuine and false miracles, and determine whether they come from God or the devil.

14. And he deceives the inhabitants on the earth because of these signs that were given him to perform in the presence of the beast. He told the inhabitants on the earth to make an image in honor of the beast that had the wound of the sword and yet lived.

For the devil and his henchmen, deception is a way of life. For them this word spells a complete abandonment of truth, honesty, integrity, righteousness, and honor as they seek to use the people living on this earth. The phrase *the inhabitants on the earth* occurs at least ten times in Revelation, and in each instance it refers to people of the world.[30] They are unbelievers who are persecutors and enemies of God's people (3:10; 6:10), antagonists who face impending judgment (8:13; 11:10), and people whose names are not written in the book of life (13:8; 17:8).

29. Sweet (*Revelation*, p. 216) writes that "the *fire from heaven* is a parody of the Holy Spirit (Acts 2:3–4), who inspires Christian prophets (Rev. 11:5)." Compare John F. Walvoord, *The Revelation of Jesus Christ* (Chicago: Moody, 1966), p. 207; Thomas, *Revelation 8–22*, p. 176.

30. Rev. 3:10; 6:10; 8:13; 11:10 (twice); 13:8, 14 (twice); 17:2, 8; compare also 13:12; 14:6.

The one who gives the beast from the earth (the false prophet) power to perform miracles is the beast from the sea (the Antichrist), who received God's permission to do so (see 19:20). John notes that these signs are to be performed in the presence of the first beast, who desires to be worshiped by the masses of humanity. This is to be done by having the people erect his image by which he acknowledges their homage.

Throughout the centuries images of one kind or another have been raised, and people have worshiped and bowed down to them. They include Nebuchadnezzar's golden image, Antiochus Epiphanes' altar of Zeus in the temple of Jerusalem, the attempt of Caligula to have his statue placed in that same temple, the statue of Domitian in the temple of Ephesus, the swastika of Hitler in Nazi Germany, and the hammer and sickle in the former Soviet Union. John reflects the historical context and culture of his age in which Christians were forced to participate in emperor worship. The pervading presence of temples and statues dedicated to Roman emperors was overpowering for the followers of Christ in the province of Asia. Only true faith in Christ could keep them from succumbing to this pressure.

The influence of the beast should not be limited to the end of the first century, because its authority is worldwide, appears in numerous forms, and lasts until the consummation. John writes that the beast had been wounded with the sword but sprung back to life. Even though many scholars see in this verse an allusion to the legend of Nero who came back to life,[31] the context of this chapter teaches that the reign of the Antichrist includes all eras. The spirit of the Antichrist suffers a mortal blow but comes back to life. Once again, this description of the beast that returns with renewed vigor is a caricature of Christ's resurrection. However, there is no comparison; the Antichrist lives to destroy life everywhere, while Christ lives to impart eternal life to all his followers.

Greek Words, Phrases, and Constructions in 13:12–14

Verse 12

ἵνα—followed by the future tense of the verb *to worship*, this particle introduces a purpose clause. The future indicative and the aorist subjunctive often are interchanged in this construction.

Verse 14

διά—this preposition followed by the accusative case should here be translated "through" (see 12:11).[32]

---

31. See, e.g., Beckwith, *Apocalypse*, p. 640; Bauckham, *Climax of Prophecy*, pp. 441–50; S. J. Scherrer, "Signs and Wonders in the Imperial Cult: A New Look at a Roman Religious Institution in the Light of Rev 13:13–15," *JBL* 103 (1984): 559–610.

32. Robert Hanna, *A Grammatical Aid to the Greek New Testament* (Grand Rapids: Baker, 1983), p. 451. See also C. F. D. Moule, *An Idiom-Book of New Testament Greek*, 2d ed. (Cambridge: Cambridge University Press, 1960), p. 55.

2. The Mark of the Beast
13:15–18

15. And he was given power to give breath to the image of the beast, so that the image of the beast might both speak and cause as many as do not worship the image of the beast to be killed.

Both the Greek text and translations feature the power of the beast coming up out of the sea (vv. 11–18). The beast out of the earth works behind the scenes without any mention of his identity. It is the beast out of the sea that receives all the attention: everything is done on his behalf and for his benefit, for he is the spirit of the Antichrist. Giving breath to the image of the beast implies animation achieved by magic. Again, giving breath to an image is a parody of God giving the breath of life to Adam (Gen. 2:7; and see Rev. 11:11). Magicians in the ancient world boasted that they could make statues speak and move; thus, Simon Magus allegedly said, "I made statues move; I gave breath to inanimate objects."[33] God allows all this mimicry and gives the beast permission to kill those who refuse to worship the image of the beast.

The Old Testament background presents the account of the three young men in the fiery furnace because they declined to obey Nebuchadnezzar's command to fall down and worship the image he had erected (Dan. 3:1–11). God rescued these three men to bring glory to his name. But the beast continues to send forth his accomplices to force everyone to worship and bow down before him, and infidels who refuse to obey are summarily killed. Christians must obey the authorities as long as there is no conflict with the teachings of Christ. John indirectly implies that there may be a time "when the act of refusing to commit high treason against Christ will be interpreted as high treason against the Antichrist."[34] The mere fact of being a Christian is sufficient evidence for enforcing the death penalty. And the persecution of God's people in today's world testifies to this grim reality. The text does not say that all the followers of Christ will be killed, but that as many as failed to worship might be executed (see v. 10; 20:4). In John's day, the temple of the Sebastoi (the family of Vespasian, Titus, and Domitian) was dedicated in Ephesus, and the local population was forced to pay homage to the emperor by worshiping him.[35]

16. And he causes all, both small and great, both rich and poor, both free persons and slaves to receive a mark on their right hand or on their forehead. 17. And no one was able to buy or sell except the one having the mark, that is, the name of the beast or the number of his name.

a. *Categories.* The second beast not only executes those who decline to worship the image of the first beast, but he also forces all categories of people to receive

33. Pseudo-Clementine *Recognitions* 3.47.2. See Aune, *Revelation 6–16*, p. 764.

34. Martin Kiddle, *The Revelation of St. John* (reprint, London: Hodder and Stoughton, 1943), p. 258.

35. S. J. Friesen, *Twice Neokoros: Ephesus, Asia, and the Cult of the Flavian Imperial Family* (Leiden: Brill, 1993), pp. 146–52; S. R. F. Price, *Rituals and Power: The Roman Imperial Cult in Asia Minor* (Cambridge: Cambridge University Press, 1984), pp. 197–99.

a distinguishing mark that sets them apart from Christians. The expression *all* does not signify that every single human being is included but rather that people from all walks of life are intended. This is clear from the various classes that are listed. "Small and great" is really an idiom that includes "people of all ages or all stations in life."[36] This expression often occurs in the Apocalypse (11:18; 19:5, 18; 20:12). Note that the categories are presented as opposites: small and great, rich and poor, free persons and slaves. These are people from all the levels of society.

b. *Mark.* The explanations for this word range from slaves being branded to people placing a tattoo on their right hand or forehead. History is replete with accounts of slaves, soldiers, or zealots being branded or tattooed. The verse, however, specifies that the purpose for bearing the mark of the beast is to be able to buy or sell merchandise, and that includes a much broader category than a small segment of the population. Some scholars put the sentence in the historical context of Caesar worship, so that only those people who had received an ink mark on either their wrist or forehead might enter the marketplace.[37] The difficulty with this interpretation is that Roman historians report nothing concerning such a practice in the empire.

If we understand John to write not for a particular moment in time as he reflects on a local incident, but for the universal church of all ages and places, then we need to interpret this verse more broadly. First, let us notice that the word *mark* appears a number of times in Revelation. John mentions it in 14:9, "If anyone worships the beast and his image and receives the mark on his forehead and his hand" (see also 19:20; 20:4). And in 14:11 he writes of "anyone who receives the mark of his name." Therefore, having the mark of the beast leads to acts of worship and the bearing of his name. It designates a person as a devotee and true follower of the beast. It indicates a person who is hostile to God, his Word, and his people; he or she bears the mark of the Antichrist on the right hand or forehead.

Next, the symbol of the *right hand* means friendship and fellowship (Gal. 2:9); it is a sign of working together in a common cause, namely, to oppose God. The mark on the *forehead* implies that these people are influenced by the same philosophy and thought patterns.[38] In their anti-Christian thinking, they glorify the beast and his achievements and attempt to destroy the work of Christ on earth.

As the devotees of the Antichrist have the mark of the beast on their forehead or right hand, so the servants of God have received the seal of the Lord and the name of both the Father and the Lamb on their foreheads (7:3; 14:1). If the mark on God's people is invisible, I interpret also the marks on the unbelievers

36. Aune, *Revelation 6–16*, p. 766.

37. Consult E. A. Judge, "The Mark of the Beast, Revelation 13:16," *TynB* 42 (1991): 158–60.

38. See the commentaries of Beale (p. 716), Caird (p. 173), Hailey (p. 296), Hendriksen (p. 150), Hughes (p. 153), and Swete (p. 173).

as invisible. And last, receiving the mark of allegiance to the beast is in itself a travesty of the pledge made at Christian baptism.

c. *Trade.* The inability to buy or sell amounts to a boycott by which the food supply is cut off and starvation lurks at the door. The first recipients of the Apocalypse could relate to these circumstances, for many of them in Smyrna lived in abject poverty (see the commentary on 2:9). But boycotts have not been confined to a certain place in history; they are common and in many cases God's people are their victims. The mark of the beast means bearing his name and number.

18. Here is wisdom. Let anyone who has a mind calculate the number of the beast. It is the number of a man, and his number is 666.

a. *Wisdom.* God's revelation, as it is presented here, can be understood only when the reader possesses wisdom given from above through the Holy Spirit. Wisdom belongs to the Lamb and to God (5:12; 7:12), but in the Apocalypse the believer must apply wisdom to this revelation. Wisdom is not scientific study and research, but insight from God which the believer receives by being in Christ Jesus (1 Cor. 1:30).

Twice in Revelation John calls for wisdom, here and 17:9, "Here is the mind that has wisdom." The context of the latter features the beast of the Abyss and the series of seven heads, seven hills, and seven kings. With respect to these two passages, minds enlightened by the Holy Spirit are able to understand their meaning with the wisdom God gives.

b. *Number.* "Let anyone who has a mind calculate the number of the beast." Persons who have intelligence enlightened by the Spirit will be able to understand. This does not mean that only intellectual people have the mental capacity to interpret this passage; everyone with the Spirit's aid will readily see its meaning in terms of Christ versus the Antichrist.

This involves calculating the number of the Antichrist. The verb *to calculate* occurs here and in Luke 14:28 (let the builder of a tower first *calculate* the cost). But how does one identify the person whose name and number is to be calculated? Solutions to this question have multiplied from the time of the early church fathers until today. Rulers, popes, causes, and items have all been suggested. In the second century, Irenaeus called attention to Titus, probably because the Roman leader destroyed Jerusalem, but this church father refrained from identifying him as the Antichrist. He alerted his readers to the danger of falsely presuming to know the name of the Antichrist.

A common interpretation applies the number 666 to the name of Emperor Nero—an interpretation that is favored by many scholars.[39] It would stand to reason that the name and number of a man in the first century calls for a person with a character of ill repute, and the name of Nero would qualify. But when did the writers begin to identify Nero with the number in this particular passage?

39. See Bauckham, *Climax of Prophecy*, pp. 384–452; Aune, *Revelation 6–16*, pp. 771–73; Kenneth L. Gentry Jr., *Before Jerusalem Fell: Dating the Book of Revelation* (Tyler, Tex.: Institute for Christian Economics, 1989), pp. 192–200; and numerous others.

There is no reference anywhere in history until the 1830s when four German scholars proposed his name.[40]

The difficulties arising from this identification are many. First, there is the method of converting the name into its numerical equivalent whereby, for example, a = 1, b = 2 c = 3 . . . j = 10, ja = 11 . . . k = 20, l = 30, m = 40, n = 50, etc. The name *Nero* by itself does not add up to 666, so it has to be expanded to Nero Caesar.

Next, if the spelling of the name is in Latin, Greek, or Hebrew or Aramaic, the sum totals differ. Indeed, if we adopt the Hebrew spelling, do we include or exclude the vowels? If we take only the consonants of Nero Caesar in Hebrew, we come to the number 616. But by adding the letter *n* to the Latin name *Nero* and dropping the *y* (Hebrew *yodh*, the equivalent of *i*) from the Hebrew spelling *qysr* (*kaisar*, the Greek form of the Latin *Caesar*) the sum is 666.[41] The problem lies not so much in the addition of the letter *n* as in the absence of the letter *y* (*yodh*) in *qysr* (*kaisar*). The method becomes questionable when letters are added and omitted to arrive at the desired number. And this calculation becomes particularly complicated when we consider that the name *Nero Caesar* must be transliterated from Latin into Greek and from Greek into Hebrew. The Apocalypse, however, is written to Greek-speaking Christians in the province of Asia. Would these hearers (1:3) readily understand that they had to transliterate a name from Latin via Greek to Hebrew (or Aramaic) to understand the number 666?

Third, if the identification of Nero Caesar with 666 is not based on solid evidence coming from the early church fathers but from nineteenth-century scholars, then names of additional Roman emperors can be considered. And other emperors have been suggested, each with appropriate titles, including Caligula, Vespasian, and Domitian.[42]

c. *Method.* In view of these difficulties I opt for a different approach. John puts the entire chapter in the framework of symbolism, so the reader may expect that the number in verse 18 must also be taken figuratively. The number seven signifies completeness; six, incompleteness. Satan, the great imitator, strives to achieve the sum total of seven but always falls short and ends up with six. God fulfilled his work of creation in seven days (Gen. 2:2); he told the Israelites to march around Jericho seven times with seven priests blowing seven trumpets on the seventh day (Josh. 6:4). And he decreed that a Hebrew servant be set free in the seventh year (Exod. 21:2; Deut. 15:12; Jer. 34:14). Satan by

40. O. F. Fritsche (1831); F. Benary (1836); F. Hitzig and E. Reuss (1837). Refer to D. Brady, *The Contribution of British Writers between 1560 and 1830 to the Interpretation of Revelation 13.16–18 (The Number of the Beast),* BGBE 27 (Tübingen: Mohr, 1983), p. 292. The early church fathers refrained from equating 666 with Neron Caesar.

41. Compare D. R. Hillers, "Revelation 13:18 and a Scroll from Murabbaʿât," *BASOR* 170 (1963): 65. This is not a Hebrew but an Aramaic document in which the Greek spelling has been transliterated into Hebrew.

42. Refer to W. G. Baines, "The Number of the Beast in Revelation 13:18," *HeythJourn* 16 (1975): 175–76; M. Oberweis, "Die Bedeutung der neutestamentlichen 'Rätselzahlen' 666 (Apk 13:18) und 153 (Joh 21:11)," *ZNW* 77 (1986): 226–41; L. van Hartingsveld, *Revelation*, pp. 56–57.

contrast faces defeat and divine judgment. In Revelation the number six points to judgment: at the end of the sixth seal, the sixth trumpet, and the sixth bowl. Satan's work always results in failure. "The number of the beast is 666, that is, failure upon failure upon failure!"[43] Although the devil has tried to eliminate all of God's people from the death of Abel to the present, he has never succeeded. In this age-old conflict not Satan but God is in charge. In conclusion, the number 666 belongs to Satan and not to one particular individual who did the devil's work in history.

Greek Words, Phrases, and Constructions in 13:15–18

Verse 15

ἵνα (second occurrence)—some manuscripts omit this particle, but it is needed for the verb ἀποκτανθῶσιν at the end of the sentence. The particle ἐάν governs the subjunctive προσκυνήσωσιν; the sentence is weighed down with subjunctives to express probability and a measure of uncertainty with respect to its message.

Verse 16

δῶσιν αὐτοῖς—the second aorist third person plural subjunctive followed by the pronoun could be interpreted reflexively, "that they give themselves a mark."[44] The absence of the preposition ἐπί calls for the indirect object "to them," and the plural is indefinite because the subject is lacking. Thus the phrase can be interpreted as a passive, "to be given."

Verse 17

καί—some leading manuscripts omit the conjunction to facilitate a smooth reading. This is true if the following ἵνα μή clause is dependent on the verb δῶσιν, but not when it depends on the preceding ποιεῖ (v. 16).[45]

Verse 18

ἑξήκοντα ἕξ—some Greek New Testaments write the Greek letters χξ (χ = 600, ξ = 60, = 6) in place of the written words that spell 666 (note that the last letter in this string is not the final *sigma* but the obsolete letter *stigma*, which once stood sixth in the Greek alphabet).[46] A variant reading is χι , which equals 616, but Irenaeus already rejected it. Metzger comments, "Perhaps the change was intentional, seeing that the Greek form Neron Caesar written in Hebrew characters is equivalent to 666, whereas the Latin form Nero Caesar is equivalent to 616."[47]

---

43. Hendriksen, *More Than Conquerors*, p. 151. He rightly observes that Revelation is a book not of riddles but of symbols (p. 151 n. 1). See also Harry R. Boer, *The Book of Revelation* (Grand Rapids: Eerdmans, 1979), p. 96.

44. Beckwith, *Apocalypse*, p. 641; Friedrich Düsterdieck, *Critical and Exegetical Handbook to the Revelation of John* (New York and London: Funk and Wagnalls, 1886), p. 381.

45. Metzger, *Textual Commentary*, p. 676.

46. See the TR, Souter, and the Majority Text.

47. Metzger, *Textual Commentary*, p. 676.

14

The Lamb and Four Messages

(14:1–20)

Outline (continued)

D. The Lamb (14:1–5)

E. Four Messages (14:6–13)

   1. The First Angel (14:6–7)
   2. The Second Angel (14:8)
   3. The Third Angel (14:9–12)
   4. A Heavenly Voice (14:13)

F. God's Wrath (14:14–20)

14 1 And I saw, and look, the Lamb standing on Mount Zion and with him 144,000 having
his name and the name of his Father written on their foreheads. 2 And I heard a sound
out of heaven like a sound of many waters and like the sound of loud thunder, and the
sound that I heard was like that of harpists playing their harps. 3 And they sang a new song
before the throne and before the four living creatures and the elders, and no one was able to learn
the song except the 144,000, those who were redeemed from the earth.

4 These are they who have not been defiled with women, for they are pure. They are the ones
who are following the Lamb wherever he goes. They are the ones redeemed from mankind—the
firstfruits to God and to the Lamb. 5 And in their mouth is found no lie, for they are blameless.

6 And I saw another angel flying in mid-heaven, having the eternal gospel to proclaim to those
who reside on the earth and to every nation, tribe, language, and people. 7 And he said in a loud
voice, "Fear God and give him glory, because the hour of his judgment has come. And worship the
one who made heaven and earth and the sea and springs of water."

8 And another angel, a second, followed and said, "Fallen, fallen is Babylon the Great, which
made all the nations drink the wrathful wine of her fornication."

9 And another angel, a third, followed them, saying in a loud voice,

> "If anyone worships the beast and his image and receives the mark on his fore-
> head or his hand, 10 he also will drink the wine of God's wrath that has been
> poured full strength into the cup of his wrath. And he will be tormented by fire
> and sulfur in the presence of the holy angels and of the Lamb. 11 And the
> smoke of their torment rises forever and ever, and they do not have rest day and
> night, they who worship the beast and his image, and anyone who receives the
> mark of his name. 12 Here is the endurance of the saints, those who are keeping
> the commands of God and the faith of Jesus."

13 And I heard a voice from heaven saying, "Write. Blessed are the dead who die in the Lord from
now on. Yes, says the Spirit, that they may rest from their toils, for their works will follow them."

14 And I saw, and look, a white cloud. And on the cloud was someone sitting like a son of man.
On his head he had a golden crown and in his hand a sharp sickle. 15 And another angel came out
of the temple crying in a loud voice to the one seated on the cloud, "Send forth your sickle and reap,
for the hour of harvesting has come, for the harvest of the earth is ripe." 16 And the one seated on
the cloud cast forth his sickle on the earth and the earth was harvested.

17 And another angel came forth out of the heavenly temple, and he had a sharp sickle. 18 And
another angel came forth from the altar. He had power over fire, and he called in a loud voice to the
one who had the sharp sickle, saying, "Send forth your sharp sickle and gather the clusters of the
grapevine of the earth, because its grapes are ripe." 19 And the angel thrust his sickle on the earth
and gathered the grapes of the earth, and he cast them into the great winepress of God's wrath.
20 And the winepress was trodden outside the city, and the blood came out of the winepress up to
the bridles of the horses for a distance of sixteen hundred stadia.

D. The Lamb
14:1–5

The contrast between God and Satan is the Apocalypse's recurring theme and strikingly so in the first few verses of this chapter compared to the preceding chapter. John describes the appearance and influence of the beast out of the earth (13:11–18), which he contrasts with the Lamb and the multitude of 144,000 on Mount Zion (14:1–5). Here in parallel columns are the differences:

Chapter 13	Chapter 14
lamb (v. 11)	Lamb (vv. 1, 4)
out of the earth (v. 11)	Mount Zion (v. 1)
worship of the beast (v. 12)	song of the 144,000 (v. 3)
beast's number 666 (v. 18)	saints' number 144,000 (v. 1)
everyone is enslaved (v. 16)	saints are redeemed (v. 3)
mark of the beast (vv. 16, 17)	name of Father and Lamb (v. 1)
deception of the beast (v. 14)	no lie in their mouth (v. 5)

After revealing the beast's attempt to force the surrender of the saints, John assures them of their security and victory. He paints a picture of the joy and happiness the saints express in following the Lamb and being in his presence. They are the 144,000 redeemed from the earth who were privileged to learn a new song of glory and joy that was heard from heaven. Not the beast out of the earth, the parody of the Lamb, not Satan the imitator, but the Lamb is King of kings and Lord of lords. He stands majestically on Mount Zion as the Victor over all the anti-Christian forces in the world. Thus the saints must take heart and not despair, for they share in the victory of the Lamb.

1. And I saw, and look, the Lamb standing on Mount Zion and with him 144,000 having his name and the name of his Father written on their foreheads.

a. "And I saw, and look, the Lamb standing on Mount Zion." The interpretation of this clause varies: some scholars take the place name literally as another name for Jerusalem, where the Lord at his coming will be with the 144,000 on Mount Zion. The projection then is futuristic but placed in the framework of having already occurred.[1] The difficulty with this view is that the Scriptures teach the return of Christ on the clouds of heaven, the resurrection of the dead, the transformation of those who are alive at that time, and the saints forever with the Lord (Matt. 24:30–31; 1 Thess. 4:16–17). Jesus and Paul portray Jesus' Second Coming with a loud command, shouting, and the trumpet call of God. But in Revelation John observes without any prior indication that the Lamb stands on Mount Zion as the battle between the forces of Satan and the followers of the

Lamb continues to rage. In brief, the Lamb has been standing there all the time.

Other scholars see the location of Mount Zion in heaven where the 144,000 reside as the redeemed from the earth (v. 3). This is the Jerusalem that is above,

1. John F. Walvoord, *The Revelation of Jesus Christ* (Chicago: Moody, 1966), p. 214; Robert L. Thomas, *Revelation 8–22: An Exegetical Commentary* (Chicago: Moody, 1995), p. 191; Robert W. Wall, *Revelation*, NIBCNT (Peabody, Mass.: Hendrickson, 1991), p. 179.

for there the church of the firstborn gathers in joyful assembly (Heb. 12:22–24). There God dwells with his people in the heavenly Jerusalem (Gal. 4:26).[2]

A third explanation is that in this book of contrasts and symbolism, John places the Lamb on Mount Zion in contrast with the lamb coming out of the earth (13:11). While the Antichrist appears to rule as the supreme commander in the world and causes the countless multitudes to worship him, the Lamb stands on Mount Zion. He is not suddenly coming to the aid of his people, but he has been there all along as the King of kings, the commander in chief, the supreme ruler in heaven and on earth (Matt. 28:18). So Moses told the Israelites: "Acknowledge and take to heart this day that the LORD is God in heaven above and on the earth below" (Deut. 4:39). When the saints on earth are persecuted by anti-Christian forces and are told that the beast is the supreme ruler on earth, they should not despair. When they open their spiritual eyes, they see the Lamb standing on Mount Zion who gives them the assurance that they are safe and secure. The days of the Antichrist are numbered because he is going down in defeat.

What then is the meaning of *Mount Zion?* Together with the term *Lamb* it should be understood symbolically. This becomes plain when we look at Psalm 2, in which the nations, peoples, kings, and rulers plot against God's Anointed One, the Christ. They want to free themselves of all the laws and rules that God has given them, but God scoffs at them and declares that he has installed his royal Son on Zion's holy hill. The Son rules the nations with an iron scepter and dashes them to pieces like pottery (Ps. 2:1–9). The rule of the Antichrist will end because of God's Son standing on Mount Zion. Not the lamb out of the earth but the Lamb of God is the King of this world. As in this psalm, so in the Apocalypse the intent of the expression *Mount Zion* is symbolic.[3] It is the place of God's dwelling as a symbol of safety and stability for his people.

b. "And with him 144,000 having his name and the name of his Father written on their foreheads." This is the second time the number 144,000 appears in Revelation (see 7:4). In both places the definite article is omitted (but not in 14:3). The two groups are identical: they are the saints who received the seal and the name of the Lamb and the Father. The seal certifying genuineness and possession signifies that all the saints belong to God.[4]

2. Robert H. Mounce, *The Book of Revelation,* rev. ed., NICNT (Grand Rapids: Eerdmans, 1998), pp. 264–65; Martin Kiddle, *The Revelation of St. John* (reprint, London: Hodder and Stoughton, 1943), pp. 262–63; John P. M. Sweet, *Revelation,* WPC (Philadelphia: Westminster, 1979), p. 221.

3. Refer to Herman Hoeksema, *Behold, He Cometh! An Exposition of the Book of Revelation* (Grand Rapids: Reformed Free Publishing Association, 1969), p. 483; G. B. Caird, *A Commentary on the Revelation of St. John the Divine* (London: Black, 1966), p. 178; Alan F. Johnson, *Revelation,* in *The Expositor's Bible Commentary,* ed. Frank E. Gaebelein (Grand Rapids: Zondervan, 1981), 12:538.

4. William Hendriksen, *More Than Conquerors* (reprint, Grand Rapids: Baker, 1982), p. 110; Gregory K. Beale, *The Book of Revelation: A Commentary on the Greek Text,* NIGTC (Grand Rapids: Eerdmans, 1998), pp. 734–35.

The unbelievers with the name and number of the beast belong to the Antichrist (13:16). But God's people with the divine names of the Lamb and the Father on their foreheads are dwelling among the followers of the beast on this earth. Together with the Lamb they are God's representatives. Their total number indicates that not one is lost of all those people the Father has given the Son (John 10:29). That is, the Antichrist is unable to lead the 144,000 astray, for their names are inscribed in the palm of God's hand (Isa. 49:16). Their number as such represents the incalculable multitude of the saints who stand in the presence of the Lamb (see commentary on 7:4, 9). The followers of the Antichrist are marked with the number 666, but the total number of believers is 144,000.

Are these 144,000 redeemed in heaven or on earth? Are they a select band? The answer to the first question is that the Lamb is always with the saints, whether they are on earth or in heaven. The second answer is that neither verse 1 nor verse 3 ("those who were redeemed from the earth") refers to a special group of saints. They are all included in the total number of God's redeemed people.[5]

2. And I heard a sound out of heaven like a sound of many waters and like the sound of loud thunder, and the sound that I heard was like that of harpists playing their harps.

John first saw the Lamb and the 144,000 on Mount Zion, and then he heard a sound coming to him out of heaven. His eye is fixed on a representative place on earth, while his ear is attuned to a sound in heaven. He fails to identify the speaker, which is common in the Apocalypse (see v. 13; 10:4, 8; 18:4). He describes the characteristics of the sound by giving comparisons taken from nature. He compares the sound with that of many waters, which is similar to the voice of Jesus addressing John on the island of Patmos: "his voice was like the sound of many waters" (1:15; 19:6; Ezek. 43:2). It is also like the sound of loud thunder, which indicates that the speaker calls everyone to pay attention (see 6:1).

In addition to the thundering loud noises heard in nature, the sound is like soft music coming from celestial harpists playing their harps (5:8; and see 15:2). John hears heavenly music entering his ears, first thunderous then soft and pleasing. It is comparable to an orchestra and choir that increase or decrease their volume at the command of the director. The sound is grand and gentle, lofty and lovely. John is privileged to hear this celestial music while he is on earth.

3. And they sang a new song before the throne and before the four living creatures and the elders, and no one was able to learn the song except the 144,000, those who were redeemed from the earth.

a. "And they sang a new song before the throne and before the four living creatures and the elders." Notice the special place the musicians and singers are allowed to occupy: they are in front of the throne, in the presence of God himself, and they stand in front of the four living creatures and the twenty-four elders who surround the throne (4:4, 6). The identity of the singers is not revealed

5. Isbon T. Beckwith, *The Apocalypse of John* (1919; reprint, Grand Rapids: Baker, 1979), p. 648.

(compare 11:15; 12:10). Their voices sing a new song that arises from hearts filled with gratitude and love to God.[6] We are not given the words of the song they sang, but we assume that they glorify the one sitting on the throne and extend thanks to the Lamb for the redemption he has accomplished on earth.

b. "And no one was able to learn the song except the 144,000." If we put it in positive terms, the intent of this clause is to include all the saints, for they are able to sing this new song; no one of the saints in heaven and on earth is excluded from joining the chorus. But no unbeliever is able to learn a song of praise to God. The saints in heaven constantly sing their praises to God. Likewise, all God's people on earth sing his praises at worship, especially on the Lord's Day. Of course, the dividing line between heaven and earth continues to exist until the last day, yet the intent of the praises of thanksgiving is similar. The perfect song of the saints in heaven reverberates to the saints on earth and strengthens them in the battle against anti-Christian forces.

What is the meaning of the number 144,000? This number is the sum of twelve times twelve times a thousand. In the Apocalypse, the number twelve refers only to God, his people, and his works (e.g., twelve tribes, twelve stars, twelve apostles, twelve gates, and twelve foundations). Twelve, symbolizing perfection, is raised to the second power in 144 and then multiplied by one thousand. One thousand is ten times ten times ten, which stands for a multitude. Thus, the number 144,000 symbolically means perfection times perfection times a multitude. This number constitutes the totality of God's people, the true Israel of God.[7]

c. "Those who were redeemed from the earth." The literal meaning of the verb in this clause is "were bought." The verb *to buy* occurs six times in the Apocalypse, but half of these have a religious connotation of Christ redeeming the saints (vv. 3, 4; 5:9). The preposition *from* means separation, and in this verse may indicate a departure of the saints from this earth to join the others in heaven. We can strengthen this interpretation by referring to 5:9, "you bought [men and women] for God out of every tribe and language and people and nation." But this explanation needs further evidence to make it complete.

First, verses 1–5 in this chapter are contrasted to the preceding context (13:11–18) in which the earth is the domain of the lamb that opposes the Father and the Lamb.

Next, the phrase *redeemed from the earth* has its parallel in "redeemed from mankind" (v. 4) so that the terms *earth* and *mankind* are synonymous. The Apocalypse uses the expression *mankind* often for those people opposed to the person and work of the Lord.[8]

---

6. Ps. 33:3; 40:3; 96:1; 98:1; 144:9; 149:1; Isa. 42:10; Rev. 5:9.

7. James L. Resseguie, *Revelation Unsealed: A Narrative Critical Approach to John's Apocalypse*, BIS 32 (Leiden: Brill, 1998), p. 66; compare Jürgen Roloff, *The Revelation of John*, trans. J. E. Alsup (Minneapolis: Fortress, 1993), p. 170.

8. Rev. 3:10; 6:10; 8:13; 11:10; 13:8, 12, 14; 14:6; 17:2, 8. Consult David E. Aune, *Revelation 6–16*, WBC 52B (Nashville: Nelson, 1998), p. 810.

Third, the redeemed on this earth are obligated to follow Jesus, who bought them, and they are willing to forsake everything for a life of wholeheartedly serving the Lord (Mark 10:28–31).

4. These are they who have not been defiled with women, for they are pure. They are the ones who are following the Lamb wherever he goes. They are the ones redeemed from mankind—the firstfruits to God and to the Lamb. 5. And in their mouth is found no lie, for they are blameless.

John gives a fourfold identification of the redeemed from the earth:

- they are pure
- they are followers of the Lamb
- they are firstfruits
- they are blameless[9]

a. "These are they who have not been defiled with women, for they are pure." First, then, let us consider the meaning of the clause "who have not been defiled with women." At first sight it appears to allude to celibates, and thus some commentators write that the clause refers to "the practice of sexual continence."[10] This view, however, is contrary to the biblical teaching of marriage which God instituted in Paradise: human beings should live together in marriage as husband and wife (Gen. 2:18–24). In fact, the New Testament indicates that the apostle Peter took his wife along on his missionary journeys (1 Cor. 9:5).

Other scholars interpret the clause to mean that the 144,000 are warriors engaged in battles for the Lord. They say that all these warriors are adult men who abstain from sexual intercourse for ceremonial purity while they are at war with their spiritual enemy. Even though Bauckham modifies this interpretation by calling ritual purity "a *metaphor* for a characteristic of Christian life,"[11] we see the restriction of a male-only army of warriors committed to lifelong celibacy as unnatural. First, it excludes from God's army all the faithful women who valiantly fight their battles against the evil one. Also, the teaching that marital relations are sinful and defiling is contrary to Scripture (see Heb. 13:4). Third, the verb *to defile* (Greek *molynein*) occurs three times in the New Testament and in each instance it is used figuratively (1 Cor. 8:7; Rev. 3:4; 14:4). The context of these passages indicates that the verb *to defile* means not falling into unfaithfulness to the

9. Refer to Elisabeth Schüssler Fiorenza, *The Book of Revelation: Justice and Judgment* (Philadelphia: Fortress, 1985), p. 871. She finds a "clearly marked composition and structure" in 14:1–5, namely, vision (v. 1), audition (vv. 2–3), and explanation (vv. 4–5).

10. Among others see Adela Yarbro Collins, "The Apocalypse [Revelation]," *NJBC*, p. 1010; and her *Apocalypse*, New Testament Message 22 (Wilmington: Glazier, 1979), pp. 99–100. Consult also D. C. Olson, "'Those Who Have Not Defiled Themselves with Women': Revelation 14:4 and the Book of Enoch," *CBQ* 59 (1997): 492–510.

11. Richard Bauckham, *The Climax of Prophecy* (Edinburgh: Clark, 1993), p. 231 Caird, *Revelation*, p. 179; G. R. Beasley-Murray, *The Book of Revelation*, NCB (London: Oliphants, 1974), p. 223.

Lord.[12] And last, four women are listed in the Book of Revelation (Jezebel [2:20]; the woman who gave birth to a male child [12:1–2, 4–6]; the great prostitute [17:1–6, 15–18]; and the bride of the Lamb [19:7]), of whom only the first and the third lead people into spiritual defilement.

A figurative interpretation of this clause fits the symbolical pattern of Revelation, namely, God's people are the bride of the Lord (19:7; 21:2, 9; 22:17). Paul tells the Corinthians: "I promised you to one husband, to Christ, so that I might present you as a pure virgin to him" (2 Cor. 11:2). This means that both men and women are included in the category of being a pure virgin; both must keep themselves from being deluded and induced by the beast to worship the image of the Antichrist. The purity of spiritual dedication to the Lord, therefore, is the first in the list of the four characteristics mentioned above that describe the 144,000.

b. "They are the ones who are following the Lamb wherever he goes." This is the second characteristic of being part of the great multitude of saints. Jesus told the disciples that "anyone who does not take his cross and follow me is not worthy of me" (Matt. 10:38). And he said that as the Shepherd he goes ahead of his people: "his sheep follow him because they know his voice" (John 10:4). Notice, first, that he expects his people to walk in his footsteps and not go astray (1 Pet. 2:21). Next, the saints look to him for leadership and direction as they travel earth's pathway and ward off the attacks of the devil. With the present tense of the verbs *to follow* and *to go* John stresses the ongoing activity of the Lamb and his followers on earth. Again, this verse shows that the 144,000 are presently following the Lord in obedience to him.

c. "They are the ones redeemed from mankind—the firstfruits to God and to the Lamb." This is the third characteristic. By shedding his blood on Calvary's cross, Jesus paid the debt to set his people free from the curse of sin and guilt. If then Christ died to redeem his people, what is the meaning of the expression *firstfruits*? There are two explanations. First, when the Israelites harvested the first ears of the grain harvest and consecrated them to the Lord, they expected the rest of the harvest to follow. So Paul writes that the members of Stephanas's household were the firstfruits in Achaia (1 Cor. 16:15), with the implication that he expected the rest of the harvest to come in the near future. A second interpretation applies the term *firstfruits* to the entire entity, the totality of the 144,000 wholly offered in thankfulness to God and the Lamb. The expression can refer to "the totality of God's people as an offering set apart to God *with no thought of more to come.*"[13] Thus, the sum total belongs to God.

d. "And in their mouth is found no lie, for they are blameless." This is the last of the four characteristics. In an anti-Christian world saturated with lies and de-

12. Refer to J. I. Packer, *NIDNTT*, 1:448–49. Consult also J. Ramsey Michaels, *Interpreting the Book of Revelation* (Grand Rapids: Baker, 1992), pp. 137–38; Gerhard A. Krodel, *Revelation*, ACNT (Minneapolis: Augsburg, 1989), pp. 262–64.

13. Beale, *Revelation*, p. 744 (his italics); Bauer (p. 81) writes that "the emphasis is less on chronological sequence than on quality."

ceit, Christians stand out as emblems of truth, honesty, and integrity. Should we turn the first clause into a positive statement with some adaptation, we would read "and truth comes from their mouth." David describes persons who are permitted to live in God's sanctuary and on his holy hill as those "who lead blameless lives and do what is right, speaking the truth from sincere hearts" (Ps. 15:2 NLT).

The first clause is taken from the writings of Isaiah and Zephaniah. The first writer portrays the Suffering Servant without deceit in his mouth (Isa. 53:9), and the second says, "The remnant of Israel will do no wrong; they will speak no lies, nor will deceit be found in their mouths" (Zeph. 3:13). The followers of Jesus, whom the prophet calls the remnant of Israel, are expected to speak the truth like their master (1 Pet. 2:22).

And the second clause, "they are blameless," is an echo of the Levitical rule to offer to God animals that were without any defect (see among other passages Lev. 1:3; 3:1, 6). Jesus presents to himself "a radiant church, without stain or wrinkle or any other blemish, but holy and blameless" (Eph. 5:27; see also Col. 1:22). These are the saints that belong to the 144,000.

In conclusion, four characteristics describe the great multitude of saints who are with the Lamb on symbolical Mount Zion (Ps. 2:6). As the forces of the Antichrist attack the church on earth, it demonstrates purity, obedience, unity, and veracity. With these traits the saints are able to overcome the evil one.

Greek Words, Phrases, and Constructions in 14:1–4

Verse 1

εἶδον καὶ ἰδού—these two verbs not only feature the activity of seeing, but they also stress the immensity of the vision itself.

τὸ ἀρνίον—the definite article referring to the Lamb is supported by leading manuscripts and its overwhelming use with the noun (27 times) in Revelation—the exception is 5:6. The Majority Text includes the definite article, but it is excluded from two translations (KJV, NKJV).

Verse 2

ὡς (second occurrence)—the presence or absence of this particle is questionable, because there is equal support for insertion and omission. The style of the Apocalypse favors the inclusion, especially when the first element in comparison is absent (compare 4:6; 6:6; 9:7; 19:1, 6 [three times]).[14]

Verses 3–4

The Greek text uses the perfect passive participle in v. 3 (ἠγορασμένοι, have been bought) and the aorist passive indicative in v. 4 (ἠγοράσθησαν, they were bought) to describe the Lamb's followers. The two forms are similar in meaning, but the perfect views the action as accomplished in the past but with continuing results.

---

14. Bruce M. Metzger, *A Textual Commentary on the Greek New Testament,* 2d ed. (Stuttgart: Deutsche Bibelgesellschaft, 1994), p. 677.

E. Four Messages
14:6–13

The contrast of chapters 13 and 14 between the followers of the beast and the followers of Christ continues in this segment. An angel proclaims the eternal gospel to all classes of people, telling them to fear God and worship him as the Creator. This message introduces not grace but judgment. Two additional angels pronounce judgment on Babylon and on all those who worship the beast by displaying the mark of his name. The converse is that the saints who obey God's commandments and faithfully follow Jesus are exhorted to be patient. They receive a blessing from the Lord, for as they rest in death their deeds continue to testify for them.

1. The First Angel
14:6–7

6. And I saw another angel flying in mid-heaven, having the eternal gospel to proclaim to those who reside on the earth and to every nation, tribe, language, and people.

John writes that he saw another angel flying in the sky between heaven and earth. First, the word *another* begs the question whether an angel has been mentioned earlier. The last reference to an individual angel was the seventh in the series of trumpet-blowing angels (11:15). Now he introduces another group of three angels in which in Greek each in turn is referred to as "another angel."[15] The first of these angels is flying in mid-heaven, much the same as the eagle in 8:13, as a portent of impending judgment. The angel's position *mid-heaven* allows his message to be heard far and wide.

This angel has to proclaim the eternal gospel to residents on this earth, that is, to all the divisions of the human race from "every nation, tribe, language, and people" (compare Matt. 24:14). The noun *gospel* appears only here in Revelation; it is preceded by the adjective *eternal* and in Greek is without the definite article. The adjective points to the timelessness and permanence of the Word of God, which people ignore to their own detriment. They are content to live on this earth without any thought of God's imminent judgment. Jesus used the illustration of the people in Noah's day, who ate, drank, and married up to the day Noah entered the ark and the flood carried them away (Matt. 24:38–39). Eating, drinking, and marrying are normal human activities, but those people performed them without any concern for God's Word or will.

The angel proclaims the gospel not necessarily as good news but as a reminder of God's abiding truth; the angel calls men and women to respond to God's message before the judgment comes. The expression "every nation, tribe, language, and people" occurs repeatedly in Revelation and alludes to unrepentant residents on this earth who are inimical to God (compare 11:9; 13:7; 17:15), to the saints who worship the Lord (see 5:9; 7:9), and to people everywhere who

---

15. R. C. H. Lenski, *The Interpretation of St. John's Revelation* (Columbus: Wartburg, 1943), p. 427.

are being called to repent (10:11). Here the angel addresses a message of repentance to all sinners who have been indifferent to God and his Word, as is evident from the angel's message.

7. And he said in a loud voice, "Fear God and give him glory, because the hour of his judgment has come. And worship the one who made heaven and earth and the sea and springs of water."

The angel speaks loudly (see 18:2) so that all the inhabitants of the earth can hear and respond to the message. Everyone who hears reacts either positively or negatively, either ardently or apathetically, either obediently or defiantly. There is no middle ground (Matt. 12:30).

Here is a command to fear God and give him glory and worship him, which on the basis of the Greek text may be interpreted as "begin to fear, give glory to, and worship God."[16] If this interpretation is correct, then the angel is addressing people who have not yet heeded God's call for reverence, glory, and worship (15:4). They have paid him no respect, were insensitive to his word and testimony, and failed to honor him. The injunction *fear God* asks from mankind reverence and praise (Eccles. 12:13). The order to *give him glory* is a Hebraic saying appearing in both Old and New Testaments: Joshua told Achan to give glory to the LORD (Josh. 7:19; see Jer. 13:16), and the Pharisees commanded the man born blind to give glory to God (John 9:24). The phrase signifies telling the truth by sinners who appear before God's judgment seat. Indeed the two commands to fear God and to give him glory are part of John's phraseology in Revelation (15:4; 19:5 and 16:9; 19:7 respectively).[17]

The reason for these commands is that the hour of God's judgment has come. Chronological time is running out for the human race, for the end is near with the Judgment Day at hand. In fact, the angel announces that the *hour* of judgment has come. John already alluded to this, writing that when God's adversaries saw his intervening action on behalf of the two witnesses, they were terrified and gave glory to the God of heaven (see commentary on 11:13). Now we hear the announcement uttered by the angel, but we are not told of its effect. The reference to the time of judgment is a repetitive theme in the Apocalypse: imminent judgment for sinners (6:16); judging the dead (11:18); the judgment has come (14:15–16); the great day of God's wrath (16:17–21); the rider coming to judge (19:11–21); and the final judgment (20:11–15).

The people are told to worship God, the maker of heaven and earth and the sea and springs of water. References to God the Creator are scarce in the Apocalypse (4:11; 10:6; 14:7) but abundant in the Old Testament, and the message of the angel echoes wording borrowed from the Old Testament (e.g., Gen. 1:1;

---

16. See Richard A. Young, *Intermediate New Testament Greek: A Linguistic and Exegetical Approach* (Nashville: Broadman, 1994), p. 143; S. Greijdanus, *De Openbaring des Heeren aan Johannes*, KNT (Amsterdam: Van Bottenburg, 1925), p. 295.

17. R. H. Charles, *A Critical and Exegetical Commentary on the Revelation of St. John*, ICC (Edinburgh: Clark, 1920), 2:3, 13; David A. de Silva, "A Sociorhetorical Interpretation of Revelation 14:6–13: A Call to Act Justly toward the Just and Judging God," *BBR* 9 (1999): 65–117, especially 88–89.

14:19, 22; 2 Chron. 2:12).[18] The point of the angel's command is to show the immense difference between worshiping God as Creator of the universe and worshiping the beast as servant of Satan (13:4, 8, 12, 15). The comparison is ludicrous, because while God is the Creator, Satan is the destroyer.

2. The Second Angel *14:8*

8. And another angel, a second, followed and said, "Fallen, fallen is Babylon the Great, which made all the nations drink the wrathful wine of her fornication."

The second angel follows the first one in mid-heaven and utters a word against Babylon, the destroyer of Jerusalem and the temple in 586 B.C. The question is how this announcement relates to the words of the first angel. The answer lies in the people's refusal to repent and give God the glory that is due him. The fall of unbelievers is unavoidable when they fail to repent, for then judgment is their just retribution.

The cry "Fallen, fallen is Babylon the Great" is taken from Isaiah 21:9 and Daniel 4:30, which mention successively the fall and the greatness of Babylon (see Rev. 18:2). In modern writing we express emphasis with italics or the use of an exclamation mark. These features were unknown in the ancient world, where writers achieved the same purpose by repeating the word that needed stress, hence the repetitious use of "fallen." The city of Babylon fell to the Assyrians in 689 B.C. and a hundred and fifty years later to the Persians in 539.

What is the meaning of *Babylon?* John writes the name six times, here and in 16:19; 17:5; 18:2, 10, 21. There are at least three interpretations for this name:

- literal Babylon, because the name of the Euphrates River also appears (9:14; 16:12);
- a code name for Rome, which Peter apparently used (1 Pet. 5:13; see also *2 Baruch* 11.1; *Sibylline Oracles* 5.143, 159, 434);
- a reference to the converging of evil in particular places throughout history.

Although a case can be made for all three explanations, the last interpretation merits attention, first, in light of the contrast of good and evil in the Apocalypse, especially in chapters 13 and 14. And second, limiting the reference to Babylon and Rome as the most typical representatives of depravity in John's day puts restrictions on the message of Revelation. This book addresses the universal church from the first century to the consummation, with hope and encouragement for all believers living in a world that is hostile to God and his people.

18. Consult W. Altink, "1 Chronicles 16:8–36 as Literary Source for Revelation 14:6–7," *AUSS* 22 (1984): 187–96; also his "Theological Motives for the Use of 1 Chronicles 16:8–36 as Background for Revelation 14:6–7," *AUSS* 24 (1986): 211–21. Beale refers to the LXX text of Dan. 4:17, 30, 34, 37 for the source of John's vocabulary (*Revelation*, pp. 751–52).

Mounce calls Babylon "a symbol of the spirit of godlessness that in every age lures people away from the worship of the Creator."[19] Babylon is God's enemy that as a world power oppresses the saints. Hence the name symbolizes the rule of the Antichrist that endures until the end of cosmic time. John is so sure of its downfall that, looking into the future, he writes the past tense: "Fallen, fallen is Babylon the Great."

The second part of this verse, "which made all the nations drink the wrathful wine of her fornication," alludes to Jeremiah 51:7, "Babylon was a gold cup in the LORD's hand; she made the whole earth drunk. The nations drank her wine; therefore they have now gone mad." The wording of this second part, which is the same as in 18:3, causes perplexity because John appears to mix the concepts of drinking wine and wrath. I suggest that John speaks symbolically and puts together two pictures in one clause; they are the pictures of wine and the wrath of God combined in the phrase "the wrathful wine." Look at these two pictures! Wine when imbibed in quantity distorts one's capability to think soberly and rationally, and fornication in God's sight is wickedness and an offense against him. To put the pictures in an everyday context, the nations of the world are intoxicated with their rejection of God and his revelation and have turned to the worship of power dominating all areas of life. What does all this mean? It points first to the potent influence evil has on the nations of the world so that people are numbed by it. And next, it points to the wrath of God people incur when they rebel against God. The second picture is the consequence of the first and therefore is the more awesome. God's wrath inevitably leads to the Judgment Day at which time his enemies will be cut off and cast into a place of torment.

3. The Third Angel
14:9–12

9. And another angel, a third, followed them, saying in a loud voice, "If anyone worships the beast and his image and receives the mark on his forehead or his hand, 10. he also will drink the wine of God's wrath that has been poured full strength into the cup of his wrath. And he will be tormented by fire and sulfur in the presence of the holy angels and of the Lamb."

a. "If anyone worships the beast and his image and receives the mark on his forehead or his hand." A third angel flying in mid-heaven cried out in a loud voice like the first angel, so that everyone in every place on earth was able to hear him. He is the last one in a group of three to utter a warning of advancing doom and destruction. God's wrath is awaiting all those who instead of worshiping him worship the beast.

The angel addresses all those who already pay homage to the beast that is coming up out of the sea of humanity and who venerate the image that has been

---

19. Mounce, *Revelation*, p. 271; see also Hoeksema, *Behold He Cometh!* pp. 496–97; Homer Hailey, *Revelation: An Introduction and Commentary* (Grand Rapids: Baker, 1979), p. 308; Philip Edgcumbe Hughes, *The Book of the Revelation: A Commentary* (Leicester: Inter-Varsity; Grand Rapids: Eerdmans, 1990), p. 161; Greijdanus, *Openbaring*, p. 296; Lenski, *Revelation*, p. 432; Luther Poellot, *Revelation: The Last Book in the Bible* (St. Louis: Concordia, 1962), pp. 187–88.

erected in his honor.[20] Those people who have the mark of the beast on their forehead and hand are able to buy and sell. But all those who refuse to worship the beast face poverty and death. Without his distinguishing mark they are banned from the marketplace (13:15, 17).

b. "He also will drink the wine of God's wrath that has been poured full strength into the cup of his wrath." The worship of the beast and his image is a direct violation of God's command not to bow down to and worship other gods and images (Exod. 20:3–6). Those people who disobey face the undiluted wrath of God.

John again uses the image of drinking wine, which is a follow-up of drinking the wrathful wine of Babylon's fornication. The act of drinking wine, in the future tense, indicates that God hands the cup to the individual himself much the same as God gave Jesus the cup of suffering in the Garden of Gethsemane (Matt. 26:42; John 18:11). The individual will be made to drink the cup of wrath; the future tense signifies the inevitability of the act.[21]

I have translated the Greek text as "God's wrath that has been poured full strength into the cup of his wrath." The words *full strength* go back to the setting of Greeks diluting their wine with water. They mixed wine and water of equal parts into a vessel that was called *kratēr,* from which we have the derivative "crater."[22] God's wrath has not been diluted but is poured full strength into the cup handed over to sinful people. God told Jeremiah, "Take from my hand this cup filled with the wine of my wrath and make all the nations to whom I send you drink it" (25:15; see also Isa. 51:17, 22; Ps. 75:8).

c. "And he will be tormented by fire and sulfur in the presence of the holy angels and of the Lamb." The wrath of God takes on frightening proportions because his adversaries are not merely objects as such; they will be tormented internally and externally. By drinking the cup of God's wrath, they burn inwardly as it affects their souls day and night, and outwardly as they experience burning fire and smell the stench of sulfur forever. Scripture describes this torment in dreadful terms. It is frightening to fall into the hands of the living God (Heb. 10:31).

The words *fire and sulfur* first appear in the account of the destruction of Sodom and Gomorrah (Gen. 19:24). Figuratively speaking, others meet a similar lot: the wicked (Ps. 11:6), Assyria (Isa. 30:33), Edom (Isa. 34:9), and Gog (Ezek. 38:22). In addition to this text, John describes the lake of fire and sulfur as the place where the devil, the beast, the false prophet, and all the wicked will be (19:20; 20:10; 21:8). While the saints are in glory, the holy angels and the Lamb acquiesce in the frightful judgment God pronounces on his enemies (see 6:16–17). They observe the administration of God's perfect justice. Henry Barclay Swete writes, "If Christians at the stake or in the amphitheater suffered in the sight of a multitude of their fellowmen, those who deny their faith must suffer

20. Worshiping the beast is paralleled by worshiping his image (see 13:4, 8, 12, 15; 16:2; 19:20; 20:4).

21. E.g., NJB, JB, KJV, RSV, NRSV, NEB, REB.

22. Aune, *Revelation 6–16*, p. 833.

before a more august assembly, composed of the holy angels and the Lamb."[23] The expression *holy angels* occurs only here in Revelation.

11. "And the smoke of their torment rises forever and ever, and they do not have rest day and night, they who worship the beast and his image, and anyone who receives the mark of his name."

The picture of torment is meant as a warning to the unbelievers, who in their daily lives reject the revelation of God and his Christ. John has taken the wording for this picture from the curse God pronounced on Edom, where pitch and sulfur will burn unquenched night and day while its smoke rises without ceasing (Isa. 34:9–10).[24] God's archenemies are forever in the smoke of this fire that is tormenting them. There is no end to their torment; they are unable to terminate it by death or annihilation (4 Macc. 13:15). It is impossible to escape God's righteous judgment except by repenting and believing in Christ during one's lifetime.

The Apocalypse is a book of contrasts from beginning to end. The smoke of the torment afflicting God's antagonists is the opposite of the smoke at the altar of incense mingled with the prayers of the saints that ascend to God (8:4). The clause "and they do not have rest day and night" refers to the wicked who suffer ceaselessly day and night in agonizing torment. This clause occurs also in the throne room scene, but there it refers to the four living creatures; they never stop singing, "Holy, holy, holy is the Lord God Almighty, who was, and is, and is to come" (4:8). While the wicked suffer, the cherubim sing praises to God. The worship of the beast leads to endless torment, but the worship of God to everlasting joy.[25]

The last part of this verse is taken from verses in the preceding chapter (13:15, 16, 17). It points to those who worship the beast and his image, and who bear the mark of his name. These people belong to the beast and worship him only. They have refused to glorify God and consequently meet him as the Judge of all the earth (19:2–3). The saints, on the other hand, suffer persecution while on earth but meet their Lord and Savior as they enter the new Jerusalem in glory.

12. "Here is the endurance of the saints, those who are keeping the commands of God and the faith of Jesus."

The text is a summary of the preceding verses and at the same time it is an elaboration of the wording in 13:10, "Here is the endurance and faith of the saints." Similarly 13:18 states, "Here is wisdom." While John writes about the wicked and God's perfect judgment, he does not forget the saints. He has a word for them, too. In the midst of hardship for not worshiping the beast and receiving his mark, the saints must employ heavenly wisdom by looking to the end and patiently endure.

---

23. Henry Barclay Swete, *Commentary on Revelation* (1911; reprint, Grand Rapids: Kregel, 1977), p. 185.

24. Consult Jan Fekkes, *Isaiah and Prophetic Traditions in the Book of Revelation: Visionary Antecedents and Their Development,* JSNTSup 93 (Sheffield: JSOT, 1994), pp. 206–8; Robert A. Peterson, *Hell on Trial: The Case for Eternal Punishment* (Phillipsburg, N.J.: Presbyterian and Reformed, 1995), pp. 196–97.

25. The text of 4 Ezra (=2 Esdras) 7:36 reads, "The place of torment will appear, and over against it the place of rest; the furnace of hell will be displayed, and on the opposite side the paradise of joy" (REB). See also *1 Enoch* 48.9.

How do Christians continue to live in a hostile pagan world? John answers that they must continue to keep God's commands and the faith of Jesus. The divine commands are summarized in the Decalogue and fully revealed in the Scriptures of the Old and New Testaments. As the world increasingly turns away from the divine commands and considers them obsolete, Christians are told to keep them. They know that in observing them is great reward (Ps. 19:11). God's law endures throughout the ages, need not be amended, is relevant in all cultures, and will never be repealed.

The last phrase in this verse, *the faith of Jesus*, is translated:

- faith in Jesus (NASB, NJB). This is interpreted subjectively as a person's faith in Jesus Christ.
- faith of Jesus (KJV, NRSV). Objective faith is reciting a Christian creed at worship or giving a defense of the gospel.
- faithful to Jesus (NIV). Faith that demonstrates dedicated loyalty is objective faith in action.

Even though there is a place for both subjective and objective faith, I favor the second choice. Those believers who put to work their faith in Jesus prove their constant faithfulness to him.[26]

4. A Heavenly Voice
14:13

This passage is read and applied at funerals to comfort those who mourn the loss of a near relative or friend. The words presented in the form of a beatitude and supported by the Spirit's testimony are precious to God's people. They convey a message of encouragement and support whenever Christians face death. Indeed, they are designed to remove the fear of death, because Christ having triumphed over death and the grave blesses his followers who die in him.

The world that is hostile toward God and his people is destined to perish; by contrast the saints who die in the Lord are entering eternal bliss. God's enemies are facing downfall and ultimate destruction (vv. 8–12), while the saints enter eternal rest in the presence of their Lord.

13. And I heard a voice from heaven saying, "Write. Blessed are the dead who die in the Lord from now on. Yes, says the Spirit, that they may rest from their toils, for their works will follow them."

John fails to identify the speaker, as is often the case in Revelation.[27] Here is a voice that utters the second beatitude in the Apocalypse out of a list of seven (1:3; 14:13; 16:15; 19:9; 20:6; 22:7, 14). The Lord, an angel, or an anonymous speaker uttered these beatitudes.

---

26. Aune (*Revelation 6–16*, p. 837) calls the phrase *kai tēn pistin Iēsou* (and faithfulness to Jesus) a gloss, but there is no evidence in Greek manuscripts to validate this suggestion.

27. See, e.g., Rev. 10:4, 8; 11:12; 12:10; 16:1; 18:4; 21:3.

The voice tells John to write. It was a command he had heard on earlier occasions when Christ ordered him to write and the Spirit uttered a promise to the churches (2:1, 8, 12, 18; 3:1, 7, 14; see also 1:11, 19; 19:9; 21:5). This beatitude is aimed at the dead, namely, those who die in the Lord. In other words, the phrase *the dead* can be used to describe unbelievers (20:5), but the qualifier *die in the Lord* clarifies its meaning. Believers whose eyes are fixed on Jesus, who is the author and perfecter of their faith (Heb. 12:2), do not fear death, while unbelievers are filled with fear of judgment and damnation (Rev. 6:15–17).

What is the significance of the phrase *from now on?* Should it be interpreted with the first clause "Blessed are the dead" or with the entire sentence?[28] Are only the saints who die a martyr's death called blessed or are all believers blessed? And when does the *now* begin?[29]

All the saints who look forward to residing in the heavenly Jerusalem, "whose architect and builder is God," are commended (Heb. 11:10). Here John adds the clarifying clause "who die in the Lord" to specify a relationship to Jesus. This relationship was a comfort to the persecuted Christians in Asia Minor in John's day. Next, it is comfort to all believers who know that Christ welcomes them at the portals of heaven. And these words encourage those Christians who even now or in the future endure the full impact of persecution, injustice, insult, and slander because of Christ's name (Matt. 5:11–12). In short, the heavenly voice speaks reassuring words not merely to those who die a martyr's death but to all God's people. Everyone who in faith looks to Jesus is in the *now* period.

The Holy Spirit affirms the words spoken by the heavenly voice, for he assures the saints that they will rest from their earthly toils that they performed on behalf of the Lord. God does not forget their works, for in heaven he crowns them with his blessing of grace and glory (Rev. 6:11; Heb. 6:10). The saints will not lose their rewards (1 Cor. 9:25; 2 Tim. 4:8). Thus through the Spirit Jesus tells the persecuted saints in Philadelphia that he will give them a new name, that is, the name of God and the name of the new Jerusalem coming down out of heaven (Rev. 3:12). And last, Jesus says that at his return he will reward everyone according to what he or she has done (22:12).

Greek Words, Phrases, and Constructions in 14:6–13

Verse 6

ἄλλον ἄγγελον—the presence of the adjective is harder to explain than its absence and therefore is likely to be the original reading. Its omission was caused by its lack of ob-

---

28. Compare Lenski, *Revelation*, p. 441.

29. At least two translations construe the words *from now on* or their equivalent with the last half of the verse. "'Henceforth,' says the Spirit, 'they may rest from their labours'" (NEB) and "'Blessed indeed,' the Spirit says: 'now they can rest for ever after their work'" (NJB). This word order may have been influenced by the Vulgate, which makes the construction part of the Spirit's utterance. The flow of the sentence, however, puts the words *from now on* at the end of the first full sentence.

vious relevance because the preceding reference to an individual angel appears way back at 11:15.[30]

εὐαγγέλιον . . . εὐαγγελίσαι—the lack of the definite article, which translators supply, shows that not the good news as such but a message of repentance is proclaimed. The aorist infinitive strengthens the concept of proclaiming a message but by itself the verb is intransitive.

Verse 7

λέγων—like the participle ἔχοντα, this present participle is the object of the verb *to see* and therefore should have been in the accusative.

Verse 8

ἔπεσεν—the repetition is for emphasis, while the aorist tense denotes the recent occurrence of its action.

Note the succession of genitives in which the governing genitive τοῦ οἴνου precedes the dependent one.[31]

Verse 13

οἱ ἀποθνῄσκοντες—"those who are dying." The present active participle refers to a single act that characterizes all people.

ἀπ' ἄρτι—Blass and Debrunner suggest the translation "exactly" or "certainly."[32]

ἵνα ἀναπαήσονται—the ἵνα clause with the aorist subjunctive may introduce "the idea of conceived result," but the context shows that it "has an imperatival meaning."[33]

F. God's Wrath
14:14–20

John takes a cyclical approach to his subject by repeatedly returning to the judgment. The next seven verses are no exception, for the reference to the harvest is a symbol of the coming judgment. This is evident from the sickles and the gathering of the clusters of grapes that are thrown into the great winepress of God's wrath.

The first part of this chapter revealed the lot of the saints, whose spiritual future is secure (vv. 1–4). The second part contains the messages of the three angels that mention the hour of judgment in which God's enemies receive the full strength of his wrath (vv. 9–13), while the saints enter into his rest. The last part of the chapter (vv. 14–20) concerns the harvest of the earth and the reaping of the grapes of God's wrath; that is, positively the ingathering of the saints and negatively the condemnation of the unbelievers.[34] These harvest pictures sym-

30. Metzger, *Textual Commentary*, p. 678.

31. Friedrich Blass and Albert Debrunner, *A Greek Grammar of the New Testament and Other Early Christian Literature*, trans. and rev. Robert Funk (Chicago: University of Chicago Press, 1961), §168.2.

32. Blass and Debrunner, *Greek Grammar*, §12.3.

33. Robert Hanna, *A Grammatical Aid to the Greek New Testament* (Grand Rapids: Baker, 1983), p. 452.

34. Bauckham, *Climax of Prophecy*, p. 296. See also his *Theology of the Book of Revelation*, New Testament Theology (Cambridge: Cambridge University Press, 1993), pp. 96–98.

bolize the judgment that is evident in both the Old and New Testaments. "Swing the sickle, for the harvest is ripe. Come, trample the grapes, for the winepress is full and the vats overflow—so great is their wickedness" (Joel 3:13; compare Isa. 63:1–6; Lam. 1:15). Similarly in the parable of the weeds Jesus depicts the Judgment Day (Matt. 13:29–30, 37–43). First the elect are harvested and afterward the wicked: first the wheat and then the weeds.

The parallelism of verses 14–16 and 17–20 is astonishing: there are two sickles, two individuals wielding sickles, two angels coming out of the temple, two angels calling in a loud voice, two commands to use the sickle, two references to ripe grain and ripe grapes, and two harvests. Also notice that the word *sickle* occurs exactly seven times in verses 14–20 to illustrate the completeness of God's judgment.

14. And I saw, and look, a white cloud. And on the cloud was someone sitting like a son of man. On his head he had a golden crown and in his hand a sharp sickle.

a. "And I saw, and look, a white cloud. And on the cloud was someone sitting like a son of man." This is now the third time in chapter 14 that John writes the words "and I saw" (vv. 1, 6), and each time he introduces a new but related topic. They are the place of the saints, the messages of the angels, and the swinging of the sickle by the Lord and an angel respectively.

The writer initiates this last segment with a reference to the prophecy of Daniel 7:13, "In my vision at night I looked, and there before me was one like a son of man, coming with the clouds of heaven" (compare Matt. 24:30). John had already alluded to this Old Testament passage when he predicted the return of Jesus "coming with the clouds" and called him "a son of man" (1:7 and 13 respectively). Here he begins by referring to the white cloud, which is the only place in Scripture where the phrase *a white cloud* appears. The color white in this instance is a symbol of holiness and judgment,[35] and these clouds are the exact opposite of dark foreboding clouds that intend to hide God's glory (Exod. 19:9; 1 Kings 8:12). Here in full view on a single cloud sits a person like a son of man. The Evangelists report Jesus' words to Caiaphas, "In the future you will see the Son of Man *sitting* at the right hand of the Mighty One and coming on the clouds of heaven" (Matt. 26:64, emphasis added; see also Mark 14:62). The term *son of man* in John's vocabulary unmistakably refers to the Lord Jesus Christ at his Second Coming (see Rev. 1:7, where the identical expression appears).

b. "On his head he had a golden crown and in his hand a sharp sickle." In addition to the Danielic title *son of man* John describes the coming Messiah as royalty. Jesus wears a golden crown on his head to show that he is a victorious conqueror (compare 6:2; 2 Sam. 12:30; 1 Chron. 20:2). He wears the royal crown as a symbol of victory; also the twenty-four elders surrounding God's throne wear golden crowns (4:4). And Jesus holds a sharp sickle in his hand as a symbol of the harvest. The sickle has been sharpened to be a ready tool in the reaper's hand to accomplish without opposition and delay the task of gathering the harvest.

---

35. Hendriksen, *More Than Conquerors*, p. 155.

15. And another angel came out of the temple crying in a loud voice to the one seated on the cloud, "Send forth your sickle and reap, for the hour of harvesting has come, for the harvest of the earth is ripe." 16. And the one seated on the cloud cast forth his sickle on the earth and the earth was harvested.

When John writes the term *another,* he is not implying that the "son of man" is angelic. In the Apocalypse John nowhere states that Jesus is an angel. In fact, the writer of Hebrews clearly shows that the Son has inherited a name that is far superior to that of angels (1:4). The expression, therefore, should be seen in the sequence of the angels mentioned earlier in verses 6, 8, and 9; this angel is the fourth one, with two more to come.

Some commentators have difficulty with the idea that an angel with a command from God tells the exalted Christ to begin the harvest. Would not Christ in whom "all the fullness of the Deity lives" (Col. 2:9) be cognizant of everything? Why would an angel have to function as an intermediary between the Father and the Son? Hence, Leon Morris queries "why the angel is closer to God than the glorious Christ."[36] In the discourse on the last things, Jesus told his disciples that apart from the Father no one, neither the Son nor the angels, knows the day or the hour of the end (Matt. 24:36; Mark 13:32; Acts 1:7). Indeed, what Jesus taught while he was on earth, John now teaches in a symbolic apocalyptic manner.[37] From the Father to the Son the angel communicates a message that the time for the harvest has come.

The angel comes forth out of the temple, from the very presence of God. From the throne room (7:15), the angel is sent forth to shout in a loud voice so that everyone far and near can hear him tell the "son of man" to harvest the ripe grain. This is the symbolic wheat harvest that is harvested at the right time when the stalks and the kernels are dry. Without delay the grain is threshed. Here the time for harvesting refers figuratively to the Judgment Day (see Jer. 51:33; Joel 3:13; Matt. 13:30, 40–42).[38] It is the time of gathering the believers into the kingdom, for the sickle goes forth to reap God's people (Mark 4:29; John 4:35–38). The "son of man" has been given the authority to put the sickle to work, though he uses his angels to assist him (Matt. 13:39; 24:31).

---

36. Leon Morris, *Revelation,* rev. ed., TNTC (Leicester: Inter-Varsity; Grand Rapids: Eerdmans, 1987), p. 178; Beale (*Revelation,* p. 772) surmises that the angel may have "authority over the Son of man, who is therefore subordinate to the angel," which he qualifies as a functional subordination. However, it is better to acknowledge with George Eldon Ladd (*Commentary on the Revelation of John* [Grand Rapids: Eerdmans, 1972], p. 199) that "the relationship between Christ and his angels is a mystery we cannot solve."

37. Louis A. Vos, *The Synoptic Traditions in the Apocalypse* (Kampen: Kok, 1965), p. 150.

38. In translation, the Hebrew text of Zech. 5:1 reads, "I looked again—and there before me was a flying scroll." But the Septuagint text—probably used by John, as is evident in the next verse—differs, "And I saw, and look, a flying sickle." The Hebrew words for scroll (*mglh*) and sickle (*mgl*) look similar.

17. And another angel came forth out of the heavenly temple, and he had a sharp sickle.

At first sight, this verse seems repetitious and superfluous. But on further reflection we notice an intricate design of the Apocalypse with respect to the last two angels of the six mentioned in this chapter.

- The fifth angel, who comes from the temple (v. 17), parallels the fourth angel, who comes from the same place (v. 15).
- The fourth angel communicates to the "son of man" that the time of the harvest has come to put in the sickle (v. 15). The sixth angel (v. 18) instructs the fifth angel (v. 17) to take the sharp sickle and harvest the ripe grapes.
- The "son of man" harvests God's elect, while the fifth angel harvests all those who throughout their lives opposed God, his Word, and his kingdom.
- The expression *firstfruits* (v. 4) refers to the harvest of God's elect; separate from them is the harvest of reaping the grapes (the depraved) destined for the great winepress of God's wrath (v. 19).

The second sickle is used not for the harvesting of grain (God's people) but for the grapes of wrath (God's enemies). It is interesting that the Septuagint text of Joel 4:13 features the plural "sickles," implying the sequence of two harvests.[39] This Old Testament passage is the background of John's design. This is obvious in Greek, for the writer of Revelation uses two different verbs for gathering grain (*therizein,* v. 15) and garnering grapes (*trygan,* v. 18). More, here threshing is a single act and is not followed by winnowing. Gathering the grapes, however, is followed by treading them out in the winepress (v. 20). Here is the difference between gathering God's people for his glory and reaping his enemies for wrath.

18. And another angel came forth from the altar. He had power over fire, and he called in a loud voice to the one who had the sharp sickle, saying, "Send forth your sharp sickle and gather the clusters of the grapevine of the earth, because its grapes are ripe."

This is the sixth angel mentioned in succession. But note that this angel comes forth from *the altar,* which is the altar of incense and prayer already discussed in preceding passages (8:2–3, 5; 9:13; 11:1; see also 16:7). Here at the altar the prayers of the saints rise up to God (6:9–10), who answers their petitions by sending forth an angel to announce the judgment. Another angel with a sickle is told to reap the grapes of God's wrath. Here is the fulfillment of Jesus' word on judgment, "I have come to bring fire on the earth, and how I wish it were al-

39. Beale, *Revelation,* p. 775; Aune, *Revelation 6–16,* pp. 799–800. Bauckham (*Climax of Prophecy,* p. 290) points out that Joel uses the Hebrew word *qṣyr* for harvesting grain and then writes about harvesting grapes. Incidentally, the Hebrew word for reaping grapes is *bṣyr.*

ready kindled" (Luke 12:49). Here fire figuratively depicts the coming judgment (8:5; compare 2 Thess. 1:7).

The rabbis taught that each angel received a specific task; that is, no angel could have a double assignment. For instance, one angel brought the message that Sarah would bear a son; another angel came to save Lot from impending doom; and a third angel was given the task of destroying Sodom and Gomorrah.[40] Does the sixth angel then have two tasks? No, he has been given power over fire, portraying judgment; and he exercises this authority by commanding the fifth angel: "Send forth your sharp sickle and gather the clusters of the grapevine of the earth, because its grapes are ripe." The command is uttered in a loud voice so that everyone in heaven and on earth is able to hear the message of judgment that begins as soon as the fifth angel puts in the sickle. The judgment is the outcome of unbelievers' continued and persistent rejection of God and his revelation and is God's answer to the numerous prayers directed to him by a multitude of suffering saints on earth and by the souls under the altar.[41]

The sharpness of the sickle indicates that the work of gathering the grapes will be accomplished in record time. These grapes, however, are not reaped for human consumption and enjoyment. The harvested clusters of grapes are destined for the great winepress of God's wrath.

19. And the angel thrust his sickle on the earth and gathered the grapes of the earth, and he cast them into the great winepress of God's wrath.

The parallel with verse 16, where Jesus flings forth his sickle on the earth and harvests the earth, is evident. Here the fifth angel casts his sickle to the earth and reaps the earth. The one gathers the sheaves and the other the clusters of grapes. The Greek text literally reads, "And the angel . . . gathered the vine of the earth." The word *vine* represents the totality of the grapes produced.

John appears to have in mind Isaiah 63:2, where the word *winepress* is placed within the context of God trampling the grapes of wrath (Lam. 1:15). The grapes are the nations, that is, God's adversaries (Joel 3:13). He stands alone trampling them under foot at a time which Isaiah calls the day of vengeance (63:4). It is the day of judgment when God metes out just punishment on the nations and grants redemption to his people. He tramples the nations in his wrath "and poured their blood on the ground" (63:6). The enemies of God and the Lamb are unable to hide themselves from their wrath. "For the great day of their wrath has come, and who is able to stand?" (6:17; see also 19:15).

20. And the winepress was trodden outside the city, and the blood came out of the winepress up to the bridles of the horses for a distance of sixteen hundred stadia.

a. "And the winepress was trodden outside the city." In August and September the harvested grapes were laid out in the sun for some time to increase the sugar content. Then they were thrown into the winepress, which was either square or

40. SB, 3:815. Compare also Aune, *Revelation 6–16*, p. 846.

41. Refer to Roloff, *Revelation*, p. 178.

round in shape with a depth of one or two feet. The press sloped to one side so that the juice flowed through an opening into a smaller vat. The grapes were crushed by trampling them underfoot, which was done by several people.

In a picture of judgment, Isaiah wrote that the Messiah, trampling the grapes in the winepress alone, trod them in his wrath as their blood stained his garments (63:3).[42] And even though John writes the verb *was trodden* in the passive voice, on the basis of the Old Testament we know that the agent is Jesus Christ. Similarly, Jacob on his deathbed blesses his sons and singles out Judah as the recipient of a messianic prophecy. He speaks of the Messiah washing "his garments in wine, his robes in the blood of grapes" (Gen. 49:11; and see Deut. 32:14). The red-colored grape juice resembles blood.

The shedding of blood might not take place within the walls of the city (Matt. 27:31; Mark 15:20; Luke 23:32; John 19:17; Acts 7:58; Heb. 13:12). Some scholars identify the place with Jerusalem, for the holiness of this city might not be violated. But in the Apocalypse the concept *holy city* refers to the saints' abode, which is separated from the dwelling place of unbelievers (11:2, 8; 20:9; 21:27; 22:14–15). The city is the presence of the Lord where the saints dwell in safety and security untouched by the wrath of God and the Lamb. "Outside the city means outside the new Jerusalem."[43]

b. "And the blood came out of the winepress up to the bridles of the horses for a distance of sixteen hundred stadia." This is the first time the word *blood* appears in the present context. It enlivens the intensity of the conflict between Christ and the anti-Christian forces that face judgment and dreadful punishment. John obviously paints a picture by using the symbolic images of grape juice from a winepress representing blood, and horses with bridles portraying warfare. He writes a similar account of this warfare in 19:11–21. There he mentions the horseman who treads the winepress of the fury of the wrath of God Almighty, whose robe is dipped in blood and whose name is the Word of God, King of kings, and Lord of lords. This rider on a white horse is a judge who judges righteously and a general who engages his enemies in warfare.

The enemy faces complete annihilation to the degree where the level of blood and gore rises as high as the horses' bridles. The length of this river of blood is 1600 stadia, that is, about 180 miles or 300 kilometers. Some commentators refer this measure to the land of Israel from north to south. Others understand the figure to mean the square of forty. Forty is the traditional number that symbolizes punishment (forty years in the desert [Num. 14:33]; forty lashes for an evildoer [Deut. 25:3]).[44] Still others take the number 1600 symbolically and

---

42. See Barry L. Bandstra, "Wine Press; Winevat," *ISBE*, 4:1072; Arnold C. Schultz, "Wine and Strong Drink," *ZPEB*, 5:936–38.

43. Krodel, *Revelation*, p. 276; Poellot, *Revelation*, p. 197. By contrast, Kiddle (*Revelation*, p. 294) and Caird (*Revelation*, pp. 193–94) assert that the city is Babylon the Great, but this interpretation appears improbable due to exegetical difficulties. Others (Mounce, Thomas, Wall, Walvoord) suggest earthly Jerusalem, which is hard to maintain in light of the distance of sixteen hundred stadia mentioned at the end of this verse.

44. Beasley-Murray, *Revelation*, p. 230.

interpret it as the square of four multiplied by the square of ten; the number four represents the earth and the number ten stands for fullness in the decimal system.

A few observations. First, in this part of the chapter filled with symbolism it is difficult to maintain that the number 1600 should be taken literally.[45] Are the adversaries of the Messiah all in one locale, namely, in the land of Israel?

Next, the number forty signifies a round number that in Scripture specifies the span of a generation, the marriageable age of Isaac and Esau, the length of David's and Solomon's reigns, an interval of fasting, and the period between Jesus' resurrection and ascension. To limit this number, therefore, to a time of punishment seems too restrictive.

Last, the kingdom of the Antichrist is worldwide in scope and not limited to any particular part of the globe. The picture John draws is one of a global conflict that envelops all the nations of the world and leads to their ultimate destruction. God's judgment is universal.[46]

Greek Words, Phrases, and Constructions in 14:14–20

Verse 14

John breaks the rules of Greek grammar in verse 14, for the first occurrence of the noun νεφέλη should have been in the accusative as object of the verb *to see*, and the noun υἱόν should have been in the dative because of the adjective ὅμοιον (see Luke 6:48). John is consistent, for the phrase ὅμοιον υἱὸν ἀνθρώπου occurs also in 1:13.

ἔχων—this nominative present participle should have been in the accusative to modify the preceding noun υἱόν. It is considered to be a nominative of apposition, which construction appears also elsewhere in Revelation (see 10:2; 19:12).

Verse 15

καὶ θέρισον—the conjunction preceding the aorist active imperative "reap!" denotes purpose. It adds a sense of urgency and finality.

Verse 18

τῆς γῆς—the genitive is appositional to the words τῆς ἀμπέλου (the vine): the vine, namely, the earth.[47]

Verse 19

τὸν μέγαν—the definite article with adjective in the masculine accusative singular modifies the feminine accusative singular τὴν ληνόν (winepress). This noun in classical and Septuagintal Greek is feminine but in some instances functions as a masculine. Al-

---

45. SB, 3:817; *1 Enoch* 100.3; 4 Ezra (=2 Esdras) 15:35. Thomas (*Revelation 8–22*, p. 224) states his preference for a literal interpretation, but he admits "this is a preference unsupported by strong argumentation."

46. See the commentaries of Roloff (p. 178), Hendriksen (p. 156), Lenski (p. 452), Poellot (p. 19), Charles (2:26), Johnson (p. 544), and Mounce (p. 281).

47. Consult Hanna, *Grammatical Aid*, p. 452.

though the grammatical construction is a solecism, the distance between the noun and the adjective leaves the distinct impression that John wanted to emphasize the enormity of the object. Also, for emphasis the adjective stands last in the sentence.[48]

Verse 20

ἀπό—the preposition in this context denotes distance away from a certain place (see John 11:18). It may be translated "for a distance of."

---

48. Friedrich Düsterdieck (*Critical and Exegetical Handbook to the Revelation of John* [New York and London: Funk and Wagnalls, 1886], p. 402) suggests that John is indicating masculine strength following the feminine weakness. But the gender of a noun has nothing to do with its strength and weakness.

15

Seven Angels with Seven Plagues

(15:1–8)

Outline (continued)

VI. Vision 5: Seven Bowls of Judgment (15:1–16:21)
   A. The Setting (15:1–8)
      1. The Saints and the Song (15:1–4)
         a. Angels and Plagues (15:1)
         b. Overcomers and Their Ode (15:2–4)
      2. Temple, Angels, and Plagues (15:5–8)

15 1 And I saw another great and marvelous sign in heaven, seven angels having seven last
plagues, for by them the wrath of God is fulfilled. 2 And I saw as it were a sea of glass mixed
with fire, and those who overcame the beast and his image and the number of his name
were standing beside the sea of glass holding harps of God. 3 And they sang the song of
Moses, God's servant, and the song of the Lamb, saying,

> "Great and marvelous are your works, Lord
> God Almighty. Just and true are your ways,
> King of the nations. 4 Who does not fear
> you, O Lord, and glorify your name? For you
> alone are holy; for all the nations will come
> and worship before you; for your righteous
> deeds have been revealed."

5 And after these things I looked, and in heaven the temple of the tent of testimony was opened.
6 And seven angels, having the seven plagues, came forth out of the temple. They were dressed in
clean, bright linen and had golden sashes around their chests. 7 And one of the four living creatures
gave to the seven angels seven golden bowls full of the wrath of God, who lives forever and ever.
8 And the temple was filled with smoke from the glory of God and from his power. And no one was
able to enter the temple until the seven plagues of the seven angels were fulfilled.

VI. Vision 5: Seven Bowls of Judgment
15:1–16:21
A. The Setting
15:1–8

Chapters 15 and 16 form a unit in which the one introduces the other.[1] Indeed, 15:1 mentions seven angels with the seven last plagues and 16:1–21 describes the angels each pouring one of the seven bowls of God's wrath on the earth. This component of seven plagues forms the last cycle in the interconnected series of sevens: seals, trumpets, and plagues. Once again we see that this

---

1. Michael Wilcock (*The Message of Revelation: I Saw Heaven Opened* [Downers Grove: InterVarsity, 1975], pp. 136–37) places 15:1 as a sixth vision and 15:2–4 as a seventh vision in a section that includes chapters 12, 13, and 14. The next division is 15:5–16:21. See also Gregory K. Beale, *The Book of Revelation: A Commentary on the Greek Text,* NIGTC (Grand Rapids: Eerdmans, 1998), pp. 784–85; Adela Yarbro Collins, *The Combat Myth in the Book of Revelation,* HDR 9 (Missoula: Scholars Press, 1976), pp. 16–19. The fact remains that chapters 15 and 16 are a unit. Placing 15:1–4 with chapter 14 creates the problem of relating "the seven angels with the seven last plagues" to the context of 14:14–20.

unit concludes with a distinct reference to God's judgment on the unbelievers. The cycle of the seals records the phrase *the fourth part of the earth* (6:8); the cycle of the trumpets uses the term *one-third* to point to partial destruction (8:7). This last cycle, however, ends in complete and total judgment. When the seventh angel has poured out his bowl, a loud voice from God's throne says: "It is done" (16:17). In short, the three cycles of seals, trumpets, and bowls follow each other with increasingly severe judgments, and the last one features finality.

There is a similarity between the opening statement of 12:1, "And a great sign appeared in heaven," and that of 15:1, "And I saw another great and marvelous sign in heaven." Also, there is a parallel between those who overcame the beast, his image, and the number of his name in 13:14–18 and the wording in 15:2. And last, 13:1, 2, and 4 mention the dragon and 13:11 the beast coming up out of the earth, that is, the false prophet. These terms correspond to 16:13, which specifies the dragon and the false prophet.[2]

In the first four verses of chapter 15, John looks to the future and foretells what will happen when the strife is over. He speaks of the victory achieved by those who have overcome the power and influence of the beast. Thus he records the song of Moses and the Lamb. And in the next four verses (15:5–8) he describes the temple and the seven angels. From this place and by these angels the plagues originate and are fulfilled.

Every time John speaks about God's judgment on the unbelieving world, he has a segment on the victorious saints.[3] For instance, after the six seals in chapter 6, he pictures the saints in chapter 7. Following the seven trumpets (chapters 10–11), he portrays God's protective care of the persecuted church (chapter 12). And the portrayal of the multitude of saints with the Lamb on Mount Zion (14:1–5) is juxtaposed with God's awesome judgments on his enemies (14:6–11). The harvest of the believers precedes that of the unbelievers (14:15–20).

1. The Saints and the Song
15:1–4
a. Angels and Plagues
15:1

1. And I saw another great and marvelous sign in heaven, seven angels having seven last plagues, for by them the wrath of God is fulfilled.

a. "And I saw another great and marvelous sign in heaven." Verse 1 is set off from the following three verses in that it provides the backdrop of verses 5–8.[4]

---

2. William Hendriksen, *More Than Conquerors* (reprint, Grand Rapids: Baker, 1982), p. 127; G. B. Caird, *A Commentary on the Revelation of St. John the Divine* (London: Black, 1966), p. 158.

3. Homer Hailey, *Revelation: An Introduction and Commentary* (Grand Rapids: Baker, 1979), p. 318.

4. J. Ramsey Michaels (*Interpreting the Book of Revelation* [Grand Rapids: Baker, 1992], p. 64) ascribes a transitional function to vv. 1–4. Leon Morris (*Revelation*, rev. ed., TNTC [Leicester: Inter-Varsity; Grand Rapids: Eerdmans, 1987], p. 182) simply regards these verses as preliminary remarks. And David E. Aune more precisely calls verse 1 a "title or superscription." See his *Revelation 6–16*, WBC 52B (Nashville: Nelson, 1998), p. 869.

Verses 2–4 form an interlude that describes the saints who have triumphed over evil and are now singing a song to worship and bring glory to God. The apparent incongruity is typical of John's style in Revelation. For instance, in 8:2 he mentions seven angels with seven trumpets, but before he enumerates each angel blowing his trumpet (8:6–9:21), he introduces another angel, who offers incense mingled with the prayers of the saints and who hurls fire from the altar to the earth (8:3–5).

Although John readily uses the adjective *another* with an angel, here the adjective puts the sign in heaven in sequence with the radiant woman (12:1–2) and her opponent the great red dragon (12:3). This is then the third time that John sees a sign in heaven.

The verb *I saw* occurs forty-two times in the Apocalypse; three of them in 15:1, 2, and 5 introduce new segments. The first one is a preliminary statement on the seven angels with the seven plagues; the second discloses the song of Moses and the Lamb that the victorious saints sing; and the third reveals the temple in heaven and the glory of God. We are not told why the sign in heaven is called "great and marvelous." But because this phrase occurs again in verse 3a, where it describes the works of God, we are confident that John saw something astounding. He saw the finality of God pouring out his wrath on the earth by employing seven angels and seven bowls.

b. "Seven angels having seven last plagues." For John this is the sign of totality. The number seven depicts completeness, so that these bowls of wrath represent the final and complete outpouring of God's anger on the world. They are the *last* plagues, in the sense of their inevitability and finality (see also 21:9).

c. "For by them the wrath of God is fulfilled." God's wrath is poured out by means of immense suffering, death, rivers of blood, fire, darkness, drought, and utter destruction (see 16:2–21). Notice the verb *fulfilled*, which indicates that the end has come and so has the judgment, even though John has much to say in the chapters preceding the scene of the great white throne (20:11–15). This means that the cycle of the seven plagues is complete and points forward to the final day. "No more plagues will come after the vial-plagues; but then the Lord himself will come to administer his final judgment."[5]

b. Overcomers and Their Ode
15:2–4

2. And I saw as it were a sea of glass mixed with fire, and those who overcame the beast and his image and the number of his name were standing beside the sea of glass holding harps of God.

a. "And I saw as it were a sea of glass mixed with fire." John once more observes the sea of glass that he saw when he recorded the scene of the throne room (4:6). He again mentions the saints who have overcome the evil one (12:11), who are now in heaven standing next to this sea of glass. The glass sea symbolizes perspicuity and transparency, so that everyone is able to observe

5. Friedrich Düsterdieck, *Critical and Exegetical Handbook to the Revelation of John* (New York and London: Funk and Wagnalls, 1886), p. 408.

God's righteousness and integrity. Thus, the saints in heaven see God's wisdom in action. They are the overcomers who have resisted following the beast, refused to worship his image, and rejected the number of his name.

Notice that in this passage the sea is mixed with fire, which symbolically directs attention to the pillar of fire that led the Israelites across the Red Sea (Exod. 13:20–14:31). The fire portrayed is a symbol of light and joy to all the saints who are standing next to the sea of glass. But the sea mixed with fire is also a symbol of God's wrath directed against his enemies. As the Egyptians drowned in the sea through which the Israelites had come safely to the shore on the other side, so the sea mixed with fire destroys the Antichrist and his hordes.

b. "And those who overcame the beast and his image and the number of his name were standing beside the sea of glass." The saints in glory are those whose task on earth is finished. They are the victors in their battle against the beast. Now this statement is remarkable indeed, because the beast "was given power to make war against the saints and to overcome them" (13:7). But they had refused to worship him and bear the number of his name (13:16–18). Numerous saints lost their lives in this warfare, yet spiritually they gained the victory. They were faithful to the end and received the crown of glory.

c. "[And they were] holding harps of God." Both the Old and New Testaments refer to the harp and lyre (2 Chron. 29:25; Ps. 33:2; 71:22; 92:3; 98:5; 147:7; 149:3; 150:3; Rev. 5:8; 14:2; 15:2). All the twenty-four elders who surround God's throne have harps to sing praises to God. Therefore, the phrase *harps of God* conveys the meaning "harps for playing to God."[6]

The saints receive heavenly harps by which they are able to sing songs of victory, for God himself has enabled the saints to triumph over the evil one. Thus they burst into song.

By the sea of crystal, saints in glory
  stand,
Myriads in number, drawn from every
  land.
Robed in white apparel, washed in
  Jesus' blood,
They now reign in heaven with the
  Lamb of God.

—William Kuipers[7]

3a. And they sang the song of Moses, God's servant, and the song of the Lamb, saying.

There are at least two questions that arise in this text: first, is the song of Moses the same as the one he taught the Israelites on the banks of the Red Sea? Inci-

6. Beale, *Revelation*, p. 791.

7. "By the Sea of Crystal," in *Psalter Hymnal* (Grand Rapids: CRC Publications, 1987), no. 620.

dentally, the other song of Moses is called the Great Song (Deut. 32). Next, are there two different songs, one of Moses and the other of the Lamb?

First, the words in this song have little in common with either of the two songs of Moses (Exod. 15 and Deut. 32). There are allusions to

- the Pentateuch (Exod. 34:10; Deut. 32:4),
- the Psalter (Ps. 86:9; 98:2; 111:2; 139:14; 145:17),
- the Prophets (Isa. 2:2; Jer. 10:7; 11:20 LXX; Amos 3:13; 4:13 LXX; Mal. 1:11).

There are no references to the Song of Moses (Exod. 15). There is only one indirect reference to the Great Song of Moses (Deut. 32:4), which in the Septuagint sets the tone for this hymn: "True are his works, and all his ways are just; God is faithful and there are no wrongs; just and holy is the Lord." Although we assume that John had in mind the Great Song of Moses, we suggest that he relied on memory and thus alluded to a number of passages taken from the three parts of the Old Testament mentioned above.[8] The Jews sang the Song of Moses (Exod. 15) in the synagogue on the Sabbath, and the possibility is not remote that the early Christians sang the hymn recorded by John in their own worship services. The hymn reflects God's mighty deeds frequently noted by Old Testament writers and is a paean of praise devoted to the Lord God.

Next, we look in vain for a song of the Lamb in the New Testament. In Revelation, however, there are hymns dedicated to the Lamb (5:9–10, 12, 13; 7:10) so that we could in fact interpret the phrase *song of the Lamb* as a song glorifying him. But because the first phrase is simply "the song *of* Moses" and not "the song *to* Moses," I favor maintaining the parallel of these two phrases. A better solution to the problem is to look at John's manner of emphasizing a certain point. When he accentuates a concept, he makes use of repetition even when the wording may differ slightly. For instance, the letter to Pergamum mentions the teachings of both Balaam and the Nicolaitans, which come from two sources, yet they are the same (2:14–15). Likewise, the song of Moses and the song of the Lamb are not two different hymns but one and the same song (15:3–4). It is the Lamb who is working through Moses the servant of God (Exod. 14:31; Heb. 3:5). Moses was a servant in the household of God, but Christ is a son over that household and is therefore the greater of the two.

3b. "Great and marvelous are your works, Lord God Almighty. Just and true are your ways, King of the nations. 4. Who does not fear you, O Lord, and glorify

8. By contrast see Richard Bauckham (*The Climax of Prophecy* [Edinburgh: Clark, 1993], pp. 296–306), who asserts that the song of Moses in Exodus 15 lies behind verses 3–4, and these verses are a "careful interpretation of the song" (p. 306). But the verbal similarities in these verses to many passages from especially the Psalter and the Prophets indicate otherwise. Writes Robert H. Mounce, "Practically every phrase of the hymn [vv. 3–4] is taken from the rich vocabulary of the O[ld] T[estament]." See his *Book of Revelation*, rev. ed., NICNT (Grand Rapids: Eerdmans, 1998), p. 286.

your name? For you alone are holy; for all the nations will come and worship before you; for your righteous deeds have been revealed."

Here we read words and phrases that are taken primarily from Old Testament hymnody, as the references to the Psalter indicate. For example, the first line, "Great and marvelous are your works, Lord God Almighty," echoes Psalm 111:2, "Great are the works of the LORD," and Psalm 139:14, "Your works are wonderful." And the phrase "LORD God Almighty" appears in Amos 3:13; 4:13. It also surfaces in numerous other places in the Apocalypse (4:8; 11:17; 16:7; 19:6; 21:22).

The second line, "Just and true are your ways, King of the nations," derives from Psalm 145:17 (144:17 LXX), "The LORD is righteous in all his ways"; also Deuteronomy 32:4 alludes to it: "And all his ways are just." The appellation "King of the nations" comes from Jeremiah 10:7.

The next line is a rhetorical question that exalts the Lord God: "Who does not fear you, O Lord, and glorify your name?" It echoes the wording of Jeremiah 10:7, "Who should not revere you?" and of Psalm 86:9, "All the nations . . . will bring glory to your name."

And the last line ("For you alone are holy; for all the nations will come and worship before you; for your righteous deeds have been revealed") reflects the words from Psalm 86:10, "You alone are God." The term *holy* in the context of "you alone are holy" appears here and nowhere else; for the use of "O Holy One" see Revelation 16:5. And the rest of the line mirrors the message from Psalm 86:9, "All the nations you have made will come and worship before you, O Lord; they will bring glory to your name." Jeremiah 16:19 expresses a similar thought: "O LORD . . . to you the nations will come from the ends of the earth" (see also Isa. 2:2), and Psalm 98:2 extols God with these words, "The LORD . . . revealed his righteousness to the nations." John frequently refers to "all the nations" in Revelation (12:5; 14:8; 15:4; 18:3, 23).

I conclude with two observations. First, the hymn that John records is a sequence of allusions to the Psalter and the prophecy of Jeremiah. Second, the hymn provides a threefold answer to the rhetorical question posed at the beginning of verse 4. This is done by three separate clauses, all beginning with *for* to express cause.

Greek Words, Phrases, and Constructions in 15:1–4

Verse 1

ἐτελέσθη—the verb means *to complete,* that is, *to end.* God's wrath is finished at the end of the seven plagues.

Verse 2

πυρί—the dative is more associative than instrumental; that is, fire is associated with the sea of glass.[9]

---

9. A. T. Robertson, *A Grammar of the Greek New Testament in the Light of Historical Research* (Nashville: Broadman, 1934), p. 529; Robert Hanna, *A Grammatical Aid to the Greek New Testament* (Grand Rapids: Baker, 1983), p. 452.

τοὺς νικῶντας ἐκ—the verb *to overcome* usually is transitive followed by an accusative; here it has the preposition ἐκ with the genitive τοῦ θηρίου (the beast). Aune construes this as a Latinism.[10] The present participle should be interpreted in the perfect tense, for the saints' task of overcoming the devil has been completed.

Verse 3

τῶν ἐθνῶν—"the nations." A variant reading is τῶν αἰώνων (the ages; NIV, NEB, RSV). The strength of the witnesses for these two readings is about the same, but the internal evidence speaks in favor of the first reading, "the nations." The variant reading may have been introduced via 1 Timothy 1:17.[11] To be complete, I mention the variant reading "the saints" (KJV, NKJV), but it has scant manuscript support.

Verse 4

οὐ μὴ φοβηθῇ—the emphatic negative with the aorist passive subjunctive functions as a future. This harmonizes with the future tense δοξάσει in the second line.

---

2. Temple, Angels, and Plagues *15:5–8*

5. And after these things I looked, and in heaven the temple of the tent of testimony was opened.

The opening clause, which also occurs in 4:1; 7:1, 9; 18:1, communicates that John's attention shifts from the vision of the saints at the sea of glass to a vision of what is about to take place in heaven. After the interlude of verses 2–4, John now continues the message of verse 1 regarding the seven angels with the seven plagues.

The scene is in heaven where John sees the open temple that gives him a view of the Holy of Holies. When Jesus died on Calvary's cross, the curtain separating the Holy Place from the inner sanctuary was split from top to bottom. God caused the tear to take place to indicate that Jesus' sacrifice had paid for the sins of his people; no substitution of animal blood was needed anymore to sprinkle the ark of the covenant. Hence the inner sanctuary was open to the view of all those who entered the temple.

The term *temple* in the phrase "the temple of the tent of testimony" signifies the inner sanctuary of the tabernacle itself. In Moses' writings the tabernacle and the tent of testimony are one and the same structure (Exod. 40:34–35; Acts 7:44). John calls this structure "the tent of testimony" and not "the tent of meeting." The expression *testimony* refers to the ark of the covenant that was placed in the Holy of Holies; the ark contained the two tablets of stone on which the Ten Commandments were inscribed (Rev. 11:19). In short, this expression alludes to the Ten Commandments, which were the basic condition of the cove-

---

10. Aune, *Revelation 6–16*, p. 872. See also his "Latinism in Revelation 15:2," *JBL* 110 (1991): 691–92.

11. Bruce M. Metzger, *A Textual Commentary on the Greek New Testament*, 2d ed. (Stuttgart: Deutsche Bibelgesellschaft, 1994), pp. 679–80.

nant God made with his people at Mount Sinai (Exod. 25:16; 40:20). These two slabs of stone were called "the two tablets of the Testimony" (Exod. 31:18).

The Ten Commandments are a witness to the people's transgressions that would call forth God's judgment and condemnation.[12] Hence from the very presence of God and from the testimony of these laws divine judgment flows forth. Passing judgment, God executes justice and righteousness on the basis of his law.[13] And as a consequence seven angels are empowered to pour out the seven plagues on the followers of the Antichrist.

6. And seven angels, having the seven plagues, came forth out of the temple. They were dressed in clean, bright linen and had golden sashes around their chests.

Once again (see v. 5) the wording of this passage is closely linked to verse 1, which speaks of angels, plagues, and the wrath of God. The seven plagues are a throwback to Leviticus 26:21, where God says, "If you remain hostile toward me and refuse to listen to me, I will multiply your afflictions seven times over, as your sins deserve." However, the stress is more on the seven angels than on the seven plagues. In this chapter John describes the angels, and in the following chapter (chap. 16) he specifies in detail the force and the extent of the plagues.

First, the angels come forth from the presence of God, that is, they leave the inner sanctuary. Next, they have been given authority over the discharging of seven plagues on the people who had rejected God. One of them also takes on the responsibility of instructing John about the punishment of the great prostitute with her followers on the one hand and the identification of the new Jerusalem with the wife of the Lamb on the other (17:1–18; 21:9–27). Third, the apparel of the angels is made out of clean and glistening linen that epitomizes holiness, and the golden sashes around their chests symbolize dignity, authority, and prominence, for God had entrusted these seven angels with a special task. They are like the "son of man," who also appeared with a golden sash around his chest (1:13; compare Dan. 10:5). And last, the golden sashes point symbolically to kings and the linen garments to priests in ancient Israel. But George Eldon Ladd rightly notes, "There is no reason to think that the golden girdles suggest priestly functions."[14]

7. And one of the four living creatures gave to the seven angels seven golden bowls full of the wrath of God, who lives forever and ever.

The four living creatures are given special roles in the progressive unfolding of the Apocalypse. They were instrumental in the opening of the first four seals (6:1–8) and in holding golden bowls of incense, which are the prayers of the saints (5:8;

12. Philip Edgcumbe Hughes, *The Book of the Revelation: A Commentary* (Leicester: Inter-Varsity; Grand Rapids: Eerdmans, 1990), p. 171; S. Greijdanus, *De Openbaring des Heeren aan Johannes*, KNT (Amsterdam: Van Bottenburg, 1925), p. 317.

13. Homer Hailey, *Revelation: An Introduction and Commentary* (Grand Rapids: Baker, 1979), p. 322; Isbon T. Beckwith, *The Apocalypse of John* (1919; reprint, Grand Rapids: Baker, 1979), p. 678.

14. George Eldon Ladd, *Commentary on the Revelation of John* (Grand Rapids: Eerdmans, 1972), p. 207. But Beale (*Revelation*, p. 807) speaks about the "priestly nature" of the angels.

and see 8:3–5).[15] But note the sequence. The golden bowls of the saints are the prayers that express praise and thanksgiving to God. Yet with these prayers the saints under the altar asked God to avenge their blood (6:9–10), and God heard them. He now sends forth his angels to cause death and destruction on his adversaries.

The four living creatures represent God's creation, and the seven golden bowls are full of the fury of his wrath. Golden bowls were used in the service of the tabernacle and the temple of Solomon (Exod. 25:29; 37:16; 2 Chron. 4:22). They were flat objects shaped in the form of a pan or saucer for holding incense. Now these bowls are filled with the wrath of God from whose anger no one is able to escape (Rev. 6:17; 14:10).

John concludes this verse with a phrase that describes God as the one *who lives forever and ever.* This phrase occurs often in the Apocalypse (4:9, 10; 10:6; see also 1:18; Dan. 4:34) and implies that idols are dead and fail to inspire awe, while God, who lives forever, ought to be feared.[16]

8. And the temple was filled with smoke from the glory of God and from his power. And no one was able to enter the temple until the seven plagues of the seven angels were fulfilled.

With the phrase "filled with smoke from the glory of God," John draws a parallel with the preceding verse, "filled with the wrath of God" (v. 7b). The smoke that emanates from God's glory and from his power permeates the inner sanctuary. The scene is reminiscent of God filling the tabernacle with the cloud of his glory (Exod. 40:34), as also took place at the dedication of Solomon's temple (1 Kings 8:10–11; 2 Chron. 5:13b-14). At the time of King Uzziah's death, Isaiah saw the Lord sitting on his throne in heaven, and "the temple was filled with smoke" (Isa. 6:4; compare Ezek. 43:5; 44:4; Num. 12:5).

The fierceness of God's wrath is so intense that no creature can enter his presence. The time of offering prayers and petitions for mercy is past, for the hour of judgment has come.[17] No one may enter the inner sanctuary until the bowls of wrath have been poured out and the destruction of the wicked has been completed, for God's mercy is forgotten, his compassion withheld, and his patience suspended.

Greek Words, Phrases, and Constructions in 15:5–8

Verse 5

ὁ ναὸς τῆς σκηνῆς—a number of translators interpret the genitive case in apposition to the nominative in the sense of an explanation, "the temple, that is, the tent" (NIV, NEB, REB, NJB).

---

15. Refer to Robert L. Thomas, *Revelation 8–22: An Exegetical Commentary* (Chicago: Moody, 1995), p. 243; Martin Kiddle, *The Revelation of St. John* (reprint, London: Hodder and Stoughton, 1943), pp. 312–13.

16. Henry Barclay Swete, *Commentary on Revelation* (1911; reprint, Grand Rapids: Kregel, 1977), p. 199.

17. Wilfrid J. Harrington, *Revelation*, SP 16 (Collegeville, Minn.: Liturgical Press, 1993), p. 161; Hendriksen, *More Than Conquerors*, p. 160.

Verse 6

ἐκ τοῦ ναοῦ—the position of this phrase gives the appearance that the seven plagues were proceeding out of the temple.

λίνον—"linen." Some leading Greek manuscripts read λίθος (stone), which probably goes back to a transcriptional error. The adjective *clean* describes the first reading better than the second.[18]

Verse 8

ἐγεμίσθη—the aorist is inceptive, "it began to be filled." The verb controls the genitive case καπνοῦ (smoke).

---

18. Metzger, *Textual Commentary*, p. 680. Beale (*Revelation*, pp. 804–5) expresses qualified support for the variant reading. And Michaels (*Interpreting Revelation*, p. 83) thinks that despite the lack of support for this reading the question "is still very much open."

16

Seven Bowls of Judgment

(16:1–21)

Outline (continued)

B. The Seven Bowls (16:1–21)
   1. The First Bowl (16:1–2)
   2. The Second Bowl (16:3)
   3. The Third Bowl (16:4–7)
   4. The Fourth Bowl (16:8–9)
   5. The Fifth Bowl (16:10–11)
   6. The Sixth Bowl (16:12–16)
   7. The Seventh Bowl (16:17–21)

16 1 And I heard a loud voice from the temple saying to the seven angels, "Go, and pour out
the seven bowls of the wrath of God on the earth." 2 And the first angel went out and
poured out his bowl upon the earth, and there appeared a bad and malignant boil on the
people who had the mark of the beast and worshiped his image.

3 And the second angel poured out his bowl on the sea, and there appeared blood as of a dead
man. And every living being in the sea died.

4 And the third angel poured out his bowl on the rivers and the springs of water, and they became
blood. 5 And I heard the angel commanding the waters say, "You are just in having judged these
things, the one who is and who was, O Holy One. 6 Because they have shed the blood of the saints
and the prophets, and blood you gave them to drink; they deserve it." 7 And I heard a voice from the
altar saying, "Yes, Lord God Almighty, true and just are your judgments."

8 And the fourth angel poured out his bowl on the sun, and he was given the power to burn the
people with fire. 9 And the people were burned with a great burning, and they blasphemed the name
of God, who has the authority over these plagues. And they did not repent to give him glory.

10 And the fifth angel poured out his bowl on the throne of the beast. And his kingdom was darkened, and the people bit their tongues because of pain. 11 And they blasphemed the God of heaven
because of their pains and their boils. And they did not repent of their works.

12 And the sixth angel poured out his bowl on the great river Euphrates, and its water dried up,
so that a road of the kings of the east was prepared. 13 And I saw out of the mouth of the dragon
and out of the mouth of the beast and out of the mouth of the false prophet three unclean spirits
like frogs. 14 For they are demonic spirits, working miracles, and they go out to the kings of the
whole world to assemble them for the war on the great day of God Almighty. 15 ("Look, I come like
a thief! Blessed is the one who stays awake and keeps his clothes on, so that he may not walk about
naked and be exposed to shame.") 16 And they brought them into the place that is called in Hebrew
Armageddon.

17 And the seventh angel poured out his bowl on the air. And a loud voice went forth out of the
temple, from the throne, saying, "It is done." 18 And there were flashes of lightning and rumblings
and peals of thunder, and there was a great earthquake, such as had not happened since humans
came on the earth, so great an earthquake. 19 And the great city became three parts, and the cities
of the nations fell. And Babylon the Great was remembered before God, and he gave her the cup of
raging wine of his wrath. 20 And every island fled and the mountains could not be found. 21 And
immense hailstones weighing about a hundred pounds each came down from the sky onto the people, and they blasphemed God because of the plague of hail, for its plague was very great.

B. The Seven Bowls
16:1–21

Throughout the Apocalypse, John bases his writing on allusions from and references to the Old Testament. In this chapter he clearly has in mind the plagues on Egypt. He is not following their sequence methodically, yet the similarity with respect to some of the plagues is obvious.

Not the sequence but the correspondence to the plagues in Egypt is significant. The first bowl causing sores on people (v. 2) parallels the plague that caused boils (Exod. 9:10). The third bowl that turned the water of rivers and springs into blood (v. 4) is identical to the plague that changed all the water of Egypt into blood (Exod. 7:19). The fifth bowl that occasioned darkness (v. 10) has its parallel in the plague that plunged all of Egypt into darkness (Exod. 10:22). The sixth bowl that dried up the Euphrates and brought forth three evil spirits appearing as frogs (v. 13) is symbolic of the plague that caused frogs to cover the land (Exod. 8:6). And the seventh bowl that hurled hailstones to the earth (v. 21) is analogous to the plague that brought hail to Egypt (Exod. 9:23–24).[1]

There is more. A comparison of the seven trumpets and the seven bowls reveals parallels that in abbreviated form appear as follows:

Seven Trumpets	**Seven Bowls**
1. earth (8:7)	1. earth (16:2)
2. sea (8:8–9)	2. sea (16:3)
3. rivers, springs (8:10–11)	3. rivers, springs (16:4–5)
4. sun, moon, stars (8:12)	4. sun (16:8)
5. pit of the Abyss (9:1)	5. throne of the beast (16:10)
6. river Euphrates (9:13–14)	6. river Euphrates (16:12)
7. lightning, hail (11:15, 19)	7. lightning, hail (16:17, 21)

The basic difference between the trumpets series and the bowls series is generally one of an increase in intensity. This becomes plain in comparing the trumpet and bowl scenes individually.

- In the first trumpet scene, the earth is affected but not the people, but in the scene of the first bowl, the people suffer from festering boils.
- The second trumpet involves only a third of the sea and its creatures, whereas the outpouring of the second bowl causes death for every living thing in the sea.
- The third trumpet is a warning, while the third bowl is God's judgment.
- The fourth trumpet ushers in partial darkness, but the result of pouring out the fourth bowl is that the people are scorched by the sun.
- The fifth trumpet releases the hordes of evil angels that torture those people who do not have God's seal on their foreheads, and the fifth bowl occasions darkness in Satan's kingdom and suffering on the people who curse God.

1. Compare Josephine Massyngberde Ford, "The Structure and Meaning of Revelation 16," *ExpT* 98 (1987): 327–30; and her *Revelation: Introduction, Translation, and Commentary*, AB 38 (Garden City, N.Y.: Doubleday, 1975), pp. 265–75.

- The sixth trumpet brings about the death of one-third of the human race in warfare, while in the scene of the sixth bowl this warfare engages the kings of the whole world.
- The seventh trumpet and the seventh bowl are almost identical except that in the bowl scene the words *It is done* sound forth from the throne to indicate finality.

A few additional comments should be made. First, as sinners harden their hearts, reject God's warnings, refuse to repent, and even curse the God of heaven (9:21; 16:9, 11), they face doom and destruction. Truly God's judgments are just (v. 7).

Second, the seven bowls form the last cycle, which needs no interlude as was the case in the preceding cycles of seals and trumpets respectively (7:1–17; 10:1–11:14).

Third, after the outpouring of the sixth and seventh bowls, John shows in detail how the followers of the Antichrist face the severity of their punishment (chapters 17 and 18).

Fourth, a degree of overlapping seems to allude to a measure of simultaneity in the pouring out of the bowls. For example, "the boils of the first plague are still active at the time of the fifth plague (v. 11)."[2] This suggests that at the end of time, haste is God's mode for accomplishing his judgments.

And last, although the parallel of trumpets and bowls is striking, we would not expect John to present mere repetition without progress. The Apocalypse from beginning to end reveals progressive parallelism.

1. The First Bowl
16:1–2

1. And I heard a loud voice from the temple saying to the seven angels, "Go, and pour out the seven bowls of the wrath of God on the earth." 2. And the first angel went out and poured out his bowl upon the earth, and there appeared a bad and malignant boil on the people who had the mark of the beast and worshiped his image.

a. "And I heard a loud voice from the temple saying to the seven angels." The Greek stresses the loudness of the voice John hears. He perceived the intensity of the sound coming from the temple (compare Isa. 66:6), which in his ears sounded majestic because it was the voice of God himself. In a typical Jewish manner John avoids using the name of God, so here and in verse 17 he mentions a loud voice coming from the temple and he intimates that God speaks. This harmonizes with the last verse in the preceding chapter where he refers to the temple and the glory of God (15:8). The voice came forth from the Holy of Holies and is none other than the voice of God, who fills the inner sanctuary with his glory and now sends forth his seven angels.

2. Robert H. Mounce, *The Book of Revelation*, rev. ed., NICNT (Grand Rapids: Eerdmans, 1998), p. 292 n. 1.

b. "Go, and pour out the seven bowls of the wrath of God on the earth." The command is direct and to the point; the angels must go forth with the bowls filled with God's wrath. They must pour out the contents of these bowls onto the earth to punish the adversaries of God and his people.

c. "And the first angel went out and poured out his bowl upon the earth, and there appeared a bad and malignant boil on the people." The angel acts in obedience to God's command and pours out his bowl. As a result, the people on the earth become ill because foul and festering boils play havoc with their bodies and afflict them with excruciating pain.

The earth, which brings forth food for mankind and on which people depend for health and well-being, is affected by the bowl poured out upon it.[3] The Greek literally reads that the angel "poured out his bowl *into* the earth." The import of this becomes evident when people consume the produce of the earth: they suffer from ulcers inside and outside their bodies. Their health is affected by the food they ingest, and they are stricken with disease (compare Exod. 9:10–11; Deut. 28:35).

d. "Who had the mark of the beast and worshiped his image." Only the anti-Christian forces that follow the beast (13:15–16) are stricken with boils, not the followers of Christ. For them the afflictions they endure are never because of God's wrath but always because of his love (Rom. 8:28).[4] The followers of the Antichrist are not limited to any particular area or nation but in their opposition to the cause of Christ they reside worldwide. Instead of repenting and turning to God, they continue to worship the image of the beast and thus suffer the consequences.

Greek Words, Phrases, and Constructions in 16:1–2

Verse 1

μεγάλης φωνῆς—although John normally writes the accusative following the verb *to hear,* now he uses the genitive case to call attention not to the content of the speech but to the volume of the voice that is speaking. The adjective precedes the noun to emphasize the loudness of the voice. This is the only place in Revelation where the adjective precedes; in all the other cases—nineteen in total—it follows the noun φωνῇ (see, e.g., 1:10; 5:2).

The adjective μέγας occurs more than eighty times in the Apocalypse, of which eleven are in this chapter. For instance, the great river Euphrates (v. 12), the great day of God (v. 14), the great city (v. 19), and Babylon the Great (v. 19) are mentioned.

Verse 2

καὶ ἐγένετο—this phrase occurs seven times in this chapter (vv. 2b, 3b, 4b, 10b, 18a, 18b with a slight variation, 19a). Notice that in the first four occurrences it is in the second half of the verse as a result of the first part.

---

3. Herman Hoeksema, *Behold, He Cometh! An Exposition of the Book of Revelation* (Grand Rapids: Reformed Free Publishing Association, 1969), p. 536.

4. William Hendriksen, *More Than Conquerors* (reprint, Grand Rapids: Baker, 1982), p. 161.

2. The Second Bowl
16:3

3. And the second angel poured out his bowl on the sea, and there appeared blood as of a dead man. And every living being in the sea died.

Also the second angel obediently follows God's command and literally pours "into" the sea the content of the bowl, that is, the wrath of God. Some commentators hint at the possibility that from John's perspective the sea is the Mediterranean.[5] But as the earth is not limited to the countries around the Mediterranean, neither is the sea.

God judges the entire world, and by having the angel pour the bowl of wrath into the sea, the food supply from the sea is taken away from the human race. While the second trumpet killed a third of the sea creatures (8:8–9), the second bowl brings death to all living beings in the sea. With the second trumpet, God still extended his grace to his creation by not depriving it of its food supply. But the effect of the second bowl is God's judgment, for this plague turns the sea into blood, which John compares to the blood of a dead man. This is impossible for us to imagine. Kendell H. Easley writes, "John is viewing a supernatural phenomenon rather than a scientific, explainable event."[6] This causes famine and death to all who depend on the bounties of the sea, for the oceans of the world become a picture of pollution.

Greek Words, Phrases, and Constructions in 16:3

ψυχὴ ζωῆς—"the soul of life" or "living being." The phrase derives from the creation account where God creates a "living being" (Gen. 1:30; 2:7). The genitive is qualitative.

τά—the Majority Text omits this definite pronoun, yet its presence specifies, namely, the things in the sea perished.[7]

---

3. The Third Bowl
16:4–7

4. And the third angel poured out his bowl on the rivers and the springs of water, and they became blood.

Here is the parallel to the third trumpet (8:10–11) and at the same time a reference to the curse that changed all the streams, canals, ponds, and reservoirs of Egypt into blood (Exod. 7:19). The people who experience the plague are like the Egyptians whose rivers God turned to blood so that "they could not drink from their streams" (Ps. 78:44). This plague differs from the preceding

5. E.g., G. R. Beasley-Murray, *The Book of Revelation*, NCB (London: Oliphants, 1974), p. 241; John F. Walvoord, *The Revelation of Jesus Christ* (Chicago: Moody, 1966), p. 233. R. C. H. Lenski (*The Interpretation of St. John's Revelation* [Columbus: Wartburg, 1943], p. 467) explains the sea as a symbol of the "antichristian world of this day" of judgment.

6. Kendell H. Easley, *Revelation*, HNTC (Nashville: Broadman & Holman, 1998), p. 285.

7. Henry Barclay Swete (*Commentary on Revelation* [1911; reprint, Grand Rapids: Kregel, 1977], p. 199) places a comma after ἀπέθανεν to make the next phrase appositional.

one, because human beings and the animal world daily depend on drinking water. When this supply is polluted and unfit to drink, they will eventually die. At this point, John could have continued the sequence with the fourth plague, but he inserts a brief interlude that reveals a hymn comparable to the song of Moses and the Lamb (15:3–4). Here an angel voices a hymn; there the saints sing a song.

5. And I heard the angel commanding the waters say, "You are just in having judged these things, the one who is and who was, O Holy One."

The angel who caused the waters of rivers and springs to become blood is now called, literally, "the angel of the waters"; he praises God for his righteous judgments. Some commentators separate these two angels by pointing out that elsewhere in Revelation there are angels who control the winds (7:1) and another angel who has power over fire (14:18). But Scripture nowhere else refers to an angel with authority over the waters.[8]

Pouring out his bowl, the angel declares the justice of God by saying: "You are just in having judged these things." Leon Morris aptly remarks, " 'The angel of the waters' sees in these proceedings an excellent example of making the punishment fit the crime."[9] The words seem to have their origin in the Great Song of Moses and the Psalter, "A faithful God . . . upright and just is he" (Deut. 32:4; see also Ps. 119:137; 145:17).

The words *who is and who was* (Rev. 11:17) are familiar; elsewhere the phrase "who is to come" completes the formula (compare 1:4, 8; 4:8). Its omission in this verse attests to the fact that God has already come in Christ and that John looks back, as it were, on the fulfillment of the consummation.

God's holiness tolerates no unrighteousness, and his judgments are always right and just. Saints who confess their sins receive his grace, but sinners who refuse to repent receive their just deserts. The song stresses holiness by placing *Holy One* at the end of the sentence following the description "who is and who was." Some translators insert the vocative "O Holy One" right after "You are just" to juxtapose the concepts *just* and *holy* (see Ps. 144:17 LXX).[10] The sequence, however, is to put the vocative as a third part of the descriptive phrase *who is and who was.* That is, the time has now come for God to exert his attribute of holiness, vindicate the saints who suffered because of his Word (6:9–10), and inflict punishment on his adversaries. Pouring the contents of the third bowl

---

8. See David E. Aune (*Revelation 6–16,* WBC 52B [Nashville: Nelson, 1998], pp. 884–85), who designates the angel of the waters as a particular angelic being in charge of that part of creation. Also, John P. M. Sweet, *Revelation,* WPC (Philadelphia: Westminster, 1979), p. 244; Philip Edgcumbe Hughes, *The Book of the Revelation: A Commentary* (Leicester: Inter-Varsity; Grand Rapids: Eerdmans, 1990), p. 171. Although apocryphal literature reveals that angels were assigned to certain parts of creation (*Jubilees* 2.2; *1 Enoch* 60.12–22; 66.2; 69.22; 75.3), in this passage we see a close connection between the third angel and the angel in charge of the waters. See SB, 3:818–20.

9. Leon Morris, *Revelation,* rev. ed., TNTC (Leicester: Inter-Varsity; Grand Rapids: Eerdmans, 1987), p. 188.

10. NRSV; see also Friedrich Düsterdieck, *Critical and Exegetical Handbook to the Revelation of John* (New York and London: Funk and Wagnalls, 1886), p. 417.

into the rivers and springs of water is God's judgment on his enemies who persecuted his people.[11]

6. "Because they have shed the blood of the saints and the prophets, and blood you gave them to drink; they deserve it."

Note that the word *blood* is mentioned twice: the spilled blood of those who were persecuted by the followers of the Antichrist, and the blood of the rivers and springs that God made the persecutors drink as their punishment. Drinking blood, which is an abhorrent act in itself, need not be taken literally; it may figuratively refer to interpersonal strife and slaughter among the oppressors themselves (Num. 23:24; Isa. 49:26). It means that the channels of communication have been clogged with conflict and carnage resulting in death.

The *saints* are all of God's people, as is evident everywhere in the Apocalypse, and the *prophets* are a special group within the church (11:18; 18:20, 24; 22:9). All these people have suffered at the hands of God's enemies.

The last clause is brief and can be translated as "they are worthy" (KJV). In that positive sense, the clause describes the saints, as in 3:4 where Jesus commends the saints in Sardis who are worthy, and 5:12 where the Lamb is called worthy. If this is the meaning, the saints are the ones who are vindicated and declared worthy.[12] But the contrary suits the context better, because the immediate antecedent refers to the anti-Christian forces that shed the blood of the saints. As their punishment they must now, figuratively speaking, drink blood. In short, the persecutors receive the just sentence they deserve.

7. And I heard a voice from the altar saying, "Yes, Lord God Almighty, true and just are your judgments."

As an appropriate response to the hymn that was sung by the angel in charge of the waters, a voice coming from the altar now sings a tribute to God. The expression *altar,* personified by functioning as the speaker, emphasizes the place where the voice originates. This is the altar where the souls of the martyrs cried out, "How long, O Sovereign Lord, holy and true, will you not judge and avenge our blood from those that dwell on the earth?" (6:10). Now that the Lord God Almighty has responded to their plea, they utter a word of praise and affirmation.

The altar is the altar of incense from which the prayers of the saints ascend to God. These prayers mingle with the aromatic smell of incense. And from this altar God casts fire on the earth by punishing the wicked (8:3–5; 14:18) and passing judgment on his adversaries.

Now these voices address the Lord God Almighty (see also 4:8; 11:17; 15:3; 19:6) and praise him for his judgments that are true and just. These voices come as an antiphonal response to the hymn of the angel (vv. 5–6).[13]

---

11. Gregory K. Beale, *The Book of Revelation: A Commentary on the Greek Text,* NIGTC (Grand Rapids: Eerdmans, 1998), p. 818. Consult also Peter Staples, "Rev. XVI 4–6 and Its Vindication Formula," *NovT* 14 (1972): 280–93.

12. Hughes (*Revelation,* p. 174) allows the possibility of applying the clause to the saints.

13. Jürgen Roloff, *The Revelation of John,* trans. J. E. Alsup (Minneapolis: Fortress, 1993), p. 186.

The Greek word *krisis* (judgment) actually signifies the process of coming to a verdict that then becomes the judge's sentence. The words "true and just are your judgments" are repeated verbatim in 19:2, and the combination "Lord God Almighty, true and just" is a copy of 15:3.

No one can accuse God of being hasty in his judgment, for the Almighty has demonstrated extraordinary patience, warning the people repeatedly while they scornfully refused to repent. No one can charge him with injustice, for he passes judgment that accords with truth and justice (Deut. 32:4; Ps. 19:9; 119:137; Dan. 3:27–28 Old Greek and Theod.).

Greek Words, Phrases, and Constructions in 16:4–7

Verse 4

εἰς—the first three bowls are poured out εἰς (*into*) the earth, the sea, and the rivers and springs of water. The last four bowls are poured out ἐπί (*upon*) the sun, the throne of the beast, the river Euphrates, and the air respectively.

Verse 7

αἱ κρίσεις—the term κρίσις may denote the manner of coming to a verdict (14:7; 18:10; 19:2), whereas the word κρίμα refers to the result of an action, namely, the sentencing (17:1; 18:20; 20:4).[14]

---

4. The Fourth Bowl
16:8–9

8. And the fourth angel poured out his bowl on the sun, and he was given the power to burn the people with fire. 9. And the people were burned with a great burning, and they blasphemed the name of God, who has the authority over these plagues. And they did not repent to give him glory.

The fourth trumpet and the fourth plague have little in common except for the reference to the sun. The fourth trumpet sounded and a third of the sun was struck so that darkness ensued (8:12). But in the fourth plague the sun is not eclipsed at all but shines in all its strength to burn the people, who are unable to protect themselves. Indeed, this plague is entirely new in the cycle of the seven bowls. The sun as the source of light and the source of heat that causes creation to flourish is now given power to destroy with torrid temperatures. The light of the sun normally provides warmth and comfort to all living beings, especially the human race; now the sun has become a destructive power. Instead of being a blessing, the sun has become a curse. The passive tense of the verb *to give* implies that God is the agent who causes this abnormality to happen.

God's people are shielded from this ordeal. In a few places of Scripture God tells his people that "they will neither hunger nor thirst, nor will the desert heat

---

14. Consult Friedrich Büchsel, *TDNT*, 3:942; Mathias Rissi, *EDNT*, 2:317. The two words can take on identical meanings.

or the sun beat upon them" (Isa. 49:10; see also Ps. 121:6; Rev. 7:16). To his followers he is a sun and shield (Ps. 84:11).

Observing the result of the affliction, John reports that unbelievers "blasphemed the name of God, who has the authority over these plagues" (compare Isa. 52:5). These people are the followers of the Antichrist, who himself blasphemes God and slanders his name and dwelling place and those who reside in heaven (Rev. 13:6). They fully know that God has the power to inflict these plagues on them, but instead of repenting of their evil ways they blaspheme him. This shows that they are completely in the power of the evil one and are unable to break away. By contrast, Jesus sets his people free from the bondage of sin. He calls his people to repentance, as is evident in the letters to the churches in Ephesus, Pergamum, Thyatira, Sardis, and Laodicea (2:5, 16, 21, 22; 3:3, 19). And even though they have to endure hardship for the sake of the gospel, their sins are forgiven because they repented.

Earlier John depicted unbelievers as refusing to listen to the trumpet calls designed to bring them to repentance (9:20–21). But when they refuse to listen, they must take full responsibility for their actions and face the unmitigated wrath of God, like Pharaoh, who hardened his heart again and again and refused to listen to God.[15] The writer of the Apocalypse concludes, "They did not repent to give him glory." This chapter's recurring theme is the refusal to repent demonstrated by sinners whose hearts are hardened by the punishments God has sent (vv. 9, 11, 21). Furthermore, failing to glorify God results in God abandoning them. Hence, Paul in Romans 1:24–28 notes three times in succession that God gives hardened sinners over to their own sins in an act of divine judgment. In summary, these people are lost forever.

Greek Words, Phrases, and Constructions in 16:8–9

Verse 8

ἐδόθη—the subject, which must be supplied, can be either the sun as the nearer antecedent or the fourth angel in the nominative case. Translators are equally divided on this issue.

Verse 9

δοῦναι—the aorist infinitive of the verb *to give* has a consecutive sense in this verse, "to give him glory." It functions as conceived result.[16]

---

15. God hardened Pharaoh's heart nine times (Exod. 4:21; 7:3; 9:12; 10:1, 20, 27; 11:10; 14:4, 8). But Pharaoh also hardened his own heart nine times (see Exod. 7:13, 14, 22; 8:15, 19, 32; 9:7, 34, 35). In the final analysis, Pharaoh was to blame because of his unbelief (Rom. 9:17–18).

16. A. T. Robertson, *A Grammar of the Greek New Testament in the Light of Historical Research* (Nashville: Broadman, 1934), p. 1001; Robert Hanna, *A Grammatical Aid to the Greek New Testament* (Grand Rapids: Baker, 1983), p. 452.

5. The Fifth Bowl
16:10–11

10. And the fifth angel poured out his bowl on the throne of the beast. And his kingdom was darkened, and the people bit their tongues because of pain. 11. And they blasphemed the God of heaven because of their pains and their boils. And they did not repent of their works.

a. "And the fifth angel poured out his bowl on the throne of the beast." The first four plagues were poured out on God's creation: the earth, the sea, the rivers, and the sun. But the fifth plague affects the throne of the beast, namely, the seat of Satan's spiritual empire. Also, the last three plagues in this series of seven are sent directly to the followers of Satan.[17] These followers blaspheme the God of heaven (v. 11), are deceived by the false prophet (v. 13), and are shaken by the forces of nature and see their world collapse (vv. 18–21).

The throne of Satan is mentioned with reference to Pergamum as representative of Rome (2:13; see also 13:2). There emperor worship had its center and there the first Roman administrative center in the province of Asia was located. Consequently some commentators place the throne of the beast in Rome, but this is too restrictive.[18] Whereas the first four bowls affected nature, the fifth one acts upon a spiritual realm. The throne of the beast is a spiritual throne described as the pit of the Abyss (9:1). Also, the rule of the Antichrist is not limited to a given era or a particular place. Wherever God rules on the face of this earth, Satan establishes his throne and claims authority (Luke 4:6). Last, all the citizens in the kingdom of the beast are stricken with fear, despair, and pain.

b. "And his kingdom was darkened, and the people bit their tongues because of pain." The plague that caused all the Egyptians to live in darkness for three days was a physical change of nature (Exod. 10:22), but the outpouring of the fifth bowl brings about spiritual darkness for all the followers of Satan. And as the Israelites had light where they lived (Exod. 10:23), so the people of God continue to live in his light.

This spiritual darkness began in the past, continues to the present, and is widespread. As a consequence, the citizens of this kingdom of darkness keep on biting their tongues because of the agonies they experience. They are restless, ill at ease, and driven to exhaustion. The Greek word *ponos*, which is translated as "pain" (vv. 10, 11; 21:4), means hard work of body and mind resulting in suffering, grief, and pain.[19] The people *bite* (literally, gnaw) their tongues to keep control of their mental and physical functions.

---

17. Wilfrid J. Harrington, *Revelation*, SP 16 (Collegeville, Minn.: Liturgical Press, 1993), p. 165.

18. Among many others see Swete (*Revelation*, p. 204), who asserts that "it is doubtless Rome"; R. H. Charles, *A Critical and Exegetical Commentary on the Revelation of St. John*, ICC (Edinburgh: Clark, 1920), 2:45; Gerhard A. Krodel, *Revelation*, ACNT (Minneapolis: Augsburg, 1989), p. 285; Mounce, *Revelation*, p. 297.

19. Liddell, p. 1448; Manfred Seitz and Hans-Georg Link, *NIDNTT*, 1:262.

c. "And they blasphemed the God of heaven because of their pains and their boils." Their bodies also suffer from the ulcers that were caused by the angel who poured out the first bowl (v. 2). Thus, their bodies are covered with festering boils from which they endure excruciating pain. In spite of the agony they have to endure, they fail to turn to God, who controls the plagues (v. 9). They refuse to seek his help; instead they curse the God of heaven (compare 11:13; Dan. 2:18, 19). The term *God of heaven* refers to the highest majesty in heaven and on earth. By cursing this majesty, the suffering earthlings show determined defiance and radical rejection of God's exalted rule.

d. "And they did not repent from their works." These works are spelled out at the end of the sixth trumpet: worship of idols, murder, magic arts, sexual immorality, and thefts (9:20–21). The people continue their sinful lifestyle and refuse to repent. Without a doubt, for these sinners the time to repent is past.[20]

Greek Words, Phrases, and Constructions in 16:10–11

Verse 10

ἐκ—in this sentence the preposition has a causal connotation: "the people bit their tongues because of pain." The verb ἐμασῶντο (they bit) is in the imperfect tense to show continued action. It is impersonal and thus refers to people in general.

Verse 11

ἐκ τῶν ἔργων αὐτῶν—"from their works." The preposition ἐκ denotes a sense of separation.

---

6. The Sixth Bowl *16:12–16*

This segment mentions geographic areas and places including the river Euphrates and Armageddon; in the next section (vv. 17–21) Babylon the Great appears. Are these names to be interpreted literally or figuratively? One is inclined to say that from John's perspective these are specific places and names that should be taken literally. This becomes plain when we note that Old Testament prophets directly and indirectly predict a drying up of the Euphrates and the waters of Babylon (Isa. 11:15; 44:27; Jer. 50:38; 51:36; see also Zech. 10:11; 4 Ezra [=2 Esdras] 13:47). This prophecy was fulfilled in the days of Cyrus king of Persia, who in 539 B.C. crossed the Euphrates with his army and defeated Babylon.[21]

The name *Armageddon* is the Hebrew equivalent of the Mount of Megiddo. But there is no mount near the place called Megiddo that overlooks the Plain of Esdraelon. Regardless of the problems surrounding the name in question, some

---

20. Richard Bauckham, *The Climax of Prophecy* (Edinburgh: Clark, 1993), p. 14.

21. Herodotus 1.190–91; Xenophon *Cyropedia* 7.5.1–36.

scholars opt for a literal interpretation.[22] They see the name *Babylon* as linked inextricably with that of *Euphrates* and discard views other than the literal one.

However, figurative explanations are viable and even preferable. First, this chapter has a few passages that should be interpreted figuratively; for instance, the drinking of blood is best understood in terms of interpersonal bloodshed among anti-Christian forces (v. 6), and keeping one's clothes on is a figurative description of being clothed with the Word of God (v. 15). On this basis, the names in the present passage can be perceived metaphorically.

Next, the Euphrates (see 9:14) was considered to be a boundary dividing east and west; this barrier has now been removed so that destructive forces can advance unhindered from place to place and cause the fall of Babylon the Great.

Third, in Revelation the name of Babylon the Great is not a localized place but is a symbol of the anti-Christian world power that lasts until the end of cosmic time (refer to the comments on 14:8).

Fourth, chapter 17 provides an explanation of Babylon by alluding to the great prostitute who sits on many waters (v. 1); this "is another way of referring to 'the Euphrates and its water' (16:12)."[23] John interprets these waters to be the "peoples, crowds, nations, and languages" (17:15); indeed these words are a commentary on the expressions *Euphrates* and *Babylon* (16:12, 19).

Fifth, in context the drying up of the Euphrates functions as a symbol to allow anti-Christian forces to go to war by deceiving, if possible, even Christians. Note that three evil spirits go out to gather the kings of the whole world to battle (v. 14), while the believers receive the warning to stay awake and not be caught unprepared (v. 15). Hence it is not so much a matter of the drying up of the Euphrates as it is of the sending forth of three evil spirits to deceive the whole world.[24] All restraints and obstacles have been removed so that the ungodly forces can do their destructive work. The moral code of God's law has ceased to influence society at large, and the mystery of lawlessness is at work in full force (see 2 Thess. 2:7).

12. And the sixth angel poured out his bowl on the great river Euphrates, and its water dried up, so that a road of the kings of the east was prepared.

This verse echoes the account of the Israelites crossing the Red Sea and the Jordan (Exod. 14:21; Josh. 3:17). The Egyptian army tried to traverse the Red Sea but drowned, while the Israelites safely crossed it (Ps. 106:9; Isa. 11:16; 51:10). Now John reveals that the kings of the east use the dry bed of the Euphrates as a road to continue their travels unimpeded by a natural barrier. But he does not indicate that the eastern kings actually invade the west. Are these kings the

---

22. Robert L. Thomas (*Revelation 8–22: An Exegetical Commentary* [Chicago: Moody, 1995], p. 269) asserts: "If 'Euphrates' is a real place, so is *Harmagedōn*." See also John F. Walvoord, *The Revelation of Jesus Christ* (Chicago: Moody, 1966), pp. 238–39; Henry Alford, *James–Revelation*, vol. 4, part 2, of *Alford's Greek Testament* (1875; reprint, Grand Rapids: Guardian, 1976), p. 702.

23. Beale, *Revelation*, p. 828.

24. Sweet, *Revelation*, p. 246; Hoeksema, *Behold, He Cometh!* pp. 546–47.

Parthians whom the Romans in John's time had not yet subdued? Although much has been written on the prowess of the Parthians and the legend of Nero's return,[25] a Parthian conquest is probably not in view. John himself provides a clue with his reference to the kings of the whole world gathered by the evil spirits for battle (vv. 13–14). This means that both the kings of the east and the kings of the world are forces pitched against Christianity; in vain these two seek to achieve the same purpose, namely, the overthrow of the church. John often mentions two slightly differing subjects which fulfill the same objective (e.g., "the song of Moses and the song of the Lamb," 15:3).

Incidentally, *the road of the kings of the east* is one phrase that has been subjected to more speculation than any other phrase in this chapter. But if there is no additional light from either the text or context, we do well to be silent.

13. And I saw out of the mouth of the dragon and out of the mouth of the beast and out of the mouth of the false prophet three unclean spirits like frogs. 14. For they are demonic spirits, working miracles, and they go out to the kings of the whole world to assemble them for the war on the great day of God Almighty.

Satan now produces a parody of God, Christ, and the Holy Spirit. God the Father is parodied by the dragon, Satan, who opposes God. The beast comes up out of the sea as the Antichrist over against Christ. And the false prophet as the beast comes up out of the earth in the place of the Holy Spirit (12:3; 13:1, 2, 11; 19:20; 20:10).

The phrase *out of the mouth of* occurs three times and should be understood symbolically as speech coming forth in triple form. Out of the mouths of the trinity of dragon, beast, and false prophet pours forth a barrage of lies and deceit. John uses the symbol of three evil spirits, who are the speakers, and he compares this trio to three frogs. Since they lack scales and fins, the Old Testament classified frogs as unclean creatures that the Israelites were to detest (Lev. 11:10). The word *frog* appears only once in the entire New Testament and in the Old only with reference to the plague of frogs in Egypt (Exod. 8:2–6; Ps. 78:45; 105:30). Although frogs are useful creatures in that they consume flies and other insects, people regarded them as unclean. In this passage John identifies frogs with *unclean spirits.* The falsehoods that come forth from the three evil spirits are slick and slippery; it is something like touching the skin of a frog. These lies, however, are abhorrent to those who are alert, vigilant, and firmly established in the Word. These saints are fully aware of the spiritual warfare the Antichrist wages against the Christ and his followers.

In addition to misrepresenting the truth, these spirits also possess the ability to perform signs and deceive the public. Earlier John wrote that the beast performed "great signs so that he even makes fire to come down out of

25. E.g., see respectively Aune, *Revelation 6–16*, pp. 891–94; and Bauckham, *Climax of Prophecy*, pp. 407–50.

heaven onto the earth before people" (13:13). This was done for the primary purpose of misleading the people (Matt. 24:24), especially "the kings of the whole world." The evil spirits direct their deception of lies and signs primarily to the rulers of the world, so that they in turn can pass on the lies to the citizens of their countries.[26] And with the deceived multitudes these kings go to war against Almighty God. John writes that the evil spirits gather the kings of the whole world "for the war on the great day of God Almighty." This war is not physical or political but rather spiritual; it is the war Satan has been waging since he led Adam and Eve astray in Paradise and will continue to wage until he is defeated and cast into the lake of fire (20:10). The Greek text features the definite article in the expression *the war* at three places that feature the final battle (16:14; 19:19; 20:8). It refers to the ultimate conflict at the end of cosmic time.

Let us have a closer look at the text (v. 14). First, the noun *kings* represents all the people in the anti-Christian gathering who engage in a spiritual warfare on a day called *the great day*.

Next, even though John mentions a specific day that he qualifies with the adjective *great*, Satan is waging war ever more fiercely as he sees time, which he knows is short (12:12), elapsing. The closer he comes to the end, the fiercer he plunges into battle. Worldwide he launches this battle against the kingdom of heaven and its King by seeking to overthrow the Christian church in an all-out war at the end. But the devil and his followers fail to realize that God brings together all the rulers of the world and their people for the purpose of defeating them.

Third, the final battle will be fought when Christ, riding on a white horse with the armies of heaven, utterly defeats his opponents (19:11–21). At that battle the kings of the earth and their armies are gathered together with the beast and the false prophet. This prophet had deluded kings and armies, but they are killed with the sword of the Lord. The expression *the kings of the earth* appears frequently in the Apocalypse and alludes to Psalm 2:2. These kings and rulers set themselves against God and his anointed Son, but the Lord treats them with scorn and derision.[27]

Finally, the adjective *great* depicts the last day when all the forces of evil are pitched against the Christ. That day indeed is the day of the Lord—a common term in both the Old and the New Testaments. Especially in the epistles of Paul and Peter, the term *the day of the Lord* means the last eschatological day.[28]

---

26. God sent a lying spirit to entice King Ahab to go to his death in battle against Syria (see 1 Kings 22:21–23).

27. Rev. 1:5; 6:15; 17:2, 18; 18:3, 9; 19:19; 21:24. The sixth seal has the expression *kings of the earth* (6:15) and the sixth trumpet has *kings of the whole world* (16:14).

28. George Eldon Ladd, *Commentary on the Revelation of John* (Grand Rapids: Eerdmans, 1972), p. 214. See 1 Cor. 3:13; 2 Thess. 1:10; 2 Pet. 3:12; and compare John 6:39; 11:24; 12:48.

15. (“Look, I come like a thief! Blessed is the one who stays awake and keeps his clothes on, so that he may not walk about naked and be exposed to shame.”)

a. “Look, I come like a thief!” This verse is an interlude in which Jesus addresses the believers on earth. Therefore, translators put it within parentheses as an aside. The question “where are the followers of Christ in this world of deception?” is now answered by the voice of Jesus calling them to be alert. He reminds them that his coming will be like a thief, which for the saints is suddenly and unexpectedly. Jesus had taught his disciples that they should be like the owner of a house who stays awake to prevent a thief from breaking in at night (Matt. 24:42–43; Luke 12:39–40). And in the letter to the church in Sardis, Jesus tells the readers that he will come like a thief (Rev. 3:3). The point Jesus makes both in teaching his disciples and in alerting the Christians in Sardis is his sudden and unexpected return. Both Paul and Peter describe the coming of the Lord as that of a thief at night (1 Thess. 5:2; 2 Pet. 3:10).

The image of the thief wanting to break into a house is juxtaposed with a beatitude that has a blessing for those who stay awake and prevent this from happening. Similarly, in Luke’s Gospel, Jesus’ parable of the thief is closely associated with the beatitude that blesses the faithful servant who stays alert (Luke 12:37, 39).[29]

b. “Blessed is the one who stays awake.” Here is the third beatitude in a series of seven (1:3; 14:13; 16:15; 19:9; 20:6; 22:7, 14). Some scholars are of the opinion that the arrangement of a warning together with a beatitude is awkward and presents proof that this passage is an intrusion or interpolation.[30] But this view cannot be sustained; manuscript evidence is lacking, and John always keeps in mind God’s people in the midst of an unbelieving world. Here with Jesus as his source he directs a word of warning to Christians to stay spiritually awake.

c. “And keeps his clothes on, so that he may not walk about naked and be exposed to shame.” The reference to keeping one’s clothes on has nothing to do with nudism but must be seen figuratively. It alludes to being spiritually clothed with the Word of God, so that when the tempter comes with lies and deceit, the believer is able to give a good account of himself or herself and thus withstand temptations, expose deceit, and ward off diabolical attacks. Walking around spiritually naked, without the garments of God’s Word, brings shame to the Christian and reproach to his Lord. This is what Jesus told the Laodiceans, “I advise you to buy from me . . . white garments to clothe yourself that the shame of your nakedness may not be revealed” (3:18). Indeed it is “a figurative way of speaking of spiritual destitution.”[31]

---

29. Louis A. Vos, *The Synoptic Traditions in the Apocalypse* (Kampen: Kok, 1965), pp. 83–84. But Bauckham (*Climax of Prophecy*, p. 105 n. 32) calls this paraphrase unconvincing.

30. Ford, *Revelation*, p. 263; Charles, *Revelation*, 2:49, 427 n. 3; James Moffatt, *The Revelation of St. John the Divine*, in *The Expositor’s Greek Testament*, ed. W. Robertson Nicholl (reprint, Grand Rapids: Eerdmans, 1956), 5:448.

31. Thomas, *Revelation 8–22*, pp. 267–68.

16. And they brought them into the place that is called in Hebrew Armageddon. The expression *Armageddon* occurs only here in the entire Bible, so that scholars struggle to present a convincing explanation. Numerous solutions have been offered,[32] but we have no absolute certainty as to what the word actually refers to. All our approaches are at best mere guesses.

Let us begin with the phrase *in Hebrew*, which by itself presents a problem because the Old Testament does not have the word *Armageddon*. By transliteration we get either Harmageddon, which is translated "mount (*har*) of Megiddo," or Armageddon, which is rendered as "city (*ar*) of Megiddo." The city was located on a plateau overlooking the Plain of Esdraelon to the northeast. In this valley many ancient and recent battles have been fought, to mention only the armies of Israel defeating Sisera and his host in the days of the prophetess Deborah (Judg. 5:19; see also 2 Kings 9:27; 23:29; 2 Chron. 35:22; Zech. 12:11) and the Six-Day War of 1967.

Further, the spelling of the word *Megiddo* varies. The Greek text has *Harmagedōn*, which apart from the prefix *har* has an *a* in place of an *e*, an *e* for an *i*, one *d* instead of two, and a final *n*. The expression is indeclinable because of its Hebrew origin. The Old Testament does not have the word in question, but John's use of Hebrew is typical of Jewish apocalyptic writings. But the writings of the church fathers never connected the name *Megiddo* with 16:16, and in contemporary literature it is never given any "eschatological significance."[33]

Another difficulty is that there is no mountain at Megiddo. Identifying this name with Mount Carmel to the west of Megiddo, which some scholars have done, finds no support in ancient writing and is therefore to be discarded. As an alternative, other scholars turned their attention to the translation "city of Megiddo." The word can then be considered a code name for a particular war, because it is common in warfare to use various code names as rallying points.[34]

Still other interpreters see the word *Armageddon* as based on the Hebrew words *har môʿēd*, translated in English as "the mountain of assembly," which appears in Isaiah 14:13. This mountain is symbolic for Mount Zion, for this place is considered to be the place from which the Christ will come to defeat his enemies. This mountain of assembly is then considered to be Mount Zion and related to the city of Jerusalem. This place serves as the gathering point for court sessions, councils,

---

32. See, e.g., Hans K. LaRondelle, "The Biblical Concept of Armageddon," *JETS* 28 (1985): 21–31, and "The Etymology of *Har-Magedon* (Rev 16:16)," *AUSS* 27 (1989): 69–73; R. E. Loasby, "'Har-Magedon' according to the Hebrew in the Setting of the Seven Last Plagues of Revelation 16," *AUSS* 27 (1989): 129–32; W. H. Shea, "The Location and Significance of Armageddon in Rev 16:16," *AUSS* 18 (1980): 157–62.

33. Joachim Jeremias, *TDNT*, 1:468. However, in an article titled "The Origin of Armageddon: Revelation 16:16 as an Interpretation of Zechariah 12:11," John Day points out that Zech. 12:11 is "the only place prior to Revelation where Megiddo is mentioned in an apocalyptic context." And that passage is the only one in the Old Testament where Megiddo is spelled with the final *n* as *mĕgiddōn* (*Crossing the Boundaries: Essays in Biblical Interpretation in Honour of Michael D. Goulder*, ed. Stanley E. Porter, Paul Joyce, and David E. Orton [Leiden: Brill, 1994], pp. 319–20).

34. See L. van Hartingsveld, *Revelation* (Grand Rapids: Eerdmans, 1985), p. 69.

command of the armed forces, and the assembly of angels and saints.[35] The difficulty with this suggestion is the absence of textual support; it is a conjecture that seeks to emend the text from the Greek to the Hebrew. Even though the proposal itself has merit, lack of textual support undermines its soundness.

I regard the term *Armageddon* as a symbol by which God delivers his people from harm and demonstrates that he has the power and might to overthrow his enemies. He repeatedly showed his faithfulness by rescuing them in both Old Testament and New Testament times. Thus, he sets them free during the final tribulation at the return of Christ. "It is for this reason that Har-Magedon is the sixth bowl. The seventh is the judgment day."[36]

Greek Words, Phrases, and Constructions in 16:14–15

Verse 14

εἰσὶν γὰρ πνεύματα—according to the grammatical rule, a neuter plural noun has a verb in the singular; here it has a plural verb. Yet in the next clause the neuter pronoun is plural and the verb is singular, ἃ ἐκπορεύεται (which went out).

Verse 15

ἵνα μή—this combination is not repeated for the second verb in the subjunctive but is understood (βλέπωσιν).

---

7. The Seventh Bowl
16:17–21

17. And the seventh angel poured out his bowl on the air. And a loud voice went forth out of the temple, from the throne, saying, "It is done."

A brief discussion on the translation of this text is in order. First, the Greek literally has "on the air," while the English idiom adopted by many translators is "into the air." But John looks not from an earthly perspective upward but from a heavenly perspective downward at the angel who is pouring out the bowl. Next, he is precise in the choice of prepositions: the voice comes *out of* the temple and *from* the throne. That is, the voice proceeds from the very presence of God and comes from the area of God's throne. Third, the translation "It is done" is not derived from the verb *to do* but from the verb *to become*. Some versions, therefore, try to express the concept that the command to pour out the bowls has been fulfilled; they read "it is over" (REB) or "the end has come" (NJB).

---

35. Meredith G. Kline, "Har Magedon: The End of the Millennium," *JETS* 39 (1996): 212–13. See Mathias Rissi, *Time and History* (Richmond: John Knox, 1966), pp. 84–85. Alan F. Johnson has a similar proposal with his conjecture that *magedōn* is a hypothetical noun formed from the Hebrew verb *gādad* and means "his place of gathering in troops." See his *Revelation*, in *The Expositor's Bible Commentary*, ed. Frank E. Gaebelein (Grand Rapids: Zondervan, 1981), 12:552.

36. Hendriksen, *More Than Conquerors*, p. 163; consult Harry R. Boer, *The Book of Revelation* (Grand Rapids: Eerdmans, 1979), p. 108.

The seventh plague affects the air that is the lifeline of all living beings on this earth. Without air everyone and everything dies. But is the concept *air* to be taken literally or symbolically? If the latter, then the word alludes to the demonic realm. According to Paul, Satan is "the ruler of the kingdom of the air" (Eph. 2:2).[37] If this interpretation is correct, we see the striking antithesis of Satan's throne (v. 10) receiving the contents of the seventh bowl of wrath and the divine voice proceeding from God's throne saying, "It is completed." Then Satan and his followers are the recipients of the last bowl of wrath.

The loud voice sounding forth from God's presence was the voice of God himself announcing the end of the plagues. The voice declared that the wrath of God poured out on all his enemies had come to an end (compare 21:6).

18. And there were flashes of lightning and rumblings and peals of thunder, and there was a great earthquake, such as had not happened since humans came on the earth, so great an earthquake.

What follows after the completion of the plagues are the signs that describe God's presence and accompany his judgment. They consist of characteristics pertaining to nature (lightning, rumblings, and thunder) and depict the throne room (4:5; see also 8:5). With the opening of the sixth seal God displays his judgment with an earthquake (6:12). But here the earthquake is of such intensity that it is not only called great but it is also said that no person has ever experienced violence of this magnitude. Truly these are the final moments predicted as "a time of distress such as has not happened from the beginning of nations until then" (Dan. 12:1).

John speaks as if all this had already taken place, whereas the scene actually refers to the future. He does this often when he looks into the future; he reports in the past tense to tell the reader of his certainty that what he says will indeed happen. Without a doubt, the great earthquake with accompanying signs in nature will occur at the time of the consummation. Note also the allusion to the worst storm that struck Egypt at the time of the plagues (Exod. 9:24). As Egypt was devastated by a hailstorm, so John predicts a plague of hail with hailstones of enormous weight (v. 21).

19. And the great city became three parts, and the cities of the nations fell. And Babylon the Great was remembered before God, and he gave her the cup of raging wine of his wrath.

a. "And the great city became three parts, and the cities of the nations fell." This is apocalyptic language that reveals the destruction of the cities of the world. The expression *the great city* refers to Babylon the Great, as is evident from the second part of this verse and the next two chapters (17:18; 18:10, 18, 19, 21). The name *Babylon the Great* already occurred in 14:8 and is the symbol of the anti-Christian world power that persecutes God's people. It is a force that will exert

37. See the commentaries of Beale (p. 841), Hailey (p. 337), Morris (p. 194), and Sweet (p. 250). Mounce (p. 303 n. 63) rules this out by saying, "There is probably no intended reference here to the air as the abode of demons (cf. Eph 2:2)."

its power until the end of time. Long before John's time, Babylon had ceased to be a world empire, and throughout the centuries it has never been able to rally again "under the formal political name of 'the Babylonian Empire.'"[38] Some scholars identify Babylon with Rome, for this is how John would have understood the force of the oppressor; others consider "the great city" to be Jerusalem; and still others see Babylon as the city along the banks of the great river Euphrates (v. 12).[39] The great city cannot be Jerusalem, for God's people dwell in the holy city, namely, the new Jerusalem. But God's enemies live in the great city (11:8), which is not a particular location but rather the quintessence of an anti-Christian force of unbelief directed by Satan against God and his people. This is Babylon the Great, the universal satanic power which God remembers and to which he hands the cup of his raging wrath.

What is the significance of this great city becoming three parts? The words *become three parts* are an idiomatic expression symbolizing complete destruction.[40] All the human arguments and philosophical allegations that have been raised against the knowledge of God are utterly demolished (2 Cor. 10:5). And all the cities of the world are destroyed; they as the centers of the anti-Christian empire fall apart and disintegrate.

b. "Babylon the Great was remembered before God, and he gave her the cup of raging wine of his wrath." God remembered the sins this empire committed against his kingdom and now pours out his anger in the form of the cup of raging wine. Who can stand in the day when God's anger is unleashed (Ps. 76:7b; Mal. 3:2; see Nah. 1:6)? John had already called attention to God's fury when he wrote that anyone who receives the mark of the beast "will drink the wine of God's wrath that has been poured full strength into the cup of his wrath" (14:10; compare Ps. 75:8; Isa. 51:17, 22; Jer. 25:15).

20. And every island fled and the mountains could not be found. 21. And immense hailstones weighing about a hundred pounds each came down from the sky onto the people, and they blasphemed God because of the plague of hail, for its plague was very great.

The sight of islands fleeing and mountains disappearing is reminiscent of the sixth seal, which is a portrayal of judgment (6:14). It means that everything on this old earth is changing instantaneously; indeed the time for the last judgment has come when the face of the earth is transformed and God is seated on the great white throne (20:11).

The plague of hail that destroyed the crops, animals, and human beings in Egypt (Exod. 9:13–26) forms the background of the hail that rains down on the people in this passage. Hail killed the Amorites during Israel's conquest of the land (Josh. 10:11), and hail mentioned by the prophets is described as an

---

38. Beale, *Revelation*, p. 830.

39. For these three differing views see successively Krodel, *Revelation*, p. 288; Ford, *Revelation*, p. 264; Thomas, *Revelation 8–22*, p. 207.

40. Lenski, *Revelation*, p. 483.

utterly destructive force (Isa. 32:19; Ezek. 13:11, 13; 38:22). The word *hail* also occurs in Revelation (8:7; 11:19). But the hail in this passage is exceptionally severe.

Hailstones weighing about a hundred pounds each are hurled down from the sky. The Greek has the word *talent,* which in terms of weight cannot be determined exactly; it varied depending on country and time. These immense chunks of ice kill every living being in their path, but instead of repenting, sinners curse God because of the hailstorm. They harden their hearts and refuse to repent (see vv. 9 and 11). In their hearts is no fear of God, no acknowledgment of their sins, and no acceptance of divine justice. Pharaoh repented as a result of the hailstorm and told Moses and Aaron that he had sinned, that God was in the right, and that he would let the Israelites go free (Exod. 9:27–28). When the storm was over, Pharaoh hardened his heart and refused to free the people of Israel. But the sinners on whom God rains hailstones of a hundred pounds each curse God while they receive his punishment.[41]

The punishment with which God strikes his enemies is so severe that John uses the Greek word *sphodra* (very much so), which is not found elsewhere in the Apocalypse. This word receives emphasis by being placed at the end of the sentence: "the plague was *very great.*" The Day of Judgment is imminent (see 19:19–21; 20:8–9).

Greek Words, Phrases, and Constructions in 16:17–19

Verse 17

ἐκ τοῦ ναοῦ ἀπὸ τοῦ θρόνου—this is the preferred reading of the text; scribes had difficulty with the concept of temple and throne in the same clause, and hence a number of variants appeared; for example, Codex Sinaiticus reads "the temple of God" and manuscript 051 has "from heaven." But the preponderant weight of witnesses supports the reading given in the text.[42]

Verse 18–19

The verb ἐγένετο appears four times in succession (vv. 18 and 19). The three in verse 18 convey the thought of "it happened," but the one in verse 19 is a Semitism. It appears in conjunction with the phrase εἰς τρία μέρη (into three parts) and reads "the great city became three parts."

ἐμνήσθη—this is a Semitism. See the parallel in Acts 10:31: Your prayer has been heard and your acts of mercy have been remembered before God.

τοῦ οἴνου . . . αὐτοῦ—here is a string of four genitives (compare 19:15) in which "the governing genitive precedes the dependent one."[43]

---

41. Swete, *Revelation,* p. 212.

42. Bruce M. Metzger, *A Textual Commentary on the Greek New Testament,* 2d ed. (Stuttgart: Deutsche Bibelgesellschaft, 1994), p. 681.

43. Nigel Turner, *Syntax,* vol. 3 of *A Grammar of New Testament Greek,* by J. H. Moulton et al. (Edinburgh: Clark, 1963), p. 218.

17

The Woman and the Beast

(17:1–18)

Outline (continued)

VII. Vision 6: Victory for Christ (17:1–19:21)
   A. Introduction (17:1–2)
   B. Conflict and Judgment (17:3–19:10)
      1. The Woman and the Beast (17:3–18)
         a. The Seductive Temptress (17:3–6)
         b. The Angel's Explanation (17:7–11)
         c. The Sovereignty of the Lamb (17:12–14)
         d. God's Purpose (17:15–18)

17 1 And one of the seven angels who had the seven bowls came, talked to me, and said,
"Come, I will show you the judgment of the great prostitute who is seated on many waters.
2 The kings of the earth have committed fornication with her, and the inhabitants of the
earth have become drunk with the wine of her fornication."

3 And he brought me in the Spirit to a desert place. And I saw a woman on a scarlet beast that
was full of names of blasphemy. The beast had seven heads and ten horns. 4 And the woman was
clothed in purple and scarlet cloth and was gilded with gold and precious stones and pearls. She had
a cup of gold in her hand full of abominations and uncleanness of her fornication. 5 And on her
forehead was a name written, a mystery,

BABYLON THE GREAT
THE MOTHER OF PROSTITUTES
AND OF THE ABOMINATIONS OF THE EARTH.

6 And I saw the woman drunk with the blood of the saints and with the blood of the martyrs of
Jesus. And when I saw her, I was greatly astounded.

7 And the angel said to me, "Why are you astounded? I will tell you the mystery of the woman and
of the beast that carries her, which has the seven heads and the ten horns. 8 The beast which you saw
was and is not and is about to go up from the Abyss and go to his destruction. And the inhabitants of
the earth will be astonished, they whose names are not written in the book of life from the foundation of the earth. They see the beast that was and is not and will come. 9 Here is the mind that has
understanding. The seven heads are seven hills on which the woman sits. 10 And they are seven
kings: five have fallen, one is, another has not yet come. And when he comes, it is necessary that he
remain for a little while. 11 And the beast that was, and is not, even he is an eighth and is of the seven,
and he goes to his destruction.

12 "And the ten horns which you saw are ten kings, who have not yet received a kingdom. But
they received authority with the beast as kings for one hour. 13 These have one purpose and they
give their power and authority to the beast. 14 These will make war against the Lamb and the Lamb
will overcome them, for he is Lord of lords and King of kings; and they who are with him are the
called, and the elect, and the faithful ones."

15 And the angel said to me, "The waters that you saw on which the prostitute sat, they are the
peoples, crowds, nations, and languages. 16 And the ten horns that you saw and the beast, these will
hate the prostitute; and they will make her desolate and naked; and they will eat her flesh and will
burn her with fire. 17 For God has placed in their hearts to do his purpose, to be of one accord, and
to give their kingdom to the beast until the words of God will be fulfilled. 18 And the woman whom
you saw is the great city which has a kingdom over the kings of the earth."

VII. Vision 6: Victory for Christ 17:1–19:21

In the sixth vision John shows the defeat of the woman called the great prostitute and Babylon the Great (chap. 17). The next chapter is an account of the fall of Babylon and its empire (chap. 18). These two chapters are followed, first, by the celebration of the wedding of the bride and the Lamb; next, by the battle the victorious Christ wages against the forces of the evil one; and last, by the beast and the false prophet who are cast into the lake of fire while the rest of Christ's opponents are killed with his sword (chap. 19).

How does this sixth vision relate to the preceding chapter? To get an overview we have to go back to the three cycles of seals, trumpets, and plagues. These cycles show similarities with respect to the seventh one in each series, because each seventh one has its location in heaven. The seventh seal introduces a period of silence in heaven (8:1); when the seventh trumpet was blown, loud voices were heard in heaven (11:15); and after the seventh bowl was poured out, a loud voice from the throne in heaven said, "It is done" (16:17). At the end of these seven-part cycles there is further information on the end of time. But even though the seventh plague is the last one for all three series, there are still more details. Hence, chapters 17 and 18 provide a detailed discussion on the sixth and seventh plagues (16:12–21). Chapter 17 presents a description of the great prostitute and the spiritual war that the kings of the earth fight against the Lamb, while chapter 18 describes the economic downfall of the world.[1]

The name Babylon the Great appears in both chapters 17 and 18. With the help of an ancient Roman coin depicting the goddess Roma sitting on seven hills and quotations from Roman historiographers (17:9), scholars interpret Babylon as a reference to Rome.[2] But identifying Babylon with Rome as the great prostitute is by itself restrictive and time-bound. To illustrate, the woman in chapter 12 is a symbol of the church and in chapter 19 she is the bride of the Lamb. By contrast, the woman in chapter 17 is called Babylon the Great, the mother of prostitutes, and the mother of the earth's abominations (v. 5). This woman is the great temptress, seducer, and liar in the service of Satan and the beast. She has been in this service not only during the days of John but from the time of the Fall and will be until the consummation. Also, at the same time this woman appears as a great metropolis that in consequence of God's judgment loses all her commercial and financial riches (18:11–24). This scene, therefore, speaks not merely of the overthrow of the Roman empire but rather of the complete and lasting defeat of the entire anti-Christian world.[3]

In view of Satan's short time on earth (12:12), I interpret chapter 17 as a picture of the beast's forces pitted against God but losing the battle in the end. The

1. Consult C. H. Dyer, "The Identity of Babylon in Revelation 17–18," *BibSac* 144 (1987): 305–16, 433–49.

2. R. Beauvery, "L'Apocalypse au risque de la numismatique: Babylone, la grande Prostituée et le sixième roi Vespasien et la déesse Rome," *RB* 90 (1983): 243–60; David E. Aune, *Revelation 17–22*, WBC 52C (Nashville: Nelson, 1998), pp. 920–28. See also Isbon T. Beckwith, *The Apocalypse of John* (1919; reprint, Grand Rapids: Baker, 1979), pp. 690–92, 711–12; Robert H. Mounce, *The Book of Revelation*, rev. ed., NICNT (Grand Rapids: Eerdmans, 1998), pp. 306–9; R. H. Charles, *A Critical and Exegetical Commentary on the Revelation of St. John*, ICC (Edinburgh: Clark, 1920), 2:54–61; Gerhard A. Krodel, *Revelation*, ACNT (Minneapolis: Augsburg, 1989), pp. 291–94.

3. Harry R. Boer (*The Book of Revelation* [Grand Rapids: Eerdmans, 1979], p. 118) remarks: "The beast constantly changes the *form* in which it manifests itself, but it never changes *itself*."

prostitute rides on this beast that has seven heads and ten horns: "[We] see the beast that was and is not and will come" (v. 8). In short, the beast has a long history, is present today, and eventually will go to his destruction. This beast transcends the successive empires of the world, including the Roman empire, while all along the prostitute is sitting on his back. "When, in Revelation 18:4, the admonition is given: 'Come forth my people, out of her, and have no fellowship with her sins,' that command was intended not only for people living close to the end of the world's history, but also for believers in John's day and age; indeed, for believers in every age."[4]

John first depicts the great prostitute who with the kings of the earth revels in her adulteries (vv. 1–2). Then he outlines her association with the beast of seven heads and ten horns (vv. 3–8). Third, he presents a time frame during which the kings of the earth war against the Lamb, who will conquer them (vv. 9–14). And last, John gives an explanation of the symbols of the waters on which the woman sits, and of the woman herself as "the great city which has a kingdom over the kings of the earth" (vv. 15–18).

A. Introduction
17:1–2

1. And one of the seven angels who had the seven bowls came, talked to me, and said, "Come, I will show you the judgment of the great prostitute who is seated on many waters. 2. The kings of the earth have committed fornication with her and the inhabitants of the earth have become drunk with the wine of her fornication."

a. "And one of the seven angels who had the seven bowls came, talked to me, and said." Here is an indication that this chapter gives a further elaboration of the sixth and seventh plagues presented in the preceding chapter (16:12–21). One of the seven angels who poured out the bowls of God's wrath addresses John. We have no indication whether this angel was the sixth or the seventh one, but this is insignificant. It is, however, meaningful that not an elder but an angel addresses John. The twenty-four elders in heaven represent the redeemed saints, and one of the elders asked John about the significance of the saints wearing white robes (7:13). But here an angel, as a messenger from God, is instructing the seer about the punishment meted out to the great prostitute. Incidentally, one of these seven angels also instructs John about the bride, the wife of the Lamb (21:9). Indeed the angel relates a tale of two women, one holy and one profane. The holy one will have Christ as her husband; the profane one has no husband—she is the great prostitute.

b. "'Come, I will show you the judgment of the great prostitute who is seated on many waters.'" The angel invited John to come with him to view the judgment scene in which the verdict had been handed down to the notorious harlot representing Babylon. The verdict indeed was an accomplished fact, for her doom

4. William Hendriksen, *More Than Conquerors* (reprint, Grand Rapids: Baker, 1982), p. 168.

was sealed. The Old Testament prophets brought God's judgments against Babylon in terms of utter destruction and being forever uninhabited (see Isa. 13:19–22; Jer. 50:39; 51:37). The prophets attached the name *prostitute* to the cities of Tyre (Isa. 23:15–17), Nineveh (Nah. 3:4), and Jerusalem (Isa. 1:21; Jer. 2:20; Ezek. 16:15), but not to Babylon. Yet here the angel portrayed Babylon the Great, called the mother of prostitutes (v. 5), not as a rebuilt city but as a symbol of all evil directed against God. Ancient Babylon was situated along the banks of the Euphrates, where numerous canals provided water for transportation and irrigation purposes (Jer. 51:13). But because this ancient city was completely destroyed and depopulated, the text should not be interpreted literally.

The text reveals symbolism, evident in the two expressions *prostitute* and *many waters.* These two should be interpreted not literally but spiritually.[5] First, the great harlot's goal is to lead people wherever possible away from Christ; hence, she is the exact opposite of the church that seeks to lead all people everywhere to Christ. Next, John explains the term *many waters* as "the peoples and the crowds and nations and languages" of the world (v. 15). They are the restless waves of humanity controlled by this vile harlot.

c. "The kings of the earth have committed fornication with her, and the inhabitants of the earth have become drunk with the wine of her fornication." Note there is repetition of the concept *fornicate,* which occurs three times in these two verses: the noun *prostitute* specifies the woman; the verb *to fornicate* describes the actions of the kings of the earth; and last, the noun *fornication* relates the medium that inebriates the inhabitants of the earth. Again, this concept must be understood spiritually; Israel and Judah were accused of being spiritual prostitutes (Ezek. 23); and Jesus labeled the religious leaders of his day "an adulterous generation" (Matt. 12:39; 16:4).

Yet the difference between fornication by unmarried persons and adultery by spouses should be noted. This unmarried woman actively engages in illicit relations with the kings of the earth who in turn lead their followers astray. These kings are the heads of "the various parts of the antichristian empire."[6] They belong to this earth and have no spiritual ties with God. Further, the inhabitants of the earth are drunk with the wine of the woman's spiritual fornication; and they are people who serve not God but Satan.[7]

The difficulty in this chapter is to understand the multiple configurations of the woman. She is called the great prostitute, is aligned with the beast, represents Babylon the Great, and personifies "the great city" (v. 18). As a spiritual prostitute she stands diametrically opposed to Christ; she serves the beast who is the

5. Robert L. Thomas (*Revelation 8–22: An Exegetical Commentary* [Chicago: Moody, 1995], p. 282) correctly observes that "it is beyond dispute that this woman of Rev. 17:1 is the epitome of spiritual fornication or idolatry."

6. R. C. H. Lenski, *The Interpretation of St. John's Revelation* (Columbus: Wartburg, 1943), p. 492.

7. The expression *inhabitants of the earth* appears frequently in the Apocalypse. See Rev. 3:10; 6:10; 8:13; 11:10 (twice); 13:8, 12, 14 (twice); 17:2, 8.

Antichrist (13:1); and she represents Babylon the Great, which is the anti-Christian empire with numerous kings of the world gathered for battle against God Almighty (16:14, 16). In other words, John is looking at this woman from various aspects in which the adjective *great* used for her and Babylon takes a significant position.

John mentioned Babylon already in 14:8, where he wrote that an angel cried, "Fallen, fallen is Babylon the Great, which made all the nations drink the wrathful wine of her fornication." Worldly Babylon should be seen as a universal force of evil that influences the multitudes of humanity to such an extent that the people are desensitized. Babylon is "the archetypal source of every idolatrous manifestation in time and space."[8]

B. Conflict and Judgment
17:3–19:10

1. The Woman and the Beast
17:3–18

The picture that John presents to his viewers is dreadful because of the blasphemy against God, the blood of the saints, the power and authority of the beast, and the prostitute who rules over the kings of the earth. But within this picture are also references to those whose names are written in the book of life, the Lamb who overcomes his enemies, the Lord of lords and King of kings with his faithful followers, and God, who accomplishes his purpose and is fully in control.

a. The Seductive Temptress
17:3–6

3. And he brought me in the Spirit to a desert place. And I saw a woman on a scarlet beast that was full of names of blasphemy. The beast had seven heads and ten horns.

a. "And he brought me in the Spirit to a desert place." The contrast between John, who is in the Spirit, and the woman, who rides the beast of blasphemy, is strikingly clear.[9] The Holy Spirit transports John to a desert much the same as he does when he takes him to heaven and to a great and high mountain (4:2; 21:10). There are Old Testament parallels, for the Spirit of God lifted Ezekiel to Jerusalem, Babylon, the valley of dry bones, and the temple of the Lord (Ezek. 3:12, 14; 8:3; 11:1, 24; 37:1; 43:5).

---

8. Alan F. Johnson, *Revelation,* in *The Expositor's Bible Commentary,* ed. Frank E. Gaebelein (Grand Rapids: Zondervan, 1981), 12:555.

9. A number of translations read "in the spirit" (KJV, NEB, NJB, NLT, NRSV), but the context affirms the meaning "in the Spirit" because of the intended antithesis. Refer to Richard Bauckham, *The Climax of Prophecy* (Edinburgh: Clark, 1993), p. 158; see Jean-Pierre Ruiz, *Ezekiel in the Apocalypse: The Transformation of Prophetic Language in Revelation 16.17–19.10* (Frankfurt am Main: Peter Lang, 1989), pp. 300–303.

What is the significance of a desert place? Various interpretations are presented, among them the following: the Arabian desert (Gal. 1:17); a place inhabited by demons (Matt. 12:43); a place of temptation (Matt. 4:1); an area shielded from the devil's lies; and a suitable region to receive visions. Although some of these interpretations have merit, I think it is better to see an Old Testament background for the term *desert* in Isaiah 21:1–10. This passage mentions a desert out of which an invader comes who brings about the fall of Babylon. Thus, Isaiah speaks about a desert where he was shown a harsh vision. "In both Isaiah and Revelation the desert is central to the vision, though in Isaiah the vision comes from the desert, while in Revelation the prophet is taken to the desert to see the vision."[10]

b. "And I saw a woman on a scarlet beast that was full of names of blasphemy. The beast had seven heads and ten horns." The focus is on the woman, who has already been identified as the great prostitute (v. 1). Now we see the supremacy of this woman, for she rides on the back of a multiple-headed beast whose horns exhibit tremendous power. First, this scarlet beast with seven heads and ten horns is described in the same terms as the red dragon, who is Satan, and as the beast coming up out of the sea (12:3, 9; 13:1). In 12:3 the Greek uses a different word for the color red, namely, *pyrros* (fiery red). The number seven denotes completeness, and ten, the number of fullness in the decimal system. Next, this language is based on the prophecy of Daniel 7:7, 20, 24 that alludes to the power of a beast with ten horns. Third, the color *scarlet* portrays sin (Isa. 1:18).[11] It also signifies pomp and power, which the soldiers mockingly sought to ascribe to Jesus by dressing him in a soldier's garb as the prince of peace (Matt. 27:28).[12] In Revelation it stands for evil exhibited by demonic power. And last, the beast is pictured as a man covered with blasphemous names directed against the Almighty. The beast in 13:1 had a blasphemous name on each of the seven heads, but here heads and horns are full of names that ridicule God, his Word, people, church, and kingdom. With his mouth the beast utters blasphemous words and slanders God, heaven, and the saints (13:5, 6).

4. And the woman was clothed in purple and scarlet cloth and was gilded with gold and precious stones and pearls. She had a cup of gold in her hand full of abominations and uncleanness of her fornication. see 18:16

The appearance of the woman is a portrait of royalty, for she is dressed in cloth of purple and scarlet dye. Royalty wore garments of those colors, as did members of the Roman senate, dignitaries, and wealthy people. Purple dye was extracted from a shellfish or the root of a Eurasian plant called "madder" and

10. Gregory K. Beale, *The Book of Revelation: A Commentary on the Greek Text,* NIGTC (Grand Rapids: Eerdmans, 1998), p. 850.

11. The dye for coloring wool or thread was made from an insect that attacks a species of an oak. The extracted hue, more crimson than scarlet, was expensive. The first mention of scarlet is in connection with the birth of Zerah (Gen. 38:28, 30). Consult W. E. Shewell-Cooper, "Scarlet," *ZPEB,* 5:292.

12. Consult Otto Michel, *TDNT,* 3:813–14.

was considered a costly product.[13] Likewise the scarlet dye was expensive to produce (see commentary on v. 3).

In addition to her dress, the prostitute adorned herself with gold jewelry to enhance the glittering of her appearance; gold thread was even woven into articles of her clothing. She also wore precious stones, diamonds and other gems, and expensive pearls. Note that the same description is given of the great city (18:16). Her outward show resembles that of a prostitute who bedecks herself with fine clothing and valuable jewelry to lure her lovers (Jer. 4:30; see also 2:20; 3:7, 8; Ezek. 23:2–3). The parody of the wife of the Lamb is clear, for the bride of the Lord is beautifully dressed for her husband (Rev. 21:2).

A parody always reveals its ugly side, for the prostitute holds in her hand a cup of gold which provides the outward aspect of riches, but the inside of the cup exhibits corruption. We would have expected that this expensive cup would contain a delicious beverage, but instead it is filled with the abominations and uncleanness of the prostitute's fornication. The word *abomination* denotes the objects and practices that are acutely offensive to God. Among others, they include the worship of idols (Deut. 27:15); the wages of prostitution (Deut. 23:18); homosexual acts and sexual perversions (Lev. 18:22; 20:13); witchcraft, casting spells, and divination (Deut. 18:10, 11).[14] The golden cup is filled with idolatry to spite and provoke God. But the cup itself is held out to the people at large, who are being seduced to drink its contents. When they do so, they suffer disastrous results, becoming victims of pornography, gambling, extravagance, power, and the craving for celebrity status. The great prostitute occupies a central position in an anti-Christian culture.

The expression *cup of gold* is an allusion to Jeremiah 51:7, "Babylon was a gold cup in the LORD's hand; she made the whole earth drunk." The next verse (51:8) predicts, "Babylon will suddenly fall and be broken." Babylon is another name for the great prostitute, who allures the world to follow her and accordingly deserves the wrath of God.

5. And on her forehead was a name written, a mystery,

BABYLON THE GREAT
THE MOTHER OF PROSTITUTES
AND OF THE ABOMINATIONS OF THE EARTH.

In Revelation, John frequently refers to the forehead on which a name is inscribed: for the unbelievers the mark of the beast; for the saints the seal or name of God and the Lamb.[15] But here the inscription on the forehead of the woman is a blatant description of her activities, shrouded in mystery but nevertheless brazenly displayed.

13. Refer to Dorothy Irvin, "Purple," *ISBE*, 3:1057; Robert North, "Thyatira," *ISBE*, 4:846.

14. Bruce K. Waltke, "Abomination," *ISBE*, 1:13–14; Josef Zmijewski, *EDNT*, 1:209–10; Werner Foerster, *TDNT*, 1:598–600. Abominations are idolatrous practices. See Bauer, pp. 137–38.

15. Rev. 7:3; 9:4; 13:16; 14:1, 9; 20:4; 22:4.

Some translations have the term *mystery* as the first word in the inscription "Mystery, Babylon the Great, Mother of Prostitutes, and of the Abominations of the Earth" (KJV, NIV, God's Word). But other versions take this term as introductory to the appellation. There are at least two reasons for leaving it out of the name and considering it a prefix. First, in verse 7 the angel explains what the mystery signifies, "I will tell you the secret of the woman and of the beast." Next, the word *mystery* refers to the hidden meaning of the prostitute's appearance. But when the inscription of the woman and the beast is disclosed, their power is destroyed and their end has come (Jer. 51:13).[16] Literal Babylon was situated along the Euphrates with many waters (Ps. 137:1), but her name is a symbol of the world's power.

Nebuchadnezzar, boasting about the city he built, used the expression *Babylon the Great* (Dan. 4:30). He exhibited inordinate pride that resulted in his immediate downfall, because not he but God is sovereign over the nations (Dan. 4:32). Similarly, this same expression adopted by the great prostitute seals her own doom. The woman called Babylon, sitting on many waters, which the angel interprets as the peoples, crowds, nations, and languages (v. 15), symbolizes the population of the entire world. The name *Babylon the Great* is a figurative description of all the godless inhabitants in the world. In the second half of the first century, the city of Rome was a cesspool of iniquity and thus became a symbol of worldly pleasure, enticement, and lust. But as I have pointed out above, to focus attention only on Rome of apostolic times is too restrictive. The name *Babylon* applies to the lasting conflict between Satan's henchmen and the people of God.

The woman calls herself "the mother of prostitutes and of the abominations of the earth." She is the mother superior over all those who commit spiritual prostitution by worshiping the beast. Her underlings proclaim the gospel of the Antichrist while she herself receives their adulation and praise. She is the source of all that is evil directed against God: slander, murder, immorality, corruption, vulgarity, profanity, and greed. And she originates these sins by putting her underlings to work. She is also the mother of all abominations in the world, for every sin originates with her. The disparity between this woman who personifies evil and the woman who is the church cannot be greater (12:1). The apostle Paul teaches that the church is the mother of believers (Gal. 4:26).[17] Blessed are those who have her as mother and God as Father. Conversely, God's enemies belong to the mother of abominations and suffer the consequences.

---

16. Günther Bornkamm (*TDNT*, 4:824) observes, "Since the power of the Antichrist possesses a *mystērion*, it enjoys present power. But this *mystērion* also indicates that its doom is sealed."

17. John Calvin judiciously observes, "And certainly he who refuses to be a son of the Church in vain desires to have God as his Father." See his *Commentaries on the Epistles of Paul to the Galatians and Ephesians*, trans. William Pringle (Grand Rapids: Eerdmans, 1948), p. 141.

6. And I saw the woman drunk with the blood of the saints and with the blood of the martyrs of Jesus. And when I saw her, I was greatly astounded.

The woman as the great temptress seeks to control the masses of humanity and persecutes those who have been redeemed by Jesus Christ. In other words, not satisfied with what she already controls and unable to deceive the elect (Matt. 24:24), she relentlessly torments and kills the saints so that their blood is spilled on the face of the earth (18:24). John now has a full view of the woman's devastating work among God's people and he sees the blood of saints and martyrs drenching the earth.

John mentions *the blood of the saints* and *the blood of the martyrs of Jesus.* He is not intimating that saints differ from martyrs. Rather the clause "the blood of martyrs of Jesus" clarifies the preceding clause "the blood of the saints." That is, the saints are the ones who bear testimony to Jesus. Six times in Revelation John writes the words "the testimony of Jesus" (1:2, 9; 12:17; 19:10 [twice]; 20:4). The phrase can refer either to Jesus' message or to the witness the saints bear to Jesus.[18]

What is the meaning of the sentence, "And when I saw her, I was greatly astounded"? John is astounded when he sees the woman's unquenchable thirst for the blood of the saints. And certainly, in the twentieth century more blood of Christians has been shed than in any previous century. John had expected to see the fall of Babylon, in accord with the prophecy, "Babylon must fall because of Israel's slain, just as the slain in all the earth have fallen because of Babylon" (Jer. 51:49). Incidentally, in this chapter and the next John repeatedly alludes to Jeremiah 51. Instead of Babylon's demise he witnesses a gorgeously arrayed woman drunk with the blood of the saints. This vision takes him by complete surprise; instead of victory for the saints he sees their physical death and destruction.[19] Instead of Babylon's demise, he looks at a beautifully adorned woman who is riding high on a beast. He is mystified.

Greek Words, Phrases, and Constructions in 17:3–5

Verse 3

γέμοντα ὀνόματα—the participle is construed as a masculine singular accusative, because the beast is given a masculine personality. The neuter singular accusative γέμον is a correction modifying the neuter noun θηρίον (the TR and the Majority Text). The verb γέμω (I fill) is normally followed by the genitive of material or content, but here ὀνόματα is in the accusative (see also verse 4, in which both the genitive and the accusative appear following the verb *to fill*).

---

18. P. Vassiliadis ("The Translation of *Martyria Iēsou*," *BibTrans* 36 [1985]: 129–34) is of the opinion that the objective genitive holds sway, "witness (unto death) to Jesus."

19. Henry Barclay Swete, *Commentary on Revelation* (1911; reprint, Grand Rapids: Kregel, 1977), p. 218; Martin Kiddle, *The Revelation of St. John* (reprint, London: Hodder and Stoughton, 1943), p. 344.

ἔχων—this masculine nominative participle is grammatically incorrect: it should be neuter and accusative to agree with θηρίον. The TR and the Majority Text solve the problem with ἔχον, but the harder reading is still preferred.

Verse 5

πορνῶν—the circumflex accent mark indicates that the word is in the feminine plural, from ἡ πόρνη. The masculine is πόρνων, from ὁ πόρνος. Ancient manuscripts were written without accent marks, so that the word could be read as either masculine or feminine. A variant reading πορνειῶν (fornications) tries to resolve the ambiguity.

---

b. The Angel's Explanation *17:7–11*

7. And the angel said to me, "Why are you astounded? I will tell you the secret of the woman and of the beast that carries her, which has the seven heads and the ten horns."

As Daniel is perplexed at the implications of Nebuchadnezzar's dream (Dan. 4:19), so John is astounded by the great prostitute called Babylon.[20] He needs someone to explain what he has observed, so that he can grasp the meaning of the woman and the beast.

The angel had invited John to see the woman on the beast and now because of John's bewilderment becomes his interpreter. He asks the rhetorical question of why he is astounded. This question is not so much a word of rebuke as a desire to help clarify the mystery of the spectacle John has observed. Looking momentarily at the bloodshed that the woman caused, John fails to see the total picture. Therefore, angelic aid is called for to clarify the mystery of the woman and the beast, and to interpret the significance of the seven heads and the ten horns (v. 3).

John should not be alarmed by the seductive appearance of the woman but rather he should understand the blasphemous power of the beast that wants to be like God. And he must see the punishment the woman and the beast will receive.[21]

8. "The beast which you saw was and is not and is about to go up from the Abyss and go to his destruction. And the inhabitants of the earth will be astonished, they whose names are not written in the book of life from the foundation of the earth. They see the beast that was and is not and will come."

a. "The beast which you saw was and is not and is about to go up from the Abyss and go to his destruction." We would have expected the angel to say something about the woman first and then discuss the beast. But the beast is more im-

---

20. Beale (*Revelation*, pp. 862–63) calls attention to similar wording in Daniel's prophecy and John's wording in Revelation 17. They are: God of gods and King of kings, mystery, astounded, beast, and Babylon the Great (Dan. 2:47; 4:9, 19, 24, 30, respectively). Similarities are evident, but they are not limited to chapter 4.

21. Beckwith, *Apocalypse*, p. 697; and John P. M. Sweet, *Revelation*, WPC (Philadelphia: Westminster, 1979), p. 255.

portant than the woman, even if she sits on his back. Satan, alias the dragon, gave him his power, throne, and authority (12:9; 13:2). This is the beast that was mortally wounded, but whose wound was healed and he lived (13:3, 12, 14).

The beast strives to be like God, "who is, and who was, and who is to come" (1:4, 8; 4:8; and see 11:17; 16:5). This expression can be applied to both God and Christ. The beast is similarly described as the one that "once was, and is not, and is about to go up from the Abyss and go to his destruction." He is the one who "was and is not and will come" (compare v. 11). Once again we see a satanic parody: the Antichrist trying to take the place of Christ.[22]

The beast controlled the nations and kingdoms of the world. God had chosen Israel as his own people out of all the nations, while Satan ruled all the others. The devil tempted Jesus by offering him all the kingdoms of the world if he would worship him (Luke 4:5–7), but Jesus refused. When the Lord was about to ascend to heaven, he uttered his enthronement speech by saying, "All authority in heaven and earth has been given to me" (Matt. 28:18). With these words he indicated that Satan had lost the battle and that Jesus rules supreme. In this battle, one of the beast's heads was fatally wounded, but it had healed (13:3, 12, 14).[23] After Pentecost, the unstoppable gospel of Christ went forth from Jerusalem to the ends of the earth. This gospel is proclaimed in every nation, and Satan is unable to restrain it. Until Pentecost, the beast as Satan's representative had power over the nations, Israel excepted, but now his authority belongs to the past. This does not mean that Satan is powerless. On the contrary, he is the roaring lion who seeks to devour anyone in his path (1 Pet. 5:8).

The beast today *is not.* What is the meaning of this enigmatic expression? God revealed himself as the "I am" (Exod. 3:14) who is without beginning and without end. But Satan is a creature with a beginning whose end is perdition. He can never be the "I am" (John 8:58), even though his stated goal is to occupy God's place (2 Thess. 2:4).

This beast is about to come up from the Abyss and go to his destruction (compare Rev. 11:7). The home of Satan is the Abyss as the exact opposite of heaven, which is the place where God dwells. The one who comes up out of the Abyss is the Antichrist, who receives authority from Satan and brings his evil acts to a climax just before the consummation. Satan is always in the background, while the beast is working for him. The Antichrist comes up from Satan's residence with the express purpose of destroying everyone and everything that promotes the cause of Christ. Ironically in the process of destroying others he himself walks the path of self-destruction (see commentary on 19:20 and 20:10).[24] While

22. Bauckham, *Climax of Prophecy,* pp. 431–32.

23. A customary interpretation is to refer to the *Nero redivivus* (Nero coming back to life) legend. Among others, see Adela Yarbro Collins, *The Combat Myth in the Book of Revelation,* HDR 9 (Missoula: Scholars Press, 1976), pp. 175–90. See also her *Apocalypse* (Wilmington: Glazier, 1979), p. 121. But if John had a legend in mind that was never fulfilled, the Apocalypse's trustworthiness would be questionable. See also my comments at 13:3a.

24. Robert W. Wall, *Revelation,* NIBCNT (Peabody, Mass.: Hendrickson, 1991), p. 207.

Christ grants his followers life eternal, Satan confers death and destruction on his captives.

b. "And the inhabitants of the earth will be astonished, they whose names are not written in the book of life from the foundation of the earth." First, the phrase *the inhabitants of the earth* points to unbelievers (see v. 2). Next, there is a close correlation with 13:3b, where the world is worshiping the beast. After receiving a fatal blow to one of his heads, the beast recovers and receives the adulation of the entire world. He appears to be the invincible force that exerts an anti-Christian influence in every segment and sector of human life. The invincibility would be terrifying were it not for the words of comfort given to those whose names are written in the book of life before creation.[25]

c. "They see the beast that was and is not and will come." The saints whose names are recorded in God's book are secure. Despite the havoc the beast wreaks, and notwithstanding the adoration the world showers on the beast, God's people are safe and free from fear. Their eternal destiny is established.

9. "Here is the mind that has understanding. The seven heads are seven hills on which the woman sits. 10. And they are seven kings: five have fallen, one is, another has not yet come. And when he comes, it is necessary that he remain for a little while."

a. "Here is the mind that has understanding." This first clause parallels an earlier statement, "Here is wisdom. Let anyone who has a mind calculate the number of the beast" (13:18). Applied wisdom is not a study of history, politics, and geography to clarify which king was in power, under what circumstances, and where he ruled. Instead John's Apocalypse must be understood theologically, for the writer depicts a reality that comprises all rulers and their times.[26] The symbolism that characterizes the entire book is also pertinent here. In this chapter notice where the woman sits: on many waters (vv. 1, 15), the beast (v. 3), and seven hills (v. 9). All three places are to be understood symbolically.

b. "The seven heads are seven hills on which the woman sits." Some commentators see in this clause a reference to Rome, which is situated on seven hills. Marcus Terentius Varro, writing in the second century before Christ, seems to have been the first to use the expression *Septimontium* (the Seven Hills) to refer to Rome; in later years many authors followed him. Aune observes: "The traditional Seven Hills are listed on an inscription from Corinth on the base of a statue erected during the first half of the second century A.D., probably depicting Dea Roma [the goddess personifying Rome] seated or standing on the Seven Hills of Rome."[27] There is no doubt that John could identify the seven hills with Rome,

25. See the commentaries of Lenski, pp. 499–500; and Beale, p. 866.

26. Johnson (*Revelation*, p. 557) observes, "When this is seen to be the case, it is unnecessary to revert to source theories." Consult Gregory K. Beale, "The Danielic Background for Revelation 13:18 and 17:9," *TynB* 31 (1980): 163–70.

27. Aune, *Revelation 17–22*, p. 945; see H. S. Robinson, "A Monument of Roma at Corinth," *Hesperia* 43 (1974): 470–84, plates 101–6; Mounce, *Revelation*, p. 315; Beckwith, *Apocalypse*, p. 698.

but the question should be asked why he would want to switch from a figurative to a literal meaning. All along, the idiom *seven heads* in Revelation has been interpreted symbolically (commentary on v. 3; 12:3; 13:1). In other words there is good reason to believe that the angel is speaking metaphorically and biblically. The parallelism is significant: seven heads are seven hills. If the one is understood symbolically, so is the other. The Old Testament indicates that mountains may symbolize political power, as is evident in these passages:

- "In the last days the mountain of the LORD's temple will be established as chief among the mountains; it will be raised above the hills, and all nations will stream to it" (Isa. 2:2).
- "'I am against you, O destroying mountain, you who destroy the whole earth,' declares the LORD" (Jer. 51:25).
- "But the rock that struck the statue became a huge mountain and filled the whole earth" (Dan. 2:35b).

Therefore, the symbolism of the seven hills points to world powers that have their place in history.[28] The woman sits not on literal hills but positions herself above world empires to direct them against God's kingdom. Throughout the ages, she has been trying to overthrow the city of God but has failed to conquer it.

c. "And they are seven kings: five have fallen, one is, another has not yet come." John is more specific because he counts five kings that belong to the past, one to the present, and the last one to the future. Many interpreters apply this sentence to Roman emperors but have difficulty agreeing on the sequence of rulers. These are the Roman emperors, ranging from Julius Caesar to Domitian:

1. Julius Caesar (49–44 B.C.)
2. Augustus (27 B.C.–A.D. 14)
3. Tiberius (14–37)
4. Gaius Caligula (37–41)
5. Claudius (41–54)
6. Nero (54–68)
7. Galba (June 68–January 69)
8. Otho (January–April 69)
9. Vitellius (April–December 69)
10. Vespasian (69–79)
11. Titus (79–81)
12. Domitian (81–96)

A number of questions arise. Where do we begin counting and where do we end? Do we begin with Julius Caesar, Augustus, Nero, or Galba? Are Galba, Otho, and

28. Consult Colin Brown, *NIDNTT*, 3:1013; Abraham Kuyper, *The Revelation of St. John,* trans. John Hendrik de Vries (Grand Rapids: Eerdmans, 1935), pp. 217–18.

Vitellius excluded because of their brief reigns? Do we omit the name of Julius Caesar since he is not part of New Testament history? If we adopt a late date for Revelation, is Domitian the sixth, the seventh, or the eighth emperor? Should we begin with Domitian and start counting backward? Scholars have tried to answer all these questions, but the numerous calculations they collectively present make it impossible to arrive at even a semblance of unanimity.[29]

John writes "Five have fallen," but apparently he is not thinking of kings who died but rather of empires that came to an end and perished.[30] In the Apocalypse, whenever saints fall, they fall in worship on their faces; but when the verb *to fall* alludes to unbelievers, it means "to perish." For instance, there is the call, "Fallen, fallen is Babylon the Great" (14:8; 18:2).

From Daniel 7:17 and 23 we know that kings represent their kingdoms, and that of the two, kingdoms are greater than kings. The Aramaic text of verse 17 in translation reads, "As for these four great beasts, four kings will arise out of the earth" (NRSV), but it is translated in the Septuagint as "kingdoms" in harmony with verse 23 (NCV, NIV, NLT, REB). While empires that raise their head against God are overthrown, God's kingdom remains forever. The five empires that have perished are, in succession, ancient Babylonia (Gen. 10:8–12), Assyria, Neo-Babylonia, Medo-Persia, Greco-Macedonia; Rome is number six, as the one that *is* during John's lifetime.[31] And then there is another, the seventh one, that has not yet come.

d. "And when he comes, it is necessary that he remain for a little while." How are we to interpret the seventh one? If this kingdom points to the rule of the Antichrist before the end, then we face a void of almost two millennia during which many empires have come and vanished. Even though this is true, the focus is on the apocalyptic expression *a little while*, which in Revelation takes on a meaning of its own. For instance, cast out of heaven, Satan knows that his time is short (12:12). This short time ought not to be taken literally but symbolically, much the same as the references to 1,260 days, forty-two months, and three and half years are understood figuratively (11:2–3; 12:6, 14; 13:5). Hence, the term *a little while* is not a chronological period but functions within a comprehensive span of time. That is, the seventh kingdom may be seen as "the collective title for all antichristian governments between the fall of Rome and the final empire of antichrist that is going to oppress the Church in the days just preceding Christ's second coming."[32]

29. Aune (*Revelation 17–22*, pp. 947–48) lists nine different ways of counting the Roman emperors. Beckwith (*Apocalypse*, pp. 704–8) discusses this subject in detail. Josephine Massyngberde Ford (*Revelation: Introduction, Translation, and Commentary*, AB 38 [Garden City, N.Y.: Doubleday, 1975], p. 289) lists four constructions.

30. Bauer (p. 660) lists the meaning as "the five have perished, disappeared, passed from the scene."

31. Hendriksen, *More Than Conquerors*, p. 171; S. Greijdanus, *De Openbaring des Heeren aan Johannes*, KNT (Amsterdam: Van Bottenburg, 1925), p. 349. Henry Alford (*James–Revelation*, vol. 4, part 2, of *Alford's Greek Testament* [1875; reprint, Grand Rapids: Guardian, 1976], p. 70) has the same sequence of kingdoms but calls ancient Babylonia Egypt and Assyria Nineveh; see William Milligan, *The Book of Revelation* (New York: Armstrong and Son, 1893), p. 285; Thomas, *Revelation 8–22*, p. 297; John F. Walvoord, *The Revelation of Jesus Christ* (Chicago: Moody, 1966), pp. 253–54.

32. Hendriksen, *More Than Conquerors*, p. 171; Beale, *Revelation*, p. 875.

The words *it is necessary* denote that God is fully in control during this little season of the seventh kingdom. God rules supreme so that the Antichrist can only do his work in the time that is allotted to him. Here indeed is comfort for the saints on earth as they go through tribulation and distress.

11. "And the beast that was, and is not, even he is an eighth and is of the seven, and he goes to his destruction."

The text appears to present a cryptic and enigmatic message, but the similarity of wording in the preceding context greatly facilitates the interpretation of this verse. Note the words *beast, is not, of the seven, the eighth,* and *destruction.* John speaks of the beast that "was and is not and is about to go up from the Abyss and go to his destruction" (v. 8; see the commentary). This beast is not one of the seven kings/kingdoms (v. 10) but personifies the totality of evil in them; therefore, he is far greater than any one individual. In short, he is absolutely depraved and works in and through each of the seven empires as an eighth.

The phrase *was, and is not, and goes* with variations occurs three times in this chapter (vv. 8a, 8b, 11) and is a clear imitation of God, "who was, and is, and is to come" (1:4, 8; 4:8). The beast, however, has a beginning and an end; and thus as a creature is limited by time and space. He is the personification of the Antichrist (2 Thess. 2:3–4), who rises from the Abyss and is on his way to destruction. Nevertheless, the beast is described as the one who is not now, so that the two terms *was* and *is not* are identical in meaning. And if he is no longer relevant, why then even mention him as an eighth king? What is the significance of this verse?

Satan, represented by the beast (13:2), lost the battle against Christ at the cross and the empty tomb. When Christ ascended to heaven, he proclaimed victory over the evil angels (1 Pet. 3:19, 22). The wound on one of the beast's heads was fatal (13:3, 12, 14), but this is not to say that his existence has ended. Far from it, for although he has lost the battle against Christ, the war itself is not over yet.

Many scholars interpret the phrase "he is an eighth and is of the seven" to refer to Domitian, who as a second Nero reintroduced persecuting the Christians.[33] Some translations (*Cassirer*, GNB, NASB, NJB, REB) even read, "he is one of the seven" in support of the view that Nero returned as a persecutor of the church. But the Greek text literally says, "and he is of the seven," in the sense of similarity. George E. Ladd offers a unique insight by writing that "the eighth is like the seven in that it succeeds them in world domination; but it stands apart in that it ascends from the abyss as the full satanic embodiment of the beast."[34]

I conclude that this verse must be interpreted in the light of the preceding context where John mentions the beast that "will come up out of the Abyss and go to his destruction" (v. 8). The beast, then, is not one of the seven rulers but is the concentration of all that is evil. And he with the false prophet will be cast

33. Among others are Aune, Beasley-Murray, Düsterdieck, Harrington, van Hartingsveld, Moffatt, Schüssler Fiorenza, Swete.

34. George Eldon Ladd, *Commentary on the Revelation of John* (Grand Rapids: Eerdmans, 1972), p. 231.

into the lake of fire that burns with sulfur, where they meet their own destruction (19:20). He is the Antichrist who is destroyed by the victorious Christ.

Greek Words, Phrases, and Constructions in 17:8–11

Verse 8

βλεπόντων—the genitive plural is explained either as taking its case from the preceding relative pronoun ὧν or as being a genitive absolute with the pronoun αὐτῶν mentally supplied.

Verse 11

αὐτός—a variant reading is οὗτος, but both are grammatically incorrect because as masculine singulars they depend on the neuter singular τὸ θηρίον (the beast).

---

c. The Sovereignty of the Lamb *17:12–14*

12. "And the ten horns which you saw are ten kings, who have not yet received a kingdom. But they will receive authority with the beast as kings for one hour. 13. These have one purpose and they give their power and authority to the beast."

John calls the attention of his readers to the picture of the beast with seven heads and ten horns (vv. 3, 7; see 12:3; 13:1). The number ten is a figurative number that in the Apocalypse always relates to Satan, his servants, and his activities. Thus, the number ten refers to

- ten days of persecution instigated by the devil (2:10);
- the dragon with ten horns (12:3);
- the beast coming out of the sea with ten horns and ten crowns (13:1);
- and the scarlet beast with ten horns (17:3, 7, 12, 16).

These ten horns are ten kings in the service of the evil one; they are united in purpose to do the bidding of the beast, that is, the Antichrist. The text precludes identifying ten kings with subordinate rulers in the Roman empire or with Parthian governors, because these kings had not yet received a kingdom.

The source for the description of the ten horns and the ten kings comes from the visions of Daniel, who depicts a beast with ten horns symbolic of his comprehensive power. Daniel explains that the ten horns are ten kings that will come from the beast's kingdom. The setting of this prophetic passage is one in which the power of an evil beast is directed against God. But God takes away his power and destroys the beast forever (Dan. 7:7, 20, 24, 26).

Therefore, in a similar vein John writes that these ten kings will receive authority with the beast for one hour. They receive their authority not from the beast but from God, even though these kings are allied with the beast, who is the Antichrist. As Paul says, "There is no authority except that which God has established" (Rom.

13:1). All along in Revelation, God gives power to Satan and his assistants and allows them to work out their evil designs within the limits that God has set.

The power these kings use against Christ lasts but for a brief period of time. The expression *one hour* should not be understood literally as sixty minutes, for here as in other places in the Apocalypse chronological time is not the issue. Rather, time is a principle that in this text merely means brevity. We are not told when these kings will receive their power, but the repeated use of the term *one hour* in the next chapter (18:10, 17, 19) suggests that the destructive forces will create havoc in the last days.

We do well not to predict who these kings will be and where they will rule, for the text itself is silent on this point. John presents a picture of the combined anti-Christian forces that in the future will be directed against the Lamb. When and where the battle eventually takes place is of no concern to him. He paints the general picture and omits the details.

John adds that the kings will be of one mind and purpose. They readily make themselves and their influence available to the Antichrist. That is, on their own accord they give their power to the beast to oppose Christ and his kingdom. They exert their opposition in all the segments and sectors of life: government, politics, law enforcement, communication, industry, business, education, legal and medical service, labor, art, sports, and entertainment.

The Antichrist will control all of life through the leaders of the world who willingly and purposefully place themselves and their people at his command. The world itself becomes one global force at the command of the Antichrist. He uses both knowledge and power in his final battle against Christ and his people in his attempt to overthrow them. Incidentally, his effort to make war against the Lord and the saints has been mentioned earlier (11:7; 13:4, 7). But here the reference is to the deciding battle in the last days (see 19:19).

14. "These will make war against the Lamb and the Lamb will overcome them, for he is Lord of lords and King of kings; and they who are with him are the called, and the elect, and the faithful ones."

a. "These will make war against the Lamb and the Lamb will overcome them." First, this sentence is an echo of Daniel 7:21, "This horn was waging war against the saints and defeating them." But there is a difference. The horn in Daniel's prophecy is a symbol of the kings who combat the Lord to defeat the saints, while in Revelation the Lord defeats the kings. Next, the sentence consists of two clauses placed in a chiastic configuration for emphasis:

these will make war against *the Lamb*
the Lamb will overcome *them*

This is the language of assurance, for Christ having triumphed over Satan by his death and resurrection is the victor. When the forces led by the Antichrist go to war against the Lamb, they are doomed to a crushing defeat. The future tense of this verse is not merely a prophecy but also a guarantee of what is going to happen.

Some commentators are of the opinion that verse 14 is out of place because it has been taken from the battle scene recorded in 19:11–21.[35] But the structure of chapter 17 with its description of the spiritual war in which the kings of the earth war against the Lamb allows for this verse. It serves as a preliminary remark to the detailed account of the rider on the white horse going to battle against his enemies. If such a preliminary remark is out of place, then not only this chapter of the Apocalypse but the entire New Testament must be rewritten.[36]

b. "For he is Lord of lords and King of kings." John uses Old Testament language that exalts the Lord God Almighty as the one and only God and King (Deut. 10:17; Ps. 136:3; Dan. 2:47).[37] The qualifiers *of lords* and *of kings* serve to express the superlative idea. Paul describes God in similar language: "God, the blessed and only Ruler, the King of kings and Lord or lords" (1 Tim. 6:15). But here the title is applied to the Lamb. The name *King of kings* denotes sovereignty and authority; the name *Lord of lords* signifies majesty and power. Every ruler, all nations, and all people are subject to him; and anyone belonging to either the angelic world or humanity who determines to fight him faces a losing battle and utter ruin.

c. "And they who are with him are the called, and the elect, and the faithful ones." Now John mentions the saints who are the Lord's followers. They have been called with an effective internal call that resulted in their salvation (Rom. 8:30). God has chosen them from before the creation of the world (Eph. 1:4), and thus as the elect they belong to him. The act of choosing his people precedes that of calling them, but here the point is that God bases calling on election. God also expects that they show him gratitude for his electing grace. Thus, they trust him by accepting his Word in faith, and they show they love him by faithfully obeying his precepts.

One last remark on this verse. The phrase *they who are with him* indicates that the saints are in the presence of the Lord. We know that because the Lord is victorious, they share in his victory. They are the overcomers who receive his blessings and will inherit all things (see, e.g., 15:2; 21:7).

d. God's Purpose *17:15–18*

15. And the angel said to me, "The waters that you saw on which the prostitute sat, they are the peoples, crowds, nations, and languages."

After instructing John for many verses (vv. 1, 7–14), the angel now addresses him with additional clarification. Note that John is not asking the angel to clarify the vision of the prostitute sitting on many waters (v. 1). On his own accord the angel interprets the vision and its meaning for John. He is not explaining the

35. Charles (*Revelation,* 2:74, 429–30) has rearranged the verses of this chapter in the following sequence: vv. 12, 13, 17, 16, 14, 18. Aune (*Revelation 17–22,* p. 953) calls verse 14 an interpolation.

36. Refer to Beckwith, *Apocalypse,* p. 701.

37. See also 2 Macc. 13:4; 3 Macc. 5:35; *1 Enoch* 9.4.

woman seated on the scarlet beast or on the seven hills, for there are additional pictures of the same prostitute.

The *waters* are representative of the human race that is under her sway. Some scholars define the multitudes to be those subjugated by Rome, but this view is too narrow. We do well to explain the waters as those masses of the world that are swayed by anti-Christian forces.

This picture of the waters presented and interpreted by the angel can only be understood as a symbol. Similarly, the number four in the four categories of peoples, crowds, nations, and languages points to the world. Throughout the Apocalypse, categories of four referring to God's creation are numerous (e.g., "peals of thunder and rumblings and flashes of lightning and an earthquake" [8:5; see also 16:18]). Thus, the use of the fourfold phrase *peoples, crowds, nations, and languages* is not restricted to one particular era but refers to all the nations of the world. "In the symbolic world of Revelation, there could hardly be a more emphatic indication of universalism."[38]

Last, the Old Testament provides numerous places where the waters symbolize the peoples of this world. The prophets use this metaphor repeatedly (see Isa. 8:7; 23:11; Jer. 47:2; 51:13).

16. "And the ten horns that you saw and the beast, these will hate the prostitute; and they will make her desolate and naked; and they will eat her flesh and will burn her with fire."

What a contrast between the woman resplendent in glory who is the bride of the Lamb (19:7–8) and the woman who is the prostitute, unmarried, vile, destitute, attacked, and forsaken.

When we read this verse, the words of Jesus immediately come to mind. "How can Satan drive out Satan? If a kingdom is divided against itself, that kingdom cannot stand" (Mark 3:23–24). The ten kings, that is, the rulers of this world, and the beast oppose God's kingdom but turn on themselves to hasten their own destruction. These kings and the beast are governed by the evil one and lack the virtues of love and respect. They are filled with hatred, and instead of being subject to the woman, they flout her authority and turn against her.

John echoes phrases and words from the prophets of the Old Testament who prophesy about Samaria and Jerusalem, that is, Israel and Judah. The Assyrians came and expressed their hatred, stripped them naked, brought them to shame, and left them desolate (Ezek. 16:39; 23:29; 26:19; Hos. 2:5–7). God took everything away from the people of Israel and Judah by sending them into exile. In fact, Ezekiel prophesied that the Assyrians and Babylonians would cut off the noses and ears of their captives and would consume by fire those who were left (23:25; 28:18). Even though God used foreign forces to accomplish the exile, the evil within Israel and Judah was the ultimate cause of their destruction.

Does John have in mind the destruction of Rome whereby subordinate vassals rise up against her? Hardly, for the imperial city never entirely fulfilled the words

38. Bauckham, *Climax of Prophecy*, p. 326.

in this verse. The splendor of Rome diminished in the course of time, and the empire came to an end in 476, but the city itself remained intact. On a broader scale, the text applies to nations pursuing economic and political goals to the detriment of others. When wealth and riches accumulate, a sudden downturn causes these nations to collapse. Likewise individuals who are enamored by fortune follow the ways of the world. When they realize that earthly possessions lose their glamour, they are unable to extricate themselves and inevitably face ultimate destruction (1 Tim. 6:9).

17. "For God has placed in their hearts to do his purpose, to be of one accord, and to give their kingdom to the beast until the words of God will be fulfilled."

All the evil and deceit we observe around us should not dissuade us from the premise that God is in full control of everything. God is sovereign and nothing happens without his will. Indeed, without their knowledge he works in the hearts and minds of earthly rulers and makes them do his bidding. He uses them as instruments in his hands, so that their hatred toward the prostitute is his design (compare Isa. 10:5–11; Jer. 34:22). The expression *placed in their hearts* is a Semitic idiom found in the Old Testament and signifies divine guidance.[39]

God has three intentions, which are that the ten horns should

- do his purpose
- be of one accord
- give their kingdom to the beast

Some commentators place the second one in brackets to indicate redundancy. But this is not necessary; there is a distinction between the first and the second objective. The first one is an objective assignment to perform God's will, while the second is a subjective intention to do his will in unity and harmony. These kings together with the beast are determined to destroy the woman who has dominated them. So all along God's purposes are fulfilled. To underscore the combined intent of the kings to be of one accord, they hand over their kingdom to the beast. The reason for this united front is to accomplish God's purpose according to his words. The words of God are his revealed will that must be done at his command.

How can a sovereign God work out his plan through the evil designs of worldly powers? This is no conflict of interest, so to speak. Rather we acknowledge that God allows evil to happen, but he uses it to further his own kingdom and to demonstrate his glory. "Does disaster befall a city, unless the LORD has done it?" (Amos 3:6 NRSV; see Isa. 14:24–27; Ezek. 24:7–8). Everything is in God's hand and he accomplishes his plan and purpose.

39. Ezra 7:27; Neh. 2:12; 7:5; 1 Esdras 8:25. See Aune, *Revelation 17–22*, p. 959.

18. "And the woman whom you saw is the great city which has a kingdom over the kings of the earth."

Here is the last explanation of symbols in this chapter. The woman, who all along has occupied a central position by sitting on many waters, a scarlet beast, and seven hills, is now the same as "the great city." There are two cities in the Apocalypse. One is the new Jerusalem that comes down out of heaven from God (3:12; 21:2, 10; 22:2–3) and the other is the city of the world controlled by Satan and known as Babylon the Great (11:8; 14:8; 16:19; 17:5; 18:2, 10). These two cities have their own citizens, their own rules and laws, and their own destinies. The one is a city of light, the other a city of darkness; the one is known because of its purity, the other because of its deceit. In the one, God and the Lamb dwell with their people; and in the other, Satan, the fallen angels, and their followers reside.[40]

The kingdom of Satan extends to the far reaches of the globe, and the rulers on earth pay him homage and submit to him. But those people with the name of the Father and of the Lamb written on their foreheads (14:1) are citizens of the kingdom of heaven. They will forever live with Christ in the new Jerusalem.

Greek Words, Phrases, and Constructions in 17:17

καὶ ποιῆσαι μίαν γνώμην—a number of manuscripts omit this phrase because of its similarity to the preceding phrase. But the inclusion of μίαν for emphasis suggests that the phrase is an idiom ("and to be of one accord") and has a legitimate place in the sentence.

---

40. Commentators present a diversity of opinions as to the identification of the great city. On the basis of 11:8 and 16:19, Ford understands it to be Jerusalem (*Revelation*, p. 292); Aune notes that it "refers clearly to Rome" (*Revelation 17–22*, p. 959); and Thomas writes that "the only viable identification . . . is Babylon on the Euphrates" (*Revelation 8–22*, p. 307). Yet the great city transcends geographic and historical boundaries. "The meaning cannot be confined to Sodom or Egypt or Jerusalem or Rome or any future city. Instead, John describes the real trans-historical system of satanic evil that infuses them all" (Johnson, *Revelation*, p. 563).

18

Songs of Doom and Destruction

(18:1–24)

Outline (continued)

2. Songs of Doom and Destruction (18:1–24)
   a. The First Lament (18:1–3)
   b. The Command to Flee (18:4–8)
   c. The Fall of Babylon (18:9–20)
      (1) The Dirge of Royalty (18:9–10)
      (2) The Lament of Merchants (18:11–17a)
      (3) The Lament of Sea Captains (18:17b–19)
      (4) Contrast (18:20)
   d. A Symbol and a Song of Doom (18:21–24)

18

1 After these things I saw another angel coming down out of heaven having great authority.
And the earth was illuminated with his glory. 2 And he cried with a mighty voice, saying,

> "Fallen, fallen, is Babylon the Great,
> And she has become the dwelling place of demons,
> and the prison of every unclean spirit,
> and the prison of every unclean bird,
> and the prison of every unclean and hated beast,
> 3 because all the nations have drunk of the wrathful
> wine of her fornication,
> and the kings of the earth have committed adultery
> with her,
> and the merchants of the earth have become rich from
> the power of her sensuality."

4 And I heard another voice from heaven saying,

> "My people, come out of her,
> so that you may not participate in her sins,
> and that you may not receive her plagues,
> 5 because her sins have piled up to heaven
> and God has remembered her crimes.
> 6 Repay her as she has repaid
> and give her back double according to her works,
> mix for her double in the cup in which she has mixed.
> 7 As much as she glorified and luxuriated herself,
> so give her torment and grief.
> For in her heart she says,
> 'I sit as a queen, and I am not a widow,
> and I will never see grief.'
> 8 Therefore, in one day her plagues will come,
> death and grief and famine,
> and she will be burned with fire,
> because the mighty Lord God is judging her.

9 "And the kings of the earth who committed adultery with her and lived in luxury will weep and
lament over her, when they see the smoke of her fiery ordeal. 10 Because of fear of her torment they
stand far off and say,

> 'Woe, woe, the great city,
> Babylon the mighty city,
> because in one hour your judgment has come!'

11 "And the merchants of the earth weep and lament over her, because no one buys their cargo
anymore. 12 They are cargoes of gold, silver, precious stones and pearls, and fine linen and purple

and silk and scarlet cloth, and all citrus-scented wood and every vessel made of ivory and every vessel
of very precious wood and bronze and iron and marble, 13 and cinnamon and spice and incense and
myrrh and frankincense, and wine and olive oil and fine wheat flour and wheat, cattle and sheep,
and horses and carriages, and bodies and souls of people.
14 "And the ripe fruit that you longed for has gone from you, and all the exquisite and elegant
things have passed away from you, never to be found again.
15 "These merchants who had become rich from her will stand far off because of the fear of her
torment, weeping and lamenting, 16 saying,

> 'Woe, woe, the great city,
> she that is clothed in fine linen and purple and scarlet,
> and gilded with gold, precious stones and pearls,
> 17 for in one hour such riches have been laid waste.'

"And every sea captain and every voyager, and sailors and as many as acquire their living from the
seas will stand far off, 18 and they cried out as they looked at the smoke of her burning, and said,
'Who is like this great city?' 19 And they cast dust on their heads and cried out and wailed, saying,

> 'Woe, woe, the great city.
> In it all those who have ships on the sea
> have become rich because of her wealth.
> In one hour she has been laid waste.
> 20 Rejoice over her, O heaven,
> and the saints and the apostles and the prophets,
> because God has given judgment for you against her.'"

21 And a mighty angel picked up a stone like a large millstone and cast it into the sea, saying,

> "Likewise Babylon the great city
> will be violently cast down
> and never be found again.
> 22 And the sound of the harps and musicians
> and flutists and trumpeters
> will never be heard in you again.
> And every craftsman of every trade
> will never be found in you again,
> and the sound of the mill
> will never be heard in you again.
> 23 And the light of the lamp
> will never shine on you again,
> and the sound of the bridegroom and the bride
> will never be heard in you again,
> because your merchants were the great ones of the earth,
> because with your sorcery you deceived all the nations.
> 24 And in her the blood of the prophets and the saints is found
> and of all who were slain on the earth."

---

2. Songs of Doom and Destruction
18:1–24

While the preceding chapter (chap. 17) described Babylon as the great prostitute, this chapter depicts her in terms of her economic downfall. Babylon is not confined to the city on the banks of the Euphrates or to Rome as the capital of the Roman empire. Babylon is the capital of the entire world, the center of the universal kingdom of darkness. It is a symbol of the whole world hostile toward God and his Christ. And this world which has taken on God as its enemy now faces the penalty of total economic collapse.

This chapter laments the fall of Babylon and is a continuation of 14:8, "Fallen, fallen is Babylon the Great." First, we notice the many hymns of judgments and lamentations over Babylon. By one count there are eight hymns (vv. 2b–3, 4b–8, 10b, 14, 16–17a, 19b, 20, 21b–24), all with appropriate introductions.[1] Next, we detect three angels who speak successively: the first one, having great authority, spoke in a loud voice (vv. 1–3); the second is introduced as "another voice from heaven" (vv. 4–20); and the third is a mighty angel who casts a millstone into the sea (vv. 21–24). Last, note the contrast of condemnation and approbation. After hymns of judgment and lament are sung in chapter 18, songs of praise are raised by a heavenly multitude (19:1–3), the twenty-four elders (19:4), a voice from the throne (19:5), and a great multitude (19:6–8).

The center section of chapter 18 is the longest and can be divided into two segments: Babylon before her fall (vv. 4–8) and after her fall (vv. 9–20). The chapter itself has four parts: the first lament (vv. 1–3), the command to flee (vv. 4–8), the second lament (vv. 9–20), and a symbol with interpretation (vv. 21–24).[2]

a. The First Lament
18:1–3

1. After these things I saw another angel coming down out of heaven having great authority. And the earth was illuminated with his glory.

The phrase *after these things* occurs at least nine times in Revelation.[3] These occurrences point not to chronological time but rather to a change from one vision to another. Here John looks first at Babylon as the great prostitute in chapter 17 and then in this chapter at the fall of Babylon.

Some interpreters identify the angel who comes down out of heaven as Jesus.[4] But this is hardly possible because of the preceding adjective *another* that points to a succession of previous angels (17:1, 3, 7, 15). It is more likely, therefore, that this angel is one of the seven mentioned earlier in 17:1, although he differs from the first angel mentioned there. Perhaps he may be identified with the mighty

---

1. Consult W. H. Shea, "Chiasm in Theme and by Form in Revelation 18," *AUSS* 20 (1982): 249–56; see also the outline of Kenneth A. Strand, "Two Aspects of Babylon's Judgment Portrayed in Revelation 18," *AUSS* 20 (1982): 53–60.

2. David E. Aune, *Revelation 17–22,* WBC 52C (Nashville: Nelson, 1998), p. 976. Aune combines the two hymns of lament and thus has three parts.

3. Rev. 1:19; 4:1 (twice); 7:9; 9:12; 15:5; 18:1; 19:1; 20:3.

4. For example, M. Robert Mulholland Jr., *Revelation: Holy Living in an Unholy World* (Grand Rapids: Zondervan, Frances Asbury Press, 1990), p. 284; Gregory K. Beale, *The Book of Revelation: A Commentary on the Greek Text,* NIGTC (Grand Rapids: Eerdmans, 1998), p. 892.

angel coming down out of heaven in 10:1. This angel has been endowed with great authority, which signifies that God has given him the task of announcing the verdict of Babylon's demise.

"And the earth was illuminated with his glory." John alludes to similar wording taken from Ezekiel, "and the earth shone with his glory" (43:2, NRSV), with the distinction that there it is the glory of Israel's God. But here the angel comes from the presence of God to brighten the earth so that everyone is able to see the extraordinary appearance.

2. And he cried with a mighty voice, saying, "Fallen, fallen, is Babylon the Great. And she has become the dwelling place of demons, and the prison of every unclean spirit, and the prison of every unclean bird, and the prison of every unclean and hated beast."

a. "And he cried with a mighty voice, saying, 'Fallen, fallen, is Babylon the Great.'" The Apocalypse is replete with angels who cry out in a loud voice so that everyone on earth is able to hear (7:2; 10:3; 14:7, 9, 15; 19:17). The word *mighty* reflects the great authority that has been given to this angel. No one can ignore the voice of an angel who announces "an event which is stupefying in its magnitude."[5] Although his announcement is similar to that of the angel who cried "Fallen, fallen is Babylon the Great, which made all the nations drink the wrathful wine of her fornication" (14:8), there are differences. In this verse he first describes the dwelling place of Babylon by referring to it three times as a prison, and then he elaborates in successive verses.

John has taken the reference to Babylon from Isaiah 21:9, "Babylon has fallen, has fallen!" (see also Jer. 50:2; 51:8).[6] The duplication of the verb *to fall* for emphasis is a typical feature in Semitic writing. Note that the past tense of the verb is given as if the actual destruction of Babylon had already taken place. The past tense states not merely the expectation but the certainty of this event.

b. "And she has become the dwelling place of demons." In desert places the goat demons dance and call to each other (Isa. 13:21; 34:14 NRSV). Evil spirits live in deserted places (Luke 8:29) and in a ruined city like Babylon.[7] This ruined place is the home of demons, whose ruler is Satan. It will become a place void of any inhabitant (Jer. 50:39; 51:37). This is a picture of a world without God that is now in the power of evil spirits who can freely vex its people.[8]

Babylon is the prison of every unclean spirit, every unclean bird, and every unclean and hated beast. In this context, the term *prison* suggests a dwelling place to which these creatures are consigned—not so much a prison, for that is the

5. Martin Kiddle, *The Revelation of St. John* (reprint, London: Hodder and Stoughton, 1943), p. 361.

6. The meaning of the word *Babylon* in chapter 17 should not be differentiated from that in chapter 18. See C. H. Dyer, "The Identity of Babylon in Revelation 17–18," *BibSac* 144 (1987): 305–16, 433–49.

7. Bauer, p. 169; Otto Böcher, *EDNT*, 1:274.

8. See S. Greijdanus, *De Openbaring des Heeren aan Johannes*, KNT (Amsterdam: Van Bottenburg, 1925), p. 359.

Abyss, but a place where they dwell. This desolate place is the home of unclean spirits and animals—a picture of a world completely devoid of God and his Word. How different is the city of God, where the Holy Spirit dwells in the hearts and lives of the saints! There the light of the gospel shines brightly and the people live in joy and happiness.

3. "Because all the nations have drunk of the wrathful wine of her fornication, and the kings of the earth have committed adultery with her, and the merchants of the earth have become rich from the power of her sensuality."

This verse is a further explanation of Babylon's ruin by mentioning three classes of people. John mentions first the broad category of nations. He repeats almost verbatim part of 14:8, "which made all the nations drink the wrathful wine of her fornication." He moves from the causative "made all the nations drink" to the perfect active, "all the nations have drunk."[9] Babylon has been successful in leading astray the masses of people (compare Jer. 25:15; 51:7). These masses followed her in symbolically drinking the wine of her fornication that has provoked God to implacable wrath (14:10; 16:19). The wine they drink, spiritually speaking, is deliberately sinning against God and acting as if he did not exist. This sin can never be forgiven, meets divine wrath, and leads to spiritual death.

The second category of people John mentions is the kings of the earth. They commit spiritual adultery with Babylon (17:2), that is, they give leadership by pursuing religious, political, and economic goals. They worship idols, rule harshly, and enrich themselves at the expense of others who are less fortunate than they. Since money is their idol, they force all their subordinates to pay homage to this god. It is no wonder that the Christians in the province of Asia lived in abject poverty: they refused to submit to the dictates of local gods and guilds (see chapters 2 and 3).

The third group are the merchants of the world. In ancient times, the merchants of Tyre were renowned throughout the world (Isa. 23:8). Similarly, traders from numerous places sailed along the shores of the Mediterranean Sea to do business in the ports of Spain, Greece, Asia Minor, Syria, Israel, and in places of Arabia (Ezek. 27:12–23). In its heyday, Rome was the storehouse of all the products and produce in the ancient world. Today multinational corporations dominate world trade and often fail to protect the environment or their own workers. As a consequence, the rich increase their assets and display their opulence while the indigent cope with poverty.

Trading goods and wares is desirable, for it meets human needs and with diligence improves the quality of life. But when greed, which Paul calls idolatry, raises its ugly head, the wrath of God comes down on those who serve this idol (Col. 3:5–6). When the rich oppress the poor, they are the violators of the downtrodden and so have become the violent (Isa. 3:14–15; Amos 2:7). But God is a

9. Aune (*Revelation 17–22*, pp. 963, 987) translates the text as "have collapsed" instead of "have drunk." For a discussion of the Greek text, see the section titled "Greek Words, Phrases, and Constructions in 18:3."

jealous God who unalterably opposes such sin and inevitably reproves the unrepentant sinner.

Greek Words, Phrases, and Constructions in 18:3

πέπωκαν—the perfect active indicative is from the verb πίνειν (to drink). One variant reading is πέπτωκαν from the verb πίπτειν (to fall). The two verbs in the perfect differ in only one letter. The variant is rejected in recent editions of the Greek New Testament and by nearly all commentators. On the basis of the Old Testament source (Jer. 25:15–17 [32:15–17 LXX]; 51:7, 39 [28:7, 39 LXX]) and the context, the verb *to drink* is demanded.[10]

---

b. The Command to Flee
18:4–8

4. And I heard another voice from heaven saying, "My people, come out of her, so that you may not participate in her sins, and that you may not receive her plagues."

John does not specifically write that the speaker is another angel. Although a case can be made that God or Christ is the speaker because of the address "My people,"[11] the context of the announcement suggests that an angel spoke these words. The next verse, "God has remembered her crimes," seems to indicate that an angel is God's messenger (v. 5).

The divine message addressed to God's people is clear and to the point: "Come out of her, so that you may not participate in her sins." This is familiar language that echoes the warnings uttered by both Isaiah and Jeremiah:

- "Leave Babylon, flee from the Babylonians!" (Isa. 48:20)
- "Depart, depart, go out from there! Touch no unclean thing!" (Isa. 52:11)
- "Come out of her, my people! Run for your lives!" (Jer. 51:45; see 2 Cor. 6:17)

The voice is not saying that God's people must live in isolation from the rest of mankind. If this were the case, they would not be able to influence the world with the gospel of salvation. Jesus prayed that his people be in the world but not of the world (John 17:14–18).

At the time of the exile when Cyrus permitted the Jews to leave Babylon, God told his people not to take along anything that was unclean or that was pertinent to idol worship. He wanted the Jews leaving Babylon to be pure and holy. Similarly, Paul exhorted the Corinthian Christians who had come out of paganism to separate themselves from idol worship and dedicate their lives to Jesus Christ (2 Cor. 6:17). For the recipients of the Apocalypse, the exhortation meant not

---

10. Bruce M. Metzger, *A Textual Commentary on the Greek New Testament*, 2d ed. (Stuttgart: Deutsche Bibelgesellschaft, 1994), p. 683. See the argument of Aune (*Revelation 17–22*, pp. 965–66).

11. Isbon T. Beckwith, *The Apocalypse of John* (1919; reprint, Grand Rapids: Baker, 1979), p. 714.

to leave the Roman world or Rome itself. Instead they were "to break with the empire's idolatrous culture and life-style and to avoid compromise," as is evident from the seven letters John addressed to the churches in the province of Asia (chaps. 2 and 3).[12] For Christians today the message is to separate themselves spiritually and morally from the secular world and not participate in its sins. While in this world, they must live in complete harmony with God's Word and the testimony of Christ as citizens of the kingdom of heaven. But if they fail to do so and adopt the ways of the world, they will also receive its plagues. These plagues are those in which God manifests his anger in the day of his wrath (16:19).[13]

5. "Because her sins have piled up to heaven and God has remembered her crimes."

The ungodly keep on sinning defiantly against God. They are like the people who built the tower of Babel to reach heaven and challenge God (Gen. 11:3–4). Now their sins have been piled up one by one until they reach heaven. John writes that their sins press against heaven, that is, there is no room left for additional sins between heaven and earth. Sinners are challenging God to do something about these sins that have come in close contact with heaven (Jer. 51:9). These sins are in the face of God, so to speak, and they have become a stench in his nostrils.[14]

God is a gracious God, and because of the sacrificial death of his Son he not only forgives the repentant sinner but also remembers his or her sins no more (Heb. 8:12; 10:17). But sins committed by unrepentant sinners he recalls one by one. They have brought him to the end of his patience and compel him to act (see Gen. 18:20).

6. "Repay her as she has repaid and give her back double according to her works, mix for her double in the cup in which she has mixed."

a. "Repay her as she has repaid and give her back double according to her works." We ask a twofold question: who is speaking and who is addressed? The first part of the question is easy, for the angel has been the speaker thus far. To answer the second part, it appears that God is the addressee, because he alone is able to dispense justice and punish evildoers. This response fits the wording of the Old Testament context on which John relies. Announcing the day of disaster that comes upon the people of Judah, God says, "I will repay them double for their wickedness and their sin" (Jer. 16:18; see Isa. 40:2). Hence, the words seem to be addressed to God in the form of an entreaty, much the same as the souls under the altar ask God to judge the inhabitants of the earth and to avenge their blood (Rev. 6:10).

12. Gerhard A. Krodel, *Revelation*, ACNT (Minneapolis: Augsburg, 1989), pp. 302–3.

13. Compare Adela Yarbro Collins, "Revelation 18," in *L'Apocalypse johannique et l'Apocalyptique dans le Nouveau Testament*, ed. Jan Lambrecht, BETL 53 (Leuven: Leuven University Press, 1980), pp. 189–92.

14. Homer Hailey, *Revelation: An Introduction and Commentary* (Grand Rapids: Baker, 1979), p. 361.

But we still have to ask why in Greek the verbs *repay* and *give back* are written as *plural* imperatives. The broader context reveals that the plural is also used in verse 4, "Come out of her!" and in verse 7, "Give such torment and grief to her!" The plural in verse 4 is addressed to God's people, but interpreting the entreaty of verses 6 and 7 as addressed to God's people flies in the face of the divine admonition not to seek revenge: "It is mine to avenge; I will repay" (Deut. 32:35; see also Rom. 12:19; Heb. 10:30). Additional suggestions are that the plural imperatives address the angels who are sent out by God to execute his judgments or that they urge the people to turn against the prostitute Babylon and ruin her (17:16–17). Both of these suggestions, however, have to account for the sudden shift from one group of addressees to another without any indication of the change.

Whatever solution is adopted, weaknesses remain. Yet consistency compels us to say that God instructs his people. At times God uses his people to execute punishment on evildoers. There are examples from both the Old and New Testaments. God revealed to Abraham that his descendants would in due time come back to the Promised Land, "for the sin of the Amorites has not yet reached its full measure" (Gen. 15:16). This sin reached its climax when the Israelites conquered the land of Canaan and then with God's help annihilated its inhabitants. Peter rebuked both Ananias and Sapphira, whereupon they collapsed and died (Acts 5:1–11). Paul reprimanded the Jewish sorcerer Bar-Jesus, alias Elymas, and struck him with blindness (Acts 13:6–12). And in Revelation the two witnesses strike their enemies with fire (11:3–6).[15]

John writes that Babylon will receive double according to her works, but the words *give her back double* go back to a Hebrew idiom that signifies "to produce a duplicate." An idiom ought not to be translated literally; therefore the translation in English should be "Give her the *very equivalent* according to her works,"[16] that is, pay her back in kind.

b. "Mix for her double in the cup in which she has mixed." That is, the exact measure should be given to her as she gave to others. What she dispensed to others will be dispensed to her. The cup is filled with the wine of God's fury, which has been stated already (14:10; 16:19). God will never forget her sins; in his wrath he will apportion to her the punishment she deserves.

---

15. Aune (*Revelation 17–22*, p. 994) writes that the practice of nonretaliation "was in all probability not uniformly espoused in early Christianity." This is questionable, however, for both Old and New Testaments clearly teach it, except where God intervenes and metes out punishment.

16. Beale, *Revelation*, p. 901 (his emphasis). William Hendriksen (*More Than Conquerors: An Interpretation of the Book of Revelation* [reprint, Grand Rapids: Baker, 1982], p. 174) says that Babylon "will receive the exact amount of punishment which she has earned." See Greijdanus, *Openbaring*, p. 363; Philip Edgcumbe Hughes, *The Book of the Revelation: A Commentary* (Leicester: Inter-Varsity; Grand Rapids: Eerdmans, 1990), p. 191.

7. "As much as she glorified and luxuriated herself, so give her torment and grief. For in her heart she says, 'I sit as a queen, and I am not a widow, and I will never see grief.'"

Because of her glory and opulence, Babylon was called "the pride of the whole earth" (Jer. 51:41 NRSV) and "the glory of the Babylonians' pride" (Isa. 13:19). For instance, the famous hanging gardens were known as one of the seven wonders of the ancient world. The city was the apex of luxury. The temple of Bel-Nebo contained a statue of the idol seated on a golden throne next to a golden altar, and on this altar, once a year, a thousand pounds of incense were burned. Yet this city, because it was filled with depravity and debauchery, was eventually brought low and destroyed. It experienced firsthand the torment and grief it had caused the nations, for the law of retribution was applied to it in full measure.

The noun *torment* signifies the agony one senses after being stung by a scorpion (9:5) or being blistered by burning sulfur (14:10). The second experience culminates in eternal punishment that deprives people of rest both day and night (14:11).

John takes his information from prophetic passages in the Old Testament, quoting almost verbatim from a passage on the fall of Babylon, "You said, 'I will continue forever—the eternal queen! . . . I am, and there is none besides me. I will never be a widow or suffer the loss of children'" (Isa. 47:7, 8; compare Ezek. 28:2; Zeph. 2:15). As Babylon speaks these words, the core of her being is filled with pride. Her words are exaggerated boasts in her self-sufficiency. She wants to occupy the throne of God and determine her own course of life. But she can never be like God and rule as queen of heaven, even though she aims to take God's place (see 2 Thess. 2:4).

The soliloquy may intentionally be an allusion "to the theme of the eternal permanence of Rome."[17] However, John resorts to using a picture of a woman who represents not only Babylon or Rome but any world city. This city signifies a world estranged from God and thus includes everyone who is inimical to God, his Word, and his church.

8. "Therefore, in one day her plagues will come, death and grief and famine, and she will be burned with fire, because the mighty Lord God is judging her."

The consequence of Babylon's pride is her downfall, here described in terms of death, grief, and famine for her citizens and burning fires for her buildings and structures. God will send this calamity upon her in one hour, which is not to be measured chronologically but rather interpreted metaphorically. One hour describes brevity, so that the plagues that strike her are devastatingly swift (vv. 10, 17, 19; see 17:12).

---

17. Aune, *Revelation 17–22*, p. 996. See Beckwith, *Apocalypse*, pp. 714–15; Robert H. Mounce, *The Book of Revelation*, rev. ed., NICNT (Grand Rapids: Eerdmans, 1998), p. 329; L. van Hartingsveld, *Revelation* (Grand Rapids: Eerdmans, 1985), p. 75.

John uses the Old Testament as his source. There he reads that God said to Babylon: "Both [the loss of children and widowhood] will overtake you in a moment, on a single day" (Isa. 47:9; see Jer. 50:31). Her buildings and earthly possessions will be burned by fire, and the people will not even "save themselves from the power of the flame" (Isa. 47:14). Suddenly, the depopulated city lies in ruins, and Babylon is left as a lonely, forsaken figure.

All this has taken place because of God's judgment against her. John describes the Lord God as *mighty,* which in this case is unique. A few times in the Apocalypse (5:2; 10:1; 18:21) angels have been called mighty, and so have political and military leaders (6:15; 19:18). John P. M. Sweet notes that this mighty city of Babylon (vv. 10, 18) "is no match for the *might* of God."[18] When the hour of judgment has come, there is no escape from the wrath of God. As the writer of the Epistle to the Hebrews observes, "It is a dreadful thing to fall into the hands of the living God" (Heb. 10:31).

c. The Fall of Babylon
18:9–20

This lengthy section contrasts the wailing of those who are doomed and the rejoicing of those who are redeemed. It can be divided into four parts:

- the kings of the earth lament the doom of Babylon (vv. 9–10);
- the merchants weep and mourn over the loss of sales and wealth (vv. 11–17a);
- the sea captains and sailors bemoan the ruin of the great city (vv. 17b–19);
- the saints and apostles in heaven respond by rejoicing over God's judgment (v. 20).

John displays a cyclical approach in this chapter. In verse 3, he mentioned the kings of the earth who had committed adultery with the great prostitute and the merchants who became rich from her luxuries. And in verses 9 and 11 he mentions these kings and merchants again. Also, the second angel who addressed the saints (vv. 4–8) apparently continues his message in the next section (vv. 9–20).

(1) The Dirge of Royalty
18:9–10

9. "And the kings of the earth who committed adultery with her and lived in luxury will weep and lament over her, when they see the smoke of her fiery ordeal."

The fall of Babylon is inevitable, and John expresses this by writing the verbs *to weep* and *to lament* in the future tense. But describing the actual ruin of the city, John writes the Greek past tense of the verb *to come,* "your judgment has come" (v. 10).

---

18. John P. M. Sweet, *Revelation,* WPC (Philadelphia: Westminster, 1979), p. 269.

The lament of the kings is an echo of the actions and lament the princes of Tyre perform and utter over their coastal city (Ezek. 26:16–17). These princes laid down their robes and ornaments and sat down on the ground trembling with fear at the sight of Tyre. John portrays the kings of the earth he mentioned earlier (v. 3). He is not alluding to the ten kings noted in the preceding chapter (17:16) but to those who, with the Babylon of earlier days and Rome in his time, pursued material riches and lived luxuriously.[19] These kings weep and lament over her because they realize the tremendous financial losses that have occurred. The shedding of tears is accompanied in typical Eastern style by beating one's chest as a sign of mourning and an expression of grief.[20]

The kings observe the smoke as Babylon goes up in flames. The emphasis is not so much on Babylon being consumed by flames but on the fire itself, the suffering, and the painful consequences. In other words, this ordeal is an all-encompassing process in which the sufferer endures pain caused by burning flames. This perverted city, whether Babylon, Rome, Jerusalem, or any place inimical to Christ, suffers immensely when God takes from her everything she idolized. Also, these kings understand that they are directly affected by the suffering of this city.

10. "Because of fear of her torment they stand far off and say, 'Woe, woe, the great city, Babylon the mighty city, because in one hour your judgment has come!'"

The rulers of this world must stand far away from the heat of the burning city for fear that they too will be tormented. But when monetary systems collapse and riches vanish, poverty knocks even at the doors of those who give leadership. This is the picture: world economies in ruins, riots and robberies a plague, disease and death rampant, and leaders filled with fear. The end is at hand. The kings too face an angry God, whose judgment will come swiftly upon them.

A twofold woe is uttered by these kings, and by the merchants and sailors in successive verses (vv. 16, 19; see the triple use in 8:13). The repetition of the word indicates emphasis. The mournful sound of the word *woe* denotes both grief and denunciation. And even though these rulers utter it, they know that the hour of judgment is coming for them, too.

The kings, the merchants, and the seafarers all describe Babylon as "the great city" (vv. 10, 16, 19), but here the text is amplified by "Babylon the mighty city." The two descriptive adjectives *great* and *mighty* pertain to her recent glory that now has faded and disappeared. And this change happened so swiftly, in *one hour*, that the merchants and sailors as well as the kings mention it (vv. 17, 19). Babylon's greatness and might suddenly end (compare v. 8).[21]

---

19. For an overview of the riches and wantonness of Rome during the first century of our era, see William Barclay, *The Revelation of John*, 2d ed. (Philadelphia: Westminster, 1960), 2:200–204.

20. Gustav Stählin, *TDNT*, 3:851 n. 128.

21. For the term *one hour*, Beale refers in his commentary to Dan. 4:19 (Old Greek and Theod.), where this expression occurs in relation to the judgment on Nebuchadnezzar (p. 908).

(2) The Lament of Merchants
18:11–17a

11. "And the merchants of the earth weep and lament over her, because no one buys their cargo anymore."

John has taken the information of merchants and their cargo from Ezekiel's lament over Tyre (Ezek. 27:1–36).[22] The prophet expresses the same grief and lament over Tyre as the kings of the earth do over Babylon. The traders see that business has come to a complete halt. They notice a total disinterest in the merchandise that comes by ship from various places around the globe—from the western shores of the Mediterranean Sea as far as Spain, from the eastern shores of that sea as far as Egypt, and from Asia and Africa. Their economic loss is indescribable, and this is their just reward. All along they have been depriving the followers of the Lamb of the right to buy and sell (Rev. 13:17). Now they themselves are denied that right, and they realize that without buyers their business is doomed. Customers are no longer buying because of the economic collapse that has made buying and selling impossible.

12. "They are cargoes of gold, silver, precious stones and pearls, and fine linen and purple and silk and scarlet cloth, and all citrus-scented wood and every vessel made of ivory and every vessel of very precious wood and bronze and iron and marble, 13. and cinnamon and spice and incense and myrrh and frankincense, and wine and olive oil and fine wheat flour and wheat, cattle and sheep, and horses and carriages, and bodies and souls of people."

Commerce in ancient times was far-flung, international, and varied. To illustrate, ships coming to Italy with cargo to be sold in Rome came from all the ports along the Mediterranean coastline. Although some ships suffered shipwreck (e.g., Acts 27:41), the volume of traffic on the sea was phenomenal. Therefore, owning a fleet of ships proved to be a profitable enterprise as long as the weather remained favorable.

The list of products presented in verses 12 and 13 is considerable: some twenty-eight articles of merchandise are mentioned, ranging from luxury items to household staples, from dry goods to livestock. Even slaves (bodies and souls of human beings) are included. Many of the items listed here also occur in a similar account of some forty different products recorded in Ezekiel 27:12–22. But John differs from the prophet in two respects: he omits the origin of these items and he fails to follow the sequence of his list. Further, the prophet's roster dates from the sixth century B.C., but John would be familiar with commercial lists circulating in his own time and reflecting the riches of Rome and other cities. At the beginning of the register are luxury items characterizing the wealth of nations and individuals. The great prostitute, for example, "was clothed in purple

22. Consult Steve Moyise, *The Old Testament in the Book of Revelation*, JSNTSup 115 (Sheffield: Sheffield Academic Press, 1995), p. 73; Ferrell Jenkins, *The Old Testament in the Book of Revelation* (Grand Rapids: Baker, 1972), pp. 54–60.

and scarlet cloth and was gilded with gold and precious stones and pearls" (17:4).

a. "Gold, silver, precious stones and pearls." Gold was imported from Spain during the first century; when those mines were depleted, it came from western Romania.[23] This metal adorned the homes of wealthy families in Rome and was used to make regal and religious objects.

Silver also originated in Spain and was used to embellish couches, cups, and plates. Precious stones generally came from India and were cut and polished in Alexandria. They were placed in rings and expensive drinking vessels.[24] Pearls were gathered from the bottom of the Red Sea, the Persian Gulf, and the Indian Ocean.

b. "Fine linen and purple and silk and scarlet cloth." This category includes expensive articles of clothing. Instead of clothing made of wool, rich people would wear linen that came from Alexandria, Scythopolis (Beth-Shean), and Laodicea. Purple was produced from a shellfish or from the root of a Eurasian plant called "madder." It was expensive to produce and therefore considered extremely valuable. Lydia was a seller of purple from the city of Thyatira (Acts 16:14). Silk produced in China, although costly, was available in abundance. Josephus remarks that the victorious armed forces parading in front of Vespasian and Titus were dressed in garments made of silk.[25] Scarlet cloth was likewise an expensive item. Scarlet produced from the berry of the kermes oak was used to dye the cloth.

c. "All citrus-scented wood and every vessel made of ivory, every vessel of very precious wood and bronze and iron and marble." Citrus-scented wood was so costly that it was only found in the form of tables in the homes of the most affluent citizens. Cicero bought such a table and reportedly paid 500,000 sesterces, an amount that was sufficient to purchase a large estate. The citron tree grew in North Africa and "was much prized for its veining, which in the best specimens simulated the eyes of a peacock's tail, or the stripes of the tiger and spots of the panther."[26]

Ivory derived from the tusks of elephants was used lavishly on countless articles ranging from household items to furniture. *Precious wood* included ebony, cedar, and cypress, because these varieties resisted decay and repelled insects. The wood was used to make furniture and panels for doors and walls. In ancient times, bronze as an alloy made of copper and tin was produced in many countries. It was highly prized, and according to one ancient writer it was regarded as even more valuable than silver or gold.[27] Iron deposits in Greece, Spain, and

---

23. Strabo 3.2.10; Tacitus *Annals* 3.53; 6.19.

24. Richard Bauckham, *The Climax of Prophecy* (Edinburgh: Clark, 1993), p. 353; Aune, *Revelation 17–22*, p. 998; Reuben G. Bullard, "Precious Stones," *ISBE*, 4:623–30.

25. Josephus *War* 7.5.4 §126.

26. Martial 14.85; Dio Cassius 61.10.3; Pliny *Natural History* 13.96. See Henry Barclay Swete, *Commentary on Revelation* (1911; reprint, Grand Rapids: Kregel, 1977), p. 233; Aune, *Revelation 17–22*, p. 1000.

27. Pliny *Natural History* 34.1.

(modern) Hungary supplied the Roman world with this metal to fashion tools and weapons. Marble came from Phrygia, Greece, and parts of Africa. It decorated the homes of wealthy citizens.

d. "Cinnamon and spice and incense and myrrh and frankincense." Here are four classes of spices that aided the rich in dispelling unpleasant odors. These spices were obtained from many countries; for instance, cinnamon was shipped in from east Africa, Arabia, and as far away as India. It was procured from the inner bark of young cinnamon tree branches. Spice as an aromatic substance also came from India. Incense was an element used for burning in cultic worship. Myrrh and frankincense were acquired from Somalia and south Arabia. All these spices were costly and considered worthy of being presented as gifts to royalty (Matt. 2:11).

e. "Wine and olive oil and fine wheat flour and wheat." These items were daily staples common in most households. Grapes were grown throughout the Middle East from Israel to Spain. In A.D. 92 a surplus of wine caused Emperor Domitian to issue an edict that no new vineyards be planted in Italy and that half of the vineyards in the Roman provinces be destroyed. Because of considerable opposition, this decree never took effect.[28] Similarly, olive trees grew in abundance and supplied the people with oil for cooking and lamps. Fine wheat flour and wheat came from Egypt, which served as the breadbasket for Rome (see Acts 27:6, 38).[29]

f. "Cattle and sheep, and horses and carriages, and bodies and souls of people." This is the last category, made up of livestock, vehicles, and slaves. The word used here for *cattle* is a general word referring to various domesticated animals, especially donkeys used for riding and carrying burdens (Luke 10:34; Acts 23:24). Wealthy Romans possessed four-wheeled carriages.

Last in the list of commodities is the item *bodies and souls of people* (slaves). It follows *carriages* to indicate the low value that was placed on slaves. The reference to humans as *bodies* comes from the Greek language in which slaves were regarded merely as bodies; while the use of *souls* comes from the Hebrew and stands for the "lives [souls] of men" (Ezek. 27:13 NASB; see also the NASB marginal reading of 1 Chron. 5:21). The combination of bodies and souls results in one category, namely, human beings, who in this case are slaves.[30]

Some slaves were people captured in war or kidnapped at sea by pirates; some had sold themselves into slavery for economic reasons; and others were born into slavery or abandoned by their parents. When in A.D. 70 the Jews lost the war against Rome, seventy thousand of them became slaves.[31] Because in the first century sla-

---

28. Suetonius *Domitian* 7.

29. Adela Yarbro Collins (*Crisis and Catharsis: The Power of the Apocalypse* [Philadelphia: Westminster, 1984], pp. 95–97) mentions that in the last years of Vespasian's reign a bread riot broke out in Rome because the price of grain had increased. Consult Bauckham, *Climax of Prophecy*, pp. 362–63.

30. Robert H. Gundry, *Sōma in Biblical Theology*, SNTSMS 29 (Cambridge: Cambridge University Press, 1976), pp. 26–28.

31. Josephus *War* 6.9.3 §420. Bauckham, *Climax of Prophecy*, pp. 365–66. Mounce estimates that there were sixty million slaves in the Roman empire (*Revelation*, p. 334). See also Scott S. Bartchy, "Slavery," *ISBE*, 4:543–46.

very was an established legal institution, the early church could only begin to emancipate slaves within the Christian community itself (see Philem. 15–16).

14. "And the ripe fruit that you longed for has gone from you, and all the exquisite and elegant things have passed away from you, never to be found again."

The speakers are not identified in this verse, but we assume that they are the merchants (vv. 11, 15) who are addressing Babylon the Great. However, there is a change from the third person plural *their* (v. 11) to the second person singular *you* (v. 14), but this abrupt break can be ascribed to John's authorial freedom.[32]

The sentence is descriptive of the harvest in the autumn when tree-ripened fruit is ready to be picked. The Greek literally reads, "the ripe fruit, the desire of your soul." And yet this desired fruit has departed from the one who was ready to harvest it. The second part of the sentence states a parallel:

A ripe fruit
B has gone from you
A′ exquisite and elegant things
B′ have passed away from you

And these riches can never, no never, be found again by anyone who longs for them.

15. "These merchants who had become rich from her will stand far off because of the fear of her torment, weeping and lamenting, 16. saying, 'Woe, woe, the great city, she that is clothed in fine linen and purple and scarlet, and gilded with gold, precious stones and pearls, 17a. for in one hour such riches have been laid waste.'"

The words *stand far off* occur three times in this chapter (vv. 10, 15, 17). These merchants are filled with fear, because they are fully aware that their doom is near and they will suffer the same torment. Presently they weep and lament, but nothing can alter their situation (see vv. 10, 11). They have lost their wealth that was their idol.

Once again the merchants wail their twofold woe over the great city (v. 10) and describe her with the same terms John uses to portray the great prostitute (17:4). Except for the addition "fine linen," the following two sentences are nearly identical:

Revelation 17:4	Revelation 18:16
clothed in purple and scarlet cloth and was gilded with gold and precious stones and pearls	clothed in fine linen and purple and scarlet, and gilded with gold, precious stones and pearls

32. There is no need to place v. 14 after v. 21. Contra R. H. Charles, *A Critical and Exegetical Commentary on the Revelation of St. John*, ICC (Edinburgh: Clark, 1920), 2:105, 351, 433.

This is another indication that the woman and the great city are the same (17:18), which means that the economic riches adorning the great city vanish. By contrast, the glory that adorns the bride of Christ and the city of God abides forever. Worldly riches disappear in *one hour*; that is, the plagues strike the woman and the great city abruptly and with devastating consequence (see vv. 10, 19; see 17:12).

Greek Words, Phrases, and Constructions in 18:12–14

Verse 12

ξύλου τιμιωτάτου—"very precious wood." This superlative adjective signifies "most rare" or "very rare." Some copyists regarded the noun ξύλου to be incongruent in the list of bronze, iron, and marble; therefore, they replaced it with λίθου (stone).[33]

Verse 14

τὰ λιπαρὰ καὶ τὰ λαμπρά— in Greek the alliteration is striking, which in English can be conveyed as "exquisite and elegant" or "glitter and glamour" (REB).

---

(3) The Lament of Sea Captains
18:17b–19

17b. "And every sea captain and every voyager, and sailors and as many as acquire their living from the seas will stand far off, 18. and they cried out as they looked at the smoke of her burning, and said, 'Who is like this great city?'"

John continues to enumerate four classes of people in language that he borrows from Ezekiel 27:27–29. First, a *sea captain* can be the shipowner or the helmsman (compare Acts 27:11). Next, a literal translation of the Greek is "and every one who sails to a place"; it means "every voyager." This phrase itself has given rise to additional translations. But if we take the term *voyager* to relate to a seafaring merchant or passenger, the text is clear. Third, the sailors are those who make up the crew of a ship, and last, there are the people who gain their living from the sea by fishing, diving for pearls, ferrying passengers, or building ships (compare Ps. 107:23).[34]

All these people look aghast at the collapse of Babylon's economic power and physical existence. They stand far off (vv. 10, 15). Notice that the verb *stand* is in the future tense, which is also true for the verbs *to weep* and *to lament* in verse 9. The tense refers to the predictability of what is going to happen: everyone generating trade via the sea or gaining products from it will stand and watch the end of Babylon.

The seafarers continue to cry out as they are looking at the billowing smoke rising from the burning city, "Who is like this great city?" This cry is an echo of

33. Bruce M. Metzger, *A Textual Commentary on the Greek New Testament*, 2d ed. (Stuttgart: Deutsche Bibelgesellschaft, 1994), p. 684.

34. Robert L. Thomas, *Revelation 8–22: An Exegetical Commentary* (Chicago: Moody, 1995), p. 339.

the question asked by travelers who observed the destruction of Jerusalem, "Why has the LORD done such a thing to this great city?" (Jer. 22:8; compare Ezek. 27:32). The question the seafarers pose is, "Who would ever have thought that this could happen to Babylon?"

19. "And they cast dust on their heads and cried out and wailed saying, 'Woe, woe, the great city. In it all those who have ships on the sea have become rich because of her wealth. In one hour she has been laid waste.'"

John has taken the cry uttered by the seafarers from the prophecy of Ezekiel. Here are the words,

> They will raise their voice and cry bitterly over you; they will sprinkle dust on their heads and roll in ashes. . . . As they wail and mourn over you, they will take up a lament concerning you: "Who was ever silenced like Tyre, surrounded by the sea?" . . . With your great wealth and your wares you enriched the kings of the earth. (Ezek. 27:30, 32, 33b)

The Book of Revelation is saturated with allusions to the Old Testament, and those from Ezekiel appear even more frequently than the references from Daniel and Jeremiah.[35] We cannot picture John exiled to the island of Patmos with a complete library of Old Testament scrolls in his possession. But he had a broad and thorough knowledge of the Scriptures, which he could quote from memory and allude to at will.

We read that the merchants whose ships ply the sea have become rich because of Babylon's wealth. They have shared in her wanton luxuries, but now as the city has been laid waste in a moment of time their source of income has vanished. It is little wonder that they are distraught, weep, lament, and cry "woe, woe."

John applies to Babylon what Ezekiel directed against Tyre, but Babylon was not a seaport; neither was Rome, which had to rely on the port of Ostia. Alan F. Johnson aptly remarks, "But in any case, it is not John's intent to describe any one city but the great harlot city, the archetype of the earth's evil cities."[36]

Greek Words, Phrases, and Constructions in 18:17b

ὁ ἐπὶ τόπον πλέων—"every one who sails to a place." The noun *place* can signify "port" and thus refer to any harbor along the Mediterranean coast. The conjecture πόντον for τόπον is unnecessary, because resorting to a conjecture is valid only when the translator faces an impossible task, which is not true in this case.

τὴν θάλασσαν ἐργάζονται—the unusual construction of the passive with a direct object can be translated as "those who work on the sea for their livelihood."[37]

---

35. Moyise, *Old Testament,* p. 16.

36. Alan F. Johnson, *Revelation,* in *The Expositor's Bible Commentary,* ed. Frank E. Gaebelein (Grand Rapids: Zondervan, 1981), 12:568.

37. Robert Hanna, *A Grammatical Aid to the Greek New Testament* (Grand Rapids: Baker, 1983), p. 454.

(4) Contrast
18:20

20. "Rejoice over her, O heaven, and the saints and the apostles and the prophets, because God has given judgment for you against her."

This verse is not part of the seafarers' lament. Looking at the collapse of Babylon and their own lack of income, they certainly would not urge the saints in heaven to rejoice over this calamity.[38] In verse 20 we hear the voice of the second angel, who began speaking to John in verse 4. This angel exhorted the people of God (vv. 4–5); then addressed God and his people (vv. 6–8); afterward he prophesied that kings, merchants, and seafarers would lament the doom of Babylon (vv. 9–19); and last he called on the saints, apostles, and prophets to rejoice.

The call to those dwelling in heaven to rejoice was also issued earlier by a heavenly voice: "Therefore, rejoice, O heavens, and they that dwell in them!" (12:12; see also Jer. 51:48). Once again the redeemed are told to be glad in the victory over God's enemies. But who are these heavenly dwellers? They are the saints, the apostles, and the prophets. The *saints* are the holy ones, whom John mentions thirteen times in the Apocalypse.[39] They are in heaven and now rejoice over God's righteous judgment pronounced on the wicked. The word *apostles* is a technical term that refers to the Twelve (21:14); for the sake of Christ the apostles had suffered persecution. The *prophets* are all those who revealed and proclaimed God's Word (see Eph. 2:20; 3:5; 4:11).

The last clause in this verse literally reads, "because God has judged judgment of you from her." Note these grammatical points: First, we have the literary figure of using a verb and a cognate noun from the root *judge*, a common Hebraism. Next, the pronoun *you* (plural) can be either subjective (belonging to you) or objective (for you). And third, the phrase *from her* can also be translated as "against her." If we incorporate these points and understand the term *judgment* to mean a verdict handed down by a judge (see 17:1), then a smooth reading is as follows: "because God has pronounced on her the judgment she wished to impose on you."[40] In effect, this is the law of retaliation (Exod. 21:24; Lev. 24:20; Matt. 5:38). The wicked passed verdicts of punishment on God's people, but now God has passed the same verdict on them (compare Jer. 51:49).

Verse 20 has been properly placed at the end of the angel's instructions, prophecies, and exhortations. It forms a triumphant conclusion to the dreary scene of Babylon's fall, which could not be concluded without a joyful response

38. Consult Bauckham, *Climax of Prophecy*, p. 341; G. R. Beasley-Murray, *The Book of Revelation*, NCB (London: Oliphants, 1974), p. 268. Some scholars think that John is the speaker, but to have a change in speakers is unnecessary. See Jürgen Roloff, *The Revelation of John*, trans. J. E. Alsup (Minneapolis: Fortress, 1993), p. 207; Charles (*Revelation*, 2:111) restores v. 20 "to its rightful place" near the end of v. 23 and ascribes it to John. And Aune (*Revelation 17–22*, p. 1007) calls this verse, together with v. 24, "a subsequent addition to the text."

39. Rev. 5:8; 8:3, 4; 11:18; 13:7, 10; 14:12; 16:6; 17:6; 18:20, 24; 19:8; 20:9.

40. Bauer, p. 451; REB, NCV, NIV, NJB.

of the martyrs. God heard the plea uttered by the saints under the altar to avenge their blood and now passed judgment on their adversaries (6:9).

Greek Words, Phrases, and Constructions in 18:20

καὶ οἱ ἀπόστολοι—some manuscripts delete the first two words, so that the sentence reads "the holy apostles" (KJV). But because the words καὶ οἱ appear three times in this verse, a scribe may accidentally have omitted them. Deletion is easier to explain than addition.

---

d. A Symbol and a Song of Doom
18:21–24

Once more John portrays the fall of Babylon but now with the aid of a symbol, the large millstone. He concludes the description of her demise in a song that verbalizes her doom. Its doleful refrain occurs six times: "never to be found (to be heard, to shine) again." The physical existence of Babylon will come to a permanent end.

21. And a mighty angel picked up a stone like a large millstone and cast it into the sea, saying, "Likewise Babylon the great city will be violently cast down and never be found again."

Throughout the last part of this chapter, John has relied on the prophecy of Jeremiah. Now once more he takes verses from this prophecy for his imagery of a symbolic stone. God says to the prophet, "When you finish reading this scroll, tie a stone to it and throw it into the Euphrates. Then say, 'So will Babylon sink to rise no more because of the disaster I will bring upon her. And her people will fall'" (Jer. 51:63–64).

The resemblance of the total picture is obvious, except that John embellishes the scene. Instead of a prophet, a mighty angel casts not a stone but a large millstone into the sea, not into a river. John symbolically portrayed the angel as mighty with respect to the tremendous task he received. Incidentally, two other angels are called mighty: the one who with a loud voice called for the opening of the scroll (5:2), and next the one who possessed the enormous power needed to execute God's purposes (10:1). This mighty angel portrays how Babylon is cast away suddenly, violently, and eternally. The large stone was like a millstone that animals pulled for grinding grain; it was extremely heavy (Mark 9:42). Yet the angel instantly lifted it up and violently whirled it through the air to the sea, where it disappeared permanently below the surface (Neh. 9:11).

This is a picture of what happens to Babylon the great city. Suddenly it will experience being picked up and cast into the sea to be seen no more. Its demise is unbelievable because of the rapidity with which it happened. Babylon typifies a world filled with evil set against Christ and all that is holy. It is submerged in the depth of the sea, and no one is ever able to find it again (Ezek. 26:21).

22. "And the sound of the harps and musicians and flutists and trumpeters will never be heard in you again. And every craftsman of every trade will never

be found in you again, and the sound of the mill will never be heard in you again. 23a. And the light of the lamp will never shine on you again, and the sound of the bridegroom and the bride will never be heard in you again."

Here is a picture of everyday life taken from the artistic, economic, and social realms. In Jeremiah 25:10 God says, "I will banish from them the sounds of joy and gladness, the voices of bride and bridegroom, the sound of millstones and the light of lamp." This is similar, except that the angel addresses Babylon with the singular pronoun *you.*

What is life without the gift of music? Day by day we are surrounded by music played by a variety of musicians. John singles out those who play the harp, flute, and trumpet, for these were the players of musical instruments in ancient times. The word *musicians* undoubtedly means lyric-poets, that is, songwriters.[41] In the city of Babylon the sound of music will forever be silenced.

Industry in John's world consisted of people working with wood, leather, metal, bricks, stone, and glass. Others were spinning wool, weaving cloth, dyeing clothes, and sewing garments. Still others were scribes and translators. All these trades and professions will suddenly come to an end. The familiar sound of the millstone grinding grain will cease, which means that the baking of bread will stop and the daily staple of life become unavailable.

The oil supply dries up, lamps no longer burn, and life is cast into darkness. Without the benefit of light, all the riches, all the jewelry, and all the fine garments are useless. The rich live in darkness because the light of a candle or lamp will forever be removed from the citizens of Babylon.

Last, the joyful voices of a bride and bridegroom about to be married will forever be silent. No more weddings, festivities, and family gatherings will take place. The prophet Jeremiah repeatedly speaks of a cessation of weddings in the towns of Judah and the streets of Jerusalem (7:34; 16:9; 25:10). But then in Jeremiah 33:11 he predicts a renewal of the sounds of joy and gladness at the time of weddings. By contrast, Babylon will forever be void of nuptial cheer, delight, and fulfillment.

23b. "Because your merchants were the great ones of the earth, because with your sorcery you deceived all the nations."

Now a twofold reason is given for the utter desolation of Babylon: the first reason is explained by the next. First, the merchants have become the rulers of the earth as the most powerful men (compare 6:15), and in their capacity they no longer needed God. They worshiped money as their idol, purposely ignoring and provocatively rejecting God's laws. John had in mind the prophecies of both Isaiah and Ezekiel, who asked the merchants of Tyre, "Who planned this against Tyre, the bestower of crowns, whose merchants are princes, whose traders are renowned in the earth?" (Isa. 23:8), and, "By your great skill in trading you have increased your wealth. . . . Will you then say, 'I am a god?'" (Ezek. 28:5, 9). These

---

41. Aune (*Revelation 17–22,* p. 1008) translates the word *mousikōn* as "singers." NJB and REB have "minstrels," NLT "songs," and NCV "other instruments."

remarks also fit Babylon, which worshiped wealth instead of the God who gave wealth.

Second, Babylon deceived the nations with sorcery. The expression *sorcery* relates to the practice of magic (9:21). While it allows a person "to control the gods, it is at the same time a gift and revelation of the gods to men."[42] This sin is an utter abomination to God (Deut. 18:10–12). All those Israelites who practiced sorcery or witchcraft were to be put to death, according to the Law of Moses (Exod. 22:18; Lev. 20:6, 27). Paul calls idolatry and witchcraft works of the flesh and not of the Spirit (Gal. 5:20). And John states that those who practice magic arts will be consigned to the lake of fire and burning sulfur (21:8; 22:15).

Sorcery and witchcraft are closely linked to prostitution and fornication (see Nah. 3:4), and the sin of substituting oneself for God is joined to sorcery (Isa. 47:9–10).[43] John paints a picture in which idolatry and immorality go together with violence and vice. With them Babylon fills all the nations of the world.

24. "And in her the blood of the prophets and the saints is found and of all who were slain on the earth."

Babylon, the world city, is no longer addressed with the singular pronoun *you* but is now referred to in the third person singular. Here then is the conclusion of the angel's message of doom with its repetitive note "never to be found again" (vv. 21–22). The verb *to find* in that message is directly related to the same verb in this verse. Because of the violence against God's people, the blood of his prophets was found in her and likewise the blood of all the saints who died for the sake of the Word of God and the testimony of the Lord (6:9–10; 16:6; 17:6; 19:2). At the time of the exile, Babylon killed innumerable Jewish people, whose blood God would avenge on her (Jer. 51:49; Ezek. 24:7). And John knew that when the Romans conquered Jerusalem in A.D. 70, in excess of one million Jews were killed.[44] The countless Christians who have been killed throughout the centuries are also included, of whom Antipas of Pergamum is a single representative (2:13).

Are only martyrs featured in this verse, and are Christians who have not been killed for the cause of Christ excluded? If this were true, then John, who presumably died a natural death in A.D. 98, is not included. We know that Stephen and the apostles James, Peter, and Paul were stoned, crucified, or beheaded, but other leaders have been spared a violent death. Every believer who faithfully follows Christ will experience suffering for his sake; and, says Jesus, "Whoever loses his life for me will find it" (Matt. 16:25b).

42. Colin Brown, "Magic," *NIDNTT*, 2:556.

43. Beale, *Revelation*, p. 922.

44. Josephus *War* 6.9.3 §420.

Greek Words, Phrases, and Constructions in 18:21–24

Verse 21

εἷς—the number has lost its significance in this context and is equivalent to the indefinite article, hence “an angel” (see 8:13; 9:13).

Verse 24

αἷμα προφητῶν—the Majority Text and the TR have the plural αἵματα. Not only textual witnesses but also the internal evidence of John’s usage of the word *blood* in the singular throughout Revelation supports this reading.

19

The Lamb's Wedding and the Final Battle against the Antichrist

(19:1–21)

Outline (continued)

3. Songs of Praise, Wedding, and Worship (19:1–10)
   a. Three Hymns and a Command (19:1–5)
   b. The Wedding (19:6–9)
   c. Worship (19:10)

C. The Decisive Battle (19:11–21)
   1. The Rider and His Armies (19:11–16)
   2. The Final Battle against the Antichrist (19:17–21)

19 1 After these things I heard as it were a loud voice of a vast multitude in heaven saying,
"Hallelujah! Salvation and praise and power belong to our God, 2 because true and just
are his judgments. Because he judged the great prostitute, who ruined the earth with her
fornication, and he avenged the blood of his servants shed by her."

3 And again they said, "Hallelujah! Her smoke goes up forever and ever." 4 And the twenty-four
elders and the four living creatures fell down and worshiped God, who was seated on the throne. And
they said, "Amen. Hallelujah!"

5 And a voice came from the throne saying, "Praise our God all you his servants, even you who
fear him, both small and great."

6 And I heard as it were the voice of a great multitude and as it were the sound of many waters
and as it were the sound of mighty peals of thunder, saying, "Hallelujah, because our Lord God Almighty rules. 7 Let us rejoice and be glad and give him glory, for the wedding of the Lamb has come
and his wife has prepared herself. 8 And fine linen that is bright and clean was given to her to clothe
herself"—for fine linen represents the righteous deeds of the saints.

9 And he said to me, "Write. Blessed are those who have been invited to the wedding banquet of
the Lamb." And he said to me, "These are the true words of God." 10 Then I fell at his feet to worship
him. And he said to me, "Don't do it. I am a fellow servant with you and your brothers [and sisters]
who hold the testimony of Jesus. Worship God. For the testimony of Jesus is the spirit of prophecy."

11 And I saw heaven opened, and look, a white horse and he that sat on it was called Faithful and
True. And he judges with justice and makes war. 12 And his eyes are as a flame of fire, and on his
head are many crowns. He has a name written that no one knows except he himself. 13 And he was
clothed in a robe dipped in blood, and his name was called the Word of God.

14 And the armies of heaven followed him on white horses; they were arrayed in fine linen, white
and clean. 15 And out of his mouth proceeds a sharp sword with which to strike the nations. And he
will rule them with an iron rod, and he treads the winepress of the fury of the wrath of God Almighty.
16 And on his robe and on his thigh he has the name written,

KING OF KINGS AND LORD OF LORDS.

17 And I saw an angel standing in the sun, and he cried out with a loud voice, saying to all the
birds that fly in mid-heaven, "Come, gather together for the great banquet of God, 18 so that you
may eat the flesh of kings and the flesh of generals, and the flesh of mighty men and the flesh of
horses and their riders and the flesh of free persons and slaves, of small and great."

19 And I saw the beast and the kings of the earth and their armies gathered to make war against
the one seated on the horse and against his army. 20 And the beast was caught and with him the false
prophet who on his authority had performed signs by which he deceived those who received the
mark of the beast and worshiped his image. These two were thrown alive into the lake of fire that
burns with sulfur. 21 And the rest were killed with the sword that proceeded from the mouth of the
rider on the horse, and the birds gorged themselves on their flesh.

---

3. Songs of Praise, Wedding, and Worship
19:1–10

Notice first that this segment belongs to the preceding two chapters (17 and 18) that describe the great prostitute and the fall of Babylon. But whereas these chapters record the demise of Babylon the Great with songs of doom and destruction, the first ten verses of chapter 19 stand in direct contrast to them. This segment contains the hallelujah choruses of the innumerable saints, the twenty-four elders, and the four living creatures. Incidentally, the Hebrew word *hallelujah* (praise the LORD) appears nowhere in the New Testament but only here in the Apocalypse (19:1, 3, 4, 6).

Next, in the first part of chapter 19 John portrays a scene in heaven where the heavenly host sings hymns of jubilation. In these hymns they observe that God judges people on the basis of truth and justice; he avenges the blood of the saints; he consigns to hell the anti-Christian forces and their smoke rises forever. And the inner circle of elders and creatures surrounding God's throne utter their consent with their "Amen, Hallelujah!" One of them even commands everyone to praise God.

The last hymn is most significant, for it relates the wedding of the Lamb and his bride, namely the saints, dressed in fine linen. Now notice the contrast. The great prostitute, who has no husband and is dressed in flashy glitter, faces irreparable loss; she is left naked and is burned (17:16). The bride of the Lamb celebrates her marriage to her husband wearing fine linen that is bright and clean (19:7–8). The church, personified as the bride, will never again have to listen to the duplicity and deceit coming from the prostitute.

The scene shifts from heaven to earth, where an angel instructs John to record the beatitude of the wedding invitation, "Blessed are those who have been invited to the wedding banquet of the Lamb." Preventing John from bowing before him, the angel tells John to worship God instead. Indeed, the duty of every saint is to worship God, summarized succinctly in the question and answer of a seventeenth-century catechism, "What is the chief end of man? Man's chief end is to glorify God, and to enjoy Him for ever."[1]

a. Three Hymns and a Command
19:1–5

1. After these things I heard as it were a loud voice of a vast multitude in heaven saying, "Hallelujah! Salvation and praise and power belong to our God."

The phrase *after these things* occurs nine times in the Apocalypse and usually denotes a shift in focus from one scene to another.[2] That is, from looking at the destruction of Babylon the Great, John now concentrates on what is happening in heaven. The break between heaven and earth is never greater than when the measure of human lawlessness is full and reaches to heaven (18:5). When God's plagues strike, nothing is left on earth except distress and devastation, but in heaven a countless multitude raises the hallelujah chorus.

After seeing Babylon's demise on earth, John now hears what appears to be a loud voice coming from a vast multitude of angels and saints in heaven. Inciden-

1. Westminster Shorter Catechism, question and answer 1.

2. Rev. 1:19; 4:1 (twice); 7:9; 9:12; 15:5; 18:1; 19:1; 20:3. The verb *I saw* is included in 4:1; 7:9; 15:5; 18:1.

tally, while recording Revelation John mentions both seeing and hearing; he readily switches from the one to the other (e.g., 1:10, 12; 5:6, 11; 14:1, 2). The *vast multitude* (see 19:6 and 7:9) in heaven represents the voice of the redeemed and the angels surrounding God's throne (compare Heb. 12:22–24). Both angels and saints form one immense chorus, perceived by John as a loud voice singing "Hallelujah!" This transliterated Hebrew word made up of *hallelu* (praise) and *yah* (an abbreviated form of Yahweh) has become a universally accepted term. In the same way, words like *amen, abba,* and *maranatha* appear in numerous languages around the globe. From Hellenistic Jews in their synagogues, early Christians adopted the expression *hallelujah* as a liturgical exclamation of joy.

The word appears only in the Psalms (twenty-four times) and in the nineteenth chapter of Revelation (four times).[3] This shout of spiritual jubilation occurs at the beginning and end of individual psalms (e.g., Ps. 104, 106, 113, 117). Psalms 113–118 are known as the Hallel.[4] Also the last five Psalms in the Psalter begin and end with the word *Hallelujah* (Ps. 146–150). "As the Heb[rew] Psalter closes with God's chosen people singing 'Hallelujah,' the N[ew] T[estament] closes with God's redeemed in heaven singing 'Hallelujah.'"[5] This is even more striking when we consider that Revelation 19 features the last series of hymns in this book.

The heavenly host continues its praise with the words, "Salvation and praise and power belong to our God." John lists three attributes of God, the first of which is *salvation.* God planned salvation and chose us in Christ before the creation of the world (Eph. 1:4–5, 11). When the human race plunged into sin, God stood ready to redeem his people. God saves body and soul of all those whom the Lamb redeems throughout the world anywhere and anytime. He receives all the praise and glory for the redemptive work the Lamb has accomplished (7:10).

The salvation that God initiated and Jesus fulfilled results in God's displaying both his glory and power (compare 5:12; 7:12). In the decisive battle against Satan, the victory belongs to God, whose glory is matchless and whose power is infinite. These three attributes of salvation, glory, and power demand songs of praise from all God's creatures, especially saints and angels.

2. "Because true and just are his judgments. Because he judged the great prostitute, who ruined the earth with her fornication, and he avenged the blood of his servants shed by her."

Here is the first reason for ascribing salvation, glory, and power to God. John writes that his judgments are true and just. The words *true and just are his judgments* are a repetition of 16:7 and are found with variation in 15:3.[6]

---

3. In addition see Tobit 13:17 [13:18 LXX]; 3 Macc. 7:18.

4. Alan F. Johnson (*Revelation,* in *The Expositor's Bible Commentary,* ed. Frank E. Gaebelein [Grand Rapids: Zondervan, 1981], 12:570) notes a close connection between the Hallel and Jesus' celebrating the Passover and the Lord's Supper.

5. Guy B. Funderburk, *ZPEB,* 3:20. See also Arthur Louis Breslich, *ISBE,* 2:600.

6. Both the Old Greek and Theod. read, "All your judgments are true" in Dan. 3:27. See also the NAB and NJB. And compare Ps. 19:9; 119:137.

The second reason is a further elaboration of the preceding clause that relates God's judgment on the great prostitute, who is also known as Babylon the Great. In the two previous chapters, John portrays her as the one who corrupted the people's morals to the point of destroying them (17:1–5; 18:3, 7–9). This destruction, then, is to be taken in a moral and religious sense with respect to seducing the human race (11:18, "And to destroy those who are destroying the earth"; see also Jer. 51:25).[7] The great prostitute who destroyed God's good creation would have to be brought to justice and stand trial before the Judge of all the earth. And his divine judgment avenges the blood of the martyrs under the altar (6:10); in fact, the prostitute has been responsible for the shedding of their blood.

The last clause in this sentence literally reads, "he has avenged the blood of his servants from her hand." Most versions translate the crucial part of the verse as "he avenged on her the blood of his servants" (see Deut. 32:43). However, I have translated the clause as "he avenged the blood of his servants shed by her" (compare NKJV, NJB). The words *from her hand* idiomatically express agency, and they parallel Elisha's words to Jehu to avenge the blood of the prophets who were killed "at the hand of Jezebel" (2 Kings 9:7 KJV). In other words, Jezebel was the cause of bloodshed.[8] Similarly, the great prostitute instigated the destruction of God's people and shed their blood. The psalmist suggests the same wording, "the revenging of the blood of thy servants which is shed" (Ps. 79:10 KJV).

3. And again they said, "Hallelujah! Her smoke goes up forever and ever."

Once more the innumerable multitude of angels and saints shouts the word "Hallelujah" at the beginning of the next hymn, praising God that the smoke of Babylon rises without ceasing. John had already used this wording in an earlier context (14:11, "And the smoke of their torment rises forever and ever"), where he borrowed the picture from the curse that God pronounced on Edom. There pitch and sulfur burn unquenched night and day and its smoke rises ceaselessly (Isa. 34:9–10). In Revelation John applies God's curse to Babylon, the representative of all the nations that have opposed God. The words "forever and ever" convey not only absolute destruction but also a picture of hell with its eternal flame. This is the imagery of Sodom and Gomorrah in which God forever destroys his enemies and by implication grants eternal peace and rest to all his people.[9]

4. And the twenty-four elders and the four living creatures fell down and worshiped God who was seated on the throne. And they said, "Amen. Hallelujah!"

This is the last time in the Apocalypse that the term *twenty-four elders* appears.[10] They are the representatives of God's redeemed people translated to glory. They

---

7. Bauer, p. 190; Günther Harder, *TDNT*, 9:103; Gregory K. Beale, *The Book of Revelation: A Commentary on the Greek Text*, NIGTC (Grand Rapids: Eerdmans, 1998), p. 927; Robert L. Thomas, *Revelation 8–22: An Exegetical Commentary* (Chicago: Moody, 1995), p. 359.

8. David E. Aune, *Revelation 17–22*, WBC 52C (Nashville: Nelson, 1998), pp. 1015, 1025–26.

9. Consult G. B. Caird, *A Commentary on the Revelation of St. John the Divine* (London: Black, 1966), p. 232; Jürgen Roloff, *The Revelation of John*, trans. J. E. Alsup (Minneapolis: Fortress, 1993), p. 211; G. R. Beasley-Murray, *The Book of Revelation*, NCB (London: Oliphants, 1974), p. 272.

10. Rev. 4:4 (twice), 10; 5:8; 11:16; 19:4; see also 5:5, 6, 11, 14; 7:11, 13; 14:3.

are elders seated on thrones who are given the privilege of ruling. They surround God's throne and are closer to it than angels. Of all God's creatures in heaven they are the ones who excel in glory and honor.[11]

The four living creatures that were first introduced in 4:6 surround the throne of God and encircle it at four equidistant points. They are the cherubim, that is, angels who have been given the task to protect, guard, and do God's bidding (see Gen. 3:24; Exod. 25:20; Rev. 15:7). They support the elders in uttering praises and the "Amen" (5:9–10, 14).

Thus with the elders they respond to the first hymn of the vast multitude by voicing their "Amen. Hallelujah!" These two words are taken from the conclusion of the Psalter's fourth book (Ps. 106:48; compare Ps. 41:13; 72:18–19; 89:52).[12] The living beings and the elders, representing both creation and the redeemed, fall down before God seated on his throne. They worship him with words of affirmation and praise. They confirm that justice has been served with respect to Babylon the Great. Together with the redeemed they glorify God and sing praises of thanksgiving. They worship God by honoring him for the work of creation and redemption, for his glory and power.

5. And a voice came from the throne saying, "Praise our God all you his servants, even you who fear him, both small and great."

Instead of a hymn, John writes a command that comes directly from the throne of God. The voice is probably not that of Jesus, because of the words "*our* God." Granted, in his letter to the church in Philadelphia, Jesus utters the words "my God" four times (3:12), and he informs his disciples that he is going to ascend to "my God and your God" (John 20:17). Nonetheless, to put the words "our God" on the lips of Jesus appears to lack authenticity. It is better to maintain that they come from the lips of a creature, possibly one of the elders, one of the cherubim, or another angelic being. In short, the unidentified voice remains anonymous.

The command addressed to all God's servants is to praise him (Ps. 150:1). In a sense, every believer is a servant of God, so that the mandate is directed to all God's people on earth (e.g., see 7:3). The saints around the throne praise him continually day and night (7:15), but the saints on earth need exhortation. The admonition for every believer is to serve God and to fear him. This means, however, that there are not two categories of people: those who serve and those who fear him. For this reason, I have provided the translation "*even* you who fear him." The italicized word conveys the sense that his servants indeed fear God. No one is excluded from serving him and no one is exempt from fearing him. Those who fear him pay respect to him and their fellow human beings; they are sensitive to God's Word and his testimony.

---

11. Refer to William Hendriksen, *More Than Conquerors* (reprint, Grand Rapids: Baker, 1982), pp. 85–86.

12. Thomas, *Revelation 8–22*, p. 361; S. Greijdanus, *De Openbaring des Heeren aan Johannes*, KNT (Amsterdam: Van Bottenburg, 1925), p. 383; Robert H. Mounce, *The Book of Revelation*, rev. ed., NICNT (Grand Rapids: Eerdmans, 1998), p. 343. R. H. Charles (*A Critical and Exegetical Commentary on the Revelation of St. John*, ICC [Edinburgh: Clark, 1920], 2:120) points out that at the conclusion of Ps. 105:48 the LXX reads, *genoito, genoito* ("may it be so, may it be so").

Fearing God means showing him reverence and rendering him praise (Eccles. 12:13). As part of his phraseology in Revelation, John writes two commands: *fear God* and *give him glory* (see 14:7; 15:4; 16:9; 19:5, 7). Indeed he teaches that regardless of one's age, gender, and status, one is required to fear, praise, and worship God.[13] Both the small and the great have equal status in his presence, and because they fear him God rewards them with his blessing (11:18 and Ps. 115:13).

Greek Words, Phrases, and Constructions in 19:1–5

Verse 1

λεγόντων—this is the present masculine genitive plural participle, but the two preceding nouns are both in the singular—*voice* is feminine and *multitude* is masculine. The plural participle is used because of the sense conveyed by the "vast multitude."

Verse 2

ἐκ χειρὸς αὐτῆς— the phrase reflects Hebrew idiom and literally means "by means of her hand." The word *hand* is superfluous, so that the phrase signifies agency, "by her," with the verb *shed* added to complete the clause.

Verse 5

αἰνεῖτε τῷ θεῷ—the verb normally takes the accusative, not the dative. But the dative reflects the influence of the Hebrew language, influence that is common in the LXX.

καὶ οἱ φοβούμενοι—the presence of the conjunction is awkward if it is translated "and," for then there are two different groups that praise God. The translation "even" averts this problem; some translations omit the conjunction.[14]

---

b. The Wedding *19:6–9*

I make two preliminary observations. First, verses 6–8 feature the last hymn in both this chapter and the New Testament. The hymn is the so-called wedding song to celebrate the coming together of bride and bridegroom for the nuptial ceremony and the supper to which invited guests may come.

Next, the sounds that introduce this wedding song John compares with three disparate groups: a vast multitude, many waters, and peals of thunder. He uses images of human life on earth that describe a scene in heaven.

6. And I heard as it were the voice of a great multitude and as it were the sound of many waters and as it were the sound of mighty peals of thunder, saying, "Hallelujah, because our Lord God Almighty rules."

John listened to a hymn that sounded as if it were sung by a vast multitude. He does not identify this throng, but because the wording is the same as in verse 1,

---

13. Horst Balz, *EDNT,* 3:432.

14. Bruce M. Metzger, *A Textual Commentary on the Greek New Testament,* 2d ed. (Stuttgart: Deutsche Bibelgesellschaft, 1994), pp. 684–85.

it appears that the multitude has the same identity.[15] They sing both the opening and the concluding hymns in this chapter; in both they sing the same notes of praise and adulation. Here are inconspicuous echoes of the hymns the multitudes sang in both chapters 5 and 7.

The voice that John hears he compares with sounds taken from nature: the sounds of many waters and of mighty peals of thunder. John describes the voice of Jesus' appearance on the isle of Patmos as a rushing sound coming from many waters (1:15; see 14:2; Ezek. 1:24; 43:2). And the phrase *mighty peals of thunder* conveys the idea of loudness that can be heard everywhere (Rev. 6:1; 14:2). These two phrases indeed point to God's power, majesty, and glory. And the mighty voice of the countless multitude attests to expressions of joy and thankfulness for the privilege of being the bride of Christ.

This voice, conveying the sound of a multitude of people talking at the same time, rises from the pleasing tones of bubbling water and then swells to the crashing crescendo of thunderclaps. These sounds are like people who begin singing softly but then culminate their hymn in resounding overtones. The first word of the song is *Hallelujah,* which has now occurred four times in these hymns. It is followed by a clause that gives the reason for this note of jubilation, "because our Lord God Almighty rules." The verb in this clause can be interpreted to read that the Lord "has begun to rule." The Lord God, as the descriptive label *Almighty* indicates, has always been the ruler over his great creation. But now the kingdom of the Antichrist has come to its anticipated end, and the Lord God is the supreme ruler in the vast universe he has created. In Revelation, the term *the Lord God Almighty* appears seven times and characterizes God's sovereignty.[16] While on earth Domitian was honored as *dominus et deus* (Lord and God), the heavenly chorus sings in triumph that God occupies the true seat of power in the world (see Ps. 93:1; 97:1; 99:1; 1 Chron. 16:31; Zech. 14:9). Last, the possessive personal pronoun *our* in "our Lord God Almighty rules" makes the chorus inclusive: the saints in heaven and on earth are one.

7. "Let us rejoice and be glad and give him glory, for the wedding of the Lamb has come and his wife has prepared herself. 8. And fine linen that is bright and clean was given to her to clothe herself"—for fine linen represents the righteous deeds of the saints.

a. *Festivity.* The exhortation to rejoice, be glad, and give glory to God is directed to all his people who receive the invitation to the wedding of the Lamb. The question now is whether God's people are portrayed as the bride and as the wedding guests at the same time. But in John's framework of symbolism pictures overlap, so that we have to conclude: "the guests and the Bride are one and the

---

15. One commentator suggests that if the multitude in verse 1 is angelic, then the one in verse 6 refers to "the great redeemed throngs" (Johnson, *Revelation,* p. 571). But another notes that in verse 6 "the redeemed can hardly be the singers, because the subject of their song is partly the bride who symbolizes . . . the redeemed in heaven" (Thomas, *Revelation 8–22,* p. 363).

16. Rev. 1:8; 4:8; 11:17; 15:3; 16:7; 19:6; 21:22. See Richard Bauckham, *The Climax of Prophecy* (Edinburgh: Clark, 1993), p. 304.

same."[17] That is, John's images flow into each other and ought not to be interpreted separately. The symbolic portrayal of the Lamb's wedding is not to be understood literally, for that results in absurdity.

John borrows his phraseology from the Psalter: "This is the day the LORD has made; let us rejoice and be glad in it" and "Ascribe to the LORD glory due his name" (Ps. 118:24 and 96:8a respectively). God not only destroys the kingdom of the Antichrist, but he also grants salvation to his people and gives them the honor of being wedded to his Son. His people rejoice because God has removed their enemy, and they express their thanks by rendering him praise and glory.

b. *Betrothal and Wedding.* Engagements and weddings differ from culture to culture and from age to age. The picture that John shows the reader is that of a Hebrew betrothal, which after a given period is followed by the wedding ceremony. The betrothal rite binds bride and bridegroom in a relationship of being promised to one another—a relationship sealed in the presence of witnesses. Paul writes that he promised the Corinthian church as a pure virgin to her husband Christ (2 Cor. 11:2). The New Testament features Christ as the bridegroom and the church as his bride.[18] Also the Old Testament mentions a similar relation between God and his people (Isa. 54:5, 6; 62:5; Jer. 3:20; Hos. 2:19).

In a Hebrew setting, there was a waiting period between betrothal and wedding while the bride and bridegroom lived separately (Deut. 22:23–24; Matt. 1:18–19). During this period the two families involved arranged the terms of the dowry. When this sum was paid, the actual wedding followed. On that day, the bridegroom in procession accompanied by friends brought the bride from her parental home to his own home. There the wedding feast was held to celebrate the wedding. William Hendriksen presents a brief sketch of this nuptial sequence as he applies it to Christ and the church.[19]

> In Christ the bride was *chosen* from eternity. Throughout the entire Old Testament dispensation the wedding *was announced.* Next, the Son of God assumed our flesh and blood: the *betrothal* took place. The price—the *dowry*—was paid on Calvary. And now, after an *interval* which in the eyes of God is but a little while, the Bridegroom returns and "It has come, the wedding of the Lamb." The Church on earth yearns for this moment, so does the Church in heaven.

I am fully cognizant of John's brevity and the risk of placing something in the text that is not there. Yet I can confidently suggest that the wedding picture John portrays must be seen against the Jewish cultural background of his day.

c. *Preparation.* John next writes, "And his wife has prepared herself." How does she ready herself for the wedding? John answers by saying that she is given fine

---

17. Charles, *Revelation,* 2:129. See also Louis A. Vos, *The Synoptic Traditions in the Apocalypse* (Kampen: Kok, 1965), pp. 164–65. Caird (*Revelation,* p. 234) asserts, "The bride is the church, but the members of the church are guests at her wedding." See also Beale, *Revelation,* p. 945.

18. Matt. 9:15; John 3:29; Rom. 7:3–4; 1 Cor. 6:15; Eph. 5:23–32; Rev. 19:7–9; 21:2.

19. Hendriksen, *More Than Conquerors,* p. 181 (his emphasis).

linen to wear that is bright and clean. The bride can prepare herself only when God provides the wedding gown for her, because this garment is beautiful and pure. Her own clothes are but filthy rags, but Christ cleanses and presents her to himself "without stain or wrinkle or any other blemish" (Eph. 5:26, 27; see Isa. 61:10). Nevertheless, what are the obligations of the bride of the Lamb while she is still on earth? These obligations are to be faithful to the bridegroom, to show him her love and devotion, and to wait expectantly for his coming. But the clothing provided for her must be seen as an unconditional gift of God.[20] This fine garment she receives is nothing but an act of grace granted her by God. There is more. The saints who washed their robes in the blood of the Lamb to make them white are now collectively called the bride.[21] And the fine linen bright and clean is the same garment the armies of heaven wear as they follow Christ in the war against the anti-Christian forces (v. 14).

The Apocalypse graphically delineates the contrast between the great prostitute, who is dressed in gaudy apparel (17:4), and the bride of the Lamb, who is given fine linen that is bright and clean. The prostitute is brought to ruin; by contrast the bride is brought to Christ to be his wife. The woman clothed with the sun and the moon under her feet who, as a symbol of the church, bore the Son (12:1–2, 5) is now the bride of the Lamb redeemed by the Son.

Last, the guests who came to the wedding banquet in the parable were given wedding clothes, a symbol of purity and holiness. But one of these guests refused to wear them and consequently was thrown outside (Matt. 22:11–13). Hence, John explains the phrase *fine linen bright and clean* as "fine linen represents the righteous deeds of the saints."

What are these righteous deeds that the saints are able to perform? Paul sheds light on this question when he writes, "We are God's workmanship, created in Christ Jesus to do good works, which God prepared in advance for us to do" (Eph. 2:10). These righteous deeds, therefore, are made possible through God's grace at work in the hearts of the saints. Set free from bondage to Satan, the redeemed dedicate their lives to serve God. They feed the hungry, give the thirsty something to drink, supply hospitality to strangers, clothe the needy, and visit the sick and those in prison (Matt. 25:37–39). Christ blesses those deeds by perfecting them through his perfect righteousness.[22]

9. And he said to me, "Write. Blessed are those who have been invited to the wedding banquet of the Lamb." And he said to me, "These are the true words of God."

The speaker again is not identified (v. 5), but the context reveals that he is an angel (v. 10). Whether he is the one who earlier had come to instruct John

---

20. Beale, *Revelation*, p. 942. See also Herman Hoeksema, *Behold, He Cometh! An Exposition of the Book of Revelation* (Grand Rapids: Reformed Free Publishing Association, 1969), p. 618.

21. Refer to Sydney Hielema, "A Perfection of Misunderstandings: John's Role as Author in the Book of Revelation," *Pro Rege* 27, no. 4 (1999): 7.

22. R. C. H. Lenski, *The Interpretation of St. John's Revelation* (Columbus: Wartburg, 1943), p. 543.

(17:1) or another angel who announced the demise of Babylon (18:1) is difficult to determine. Certainly, the speaker is not Jesus, even though the Lord had told John earlier to write (1:11, 19). The numerous commands to write in the Apocalypse are uttered by Jesus, an angel, or an unidentified voice. The speaker now directs John to write the fourth of the seven beatitudes, "Blessed are those who have been invited to the wedding banquet of the Lamb."

Who are those invited to the banquet? They are all those who have responded, have received the gift of salvation, and have been clothed in white garments to be seated at the table of the Lamb. These individuals are the saints in heaven. The writer of 4 Ezra (=2 Esdras) 2:38–41 depicts a heavenly setting of the entire company who may sit at the banquet, who are arrayed in shining robes of white, who fulfilled the law of the Lord, and whose number is complete.

The words *have been invited* reveal that the initial invitation was issued in the past, that the guests responded favorably, and that they now have the privilege of being seated at the banquet. While others who received the invitation refused to accept it (Matt. 22:3), those who responded are called "blessed."

The speaker continues by emphatically noting, "These are the true words of God." God has extended his invitation to the guests, and his words are true without fail. All that God has revealed in his Word is infallible, and all the words that the angel at God's command has communicated are true. Commentators differ on the application of the above-mentioned clause, linking it either it to the preceding beatitude[23] or to the entire section in which the angel has communicated what must take place (17:1–19:9a). I opt for the latter and find a parallel in 22:6.[24] Thus, at the conclusion of this section, the angel states that these words are true, which as a fitting response is the equivalent of a solemn "Amen."

Greek Words, Phrases, and Constructions in 19:6–9

Verse 6

λεγόντων—the genitive masculine/neuter plural form of the participle has no near antecedent with which it harmonizes. The noun *multitude,* although far from the participle, must serve here as a collective plural; that is, the gender and number of the participle are determined by the sense of the passage.

Verse 9

οἱ . . . κεκλημένοι—the lengthy prepositional clause "to the wedding banquet of the Lamb" has been placed between the definite article and the perfect passive participle. This occurs also in the introductions of the seven letters to the seven churches (2:1, 8, 12, 18; 3:1, 7, 14).

---

23. See Philip Edgcumbe Hughes, *The Book of the Revelation: A Commentary* (Leicester: Inter-Varsity; Grand Rapids: Eerdmans, 1990), p. 201. But others limit it to the immediate context of vv. 7–9a, so Beale (*Revelation,* p. 945).

24. Beasley-Murray, *Revelation,* p. 275.

c. Worship
19:10

10. Then I fell at his feet to worship him. And he said to me, "Don't do it. I am a fellow servant with you and your brothers [and sisters] who hold the testimony of Jesus. Worship God. For the testimony of Jesus is the spirit of prophecy."

a. *Duplicate.* This text is duplicated almost verbatim in 22:8b–9: "I fell before the angel at his feet to worship him who showed me these things. And he said to me, 'Don't do this. I am a fellow servant of you and your brothers the prophets and of those who keep the words of this book. Worship God.'" Presumably, John wrote these words twice in order to emphasize his point. Also, he purposely designed them as conclusions to two visions (17:1–19:10 and 21:9–22:9).[25] That is, John first writes a conclusion to the vision of Babylon's destruction and then a conclusion to the vision of the new Jerusalem.

b. *Angel worship.* Although angel worship did exist in Jewish circles during apostolic times (Col. 2:18), John is emphasizing that God's people must worship no one except the triune God. He stresses that to worship an angel is absolutely forbidden, even if angels convey messages directly from God. But note that the author of Hebrews assigns a place to angels that is not higher but lower than that of the saints on earth: "Are not all angels ministering spirits sent to serve those who will inherit salvation?" (Heb. 1:14). If John is forbidden to worship an angel who ministered to him, it would be perverse for the early Christians to engage in the worship of angels, emperors, or beasts.[26] Homage may never be paid to a creature—only to God (Acts 10:25–26; 14:11–15).

c. *Fellow servant.* After preventing John from worshiping him, the angel identifies himself as a fellow servant; this means that he and the apostle have a similar status. He stands in the presence of God Almighty but places himself on the level of God's people, whom he calls his brothers (and that includes his sisters). He characterizes all of them as those who hold the testimony of Jesus (see 1:2, 9; 6:9; 12:11, 17; 20:4). The phrase *testimony of Jesus* can be interpreted subjectively, as the testimony Jesus himself gives, or objectively, as the testimony God's faithful servants give about Jesus. In this instance, both the subjective and objective interpretations are valid. Subjectively Jesus is God's messenger (John 3:34), and objectively God's people are witnesses for the Lord. But the phrase *testimony of Jesus* occurs twice. John clarifies the first occurrence with the clause "for the testimony of Jesus is the spirit of prophecy." This means that the Holy Spirit has inspired prophets in both Old Testament and New Testament eras to bear witness

---

25. Bauckham, *Climax of Prophecy*, p. 133. By contrast, Charles (*Revelation*, 2:128) thinks that "xix.10 is rewritten from xxii.8–9 by the editor and given a less general meaning." He considers 19:20 an interpolation and has rearranged chapter 22 by placing verses 8–9 in their "right context at the close of the Book." His views are highly improbable.

26. Gerhard A. Krodel, *Revelation*, ACNT (Minneapolis: Augsburg, 1989), p. 316. See also Henry Barclay Swete, *Commentary on Revelation* (1911; reprint, Grand Rapids: Kregel, 1977), p. 248; Isbon T. Beckwith, *The Apocalypse of John* (1919; reprint, Grand Rapids: Baker, 1979), p. 729.

to Jesus Christ through the spirit of prophecy. Thus this spirit refers to both the testimony from Jesus and the testimony about him. All believers receive the gospel of salvation through the working of the Holy Spirit and in turn make it known to others. Beale suggests the following paraphrase, "those giving the testimony to [and from] Jesus are prophetic people."[27]

One last remark. Between the two occurrences of *the testimony of Jesus,* John places the imperative "Worship God." This imperative is given as a single command that comprises worship without temporal and local limits. The command is for everyone to worship God anytime and everywhere regardless of circumstances. The early recipients of the Apocalypse realized that by giving their testimony about Jesus they placed themselves in open conflict with pagan and Roman authorities that compelled them to worship idols and Caesar. Now they are told to worship God and by implication to be his witnesses (compare Matt. 4:10; Acts 1:8).

Greek Words, Phrases, and Constructions in 19:10

ὅρα μή—the word order is significant, for the negative particle follows the verb in the present imperative, giving the English idiomatic equivalent "Don't do it!" After the negative particle, we should supply an unexpressed subjunctive such as ποιήσῃς. Hence the particle negates not the verb *to see* but the implied verb *to do.*

C. The Decisive Battle 19:11–21

In the preceding section (17:1–19:10), John related the demise of worldly Babylon the Great. But Babylon is only the first of God's enemies to perish. The next two are the beast that came up out of the sea and the beast that came up out of the earth, also known as the false prophet (13:1, 11). John relates the defeat and destiny of Satan in the next chapter (20:1–10).

The author introduced Satan first (chap. 12), then the beast out of the sea and the beast out of the earth (chap. 13), and last the great prostitute (chap. 17). In reverse order, the prostitute who suffers defeat and destruction in the form of Babylon is mentioned first (chap. 18), then the beast and the false prophet (chap. 19), and last Satan (chap. 20).[28]

The Lord Jesus now appears not as the Bridegroom and the Lamb (vv. 7, 9) but as the King of kings and Lord of lords. The armies of heaven accompany him to wage war against his enemies, who are led into battle by the beast and the false

---

27. Beale, *Revelation,* p. 947. Bauckham (*Climax of Prophecy,* p. 161) succinctly writes, "Those who bear the witness of Jesus are certainly not just the prophets (19:10) but Christians in general (12:17)." Refer to Frederick D. Mazzaferri, *The Genre of the Book of Revelation from a Source-Critical Perspective,* BZNW 54 (Berlin and New York: de Gruyter, 1989), pp. 306–13.

28. Homer Hailey, *Revelation: An Introduction and Commentary* (Grand Rapids: Baker, 1979), p. 381; Lenski, *Revelation,* p. 547.

prophet. These two are utterly defeated and thrown alive into the lake of fire and brimstone; the rest of their followers are killed with the sword. Here is a picture of the ultimate defeat of both the beast and the false prophet, and their eternal reward. John vividly portrays the destruction of all wickedness and the Christ who triumphs over his enemies. Therewith he presents the last section of the sixth vision that began at 17:1.

1. The Rider and His Armies
19:11–16

11. And I saw heaven opened, and look, a white horse, and he that sat on it was called Faithful and True. And he judges with justice and makes war.

This is the second time in Revelation that John writes that he saw heaven opened (4:1; see Ezek. 1:1). Now there is no open door that allows him a view or an entry into heaven. This time heaven is opened not for John to enter but for the Lord and his armies to exit. They leave heaven to engage in a spiritual battle against enemy forces. These words introduce the conflict at the end of cosmic time. Considering this complex imagery, we should not consult chronology "to determine how truth can best be expressed."[29] Rather we focus attention on the reality of this battle and its inevitable outcome.

At Jesus' baptism, heaven was opened and the Spirit of God came down (Matt. 3:16). Now heaven is opened and a rider on a white horse appears whose name is Faithful and True, namely, Jesus. The color white symbolizes victory, for this rider goes forth to be the victorious conqueror (compare 6:2).[30] He rides on a white horse as a symbol of warfare and is identified by two names: Faithful and True. The names are familiar, for Jesus in his letter to the church in Laodicea introduced himself as the "Amen, the faithful and true witness" (3:14; refer also to 1:5; 3:7; 6:10). Christ is faithful because he fulfills everything the Scriptures reveal of and about him, and he is true because he personifies truth (John 14:6). The contrast with Satan the father of the lie is obvious (John 8:44).

Christ also appears as the Judge, for "he judges with justice and makes war." At the beginning of this conflict, he is identified as the Judge. By waging war against his enemies, he administers justice that results in the total defeat of his opponents. God has ordained that divine judgment precedes victory with the assurance that justice will inevitably triumph. Notice the present tense of the verbs *to judge* and *to make war* conveying a progressive sense.[31] In contemporary terms, John sees within the entire vision a fragment like a newsreel clip of these two activities; they convey a symbolic representation of the great conflict between Christ and his enemies. Yet the concept of judging with justice also has a positive

---

29. Mounce, *Revelation*, p. 351.

30. Compare John P. M. Sweet, *Revelation*, WPC (Philadelphia: Westminster, 1979), p. 282; George Eldon Ladd, *Commentary on the Revelation of John* (Grand Rapids: Eerdmans, 1972), p. 253.

31. Swete, *Revelation*, p. 251; Thomas, *Revelation 8–22*, pp. 383–84.

connotation, as is evident in the many Old Testament references applied to God's people and the nations (see Ps. 9:8; 72:2; 96:13; 98:9; Isa. 11:3–4).[32]

12. And his eyes are as a flame of fire, and on his head are many crowns. He has a name written that no one knows except he himself.

This verse describes three aspects of Christ: his eyes, his head, and his name. The first two are visible and known, but the third, although written, only he himself knows. The description of Jesus' eyes as flames of fire resembles a clause in Daniel 10:6, "his eyes like flaming torches." And John's portrayal of Jesus on Patmos has similar wording, "His eyes were like a flame of fire" (1:14; 2:18). These flames of fire convey Christ's holy anger toward his enemies and his wrath against sin that is piled up to heaven (18:5).

The second aspect is that Christ wears *many crowns*, which the Greek text conveys as diadems (see 12:3; 13:1, where this word is applied to Satan and the beast as they imitate Christ). Diadems in John's day were individual ribbons tied around someone's head. Here the many diadems represent Christ's supremacy in countless areas. The picture is purely symbolic of his complete sovereignty in the universe and does not lend itself to literalism. We assume that these diadems on Christ's head displayed names to indicate the areas of his sovereignty (compare Isa. 62:2–3).

The third aspect is the name that no one knows except Christ. This sentence has caused at least one commentator who examined the parallel lines in verses 12 and 13 to assert that the sentence "He has a name written that no one knows except he himself" is a gloss. By deleting this line, he says that the parallelism of verses 12 and 13 is restored.[33] But is there really a contradiction in these two verses, where verse 12c states an inability to know the name of Christ and verse 13b divulges this name as "the Word of God"? To be sure, the names for Christ are numerous in the New Testament; the Apocalypse calls him the Lamb, Faithful and True, Lord of lords and King of kings, Root, offspring of David, Morning Star, and others. In verse 13 the written name of the rider on the white horse is "the Word of God." A name refers to the very being of a person; for instance, an overcomer is given a white stone on which "is written a new name which no one knows except the one who receives it" (2:17). When on the island of Patmos John hears a divine voice and describes the speaker as "a son of man" (1:13), he declines to identify Jesus by name. In fact, he is unable to utter the name of this divine person. This corresponds with the mysterious wording in an early Christian hymn, "God . . . gave him the name that is above every name" (Phil. 2:9). We know that the appellation *Jesus* is his earthly name and *Christ* his official designation, but he still has another name that remains hidden from us. This mysterious name will be revealed to his people when his redemptive work has been brought

32. Aune, *Revelation 17–22*, p. 1053; Jan Fekkes, *Isaiah and Prophetic Traditions in the Book of Revelation*, JSNTSup 93 (Sheffield: JSOT, 1994), pp. 117–22.

33. Charles, *Revelation*, 2:132, 436. Aune (*Revelation 17–22*, p. 1055) calls it a later addition.

to completion. Certainly at the wedding banquet of the Lamb (v. 9) when his bride enjoys perfect blessedness, the Lord will reveal the mystery of his name.[34]

There is still another explanation, namely, that God shares his name with Christ, whereby the divinity of Christ is expressed.[35] At three other places in the Apocalypse, John identifies Christ with God by ascribing divinity to Jesus when he mentions him together with God with reference to God's kingdom and throne. There is one kingdom, not two; and one throne, not two (11:15; 20:6; 22:3).

13. And he was clothed in a robe dipped in blood, and his name was called the Word of God.

a. "And he was clothed in a robe dipped in blood." Once again (v. 12), John borrows imagery from the prophecy of Isaiah that mentions garments that are blood-spattered and stained "like those of one treading out the winepress" (63:2–3). He portrays Jesus as having been clothed in a robe, with the implication that he had wrapped this garment around him in times past. Treading out the grapes in the winepress is an Old Testament portrayal of God who in his anger against sin tramples on the grapes of wrath. It refers to God's day of vengeance when he alone worked for the salvation of his people and then expended his wrath on the wicked (Isa. 63:4–6). The picture, then, is a robe spattered with the blood of his enemies; that is, God pronounced and passed judgment with the result that the evidence is visibly displayed on his garments.

The image is not of the Lamb whose blood was shed on Calvary's cross for the remission of sin. Here we see the Judge of all the earth, the Captain of his armed forces, and the King of kings and Lord of lords. The red spots on his robe are not of his own blood but that of his enemies.

Some scholars raise two objections to this interpretation. The first is that the final battle has not yet begun and already his garment is stained with blood; therefore it must depict the blood of the Lamb that was slain, as is evident from its many references in Revelation (1:5; 5:6, 9; 7:14; 12:11).[36] However, the picture John borrows from Isaiah's prophecy is symbolic and presents God as the executioner of his enemies. In John's Apocalypse, Christ is executioner and commander-in-chief. He fought his opponents throughout the ages before engaging the last battle.[37]

---

34. Friedrich Düsterdieck, *Critical and Exegetical Handbook to the Revelation of John* (New York and London: Funk and Wagnalls, 1886), p. 458. See also Aune (*Revelation 17–22*, p. 1055), who calls attention to the *Ascension of Isaiah* 9.5 and notes that the real name of Jesus "cannot be known by his followers until they have ascended out of the body." Beale (*Revelation*, p. 956) joins vv. 12 and 16 chiastically and avers that the title in v. 16 "is intended to be the most formal explanation of the name in v. 12."

35. Consult Thomas B. Slater, *Christ and Community: A Socio-Historical Study of the Christology of Revelation*, JSNTSup 178 (Sheffield: Sheffield Academic Press, 1999), p. 216.

36. See the commentaries of Johnson (p. 574), Krodel (p. 323), and Lenski (p. 547).

37. Consult Hoeksema, *Behold, He Cometh!* p. 631; Thomas, *Revelation 8–22*, pp. 386–87; Beasley-Murray, *Revelation*, p. 280; Ladd, *Revelation*, pp. 254–55.

Another objection is that the robe is not spattered with blood (Isa. 63:3) but rather is dipped in blood. But John is not necessarily borrowing only from Isaiah and excluding other Old Testament passages. For instance, Jacob in blessing Judah said, "he will wash his garments in wine, his robes in the blood of grapes" (Gen. 49:11).

b. "And his name was called the Word of God." The appellation *the Word of God* calls to mind John 1:1, 14 and 1 John 1:1, where the apostle introduces Jesus accordingly, and it is reminiscent of the superscript of the letter to the Laodiceans, "The Amen, the faithful and true witness, the origin of God's creation" (3:14). In Revelation, John writes the term *the word(s) of God* exactly seven times to express completeness (1:2, 9; 6:9; 17:17; 19:9, 13; 20:4). It often occurs with the expression *the testimony of Jesus* and similarly can be interpreted as the word that comes from God to mankind or the word that reveals God. Here it is Jesus bringing God's revelation, whose words are faithful and true. Jesus slays his enemies with that Word. Thus, John identifies Jesus with the Word of God.

14. And the armies of heaven followed him on white horses; they were arrayed in fine linen, white and clean.

The warrior coming to avenge the blood of the saints slain for the Word of God (6:9–10) is accompanied by the armies of heaven advancing on white horses. Earlier John described the battle in heaven which Michael and his angels waged against Satan and his hosts (12:7–9). But are these forces composed of angels (Deut. 33:2; Ps. 68:17) or of glorified saints who accompany the victorious Christ (17:14)? The saints had washed their robes in the blood of the Lamb and made them white (7:14). They wear linen garments that are fine, white, and clean as symbols of their righteous deeds (v. 8). But the seven angels who come out of the temple are also dressed in linen that is shining and clean (15:6). It is best to include in the armies of heaven both angels and saints, for both accompany Jesus on his return and both will be present at the judgment (Matt. 24:31; Mark 13:27; Luke 9:26; 1 Thess. 4:13–18; 2 Thess. 1:7–10).

Notice that the armies are not supplied with weaponry and no battle plans are drawn, yet they are attacked by the armies of the beast and the kings of the earth (v. 19).[38] John writes that they appear in fine linen that is white and clean. We read that not the angels but the commander of the armies engages the enemy with the sword coming out of his mouth, namely, the Word of God. That Word is alive, active, and sharper than a two-edged sword (Heb. 4:12); with it the warrior of heaven will destroy his opponents.[39] All his followers are seated on white horses, which are symbols of victory in the final battle (see 6:2).

38. See Leon Morris, *Revelation*, rev. ed., TNTC (Leicester: Inter-Varsity; Grand Rapids: Eerdmans, 1987), p. 225; Beasley-Murray, *Revelation*, p. 281.

39. Compare Wisdom 18:15–16, "when your all-powerful word leapt from your royal throne in heaven . . . like a relentless warrior, bearing the sharp sword of your inflexible decree" (REB). Refer to Elisabeth Schüssler Fiorenza, *The Book of Revelation: Justice and Judgment* (Philadelphia: Fortress, 1985), p. 98.

15. And out of his mouth proceeds a sharp sword with which to strike the nations. And he will rule them with an iron rod, and he treads the winepress of the fury of the wrath of God Almighty.

The image of a sharp sword coming out of Jesus' mouth is familiar because of John's description of Jesus on the island of Patmos (1:16). Paul writes that at Christ's return Christ will destroy the lawless one with the breath of his mouth (2 Thess. 2:8), for the battle that the Lord fights is not with a sword but with his word. This is spiritual warfare in which he battles spiritual forces of darkness in heavenly places (Eph. 6:12). This word coming forth from the mouth of Jesus carries out divine judgment to strike down the wicked (Rev. 19:21; see also 2:12, 16; Isa. 11:4; 49:2). Thus single-handedly Jesus strikes down his enemies.

The nations that rise up against the Lord will be struck down with his sword, which is a verbal sword, and with the rod of iron he will dash them to pieces as if they were an earthen pot. John quotes the Psalter, "You will rule them [the nations] with an iron scepter [rod of iron]" (Ps. 2:9). But here we encounter a difficulty, for in the Greek of Revelation the verb *to rule* is *poimainein,* which signifies "to shepherd" (see Rev. 2:27; 12:5).[40] Consequently, the rod of iron appears to be misplaced in the hand of the shepherd. But note that the Lord rules the nations as a shepherd-king who with this rod protects his own people and destroys his enemies. The rod of iron is as deadly a weapon as the word of God that comes from Jesus' mouth. And at the same time that word strengthens the believer. But if anyone does not accept this word of Jesus, it will condemn him at the last day (John 12:48).

The Greek is emphatic, for it literally reads: "he *himself* treads the winepress." Note also that John writes the present tense of the verb *to tread* to indicate a process. The Lord tramples the grapes, that is, the nations, under foot. John once more relies on Isaiah 63:2–3, where the word *winepress* refers to God's trampling the grapes of wrath (see also Lam. 1:15). And he returns to his discussion of the wine of God's fury (14:10) and the winepress of God's wrath (14:19–20). He combines these two metaphors of wine and winepress in one picture, which means that his enemies who have shed the blood of his saints (16:6; 17:6; 18:24) must now drink the wine of God's fury. There is one more image in this picture of the winepress: the Lord himself treads the grapes of God's wrath and while doing so soaks his garment in the blood of his enemies.[41]

16. And on his robe and on his thigh he has the name written,

KING OF KINGS AND LORD OF LORDS.

This verse presents a difficulty. John reveals a royal title, while in verse 12 he states that no one but the Lord knows his name. But this title has been revealed earlier albeit in reverse order (17:14) and has been a well-known designation in Old and New Testament times.[42] The title conveys the equivalent of superlative nouns, as if they

40. See the linguistic explanation of this point in the footnote on 2:27.

41. Compare Caird, *Revelation,* p. 246.

42. Refer to 1 Tim. 6:15; Deut. 10:17; Ps. 136:2–3; Dan. 2:47; 2 Macc. 13:4; 3 Macc. 5:35; *1 Enoch* 9.4. See Adolf Deissmann (*Light from the Ancient East,* trans. Lionel R. M. Strachan [reprint, Grand Rapids: Baker, 1978], p. 363), who notes its use in "very early Eastern history" but also in John's day "according to the evidence of parchments, coins and inscriptions."

were written as "the greatest King" and "the greatest Lord." Jesus Christ is the highest exalted Sovereign, who reigns with majesty, power, and authority.

Interpretations of the precise location of the words *robe* and thigh are many. These interpretations range from identifying robe and thigh—because the one covers the other—to having the name written on a sword in the place of a thigh. Whether we interpret the phrase to mean "on his robe, that is, on his thigh" or marshal evidence of ancient statues with names written on thighs, the fact remains that the picture is purely symbolic. The thigh is a figure of power and the robe a symbol of royal majesty. The majestic inscription applies to both places.

Last, the contrast between the Antichrist and the Christ is evident in regard to their names. The beast as the personification of the Antichrist wears on his heads blasphemous names (13:1), indeed he is covered with these names (17:3). But Jesus Christ wears outwardly on his robe and inwardly on his thigh the highest possible name in heaven and on earth: KING OF KINGS AND LORD OF LORDS.

Greek Words, Phrases, and Constructions in 19:11–16

Verse 11

ἐν δικαιοσύνῃ—this prepositional phrase "with justice" expresses manner and thus can be translated adverbially as "justly."

Verse 12

ἔχων—the masculine singular participle refers not to a name written on a diadem but to the name ascribed to the rider on the white horse.

Verse 13

βεβαμμένον—the perfect passive participle from the verb βάπτω (to dip) caused some copyists, in view of Isaiah 63:3, to change the reading to the perfect passive participle of either the verb ῥαίνω or ῥαντίζω (I sprinkle). The most difficult reading βεβαμμένον has given rise to the variants, and therefore, the rule that the harder reading is the original holds true.[43]

Verse 15

There are five successive genitives in the literal translation of the phrase "the wine-press of the *wine* of the *fury* of the *wrath* of *God* of the *Almighty*." This is the longest sequence of genitives in the Apocalypse.

Verse 16

Aramaic scholar Charles C. Torrey proposes that the Apocalypse was translated from Aramaic into Greek and that the translator inadvertently read the Hebrew and Aramaic

---

43. Metzger, *Textual Commentary*, pp. 686–87.

word *digĕleh* (his banner) as *ragĕleh* (his thigh).[44] This is an interesting observation, but there is no proof of the existence of an Aramaic manuscript of the Apocalypse.

Compare also Patrick W. Skehan, who contrasts the beast whose number is 666 (13:18) with the numerical value of the name "King of kings and Lord of lords" and calculates that the number is 777. He had to translate the title from Greek into Aramaic and delete the copulative *and* to arrive at this number.[45] But John does not speak of mystery in this text, for he indicates not a hidden but a revealed name.

---

2. The Final Battle against the Antichrist *19:17–21*

This is a battle in which evil is conquered and the beast and the false prophet are consigned to the lake of fire and sulfur. Christ fights without weapons of warfare against the agents of Satan and their followers. The saints are not engaged in this final battle against evil, which is banished forever.

17. And I saw an angel standing in the sun, and he cried out with a loud voice, saying to all the birds that fly in mid-heaven, "Come, gather together for the great banquet of God, 18. so that you may eat the flesh of kings and the flesh of generals, and the flesh of mighty men and the flesh of horses and their riders and the flesh of free persons and slaves, of small and great."

John saw an angel illumined by the sun (compare 12:1) who with a powerful voice addressed all the scavenger birds flying in the sky. By standing in the sun, the angel could be seen by all these birds, and his booming voice could be heard everywhere.

The writer borrowed a vision from the prophecy of Ezekiel, where the birds and beasts of prey are summoned by God to consume the flesh and blood of mighty men, princes, horses and riders, and soldiers (Ezek. 39:4, 17–20). The birds of prey who have been created to consume carcasses and thus remove unsightly scenes and dreadful smells have been called to be present at the aftermath of Christ's battle against the Antichrist and his followers. This, then, is the exact fulfillment of Ezekiel's prophecy against Gog in the land of Magog (Ezek. 38–39).

John paints a picture of contrasts with respect to the banquets mentioned in this chapter. The first banquet is that of the Lamb's wedding supper to which all the saints have been invited (vv. 7–9). The second is that of the vanquished to which all the birds of prey are summoned to do their task of removing the repulsive remains of the slain kings, generals, mighty men, horses and horsemen, and people of every level of society. This is an imitation, which now is not initiated by Satan but by God himself.

The magnitude of this second banquet is revealed in its description as the great banquet of God. It really pictures all God's opponents slain on the battle-

---

44. See C. C. Torrey, *The Apocalypse of John* (New Haven: Yale University Press, 1958), pp. 153–54; and his article "Armageddon," *HTR* 31 (1938): 237–48.

45. Patrick W. Skehan, "King of Kings and Lord of Lords (Apoc. 19:16)," *CBQ* 10 (1948): 398.

field of life; they are lying lifeless everywhere on the surface of this earth. No mention is made of the battle itself; only its outcome is important. God's final battle is against all the people who have followed the Antichrist and against all unrighteousness and deceit perpetrated by the evil one on all levels of society. In brief, the number of the slain includes everyone who is evil. All earthly power has come to an end, for Christ the King is Victor.

19. And I saw the beast and the kings of the earth and their armies gathered to make war against the one seated on the horse and against his army.

In the two previous verses (vv. 17–18), John painted a broad picture of the battle and its anticipated outcome. But in this verse, he has a close-up frame that clearly draws the battle lines between the Antichrist with his kings and armies (plural) and the Christ with his army (singular). The kings of the earth are those ten kings who are in the service of the Antichrist (see the commentary on 17:12).

In an earlier passage (17:13–14), John predicted that the forces of the beast, namely, the Antichrist, would fight the Lamb and his followers. And he said that the Lamb as Lord of lords and King of kings would conquer them as foretold in Psalm 2:2, "The kings of the earth take their stand and the rulers gather together against the LORD and against his Anointed One."

This is the great day of God Almighty on which the final battle against all the forces of evil is fought (see Rev. 16:14). All the armies of the Antichrist are pitched against the Christ and his heavenly army, while the outcome of the battle is never in doubt. We are not given any indication the army itself participates in this battle. Even though the term *war* appears in this verse, nothing is reported about the conflict itself. In the Greek text, the definite article precedes that term to indicate that this war conclusively determines the future of the beast and his ally the false prophet.

20. And the beast was caught and with him the false prophet who on his authority had performed signs by which he deceived those who received the mark of the beast and worshiped his image. These two were thrown alive into the lake of fire that burns with sulfur.

After the destruction and demise of the great prostitute (17:16), the beast and the false prophet are next. The beast is the Antichrist, and the beast coming up out of the earth is the false prophet (see commentary on 13:11; 16:13; 20:10). They are the two leaders and instigators in the service of Satan (13:1, 11). Throughout history, the false prophet led astray all the people who were deceived by the signs he performed. He forced all his followers to worship the beast—all those who had the mark of the beast on their right hand and forehead (13:13–16).

Now the beast and the false prophet are captured. Although John provides no details of this arrest, the verb *to capture* can be interpreted as someone forcefully laying hands on them. They are arrested because of their craftiness to deceive the multitudes on the face of the earth. The false prophet displayed miracles so that men, women, and children worshiped the Antichrist and as his loyal servants paid him obeisance. The beast coming up out of the sea holds political power over the masses of humanity; and the beast coming up out of the earth retains philosophical power over the human mind.

John writes that these two were thrown alive into the lake of fire that burns with sulfur. First, John presents an image taken from the prophecy of Daniel 7:11b, "I kept looking until the beast was slain and its body destroyed and thrown into the blazing fire." Daniel refers to a river of fire in the preceding verse (7:10); John turns the river into a lake of fire. The great prostitute was burned with fire, presumably in the same place (17:16). Likewise Satan will be thrown into the lake burning with sulfur (20:10), as will all those who worshiped the beast and his image and who had received the mark of the beast on their forehead and hand (14:9–10; 21:8).

Next, nothing is said about the identity of the Antichrist and the false prophet, so that we are unable to look for two distinct persons. We read that these two are thrown alive into the lake of fire, with the implication that they are spiritual beings whose immortality makes them suffer forever and ever. In their opposition to Christ these two were united throughout time, and now in their punishment they will endlessly be together.[46]

Third, the two leaders are not locked up in the Abyss, from which they can be released for a time (see 9:1; 11:7; 17:8; 20:3, 7). They are cast into a lake of fire in which all Christ's opponents and even the devil will remain eternally (20:10, 14–15; and 21:8). The term *lake* reveals a far broader area than the Abyss, which is a bottomless shaft. This lake is a vast area of fire that burns ceaselessly with the nauseating smell of sulfur. The impossibility of ever leaving this burning pool is self-evident, and everlasting pain and horror are the lot of those consigned to hell.[47] There is no indication anywhere in the Apocalypse that the wicked are annihilated upon completing a time of punishment. The scene is reminiscent of the destruction of Sodom and Gomorrah (Gen. 19:24; Ps. 11:6; Isa. 30:33; Ezek. 38:22).

21. And the rest were killed with the sword that proceeded from the mouth of the rider on the horse, and the birds gorged themselves on their flesh.

There are differences between the twosome (the beast and the false prophet) and their followers. First, these two leaders are thrown alive into the lake of fire and burning sulfur, that is, they are not going there through the gates of death. But their followers are killed with the sword, even though the language is symbolical. The sword of the Lord is the breath of his mouth (2 Thess. 2:8; see Rev. 19:15; 1:16).

Next, the remnant is slain with the word of God that testifies against them and puts them in a position of enduring shame and everlasting abhorrence. They are

---

46. Swete, *Revelation*, p. 258.

47. Consult Greijdanus, *Openbaring*, pp. 398–99; Beale (*Revelation*, p. 969) notes that 14:10–11 with its temporal phrases *forever and ever* and *day or night* and its descriptions of fire and sulfur "refer to eternal conscious torment and not ontological annihilation at one point in time." See Robert A. Peterson, *Hell on Trial: The Case for Eternal Punishment* (Phillipsburg, N.J.: Presbyterian and Reformed, 1995), pp. 195–98.

killed, which signifies that their power is forever taken from them. Their eternal destiny is the lake of fire.

And last, their slain bodies are not given a decent burial; instead, the birds of prey devour their flesh. The number of those who are slain is so large that all the birds that feed on carrion could stuff their craws with flesh to the point of overfill. Here is a picture of utter loathsomeness (Isa. 66:24).

Greek Words, Phrases, and Constructions in 19:17–21

Verse 17

ἕνα—the number one preceding a noun in the Apocalypse is equivalent to the indefinite article, hence "an angel" (compare 8:13; 9:13; 18:21).

Verse 18

σάρκας—this accusative plural noun occurs five times in verse 18 (the genitive plural in verse 21). The plural form conveys the totality of the slaughter.

Verse 20

ἐνώπιον—usually translated "in the presence of," but it can mean "on his behalf" or "on his authority."[48]

Verse 21

τὰ ὄρνεα ἐχορτάσθησαν—"the birds gorged themselves." In New Testament Greek, the neuter plural noun is usually followed by a verb in the singular when the noun is nonpersonal and abstract. Nouns referring to persons or living beings are often followed by the plural verb.[49]

---

48. Bauer, p. 271; Aune, *Revelation 17–22*, p. 1045.

49. Friedrich Blass and Albert Debrunner, *A Greek Grammar of the New Testament and Other Early Christian Literature*, trans. and rev. Robert Funk (Chicago: University of Chicago Press, 1961), §133.1.

20

Satan's Defeat and the Judgment Day

(20:1–15)

Outline (continued)

VIII. Vision 7: New Heaven and New Earth (20:1–22:5)
- A. Defeat of Satan and Death (20:1–15)
    1. The Binding of Satan (20:1–3)
    2. The Saints in Heaven (20:4–6)
    3. Satan's Defeat and Demise (20:7–10)
    4. The Judgment Day (20:11–15)

20 1 And I saw an angel coming down out of heaven who had the key of the Abyss and a great
chain in his hand. 2 And he took hold of the dragon, the ancient serpent, who is called
the Devil and Satan, and he bound him for a thousand years. 3 And he cast him into the
Abyss and closed and sealed it above him, so that he might no longer deceive the nations
until the thousand years were completed. After these things it is necessary to release him for a short
time.

4 And I saw thrones and they that sat on them. And judgment was given to them. And I saw the
souls of those who were beheaded because of their testimony of Jesus and the Word of God, and
those who had not worshiped the beast or his image and had not received his mark on their forehead
and on their hand. And they lived and reigned with Christ a thousand years. 5 (And the rest of the
dead lived not until the thousand years were completed.) This is the first resurrection. 6 Blessed and
holy is the one who has part in the first resurrection. Over these the second death has no authority,
but they will be priests of God and of Christ and will reign with him a thousand years.

7 And when the thousand years are completed, Satan will be released from his prison. 8 And he
will go forth to deceive the nations which are in the four corners of the earth, Gog and Magog, to
gather them for war, whose number is as the sand of the sea. 9 And they went up over the breadth of
the earth and encircled the camp of the saints and the beloved city. And fire came down from heaven
and devoured them. 10 And the devil who deceived them was cast into the lake of fire and sulfur,
where both the beast and the false prophet are. And they will be tormented day and night forever
and ever.

11 And I saw a great white throne and him who sat on it, from whose face earth and heaven fled,
and their place was not found anymore. 12 And I saw the dead, both great and small, standing before
the throne. And the books were opened, and another book was opened, which is the book of life,
and the dead were judged according to their works by the things written in these books. 13 And the
sea gave up the dead that were in it, and Death and Hades gave up the dead that were in them, and
each one was judged according to his works. 14 And Death and Hades were cast into the lake of fire.
This is the second death, the lake of fire. 15 And if anyone is not found written in the book of life,
he is cast into the lake of fire.

VIII. Vision 7: New Heaven and New Earth 20:1–22:5

The last half of the preceding chapter (19:11–21) revealed the removal of the Antichrist and the prophet of falsehood from this earth and the demise of their followers. John's message in that chapter is that Christ Jesus is victorious and so are the saints. Also, the defeat of the anti-Christian forces signifies the cessation of evil. All that remains for John to relate in chapter 20 is the removal of Satan and the end of Death and Hades.

In the first part of this chapter (vv. 1–10), John presents an additional aspect of the end of time. In it John directs full attention to Satan's imprisonment, release, defeat, and damnation. Afterward John focuses his attention on the last judgment, which eventuates in the elimination of Death and Hades and the dispatch of unbelievers to a place prepared for them (vv. 11–15).

We note that chapter 20 presents a picture that is concurrent with preceding chapters that relate repetitive scenes on the judgment. Thus, the twenty-four elders announce the time of judgment (11:18) and the Son of Man inaugurates the Judgment Day (14:14–20). God pours out his wrath in anticipation of the final judgment (16:17–21), the rider on a white horse judges with justice to defeat his enemies (19:11–21), and God opens the books to judge each person at the last judgment (20:11–15). In short, Revelation is a volume of parallels that progress with each successive cycle.

The cyclical method of interpreting Revelation 20 can be illustrated exegetically. First, the Greek text, but not the translation, features the definite article in the expression *the war* at three places that feature the final battle (16:14; 19:19; 20:8). Next, the word *war* (Greek *polemos*) occurs nine times in the Apocalypse, but only the last three have the definite article and thus stress the ultimate conflict at the end of cosmic time. Last, the literal wording of the Greek text is nearly identical in all three places: "to gather them for the war" (16:14); "gathered to make the war" (19:19); and "to gather them for the war" (20:8).[1] These three chapters cyclically refer to the end of time when the last battle is fought.

There is a close connection between chapters 12 and 20 in regard to the binding of Satan. Satan lost the battle against the archangel Michael and his warriors when he and his angels were cast out of heaven (12:7–9). Consequently Satan was restricted in his activities, for God himself protected the woman representing the saints who obey his commands and believe Jesus' testimony (12:13–17). God binds Satan in such a way that he cannot deceive the nations anymore (20:3). The devil is unable to stop the advance of Christ's gospel across the globe. Therefore, the decision to bind Satan was first made in chapter 12 and not in chapter 20.[2]

A linear interpretation of chapters 19 and 20 encounters a difficulty with respect to the anti-Christian forces that were completely destroyed in 19:18, 21 and reappear in 20:8. Chapter 19 offers no indication that, at the conclusion of the final battle, survivors were able to regroup for another confrontation. Instead it conveys the concept of finality, for Christ as King of kings and Lord of lords is victorious.

1. William Hendriksen, *More Than Conquerors* (reprint, Grand Rapids: Baker, 1982), p. 195; R. Fowler White, "Reexamining the Evidence for Recapitulation in Rev. 20:1–10," *WTJ* 51 (1989): 319–44, especially 328–30; Gregory K. Beale, *The Book of Revelation: A Commentary on the Greek Text,* NIGTC (Grand Rapids: Eerdmans, 1998), p. 980.

2. Abraham Kuyper, *The Revelation of St. John,* trans. John Hendrik de Vries (Grand Rapids: Eerdmans, 1935), pp. 280–81; Herman Bavinck, *The Last Things: Hope for This World and the Next,* ed. John Bolt and trans. John Vriend (Grand Rapids: Eerdmans, 1996), p. 112; Hendriksen, *More Than Conquerors,* pp. 188–90; Philip Edgcumbe Hughes, *The Book of the Revelation: A Commentary* (Leicester: Inter-Varsity; Grand Rapids: Eerdmans, 1990), p. 209; R. C. H. Lenski, *The Interpretation of St. John's Revelation* (Columbus: Wartburg, 1943), pp. 574–77.

A last preliminary remark. As is evident, Revelation on the whole and chapter 20 in particular demonstrate symbolism. For instance, the chain with which the angel binds Satan is not a customary string of metal links; neither is the key to the Abyss a metallic object nor are the thousand years chronologically ten centuries. The term *key* appears in 1:18, where Jesus notes that he holds the keys of Death and Hades; in 3:7 Jesus says that he holds the key of David; and in 9:1 an angel described as a star holds the key to the Abyss. In all these passages the word signifies authority. It is clear that a spirit cannot be shackled with a chain but can be restricted by a divine command. And the expression *one thousand* in a book that is filled with symbolic numbers intimates a multitude, that is, a large number.

A. Defeat of Satan and Death
20:1–15

This chapter can be divided into four parts: the binding of Satan (vv. 1–3); the saints with Christ (vv. 4–6); Satan's defeat and demise (vv. 7–10); and the last judgment (vv. 11–15). The chapter actually presents four pictures that differ from each other but are intimately related. The first one shows the binding of Satan. Then after Satan is bound, we see a picture of what happens to the saints. The third one portrays Satan's release and ruin, and the last one depicts the Judgment Day. The first and the second occur contemporaneously; the third and fourth follow each other sequentially. John opens his photo album, as it were, and shows us various images of the end time. They are synchronic, describing events that happen simultaneously in a designated period.[3]

The first three verses of the chapter present an earthly aspect of the millennium. The second segment (vv. 4–6) depicts a heavenly aspect of that period. The next few verses (vv. 7–10) once again portray an earthly aspect, and the last five verses (vv. 11–15) picture a heavenly aspect of the Judgment Day.

1. The Binding of Satan
20:1–3

1. And I saw an angel coming down out of heaven who had the key of the Abyss and a great chain in his hand.

John's term *I saw* need not be seen as a chronological succession. The expression refers to one of the numerous pictures he received and recorded (e.g., 19:11, 17, 19; 20:4, 11, 12). The one here describes an angel coming down out of heaven (compare 10:1; 18:1). God sends him to the Abyss (9:1) with a key to open it and with a great chain in his hand to lay hold of the archenemy Satan. Notice that in this and subsequent verses nothing is said about the victorious

3. Elisabeth Schüssler Fiorenza, *The Book of Revelation: Justice and Judgment* (Philadelphia: Fortress, 1985), p. 47. She comments that Revelation is not a continuous development of events from beginning to end, but rather it "consists of pieces or mosaic stones arranged in a certain design, which climaxes in a description of the final eschatological event."

Christ. The verse is reminiscent of the warfare in heaven when Michael and his angels defeated Satan and his horde and dispatched them to the earth (12:7–9). Now in this scene an angel descends to limit Satan's influence by consigning him to the bottomless pit, also known as hell. The Abyss is the place where demons are kept, but at times they are released from it (see 9:1; Luke 8:31). At the end of time they will have to exchange it permanently for the lake of fire and burning sulfur.

2. And he took hold of the dragon, the ancient serpent, who is called the Devil and Satan, and he bound him for a thousand years. 3. And he cast him into the Abyss and closed and sealed it above him, so that he might no longer deceive the nations until the thousand years were completed. After these things it is necessary to release him for a short time.

a. "And he took hold of the dragon." The object of the angel's mission is to make an arrest. This is no ordinary arrest but the apprehension of the dragon himself, who is also known as the ancient serpent (Gen. 3:1–7), the Devil, and Satan (see commentary on 12:9). Satan's trajectory is from heaven, to earth, to the Abyss.

b. "And he bound him for a thousand years." The angel overpowered Satan and bound him. But this binding refers to restrictions God placed on the evil one in the form of depriving him of power and authority. Satan and his fallen angels are "bound as to a rope, which can be more or less lengthened."[4] They can try to free themselves, but it is impossible for them to be released. John intended not a literal binding but a figurative restraint whereby Satan is unable to perform his wickedness as he did prior to his restriction. From Jesus, John learned that to enter the house of the strong man, who is Satan, binding him had to be done first (Matt. 12:26–29; Mark 3:26–27). Jesus told him that he had seen Satan falling as lightning from heaven (Luke 10:18). Simon Peter writes that God did not spare fallen angels, among whom was Satan, but cast them into hell, binding them with chains of darkness to await their judgment (2 Pet. 2:4). Peter is fully aware of Satan's wrath (Rev. 12:17). The devil is still active, prowling like a roaring lion seeking erring sinners whom he may devour (1 Pet. 5:8).[5] But Satan can go only as far as God permits (compare Job 1:12; 2:6). Paul writes about the man of lawlessness, who, as the leader of evil forces, is being restrained (2 Thess. 2:6). Even though these words are cryptic, they reveal that the evil one is kept in check.

If the binding of Satan is a symbolic act, then it is reasonable to assume that the term *a thousand years* may also be interpreted symbolically. The literature on this term is open to either a literal or a symbolical interpretation with roots in

4. Oscar Cullmann, *Christ and Time: The Primitive Christian Conception of Time and History*, trans. Floyd V. Filson (London: SCM, 1951), p. 198.

5. Consult W. J. Grier, *The Momentous Event* (London: Banner of Truth Trust, 1970), pp. 11–13. Beale (*Revelation*, p. 985) observes that Satan's binding became effective after Christ's resurrection "and it lasts throughout most of the age between Christ's first and second comings." See also Augustine *City of God* 20.7.

various settings.[6] In the early church, the number one thousand was explained in the light of Psalm 90:4, "For a thousand years in your sight are like a day that has just gone by, or like a watch in the night" (see also 2 Pet. 3:8).

Numerous theologians espouse a literal explanation of exactly one thousand years as the interval between Jesus' return to earth and the end of time. But there are objections to this view. First, the word *millennium*, derived from the Latin words *mille* (thousand) and *annus* (year), occurs six times in this chapter and nowhere else in any other New Testament eschatological teachings (vv. 2, 3, 4, 5, 6, 7). In his eschatological discourse (Matt. 24), Jesus says nothing about a thousand-year reign with the saints on this earth. In their respective epistles, Paul and Peter mention no millennial interim reign of Christ on earth. Next, the New Testament teaches but one return of Christ and not two. Third, the first mention of a thousand-year period (v. 2) is "the devil's millennium" extending from Satan's stay in the Abyss until he is consigned to the lake of fire forever.[7] Fourth, a literal interpretation of this number in a book of symbolism and especially in this chapter filled with symbols is indeed a considerable obstacle. And last, one thousand is ten to the third power and denotes fullness. It is therefore more in line with the tone and tenor of Revelation to interpret the term metaphorically.

c. "And he cast him into the Abyss and closed and sealed it above him." How is it possible for Satan to be active on this earth when the angel hurls him into the bottomless pit and closes it with a seal? For Satan to be set free is unattainable. But that is not the point, for the three verbs *to cast, to close,* and *to seal* express finality in depriving Satan of his erstwhile power. In fact, these three actions may be idiomatic and equivalent to our expression "signed, sealed, and delivered."[8] When Satan was cast out of heaven and hurled to the earth, he lost the authority he once possessed (12:9).

d. "So that he might no longer deceive the nations until the thousand years were completed." Throughout the Old Testament era, only the nation of Israel received God's revelation (Rom. 3:2). Although the names of individual non-Jews were recorded in God's register and adopted into his family (Ps. 87:4–6), Gentile nations were devoid of his Word. But all that changed after Jesus' resurrection when he instructed his followers to make disciples of all nations (Matt. 28:19–20). Since Jesus' ascension, Satan has been unable to stop the advance of the gospel of salvation. He has been bound and is without authority, while the

6. Apocryphal and pseudepigraphical literature alludes to a messianic kingdom; see *1 Enoch* 91.12–13; 93.1–14; *2 Enoch* 32.2–33.2; *Sibylline Oracles* 3.1–62; 4 Ezra (=2 Esdras) 7:28–29; 13:32–36; *2 Baruch* 29.4–30.1; 39.7; 40.3; 72.2–4. Also see *Barnabas* 15.3–9; Irenaeus *Against Heresies* 5.32–36; Justin Martyr *Dialogue with Trypho* 81.

7. Gerhard A. Krodel, *Revelation,* ACNT (Minneapolis: Augsburg, 1989), p. 70.

8. M. Eugene Boring, *Revelation,* Interpretation (Louisville: Knox, 1989), p. 200; see also Wilfrid J. Harrington, *Revelation,* SP 16 (Collegeville, Minn.: Liturgical Press, 1993), p. 196. David E. Aune (*Revelation 17–22,* WBC 52C [Nashville: Nelson, 1998], p. 1083) notes that the binding and sealing of an evil spirit with incantations from Jewish Aramaic texts means that "the demon is conquered."

nations of the world around the globe have received the glad gospel tidings. The Son of God has taken possession of these nations (Ps. 2:7–8) and has deprived Satan of leading them astray during this gospel age. Christ is drawing to himself people from all these nations, and out of them God's elect will be saved and drawn into his kingdom. These nations receive the light of the world (John 8:12) and are no longer living in darkness and deceit. Satan is unable to check the mission outreach of the church, for he cannot prevent the nations from knowing the Lord. "By means of the preaching of the Word as applied by the Holy Spirit, the elect, from all parts of the world, are brought from darkness to the light."[9]

The Apocalypse records the word *nation* twenty-three times. Of these, sixteen feature the plural with the definite article: *the nations.*[10] Of these sixteen, the last three (21:24, 26; 22:2) refer to the redeemed nations in glory, whereas the other thirteen occurrences suggest that they belong to the class of Gentile nations. The meaning of the word in this verse is that Satan has lost his deceptive power over the nations of the world during the millennium. It seems best to take the term *one thousand* symbolically to refer to an indefinite period between the ascension of Jesus and his return. In brief, the passage teaches an eschatology that presently is in the process of being realized.[11]

e. "After these things it is necessary to release him for a short time." This is now the third time in Revelation that John speaks of *a short time* (6:11; 12:12). How long is this period? We note first the reading *it is necessary,* which speaks of divine necessity. That is, God the Father knows the exact time of Jesus' return (Matt. 24:36), and from his heavenly perspective the period of chronological time is brief. Next, the expression *short time* should be understood in relation to the thousand years. The one is short, the other long. John's message to the saints on earth is that there will come a brief interval during which Satan will be released. Jesus promises that "for the sake of the elect those days will be shortened" (Matt. 24:22). He ensures their safety, for Satan is unable to destroy them spiritually.

Greek Words, Phrases, and Constructions in 20:2

ὁ ὄφις ὁ ἀρχαῖος—the nominative case has its antecedent in τὸν δράκοντα, which is in the accusative. Some Greek manuscripts (adopted by the TR and the Majority Text) read

---

9. Hendriksen, *More Than Conquerors,* pp. 188–89. Consult S. Greijdanus, *De Openbaring des Heeren aan Johannes,* KNT (Amsterdam: Van Bottenburg, 1925), p. 403; Lenski, *Revelation,* pp. 575–76; Hughes, *Revelation,* pp. 209–11.

10. Rev. 2:26; 11:2, 18; 12:5; 14:8; 15:3, 4; 16:19; 18:3, 23; 19:15; 20:3, 8; 21:24, 26; 22:2. Note that 2:26; 12:5; and 19:15 are linked to Ps. 2:9 in which Christ rules the nations with an iron scepter, dashing them to pieces like pottery; 15:3 has a variant reading "King of the ages," while 15:4 derives from Psalm 86:9, "All the nations . . . will bring glory to your name"; 15:4 expresses God's universal sovereignty over the Gentile nations whom the Lord in his time will subdue. And last 11:2 is translated as "the Gentiles."

11. Colin Brown, *NIDNNT,* 2:702–3; Anthony A. Hoekema, *The Bible and the Future* (Grand Rapids: Eerdmans, 1979), pp. 173–74; Stanley J. Grenz, *The Millennial Maze: Sorting Out Evangelical Options* (Downers Grove: InterVarsity, 1992), p. 173.

the accusative case in conformity with the antecedent. But the rule of the harder reading prevails, for a change to conform is easier to explain than the opposite. Also, the use of the nominative in apposition with another case occurs often in the Apocalypse (e.g., 1:5; 2:13). Note the occurrence of participles as nominatives in apposition (2:20; 3:12; 8:9; 9:14; 14:12, 14).

---

2. The Saints in Heaven
20:4–6

Of the four pictures in this chapter, here is the second. Although John fails to report the place where the portrayal occurred, the context shows that the location is not earth but heaven. The vocabulary of thrones, judgment, and souls depicts a heavenly scene. Further, the term *throne* occurs forty-seven times in the Apocalypse. Apart from the references to Satan's throne and that of the beast (2:13; 13:2; 16:10), this term alludes to heaven. And the souls of decapitated bodies are in heaven with God.

Leon Morris notes that John is taking the reader behind the scenes and reveals what has happened to the martyrs who have died a physical death. They are alive because of their first resurrection, and in the presence of Christ they reign with him while Satan is bound.[12] John describes his vision in a Semitic literary style that coordinates relatively short clauses each beginning with the conjunction *and.*

4. And I saw thrones and they that sat on them. And judgment was given to them. And I saw the souls of those who were beheaded because of their testimony of Jesus and the Word of God, and those who had not worshiped the beast or his image and had not received his mark on their forehead and on their hand. And they lived and reigned with Christ a thousand years.

a. "And I saw thrones and they that sat on them. And judgment was given to them." This lengthy verse reveals at least three points: thrones of judgment; souls of martyrs; and a millennium of living and ruling with Christ. Let us begin with the thrones on which God's people sit for the purpose of judging. There are references to thrones and judging in the Old Testament (Dan. 7:9, 22) and the New Testament (Matt. 19:28; Luke 22:30; 1 Cor. 6:2). The saints in heaven have the honor and duty to judge the twelve tribes of Israel, the world, and angels; and they will rule with Christ. Indeed, God highly exalts the redeemed saints by giving them the privilege of judging human beings and angels. This judging alludes not to the final judgment but rather to the authority that the saints receive to rule as the Old Testament judges did.

John refers to thrones in connection with the twenty-four elders who function as representatives of God's people in heaven. They appear in the presence of God around the throne of God, reigning with the Lamb and worshiping the

---

12. Leon Morris, *Revelation,* rev. ed., TNTC (Leicester: Inter-Varsity; Grand Rapids: Eerdmans, 1987), p. 228.

one seated on the throne. They continue doing this, and there is no indication that they are told to cease reigning.[13] In other words, they are ruling on their thrones with Christ in heaven while Satan is bound on earth. Jesus promises the overcomers to sit with him on his throne (3:21), and this promise of reigning with him appears frequently in the Apocalypse (5:10; 20:4, 6; 22:5; and see 2 Tim. 2:12).

b. "And I saw the souls of those who were beheaded because of their testimony of Jesus and the Word of God." Next, let us consider the topic of the souls of martyrs. John is descriptive and precise in his wording, for he is not writing the expression *souls* as a synonym for persons; he refers to souls without bodies. He describes martyrs beheaded by Roman executioners. Their bodies returned to the dust of the earth and their souls to God in heaven; and these saints are forever with Christ. They are martyrs killed for their courage in witnessing for Jesus and proclaiming the Word of God. The parallel of 6:9 is significant: "I saw under the altar the souls of the ones slain because of the Word of God and because of the testimony they were holding." Throughout the Apocalypse John writes the phrases *Word of God* and *testimony of Jesus* (1:2, 9; 12:11, 17; 19:10; 20:4). Are only beheaded martyrs in view in this text? Certainly, John the Baptist was beheaded for teaching and preaching God's revelation, and James the son of Zebedee (Matt. 14:3–12; Acts 12:2). According to tradition, Paul was beheaded outside the city wall of Rome, but Peter was crucified upside down, and James the half-brother of Jesus was thrown from the temple. Surely they are included here. The apostle John lived to the end of the first century (A.D. 98) and died a natural death. Yet because he faithfully proclaimed Christ's gospel and taught the Scriptures, he was exiled to Patmos.

c. "And those who had not worshiped the beast or his image and had not received his mark on their forehead and on their hand." Does this verse mention two groups of saints (martyrs and other saints) or only one group? That is, does it suggest two groups of saints: those who were beheaded and those who died a natural death while being faithful to Jesus by their refusal to pay homage to the beast? No, not really. Wherever John mentions the concept of martyrdom for the sake of Jesus, the context seems to indicate the inclusion of all believers who have been obedient to their Lord. John does not imply that faithful saints differ from suffering martyrs (see commentary on 6:9; 17:6). Rather with the one clause he seeks to clarify the preceding clause. Satan and his henchmen do not exempt any true follower of Christ from oppression, hardship, and temptation. And, last, all true believers are overcomers who are invited to sit with Christ on his throne (3:21).[14]

By repeating the reference to the worship of the beast and the bearing of his mark on right hand and forehead (14:9, 11; 15:2; 16:2; 19:20), John states that

13. Floyd E. Hamilton, *The Basis of Millennial Faith* (Grand Rapids: Eerdmans, 1952), pp. 124–25.

14. John P. M. Sweet, *Revelation*, WPC (Philadelphia: Westminster, 1979), p. 288. Krodel (*Revelation*, p. 334) points to v. 9, which mentions the camp of the saints without restricting it to martyrs.

none of the saints has engaged in his worship and borne his mark. With this explanation he includes all the saints who have suffered for Christ in one way or another: abuse, banishment, deprivation, imprisonment, confiscation of goods and possessions. They have been barred from the marketplace and forbidden to buy or sell.

d. "And they lived and reigned with Christ a thousand years." The third aspect in this text is a millennium of living and ruling with Christ. The Greek verb *ezēsan* (they lived) occurs also in verse 5 with reference to the rest of the dead (see the commentary). Besides these two occurrences, the verb (in the singular) appears twice more in the Apocalypse: the one describes the resurrected Christ (2:8) and the other describes the beast who was wounded by the sword but lived in a parody of Jesus' resurrection (13:14). This same verb also appears in the parable of the lost son, where the father rejoices that his son who was dead is alive again (Luke 15:24, 32). The father states that his lost son has experienced a spiritual rebirth; similarly the saints have come to life spiritually.[15] When the saints depart from this earthly scene, they enter eternal life. They remain without their resurrected bodies until the return of Christ.

The saints live and rule with Christ a thousand years, but where is Christ? He is in heaven, where he sits on the throne and rules; all authority to rule in heaven and on earth has been given to him (Matt. 28:18). And the saints redeemed from sin and death are seated on heavenly thrones and are privileged to rule as royalty with Christ in heaven.

5. (And the rest of the dead lived not until the thousand years were completed.) This is the first resurrection.

Some translations (GNB, NCV, NIV) consider verse 5a a parenthetical interlude between verses 4 and 5b to express contrast. The Book of Revelation is filled with contrasts between good and evil, holy and profane, life and death. In this chapter the souls that enjoy eternal life are contrasted with the rest of the human race, who remain dead. Notice that John devotes much attention to the saints who receive eternal life but only one line to the unbelievers. God never grants "the rest of the dead" eternal life; they are cut off forever from the source of life and are condemned to remain forever separated from God. The emphasis in verse 5a is on the negated verb *to live*, which indicates that all those who have worshiped the beast and have his mark are devoid of spiritual life.

Verse 5a is not speaking about a resurrection that unbelievers will experience; they are dead and remain in that state. Nonetheless, both the Old and the New Testament speak about the resurrection of unbelievers.

- "Multitudes who sleep in the dust of the earth will awake: some to everlasting life, others to shame and everlasting contempt" (Dan. 12:2).

15. Robert H. Mounce (*The Book of Revelation*, rev. ed., NICNT [Grand Rapids: Eerdmans, 1998], p. 366 n. 10) notes that the New Testament lists forms of the verb *zaō* (I live) 140 times, "each of which determines its specific meaning in that instance."

- "Do not be amazed at this, for a time is coming when all who are in their graves will hear his [Jesus'] voice and come out—those who have done good will rise to live, and those who have done evil will rise to be condemned" (John 5:28–29).

John writes "until the thousand years were completed" and intimates that during the thousand-year period until the final judgment the wicked remain separated from God. When that period has come to an end, they appear before God at the final judgment and are consigned to "the second death." This means that they remain forever cut off from God in respect to body and soul.

The short sentence "This is the first resurrection" should be seen as the conclusion to verse 4, where the enthroned saints in heaven reign with Christ. The first resurrection, then, is a spiritual resurrection much the same as the second death is a spiritual death. The first one means eternal life in the presence of God, the second, complete separation from God. There is no doubt that the second resurrection, which John omits from this discussion, is a bodily phenomenon. And by comparison, if the second death is a spiritual death for the unbeliever, then the first death, which is not mentioned, refers to the physical death of the believer.

Here is a table showing the contrasts:[16]

Saints	Wicked
first (physical) death	first (physical) death
first (spiritual) resurrection	
	second (spiritual) death
second (physical) resurrection	second (physical) resurrection

We need not infer a first spiritual resurrection of the wicked, for without regeneration they remain dead in their transgressions and sins (Eph. 2:1; Col. 2:13). Their second spiritual death is in effect their eternal death, since they are forever cut off from God's grace extended to them during their life on earth.

The contrast is striking, because what is gain for the saints is loss for the wicked: the saints receive eternal life, but the wicked eternal death. Notice these points:

- the first (physical) death of the saints underlines their spiritual resurrection, which is eternal life;
- the first (physical) death of the wicked is separation from God, who is the source of life;

16. Consult Meredith G. Kline, "The First Resurrection," *WTJ* 37 (1975): 366–75; see also Meredith G. Kline, "The First Resurrection: A Reaffirmation," *WTJ* 39 (1976): 110–19; Beale, *Revelation*, p. 1005.

- the first (physical) death of the saints results in their entering heaven and exempts them from suffering a second spiritual death;
- the second (physical) resurrection of the wicked underlines their spiritual death;
- the second (spiritual) death of the wicked is eternal separation from God.

Those who belong to Christ die once but rise twice (spiritually and physically), whereas those who have rejected him rise once but die twice (physically and spiritually).[17]

6. Blessed and holy is the one who has part in the first resurrection. Over these the second death has no authority, but they will be priests of God and of Christ and will reign with him a thousand years.

John writes the fifth beatitude in a series of seven.[18] This is the only beatitude that has a double predicate: *blessed and holy.* Also, it is a beatitude that is in the singular but applies to all God's holy people. Holiness separates believers from the rest of humanity, for all believers will be priests of God and of Christ. Note that with the words *of God and of Christ* John places Christ once again on the same level as God and stresses his divinity (see 11:15; 21:22; and 22:3).

Because the saints are declared holy, they can never be subject to the second death. They will serve God and Christ as priests, and as kings they will reign with him. In two earlier passages (1:6; 5:10), John writes that the saints have been made priests, that is, they are priests in the kingdom now and in the future. He borrows the concepts *priests* and *kingdom* from the Old Testament, "Although the whole earth is mine, you will be for me a kingdom of priests and a holy nation" (Exod. 19:5b–6a; Isa. 61:6). The saints are a royal priesthood as they serve God as priests and with Christ rule in the kingdom (1 Pet. 2:9). Upon leaving this earthly scene and entering heaven, they will continue to function as priests and kings, because their intimate communion with Christ will last indefinitely (see v. 4).

Greek Words, Phrases, and Constructions in 20:4–5

ἔζησαν—this is the ingressive aorist (stressing the beginning of an action), "they came to life" (compare Luke 15:32). By contrast the aorist tense in ἐβασίλευσαν (they reigned) is constative (viewing the action as a whole).

---

3. Satan's Defeat and Demise
20:7–10

This is the third picture that John shows to his readers. It is a portrayal of Satan waging war against God. He not only loses this battle but he, too, like the beast and the false prophet, is thrown into the place of everlasting torment from which he can never escape. He is the first member of the trio, for Satan as the

17. Geoffrey B. Wilson, *Revelation* (Welwyn, England: Evangelical Press, 1985), p. 163.
18. Rev. 1:3; 14:13; 16:15; 19:9; 20:6; 22:7, 14.

father of the lie has been the instigator. But here he is the last one of the trio, because he must realize that he as the worst of the three is unable to escape the punishment God has reserved for him.

7. And when the thousand years are completed, Satan will be released from his prison. 8. And he will go forth to deceive the nations which are in the four corners of the earth, Gog and Magog, to gather them for war, whose number is as the sand of the sea.

By showing the reader different illustrations, John first reveals what happened to the beast and the false prophet who fought a battle against Christ and lost. They were thrown into the lake of fire and burning sulfur (19:19–21). This picture reveals nothing of Satan, but a second one taken from a different point of view exhibits Satan participating in that same battle and losing it. Satan suffers the same fate by being thrown into the lake of burning sulfur. This is the same battle we read of in 19:19, and John is providing two sketches of the same event (see also 16:14).

Near the end of the period between the ascension and return of Christ, Satan will be released from his restrictions. He himself will not break loose from his prison, but God will allow him to freely deceive the nations once more as in the ages prior to the Christian era. This means that he can muster his forces to disperse falsehood worldwide, lead the masses of mankind astray, and wage war against God's people. At present non-Christian religions together with secularism are spearheading the lie, causing humanity to live in spiritual darkness, and fiercely persecuting Christians on every continent.

John writes that Satan "will go forth to deceive the nations which are in the four corners of the earth." The devil gathers his followers from everywhere on the face of this earth, and he controls the masses with the lie. His forces are numberless and a vast army reflects his awesome power. The entire non-Christian world from east to west and north to south is at his command.

These forces like those of *Gog and Magog* mentioned in Ezekiel 38 and 39 are pitted against God's faithful people.[19] Ezekiel predicted that a vast army from the north would come and invade Israel. The multitude of soldiers would be so large that it would cover the countryside like sand on the seashore (Josh. 11:4; Judg. 7:12; 1 Sam. 13:5). The phrase *as sand on the seashore* is an idiomatic expression signifying an innumerable multitude.

According to Ezekiel, the invasion takes place during the messianic age, while in Revelation John places the war of Gog and Magog at the conclusion of this gospel age. Gog is the personal name of the prince of Meshech and Tubal in Asia Minor (Ezek. 39:1) and of a descendant of Reuben (1 Chron. 5:4), and the *ma* in Magog may mean "*land* of Gog" (see Gen. 10:2). The names do not refer to particular nations, for neither Gog nor Magog can be identified with any degree of certainty. They are symbolic terms that allude to extensive forces assembled from "the four corners of the earth," not from one or two nations.

19. Consult SB, 3:831–40; Dieter Sänger, *EDNT*, 1:267; Karl Georg Kuhn, *TDNT*, 1:789–91.

According to Augustine, these nations will rise up against the church in a final worldwide protest.[20]

9. And they went up over the breadth of the earth and encircled the camp of the saints and the beloved city. And fire came down from heaven and devoured them.

The construction *and they went up* is generally used of Jerusalem, which is located at an elevation of about 2,500 feet. Although the Mount of Olives is higher by 150 feet, the expression always applies to the city of David (e.g., Ezra 1:3; Ps. 122:4; Jer. 31:6; John 2:13; 11:55; Acts 11:2; Gal. 2:1). Here there is no reference to Jerusalem but instead to *the breadth of the earth.* The wording by itself is unfamiliar and occurs only here (but see the Septuagint of Hab. 1:6; Dan. 12:2; Sirach 1:3). The entire clause indicates that these hostile forces come from the ends of the earth, that is, from everywhere, to fight their battle against God's people. This is not a new battle, for it is the same battle John described in 16:12–16; 17:14–18; and 19:11–21.

The battleground is the "camp of the saints and the beloved city" which the anti-Christian forces encircle. The words *camp* and *city* are a double symbol describing the saints on earth who face their spiritual enemies on a daily basis. The *camp* is a military term as in the encampment of the Israelites in the desert (e.g., Num. 5:1–4; Deut. 23:14). But here the "camp of the saints" includes true Christians from all peoples, nations, languages, and races.[21] The reference is to the church that faces the spiritual enemy of Satan's armies. A camp connotes a temporary abode and a city denotes a permanent dwelling. The expression *beloved city* (Sir. 24:11) likewise refers to God's people in whose heart the Holy Spirit dwells. "There are only two cities or kingdoms in the Apocalypse—the city of Satan, where the beast and harlot are central, and the city of God, where God and the Lamb are central."[22] Elsewhere in the Apocalypse we see that where the saints gather, there is the city of God; and where immorality and profanity abound, there is the city of Satan (11:2, 8). Indeed Jesus calls the overcomers "the city of my God" (3:12). The beloved city is the spiritual dwelling place of the saints.

God sends down fire from heaven to devour his enemies. The incalculable multitude gathered to wage war against the saints ought not to frighten them because God is their protector. God's enemies are unable to escape when the cup

20. Augustine *City of God* 20.11. See Henry Barclay Swete, *Commentary on Revelation* (1911; reprint, Grand Rapids: Kregel, 1977), p. 268. Harry R. Boer (*The Book of Revelation* [Grand Rapids: Eerdmans, 1979], p. 133) observes that apart from Ezekiel, "the Old Testament does not know a nation by the name of Magog nor a king by the name of Gog." In Revelation the names are genealogical and do not refer to a specific country and ruler.

21. The expression "the peace of God in the camps of his saints" appears in the War Scroll of Qumran (1QM 3.5). The word *camps* is a Hebrew plural that represents the singular. See Aune, *Revelation 17–22,* p. 1098.

22. Alan F. Johnson, *Revelation,* in *The Expositor's Bible Commentary,* ed. Frank E. Gaebelein (Grand Rapids: Zondervan, 1981), 12:588.

of his wrath is full. He will destroy them with fire from heaven (2 Kings 1:10, 12; Ezek. 39:6).

10. And the devil who deceived them was cast into the lake of fire and sulfur, where both the beast and the false prophet are. And they will be tormented day and night forever and ever.

There is a purposeful repetition in the Apocalypse with reference to the lake of fire and sulfur. This is the presumed place where the great prostitute was burned with fire (17:16); the beast and the false prophet are cast into this fiery lake (19:20); and as the last one, Satan shares a similar destiny. In the second half of Revelation (chaps. 12–22), Satan is mentioned first (chap. 12), then the beast out of the sea and the beast out of the earth (chap. 13), and last the great prostitute (chap. 17). With respect to their destruction, Babylon the Great as the prostitute who suffers defeat and destruction is mentioned first (chap. 18), then the beast and the false prophet (chap. 19), and last Satan (chap. 20). Satan being first and last reflects an imitation of Christ, who is the first and the last, the beginning and the end (1:17; 2:8; 22:13). The difference, however, is one of life and doom.

I interpret the picture of Satan's demise as one that is taken at the same time as when the beast and the false prophet are cast into the lake of fire. These three were waging the same war in which all of them were defeated and destroyed. John portrays Satan as the loser, the one who sought to destroy the male child but failed (12:5). Satan fought a war in heaven and lost (12:9), was bound and kept in the Abyss (20:3), and was dispatched to his final destiny by being cast into the lake of fire and burning sulfur.

The infamous trio (Satan, the beast, and the false prophet) will be tormented day and night forever and ever. First, notice that the expression *day and night* also occurs in the throne room scene where the four living creatures sing praises to God day and night without ceasing (4:8). By contrast those who are cast into the lake of fire are tormented day and night forever and ever (see also 14:11). Next, all they whose names are not recorded in the book of life suffer a similar fate and will be eternally with Satan and the two beasts (v. 15). Third, Scripture nowhere teaches that their torment will eventually come to an end. On the contrary, Jesus said, "Depart from me, you who are cursed, into the *eternal* fire prepared for the devil" (Matt. 25:41, emphasis added).[23] Last, the torment that this trio must suffer is one of spiritual and mental agony. They enter this eternal state of suffering at the time when all the ungodly appear before the judgment seat. At that moment all of them enter their "second death," which means that they are forever separated from the living God.

23. Robert A. Peterson, *Hell on Trial: The Case for Eternal Punishment* (Phillipsburg, N.J.: Presbyterian and Reformed, 1995), pp. 89–90.

Greek Words, Phrases, and Constructions in 20:8–10

Verse 8

αὐτῶν—the pronoun is superfluous because of the relative pronoun ὧν at the beginning of the clause. This construction is common in the Apocalypse (3:8; 7:2, 9; 13:8, 12).

Verse 10

ὁ πλανῶν—the main verb is in the past tense, while this participle that precedes it is in the present. The participle signifies repetitiveness and reveals Satan's character.

4. The Judgment Day
20:11–15

The fourth picture reveals a heavenly aspect of the final judgment. In five verses John discloses the end of cosmic time and thus the end of world history. God's plan has been fulfilled and everything that had to be taken care of has been completed. God now calls everyone into his courtroom, and as the books are opened, everyone is judged in accord with divine justice. The division between the saints and the ungodly is irrevocable and final. The ones whose names are recorded in the book of life are forever with the Lord, but those who have spurned him are forever cut off.

11. And I saw a great white throne and him who sat on it, from whose face earth and heaven fled, and their place was not found anymore.

a. "And I saw a great white throne and him who sat on it." The uncomplicated description of the throne is preceded by two adjectives, *great* and *white*. John writes the Greek adjective *megas* (great) eighty times in Revelation to denote something that is larger than life. In this verse, John portrays God's throne in eschatological dimensions, because human beings are unable to fathom heavenly proportions. Further, the throne is *white*, the color depicting purity, holiness, and victory. But here it has the additional meaning of divine justice that eminently describes this throne. It means that not even one speck or wrinkle mars the whiteness of God's perfect justice.

When John portrays God, he avoids referring to him by name. In typical Jewish fashion, he circumscribes him with the words "him who sat on it [the throne]." Similarly, with reference to the throne room scene, John uses the same phraseology (4:2–3, 9–10; 5:1, 7, 13; 6:16). God is too awesome to be described in human terms. John undoubtedly had in mind "the Ancient of Days" taking his seat in the throne room to render judgment (Dan. 7:9–10). But also the Son of Man, namely, Jesus, sits on the throne of his Father to judge the living and the dead, spiritually speaking. In fact, there are numerous passages in the New Testament that testify to the fact that God has given the Son authority to pass judgment.[24] God judges the human race in and through his Son.

24. See Matt. 16:27; John 5:22; Acts 10:42; 17:31; Rom. 2:16; 14:9; 2 Cor. 5:10; compare *Sibylline Oracles* 2.230–44.

b. "From whose face earth and heaven fled, and their place was not found anymore." When the Judgment Day comes, God's creation will be affected in such a way that the earth will undergo a complete change. At that moment catastrophic events of enormous proportions will happen, for the atmosphere will be rolled up like a scroll to be replaced by the new heavens and the new earth (6:14; 16:20; 21:1; 2 Pet. 3:7, 10, 12–13). The old order disappears to give place to the new. The substance and the existence of this earth does not disappear, but its external form dissolves.[25] Although a literal interpretation would suggest the complete destruction and annihilation of the heavens and earth, Scripture teaches a meltdown of the elements but not their elimination (2 Pet. 3:10, 12). That is, they are renewed rather than replaced. In his sermon at Solomon's Colonnade, Peter spoke of a time when God would "restore everything" (Acts 3:21). Also Paul does not speak of a dissolution of creation but of its deliverance from bondage (Rom. 8:21). Not creation itself but the defects of the old order are removed to make place for the new.[26]

12. And I saw the dead, both great and small, standing before the throne. And the books were opened, and another book was opened which is the book of life, and the dead were judged according to their works by the things written in these books.

John is given a view of the last judgment, and he notices the dead standing before God's throne. All those who have died since God pronounced the curse on the human race appear before the Judge of all the earth. All of them are raised from the dead to receive a sentence of acquittal or condemnation, of life or "second death." All people great and small, that is, all human beings, appear before the Judge.

Repeatedly, John returns to Daniel's prophecy that portrays the Judgment Day with multitudes standing before the court of heaven; when the court is seated, the books are opened (Dan. 7:10; 12:1–2).[27] The books contain records of everyone's deeds of good and evil, for God knows everything that has been said and done and rewards each one accordingly (Rev. 2:23; 18:6; 22:12; Ps. 28:4; 62:12; Rom. 2:6). Thus, everyone is judged in accordance with the records, but this does not imply a doctrine of works righteousness. A person is judged and declared absolved on the basis of whether his or her name is recorded in the book of life. Scripture often refers to the book of life or a similar record.[28] In Revelation this book is of greater importance than the books that have recorded a per-

---

25. Irenaeus *Against Heresies* 5.36.1; Swete, *Revelation,* p. 271.

26. Hendriksen, *More Than Conquerors,* p. 196; George Eldon Ladd, *Commentary on the Revelation of John* (Grand Rapids: Eerdmans, 1972), p. 272; Wilson, *Revelation,* p. 165; G. B. Caird, *A Commentary on the Revelation of St. John the Divine* (London: Black, 1966), p. 259. For the view that the earth will be annihilated to be followed by a new creation, see Robert L. Thomas, *Revelation 8–22: An Exegetical Commentary* (Chicago: Moody, 1995), pp. 429, 439–40; John F. Walvoord, *The Revelation of Jesus Christ* (Chicago: Moody, 1966), pp. 305–6.

27. See also *1 Enoch* 89.61–63; 90.20; *2 Baruch* 24.1; *Ascension of Isaiah* 9.22.

28. See Exod. 32:32; Deut. 29:20; Dan. 12:1; Mal. 3:16; Luke 10:20; Phil. 4:3; see also *1 Enoch* 47.3.

son's deeds. The term *book of life* appears six times (3:5; 13:8; 17:8; 20:12, 15; 21:27), and the expression *books* occurs twice (v. 12). It is not because of anyone's works but because of God's electing grace that one's name is recorded in the book of life.[29] What then is the purpose of opening the books? Paul supplies the answer by saying, "For we must all appear before the judgment seat of Christ, that each may receive what is due him for the things done while in the body, whether good or bad" (2 Cor. 5:10). Although believers are responsible for their actions, they are forgiven through Christ. But those who have rejected Christ are held accountable for their words and deeds that testify against them.

For believers, God's grace goes hand in hand with human responsibility. Paul exhorts his readers to "continue to work out your salvation with fear and trembling, for it is God who works in you to will and to act according to his good purpose" (Phil. 2:12a–13). Scripture puts divine election on the one hand and human responsibility on the other, but it refrains from solving the mystery of where these two meet. God has graciously chosen his people through Christ, which is evident in the names of his people recorded in the book of life. They keep the Word of God and live by the testimony of Jesus, and they love God's commandments and cherish his precepts (Ps. 19:7–11; 119:127–28). They are the Lord's faithful witnesses even to the point of death (2:13; 6:9), and they perform good works to show their thankfulness to God, so that his name is honored and praised. By contrast, the incriminating evidence the opened books present against the unbelievers results in their banishment and never-ending separation from the living God (Matt. 25:46).

13. And the sea gave up the dead that were in it, and Death and Hades gave up the dead that were in them, and each one was judged according to his works.

a. "And the sea gave up the dead that were in it." The Bible views the sea as a source of fear.[30] Jonah overcame his fear when through willful disobedience he boarded a ship that set sail in a westerly direction directly opposite from Nineveh to which God had instructed the prophet to go (Jonah 1:3). Paul traveled mostly by land and occasionally sailed by ship, prompted by either haste or necessity. And John writing about the new heavens and the new earth, remarks that "the sea was no more" (21:1). The capricious and unpredictable sea has no place in the new creation.

Having claimed the lives of countless multitudes, the sea at God's command gave up the dead that were in it. The sea is symbolic of a demonic power that holds the invisible graves of its victims.[31] The ancients attached great importance to burial, which was denied those whom the sea had swallowed, and whose bodies decomposed. For a corpse to be left unburied, here because of the sea's power, was

29. Johannes Behm, *Die Offenbarung des Johannes,* Das Neue Testament Deutsch 11 (Göttingen: Vandenhoeck & Ruprecht, 1953), p. 104.

30. Consult John H. Paterson, "Sea," *ZPEB,* 5:316.

31. Jürgen Roloff, *The Revelation of John,* trans. J. E. Alsup (Minneapolis: Fortress, 1993), p. 232. *First Enoch* 61.5 states, "These measures shall reveal all the secrets of the depths . . . and those who have been devoured by the fish of the sea, that they may return." See also Isbon T. Beckwith, *The Apocalypse of John* (1919; reprint, Grand Rapids: Baker, 1979), p. 749.

an act of irreverence (compare Jer. 8:1–2; 14:16; Ezek. 29:5). Some scholars note that the disappearance of heaven and earth (v. 12) seems to conflict with the presence of the sea. But this is a matter of authorial freedom of placing "events in the reverse of their logical order (see 3:3, 17; 5:5; 6:4; 10:4, 9; 22:14)."[32]

b. "And Death and Hades gave up the dead that were in them, and each one was judged according to his works." If the sea is a power that holds the dead, so are Death and Hades, which are always mentioned together in the Apocalypse (v. 14; 1:18; 6:8).[33] Jesus holds the keys of both Death and Hades, depriving them of their authority. Now is the time for judging to determine the eternal destiny of every individual, regardless of whether death was by drowning, murder, or natural causes. Aside from the fact that multitudes of sinners stand before God's judgment seat, the records of each person will be carefully reviewed with verdicts of either innocent or guilty. There is neither time nor place for repentance, because repentance belonged to the cosmic era. The verdicts are irrevocable.

14. And Death and Hades were cast into the lake of fire. This is the second death, the lake of fire. 15. And if anyone is not found written in the book of life, he is cast into the lake of fire.

The phrase *lake of fire* occurs only in Revelation, and that for a total of six times (19:20; 20:10, 14 [twice], 15; 21:8). John explains the significance of this phrase by identifying it as *the second death.* This is the place where the wicked are forever separated from the living God to suffer eternally the torments of hell. It is the place in which the wicked spend eternity. But how do we understand the terms *Death* and *Hades*? First, Death is a state and Hades a place. Next, these two are intricately connected, as in the fourth seal where the rider on the pale horse is Death, and Hades is following closely behind him (6:8). Hades as the place where the souls of unbelievers are kept is not to be identified as the grave in which the bodies of both believers and unbelievers repose. By contrast, hell is the place of endless suffering. When both Death and Hades are cast into the lake of fire, the authority they exercised in cosmic time has ended.[34]

If Death and Hades are cast into the lake of fire, which is the same as the second death, will their authority continue in that state and place? Their temporary power will become a permanent power in the lake of fire over the unbelievers suffering in hell.[35] The anguish and distress of the wicked in hell is unimagin-

32. Aune, *Revelation 17–22,* p. 1102. R. H. Charles (*A Critical and Exegetical Commentary on the Revelation of St. John,* ICC [Edinburgh: Clark, 1920], 2:194–95) calls this stanza "a hopeless confusion of thought, which can only be due to deliberate change of the text." So he changes the wording, without manuscript proof, from "and the *sea* gave up the dead" to "and the *treasuries* gave up the dead" (pp. 196, 442).

33. Richard Bauckham, *The Climax of Prophecy* (Edinburgh: Clark, 1993), pp. 69–70.

34. Consult John M. Court, *Myth and History in the Book of Revelation* (Atlanta: John Knox, 1979), p. 65.

35. Beale, *Revelation,* p. 1035; J. Webb Mealy, *After the Thousand Years,* JSNTSup 70 (Sheffield: Sheffield Academic Press, 1992), p. 181. By contrast, Harrington (*Revelation,* p. 206) states that the second death does not mean eternal torture but only that someone no longer exists at death.

able. The parable of the rich man (Luke 16:19–31) describes hell as agony, fire, and a place of torment. There the rich man was cut off from Abraham and Lazarus in heaven, and there he suffered the second death that is both spiritual and physical.

John comes to the conclusion of his judgment vision, and once more he stresses the lot of the wicked. Their names are not recorded in the book of life, and therefore they are thrown into the lake of fire. "Not every lost person will undergo the sufferings of a Judas! God will be perfectly just, and each person will suffer precisely what he deserves."[36]

The comfort God's people receive is that their names are recorded in the book of life; they are the possession of the Lamb who was slain for them. John links the expression *book of life* to the Lamb (13:8; 21:27). To be forever with the Lord is the reward he grants his people whose names are in this book.

Greek Words, Phrases, and Constructions in 20:11–13

Verse 11

οὗ ἀπὸ τοῦ προσώπου—the construction is disputable because the normal flow would be to place the possessive personal pronoun αὐτοῦ following the noun instead of the genitive relative pronoun at the beginning (compare Jer. 22:25 LXX).

Verse 13

ἐκρίθησαν ἕκαστος—the plural verb is followed by the singular subject, which is understood as distributive.

---

36. Hoekema, *The Bible and the Future,* p. 273.

21

The New Jerusalem

(21:1–27)

Outline (continued)

B. The New Jerusalem and the Tree of Life (21:1–22:5)
   1. God and His People (21:1–8)
   2. The Holy City (21:9–14)
   3. The Adornment of the City (21:15–21)
   4. The Light of the City (21:22–27)

21 1 And I saw the new heaven and the new earth, for the first heaven and the first earth went
away; and the sea was no more. 2 And I saw the holy city, the new Jerusalem, coming down
out of heaven from God prepared as a bride adorned for her husband. 3 And I heard a
loud voice from the throne saying, "Look, the tabernacle of God is with people, and he
will dwell with them, and they will be his people, and God himself will be with them and be their God.
4 And he will wipe away every tear from their eyes, and there will no longer be death, or grief, or
crying, nor will there be pain anymore, because the first things passed away."

5 And the one seated on the throne said, "Look, I am making all things new," and he said, "Write,
for these words are faithful and true." 6 And he said to me, "It is done. I am the Alpha and the
Omega, the Beginning and the End. I will give freely to the one who is thirsty from the fountain of
water of life. 7 He that overcomes will inherit these things, and I will be a God to him, and he will be
a son to me. 8 To the cowardly and the unbelievers and those who are detested and the murderers
and the fornicators, and the sorcerers and idolaters, and to all who are deceivers, their part is in the
lake of fire and sulfur, which is the second death."

9 And there came one of the seven angels who held the seven bowls full of the last seven plagues.
He talked with me and said, "Come, I will show you the bride, the wife of the Lamb." 10 And he brought
me in the Spirit to a great and high mountain, and he showed me the holy city Jerusalem that came
down out of heaven from God. 11 It had the glory of God, and its brilliance was like a precious stone,
as a crystallized jasper stone. 12 It had a great, high wall with twelve gates and at the gates twelve angels,
and on the gates the names of the twelve tribes of Israel were inscribed: 13 on the east three gates, and
on the north three gates, and on the south three gates, and on the west three gates. 14 And the wall of
the city had twelve foundations and on them were the twelve names of the twelve apostles of the Lamb.

15 And the one who spoke with me had a golden measuring reed to measure the city and its gates
and its walls. 16 And the city was foursquare and its length was like its breadth. And he measured the
city with a reed at twelve thousand stadia; its length and breadth and height were equal. 17 And he
measured its wall, 144 cubits, according to the human measure, which the angel used. 18 And the
wall was built of jasper, and the city was of pure gold like clear glass. 19 The foundations of the wall
of the city were adorned with every kind of precious stone. The first foundation was jasper, the second sapphire, the third chalcedony, the fourth emerald, 20 the fifth sardonyx, the sixth carnelian,
the seventh chrysolite, the eighth beryl, the ninth topaz, the tenth chrysoprase, the eleventh jacinth,
and the twelfth amethyst. 21 And the twelve gates had twelve pearls, each one of the gates was a single
pearl. And the street of the city was pure gold like transparent glass.

22 And I did not see a temple in it, for the Lord God Almighty and the Lamb are its temple. 23 And
the city did not need the sun or the moon to illumine it, for the glory of God illumines it and the Lamb
is its lamp. 24 And the nations will walk through its light, and the kings of the earth bring their glory
into it. 25 And its gates are never closed during the day, for there is no night there. 26 And they will
bring the glory and honor of the nations into it. 27 And nothing unclean will ever enter it, neither he
that does detestable and deceitful things, except those [names] written in the book of life of the Lamb.

B. The New Jerusalem and the Tree of Life 21:1–22:5

After the final judgment, John shows his readers a picture of perfection that differs radically from the present world. The old order has passed away and all things are new. Cosmic time has been turned into eternity; separation from God has become intimate communion with him. Death belongs to the past, for the saints drink the water of life. The wicked are in the lake of fire, while the saints are with God and belong to his family. The new Jerusalem is a picture of perfection with respect to measurement, adornment, and glory. This picture reveals a river of life flowing from the throne of God and the Lamb with fruit-bearing trees on either side of this river. With the curse removed God's servants serve him and the Lamb. This is Paradise restored. Note the connection between the first creation recorded in Genesis and the new creation of heaven and earth in Revelation. In Paradise before the Fall, God intimately communed with Adam, gave him instructions, and provided for his needs (Gen. 2:15–25). On the new earth, God dwells with his people in intimate fellowship: "Look, the tabernacle of God is with people, and he will dwell with them" (v. 3a). After the Fall, Adam and Eve hid themselves from the presence of God (Gen. 3:8); at the restoration God dwells with them forever in his tabernacle.[1] The Garden of Eden was a place without fear, pain, crying, and death; the new creation is a place where "there will no longer be death, or grief, or crying, nor will there be pain anymore" (v. 4).

The second half of the chapter (vv. 9–27) is a description of the new Jerusalem regarding its holiness, perfection, adornment, and glory. This portrait of the city related in human language of time and space depicts, be it inadequately, the beauty of the new heaven and the new earth. The somewhat disjointed flow of thought shows that the writer is attempting to transmit as many details as he is able. Nonetheless, throughout his discourse John develops his basic theme that God is with his people in a holy and perfect setting.[2]

1. God and His People
21:1–8

1. And I saw the new heaven and the new earth, for the first heaven and the first earth went away; and the sea was no more.

John relies on the Old Testament Scriptures by alluding to Isaiah 65:17 and 66:22, where God says that he will create new heavens and a new earth, and the things belonging to the past will not be remembered or come to mind. The apostle had already noted that from God's presence earth and heaven had fled and their place was no more (see commentary on 20:11). God will not annihilate heaven and earth and then create them anew out of nothing. Instead he will transform

---

1. William Hendriksen, *More Than Conquerors* (reprint, Grand Rapids: Baker, 1982), pp. 196–97.

2. Jürgen Roloff, *The Revelation of John*, trans. J. E. Alsup (Minneapolis: Fortress, 1993), p. 233. By contrast, R. H. Charles (*A Critical and Exegetical Commentary on the Revelation of St. John*, ICC [Edinburgh: Clark, 1920], 2:147) writes that after the death of John, "materials . . . were put together by a faithful but unintelligent disciple in the order which he thought right." Charles then proceeds to rearrange the text of Revelation in a perplexing sequence that needs a special key to make it intelligible. J. Massyngberde Ford (*Revelation: Introduction, Translation, and Commentary*, AB 38 [Garden City, N.Y.: Doubleday, 1975], pp. 331–46, 360–61) follows Charles in rearranging the text of the Apocalypse according to her insights. But the message John conveys is sufficiently clear and convincing, and the integrity of the book remains intact.

them in a process that is the same as calling forth the lowly bodies of the saints to make them like the glorious body of the Lord (Phil. 3:21). Just as Jesus' body was transformed at his resurrection, so at the coming of the Lord the bodies of his people will be not annihilated but completely changed and glorified.[3] The melting of the elements with fire occurs in preparation for a renewed earth (2 Pet. 3:10, 12).

John writes the expression *new* nine times in Revelation; four of them appear in chapter 21:1 (twice), 2, and 5. This adjective conveys the meaning of something that is new but has its origin in the old. The new covenant came forth out of the old; the new command came from the old one; the new Jerusalem has its source in the old; the new man is a transformation of the old man; and the new heaven and the new earth are based on the old.[4]

Hence the new heaven and earth that will appear at the consummation are not to be identified as a second heaven and earth. They are qualitatively different from the old in that they picture the holy and perfect abode of God and his people. Peter, writing about the destruction of the heavens by fire, says, "But in keeping with his promise we are looking forward to a new heaven and a new earth, the home of righteousness" (2 Pet. 3:13). Peter visualizes a renovation by fire to bring about a change from old to new, but John writes not a single word in this chapter about a destructive fire.[5]

The interesting phrase *and the sea was no more* may signify that just as the former configurations of heaven and earth pass away so the sea no longer will exist with its present boundaries. But the term *sea* may also have a figurative connotation referring to afflictions God's people endured in a sinful world. John himself appears to point to a symbolic interpretation by writing a parallel clause that reiterates the same wording: "the sea *was no more*" and "death, grief, crying, and pain *will be no more*."[6]

2. And I saw the holy city, the new Jerusalem, coming down out of heaven from God prepared as a bride adorned for her husband.

John mentions the holy city in passing, for later in the chapter (vv. 9–14) he gives a detailed description of this city. The term *the holy city* appears in the Old

---

3. Refer to R. C. H. Lenski, *The Interpretation of St. John's Revelation* (Columbus: Wartburg, 1943), p. 615; Philip Edgcumbe Hughes, *The Book of the Revelation: A Commentary* (Leicester: Inter-Varsity; Grand Rapids: Eerdmans, 1990), p. 222; Luther Poellot, *Revelation: The Last Book in the Bible* (St. Louis: Concordia, 1962), pp. 273–74; S. Greijdanus, *De Openbaring des Heeren aan Johannes*, KNT (Amsterdam: Van Bottenburg, 1925), p. 416.

4. The word *kainos*, meaning "qualitatively new," generally differs from the term *neos*, signifying "not previously in existence." John uses the first term in Revelation but never the second. See Jörg Baumgarten, *EDNT*, 2:229; Hermann Haarbeck, Hans-Georg Link, and Colin Brown, *NIDNTT*, 2:670–76; Johannes Behm, *TDNT*, 3:447; Richard Bauckham, *The Theology of the Book of Revelation*, New Testament Theology (Cambridge: Cambridge University Press, 1993), pp. 49–50.

5. David E. Aune (*Revelation 17–22*, WBC 52C [Nashville: Nelson, 1998], pp. 1117–19) has compiled all the possible references to a fiery destruction of heaven and earth from Jewish, early Christian, and pagan sources.

6. Gregory K. Beale, *The Book of Revelation: A Commentary on the Greek Text*, NIGTC (Grand Rapids: Eerdmans, 1998), pp. 1042–43.

Testament in Nehemiah 11:1, 18; Isaiah 48:2; 52:1; and Daniel 9:24 as an appellation of Jerusalem. The New Testament, however, features the expression only in the Gospel of Matthew (4:5 and 27:53) and in the Apocalypse (11:2; 21:2, 10; 22:19). The absence of this term in the rest of the New Testament is significant. After the tearing of the curtain separating the Holy of Holies from the Holy Place, God no longer dwelled in the temple of Jerusalem but in the church. And note that the Holy Spirit filled not the temple or Jerusalem at Pentecost but the apostles and all those who repented and were baptized (Acts 2:1–4, 38–39). Paul writes that believers are the temple of God because in them his Spirit dwells (1 Cor. 3:16–17; see 6:19). The temple of God is the church, namely, the body of believers. Accordingly, when John uses the term *holy city* in Revelation, he intimates that the new Jerusalem is the place where God is dwelling with his people (v. 3).

The new Jerusalem is "coming down out of heaven from God." The writer of Hebrews speaks about a heavenly Jerusalem, Mount Zion, and the city of the living God (12:22; see also 11:10, 16; Gal. 4:26; 4 Ezra [=2 Esdras] 7:26, 75; *2 Baruch* 4.2–6). This city projects permanence, security, beauty, and fullness. It originates in heaven and derives from God, who is pleased to dwell with his people. In Revelation the name *Jerusalem* occurs only here and in 3:12, and is an allusion not to the capital of Israel but to the spiritual city of God. This new Jerusalem filled with God's people comes down to earth, whereby heaven and earth are made one.[7]

Describing the intimacy of God and his people, John uses the metaphor of a wedding ceremony in which a bride is prepared and adorned for her husband (compare 19:7; Isa. 49:18; 61:10).[8] The one who has prepared and adorned the bride cannot be the bride, that is, the church herself. No, it is Christ Jesus who has cleansed her and then presented her without stain or wrinkle or blemish to himself (Eph. 5:26–27). The wedding ceremony is now about to begin, and from this time on bride and bridegroom will be together forever.

3. And I heard a loud voice from the throne saying, "Look, the tabernacle of God is with people, and he will dwell with them, and they will be his people, and God himself will be with them and be their God."

The expression *a loud voice* occurs frequently in Revelation and implies that everyone is able to hear the message coming from God's throne (16:17 and 19:5). John fails to identify this voice, which may be that of God. If we assume that he tries to avoid the use of the divine name, we see further evidence in verse 5 where John circumscribes the name of God with the words "the one seated on the throne." Even so, the emphasis is not on the speaker but on the joyful mes-

7. Gerhard A. Krodel (*Revelation*, ACNT [Minneapolis: Augsburg, 1989], pp. 344–45) remarks that Paul describes his vision of Christians being "caught up" in the clouds (1 Thess. 4:17), but John indicates an opposite movement of resurrected saints coming down from heaven to the new earth.

8. The combination of the double metaphor of a woman and a city turns up in the context of 4 Ezra (=2 Esdras) 10:27, "I looked up and saw no longer a woman but a city."

sage. The voice calls attention to the unity of God and his people expressed in the image of the Old Testament tabernacle. John alludes to a well-known passage, in which God, speaking about an everlasting covenant with his people, says: "I will put my sanctuary among them forever. My dwelling place will be with them; I will be their God and they will be my people" (Ezek. 37:26–27). This text is a golden thread woven into the fabric of Scripture from beginning to end (Gen. 17:7; Exod. 6:7; Lev. 26:12; Ezek. 11:20; Zech. 2:10–11; 2 Cor. 6:16; Rev. 21:3, 7).[9] It is the thread of God's abiding love toward his covenant people.

In an earlier passage (13:6), John had used the illustration of the scene of God dwelling in his heavenly tent (Greek *skēnē*) surrounded by his people. The tabernacle in the desert had the Holy of Holies where God dwelled. The temple in Jerusalem likewise had the sacred place behind the curtain as God's dwelling. But neither in the desert nor in Jerusalem did God and his people live under one roof. Now notice that when Jesus came, he dwelled among his people; literally, "he pitched his tent" among them (John 1:14). This is also the case in the new Jerusalem, where God and his people live together in perfect peace and harmony. The people will fully know him, love and serve him, and forever taste his goodness. The symbolic tent in which God and his people dwell is not a picture of their dwelling in a temporary shelter.[10] The symbolism points to the privilege his people have in contrast to the Old Testament saints. From them only the high priest once a year might enter the Holy of Holies on the Day of Atonement. Now his people are always in his presence. The emphasis in this verse is on God, for he has made it possible for human beings to dwell with him, he is their God, and he is forever with them.

The literal translation of the Greek text is "and they will be his peoples," but in most translations it is given in the singular as "people." The text, however, intimates that they come from "every tribe, tongue, people, and nation." All of them are accommodated as priests in the presence of God. "Therefore, this is the first hint that there is no literal temple in the new Jerusalem" (v. 22).[11]

One last remark. The phrase *and God himself will be with them* is reminiscent of the name given to Jesus, Immanuel, which means, "God with us" (Matt. 1:23; Isa. 7:14).

4. "And he will wipe away every tear from their eyes, and there will no longer be death, or grief, or crying, nor will there be pain anymore, because the first things passed away."

This is now the second time (7:17) that John alludes to Isaiah 25:8 (see Jer. 31:16), "The Sovereign LORD will wipe away the tears from all faces." Like a mother who bends down and tenderly wipes away the tears from the eyes of her weeping child, so the Lord God stoops down to dry the tear-filled eyes of his chil-

9. Consult Simon J. Kistemaker, *Exposition of the Second Epistle to the Corinthians,* NTC (Grand Rapids: Baker, 1997), pp. 231–32.

10. Wilhelm Michaelis, *TDNT,* 7:382.

11. Beale, *Revelation,* p. 1048.

dren. Here is a telling portrait of God's tender mercies extended to the suffering members of his household. Ever since the fall into sin, mankind has shed countless tears, so that this present world indeed can be called a vale of tears. The shedding of tears is the result of anguish, oppression, persecution, sorrow, and death.

Death rules supreme until the final judgment (20:14). But that power will have effectively come to an end when God and his people are together. Jewish literature also states that at the time of the Messiah death will cease forever.[12] With the departure of death, mourning, crying, and disease also disappear, for all these have been caused by the curse of sin affecting God's creation (Gen. 2:17; Rom. 8:20–23). None of them have any part in God's renewed creation, which is marked by peace and harmony, joy and mirth, pleasure and delight (Isa. 35:10; 51:11; 65:19). Indeed the first things have passed away and all things are new (Isa. 43:18; 65:17).

5. And the one seated on the throne said, "Look, I am making all things new," and he said, "Write, for these words are faithful and true."

The phrase *the one seated on the throne* is a circumscription of the divine name that recalls the throne room setting (chapter 4). It is a recurring phrase in Revelation and Old Testament passages.[13] Avoiding the use of God's name, John allocates the origin of the voice to the throne. Now not an angel but God himself speaks and instructs John (vv. 5–8). Several times from his throne God directs a message to his people (v. 3; 1:8; 16:1, 17), but this is the last time in Revelation that he directly utters an announcement.[14]

God tells the readers of the Apocalypse that he is *making all things new* (compare Isa. 43:19, which lacks the words *all things*). But here is the glorious outcome of God's redemptive plan that Christ fulfilled: the renewal of all things. Notice that God calls attention to the fact that he is presently doing it, not that he will eventually do it. This utterance, therefore, is a direct revelation from God, who recreates, and as such it is one of the most important verses in Revelation.[15] God renews sinful human beings through the work of Christ and makes them into a new creation (2 Cor. 5:17). In addition to human beings all things are renewed. This is God's promise that points forward to the consummation, the transformation of heaven and earth, and the renewal of his entire creation (see 4 Ezra [=2 Esdras] 7:75).

---

12. *Exodus Rabbah* 15.21; Targum to Isaiah 65:20; 4 Ezra (=2 Esdras) 8:53; *2 Enoch* 65.10.

13. Rev. 4:2, 9, 10; 5:1, 7, 13; 6:16; 7:10, 15; 19:4; 20:11. See also 1 Kings 22:19; 2 Chron. 18:18; Ps. 47:8; Isa. 6:1; also Sirach 1:8.

14. Some commentators, however, understand the speaker to be Christ or an angel. E.g., Lenski, *Revelation*, pp. 620–21; Greijdanus, *Openbaring*, p. 419. Ernst Lohmeyer (*Die Offenbarung des Johannes*, HNT 16 [Tübingen: Mohr, 1970], p. 166) observes that in chapters 21 and 22 there are three parts: in the first one God speaks (21:5–8), in the second one an angel (21:9–22:5), and in the third one Christ (22:6–7).

15. Krodel (*Revelation*, p. 348) calls verse 5a "the most important pronouncement in the whole letter." See also his *Revelation*, pp. 236–37.

Once again John is told to *write* (1:11; 14:13; 19:9), so that the content of Revelation may be preserved for countless generations. The reason for recording these words is that they are *faithful and true.* They are not hollow sounds, nor words that in time lose their meaning, but they express unqualified and lasting trustworthiness. God, who in Christ is the Savior and Redeemer of this world, will honor his word in bringing about a new heaven and a new earth. The words *faithful and true* are repeated in 22:6 (compare 19:9).

6. And he said to me, "It is done. I am the Alpha and the Omega, the Beginning and the End. I will give freely to the one who is thirsty from the fountain of water of life."

a. "It is done." In his coordinated Semitic style of starting nearly every sentence with the conjunction *and,* John continues his account and records the words God speaks. The first item, in Greek one word, *gegonan,* is translated "It is done," literally, "They have become reality." The term derives not from the verb *to do* but from the verb *to become.* This word was also spoken when the seven angels had poured out the seven plagues (16:17). But note the difference of the seven angels pouring out God's wrath on the wicked and God uttering the words "It has been done" to announce the completion of recreating heaven and earth. The first one comprises judgment on the wicked, the other the renewal of all things. God speaks these words as if everything is already renewed; and in a vision he shows John their fulfillment.

b. "I am the Alpha and the Omega, the Beginning and the End." First, the words "I am" refer to God telling Moses at the burning bush near Mount Sinai to go to the Israelites in Egypt with the message "I AM has sent me to you" (Exod. 3:14). Jesus claimed this name for himself when he told the Jews, "Before Abraham was born, I am" (John 8:58). Hence, both God and Christ use this name. In the Apocalypse, we encounter the same designations for God and Christ, for both can say "I am the Alpha and the Omega, the first and the last, the beginning and the end" (see commentary on 1:8).[16]

God through Christ is fully in control of every situation, so that the words spoken here are a source of comfort for believers who endure hardship and persecution for the sake of the gospel. From beginning to end God is the Sovereign ruler in the universe that he has made and upholds by his power. He is Lord of the future that points beyond the final judgment to a new creation. He is the first and the last letter of the Greek alphabet; in Christ he is the Word of God. Therefore, God's words spoken in this passage are meant to strengthen the faith of Christians in their turmoil and distress.

c. "I will give freely to the one who is thirsty from the fountain of water of life." The first word and the last word in a Greek sentence are stressed; here both the pronoun *I* and the adverb *freely* are emphasized. God offers the water of life, which is eternal life, to anyone who is thirsty. He makes it available free of charge. This is evident in the words Jesus spoke to the Samaritan woman at Jacob's well, "But who-

16. Richard Bauckham, *The Climax of Prophecy* (Edinburgh: Clark, 1993), p. 34.

ever drinks the water that I give him will never thirst. Indeed, the water I give him will become in him a spring of water welling up to eternal life" (John 4:14). The Old Testament interprets water spiritually as God's free gift, for example, in Isaiah 55:1 God offers it "without money and without cost."[17] This free gift comes directly from the source of life, namely, from God himself.

7. "He that overcomes will inherit these things, and I will be a God to him, and he will be a son to me."

The text looks at the present reality of God's people living for him in a world of sin and oppression. They know that Christ has won the battle but the war has not yet ended. Every believer must fight daily against sin, the devil, and the world. And everyone who follows Christ receives the promise of eternal life and inherits all the good things that are coming (compare Heb. 10:1).

This verse consists of two parts, a promise of inheritance and a messianic allusion applied to believers. First, the verb *to inherit* occurs only here in the Apocalypse and doctrinally is in complete harmony with the teachings of Paul.[18] For instance, Paul confidently writes, "Now if we are children, then we are heirs—heirs of God and co-heirs with Christ" (Rom. 8:17; and see Gal. 3:29; 4:7; Eph. 3:6; Titus 3:7). We as followers of Christ inherit all the blessings of a new heaven and a new earth. For us, the link between being children of God and being heirs is unbreakable. Whereas Jesus is the one and only Son, we are adopted sons and daughters. And whereas Jesus inherits all things (Heb. 1:2), we as co-heirs share in all his blessings.[19]

Next, John quotes 2 Samuel 7:14 but modifies the wording to suit his theological purpose. God's promise given by Nathan to King David concerning Solomon as his successor to the throne prophetically pointed to the Son of God: "I will be his father, and he will be my son." But John in the Apocalypse writes, "And I will be a God to him, and he will be a son to me." Notice that he replaces the word *father* with *God*, because in Jesus Christ God has adopted us as his sons and daughters and made us members of his family (compare 2 Cor. 6:18). In Revelation, John never calls God the father of believers; yet he is the Father of Christ (1:6; 2:27).[20]

8. "To the cowardly and the unbelievers and those who are detested and the murderers and the fornicators, and the sorcerers and idolaters, and to all who are deceivers, their part is in the lake of fire and sulfur, which is the second death."

The contrast between God's people and the wicked appears once again. The preceding verses (vv. 5–7) were addressed to the persevering saints on earth, but

---

17. Consult Isa. 44:3; 49:10; Jer. 2:13; 17:13; Zech. 14:8. See John 7:37–38; Rev. 7:17; 22:1, 17.

18. Henry Barclay Swete, *Commentary on Revelation* (1911; reprint, Grand Rapids: Kregel, 1977), p. 281; Isbon T. Beckwith, *The Apocalypse of John* (1919; reprint, Grand Rapids: Baker, 1979), p. 752; Robert L. Thomas, *Revelation 8–22: An Exegetical Commentary* (Chicago: Moody, 1995), p. 449.

19. Hughes, *Revelation*, p. 225.

20. John P. M. Sweet, *Revelation*, WPC (Philadelphia: Westminster, 1979), p. 300.

this verse lists the people whom God consigns to the lake of fire and sulfur. In summary, this segment looks ahead to the renewal of all things, and at the same time it focuses attention on the reality of this pre-consummation age. This dual focus also occurs in two additional passages (v. 27; 22:14–15). Here John lists a long catalog of those who are not part of God's kingdom.

a. *Cowardly.* The first are those who are spineless. They are placed at the top of the list in contrast to all the believers on earth who suffer persecution and hardship for the sake of Christ. Instead of living a life of dedication to the Lord, they fear danger and flee the consequences of confessing the name of Jesus. They are the people whom John describes as leaving us but not belonging to us (1 John 2:19).

b. *Unbelievers.* These people are similar to the cowards in that they have been unfaithful to God and his commands and thus have fallen into skepticism and agnosticism. Whereas God's words are faithful and true (v. 5), theirs are the exact opposite—untrustworthy.

c. *Detestable people.* This Greek word (*ebdelygmenoi*) with its cognates points to those people who have become polluted by the world.[21] They pursue a lifestyle that is diametrically opposed to biblical teaching, and they are an abomination in God's sight. They worship the beast (17:4).

d. *Murderers.* John mentions this word twice, here and in 22:15. But the concept of the enemies shedding the blood of God's people appears repeatedly; the saints are martyrs for the sake of Christ (2:10, 13; 6:10; 16:6; 17:6; 18:24; 19:2).

e. *Immoral persons.* The sins of murder and sexual immorality are frequently connected, as the one sin leads to the next. If prostitution was rampant in John's time, so it is today. Fornication is the order of the day and so is adultery. The world is gradually sinking ever deeper into the morass of sexual immorality, including homosexuality.

f. *Sorcerers.* The Greek term *pharmakoi* has given rise to the derivative *pharmacy* (22:15; and related words in 9:21; 18:23). The word means the use of drugs to cast spells for practicing witchcraft and deceiving the people (Exod. 22:18; Lev. 20:6, 27). God condemns magic spells and witchcraft; he told Moses to kill those who consulted soothsayers; and the prophet Nahum links sorcery and witchcraft to sexual immorality (Deut. 18:10–12; Nah. 3:4 respectively).

g. *Idolatry.* Paul writes that idolatry and witchcraft are works of the flesh (Gal. 5:20). And John puts idolaters with sorcerers, fornicators, and murderers outside the gates of the new Jerusalem and consigns them to everlasting doom (22:15).

h. *Liars.* All people who turn the truth into a lie God dispatches with the other sinners to the lake of fire and sulfur. They are forever cut off from the living God and suffer the second death.

---

21. Consult Werner Foerster, *TDNT,* 1:598–600; Josef Zmijewski, *EDNT,* 1:209–10; and G. R. Beasley-Murray, *The Book of Revelation,* NCB (London: Oliphants, 1974), p. 314.

Greek Words, Phrases, and Constructions in 21:2–3

Verse 2

The spelling of Jerusalem as Ἰερουσαλήμ, occurring three times in the Apocalypse (3:12; 21:2, 10), differs from the more common Ἰεροσόλυμα. The first one transliterates the Hebrew word, while the second is a Hellenistic spelling of the name.

Verse 3

θρόνου—The TR and the Majority Text read οὐρανοῦ as a variant resulting from assimilation to ἐκ τοῦ οὐρανοῦ in the preceding verse.

λαοί—the plural is the preferred reading in Greek New Testaments (Nes-Al[27], UBS[4], BF[2], Merk), and the NRSV also reads "peoples." The TR and the Majority Text have the singular, but the choice between singular and plural is difficult to determine. The plural has slightly better textual support.[22] In English, however, the word *people* is commonly used collectively, while *peoples* is uncommon.

αὐτῶν θεος—"[and be] their God." These words appear to be superfluous after the phrase "and God himself will be with them." Nevertheless the expanded text is the more difficult reading.

2. The Holy City
21:9–14

This segment clearly shows, first, John's cyclical approach by repeating the reference to the bride, the wife of the Lamb, and the new Jerusalem (19:7 and 21:2, 9). And second, in nearly identical wording John demonstrates the contrast between the great prostitute and the wife of the Lamb, the blasphemous beast and the holy city. Here is the parallel of these two segments:[23]

Revelation 17:1, 3	**Revelation 21:9, 10**
And one of the seven angels who had the	And one of the seven angels who held the
seven bowls came	seven bowls full of the last seven plagues came
and talked to me and said,	and talked with me and said,
"Come, I will show you	"Come, I will show you
the judgment of the great prostitute."	the bride, the wife of the Lamb."
And he brought me to the desert	And he brought me
in the Spirit.	in the Spirit
There I saw a woman sitting on a	to a great and high mountain
scarlet beast that was full of	and he showed me the holy city, Jerusalem,
names of blasphemy.	that came down out of heaven from God.

22. Bruce M. Metzger, *A Textual Commentary on the Greek New Testament,* 2d ed. (Stuttgart: Deutsche Bibelgesellschaft, 1994), p. 688.

23. Adapted from Aune, *Revelation 17–22,* pp. 1144–45. See also Beale, *Revelation,* p. 1063; Krodel, *Revelation,* pp. 352–54.

9. And there came one of the seven angels who held the seven bowls full of the last seven plagues. He talked with me and said, "Come, I will show you the bride, the wife of the Lamb."

The above-mentioned parallel seems to indicate that John refers to the same angel who talked to him earlier (17:1). There the focus was on the great prostitute who received God's judgment and punishment, but here it is on the bride of the Lamb. The contrast is striking and painted in vivid colors. This angel attired in clean, bright linen with a golden sash around his chest poured out the bowl of God's wrath on Babylon the Great (15:6; 16:19). Now he is privileged to reveal to John the glory of the holy city, the new Jerusalem.[24]

The great prostitute who is riding on the beast personifies the wicked city of Babylon the Great. The bride, however, is the wife of the Lamb and symbolizes the holy city. The prostitute is without a husband and is destroyed by the beast and his followers (17:15–18). But as husband, the Lamb supplies his wife with everything she needs, honors her with great respect, and adorns her with attractive attire and exquisite accessories. In the remaining verses of Revelation the Lamb is mentioned seven times (vv. 9, 14, 22, 23, 27; 22:1, 3).[25]

John is asked to come along with the angel who is ready to show him the bride, the wife of the Lamb. The words *the bride, the wife* are not to be read as if the wedding had already taken place (compare 19:7), but rather as a first-century Jewish betrothal of a woman to a man. The betrothal ceremony was equivalent to the wedding itself, with the understanding that the couple had no sexual relations during the period between betrothal and wedding. During this intervening period, the bride was considered to be the wife of her future husband.[26] This means that the church is already the wife of the Lamb, even though the wedding has not yet taken place.

The imagery used in this text derives from Isaiah 61:10, where the prophet speaks about the bridal couple as the bridegroom adorns his head and the bride enhances her appearance with jewels. What the angel reveals to John is not a beautiful, marriageable young lady but the holy city, the new Jerusalem, coming down out of heaven. The Jerusalem that descends to earth from heaven is the church of the Lord Jesus Christ, now coming down in a vision and at the appropriate time in reality. The full beauty of this church will not be evident until the Lord returns in glory. It is the imagery of the holy city and the bride mentioned earlier (v. 2) that brings the people of the new Jerusalem and their Lord into an inseparable husband-wife relationship.

24. Refer to Hendrik R. van de Kamp, *Israël in Openbaring* (Kampen: Kok, 1990), p. 277.

25. Robert H. Mounce, *The Book of Revelation*, rev. ed., NICNT (Grand Rapids: Eerdmans, 1998), p. 389; Aune, *Revelation 17–22*, p. 1151.

26. Joachim Jeremias, *TDNT*, 4:1105; Walther Günther, *NIDNTT*, 2:585; Beasley-Murray, *Revelation*, p. 318.

10. And he brought me in the Spirit to a great and high mountain, and he showed me the holy city Jerusalem that came down out of heaven from God.

The prophecy of Ezekiel teaches that the Holy Spirit repeatedly took the prophet and lifted him up. Thus, the Spirit took Ezekiel to Jerusalem, Babylon, the valley of dry bones, and the temple of the Lord (Ezek. 3:12, 14; 8:3; 11:1, 24; 37:1; 43:5). "In visions of God he took me to the land of Israel and set me on a very high mountain" (Ezek. 40:2).[27]

The parallel of this verse with Revelation 17:3 is evident, but notice the difference. There the Spirit drove John into the desert to see the great prostitute, while here he took him to a high mountain to show him the holy city Jerusalem descending from heaven. "The Harlot City is seen in a wilderness, the Bride City from a mountain."[28]

Note also the difference between Ezekiel's account (40:2) and that of John. In Ezekiel the city is on the south side of the mountain; in Revelation it descends from heaven, that is, from God, without indicating that it settles on the high mountain. Further, the vision of Ezekiel reveals a wall surrounding the temple area (40:5), but in the Apocalypse there is no temple in the holy city, for the presence of God and the Lamb is the temple.

The new Jerusalem is called *holy,* which means that the city has been consecrated by God as a place without sin; in other words, it is perfect in every respect. The privilege of living forever in the presence of God is his gracious gift to us. At one time in human history, people started building the tower of Babel to reach heaven, but God frustrated their efforts (Gen. 11:1–9). By contrast, God takes the initiative to bring the new Jerusalem down to earth. It is the city of God that descends to earth, not human beings who decide to link their city to heaven. The old Jerusalem ravaged by sin could no longer be called holy after the death of Jesus (see commentary on 11:2). The new Jerusalem is free from sin and resumes the name *the holy city.*[29]

11. It had the glory of God, and its brilliance was like a precious stone, as a crystallized jasper stone.

Standing on a high mountain, John is able to see the entire scope of the descending city. So the believer who stands on a mountaintop of faith is able to see the extent of God's church. This church portrayed here as the holy city Jerusalem is filled with glory. The city itself has no source of light but depends for its brilliance on the glory of God. Just as the sun beams its light to the moon, which in turn reflects the light of the sun, so God's glory illumines the church, which in turn diffuses the light. "And the city did not need the sun or the moon to illumine it, for the glory of God illumines it and the Lamb is its lamp" (v. 23; see Isa. 58:8; 60:1–2, 19; Ezek. 43:4–5). It is the diffused light of God that illumines the

27. Four times in Revelation the phrase *in the Spirit* occurs (1:10; 4:2; 17:3; 21:10). Many translations feature the lower case letter for "in the spirit" (KJV, NEB, NJB, NLT, NRSV).

28. Swete, *Revelation*, p. 284.

29. Van de Kamp, *Israël in Openbaring*, pp. 269, 278.

city. Paul uses similar terminology when he describes the children of God living in a crooked and perverse generation. He commends them by saying, "You shine like stars in the universe" (Phil. 2:15).

John compares this brilliant light of God's glory to that of a precious stone, namely, a crystallized stone called jasper. Crystallized jasper is quartz appearing in a variety of colors that may be compared to the radiance of a diamond (Exod. 28:20; 39:13; Ezek. 28:13).[30] It reproduces indescribable splendor that John conveys in greater detail in the rest of the chapter. We should bear in mind that he is describing what he is permitted to see by comparing it to that which human beings are able to comprehend.

12. It had a great, high wall with twelve gates and at the gates twelve angels, and on the gates the names of the twelve tribes of Israel were inscribed: 13. on the east three gates, and on the north three gates, and on the south three gates, and on the west three gates.

John's description of the holy city communicates safety, for the wall that is both great and high imparts security. In addition the twelve angels that guard the twelve entrances are there to keep an eye on the traffic moving in and out. On the other hand, the totality of twelve gates in this city allows for free and easy traffic moving in and out of it. The number twelve occurs ten times in this chapter and the next one (vv. 12 [three times], 14 [three times], 16, 21 [twice]; 22:2). In the Apocalypse, this number always illustrates God, his people, and their dwelling places. It describes the elect of the twelve tribes (7:5–8) and the woman, symbolizing the church, with twelve stars on her head (12:1). It depicts the new Jerusalem with twelve gates, twelve angels, and twelve tribes of Israel (21:12); it lists the twelve names of the apostles written on the city's twelve foundations (21:14). And it measures in length, breadth, and height twelve thousand stadia (21:16). Last, along both sides of the river flowing from the throne of God are twelve fruit-bearing trees (22:2), collectively referred to as the tree of life. This number never applies to Satan, his works, and his followers. I conclude that, like seven and ten, twelve is the number of perfection.

The background for John's description of the holy city comes from the prophecy of Ezekiel, where the prophet presents a picture of Jerusalem with its walls and gates (40:5; 48:30–35). Nevertheless the measurements are completely different.

On the twelve gates were written the names of the twelve tribes of Israel, and on the twelve foundation stones were the names of the twelve apostles (v. 14). Here John shows the link between the Old and New Testament believers, which he did earlier by mentioning the twenty-four elders (4:4).[31] John refrains from listing the names of the twelve tribes and of the twelve apostles. In an earlier

30. Bauer, p. 368; Norman Hillyer, *NIDNTT*, 3:398; Reuben G. Bullard, "Stones, Precious," *ISBE*, 4:627–28. The NJB consistently translates the Greek *iaspis* (jasper) as "diamond" in Revelation.

31. Greijdanus, *Openbaring*, p. 424; Abraham Kuyper, *The Revelation of St. John*, trans. John Hendrik de Vries (Grand Rapids: Eerdmans, 1935), pp. 324–25.

chapter he noted the names of the twelve tribes of Israel (7:5–8). Ezekiel, however, lists the names of the twelve tribes on the twelve gates. The three gates on the north had Reuben, Judah, and Levi; the three on the east had Joseph, Benjamin, and Dan; the three on the south had Simeon, Issachar, and Zebulun; and the three on the west had Gad, Asher, and Naphtali (Ezek. 48:31–34). Without mentioning the names of either the tribes or the apostles, John wants to show that the Christian church and the Old Testament people of God are united in perfect unity and harmony.[32]

Instead of showing a clockwise movement from north to east to south and to west as in Ezekiel 48, John gives a random movement from east to north to south and to west (see Ezek. 42:16–19). I am unable to account for the order and see no special significance. There is a difference, however, between the view of Ezekiel 48:30 that the gates of the city are exits and that of Revelation 21:25–27, which sees the gates as entrances. These entrances are never shut, for anyone who is holy may enter them.

14. And the wall of the city had twelve foundations and on them were the twelve names of the twelve apostles of the Lamb.

The city wall itself was built on a total of twelve foundation stones, which were partially above ground and exhibited the names of the twelve apostles. With the names of the apostles at ground level and the names of the twelve tribes at the gate level, believers belonging to either the Old Testament or New Testament era were given entrance into the city. Paul relates that all these people as members of God's household are "built on the foundation of the apostles and prophets with Christ Jesus himself as the chief cornerstone" (Eph. 2:20). Jesus told his disciples, "On this rock I will build my church" (Matt. 16:18). And the writer of Hebrews notes that by faith Abraham looked "forward to the city with foundations, whose architect and builder is God" (Heb. 11:10). Here is an example of Scripture's unity and harmony, for all these passages convey a similar message. John stresses that the twelve apostles are of the Lamb, implying that Jesus by his sacrificial death on the cross set his people free from sin and guilt. The twelve apostles were commissioned as messengers of Christ's gospel to the world at large (Matt. 28:19–20).

There is no need to supply the names of the twelve apostles, just as there is no need to write down the names of the twelve tribes of Israel. The number twelve is symbolic of the beginning of the nation Israel and the beginning of the church. Indeed, after the church was established, it was customary to speak of "the Twelve" without specifying the names of the apostles. So Paul in his list of Jesus' appearances simply writes, "and that he appeared to Peter, and then to the Twelve" (1 Cor. 15:5).

32. Refer to Swete, *Revelation*, p. 286; David E. Holwerda, *Jesus and Israel: One Covenant or Two?* (Grand Rapids: Eerdmans; Leicester: Inter-Varsity, 1995), p. 110.

Greek Words, Phrases, and Constructions in 21:9–14

Verse 9

τῶν γεμόντων—although this is the better-attested reading, the case should have been the accusative instead of the genitive. This is one of the solecisms in the Apocalypse.

Verse 10

ἐκ τοῦ οὐρανοῦ ἀπὸ τοῦ θεοῦ—here is a recurring phrase in Revelation (3:12; 21:2).

Verse 11

ὁ φωστήρ—this noun differs little from the noun φῶς, except that it signifies the radiance of a beam of light. The nominative case breaks the flow of the sentence and in effect introduces an independent grammatical structure, probably due to John's coordinate Semitic style.

Verse 12

ἔχουσα—the nominative case is due to the case of φωστήρ in the preceding verse (v. 11). The present participle (twice) may be translated as the present finite verb *has.* The feminine gender depends on the noun πόλιν in verse 10.

Verse 14

ἔχων—the participle follows τὸ τεῖχος, which is neuter; that is, the participle should have been in the neuter case instead of the masculine. This is a case of an error of the ear that failed to distinguish between the sound of an *omega* and an *omicron.*

3. The Adornment of the City *21:15–21*

15. And the one who spoke with me had a golden measuring reed to measure the city and its gates and its walls.

The one who spoke with John is one of the seven angels, who had told him that he would show him the bride, the wife of the Lamb (v. 9). Now this angel continues to reveal to John the extent of the city of God.

Whereas earlier John was given a reed and told to measure the temple of God, the altar, and those who worshiped (11:1), now the angel takes in hand a *golden measuring reed.* The golden reed harmonizes with heavenly items that are made out of gold: lampstands, harps, bowls, crowns, and incense altar. Even the streets are made out of pure gold. Not John but the angel measures the city with its gates and walls. Here the measurements are listed (v. 16), which was not the case in John's measuring the temple and the altar. Also, there is a similar reference to measuring the city, the wall, and the gates in Ezekiel 40:5–15 and 45:1–2, but the measurements differ from those of the new Jerusalem.

16. And the city was foursquare and its length was like its breadth. And he measured the city with a reed at twelve thousand stadia; its length and breadth and height were equal.

The city of the new Jerusalem is foursquare, but in addition to the length and breadth its height is given in equal measurement. The length is twelve thousand stadia, so is the width, and likewise the height. Here then is a picture of a perfect cube that reminded a person familiar with the Old Testament of the Holy of Holies in Solomon's temple. "The inner sanctuary was twenty cubits long, twenty wide and twenty high" (1 Kings 6:20). A cube is a symbol of perfection.

Notice the difference between the Holy of Holies in Solomon's temple, where God dwelled among his people on a sinful earth, and the holy city Jerusalem coming down out of heaven, where God dwells with his sinless people. The size of the city in human computation is staggering indeed, for twelve thousand stadia is more than fourteen hundred miles (twenty-three hundred kilometers). We can measure the length and the breadth and come to some understanding, but its height is incredible. Instead of taking these measurements literally, I suggest regarding them symbolically as a means of describing heaven in terms of symmetry and perfection.[33] Some scholars wish to bring down the dimensions of the city to more acceptable terms. An emendation of changing stadia to cubits makes the total distance of each side three and a half miles (5.6 kilometers).[34] But John is not interested in making the dimensions acceptable to human norms, because for him the measurements are figurative. For instance, a cube has twelve edges: four at the top, four at the bottom, and four on the sides. Each edge is twelve thousand stadia, which multiplied by twelve comes to 144,000. This is the same number as that of the Lamb's followers (14:1).[35] For John, the matter is one of symbolism.

17. And he measured its wall, 144 cubits, according to the human measure, which the angel used.

John provides the measurement of the wall that he had described as great and high (v. 12). He states that it is according to human calculations used by the angel measuring 144 cubits (about 220 feet). The length of a cubit varied from 18 to 21 inches (45 to 52 centimeters) measured from the elbow to the tip of one's middle finger. However, John does not reveal whether the measurement refers to width or height, and thus he leaves it an open question.[36] The city's height of 12,000 stadia could never be supported by a thickness of 144 cubits, and interpreting 144 cubits as its height runs into conflict with the 12,000 stadia.

I observe that whether John has in mind a thick or high wall, the structure itself appears to be out of proportion with the dimensions of the rest of the city. I do not take the wall to be a defensive structure that surrounds the city proper,

---

33. See George Eldon Ladd, *Commentary on the Revelation of John* (Grand Rapids: Eerdmans, 1972), p. 282. Hughes (*Revelation*, p. 228) applies the symbolic number twelve thousand of the city's size to "the great concourse of its population," but the symmetry points to perfection. Compare Craig S. Keener, *Revelation*, NIVAC (Grand Rapids: Zondervan, 2000), p. 494.

34. Consult M. Topham ("The Dimensions of the New Jerusalem," *ExpT* 100 [1989]: 417–19), who suggests that the expression *Son of God* in Hebrew letters adds up to 144, as a designation of the Messiah.

35. Refer to Kendell H. Easley, *Revelation*, HNTC (Nashville: Broadman & Holman, 1998), p. 399.

36. Translations that have adopted width are NIV, REB, NLT, and *Peterson*. Those that have adopted height are NJB, GNB, NEB, and *Phillips*.

for the holy city has no need of defenses.[37] All God's enemies have been consigned forever to the lake of fire (v. 8).

The point is not the width or height of the wall itself but the number 144 as the square of twelve. It is the multiplication of the representative twelve tribes on the gates and the representative twelve apostles on the foundation of the city. Therefore, this number should be understood as a symbolic figure.

18. And the wall was built of jasper, and the city was of pure gold like clear glass.

In this verse and those that follow (vv. 19–21) John depicts the beauty of the holy city. He speaks of the city wall and the appearance of the city. First, he mentions that jasper is built into the wall's construction; the word *jasper* occurs four times in Revelation (4:3; 21:11, 18, 19). For the throne room scene John portrays as jasper the one occupying the throne (4:3). This jasper probably is a variety of quartz in the various colors of green, yellow, brown, and mottled red.[38] It reflects God's glory through this stone; it is truly a picture of indescribable beauty. The Old Testament refers to the jasper stone (see Exod. 28:20; 39:13; Ezek. 28:13), but we assume that the stone differs from what we mean by jasper today, a green semiprecious stone. As an alternative John pictures utter brilliance, that is, the radiance of God himself in dazzling light.

John writes, "The city was of pure gold like clear glass." Gold is a metal and is not transparent like glass. It is possible that John has in mind the gleaming splendor of this metal, because for him gold signifies heaven's perfection. Also, he uses the word *like* to indicate that gold was similar to clear glass as a shiny substance. Although in ancient times glass was opaque, in a subsequent verse he again writes about its perspicuity: "the street of the city was pure gold like transparent glass" (v. 21). The writer highlights not apparent inconsistencies, such as transparent gold, but rather perfection in the sense of the perspicuity of glass in its purest form.

19. The foundations of the wall of the city were adorned with every kind of precious stone. The first foundation was jasper, the second sapphire, the third chalcedony, the fourth emerald, 20. the fifth sardonyx, the sixth carnelian, the seventh chrysolite, the eighth beryl, the ninth topaz, the tenth chrysoprase, the eleventh jacinth, and the twelfth amethyst.

The emphasis on the number twelve relates to both the foundation stones and the precious stones, which are a reminder of the breastplate the high priest wore when he entered the Holy of Holies. Each of the twelve stones had the name of one of the twelve tribes of Israel, so that when the high priest entered the Holy of Holies he represented all God's people. The breastplate was a square, a span long and a span wide (Exod. 28:16; 39:9). Many of the stones mentioned here are part of the high priestly breastplate, which had four rows of

37. Contra Charles, *Revelation*, 2:164.

38. Reuben G. Bullard, *ISBE*, 4:627.

three stones each (Exod. 28:17–21; 39:10–14; compare Ezek. 28:13).[39] From the list in Exodus, the eight names in italic appear also in John's account.

ruby, *topaz, beryl*
turquoise, *sapphire, emerald*
jacinth, agate, *amethyst*
chrysolite, onyx, *jasper*

I am unable to explain why John's list differs from that in the Exodus account of the high priestly breastplate. The connection of the breastplate to the foundation stones of the holy city appears to lie in the prophecy of Isaiah 54:11–12 concerning the restoration of Jerusalem. "O afflicted city . . . I will build you with stones of turquoise, your foundations with sapphires. I will make your battlements of rubies, your gates of sparkling jewels, and all your walls of precious stones" (see also Tob. 13:16–17).[40] In context, the LORD Almighty is the husband who takes back his wife with deep compassion and then lavishes upon her sparkling jewels and precious stones (Isa. 54:5–7, 11–12). John adopts Isaiah's symbolism of wife and city in terms of God's people and the new Jerusalem.

Between the twelve gates of the holy city were twelve foundation stones. Each one of these stones had a name of one of the twelve apostles written on it (see v. 14). The embellishing of these foundations with twelve kinds of precious stones is not so much a reference to the splendor and wealth of the holy city as to the glory and holiness of God.[41]

There are no hidden meanings in the individual precious stones. Jasper is associated with the wall and now also with the first foundation stone. Sapphire adorning the second foundation is a blue-colored stone (*lapis lazuli,* REB) mentioned often in Scripture.[42] The third stone is chalcedony, which is translated as "agate" (GNB, NLT, NRSV) or as "turquoise" (NJB). The fourth is emerald, a green-colored stone, the same as emerald today. Fifth is sardonyx, which some versions have translated as "onyx" (GNB, NCV, NLT, NRSV) or as "agate" (NJB); it has streaks of reddish-brown in a white setting. Number six is carnelian, translated as "sardius" (ASV, KJV, NASB) or "ruby" (NJB), which has bands of color ranging from orange-red to dark brown. The seventh is chrysolite, which is "gold-

39. Charles (*Revelation,* 2:165–69) claims that the order is the opposite of that of an ancient zodiac scheme. But this theory lacks confirmation; see T. F. Glasson, "The Order of the Jewels in Revelation xxi.19–20: A Theory Eliminated," *JTS* 26 (1975): 95–100. Consult also W. W. Reader, "The Twelve Jewels of Revelation 21:19–20: Tradition History and Modern Interpretations," *JBL* 100 (1981): 433–57; M. Wojciechowski, "Apocalypse 21.19–20: Des Titres Christologiques Cachés dans la Liste des Pierres Précieuses," *NTS* 33 (1987): 153–54.

40. Beale, *Revelation,* pp. 1083–84; Krodel, *Revelation,* pp. 360–61. And see Jan Fekkes, "'His Bride Has Prepared Herself': Revelation 19–21 and Isaianic Nuptial Imagery," *JBL* 109 (1990): 269–87.

41. Alan F. Johnson, *Revelation,* in *The Expositor's Bible Commentary,* ed. Frank E. Gaebelein (Grand Rapids: Zondervan, 1981), 12:597.

42. Exod. 24:10; 28:18; 39:11; Job 28:6, 16; Song 5:14; Isa. 54:11; Lam. 4:7; Ezek. 1:26; 10:1; 28:13; Rev. 21:19. For details on the individual stones, consult Bullard, *ISBE,* 4:625–30.

stone" (*Phillips*) or "gold-quartz" (NJB). Eighth is beryl of a green, blue, or bluish-green variety. The ninth is topaz, which comes in a variety of colors ranging from white to yellow, blue, and green. Number ten is chrysoprase, apple-green in color, translated as "emerald" (NJB). The eleventh is jacinth, also given as "turquoise" (GNB, REB) or "zircon" (*Phillips*), which varies from gray to brown, yellow, green, and red. And number twelve is amethyst, varying from lilac to deep purple. These precious stones are a bright display of a multiplicity of hues that portray the new Jerusalem. I surmise that these colors are indescribable from an earthly perspective.

21. And the twelve gates had twelve pearls, each one of the gates was a single pearl. And the street of the city was pure gold like transparent glass.

John turns his attention once again to the gates of the city (vv. 12–13), describing them in the light of Isaiah 54:12, "I will make . . . your gates of sparkling jewels."[43] The jewels of these gates are pearls, one for each of the twelve gates. And again he expects the reader to understand his description symbolically: twelve gates and twelve pearls. In addition to the precious stones for the walls of the city, the builder has used pearls to construct its gates. Pearls in Scripture are highly valued, as is evident in the parable of the pearl of great price (Matt. 13:45–46; compare Matt. 7:6; see also 1 Tim. 2:9; Rev. 18:12). To enter the kingdom of heaven, the merchant sold all his possessions and bought the pearl of great value.

The emphasis ought not to be placed on the literal size of a single pearl from which a gate was made nor on the monetary value of this pearl. John is speaking figuratively and conveys a picture of perfection. "Gates of pearl are a symbol of unimaginable beauty and unassessable riches."[44]

The street of the city appears to be the main corridor and is used here as an example of all the streets (see 22:2). This street was made of pure gold symbolizing heaven's perfection (see v. 18). John compares it with transparent glass denoting perfect purity. Its clarity was of such a degree that it was completely free from any defect. All the inhabitants of this city were without flaw. Whereas only the priests were allowed to walk on the gold-covered floor of Solomon's temple (1 Kings 6:30), in the new Jerusalem all the saints walk the streets of gold.

Greek Words, Phrases, and Constructions in 21:16–21

Verse 16

τῷ καλάμῳ—the dative case is instrumental, "he measured with the reed." And the genitive case in δώδεκα χιλιάδων functions as a genitive of measure.

---

43. The Jews understood the jewels (carbuncles) to be pearls. See the Babylonian Talmud, in which Rabbi Jochanan says, "The Holy One, blessed be He, will in the time to come bring precious stones and pearl which are thirty [cubits] by thirty and will cut out from them [openings] ten [cubits] by twenty, and will set them up in the gates of Jerusalem" (*Baba Bathra* 75a; and see *Sanhedrin* 100a). Consult SB, 3:851–52.

44. William Barclay, *The Revelation of John*, 2d ed. (Philadelphia: Westminster, 1960), 2:275.

Verse 18

ἡ ἐνδώμησις—the word can be translated as "building material" or as "foundation." But because the word occurs only here in the New Testament and rarely elsewhere, the meaning is uncertain. It can mean that the construction material built into the wall was the precious jasper stone.

Verse 19

χαλκηδών—the name of Chalcedon lies behind this stone, which was mined near this city. The city's name, however, derives from the word χαλκός (copper).[45]

Verse 21

ἀνὰ εἷς ἕκαστος—the preposition ἀνά is distributive like κατά and signifies "each individual."[46]

---

4. The Light of the City
21:22–27

22. And I did not see a temple in it, for the Lord God Almighty and the Lamb are its temple. 23. And the city did not need the sun or the moon to illumine it, for the glory of God illumines it and the Lamb is its lamp.

Throughout the Apocalypse, John has mentioned the presence of a heavenly temple.[47] He repeatedly depicted the temple as the very place where God dwells, but now when God takes up residence in the new Jerusalem, John writes that the holy city itself has become the temple. The Holy of Holies in Solomon's temple was constructed in the form of a cube (1 Kings 6:20); now the holy city itself is a cube where God dwells and which he fills completely with his sacred presence. The saints in this city are never outside his presence, for God never departs from his people. They have immediate and direct access to him and no longer need Christ as the intermediary (Heb. 9:24). Christ's mediatorial role as the Lamb has come to an end, for now he functions as bridegroom in a marital relationship with his people (19:7).

Ezekiel devoted seven chapters to the new temple, the priests, and religious services (Ezek. 40–46), but the construction of the second temple never fulfilled the ideal. Aged men who recalled the beauty of Solomon's temple wept at the sight of the second (Ezra 3:12). The fulfillment of the ideal temple is reflected in God's promise to live among his people forever and in the subscription "the LORD is there" (Ezek. 43:7 and 48:35, respectively).[48] Jesus told the Samaritan woman that true worshipers would worship God anywhere (John 4:21, 23), and

---

45. J. H. Moulton and W. F. Howard, *Accidence and Word-Formation*, vol. 2 of A *Grammar of New Testament Greek*, by J. H. Moulton et al. (Edinburgh: Clark, 1929), p. 376.

46. Friedrich Blass and Albert Debrunner, *A Greek Grammar of the New Testament and Other Early Christian Literature*, trans. and rev. Robert Funk (Chicago: University of Chicago Press, 1961), §248.1.

47. Rev. 3:12; 7:15; 11:1–2, 19; 14:15, 17; 15:5–6, 8; 16:1, 17.

48. Holwerda, *Jesus and Israel*, p. 65.

Paul taught his readers that they as the church were God's temple (1 Cor. 3:16–17; 2 Cor. 6:16; Eph. 2:21–22).[49]

John mentions the Lord God Almighty and the Lamb in the context of the temple. When God and his people are forever together, then the Old Testament prophecies concerning the ideal temple will be completely fulfilled in Jesus Christ. Then the presence of God and Christ serves as their temple. God is their sovereign Lord, the Almighty (1:8; 4:8; 11:17; 15:3; 16:7, 14; 19:6, 15), who dwells with them in the new Jerusalem.

The temple and the holy city are one and the same; John mentions these places sequentially. John clearly relies on Isaiah 60:19 (compare Isa. 24:23), which he freely adapts.

Isaiah 60:19	Revelation 21:23
The sun will no more be your light by day,	And the city did not need the sun
nor will the brightness of the moon shine on you,	or the moon to illumine it,
for the LORD will be your everlasting light,	for the glory of God illumines it
and your God will be your glory.	and the Lamb is its lamp.

Isaiah writes his prophecy in the context of "the City of the LORD, Zion of the Holy One of Israel" (Isa. 60:14), and John pens his words following the description of the new Jerusalem. John turns Isaiah's clause "your God will be your glory" into a messianic fulfillment "the Lamb is its lamp."[50] The LORD God and the Lamb share the same glory (see John 1:14), for here the Lamb is the source of light and in 22:5 it is God himself. This divine light dims all other sources and renders them irrelevant. Further, sun and moon, created to mark cosmic time, cease to function in eternity. Hence, John writes "there is no night there" (v. 25; compare Zech. 14:7). Last, the wording of this text is repeated, although not verbatim, in 22:5, "and they have no need of the light of a lamp and of the light of the sun, because the Lord God will illumine them."

24. And the nations will walk through its light, and the kings of the earth bring their glory into it. 25. And its gates are never closed during the day, for there is no night there. 26. And they will bring the glory and honor of the nations into it.

a. "And the nations will walk through its light, and the kings of the earth bring their glory into it." John continues to rely on Isaiah 60 and selects verses 3 and 5, "Nations will come to your light, and kings to the brightness of your dawn. . . . To you the riches of the nations will come." Throughout the Apocalypse, the term *the nations* normally alludes to the Gentiles, who because of

49. Refer to Mounce, *Revelation*, p. 395.

50. Beale, *Revelation*, p. 1093.

their opposition to God deserve his wrath. In three occurrences (vv. 24, 26; 22:2) the term refers to the redeemed nations in the new Jerusalem. In light of the passage from Isaiah's prophecy, John gives a new meaning to the concepts *nations* and *kings,* removing the idea of enmity against God and his people (e.g., 18:3, 9, 23; 19:19). He notes that these nations and kings are part of God's family.[51] They joyfully bring their sacrificial gift of praise, "the fruit of lips that confess his name" (Heb. 13:15).

The inhabitants of the new Jerusalem originate from every tribe, language, people, and nation; they were purchased with the blood of the Lamb (5:9). They are part of the great multitude that no one could number (7:9). The kings of the earth are among those who have the privilege of ruling with Christ because they did not receive the mark on their foreheads or their hands (20:4, 6). Certainly, these nations and kings are citizens in God's kingdom and do not live outside the city, "for outside the city of God there is nothing—except the lake of fire."[52]

The nations walk through the divine light that illumines the holy city, and the kings of the earth glorify God. They live in the light and as a result offer glory and honor to God (v. 26).

These inhabitants seek not their own glory, but in continual worship they render it to God.[53]

b. "And its gates are not closed during the day, for there is no night there." John continues to borrow from Isaiah's prophecy:

Isaiah 60:11	**Revelation 21:25–26**
Your gates will always stand open, they will never be shut, day or night, so that men may bring you the wealth of the nations	And its gates are never closed during the day, for there is no night there. And they will bring the glory and honor of the nations into it.

In ancient times, the city gates were shut at nightfall for the security and safety of the citizens. But here John changes the wording of Isaiah and says, "And its gates are never closed during the day," and then adds, "for there is no night there." He implies that because sun and moon have ceased to function, the holy

51. G. B. Caird (*A Commentary on the Revelation of St. John the Divine* [London: Black, 1966], p. 279) interprets "the nations" as those who had trampled the holy city underfoot, whom the great whore had seduced, and "who were finally reduced to subjection by the armies of Christ." Also, Christ subdued "the kings," who had caused untold suffering to God's people. Compare Sweet, *Revelation,* p. 308; and Mathias Rissi, *The Future of the World,* Studies in Biblical Theology 23, 2d series (London: SCM, 1972), pp. 73–74. But this exegesis comes up short because these kings and armies were killed by the sword of Christ and perished (19:18, 21). Also, the prophecy of Isaiah notes that nations and kings drawn by the brightness of God's light bear gifts and proclaim praises to the LORD (60:3, 6).

52. Krodel, *Revelation,* p. 365.

53. Bauckham, *Climax of Prophecy,* pp. 314–16.

city is in eternal daylight and enjoys the light of God and the Lamb. In fact, the Greek uses the emphatic negative: "its gates are *never* closed."[54]

The saints in the holy city never need rest, and there is no darkness anymore within its walls. Angels who partake of eternity worship God day and night without resting (4:8); by contrast, worshipers of the beast in hell have no rest day and night (14:11). John uses the cosmic terms of day and night, but he points out that in eternity the saints bask in eternal light and implies that they never experience the eternal darkness of those who die a second death.

Everlasting openness of the city gates signifies not that some undesirable beings, human or angelic, can enter it. On the contrary, the open doors suggest that the residents are absolutely safe from all the evil forces that have been consigned to the lake of burning fire.

c. "And they will bring the glory and honor of the nations into it." The subject, here indicated as *they*, goes back to verse 24, "The nations . . . and the kings of the earth." These nations and kings collectively have bent their knees in worship, acknowledging Jesus as Lord of lords and King of kings. They are the kings of Tarshish, of distant lands, of Sheba and Seba. They will bring their tribute by glorifying and honoring the Lord; and they bow down before him and serve him (Ps. 72:10–11).

When John mentions city, nations, kings, gates, day, night, glory, and honor, he uses figurative language. His symbolism implies that the new Jerusalem encompasses the new heaven and the new earth.[55] God and the Lamb dwell forever with the saints in a renewed creation of heaven and earth, called the holy city.

27. And nothing unclean will ever enter it, neither he that does detestable and deceitful things, except those [names] written in the book of life of the Lamb.

While the preceding verses reveal the life of the saints following the last judgment, this verse is directed to the people living on earth before this judgment. John issues a warning by telling his readers that they are still living in the day of grace. When the consummation comes, no opportunity will be given for repentance and acceptance into heaven. Spiritual renewal takes place in the present life, not in the afterlife. Now is the time to heed the warning, repent, and wholeheartedly follow the Lord by doing his will.

What is the meaning of the word *unclean*? It refers to any unholy being or anything impure.[56] It is a ritual expression transmitted from Judaism to Christianity. Old Testament rules and regulations forbade anyone who was physically or spiritually unclean to enter the temple courts, and in New Testament times anyone

54. In their respective commentaries, Aune (*Revelation 17–22,* p. 1173), Charles (*Revelation,* 2:173, 439 n. 5), and Lohmeyer (*Offenbarung,* p. 175) consider the text a "redactional insertion" and the second clause "a corruption due in part to xxii.5." Their revisions of the text are pointless if we consider John to be indicating everlasting daylight when cosmic time has ceased.

55. Lenski, *Revelation,* p. 647.

56. Jan Fekkes, *Isaiah and Prophetic Tradition in the Book of Revelation,* JSNTSup 93 (Sheffield: JSOT, 1994), p. 274.

who refuses to acknowledge Jesus as Lord is barred from receiving baptism and partaking of communion; and any member who refuses to repent faces discipline.

John has in mind the words from Isaiah 52:1b, "O Jerusalem, the holy city. The uncircumcised and defiled will not enter you again." The writer of the Apocalypse specifies in another passage what he includes in "unclean." An unclean person who practices detestable things has as companions "sorcerers, fornicators, murderers, idolaters, and everyone who loves and practices deceit" (22:15; see 21:8). And those who speak deceitfully have Satan as their father (John 8:44); they are excluded from God's kingdom.

By contrast, those people whose names are recorded in the Lamb's book of life are free to enter the holy city; they possess life eternal and belong to their faithful Savior Jesus Christ. The Lamb, who bought them with his blood (5:9), will never blot out their names from his book (3:5) and will grant them the right to the tree of life and entrance into the city (22:14).

Greek Words, Phrases, and Constructions in 21:23–27

Verse 23

ἵνα—with the subjunctive φαίνωσιν the particle places limitations on the preceding nouns "sun" and "moon."

Verse 24

τὰ ἔθνη—this neuter plural, according to the classical rule, should have been followed by a verb in the singular, but here περιπατήσουσιν is in the plural. This happens more often in New Testament Greek.

Verse 26

οἴσουσιν—the future tense of the verb φέρω (I bring) has as subject either the kings of the earth (v. 24) or an indefinite plural as the pronoun "they." If verse 25 is an interruption of the flow of thought, then the subject of verse 24 is the preferred reading.

Verse 27

Some manuscripts have the neuter singular participle ποιοῦν instead of the masculine ποιῶν to agree with the neuter subject πᾶν κοινόν. But the sentence conveys not the sense of the neuter but that of the masculine, as is evident from the direct objects "detestable and deceitful things" practiced by people.

22

The Tree of Life and Conclusion

(22:1–21)

Outline (continued)

   5. The Tree of Life (22:1–5)

IX. Conclusion (22:6–21)
   A. Jesus' Return (22:6–17)
   B. Warning (22:18–19)
   C. Promise and Blessing (22:20–21)

22 1 And he showed me the river of the water of life, sparkling like crystal. It proceeds from
the throne of God and the Lamb, 2 down the middle of the city's main street. And on either side of the river is the tree of life bearing twelve kinds of fruit, according to each
month of the year it gives its fruit. And the leaves of the tree are for the healing of the nations. 3 And no longer will there be any curse. And the throne of God and of the Lamb will be in it,
and his servants will serve him, 4 and they will see his face. And his name will be on their foreheads.
5 There will be no night there, and they have no need of the light of a lamp and of the light of the
sun, because the Lord God will illumine them. And they will reign forever and ever.

6 And he said to me, "These words are faithful and true, and the Lord God of the spirits of the
prophets has sent his angel to show his servants what must soon take place. 7 And look, I am coming
soon. Blessed is the one who keeps the words of the prophecy of this book."

8 I, John, am the one who hears and sees these things. And when I heard and saw, I fell before
the angel at his feet to worship him who showed me these things. 9 And he said to me, "Don't do it.
I am a fellow servant of you and your brothers the prophets and of those who keep the words of this
book. Worship God."

10 And he said to me, "Do not seal the words of the prophecy of this book, for the time is near.
11 Let the evildoer continue to do evil, and let the filthy continue to be filthy, and let the just continue to do righteousness, and let the holy one continue to be holy."

12 "Look, I am coming soon. And my reward is with me to give to each according to his work.
13 I am the Alpha and the Omega, the First and the Last, the Beginning and the End.

14 "Blessed are they who wash their robes, so that they may have the right to the tree of life and
by the gates they may enter the city. 15 Outside are the dogs and the sorcerers and the fornicators
and the murderers and the idolaters and everyone who loves and practices deceit.

16 "I, Jesus, have sent my angel to you to testify to these things in the churches. I am the Root and
Descendant of David, the bright Morning Star."

17 "And the Spirit and the bride say, 'Come!' And let the one who hears say, 'Come!' And let the
one who is thirsty come, and let the one who desires take freely of the water of life."

18 "I testify to everyone who hears these words of the prophecy of this book. If anyone adds anything to them, God will add to him the plagues written in this book. 19 And if anyone takes anything
away from the words of the prophecy of this book, God will take away his share in the tree of life and
the holy city, which are described in this book."

20 He who testifies to these things says, "Yes, I am coming soon." Amen, come Lord Jesus.

21 The grace of the Lord Jesus be with all.

---

5. The Tree of Life
22:1–5

The first five verses of chapter 22 are part of the preceding section and not part of the conclusion (22:6–21). They belong to the description of the new Jerusalem, where from God's throne a life-giving river flows forth, with the tree of life along its banks. In this section are the concluding references to the throne in the city, the cessation of night, and the divine light that shines forever. The saints fully enjoy the beauty of the new creation in which they reign eternally.

Here is a picture of the new Garden of Eden. God's revelation begins with Adam and Eve in Paradise, with the tree of life and a river to water this garden, and his revelation concludes with a picture of the redeemed in that renewed garden with the tree of life and the river of life flowing from the throne of God and the Lamb.

This is heaven on earth. In a few lines an anonymous author expressed the thought that being with Jesus is heaven indeed.

Heaven

The light of heaven is the face of Jesus.
The joy of heaven is the presence of Jesus.
The melody of heaven is the Name of Jesus.
The employment of heaven is the service of Jesus.
The harmony of heaven is the praise of Jesus.
The theme of heaven is the work of Jesus.

Paul put it candidly, "We are confident, I say, and would prefer to be away from the body and at home with the Lord" (2 Cor. 5:8).

1. And he showed me the river of the water of life, sparkling like crystal. It proceeds from the throne of God and the Lamb.

The pronoun *he* alludes to the angel (21:9) who has the task of revealing to John the holy city. Central to the city is the throne that is depicted as the source of life. The throne belonging to God and the Lamb is the source of the river that supplies the water of life. But the emphasis is not so much on the river or the water as on the word *life.* Jesus offered the Samaritan woman at Jacob's well living water (John 4:10–11; 7:38), that is, water whose very essence is life.[1] The angel tells John that there is a river with an abundance of that life-giving water originating in the throne of God and the Lamb and flowing from it. This water of life signifies a steady stream of blessings to all the saints. Recording a heavenly anthem, John had written, "Because the Lamb at the center of the throne will shepherd them, and he will lead them to springs of living water" (Rev. 7:17; compare 21:6; 22:17).

Also the prophets portrayed a river flowing from the temple in Jerusalem. Ezekiel depicts a river flowing from the temple that became "deep enough to swim in—a river that no one could cross" (47:5), which was a source of life to

1. R. C. H. Lenski, *The Interpretation of St. John's Revelation* (Columbus: Wartburg, 1943), p. 649; Herman Hoeksema, *Behold, He Cometh! An Exposition of the Book of Revelation* (Grand Rapids: Reformed Free Publishing Association, 1969), p. 710; David E. Holwerda, *Jesus and Israel: One Covenant or Two?* (Grand Rapids: Eerdmans; Leicester: Inter-Varsity, 1995), pp. 78–79.

trees and fish (47:7–9). Zechariah writes, "On that day living water will flow out of Jerusalem" (14:8). Likewise, at the dawn of human history, "a river watering the garden flowed from Eden" (Gen. 2:10).

Sparkling clear water surges forth not from the temple but from the throne—there is no temple in the holy city. The stream initiates from the throne of both God and the Lamb. In the throne room the Lamb stands in or at the center of the throne (5:6; 7:17), but in the last of his seven letters Jesus invites the Laodiceans to sit with him on his Father's throne (3:21). That is, Father and Son as two divine persons occupy the same throne. John avoids designating Jesus as God in order not to leave the impression that he is teaching the existence of two Gods. The Father and the Son are one (John 14:20; 17:22).

2. Down the middle of the city's main street. And on either side of the river is the tree of life bearing twelve kinds of fruit, according to each month of the year it gives its fruit. And the leaves of the tree are for the healing of the nations.

The river gushes forth down the center of the main street mentioned earlier and described as made of gold (21:21). John's description is compact, yet the picture is clear; his focus is not on the street but on the river. On either side of the river are rows of trees, which he presents collectively as the tree of life. God planted this tree and the tree of the knowledge of good and evil in the Garden of Eden (Gen. 2:9), and cherubim guarded this tree of life with a flaming sword (Gen. 3:24). With the river and the tree of life, John paints a picture of a renewed Paradise to complete the biblical account of human history. Adam and Eve driven from the Garden of Eden were prevented from touching the tree of life, but in the garden of the holy city all the inhabitants have a right to that tree (22:14; 2:7).

The tree of life bears twelve kinds of fruit, one for each month of the year. John resorts to chronological divisions of time to express to human beings what otherwise would be incomprehensible. Standing on the threshold of eternity, he has to express himself in temporal terms of month and year. The significance of the tree bearing fruit is the abundant yield, and this food sustains the everlasting life of all those who eat.

The last part of the verse is problematic: "And the leaves of the tree are for the healing of the nations." If the sentence is interpreted to mean that illness and pain are present in the new Jerusalem, the concept *perfection* has lost its validity. The wording of the next verse (v. 3a) prohibits this interpretation, "And no longer will there be any curse." Some commentators view the words *for the healing of the nations* to refer to the effect of the gospel on the nations in the preconsummation era.[2] But the context demands an explanation not of the gospel age but of eternity. Still others present a plausible elucidation by looking at the Greek word for healing (*therapeian*) and suggest that this word refers to a thera-

2. S. Greijdanus, *De Openbaring des Heeren aan Johannes,* KNT (Amsterdam: Van Bottenburg, 1925), p. 432; Henry Barclay Swete, *Commentary on Revelation: The Greek Text with Introduction, Notes, and Indexes* (1911; reprint, Grand Rapids: Kregel, 1977), p. 300.

peutic healing understood as health-giving.[3] I add that the language is symbolic and implicitly points to the curse that rested on the human race because of the tree in Paradise and that brought sickness, pain, and death. But the tree in the renewed Paradise provides healing for the nations, which means that its inhabitants can enjoy eternal life free from physical and spiritual needs.[4]

John takes the wording from Ezekiel 47:12, where fruit trees are mentioned: "Their fruit will serve for food and their leaves for healing." This accords with a comment in 4 Ezra (=2 Esdras) 7:123: "What good is the revelation to us of paradise and its imperishable fruit, the source of perfect satisfaction and healing?" (REB).

3. And no longer will there be any curse. And the throne of God and of the Lamb will be in it, and his servants will serve him.

a. "And no longer will there be any curse." John borrows the wording from a prophecy on the eschatological restoration of Jerusalem, "And people will live in it, and there will be no more curse, for Jerusalem will dwell in security" (Zech. 14:11 NASB). After Adam and Eve sinned in Paradise, God pronounced a curse on creation and the human race (Gen. 3:17–19). And this curse remains in effect until the restoration takes place and everyone can freely take fruit from the tree of life. Then the sad history of sin and its consequences will have ended, never to be repeated. The curse will forever be lifted through the sacrificial death of the Lamb on Calvary's cross.

b. "And the throne of God and of the Lamb will be in it, and his servants will serve him." Once again John mentions that the throne of God and of the Lamb will be in the holy city. Again he indirectly stresses the deity of Christ as equal to God. This becomes evident with the use of the personal pronouns *his* and *him* in the second clause (see 22:4; see also 11:15; 20:6). God and the Lamb occupy one throne, while the citizens of the holy city in the capacity of priests will serve them. John expresses similar wording in 7:15, "Therefore, they are before the throne of God and serve him day and night in his temple, and he who is seated on the throne will spread his tent over them."

4. And they will see his face. And his name will be on their foreheads.

The first clause has a remarkable message, for throughout Scripture we read that no one can see the face of God and live. Moses was permitted to see his back but not his face (Exod. 33:20, 23). No one has ever seen God (John 1:18; 6:46; 1 John 4:12), but here John writes that the glorified saints will see his face. He mentions this elsewhere: "But we know that when he appears, we shall be like him, for we shall see him as he is" (1 John 3:2b; compare Heb. 12:14). God has a relationship with his people that is the same as before the fall in Paradise when he walked and talked with Adam and Eve in the cool of the day.

---

3. John F. Walvoord, *The Revelation of Jesus Christ* (Chicago: Moody, 1966), p. 330; Leon Morris, *Revelation*, rev. ed., TNTC (Leicester: Inter-Varsity; Grand Rapids: Eerdmans, 1987), p. 249; Robert L. Thomas, *Revelation 8–22: An Exegetical Commentary* (Chicago: Moody, 1995), p. 485.

4. Consult Robert H. Mounce, *The Book of Revelation*, rev. ed., NICNT (Grand Rapids: Eerdmans, 1998), pp. 399–400.

All those who have the name of the Lamb and of the Father written on their foreheads (14:1) will see him. The Lamb redeemed his people and brought them into the presence of the Father. It is through Christ that the saints have the privilege of seeing God in eternity. The imprint of the divine name on the foreheads of the saints signifies that as residents of the new Jerusalem they belong to God, bear his image and likeness, and are citizens of his kingdom.

5. There will be no night there, and they have no need of the light of a lamp and of the light of the sun, because the Lord God will illumine them. And they will reign forever and ever.

This verse is the concluding passage that summarizes what John has been saying in the last part of chapter 21. By repeating the wording of this last part, John seeks to emphasize his message. First, he repeats 21:25 word for word by saying that in the new creation the cosmic division of night and day will have ceased to function (Zech. 14:7). There will always be light in the holy city, which means that everything belonging to the old creation has vanished. Next, it teaches that in the renewed world God's people will never need to rest and sleep; they will have boundless energy to serve God and praise his name forever and ever.

John reiterates the wording of 21:23 when he writes that the saints will have no need of the light of lamp or sun. He again stresses the equality of God and the Lamb by stating that each of them serves as a lamp to his people. In the words of Isaiah, "The LORD will be your everlasting light" (60:19).

Last, "and they will reign forever and ever" is an echo of Daniel's prophecy, "But the saints of the Most High will receive the kingdom and will possess it forever—yes, forever and ever" (Dan. 7:18; see also Dan. 7:27). John provides no details, but earlier he wrote that the saints sit with Christ on the throne of his Father (Rev. 3:21).

Greek Words, Phrases, and Constructions in 22:1–2

ὕδατος ζωῆς—the second noun clarifies the first one: "water, that is, eternal life." This interpretation accurately renders John's intention.

Instead of placing a period at the end of verse 1, as in Greek New Testaments, it is better to regard it as a comma and place the period after the first clause of verse 2. "It proceeds from the throne of God and the Lamb, down the middle of the city's main street."

ἐντεῦθεν καὶ ἐκεῖθεν—John 19:18 has a similar expression ἐντεῦθεν καὶ ἐντεῦθεν, "one on either side" (see Dan. 12:5 Theod.).

IX. Conclusion
22:6–21

The similarities between the first chapter and the last chapter of the Apocalypse are striking.[5] Both passages refer to God's revelation, obedience to the Word, the identity of the Lord, and the testimony to the churches.

---

5. Consult David E. Aune, *Revelation 17–22,* WBC 52C (Nashville: Nelson, 1998), pp. 1205–6; Gerhard A. Krodel, *Revelation,* ACNT (Minneapolis: Augsburg, 1989), pp. 368–69.

Revelation 1:1	Revelation 22:6
God gave Jesus [his revelation] to show his servants what must soon take place by sending his angel	the Lord God has sent his angel to show his servants what must soon take place

Revelation 1:3	Revelation 22:7, 10
Blessed are the ones who hear the words of this prophecy and who heed the things written in it. For the time is near.	Blessed is the one who keeps the words of the prophecy of this book. For the time is near.

Revelation 1:8, 17	Revelation 22:13
I am the Alpha and the Omega the First and the Last.	I am the Alpha and the Omega the First and the Last.

Revelation 1:1	Revelation 22:16
And he made it known by sending his angel to his servant John who testified.	I, Jesus, have sent my angel to you to testify these things in the churches.

John mentions his name three times in chapter 1 (vv. 1, 4, 9), and then once more in chapter 22 (v. 8). Also, in the first chapter John records words of Jesus, who instructed John to write seven letters (chaps. 2 and 3); Jesus' voice is heard again in chapter 22 (vv. 7, 12–16, 18–20). The Holy Spirit speaks at the conclusion of each of the seven letters (2:7, 11, 17, 29; 3:6, 13, 22) but also in 14:13 and 22:17. The prologue (1:3) features the first beatitude, and chapter 22 completes the series with the sixth and seventh (vv. 7, 12). And last, in 22:18–19 God utters a warning that is comparable to a copyright notice in a modern book. In other words, God is saying that this book belongs to him and must be treated with utmost respect.

A. Jesus' Return
22:6–17

6. And he said to me, "These words are faithful and true, and the Lord God of the spirits of the prophets has sent his angel to show his servants what must soon take place."

The glory of the heavenly scenes has come to an end, but John, who has come back to cosmic reality, is still in the presence of the angel. The Greek text briefly reads, "And he said to me," while it is evident that the angel is the speaker (see 22:1). There are multiple witnesses in the conclusion of the Apocalypse. There is the angel who addresses and corrects John. Then there is John himself, Jesus, and last the Holy Spirit and the bride (the church).[6]

Both the angel and John testify to the genuineness of the book, which is absolutely trustworthy because God is its author. This does not mean that for the composition of the book John was a mere writing instrument in the hand of God. He functioned as a first-century Jew who wrote the Koine Greek spoken by his contemporaries. And God used John with his talents, insight into the Scriptures, and authorial ability to compose Revelation. Nonetheless, God is the primary author and John the secondary.

a. "These words are faithful and true" is a repeat of 21:5 (see also 19:9). By reiterating these same words, John emphasizes their indisputable reliability. Some scholars have attempted a restructuring of the Apocalypse to make the text more acceptable for modern readers, but the fact of the matter is that God as the great architect has constructed this book. John writes, "The Lord, the God of the spirits of the prophets, has sent his angel to show his servants" (compare Num. 27:16). John has in mind the work of the Holy Spirit, who inspired the prophets of the Old and New Testaments not only to speak but also to write the living Word of God (Rev. 19:10; 1 Cor. 14:32). And John has relied on both Testaments to formulate his thoughts in the Apocalypse.

God sent his angel to John to show his servants what was coming, but Jesus is also named as the sender (cf. vv. 6, 16). This fact by itself once more illustrates the divinity of Christ. John notes that the servants who receive this divine message are all God's people who implicitly obey his Word (see v. 3; 1:3; 2:20; 7:3; 19:2, 5).

b. "What must soon take place." These words also appear in 1:1 and echo Daniel's answer to King Nebuchadnezzar (2:28–29 Old Greek and Theod.). But even though the message is no doubt urgent, in view of the passing of time the question concerning its imminence cannot be suppressed. It is clear that Jesus anticipated this query. In the succeeding verses he repeatedly assures the reader that he is coming soon (vv. 7, 12, 20; see also 2:5, 16, 25; 3:3, 11). From a human perspective, the fulfillment of this promise seems to have been postponed. But from a divine perspective, the things that have been predicted are taking place even now, so that the consummation itself is imminent indeed. The term *soon* expresses the sober reality that the consummation is at hand. When the sins of this evil world reach to heaven and leave no room for additional sins between heaven and earth (18:5), then the cup of wrath is full and the end has come.

7. "And look, I am coming soon. Blessed is the one who keeps the words of the prophecy of this book."

Who is the speaker? Certainly, the first person singular pronoun *I* points to Jesus, for he has promised his return all along. But even though these words belong to Jesus, it is possible to interpret them as quoted by the angel. This is the

6. William Hendriksen (*More Than Conquerors* [reprint, Grand Rapids: Baker, 1982], p. 209) mentions three: the angel, John, and Jesus.

position of many commentators,[7] yet Christ himself could have spoken these very words directly to John (see vv. 12, 20).

The early Christians in the first century when celebrating the Lord's Supper would conclude the sacrament with a prayer that ended with the word *Maranatha* (Our Lord, come!; *Didache* 10.6; see 1 Cor. 16:22).[8] They knew that Jesus as their host was in the midst of them spiritually, but their desire was to have him return physically.

The sixth beatitude repeats in abbreviated form the words of the first beatitude. "Blessed is the one who keeps the words of the prophecy of this book" and "Blessed is the one who reads aloud and the ones who hear the words of this prophecy and who heed the things written in it" (1:3). There is an obvious connection between *the one who keeps* and *the one who heeds.* The Greek text has a present participle in "the one who is keeping" to indicate the continuing task of voluntarily and joyfully obeying the divine words written in this book. And the phrase "the words of the prophecy of this book" appears three times (vv. 10, 18, 19). These words point to the contents of Revelation.

8. I, John, am the one who hears and sees these things. And when I heard and saw, I fell before the angel at his feet to worship him who showed me these things.

John provides a personal identification with the pronoun *I* (see 1:9) in an effort to make sure that his readers will know that he as their well-known spiritual leader is indeed the author of this book. He uses a formula ("I, [and personal name]") that was common in his day, for both Paul ("I, Paul," Gal. 5:2; Eph. 3:1; Col. 1:23; 1 Thess. 2:18; Philem. 19) and Jesus employ it ("I, Jesus," Rev. 22:16). It also appears in the prophecy of Daniel 7:15, 28; 8:1.

The writer is a witness by ear and eye. Hence, his testimony is not based on human imagination but on divine revelation. He has now recorded in the Apocalypse all that he has heard and seen, and that is not limited to the vision of the new Jerusalem.[9] The Book of Revelation includes his vision of Jesus, the letters to the seven churches, the seals, the trumpets, the plagues, the final judgment, and the new Jerusalem. John testifies to the trustworthiness of what he personally has written down (compare John 21:24).

John falls at the feet of the angel who revealed these overwhelming things to him. This is the same phenomenon described in 19:10, where John, upon seeing

---

7. Swete, *Revelation,* p. 303; Isbon T. Beckwith, *The Apocalypse of John* (1919; reprint, Grand Rapids: Baker, 1979), pp. 773–74; Thomas, *Revelation 8–22,* p. 497. M. Robert Mulholland Jr. (*Revelation: Holy Living in an Unholy World* [Grand Rapids: Zondervan, Frances Asbury Press, 1990], pp. 332–33) identifies Christ with the angel by writing that Christ appears in angelic form. This interpretation meets difficulty in the next two verses, for there the identification fails. Homer Hailey (*Revelation: An Introduction and Commentary* [Grand Rapids: Baker, 1979], p. 426) suggests that God is the speaker.

8. Michael Wilcock, *The Message of Revelation: I Saw Heaven Opened* (Leicester: Inter-Varsity; Downers Grove: InterVarsity, 1975), p. 214.

9. Richard Bauckham, *The Climax of Prophecy* (Edinburgh: Clark, 1993), p. 256.

the wedding banquet of the bride and bridegroom, falls at the feet of the angel. Although the two instances are identical except for the wording, they occupy different positions in the Apocalypse. The first incident relates to the wedding banquet, at which time the church and Jesus come together as bride and bridegroom. The second occurs in the conclusion of Revelation, where John conveys the same account for the sake of emphasis.

9. And he said to me, "Don't do it. I am a fellow servant of you and your brothers the prophets and of those who keep the words of this book. Worship God."

The words of the angel are almost the same as those spoken by him and recorded in 19:10, "And he said to me, 'Don't do it. I am a fellow servant with you and your brothers [and sisters] who hold the testimony of Jesus. Worship God.'" But now the angel expands the sentence by adding the words "the prophets and of those who keep the words of this book." Bauckham notes, "The angel's rejection of worship now functions, therefore, to claim for the whole book the authority, not of the angel, but of God himself (hence 22:18–19), to whom alone worship is due"[10] (Exod. 20:5; Deut. 5:9). The repetition is not an oversight of the author but rather a deliberate decision to stress the divine inspiration of the entire book, whose primary author is God, who is worthy of worship and praise.

The admonition is meant for John and all God's people. John and the prophets are not on a level that is separate from and above ordinary believers; they are part of them. God teaches that the worship of any creature, whether angel, human being, animal, or inanimate object, is absolutely forbidden. Ultimately there are only two categories of being in the universe: the Creator and his creation. Nothing in God's entire creation may ever be placed above the Creator and receive homage. Thus, Jesus rebuffed Satan, because the devil asked the Lord to worship him. On the basis of Scripture, Jesus told him to worship only the LORD God (Deut. 6:13; Matt. 4:10; Luke 4:8).

10. And he said to me, "Do not seal the words of the prophecy of this book, for the time is near."

Once again John fails to identify the speaker (see v. 7), who probably is the angel who speaks on behalf of Jesus. Thus, the primary source is the Lord, who addresses John with a negative command never to seal the words of this prophecy. The positive side of this command, therefore, is to publish them as a document and to proclaim them to all people.[11] The difference between the prophecy of Daniel and the Apocalypse of John is clear. The former is told to close up and seal the words of his prophecy until the end of time (Dan. 8:26; 12:4, 9; compare Rev. 10:4), but John's book must be left unsealed and available to anyone who wishes to read and hear its message. Also, the Jewish apocalypses were kept

10. Bauckham, *Climax of Prophecy*, p. 134. See Gregory K. Beale, *The Book of Revelation: A Commentary on the Greek Text,* NIGTC (Grand Rapids: Eerdmans, 1998), p. 1128.

11. Ernst Lohmeyer, *Die Offenbarung des Johannes,* HNT 16 (Tübingen: Mohr, 1970), p. 179.

sealed to the uninitiated.[12] But God's Word is not chained, for it is sent forth to accomplish his plan and purpose (Isa. 55:11; 2 Tim. 2:9).

The time is near. This is not a reference to a calendar or to clock time; rather it means an opportune moment or a time of decision. The words are identical to 1:3, so that at the beginning and at the end of the Apocalypse, the same note of urgency is sounded. God is alerting his people to be prepared in the end time.

11. "Let the evildoer continue to do evil, and let the filthy continue to be filthy, and let the just continue to do righteousness, and let the holy one continue to be holy."

John's practice of making contrasts is obvious in these four clauses. The first two present negative aspects and the last two positive aspects. The first and the third clauses correspond, as do the second and the fourth. That is, doing evil is placed over against doing righteousness, and being filthy is the opposite of being holy.

1. let the evildoer continue to do evil	3. and let the just continue to do righteousness
2. and let the filthy continue to be filthy	4. and let the holy one continue to be holy

The first and third lines stress one's deeds, while the second and fourth lines emphasize one's character.[13] The second, third, and fourth clauses begin with the conjunction *and*, which is characteristic of John's coordinate style of writing.

The Greek third-person imperatives appearing four times in the clauses are marked in English by the word *let*. This word can be either "the 'let' of positive exhortation" (as in "let the wicked forsake his way") or "the 'let' of withdrawal" (as in "let him be").[14] An objection to this interpretation is that the four lines feature the same command and therefore must be understood "in the same imperatival manner."[15] But John has divided humanity into the two groups of those who do evil and are filthy and those who practice righteousness and are holy. The word *continue* occurring in all four clauses indicates a process that is ongoing. It leads to either a life of degradation or a life of holiness. "One either grows in grace and stature as a Christian or sinks deeper into hardness and indifference as a sinner; there is no standing still."[16] The sinner and the saint either regress or progress in their spiritual life. The sinner regresses from unbelief to disobedience, from disobedience to neglect, from neglect to apostasy, and from apostasy to hardening of the heart. The saint continues to make progress in a life

12. In 4 Ezra (=2 Esdras) 12:37–38; 14:5–6, 45–47, the command to hide the book and to disclose its contents only to the wise is plain. See Aune, *Revelation 17–22*, p. 1216.

13. Kendell H. Easley, *Revelation*, HNTC (Nashville: Broadman & Holman, 1998), p. 419.

14. Hendriksen, *More Than Conquerors*, p. 208.

15. Beale, *Revelation*, p. 1132; Mounce, *Revelation*, p. 406 n. 18.

16. Hailey, *Revelation*, p. 428.

that leads from faith to practicing obedience, from obedience to joy, and from joy to unending bliss in the Lord. The character of the hardened sinner is decidedly anti-Christian, but that of the saint is marked by righteousness and holiness.

There are echoes from the Old Testament in this series of contrasts. At the end of Daniel's prophecy we read,

> Many will be purified, made spotless
> and refined,
> but the wicked will continue to be
> wicked.
> None of the wicked will understand,
> but those who are wise will understand.
> (Dan. 12:10; compare Ezek. 3:27)

This is not to say that God fails to call the sinner to repentance. "Repentance is always a live option as long as a person is living."[17] Ezekiel devotes an entire chapter to the life of the righteous versus the life of the wicked, and at its conclusion he writes, "For I take no pleasure in the death of anyone, declares the Sovereign LORD. Repent and live!" (Ezek. 18:32).

12. "Look, I am coming soon. And my reward is with me to give to each according to his work. 13. I am the Alpha and the Omega, the First and the Last, the Beginning and the End."

The words of verse 12 are a confirmation of the preceding verse (v. 11). Jesus says that he is coming soon (see vv. 7, 20) and will then reward every human being according to his or her works. But can the word *reward* be interpreted as a payment for work performed?

First, the promise of Jesus' return means joy and happiness for the believer but fear and remorse for the unbeliever. His return must be seen against the background of the last judgment at which time the righteous will enter into their heavenly reward and the unrighteous into outer darkness (Matt. 25:31–46).

Next, in Scripture there is no works righteousness, "no petty calculation of reward, no counting of good works (and bad), no correspondence between achievement and reward."[18] The term *reward* has no connection with the concept "treasure in heaven" (Matt. 6:19), for any reward that God gives is on the basis of unmerited grace. The gift of salvation is pure grace, undeserved, and unearned.

When Jesus says that he is coming soon and his reward is with him, he rephrases words recorded in the Old Testament Scriptures. "See, the Sovereign LORD comes with power, and his arm rules for him. See, his reward is with him, and his recompense accompanies him" (Isa. 40:10; see also Ps. 28:4; Jer. 17:10). In his letter to the church in Thyatira, Jesus says that he will repay each of them

17. Alan F. Johnson, *Revelation*, in *The Expositor's Bible Commentary*, ed. Frank E. Gaebelein (Grand Rapids: Zondervan, 1981), 12:601.

18. Wilhelm Pesch, *EDNT*, 2:433. See also Paul Christoph Böttger, *NIDNTT*, 3:141–44; Herbert Preisker, *TDNT*, 4:716–19.

according to their deeds (Rev. 2:23; compare 18:6; and 20:12–13). These passages refer to the coming of Jesus as the judge of all the earth.

Jesus identifies himself with the first and the last letter in the Greek alphabet, the Alpha and the Omega, and as the First and the Last, the Beginning and the End (see 21:6). In this summary statement, he utters three clauses that convey the concept that he is everlastingly divine. Note that in the first chapter God identified himself with the letters Alpha and Omega, but Jesus identified himself as "the First and the Last" (1:8 and 17, respectively). Now in the conclusion to the Apocalypse, Jesus clearly places himself equal to God with the same words of identification. He is equal with God in power and authority.

14. "Blessed are they who wash their robes, so that they may have the right to the tree of life and by the gates they may enter the city."

a. "Blessed are they who wash their robes." With this last and seventh beatitude Jesus addresses the saints on earth by calling blessed those people who wash their robes. He implies that their robes are filthy because of sin, which can be removed only through the blood of Christ. The verb *to wash* is a participle in the present tense to indicate that sin is a continual polluting agency that needs repeated cleansings. Earlier John recorded the words of an elder who instructed him concerning the status of the saints in heaven. "These are they who have come out of the great tribulation and have washed their robes and have made them white in the blood of the Lamb" (7:14). Whereas the words of the elder are addressed to celestial saints, whose robes have been washed once for all (aorist tense), Jesus speaks to the saints on earth and by implication urges them to wash their robes again and again (present tense). Moses instructed the Israelites at Mount Sinai to wash their clothes prior to coming before God to hear the Law (Exod. 19:10, 14). This means that no one can enter the presence of God in filthy garments, for such an act is abominable to him. Only those who are covered with the robe of righteousness may enter God's holiness (Isa. 61:10). Clothed in pure linen, they are permitted to sit at the table of the Lord (19:8; compare Matt. 22:11–13).

b. "So that they may have the right to the tree of life." Adam and Eve were driven out of the Garden of Eden, and cherubim prevented them from approaching the tree of life (Gen. 3:24). But now the saints have perfect freedom to take the fruit of this tree (2:7; 22:2). Indeed Jesus grants them the right to do so. Delivered from the bondage of sin and guilt through his sacrifice, they now enjoy life eternal with unhindered access to the tree of life.

c. "And by the gates they may enter the city." They are God's people who have the right to enter the holy city and enjoy never-ending residency. Their names are recorded in the book of life that grants them citizenship in the new Jerusalem (21:27b).

15. "Outside are the dogs and the sorcerers and the fornicators and the murderers and the idolaters and everyone who loves and practices deceit."

Addressing the people on earth, Jesus once again shows contrast between the believer and the unbeliever. Believers are dressed in clean garments and have the right to the tree of life and to heavenly citizenship. But unbelievers are excluded, because their lifestyle is compared to "those who are detested and the murderers and the fornicators, and the sorcerers and idolaters, and to all who are deceivers" (21:8). These six categories are identical, with the exception that the detested ones are now called dogs. In Old Testament times street dogs were despised (e.g., 1 Kings 14:11; 2 Kings 8:13), and a male prostitute was called a dog (Deut. 23:18). In New Testament times the rabbis would refer to Gentiles as dogs, and Paul even designated his opponents as such (Phil. 3:2).[19] In brief, the word *dog* was a pejorative term denoting someone to be shunned.

The sorcerers, murderers, idolaters, fornicators, and deceitful persons are mentioned and discussed in 21:8. The repetition of these categories in the concluding verses of the Apocalypse is for emphasis. This fact is stressed with the addition of the verbs *to love* and *to practice* in the phrase "everyone who loves and practices deceit." The addition underscores the depth of sin when a sinner turns the truth into a lie and takes great delight in doing so. A plausible suggestion is to view this vice list as a warning to repent directed to Christians who are in danger of drifting away (Heb. 2:1; 3:12–13; 4:1, 11).[20]

16. "I, Jesus, have sent my angel to you to testify to these things in the churches. I am the Root and Descendant of David, the bright Morning Star."

Jesus identifies himself as the speaker with the use of the personal pronoun *I*, common in Paul's epistles ("I, Paul," Gal. 5:2; Eph. 3:1; Col. 1:23; 1 Thess. 2:18; Philem. 19) and in Revelation ("I, John," 1:9 and 22:8). Jesus says that he has sent his angel, which once more is an indication of his divinity. In 1:1 God sent his angel to John, while here Jesus claims that he has dispatched his angel. Notice also that the message of the angel is for the recipients given here in the second person plural *you*, which refers to the readers and hearers of the Apocalypse (1:3).

The verb *to testify* appears three times in these concluding verses (vv. 16, 18, 20) and means the act of bearing witness to the prophetic word that God passes on to his people (1:2). It signifies to confirm "these things" (that is, the Apocalypse) passed on and delivered to the recipients.[21] The addressees are the members of the seven churches, but these churches represent symbolically the universal church that is present throughout the world in time and place.

In the salutation John writes, "John to the seven *churches* that are in [the province of] Asia. Grace to *you*" (1:4, emphasis added). Thus, the plural noun and pronoun *churches* and *you* respectively appear in the same context, be it in reverse order. The parallel structure in the salutation (1:4) and in the conclusion (22:16) is clear; it confirms the interpretation that the noun and the pronoun indeed are the same category.[22]

---

19. Refer to Otto Michel, *TDNT*, 3:1101–4.

20. Thomas, *Revelation 8–22*, p. 507; Robert W. Wall, *Revelation*, NIBCNT (Peabody, Mass.: Hendrickson, 1991), p. 266.

21. Bauer, pp. 492–93; Hermann Strathmann, *TDNT*, 4:499. Aune (*Revelation 17–22*, p. 1225) argues that the plural *you* "refers to a circle of Christian prophets whose task it was to transmit John's revelatory message to the churches." See also his "Prophetic Circle of John of Patmos and the Exegesis of Revelation 22.16," *JSNT* 37 (1989): 103–16.

22. Consult Beale, *Revelation*, pp. 1145–46.

Five times in Revelation Jesus uses the "I am" to identify himself (1:8, 17; 2:23; 21:6; 22:16). Here he names himself "the Root and Descendant of David, the bright Morning Star." The Old Testament provides the background for these names; the phrase "the Root and Descendant of David" originates in Isaiah 11:1, 10 and 53:2; and "the bright Morning Star" is an echo of Numbers 24:17, "A star will come out of Jacob." In his letter to the church in Thyatira, Jesus promises the morning star to every overcomer (2:28); and mentioning the day of Christ's return, Peter informs his readers that this happens when "the morning star rises in your hearts" (2 Pet. 1:19). With the use of this expression, Peter points to Christ.[23]

17. "And the Spirit and the bride say, 'Come!' And let the one who hears say, 'Come!' And let the one who is thirsty come, and let the one who desires take freely of the water of life."

Jesus appears to be the speaker and now announces that the response to his words comes from two sources, namely, the Holy Spirit and the church on earth. These two continue to utter their appeal for Jesus' return with a request in the present tense that signifies "Carry out your plan in history with a view toward your coming."[24] The call for the coming of the Lord is repeated in verse 20 as the last petition in the Apocalypse, "Amen, come Lord Jesus." The Spirit of Christ is the Spirit of the bridegroom; and this Spirit has his abode in the bride, that is, the church. Hence, at the powerful urging of the Spirit, the church expresses her longing for the return of Christ, her bridegroom. Not only the organic body of the church but also every individual believer who obediently responds to the prompting of the Spirit articulates this yearning. The invitation "Come!" occurs twice to stress urgency.

However, the third invitation, "Let the one who is thirsty come," is not addressed to Christ but to the people as a call to come to him. This causes confusion, especially as the last exhortation, "Let the one who desires take freely of the water of life," is also an evangelistic address. This inconsistency can be solved when we interpret the double meaning of the verb *to come.* First, the church at worship and at the celebration of the Lord's Supper petitions Christ to return (*Maranatha;* see *Didache* 10.6). Next, at the same time the church extends to everyone the invitation to come to Christ. Writing about the coming of the Lord, Peter instructs his readers to live holy and godly lives "as you look forward to the day of God and speed its coming" (2 Pet. 3:12a), thus indicating that God's people have a part in shortening the time before Jesus' return. Addressing the crowd after healing the crippled beggar, Peter told the people to repent in order to hasten the coming of Christ (Acts 3:19–21). Similarly about A.D. 300, a Jewish rabbi wrote, "If the Israelites were to repent for one day, then the Son of David [the Messiah] would come."[25] This

23. See Simon J. Kistemaker, *Exposition of the Epistles of Peter and of the Epistle of Jude*, NTC (Grand Rapids: Baker, 1987), p. 270.

24. Hendriksen, *More Than Conquerors*, p. 209; Lenski, *Revelation*, p. 670.

25. SB, 1:164. See Kistemaker, *Epistles of Peter*, pp. 338–39.

means that the church must bring the gospel to the world, lead people to faith and repentance, and fill the house of God. Then the end will come and Christ will return.

Everyone who desires to drink from the water of life may freely come and take. There is an Old Testament invitation, recorded in Isaiah 55:1, "Come, all you who are thirsty, come to the waters; and you who have no money, come, buy and eat! Come, buy wine and milk without money and without cost" (see also John 7:37; Rev. 21:6).

Greek Words, Phrases, and Constructions in 22:14–16

Verse 14

πλύνοντες τὰς στολὰς αὐτῶν—"washing their robes." Leading Greek manuscripts support this phrase, but the TR and the Majority Text have a different reading, ποιοῦντες τὰς ἐντολὰς αὐτοῦ ("doing his commandments"). The sound of the two phrases is similar, but the second appears "to be a scribal emendation," because John uses the expression τηρεῖν τὰς ἐντολάς (12:17; 14:12).[26]

ἵνα—when followed by the future tense of the verb *to be*, the clause is more result than purpose. It expresses certainty that what is promised will take place.

Verse 16

ἐπί—a common translation is "for." Variants are either ἐν (in) or the omission of any preposition. I prefer the reading ἐν.

B. Warning
22:18–19

18. "I testify to everyone who hears these words of the prophecy of this book. If anyone adds anything to them, God will add to him the plagues written in this book. 19. And if anyone takes anything away from the words of the prophecy of this book, God will take away his share in the tree of life and the holy city, which are described in this book."

Jesus most likely is the speaker because the personal pronoun *I* harmonizes with verse 16, and the verb *to testify* appears in verse 20 where Jesus is the speaker. In the introductory part and the conclusion Jesus directly addresses the readers and hearers, but for the rest of Revelation he sent his angel.[27] His address to the person who hears the words of the prophecy of this book repeats

---

26. Bruce M. Metzger, *A Textual Commentary on the Greek New Testament*, 2d ed. (Stuttgart: Deutsche Bibelgesellschaft, 1994), p. 690.

27. Swete, *Revelation*, p. 311; Thomas, *Revelation 8–22*, p. 513; Mounce, *Revelation*, p. 410; Luther Poellot, *Revelation: The Last Book in the Bible* (St. Louis: Concordia, 1962), p. 301; Greijdanus, *Openbaring*, p. 446. Some scholars designate John as the speaker. See Jürgen Roloff, *The Revelation of John*, trans. J. E. Alsup (Minneapolis: Fortress, 1993), p. 253; Wilfrid J. Harrington, *Revelation*, SP 16 (Collegeville, Minn.: Liturgical Press, 1993), p. 226.

similar wording in verses 7 and 10. Hearing must be accompanied by understanding (compare 1:3).

The solemn warning not to add to or detract from the words of this book is common in ancient literature. For instance, Moses warns the Israelites not to add to or subtract from the decrees and laws God gave them (Deut. 4:2; 12:32). This formula was attached to documents much the same as modern manuscripts are protected by copyright laws.[28] In addition, curses were added in the form of a conditional sentence, "If anyone adds or takes away anything from this book, a curse will rest upon him." Paul wrote a similar condemnation when he told the Galatians that if anyone preached a gospel which was not the gospel of Christ, "let him be eternally condemned" (Gal. 1:6–8). Now Jesus pronounces a curse on anyone who distorts his message.[29]

What are these curses? The plagues written in this book include not only temporal penalties but also eternal separation from the living God and exclusion from eternal life and the holy city. They are applied not to anyone making a clerical error in copying the manuscript but to the one deliberately distorting the text.[30] Copyists who unintentionally made errors of the eye or ear are not addressed. If this were the case, I venture to say that no one would have dared to make a copy of the Apocalypse.

Twice in this passage the word *prophecy* occurs, which signifies that the words recorded in this Apocalypse are being fulfilled in the course of time and point to fulfillment when Jesus returns. What he has promised he will certainly fulfill in the time set by the Father (Matt. 24:36; Acts 1:7). Note that the word *prophecy* appears seven times in Revelation, and four of them are in the last chapter (1:3; 11:6; 19:10; 22:7, 10, 18, 19).

Greek Words, Phrases, and Constructions in 22:19

ἀπὸ τοῦ ξύλου—the TR reads ἀπὸ βίβλου, which lacks Greek manuscript support. In 1516 Erasmus translated these words from the Latin Vulgate into Greek. "The corruption of 'tree' into 'book' had occurred earlier in the transmission of the Latin text when a scribe accidentally miscopied the correct word *ligno* ('tree') as *libro* ('book')."[31]

---

28. Aune (*Revelation 17–22*, pp. 1208–13) lists a number of examples taken from many sources. One of them appears in 1 Maccabees 8:30 in connection with a treaty the Romans made with the Jews, "But if, hereafter, both parties agree to add or to rescind anything, what they decide shall be done; any such addition or rescindment shall be valid" (REB).

29. According to the *Letter of Aristeas* 310–11, after the Hebrew Scriptures had been translated into Greek, a curse was pronounced on anyone who would make alterations to the translation by adding or omitting any of the words that had been written.

30. R. H. Charles (*A Critical and Exegetical Commentary on the Revelation of St. John*, ICC [Edinburgh: Clark, 1920], 2:223) comments, "The plagues are concerned with temporal punishments, not with eternal." Then he asserts that verses "18b–19 introduce a wrong note in these last verses." He considers them an interpolation and places them in a footnote (p. 445).

31. Metzger, *Textual Commentary*, p. 690.

C. Promise and Blessing
22:20–21

20. He who testifies to these things says, "Yes, I am coming soon." Amen, come Lord Jesus.

Here is the earnest declaration from the lips of Jesus that he indeed will return as he has promised (v. 12). The Spirit and the bride implore him to come, and every sincere believer likewise entreats him to return (v. 17). Now Jesus assures everyone that he is coming soon. But how soon will he make his appearance? We can safely say that his return is closer now than ever, since nearly two thousand years have passed. Nonetheless, the meaning of this adverb is "without delay, quickly, at once, in a short time."[32]

The response to Jesus' promise is formulated in a prayer that is the last petition in Scripture, "Amen, come Lord Jesus." That is, the believer is convinced of the veracity of this promise and confirms it with a hearty "Amen."

21. The grace of the Lord Jesus be with all.

This benediction is short and is reminiscent of the epistolary literature of Paul. It confirms that the Apocalypse is sent as an epistle to the churches and therefore needs an appropriate parting blessing. The benediction is expressed as a prayer or wish much the same as the greeting in the introduction (1:4).

The variants reflected in translations concern the recipients of this book. In view of the benediction itself, these variations are of little importance. The grace of the Lord Jesus is with all those who love him, serve him, and long for his return.

Greek Words, Phrases, and Constructions in 22:21

μετὰ πάντων—"with all." Other readings have "with all the saints" and "with you all." Of these three, the shortest reading is preferred.

Soli Deo Gloria

32. Bauer, p. 807.

Bibliography

Commentaries

Alford, Henry. *James–Revelation*. Vol. 4, part 2 of *Alford's Greek Testament: An Exegetical and Critical Commentary*. 1875. Reprint, Grand Rapids: Guardian, 1976.
Allo, Ernest B. *Saint Jean l'Apocalypse*. Études bibliques. Paris: Gabalda, 1921.
Aune, David E. *Revelation 1–5*. Word Biblical Commentary 52A. Dallas: Word, 1997.
———. *Revelation 6–16*. Word Biblical Commentary 52B. Nashville: Nelson, 1998.
———. *Revelation 17–22*. Word Biblical Commentary 52C. Nashville: Nelson, 1998.
Barclay, William. *The Revelation of John*. 2d ed. 2 vols. Philadelphia: Westminster, 1960.
Barnes, Albert. *Notes on the New Testament: Revelation*. Edited by Robert Frew. Reprint, Grand Rapids: Baker, 1949.
Beale, Gregory K. *The Book of Revelation: A Commentary on the Greek Text*. New International Greek Testament Commentary. Grand Rapids: Eerdmans, 1998.
Beasley-Murray, G. R. *The Book of Revelation*. New Century Bible. London: Oliphants, 1974.
Beckwith, Isbon T. *The Apocalypse of John: Studies in Introduction with a Critical and Exegetical Commentary*. 1919. Reprint, Grand Rapids: Baker, 1979.
Behm, Johannes. *Die Offenbarung des Johannes*. Das Neue Testament Deutsch 11. Göttingen: Vandenhoeck & Ruprecht, 1953.
Blomberg, Craig L. *Matthew*. New American Commentary 22. Nashville: Broadman, 1992.
Boer, Harry R. *The Book of Revelation*. Grand Rapids: Eerdmans, 1979.
Boring, M. Eugene. *Revelation*. Interpretation: A Bible Commentary for Teaching and Preaching. Louisville: John Knox, 1989.
Caird, G. B. *A Commentary on the Revelation of St. John the Divine*. Harper's New Testament Commentaries. New York: Harper and Row, 1966.
Calvin, John. *Commentaries on the Catholic Epistles*. Reprint, Grand Rapids: Baker, 1981.
———. *Commentaries on the Epistles to the Philippians, Colossians, and Thessalonians*. Reprint, Grand Rapids: Baker, 1981.
Charles, R. H. *A Critical and Exegetical Commentary on the Revelation of St. John*. 2 vols. International Critical Commentary. Edinburgh: Clark, 1920.
Chilton, David. *The Days of Vengeance: An Exposition of the Book of Revelation*. Fort Worth, Tex.: Dominion, 1987.
Collins, Adela Yarbro. *The Apocalypse*. Wilmington: Glazier, 1979.
Düsterdieck, Friedrich. *Critical and Exegetical Handbook to the Revelation of John*. New York and London: Funk and Wagnalls, 1886.

Consult the index of authors and the footnotes for references to the numerous articles mentioned in the commentary.

Easley, Kendell H. *Revelation.* Holman New Testament Commentary. Nashville: Broadman & Holman, 1998.

Ellul, J. *Apocalypse: The Book of Revelation.* Translated by George W. Schreiner. New York: Seabury, 1977.

Fairbairn, Patrick. *Ezekiel and the Book of His Prophecy.* Edinburgh: Clark, 1876.

Ford, Josephine Massyngberde. *Revelation: Introduction, Translation, and Commentary.* Anchor Bible 38. Garden City, N.Y.: Doubleday, 1975.

Greijdanus, S. *De Openbaring des Heeren aan Johannes.* Kommentaar op het Nieuwe Testament. Amsterdam: Van Bottenburg, 1925.

Hailey, Homer. *Revelation: An Introduction and Commentary.* Grand Rapids: Baker, 1979.

Harrington, Wilfrid J. *Revelation.* Sacra Pagina 16. Collegeville, Minn.: Liturgical Press, 1993.

Hartingsveld, L. van. *Revelation.* Grand Rapids: Eerdmans, 1985.

Hendriksen, William. *Exposition of Philippians.* New Testament Commentary. Grand Rapids: Baker, 1962.

———. *More Than Conquerors: An Interpretation of the Book of Revelation.* Reprint, Grand Rapids: Baker, 1982.

Hoeksema, Herman. *Behold, He Cometh! An Exposition of the Book of Revelation.* Grand Rapids: Reformed Free Publishing Association, 1969.

Hughes, Philip Edgcumbe. *The Book of the Revelation: A Commentary.* Leicester: Inter-Varsity; Grand Rapids: Eerdmans, 1990.

Johnson, Alan F. *Revelation.* In vol. 12 of *The Expositor's Bible Commentary,* edited by Frank E. Gaebelein. 12 vols. Grand Rapids: Zondervan, 1981.

Keener, Craig S. *Revelation.* NIV Application Commentary. Grand Rapids: Zondervan, 2000.

Kiddle, Martin. *The Revelation of St. John.* Reprint, London: Hodder and Stoughton, 1943.

Kistemaker, Simon J. *Exposition of the Epistle of James.* New Testament Commentary. Grand Rapids: Baker, 1986.

———. *Exposition of the First Epistle to the Corinthians.* New Testament Commentary. Grand Rapids: Baker, 1993.

Krodel, Gerhard A. *Revelation.* Augsburg Commentary on the New Testament. Minneapolis: Augsburg, 1989.

Kuyper, Abraham. *The Revelation of St. John.* Translated by John Hendrik de Vries. Grand Rapids: Eerdmans, 1935.

Ladd, George Eldon. *A Commentary on the Revelation of John.* Grand Rapids: Eerdmans, 1972.

Lenski, R. C. H. *The Interpretation of St. John's Revelation.* Columbus: Wartburg, 1943.

Lohmeyer, Ernst. *Die Offenbarung des Johannes.* Handbuch zum Neuen Testament 16. Tübingen: Mohr, 1970.

Lohse, Eduard. *Die Offenbarung des Johannes.* Das Neue Testament Deutsch 11. Göttingen: Vandenhoeck & Ruprecht, 1960.

Luther, Martin. *The Catholic Epistles.* Vol. 30 of *Luther's Works,* edited by Jaroslav Pelikan. St. Louis: Concordia, 1967.

Michaels, J. Ramsey. *Revelation.* IVP New Testament Commentary series. Downers Grove: InterVarsity, 1997.

Milligan, William. *The Book of Revelation.* New York: Armstrong and Son, 1893.

Moffatt, James. *The Revelation of St. John the Divine.* In vol. 5. of *Expositor's Greek Testament,* edited by W. Robertson Nicholl. Reprint, Grand Rapids: Eerdmans, 1956.

Morris, Leon. *Revelation.* Rev. ed. Tyndale New Testament Commentaries. Leicester: Inter-Varsity; Grand Rapids: Eerdmans, 1987.
Mounce, Robert H. *The Book of Revelation.* Rev. ed. New International Commentary on the New Testament. Grand Rapids: Eerdmans, 1998.
Mulholland, M. Robert, Jr. *Revelation: Holy Living in an Unholy World.* Grand Rapids: Zondervan, Francis Asbury Press, 1990.
Parker, T. H. L. *Calvin's New Testament Commentaries.* Grand Rapids: Eerdmans, 1971.
Poellot, Luther. *Revelation: The Last Book in the Bible.* St. Louis: Concordia, 1962.
Roloff, Jürgen. *The Revelation of John.* Translated by J. E. Alsup. Minneapolis: Fortress, 1993.
Seiss, Joseph A. *The Apocalypse.* Grand Rapids: Zondervan, 1957.
Summers, Ray. *Worthy Is the Lamb: An Interpretation of Revelation.* Nashville: Broadman, 1951.
Sweet, John P. M. *Revelation.* Westminster Pelican Commentaries. Philadelphia: Westminster, 1979.
Swete, Henry Barclay. *Commentary on Revelation: The Greek Text with Introduction, Notes, and Indexes.* 1911. Reprint, Grand Rapids: Kregel, 1977.
Thomas, Robert L. *Revelation 1–7: An Exegetical Commentary.* Chicago: Moody, 1992.
———. *Revelation 8–22: An Exegetical Commentary.* Chicago: Moody, 1995.
Wall, Robert W. *Revelation.* New International Biblical Commentary on the New Testament. Peabody, Mass.: Hendrickson, 1991.
Walvoord, John F. *The Revelation of Jesus Christ.* Chicago: Moody, 1966.
Wilcock, Michael. *The Message of Revelation: I Saw Heaven Opened.* Leicester: Inter-Varsity; Downers Grove: InterVarsity, 1975.
Wilson, Geoffrey B. *Revelation.* Welwyn, England: Evangelical Press, 1985.
Zahn, Theodor. *Die Offenbarung des Johannes.* 2 vols. Kommentar zum Neuen Testament 18. Leipzig: Deichert, 1924–26.

Studies

Barclay, William. *Letters to the Seven Churches.* New York: Abingdon, 1957.
Bauckham, Richard. *The Climax of Prophecy: Studies on the Book of Revelation.* Edinburgh: Clark, 1993.
———. *The Theology of the Book of Revelation.* New Testament Theology. Cambridge: Cambridge University Press, 1995.
Bavinck, Herman. *The Last Things: Hope for This World and the Next.* Edited by John Bolt. Translated by John Vriend. Grand Rapids: Baker, 1996.
Beale, G. K. *The Book of Revelation and the Johannine Apocalyptic Tradition.* Journal for the Study of the New Testament: Supplement Series 190. Sheffield: Sheffield Academic Press, 2000.
———. *John's Use of the Old Testament in Revelation.* Journal for the Study of the New Testament: Supplement Series 166. Sheffield: Sheffield Academic Press, 1998.
———. *The Use of Daniel in Jewish Apocalyptic Literature and in the Revelation of St. John.* Lanham, Md. University Press of America, 1984.
———, ed. *The Right Doctrine from the Wrong Texts? Essays on the Use of the Old Testament in the New.* Grand Rapids: Baker, 1994.
Bock, Darrell L., ed. *Three Views on the Millennium and Beyond.* Grand Rapids: Zondervan, 1999.
Bowman, J. W. *The Drama of the Book of Revelation.* Philadelphia: Westminster, 1955.

Brady, D. *The Contribution of British Writers between 1560 and 1830 to the Interpretation of Revelation 13.16–18 (the Number of the Beast): A Study in the History of Exegesis.* Beiträge zur Geschichte der biblischen Exegese 27. Tübingen: Mohr, 1983.

Charles, R. H. *Studies in the Apocalypse.* 2d ed. Edinburgh: Clark, 1915.

Clouse, Robert G., ed. *The Meaning of the Millennium.* Grand Rapids: Eerdmans, 1977.

Collins, Adela Yarbro. *The Combat Myth in the Book of Revelation.* Harvard Dissertations in Religion 9. Missoula: Scholars Press, 1976.

———. *Crisis and Catharsis: The Power of the Apocalypse.* Philadelphia: Westminster, 1984.

Collins, John J. *The Apocalyptic Imagination.* New York: Crossroad, 1992.

Court, John M. *Myth and History in the Book of Revelation.* Atlanta: John Knox, 1979.

Cullmann, Oscar. *Christ and Time: The Primitive Christian Conception of Time and History.* Translated by Floyd V. Filson. London: SCM, 1951.

Farrer, Austin. *A Rebirth of Images: The Making of St. John's Apocalypse.* Glasgow: University Press, 1949.

Fekkes, Jan. *Isaiah and Prophetic Traditions in the Book of Revelation: Visionary Antecedents and Their Development.* Journal for the Study of the New Testament: Supplement Series 93. Sheffield: JSOT, 1994.

Friesen, S. J. *Twice Neokoros: Ephesus, Asia, and the Cult of the Flavian Imperial Family.* Leiden: Brill, 1993.

Gentry, Kenneth L., Jr. *Before Jerusalem Fell: Dating the Book of Revelation.* Tyler, Tex.: Institute for Christian Economics, 1989.

Goppelt, Leonhard. *The Typological Interpretation of the Old Testament in the New.* Translated by Donald H. Madvig. Grand Rapids: Eerdmans, 1982.

Grenz, Stanley J. *The Millennial Maze: Sorting Out Evangelical Options.* Downers Grove: InterVarsity, 1992.

Grier, W. J. *The Momentous Event.* London: Banner of Truth Trust, 1970.

Gundry, Robert H. *The Church and the Tribulation: A Biblical Examination of Posttribulationism.* Grand Rapids: Zondervan, 1973.

Hamilton, Floyd E. *The Basis of Millennial Faith.* Grand Rapids: Eerdmans, 1952.

Hemer, Colin J. *The Letters to the Seven Churches of Asia in Their Local Setting.* Journal for the Study of the New Testament: Supplement Series 11. Sheffield: JSOT, 1986.

Hill, Charles E. *Regnum Caelorum: Patterns of Future Hope in Early Christianity.* Oxford: Clarendon,1992.

Hoekema, Anthony A. *The Bible and the Future.* Grand Rapids: Eerdmans, 1979.

Holwerda, David E. *Jesus and Israel: One Covenant or Two?* Grand Rapids: Eerdmans; Leicester: Inter-Varsity, 1995.

Hunter, Archibald M. *Probing the New Testament.* Richmond, Va.: John Knox, 1971.

Hunter, Stephen A. *Studies in the Book of Revelation.* Pittsburgh: Pittsburgh Printing, 1921.

Kuyvenhoven Andrew. *The Day of Christ's Return.* Grand Rapids: CRC Publications, 1999.

Lawlor, Hugh Jackson. *Eusebiana: Essays on the Ecclesiastical History of Eusebius Pamphili, ca 264–349 A.D. Bishop of Caesarea.* 1912. Reprint, Amsterdam: Philo, 1973.

Mazzaferri, Frederick David. *The Genre of the Book of Revelation from a Source-Critical Perspective.* Beiheft zur Zeitschrift für die neutestamentliche Wissenschaft 54. Berlin and New York: de Gruyter, 1989.

Mealy, J. Webb. *After the Thousand Years.* Journal for the Study of the New Testament: Supplement Series 70. Sheffield: JSOT, 1992.

Metzger, Bruce M. *Breaking the Code: Understanding the Book of Revelation.* Nashville: Abingdon, 1993.

Michaels, J. Ramsey. *Interpreting the Book of Revelation.* Grand Rapids: Baker, 1992.

Milligan, William. *The Revelation of St. John.* London: Macmillan, 1886.

Morris, S. L. *The Drama of Christianity: An Interpretation of the Book of Revelation.* Reprint, Grand Rapids: Baker, 1982.

Moyise, Steve. *The Old Testament in the Book of Revelation.* Journal for the Study of the New Testament: Supplement Series 115. Sheffield: Sheffield Academic Press, 1995.

Murray, George L. *Millennial Studies: A Search for Truth.* Grand Rapids: Baker, 1960.

Pate, C. Marvin, ed. *Four Views on the Book of Revelation.* Grand Rapids: Zondervan, 1998.

Paulien, Jon. *Decoding Revelation's Trumpets: Literary Allusions and the Interpretation of Revelation 8:7–12.* Andrews University Seminary Doctoral Dissertation Series 11. Berrien Springs, Mich.: Andrews University Press, 1987.

Peterson, Robert A. *Hell on Trial: The Case for Eternal Punishment.* Phillipsburg, N.J.: Presbyterian and Reformed, 1995.

Pippin, Tina. *Death and Desire: The Rhetoric and Gender in the Apocalypse of John.* Louisville: Westminster/John Knox, 1992.

Price, S. R. F. *Rituals and Power: The Roman Imperial Cult in Asia Minor.* Cambridge: Cambridge University Press, 1984.

Ramsay, William M. *The Cities and Bishoprics of Phrygia.* Vol. 1, parts 1 and 2. 1895. Reprint, New York: Arno, 1975.

———. *The Letters to the Seven Churches of Asia and Their Place in the Plan of the Apocalypse.* London: Hodder and Stoughton, 1904. Reprint, Grand Rapids: Baker, 1979.

Resseguie, James L. *Revelation Unsealed: A Narrative Critical Approach to John's Apocalypse.* Biblical Interpretation Series 32. Leiden: Brill, 1998.

Rissi, Mathias. *The Future of the World: An Exegetical Study of Revelation 19.11–22.15.* Studies in Biblical Theology 23, 2d series. London: SCM, 1972.

———. *Time and History: A Study on the Revelation.* Translated by Gordon C. Winsor. Richmond: John Knox, 1966.

Robinson, John A. T. *Redating the New Testament.* Philadelphia: Westminster, 1976.

Ruiz, Jean-Pierre. *Ezekiel in the Apocalypse: The Transformation of Prophetic Language in Revelation 16.17–19.10.* Frankfurt am Main: Peter Lang, 1989.

Schüssler Fiorenza, Elisabeth. *The Book of Revelation: Justice and Judgment.* Philadelphia: Fortress, 1985.

———. *Invitation to the Book of Revelation: A Commentary on the Apocalypse.* Garden City, N.Y.: Doubleday, 1981.

Slater, Thomas B. *Christ and Community: A Socio-Historical Study of the Christology of Revelation.* Journal for the Study of the New Testament: Supplement Series 178. Sheffield: Sheffield Academic Press, 1999.

Stauffer, Ethelbert. *Christ and the Caesars.* Translated by K. and R. Gregor Smith. London: SCM, 1955.

Stonehouse, Ned B. *The Apocalypse in the Ancient Church.* Goes, Netherlands: Oosterbaan & Le Cointre, 1929.

———. *Paul before the Areopagus and Other New Testament Studies.* London: Tyndale, 1957.

Tenney, Merrill C. *Interpreting Revelation.* Grand Rapids: Eerdmans, 1957.

Thompson, Leonard L. *The Book of Revelation: Apocalypse and Empire.* New York and Oxford: Oxford University Press, 1990.

Torrey, C. C. *The Apocalypse of John.* New Haven: Yale University Press, 1958.

Ulfgard, H. *Feast and Future: Revelation 7:9–17 and the Feast of Tabernacles.* Coniectanea biblica, New Testament Series 22. Stockholm: Almqvist & Wiksell, 1989.

Van der Meulen, Ruurd Jan. *De Openbaring in het Laatste Bijbelboek.* Utrecht: Den Boer, 1948.

Vos, Louis A., *The Synoptic Traditions in the Apocalypse.* Kampen: Kok, 1965.

Tools

Aland, Kurt, et al., eds. *The Greek New Testament.* 4th ed. Stuttgart: Deutsche Bibelgesellschaft and United Bible Societies, 1993.

Balz, Horst, and Gerhard Schneider, eds. *Exegetical Dictionary of the New Testament.* 3 vols. Grand Rapids: Eerdmans, 1990–93.

Bauer, Walter. *A Greek-English Lexicon of the New Testament.* Edited by William F. Arndt and F. Wilbur Gingrich. 2d ed. Revised and augmented by F. Wilbur Gingrich and Frederick W. Danker. Chicago and London: University of Chicago Press, 1979.

Blass, Friedrich, and Albert Debrunner. *A Greek Grammar of the New Testament.* Translated and revised by Robert Funk. Chicago: University of Chicago Press, 1961.

Bromiley, Geoffrey W., ed. *The International Standard Bible Encyclopedia.* Rev. ed. 4 vols. Grand Rapids: Eerdmans, 1979–88.

Brown, Colin, ed. *New International Dictionary of New Testament Theology.* 3 vols. Grand Rapids: Zondervan, 1975–78.

Brown, Raymond E. *An Introduction to the New Testament.* Anchor Bible Reference Library. New York: Doubleday, 1996.

Carson, D. A., Douglas Moo, and Leon Morris. *New Testament Introduction.* Grand Rapids: Zondervan, 1992.

Charlesworth, James H., ed. *The Old Testament Pseudepigrapha.* 2 vols. Garden City, N.Y.: Doubleday, 1983.

Clement of Alexandria. *Who Is the Rich Man That Shall Be Saved?* In vol. 2 of *The Ante-Nicene Fathers,* edited by Alexander Roberts and James Donaldson. Reprint, Grand Rapids: Eerdmans, n.d.

Dana, H. E., and Julius R. Mantey. *A Manual Grammar of the Greek New Testament.* 1927. Reprint, New York: Macmillan, 1967.

Deissmann, G. A. *Bible Studies.* Reprint, Winona Lake, Ind.: Alpha, 1979.

———. *Light from the Ancient East.* Translated by Lionel R. M. Strachan. Reprint, Grand Rapids: Baker, 1978.

Elwell, Walter A., ed. *Baker Encyclopedia of the Bible.* Grand Rapids: Baker, 1988.

———. *Evangelical Dictionary of Theology.* Grand Rapids: Baker, 1984.

Epstein, Isidore, ed. *The Babylonian Talmud.* London: Soncino, 1935.

Eusebius. *Ecclesiastical History.* Translated by Kirsopp Lake and J. E. L. Oulton. 2 vols. Loeb Classical Library. London: Heinemann; Cambridge, Mass.: Harvard University Press, 1980.

Guthrie, Donald. *New Testament Introduction.* 4th ed. Downers Grove: InterVarsity, 1990.

———. *New Testament Theology.* Downers Grove: InterVarsity, 1981.

Hanna, Robert. *A Grammatical Aid to the Greek New Testament.* Grand Rapids: Baker, 1983.

Irenaeus. *Against Heresies.* In vol. 1 of *The Ante-Nicene Fathers,* edited by Alexander Roberts and James Donaldson. Reprint, Grand Rapids: Eerdmans, n.d.

Josephus, Flavius. *Jewish Antiquities.* Translated by H. St. J. Thackeray et al. 7 vols. Loeb Classical Library. Cambridge, Mass.: Harvard University Press; London: Heinemann, 1930–65.

———. *The Jewish War.* Translated by H. St. J. Thackeray. 2 vols. Loeb Classical Library. Cambridge, Mass.: Harvard University Press; London: Heinemann, 1927–28.

Justin Martyr. *Dialogue with Trypho.* In vol. 1. of *The Ante-Nicene Fathers,* edited by Alexander Roberts and James Donaldson. Reprint, Grand Rapids: Eerdmans, n.d.

Kittel, Gerhard, and Gerhard Friedrich, eds. *Theological Dictionary of the New Testament.* Translated by Geoffrey W. Bromiley. 10 vols. Grand Rapids: Eerdmans, 1964–76.

Liddell, H. G., R. Scott, H. S. Jones, and R. McKenzie. *A Greek-English Lexicon.* 9th ed. With revised supplement. Oxford: Clarendon, 1996.

Metzger, Bruce M. *A Textual Commentary on the Greek New Testament.* 2d ed. Stuttgart: German Bible Society, 1994.

Moule, C. F. D. *An Idiom-Book of New Testament Greek.* 2d ed. Cambridge: Cambridge University Press, 1960.

Moulton, James H., W. F. Howard, and Nigel Turner. *A Grammar of New Testament Greek.* 4 vols. Edinburgh: Clark, 1908–76.

Nestle, Eberhard, and Erwin Nestle, eds. *Novum Testamentum Graece.* Rev. Barbara and Kurt Aland et al. 27th ed. Stuttgart: Deutsche Bibelgesellschaft, 1993.

Roberts, Alexander, and James Donaldson, eds. *The Ante-Nicene Fathers: Translations of Writings of the Fathers down to A.D. 325.* 10 vols. Reprint, Grand Rapids: Eerdmans, n.d.

Robertson, A. T. *A Grammar of the Greek New Testament in the Light of Historical Research.* Nashville: Broadman, 1934.

Schneemelcher, Wilhelm, ed. *New Testament Apocrypha.* English translation edited by R. McL. Wilson. Rev. ed. 2 vols. Cambridge: James Clarke; Louisville: Westminster/John Knox, 1991–92.

Strack, H. L., and P. Billerbeck. *Kommentar zum Neuen Testament aus Talmud und Midrasch.* 5 vols. Munich: Beck, 1922–28.

Tenney, Merrill C., ed. *The Zondervan Pictorial Encyclopedia of the Bible.* Grand Rapids: Zondervan, 1975.

Thayer, Joseph Henry. *Greek-English Lexicon of the New Testament.* New York: American Book, 1886.

Trench, Richard C. *Synonyms of the New Testament.* Edited by Robert G. Hoerber. Grand Rapids: Baker, 1989.

Young, Richard A. *Intermediate New Testament Greek: A Linguistic and Exegetical Approach.* Nashville: Broadman & Holman, 1994.

Index of Authors

Index of Authors

Index of Authors

Index of Scripture and Other Ancient Writings

Old Testament

New Testament

Acts

Romans

Old Testament Apocrypha

Old Testament Pseudepigrapha

Index of Scripture and Other Ancient Writings

Josephus and Philo

Other Jewish Writings

Classical Writings

Index of Scripture and Other Ancient Writings

Early Christian Writings